1984

W9-CLF-735

A Handbook of
CLASSICAL
DRAMA

A Handbook of

CLASSICAL DRAMA

By

PHILIP WHALEY HARSH

STANFORD UNIVERSITY PRESS
Stanford, California

PREFACE

Greek tragedy, one of the greatest achievements of the human genius, exerts a more vital influence on modern literature and can be more readily appreciated than perhaps any other ancient genre. Still, the modern reader unacquainted with ancient thought is likely to miss some of the greatness of the *Agamemnon;* he is almost sure to be puzzled by the *Bacchae* and to misinterpret the *Hippolytus.* The comedies of Aristophanes are even more difficult for him to understand. Important problems arise concerning the Roman plays also. For such a reader the present work is designed to be a general introduction. For the reader already acquainted with the field it is designed to be a modern appreciation of the plays as literature and a convenient brief guide to further critical material. In order best to serve these ends it has seemed advisable to treat the more important plays in some detail and the less important ones very summarily rather than to divide the space available among important and unimportant alike.

The more elaborate treatments have been broken up into sections with clearly marked headings. Factual material, in which an effort has been made to distinguish between the authenticated and the conjectural, has been placed first. Under the heading "Sources" all plays known to have been written previously on the same subject are mentioned, but from this mere heading the reader should draw no inferences concerning the poet's actual indebtedness. Where evidence of indebtedness exists, it is usually cited specifically.

The critical discussion, which follows the factual material, is concerned primarily with dramatic technique. Since the plays themselves differ so widely, however, no rigid procedure can be maintained. More than half the space devoted to the *Antigone,* a tragedy of character and decision, is concerned with the characters; whereas in the treatment of the *Iphigenia in Tauris,* a melodramatic play of action, almost nothing is said about the characters.

In each treatment it is assumed that the reader is well acquainted with the play. A student should, if possible, read a given play both before and after reading a critical appreciation of it.

Technical terms are defined upon their first occurrence, which may readily be located by the use of the Index.

Asterisks are here used, as in other guidebooks, to indicate important works. Two asterisks indicate that the play, in the opinion of the present writer, deserves its generally recognized status as a masterpiece; one asterisk indicates that it is a successful and important work.

No effort has been made to outline the mere events of a play; this is usually done in the introduction to a translation.

English titles of the plays and names of some characters vary with the translator. For the reader's convenience the present writer has, with few exceptions, used the titles and names appearing in the latest complete collections of translations—*The Complete Greek Drama* by Oates and O'Neill and *The Complete Roman Drama* by Duckworth. The order of the plays, also, is the same as in these collections, with minor variations. This is the conventional order in all editions. For the Greek dramatists and for Terence, this order is based on chronology; for Plautus, the chronology of whose plays is very uncertain, this order is alphabetical according to the original Latin titles; for Seneca, where chronological data are almost wholly lacking, this order is based on the order of the chief manuscript.

In citing modern works, author and title only are given, sometimes in abbreviated form, if the work is listed in the Bibliography. Translations of ancient authors quoted are made by the present writer unless otherwise accredited.

The problem of securing a good translation is the most serious one which the modern reader faces and is almost insurmountable. A poor translation has often ruined the simple prose of Ibsen. Even the best translation falls far below the grand poetry of Aeschylus. Precise and profound appreciation of any literary work, of course, can be obtained only from the original text.

It would require a lifetime to become thoroughly acquainted with the scholarly material on almost any one of the eight major authors covered in the present work. The writer is acquainted with only a small part of all this material; he hopes that he is acquainted with the most important part and that the obvious advantages of a study appreciating all classical drama from a single critical point of view will compensate for shortcomings in given fields. In regard to many of the plays, of course, there are various interpretations different from the ones here presented or even cited. A mere guidebook should confine itself to the widely accepted views, especially where Greek tragedy is concerned; for no richer collection of critical opinion can be found than that on Greek tragedy. But this collection is rich in error—though even the error is enlightening—as well as in sound doctrine. The last indisputable word has been written on few if any of the plays, and one must often grope for a satisfactory interpretation of his own.

The writer has invariably formulated and composed his own treatments of the plays before further consultation of modern works of criticism. Important changes and additions subsequently introduced on the basis of such works have been duly accredited. It goes without saying, however, that he is far more indebted to certain great authorities than becomes evident in this process or than would be possible to record in a mere synthesis. These authorities have been for Aeschylus especially Wilamowitz and Smyth; for Sophocles, Jebb; for Euripides, Wilamowitz and Gilbert Murray; for Aristophanes, Starkie; for New Comedy, Legrand, Leo, Lindsay, and Prescott; and for the general field, especially Haigh, Flickinger, and Wilhelm Schmid.

The writer wishes to thank his colleagues and friends for their numerous helpful criticisms, especially James Turney Allen, Hardin Craig, O. Curtis Crawford, James V. Cunningham, Eugene G. O'Neill, Jr., Oscar S. Powers, and, most of all, Hermann F. Fränkel and Virgil K. Whitaker, who have read parts of the manuscript, and Hubert C. Heffner, who has read the whole of it. The writer alone, however, is responsible for the shortcomings which remain. Stimulating discussions with many students in the writer's classes at Stanford University have provided more than one important contribution. The writer is indebted also to Professor Willy Gierlichs of the University of Cologne, Germany, who, without thought of remuneration, sent a copy of Schmid's most recent volume containing his monumental work on Euripides at a time when German books could no longer be secured through commercial channels.

P. W. H.

STANFORD UNIVERSITY,
March 1, 1944

CONTENTS

PART ONE. GREEK TRAGEDY

PART THREE. NEW COMEDY

Part One

GREEK TRAGEDY

I
INTRODUCTION TO GREEK TRAGEDY

A Greek tragedy is a dramatic and choral presentation of an action usually taken from legend or remote history and involving incidents of a certain magnitude. The action is complete in itself, is treated in a serious manner, and is normally interpreted so as to exhibit some religious, moral, or political significance. Tragedy, like almost all ancient drama, is written in verse, and the scenes of spoken verse are marked off by choral songs or other lyrics. No intermissions occur within a play. The ending may be a happy solution, but usually it involves a reversal of fortune from good to bad and is tragic in the modern sense of that word.

In the present work, the action or story is termed the subject of the play, the significance the theme of the play. An appreciation of this significance is usually essential to any profound interpretation, for the dramatists in bold and honest fashion presented the great problems of ethics and religion.[1]* They could hardly be said definitively to have solved these problems. Their activity was the brilliant effervescence which preceded and in part, no doubt, resulted in the development of systematic Greek philosophy. They were, above all, poets and dramatists of an intensely alive contemporary theater.

The political implications of Greek tragedy are veiled, for tragedy was required to maintain a high dignity, and they usually escape the modern reader unless he is intimately acquainted with the history of the period. Such implications, but not narrow partisanship, can frequently be discerned, however, especially in the plays of Aeschylus and Euripides.

This emphasis upon serious significance does not impair the vitality of the drama. Significance, indeed, is wholly lacking in any literature only when that literature becomes so romanticized that it is no longer a true representation of life, or when it becomes utterly frivolous. If the religious and moral and political conceptions of the Greeks had genuine validity in their actual life, then these conceptions must inevitably appear in any honest and serious dramatization of their life.

---

* Notes, numbered consecutively for each chapter, will be found following the entire text; see page 441, below.

ORIGIN

Aristotle (*Poet.* 1449 a) says that both tragedy and comedy began in improvisations, tragedy arising from the dithyramb, a choral poem properly in honor of the god Dionysus, and comedy arising from the phallic songs. He further intimates that tragedy originally had only one actor, and was a short, ludicrous satyric play employing the gay and dancing trochaic meter. Modern scholars have debated the question of these origins endlessly.[2]

All drama at Athens was a part of the worship of Dionysus. Dionysus was a divinity of fertility.[3] He was also the god of wine, which he was said to have brought to Greece. During two of his festivals, the Lenaea in January–February and the Great or City Dionysia in March–April, plays were produced in the theater sacred to him located on the southeast side of the Acropolis. It may be that women of respectable position did not, at least in the fifth century, attend the performances.[4] Each play was produced only once during the festival, but later it might be reproduced in other towns of Attica or elsewhere.

The ancient theater was not a commercial enterprise, therefore, but a religious institution under the direction of the state; the plays for a given festival were chosen by a state official selected by lot from the Athenian populace; the state furnished the actors for the plays and assigned wealthy citizens, then called the "choregi," to provide and train the choruses at their own expense. It was the custom that on a given day one dramatist should present three tragedies and a satyr-play and that only three actors should be furnished for a given set of plays. Three dramatists participated in each festival, and three prizes were awarded them by a panel of judges chosen in a very elaborate manner in order to prevent bribery or intimidation.[5] Since Aeschylus and Sophocles usually won the first prize when they competed, it is safe to assume that the best series of plays usually was ranked first by such judges; but there were many factors in this method of awarding prizes which might easily cause a miscarriage of justice in a given instance. We should feel no surprise, therefore, when we learn that Sophocles received the second prize for his series of tragedies which contained the *Oedipus* or that Euripides received third prize for a series which contained the *Medea.*

LEGENDARY SUBJECTS

The subject matter of Greek tragedy from the very beginning was taken from legend or myth. The choral dithyramb out of which tragedy developed seems originally to have been concerned with the birth of Dionysus, if we may so interpret a remark of Plato (*Laws* 700 B). Possibly the original subject of tragedy was the passion of Dionysus, or his death and rebirth, which were symbolic of the yearly cycle of the disappearance of the seed beneath the ground in the fall of the year and its re-emergence in the spring. But even before tragedy had developed under Aeschylus from an essentially choral to an essentially dramatic form, any legendary subject was considered acceptable for tragedy and some few plays were being written on contemporary events.

Since it was in this early period that the conventions were being established, these early plays on contemporary events deserve careful attention. Phrynichus, the older contemporary of Aeschylus, wrote at least two such plays. The first of these concerned the capture and destruction of Miletus by the Persians in 494 B.C. The Athenians, who had attempted to save Miletus, were so pained by this portrayal of the sufferings of their friends and allies that they fell to weeping in the theater and later levied a heavy fine upon the dramatist. They also decreed that no one should ever "use this drama again."[6] From this unpleasant experience the poet rightly concluded that if a friendly nation's defeat pained the audience a hostile nation's defeat would please them, and so he later brought out a play on the Persian defeat at Salamis. This play was laid at the faraway Persian capital, and its chorus consisted of Phoenician women whose husbands had gone with the army against Greece. Greek religious feeling, which warned against too great delight in good fortune, made it obviously unwise to dramatize the battle of Salamis as an Athenian victory. This play was a success. It was followed and to some extent imitated by Aeschylus' famous *Persians* (472 B.C.). Again the scene was laid at the Persian court in Susa. In these two plays, therefore, the remoteness of the locale of the play and the royalty of the characters furnish an atmosphere not unlike that of the plays written on legendary subjects, and we may perhaps assume that the audience would view plays written about Priam and the fall of Troy as essentially no less historical or realistic than such plays written about the Persian Wars, especially since the scene of these plays was laid in Persia and since Aeschylus included the ghost of Darius as one of the characters. Somewhat analogous would be the attitude of an Elizabethan audience in viewing *King Lear* or *Macbeth* as perhaps not so very much less historical than *Richard II*.

It may be significant that both these plays on the defeat of the Persians were produced, as it seems, with famous politicians as choregi. Themistocles, himself the great hero of Salamis, was choregus for Phrynichus in 476, and it is usually assumed that the *Phoenician Women* was produced at this time. The choregus for Aeschylus when the *Persians* was produced was none other than the rising young Pericles.[7]

The use of contemporary history as a source for dramatic themes, however, did not become popular among the Greeks—these are the only historical plays of which we hear in the fifth century—and it has never been a very successful practice in serious drama. Events which are recent and well known obviously circumscribe and curtail the dramatist's license.[8]

Incidentally we may note that the Renaissance dramatists were fond of writing on subjects taken from Greek and Roman history, which occupied somewhat the same relative position to Renaissance times that Greek legendary history did to the Periclean Age. So Trissino wrote his *Sofonisba* (1515) and Jodelle his *Cléopâtre* (1552). Many another dramatist wrote on the same subjects—for they were obviously common property—or on similar ones. The practice was continued by Shakespeare, Corneille, and Racine. Renaissance art, also, was founded on the same principles.

The appearance of fiction was generally avoided in serious Greek literature, but actually invention and innovation were freely practiced and were advocated by Aristotle (*Poet.* 1451 b). Even though Greek legend presented an incomparable and obvious source of dramatic plots, we must not assume that these plots were ready-made and required little or no adaptation. On the contrary, Greek legend was an amorphous mass of vague and often contradictory stories, with few details that could not be changed. It was the duty of the dramatist to focus the stories and construct them into unified and sharply climaxed plots. How wide a choice of incident and motivation lay at hand is well shown by the legends of Medea at Corinth and by the various explanations of Apollo's servitude in the house of Admetus. But originality had even more scope. Legends were rewritten to suit the author's purpose. The whole story of Antigone's burying her brother Polyneices, for instance, was not crystallized by Sophocles' masterly presentation of his version. Euripides in his *Antigone*—which is assumed to be later than that of Sophocles, although definite evidence on this point is lacking—produced a very different version of the story in which the heroine was not immediately put to death for burying Polyneices but was married, perhaps secretly, to Haemon. Minor details even of the best-known legends were varied endlessly. In the *Phoenissae* of Euripides, Jocasta is still alive at the time of the duel between Eteocles and Polyneices; this contradicts not only Aeschylus and Sophocles but Homer also (*Odyssey* 11. 277). So great are the divergences found in the various authors that many of these changes must have been recognized as innovations. No greater consistency should be expected in the various plays of the same author. Creon, king of Thebes, has an important role in three plays of Sophocles, but in each he is given a different character. In the *Antigone* he is the new king solicitous for his throne, primarily a good man but driven by fear of overthrow and by pride to commit a great wrong; in the *Oedipus* he is a loyal subject falsely accused, and later a wise and pious ruler; in the *Oedipus at Colonus* he is a cruel tyrant. The peculiar interests of each play determine the characterization of Creon there to be adopted. Again, in Euripides' *Iphigenia in Tauris* Iphigenia has not actually been sacrificed at Aulis by her father; but in his *Electra* and his *Orestes*—plays written in the same general period— she is always thought of as actually having been sacrificed. The reason for this inconsistency is obvious: those plays which deal with the vengeance of Orestes in a serious manner must of course assume that Agamemnon actually sacrificed his daughter so that Clytemnestra may have some justification for the murder of Agamemnon. In each play, therefore, the author adopts that form of the legend which is most effective for his immediate purpose and carefully discards all reference to alternate versions..

Fictitious names for main characters are avoided in Greek tragedy. Even when the events dramatized are of the poet's own creation, the historical names in themselves lend a certain credibility,[9] and it is for this reason, Aristotle intimates, that they are used.[10] Similarly in a modern historical drama few of the audience can distinguish between history and fiction, and most spectators accept the whole action as the dramatist presents it.

Where well-established legends are concerned, plausibility extends to the miraculous and the marvelous.[11] In the *Alcestis* of Euripides, for instance, a modern reader might feel that the bringing of Alcestis back to life by Heracles is an outrageous abuse of belief in the supernatural, forgetting that her resurrection was an essential feature of a well-established tradition. Such events, though obviously impossible in real life, were acceptable to the Greeks for literary and artistic purposes just as many impossible miracles of the Old Testament are acceptable today for the same purposes. Where such legends are concerned one is accustomed to a "willing suspension of disbelief."

The employment of supernatural events, furthermore, sometimes has other distinct **advantages**. In the *Alcestis,* for instance, Euripides is enabled to depict the profound emotions and the extraordinary developments of character which are the main concern of the play. Essentially the same arbitrary disregard for reality is employed as an artistic device in modern literature and for the same purpose. The Russian novelist, Dostoevski, for instance, places his novels in a world which is strange and wild beyond all reality as we know it, perhaps even beyond the world of Greek mythology. Although Dostoevski's world does not transcend the realm of possibility, still, as Aristotle (*Poet.* 1461 b) intimates, the impossible told in a plausible manner—the way of Homer and Greek tragedy—violates the illusion of reality less offensively than does the possible told in an implausible manner—perhaps the way of Dostoevski. These mythological and fanciful worlds, however, should be viewed as psychological laboratories in which the author places his characters in order that they may be observed and described under conditions that are more severe and more intense than those of our ordinary life, and the artistic use of such devices makes it possible to point the significance of actions with a lucidity and an emphasis that are lacking in ordinary life. In many literary and artistic productions of our own day, lucidity and emphasis are lacking because their authors have sacrificed profound significance to factual reality.

The dignity and power of Greek tragedy, also, are due in part to the legendary subjects. The dramatists seem to have felt, as Aristotle certainly did (*Poet.* 1448 b, 1453 a), that to be most effective tragedy must deal with illustrious persons and significant events. Only a catastrophe of great import can overwhelm us and thus have the most powerful tragic effect. Such persons and such events are found in legend or history.

A certain artistic detachment and perspective, furthermore, is attained by the Greek dramatist, as by the Greek artist, in the use of legendary subjects as the framework of his creations. It was as a result of this perspective that Greek drama and Greek art achieved a universality which makes them as interesting and significant today as they were when they were first produced.

In accounting for the use of these subjects to the exclusion of all others and for their unfailing popularity in Greek drama as in other types of Greek poetry and art, one must not overlook the peculiar excellence of Greek legend and myth. A colorful and glorious past was blended with productive imagination to form a result far superior to Hebraic or Germanic myth and legend. The gods of Greek mythology were the most thoroughly human gods—and therefore the most interesting—that man has ever conceived. Even a lively sense of humor is possessed by these gods and their devotees, as may be seen in Homer's tale of Ares and Aphrodite (*Odyssey* 8. 266–366) and in Aristophanes' portrayal of Dionysus himself, the patron divinity of drama, as a cowardly and effeminate debauchee. This portrayal in the *Frogs* had not the slightest tinge of sacrilege in the eyes of the original audience, first, because Aristophanes was only joking and, secondly, because Dionysus was popularly conceived as actually an effeminate debauchee. The heroes and heroines of Greek myth and legend, furthermore, are free from the artificiality and affectation which often characterize other legend; they are invariably human, with human faults as well as human virtues, and with faults and virtues combined in thoroughly human proportions.

The origin and the original significance of the legends or myths are matters of great interest only to students of folklore and religion. To students of Greek drama these speculations are of no more concern than they were to the Greek dramatists themselves. Some critics, however, have failed to realize the poet's artistic purposes and results in the use of legends. Fundamental misinterpretations have resulted. Thus many plays of Euripides have been misinterpreted as covert satires on popular religion.[12] Explanations of contemporary cults and history, it is true, frequently occupy an important place in Greek tragedy. In the *Eumenides* of Aeschylus, for instance, the fate of Orestes, which should be the main subject of the play, becomes subordinated to the portrayal of Athena and the glorification of Attica. Even in the *Bacchae* of Euripides, however, the dramatist seems to be little concerned with contemporary popular religion, and any attempt to find there the primitive Dionysiac ritual or a "heartfelt glorification of 'Dionysus' " seems futile.[13] The *Bacchae,* like other Greek tragedies, seems to have been written primarily not for religious but for dramatic purposes.

A natural consequence of the use of plots taken from legend or history is the continual reworking of the same subjects by various dramatists. Even today, in spite of modern copyright laws, one play about Lincoln or Elizabeth, if successful, is likely to be followed by another. Reworking the same subject was even more natural in Athens of the fifth century, where a given play was normally performed only once. Obviously Aeschylus was not deterred from writing a play on the defeat of the Persians at Salamis by the mere fact that Phrynichus had already written on this subject. Such a subject from history and legend is a national and not a personal possession.

The dramatists were fond of reinterpreting even the most famous stories and of improving upon the technique of earlier plays. Each of the three great tragic poets dramatized the story of Orestes slaying his mother, and fortunately all three plays are extant. The deception employed in the actual slaughter differs somewhat in each, and clever intrigue of this sort—the vengeance of Odysseus is the classic example —never failed to arouse the keen interest of a Greek audience. Other important variations in these same plays are found in the characterizations. The actions of Orestes are essentially the same in each, but his character is very different. His secondary motivations, his attitude toward the slaying of his mother, and especially the effect of this act upon his mind—all these are significantly varied. Even more important than the psychology of the characters concerned, but inextricably bound in with it, is the final judgment of the author on the moral problem. Aeschylus concludes that Orestes has done a necessary but very dreadful deed; Euripides, that he has done a very dreadful deed which never should have been committed; Sophocles, that Orestes has done a glorious deed. Nor did these three plays exhaust the possibilities of this subject, as we may see from the fragmentary remains of still other versions.[14]

Open criticism of the signs by which Orestes is recognized in the *Choephoroe* of Aeschylus, furthermore, is found in the *Electra* of Euripides (527–44). The younger poet obviously thought that he was improving the technique of the older one. Neophron in his *Medea,* to cite another example, was probably criticizing and improving upon Euripides when he motivated the appearance of Aegeus much better than Euripides had done. Plays were often heavily indebted to previous ones on the same theme, and a very few changes were sufficient to avoid the stigma of plagiarism.

This reworking of the same plots was not, however, a process which could profitably be continued indefinitely.[15] Three such masters as Aeschylus, Sophocles, and Euripides left little room for improvement. Technical evolution practically ceased with Sophocles, and evolution of character treatment and philosophical outlook with Euripides. Agathon, it is true, showed signs of real originality, and it was very unfortunate for the development of the drama that his innovation of writing an entirely fictional tragedy did not introduce a new era, also that his use of interlude choral songs unconnected with the theme of the play did not lead to an early abandonment of the chorus in tragedy.[16] The Roman dramatists at times employed subjects taken from history and from contemporary events but never with any noteworthy success. Tragedy as great literature in ancient times began with Aeschylus and died with Euripides and Sophocles, and the legendary subjects that were in part responsible for its greatness were in part responsible for its atrophy and death.

METER AND MUSIC

With the exception of some occasional lines of prose in Aristophanes, all ancient tragedy and comedy are written in verse. The dramatic scenes of tragedy are almost invariably written in the simplest of all Greek meters and the one most closely approaching natural conversation, the six-foot iambic verse technically known as iambic trimeter.[17] This verse was spoken without musical accompaniment of any kind; and it corresponds roughly to blank verse in English, though all Greek verse is quantitative and not accentual. Presuming that the reader cannot pronounce Greek, we may quote an iambic line from a lost Latin tragedy by Ennius, marking off the feet by vertical lines:

Exsúr|ge, praé|co; fác| populo aú|dién|tiám.[18]

The first foot, it will be noted, is not a pure iamb—for an iamb is a short syllable followed by a long one—but a spondee, two long syllables. Such substitution, though "irrational" because it should lengthen the time taken for pronunciation, is extremely common in all iambic verse —commoner in Latin than in Greek, where it is allowed only in the odd feet of this verse. Spondees retard the measure and make a weighty and dignified line. The fourth foot of this verse from Ennius is neither an iamb nor a spondee but a cyclic anapest, or two short syllables in the same word followed by one long syllable (the final vowel of *populo* is elided). This substitution, in which one long syllable of the irrational spondee has been "resolved" into two short syllables, tends to accelerate the measure. An "apparent" dactyl or one long syllable followed by two short syllables may also be substituted as another resolution of an irrational spondee; this, too, accelerates the measure. It is of a somewhat gayer tone than the anapest. Lastly the long syllable of a pure iamb itself may be resolved into two short syllables. The resultant foot of three short syllables is called a tribrach, a light and rapid foot.

Resolutions tend to make the verse less formal and dignified. A comparison of the frequency of such resolutions, therefore, gives some idea of the formality or informality of the spoken verse of the several dramatists. Sophocles and Aeschylus are both extremely severe in this regard, though the *Philoctetes* shows a marked relaxation. Euripides, however, began with the same type of severity, which is exhibited in the *Alcestis,* the *Medea,* the *Heracleidae,* and the *Hippolytus;* but he soon entered upon a steady development of relaxation.[19] The informality of his later iambic verse approaches that of Aristophanes and Menander, though there are still various licenses admitted in comedy which are infrequent or wholly lacking in tragic verse. Euripides' development toward a more informal verse is vaguely comparable to the development of Shakespeare.

On occasion, the iambic trimeter may yield to some other meter. So at moments of great excitement, it may be replaced by trochaic lines of seven and one-half feet (tetrameter catalectic). From the same play of Ennius:

Mále vo|léntes | fámam | tóllunt, | béne vo|léntes | glóri|ám.[20]

This excited, "dancing" meter was the measure of satyric tragedy.[21] It was not normally spoken but was delivered as recitative, at least sometimes accompanied by the flute. In general, it admits the same resolutions and substitutions as the iambic trimeter; but it never resembles natural conversation. This verse is frequently used in early tragedy, and it re-emerges in the later plays of Euripides and Sophocles. It is naturally well adapted to Latin. Plautus and apparently his contemporary Ennius used it more frequently than any other verse, including the iambic trimeter itself.

The purpose of this trochaic verse in tragedy is to emphasize excitement. Thus in the *Agamemnon* of Aeschylus, when the tension rises to such a pitch of excitement that both Aegisthus and the chorus decide to resort to arms, there is a shift to this meter. Again, it is effectively used in Sophocles' *Philoctetes* (1402–8) and repeatedly in Euripides' *Iphigenia at Aulis*. This meter, though occurring at the end of *Oedipus the King,* is almost wholly absent from the masterpieces of the most severe period of Sophocles and Euripides. Perhaps it was then felt to be too sensational for tragedy.

Another meter delivered as recitative, the anapestic, is frequent in tragedy. Thus in the alternate dialogue opening of the *Iphigenia at Aulis,* anapestic recitative is employed to give a more spirited and poetic opening to the play. Primarily, however, this is a marching meter.

The lyric meters employed in the choral songs are so elaborate that no attempt will here be made to explain them. Suffice it to say that they are very subtly adapted to produce whatever mood and atmosphere the poet wishes for a given situation. That the audience responded to the mood of the music is attested by ancient writers.[22] The lyre or the double flute was used for accompaniment.[23]

Most choral songs are responsive; that is, a series of lines, constituting the "strophe," is followed by a second series precisely equivalent metrically to the former and constituting the "antistrophe." Such a responsive lyric is termed a complete choral song or "stasimon." During such a song the chorus went through certain dance figures or movements, which took in the whole body and especially the hands.[24]

Occasionally the chorus use anapests or a short lyric that is not responsive. Frequently they join with a character in a lyric exchange or "kommos," and this, too, is usually constructed in a responsive series. Also a character may sing a monody, which may or may not be responsive. The considerations governing the choice of these various forms and their functions are best discussed in connection with the chorus and the structure of episodes. Suffice it here to say that none of these forms is called a stasimon.

STRUCTURE OF TRAGEDY

Greek tragedies vary so greatly in subject material that their plots cannot, of course, be reduced to a single basic type. *Oedipus the King* is often taken as a typical play; but actually this play, having a plot of tragic discovery, is very unusual. The plot of tragic decision is much more frequent and can be reduced to features that are typical of many plays. The opening situation is crucial and ominous but not absolutely hopeless.[25] The main tragic character is determined upon a certain course of action. Thus Pentheus in Euripides' *Bacchae* is determined to stamp out the worship of Dionysus. In the early episodes of the play various characters bring pressure upon this main person in an effort to dislodge him from his determination and so avert the tragedy. These scenes usually build up to an emotional climax at which by word or overt act the main character carries into effect his fatal determination, and his downfall immediately follows. Pentheus calls out his armed forces against the worshipers, and Dionysus drives him mad. The remaining scenes often begin with a messenger's report of the catastrophe. A lyric exchange or "kommos" between the chorus and an important character may follow, and a final scene may evaluate the main character and dwell upon his ruin.

Prologos.—The two earliest extant plays of Aeschylus, the *Suppliants* and the *Persians,* have no introductory scene or "prologos" but begin immediately with the entrance of the chorus or "parodos." That was probably the original type of opening; but even the play of Phrynichus after which Aeschylus modeled his *Persians* began with an iambic monologue by one of the characters. Almost all later tragedies begin with an iambic scene, which may be either a monologue or a dialogue. Thus the play, as the iambic meter indicates, began on a low emotional note.

In content, of course, this first scene or prologos is devoted mainly to exposition; but portrayal of character also is often an important consideration here, especially in Sophocles, and the action of the plot may be initiated during this section. In *Oedipus the King*, for instance, action begins here with the arrival of Creon.

Parodos.—The prologos is followed by the entrance of the chorus or parodos. The chorus may enter chanting anapests, but they usually begin immediately with their first lyric. This varies in length from twenty to some two hundred lines, according to the period of the play and to the effect which the poet wishes to produce. In general the first choral lyric normally gives further expositional background and strikes the proper emotional tone. Indeed this song may often be termed the emotional exposition of the play.

Episodes.—After the parodos there follows another section in spoken iambic verse or an episode. The first episode is normally concerned with the beginning of the action and the complication of the plot. This episode is usually followed by another complete choral song, the first "stasimon," after which, of course, another episode occurs. Thus the choral songs interrupt the dramatic action and mark off the tragedy into various "chapters" of action.

The number of these chapters of action varies from play to play. The *Oedipus the King* has six such chapters: the prologos, four episodes (only those sections coming between whole choral songs are called episodes), and the exodos or final section. Most of the extant plays of Aeschylus have five chapters of action. Eventually it became customary, perhaps by the time of Menander and certainly before the time of Seneca, to limit the number to five—the origin of the later rule of five acts.[26]

The relation of the plot structure to these formal chapters of action also varies, and its details are most profitably studied in connection with a given play such as the *Oedipus the King* or the *Bacchae*. In the detailed discussions of these two plays, the formal chapters of action have been noted. So have they been also in the discussions of certain other plays formally typical of their genres and of their periods, especially Aristophanes' *Wasps*, Menander's *Arbitration*, Plautus' *Captives*, and Seneca's *Phaedra*. Still, some generalizations have already been made concerning Greek tragedy, and a few others can be added. The episodes are artistically constructed usually as distinct phases of the action. No consistent effort is made to have them, like acts in a modern play, end in a climax. The climax of a Greek tragedy often comes well within a section, as the climax at verse 810 in the *Bacchae*. But a special emphasis inevitably attaches itself to the ending of each episode, and the poet is careful to exploit this emphasis by having the final note significant in view of the past action or suggestive of the future.

The peripety, or the reversal of fortune, normally occurs not in the final section of the play but in the episode preceding the last complete choral song. This gives the chorus an opportunity to comment on the tragedy and allows the play to end on a low emotional pitch befitting finality.

The division of the play into episodes sharply marked off by choral songs is sometimes artistically inadvisable. But relief from the monotony of the iambic lines is apparently demanded in all Attic drama, and in tragedy emotional relief from harrowing action is sometimes advisable. Lyrics may not be dispensed with, therefore, but various other manners of inserting them may be employed. The strophe of a choral lyric may be immediately followed not by the antistrophe but by a series of iambic lines spoken by one or more characters. When the antistrophe finally does occur, it too is followed by a similar series of iambic lines. (The relative position of the iambic lines may be reversed, one series occurring before the strophe and another before the antistrophe.) This type of construction occurs in the earliest extant plays, and some scholars assume that it is the original type: the chorus sings, the actor responds.[27] This is characteristic of the first part of an Aristophanic comedy; it is found in an early satyr-play of Sophocles (the *Ichneutae*), fragments of which have recently been discovered; it also re-emerges in various tragedies. The effect of this construction is obvious: the choral lyrics do not mark off chapters of action but play an intimate accompaniment for the spoken lines, and thus they bind rather than interrupt the action.

A simple and clear example of this type of construction, which may be termed composition with interlarded lyrics (epirrhematic), occurs in the *Philoctetes*. After the entrance song of the chorus, there is only one complete and uninterrupted choral song in the remainder of the play (676–729). The action of this play of intrigue must be rapid and intense; hence only one real break is allowed, coming at the center of the play. The first long section of action (219–675) is here maintained by means of composition with interlarded lyrics.

In the second half of the *Philoctetes*, still another type of construction is used. Instead of allowing complete choral songs, lyric exchanges between a character and the chorus, or "kommoi" (singular, "kommos"), relieve the monotony of the iambic scenes without interrupting the exciting tension. Thus when Philoctetes faints, there is a lyric exchange between the chorus and Neoptolemus. Although the few lines of Neoptolemus here are merely chanted dactylic hexameters, the words of the chorus (after a short invocation to Sleep) are addressed directly to Neoptolemus, who obviously retains the spotlight of interest. Later

Philoctetes himself indulges in a much longer and truly lyric kommos (1081–1217).

From the standpoint of dramatic technique, these lyric exchanges perform much the same function as the interlarded construction. They not only avoid too sharp a break in the development of an action which the poet wishes to be continuous, but also—and this is perhaps even more important—allow a character of the drama to retain the center of the "stage" rather than yield his position and importance to the chorus.

Lyric monodies or duets have these same dramatic advantages and give even more prominence to the actors at the expense of the chorus. Thus the first two-thirds of the *Iphigenia at Aulis* contain four complete responsive choral songs, while the final third, at least in its present state, contains none. Instead, Iphigenia, the center of the dramatic interest, is here given two monodies. As she makes her final exit, she exchanges a very few lyric lines with the chorus, and after she has gone the chorus continues for a brief period; but as long as Iphigenia remains she commands the interest of the audience unchallenged.

Exodos.—The section after the last stasimon is called the "exodos." Two characteristic features here are especially noteworthy, the messenger's speech—though this may occur in earlier sections of the play— and the *deus ex machina.*

The messenger first appears in the *Persians* of Aeschylus, where he magnificently describes the battle of Salamis. Such an event obviously must, in any theater, be described rather than portrayed. The awkwardness of changing scene in the Greek theater, the paucity of actors there used, the simplicity of presentation in an open theater without curtain or shadows, and frequently the indispensability of supernatural phenomena in the legends dramatized all made the messenger's speech an extremely important technical device. But an artistic *raison d'être*, also, explains the retention of this device throughout Greek tragedy. During the fifth century the Athenians were just awakening to the beauty and utility of rhetorical composition—a discipline of the utmost importance in the courts and deliberating bodies of any democracy, especially a pure rather than a representative democracy. The many debates in Greek drama reflect this interest. The Athenian audience, therefore, was predisposed to the sympathetic reception of long, elaborate, and forceful speeches. Indeed any audience would be enthralled by Aeschylus' description of Salamis or Euripides' description of the fate of Pentheus in the *Bacchae,* for these are masterly compositions.

At the end of a Greek tragedy, especially one of Euripides, a divinity may appear.[28] The actor taking this role was brought on perhaps supported by some mechanical device high above the heads of the chorus and other characters. This *deus ex machina,* as it is called, may on rare occasion solve a plot that otherwise seems impossible of solution. This is the case in Euripides' *Orestes.* But the god is not brought in primarily to furnish a solution in his *Iphigenia in Tauris* or in Sophocles' *Philoctetes,* for in these plays the author by slightly changing the final scenes could wholly dispense with the *deus ex machina.* The reasons for employing the device in these instances are best included in the detailed consideration of each of these plays. In general, however, it may be said that the *deus ex machina* is employed primarily not to bring about or materially affect the solution of the plot but to produce other effects. Often the poet wishes to foretell the future of the characters, at times to point out the relationship between the events of the play and the customs of Attica. This can be done directly only by one with supernatural knowledge. A deity, furthermore, can explain or interpret the action with an authority far beyond that of the chorus. In plays like the *Hippolytus* or the *Bacchae,* deities are concerned in the action and divine explanation is of the utmost importance for the theme. Deities can also place the seal of utter finality and divine approval upon the solution of a play. Lastly, the appearance of a deity makes a highly spectacular closing tableau.

CERTAIN FEATURES OF DRAMATIC METHOD

Functions of the chorus.—Tragedy is said to have developed out of the dithyrambic chorus of fifty members, and in the earliest of all extant dramas, the *Suppliants* of Aeschylus, the chorus actually consists of fifty persons.[29] The number fifty is quite natural in this particular play, however, since its plot is concerned with the fate of the fifty daughters of Danaus. In the subsequent plays of Aeschylus the chorus was reduced to twelve members, but Sophocles increased this number to fifteen. Masks were worn by the chorus as well as by the actors, but the heroic costumes of the actors sharply contrasted with the simple Athenian dress of the chorus.[30] The movements of the chorus during their lyrics have been mentioned in connection with meter and music. During the dialogue scenes they stood in various formations in the orchestra, where the actors, too, normally took their positions.[31]

The individuals of the chorus were ordinary Athenian citizens, and many choruses were trained and exhibited each year. The dithyrambic choruses alone at each City Dionysia contained five hundred members. Even though the dramatic choruses, at least in the time of Aristotle (*Politics* 3. 3 [1276 b]), had a more professional aspect, the same individuals often appearing in both comic and tragic choruses, still choral performances constituted a truly national art at Athens. A considerable number of spectators in every audience, therefore, must at some time in their lives have participated in such performances, and this excellent training of large numbers of citizens doubtless contributed in no small degree to the surprisingly keen appreciation of the Athenian audience. Since without such an audience Greek drama could never have achieved its great heights, this training should perhaps be listed as the first important though indirect contribution of the chorus to drama.[32]

Greek tragedy, originating from the chorus, always remained something more than a purely dramatic presentation. Elements of the modern opera and of the ballet are inherent in the chorus. Their lyrics and choral dancing, accompanied by the lyre or flute, made contributions which have no counterpart in our own contemporary drama. Greek tragedy cannot, therefore, be judged wholly by dramatic criteria.

Poetic beauty was the chief contribution of the tragic chorus and one of the glories of the Greek genius. Approximately one-half of the *Suppliants* of Aeschylus consists of choral lyrics; but in subsequent plays this proportion was soon reduced to about one-fourth or less. Although the beauty of these lyrics is mutilated and dimmed even in the best translations, it cannot be wholly obscured; and the modern reader who wishes to approach Greek tragedy from the Athenian point of view must attempt to appreciate the beauty of the choral songs and to understand their relationship to the dramatic action. The original audience consciously appreciated this poetry, and their reception of the dramatic action, consciously or unconsciously, was profoundly affected by it.

These choral songs may build up tragic atmosphere, as they do so effectively in the *Agamemnon* of Aeschylus, or they may otherwise modulate the tone of the play. Frequently they bring a poetic relief from overcharged emotions. Such relief is at once harmonious with the dignity of Greek tragedy and in accordance with that consistency of tone and style which played such an important role in all Greek literature and art.[33]

These are the chief poetic effects of the choral songs, and choral drama is seen at its peculiar best when these effects are of the greatest importance as in the *Agamemnon* or in Euripides' *Trojan Women* or *Bacchae*. In these plays an atmosphere is created and a poetic effect produced which is quite beyond the reach of realistic prose drama.

In content, the choral lyrics usually have a significance directly pertinent to their dramatic context. They regularly generalize the particular events and interpret the action of the play as the poet would have it interpreted.[34] Thus in the *Oedipus,* after Oedipus has insolently quarreled with Creon and after Oedipus and Jocasta have expressed skepticism of oracles and have discussed incest and murder, the chorus in their following lyrics pray for reverent purity in word and deed, condemning insolence and skepticism and sacrilege. Also in the final lines of the play, which are sometimes considered spurious, the chorus reiterates the old Greek maxim that no man should be judged fortunate until he has finished his life in happiness, thus emphasizing the irony of fate—perhaps the fundamental theme of the play. It is owing to these functions that the chorus has often been called the poet's ideal spectator of the play. Since the chorus is usually composed of ordinary good citizens, it is well fitted to fill this role. As ordinary good citizens the chorus may be called the social background of the action also, and this background is all the more desirable since the main characters of a Greek tragedy are invariably figures of high station. Social background, furthermore, is an essential feature in many plays. In the *Agamemnon* the popular resentment over the heavy toll of life which the war has taken and the resultant popular hatred of Agamemnon must be brought out. In the plays dealing with the vengeance of Orestes, likewise, the hatred and contempt of the people for their murderous and lecherous rulers must be depicted. The historical background of the action, also, may be furnished by the chorus. Accordingly, in the *Phoenissae* of Euripides, the choral songs emphasize the early history of Thebes and the house of Oedipus, for the poet wishes the play to cover not merely the quarrel of the sons but the complete saga. In accordance with this role of the social or historical background, the chorus usually lacks distinctive, personalized character.

Sometimes the chorus has a very definite character, however, and interprets the action from its own peculiar point of view. In the *Bacchae* of Euripides, for instance, the chorus consists of devotees of Bacchus. They exalt Bacchus and condemn Pentheus with a passionate fervor that should not be mistaken for the poet's own feelings. At the other extreme, the chorus may drop all pretense of characterization and dramatic illusion to express philosophical or political ideas which are obviously those of the poet himself. This was a regular practice in the informality of Old Comedy; but in tragedy, too, it is occasionally found. One of the most obvious examples of such a lapse in the dramatic illusion, noted even in ancient times, is the famous chorus on Necessity in the *Alcestis* (962–83), where the speaker is clearly the philosophical Euripides and not the group of simple Thessalian elders who constitute the chorus. But there is no certain criterion for deter-

mining when the chorus is speaking in character and when it is expressing the views of the poet.

It is obvious that the characterization of the chorus, therefore, was
much less formal and consistent than the characterization of the individual roles of the play. This dramatic license is observable in all periods of Greek tragedy, and it is particularly noticeable in certain plays.
In the *Agamemnon,* for instance, the chorus in their opening songs
have the pathos and profundity of Aeschylus himself; but again, as in
their scene with Cassandra, they are almost stupid. When the cries of
the stricken Agamemnon are heard behind the scenes, the chorus com-
prises twelve pitifully ineffectual old men; but when they are insulted
by Aegisthus, they apparently seize their arms and are ready to risk
their lives in opposing him. So inconsistent is the character of the
chorus. But rash indeed would be the critic who would have the role
of the chorus changed in any of these scenes in the *Agamemnon* merely
to maintain consistency. Here in each scene they have precisely that
character which makes the scene artistically most effective. Since the
chorus have little or no bearing upon determining the action of the plot,
there is not much more necessity for them to maintain a consistent
character—except that they are animate beings—than there is for maintaining the same backdrop in a modern play or the same lighting effects
throughout. Still, in most tragedies the changes of the chorus are slight
and inconspicuous.

The comparison of the chorus to a backdrop or to lighting effects
is not so impertinent as it may at first seem, for the chorus frequently
serves as the chief character's accompaniment or foil. Its composition,
indeed, is usually determined by a consideration of the chief character.
If this character is a woman, the chorus normally represents women
(although actual performers of all female roles in tragedy and comedy
were men). Still, many exceptions to this rule are introduced for
artistic effect. In the *Agamemnon,* Clytemnestra, of course, carries
the leading role from a dramatic point of view; but, since this specific
character calls for a foil rather than for a support, and since the fate
of Agamemnon is the center of interest in the play, the chorus consists
of men. Again, in the *Antigone* and in the *Bacchae,* the leading character is deliberately isolated from sympathy and support, and so the
chorus is made up of the opposite sex. The composition of the chorus
in still other plays may be determined by the nature of the action. Thus
in the *Iphigenia in Tauris,* the chorus must be thoroughly devoted to
Iphigenia, since she plans and executes an intrigue against the king of
the land in their presence.

The continuous presence of the chorus entailed certain disadvan-

tages and limitations, and these became more and more obvious as
tragedy developed from an essentially lyric to an essentially dramatic
form and as its subject matter was broadened to include intrigue and
intimate action. In the *Hippolytus,* for instance, the chorus could save
the life of Hippolytus and the future of Theseus by revealing the truth,
but they do not do so. The situation is somewhat mitigated by their
previous oath of silence and by the conventional passivity of the chorus.
In the *Agamemnon* and in the *Heracles* the choruses are wholly unable
to prevent dreadful crimes from being committed.[35] In both plays they
are represented as in extreme old age. Change of scene and passage of
time, also, as the discussion of the unities below will reveal, were hindered by the presence of the chorus.

The continuous presence of the chorus did impose obvious limitations; but the Greek tragic poets showed great ingenuity in circum-
venting these and in exploiting the chorus in innumerable ways. The
chorus is almost invariably so constituted that it has reason to be keenly
interested in the outcome of the drama. Sometimes, as in the *Suppliants* of Aeschylus and the *Suppliants* of Euripides, the chorus is the
leading character, and the action concerns its fate. But even in these
plays, the chorus tends to be passive rather than active. In the *Eumenides,* however, the chorus plays a leading and very active role. In the
other tragedies, the chorus does not play a leading role and is not normally concerned with forwarding the dramatic action. There are exceptions. In the *Choephoroe* of Aeschylus the chorus persuade the old
Nurse, who has been sent to fetch Aegisthus with his guard, to change
the message and summon Aegisthus alone and unprotected. In the *Ion*
of Euripides the chorus of female slaves have been strictly charged by
their master to keep a secret which has been revealed in their presence.
Such a charge is a conventional device in plays of intrigue and is almost
invariably honored. But here, though the charge has been reinforced
with a threat of death, the slaves are true women and more loyal to
mistress than to master. They reveal this secret to her, and she immediately acts upon their information.

The incidental dramatic functions of the chorus are many and various. The earliest one was to play the role of an interlocutor for the
actor present. This function, we assume, was performed by the leader
of the chorus, the "coryphaeus," who alone, it seems, spoke the iambic
lines assigned to the chorus. Obviously it is more dramatic for an actor
to address an informative speech ostensibly to the chorus rather than
directly to the audience. This function of interlocutor was retained
throughout the history of Greek tragedy, although there is a tendency
in the later plays of Euripides to reduce the importance of the chorus

in this as in other respects. Asides, furthermore, are almost unknown in
Greek tragedy—perhaps the best examples are in the *Hecuba* (736–51)
—although in later comedy, when the chorus no longer was present
continuously, asides became very common and doubtless seemed quite
natural in the huge ancient theater.

The chorus regularly introduces a character entering the scene for
the first time—a natural function, since in the Greek theater an entering character would presumably pass near some members of the chorus
before approaching the other characters present. Some form of introduction was usually necessary, furthermore, because there were no
handbills to aid in identifying new characters, though the use of distinctive masks and costumes, as in the case of a messenger, might furnish sufficient identification. At this introduction of an entering character, even if it was made by the coryphaeus alone, the whole chorus
probably turned toward the new character, thus focusing the attention
of the theater upon him. Similarly, when two or more characters were
on stage, the chorus might focus on one to the exclusion of the others.[86]

The chorus, often with intuition approaching clairvoyance, may
relate action that is taking place at the same time "off stage." So in the
Bacchae, when Dionysus leads Pentheus out to Mount Cithaeron to
destroy him, the chorus enthusiastically sings of Pentheus' mother discovering him and mistaking him for a mountain lion—as she actually
does.

Periods during which no actor is present are effectively taken up by
choral songs. Thus time is allowed for the accomplishment of action
"off stage" and for the actors' changes of costume in order to assume
different roles.

As a summary of the dramatic functions of the chorus, we may
quote the generalizations of the best Greek practices which Horace
makes in his *Ars Poetica* (193–201):

Let the chorus take the part of an actor and uphold the duty of a man
and not sing mere interludes which have no contribution for or close connection with the subject of the plot. Let it both favor the good and counsel
them as a friend; let it check him who is quick to wrath and love the man
who fears to sin; let it commend the simple way of life, wholesome justice
and decrees, and peaceful security; let it keep the secrets committed to it,
and let it beseech the gods that Fortune return to the wretched and depart
from the proud.

In certain of the later plays of Sophocles and Euripides the role of
the chorus is notably reduced. Sophocles tends to develop it into a
minor supporting character, as in the *Philoctetes.* Euripides is inclined
to detach it from the action and develop a mere interlude. One of the

earliest occurrences of an interlude lyric is found in the *Iphigenia in Tauris* at the point where Iphigenia, having deceived the king, takes her brother and Pylades down to the sea to make their escape. The other most frequently cited interlude lyric occurs in the *Helen*. These two plays have practically the same plot, and the remarkable point here is that the interlude lyric in each play occurs precisely at its climax.[37] Critics have overlooked this fact and accredited the use of interlude lyrics to mere carelessness or Euripidean perversity. But at least in these early instances the poet has been keener than his critics, possibly including Aristotle; for the use of an impertinent interlude at the climax of these melodramatic plays apparently is designed to avoid jeopardizing the suspense at this point and closely resembles the modern practice of reaching the climax immediately before an intermission—at the very end of the second act in a modern play of three acts. Such interlude lyrics in Euripides clearly resemble an intermission.

Euripides' younger contemporary, Agathon, according to the frowning Aristotle (*Poet.* 1456 a), was the first to introduce the practice of employing interlude lyrics which have nothing to do with the dramatic context. Some scholars think that Agathon, like the writers of comedy in the fourth century, may have been content merely to indicate in his text the places where interludes should be inserted.[38] It seems probable from certain papyrus fragments that this practice was followed occasionally by later writers of tragedy.[39] But, if we may judge from the scanty evidence and from Seneca, tragedy as a rule did not develop beyond the stage of an unhappy compromise between a pertinent and an interlude chorus.

The interlude was a necessary development, of course, before the chorus could be entirely eliminated. It nevertheless constituted an awkward stage in the transition of drama, since any interlude is obviously a distraction and a blemish from the artistic point of view. It was severely criticized by Aristotle and other theorists. But the critics should have realized that choral drama, though it had made one of the most brilliantly successful displays that the theater has ever seen, by the end of the fifth century had run its natural course.

Trilogy.—In the time of Aeschylus, it seems to have been the normal practice for the poet to write his required three tragedies all on the same subject. Such a series of three plays is termed a trilogy. Only one complete trilogy has been preserved, the trilogy on Orestes (*Oresteia*) of Aeschylus. The first play concerns the return of Agamemnon from Troy and his murder by Clytemnestra, the second the vengeance which his son Orestes took on his own mother and her accomplice, and the third the final purification of Orestes. The first play of this trilogy is often considered the greatest of all Greek dramas. During this period a satyr-play apparently always followed the three tragedies, and if its subject had a connection with the same legend the whole four plays constituted a tetralogy. The satyr-play which followed this trilogy of Aeschylus has not been preserved; but we know that its title was *Proteus,* and it was doubtless a parody of Menelaus' experiences with Proteus as related in the *Odyssey* (4. 351–570), just as Euripides' extant *Cyclops* is a parody of Odysseus' experiences with the Cyclops. The form of the trilogy in certain aspects appears beyond the technical powers of Aeschylus; and, although we may deplore the failure of the trilogy to develop into a grand and complex form resembling a modern play in three acts, we can easily understand why such a development did not take place.

Even in the time of Aeschylus the three tragedies presented on a given day apparently might be written on different subjects. His *Persians* seems to be an example of such a single play. Sophocles, before the period in which his earliest extant plays were written, abandoned the unwieldy and difficult form of the trilogy and turned all his attention to perfecting the single play. Euripides did likewise. When these two men began to produce, dramatists were still struggling with elementary problems of technique. Even the single play, therefore, offered an ample field for development, and its perfection was obviously the immediate task.

Unity of action.—Unity of action exists when nothing included in the play can be omitted and nothing really pertinent to it can be added. It seems to have been the rule of the trilogy as a whole. Each of the three plays of Aeschylus' extant trilogy covers a definite phase of the action, however, and so achieves a partial unity of its own. Each play also has its own chorus. But the solutions of the first and second plays are solutions only of their immediate problems and obviously lead up to the following play. Definite finality is achieved only in the last play. The first play contains very elaborate exposition. The opening scene of the second play is devoted in part to explaining what has happened in the interval between the first and second plays—for several years have elapsed—and in part to foreshadowing the coming action. The third play, also, has its own exposition. But one group of characters, whose fates are closely bound together, and one theme are carried through the whole series. There are no minor plots; and the development of the action is essentially simple, precisely as we should expect in the early period of dramatic activity.

With such a tradition, it is not surprising that Sophocles and Euripides, turning their efforts to perfecting the individual play, normally maintained strict unity of action. By employing an elaborate prologue and an equally elaborate epilogue, which in some cases take the places of what might have been the first and last plays of a trilogy, the poet may still make his play cover an incident of some magnitude. Since a tetralogy and a comedy also, at least in certain periods, seem to have been presented on a single day, the length of each tragedy was necessarily limited.[40] Short as each was, a large portion of it was devoted to choral lyrics. Only three actors, furthermore, seem to have been employed in the actual production of a given play. Such external conditions, however, should not be stressed, for they were doubtless maintained because they were harmonious with the artistic purposes of the poet. It was a characteristic of the Greek genius to be as conservative with artistic means as possible. Simple unity of form and its resultant emphasis of purpose, furthermore, were perhaps the most effective achievements of Periclean art and literature. But at least there was no external pressure upon the dramatist for expansion of the single play. Such pressure has been present in the Renaissance and in the modern theater, where dramas are required to be perhaps twice as long as the dramatic scenes of the average Greek play. Modern dramatists have frequently complained of this pressure. Noteworthy are Voltaire's remarks in his *Oedipe*;[41] and in the preface to the *Oedipus* of Dryden and Lee (edition of Walter Scott and George Saintsbury), we read as follows:

. . . . Sophocles, indeed, is admirable everywhere; and therefore we have followed him as close as possibly we could. But the Athenian theatre (whether more perfect than ours, is not now disputed) had a perfection differing from ours. You see there in every act a single scene (or two at most), which manage the business of the play; and after that succeeds the chorus, which commonly takes up more time in singing than there has been employed in speaking. The principal person appears almost constantly through the play; but the inferior parts seldom above once in the whole tragedy. The conduct of our stage is much more difficult, where we are obliged never to lose any considerable character which we have once presented. Custom likewise has obtained that we must form an under-plot of second persons, which must be depending on the first; and their by-walks must be like those in a labyrinth, which all of them lead into the great parterre; or like so many several lodging chambers, which have their outlets into the same gallery. Perhaps, after all, if we could think so, the ancient method, as it is the easiest, is also the most natural, and the best. For variety, as it is managed, is too often subject to breed distraction; and while we would please too many ways, for want of art in the conduct, we please in none . . . .

Unities of time and place.—Greek tragedy, according to Aristotle (*Poet.* 1449 b, Bywater), endeavors to keep as far as possible within a single circuit of the sun, or something near that, although at first the practice in this respect was just the same in tragedies as in epic poems. Within the extant trilogy of Aeschylus, considerable time passes and the scene changes twice. The intermission between plays facilitated these changes just as the intermission between acts does in the modern theater. The whole series of three plays, furthermore, was of a length adequate for such representation of the passage of time. But within a single Greek tragedy, passage of time or change of scene was hindered by lack of an intermission and by the short compass of the play. Even more embarrassing was the continuous presence of the chorus—the one most important external factor. Obviously the scene could not be changed, nor could more than a few hours be supposed to elapse while fifteen men who were an indispensable part of the play remained before the eyes of the audience. The difficulties of indicating a change of scene visually (or conceivably the aesthetic objection to such change without visual indication) may have played a part after tragedy lost its early informality.

This short compass of time imposed a limitation in the type of plot which could be used in the single play. Apparently the Prometheus trilogy of Aeschylus had as its theme the gradual tempering of Prometheus and the gradual enlightenment of Zeus, in other words the gradual evolution of Man and of God. But this process extended over the thousands of years which passed between the first and second plays. A single play, in which the action covers only a few hours, however, obviously could not deal with development of character. Although there may be some basic change of character in the *Alcestis* or in the *Medea*, consistency and stability of character are the rule. Aristotle (*Poet.* 1454 a) insists upon the necessity of consistency and criticizes Euripides' *Iphigenia at Aulis* because to him Iphigenia seems one person when she supplicates her father to spare her life and quite a different person after she has made her heroic decision to die willingly. Certainly unity of time is not conducive to portraying development of character.

The unities of time and place, however, were normally very compatible with the poet's desire for dramatic concentration and with the short and strictly unified action of an individual tragedy. Still, there are a few cases where the scene is changed or where many days pass within a single play. The *Eumenides* of Aeschylus, for instance, opens with two scenes at Delphi; but afterward the chorus leaves the theater in pursuit of Orestes. A vacant scene follows, and then Orestes re-enters with lines which indicate that he is now in Athens. An indefinite period of time has elapsed. In the *Ajax* of Sophocles, also, the chorus withdraws to go in search of Ajax; Ajax re-enters with lines which, in the light of the previous action, indicate that he is now upon the deserted seashore—his suicide seems to require solitude. There are a few other cases where the chorus is withdrawn but no change of scene occurs and no length of time elapses.[42] In later comedy after the chorus has been reduced to a mere interlude and does not remain continuously on the scene, the passage of a night is allowed.[43] These facts clearly show that the dramatists had no great prejudice against a change of scene or the passage of time. The removal of the chorus and the consequent vacant scene, however, were obligatory in such cases, and obvious artistic considerations prevented the development of such an awkward procedure as long as the chorus remained an integral part of the play.

The necessity of allowing intervals for the passage of time during the action is often avoided in Greek tragedy by a device which may be termed double chronology. This was a well-established convention even in the time of Aeschylus. Action which occurs "on stage" goes forward approximately as the play itself. This action often begins about dawn and is completed by dusk or before. But the action which is supposed to occur "off stage" is handled with extreme freedom, especially while a choral lyric is being sung. Thus the *Agamemnon* of Aeschylus opens before dawn on the night when Troy is being taken, but Agamemnon returns from Troy in the course of the play. Again, in the *Suppliants* of Euripides, Theseus leaves the scene (Eleusis) to go to Thebes with all his forces and do battle. After a choral song of only thirty-six lines, a messenger enters and announces the victory of Theseus over the Thebans. By the use of such double chronology, therefore, the Greek dramatists avoid some of the difficulties inherent in the observance of the unity of time.

Still other devices were employed by the dramatists to circumvent the difficulties inherent in the unity of place. The lack of ability to portray an interior scene was made up in part by throwing the wide doors of the palace or temple open and at times by rolling out a platform with an interior tableau upon it. Another device, even more characteristic of Greek tragedy, is the messenger's speech, by which events which could not conveniently be portrayed are related to the chorus and the audience.

Foreknowledge and suspense.—Since Greek tragedy was written on legendary themes, the audience usually had some foreknowledge of the events, and of course the author had to take this foreknowledge into account in composing his play. But Aristotle (*Poet.* 1451 b) observes that even the known stories were known only to a few.[44] A recent comparison between the plays of Seneca and the extant Greek tragedies on the same subjects has conclusively shown that Seneca, writing for a highly educated and sophisticated audience, took for granted a detailed knowledge of the legends, whereas the Greek plays are usually self-contained and intelligible to the most uninformed spectator.[45] The modern reader also finds himself going to the mythological dictionary much more frequently when he is reading Seneca. In order that the whole audience may view the play with precisely the same degree of enlightenment, the Greek poet usually restates the basic facts of the legend as he has accepted it for his present play, and then he constructs the action so as to exploit as fully as possible this foreknowledge.

The Greek dramatist had at his disposal means of imparting foreknowledge that our own contemporary dramatists can hardly employ —divinities, oracles, and the supernatural. The personal appearance of a god, such as Apollo in the *Alcestis,* was offensive neither to the believer nor to the skeptic. The believer still regularly consulted oracles, as did practically all Greek states, with the conviction that thus he might discover the will of the gods, although even the believer in Athens of the later fifth century expended his most ardent worship not on Apollo and Dionysus but on the mystery cults at Eleusis. The skeptic viewed the divinities of the theater primarily as poetic abstractions of basic forces of nature. For both believer and skeptic, divinities and oracles and the supernatural were firmly established by a long and glorious poetic tradition, ingrained in the Greek character by the use of the Homeric poems as the basis of all education. For both believer and skeptic, the use of such divinities lent an Olympic grandeur and dignity to the play. With regard to the special effects which such a framework might achieve for a composition, we may note that the divinities in the *Hippolytus* help to relieve Phaedra of the onus which she would normally bear and that they impart a lofty cosmic significance to what otherwise would be a sordid story. It was the skeptic Euripides who made the freest use of divinities to open and close his plays, and we may be sure that he did so primarily because of the poetic and artistic effects which divinities alone made possible.

Aeschylus and Sophocles were no skeptics. But it was doubtless for the theatrical effect and not because of belief in the supernatural that Aeschylus brought the ghost of Darius on stage in the *Persians.* Aristophanes attests the power of this effect upon the audience (*Frogs* 1028). Every extant play of Sophocles contains one or more oracles or prophecies, but none of these is cited that does not make an important contribution to the drama. When it is reported in the *Ajax* that, according to Calchas, Ajax will be saved if he survives this day, the climactic emergency of the situation receives a powerful emphasis. Similar is the oracle at the opening of the *Trachiniae*. The use of oracles in the *Oedipus* for purposes of dramatic irony—they are also an essential part of the legend—is quite different but none the less effective. The supernatural in Greek tragedy is largely a dramatic phenomenon.

Foreknowledge of an action's outcome may have distinct artistic advantages. Elaborate foreshadowing and foretelling are employed in the Homeric poems. The death of Hector is repeatedly foretold in the *Iliad,* as is the death of Patroclus and even that of Achilles. The account of the death of Achilles is not an actual part of the poem, but this foretelling adds a very effective pathos and irony to the final books. Similar to this is the foreshadowing of the divine vengeance to fall upon the Greeks in the prologue of the *Trojan Women* of Euripides. Though this vengeance is not a part of the action of the tragedy, its foreshadowing adds powerful dramatic irony to the triumph of the Greeks.

In the *Alcestis* of Euripides the bringing of Alcestis back to life must be foretold because the author wishes the whole action of the play to be interpreted in the light of this knowledge, without which the spectator would view the first of the play with very different emotions and would consider the solution—Alcestis' return to life—a rude and indecent shock.[46] But, since the outcome is known, dramatic irony—in which the lines or action of a character have one meaning for him or for another character and an additional, more significant meaning for the audience—fills almost every scene of the play. Irony and surprise, of course, tend to be mutually exclusive; for irony depends on knowledge, surprise on ignorance of the true situation or its outcome. The Greek dramatist in his serious plays almost invariably prefers irony, as being the more dignified and the more tragic. The pathetic discrepancy between the intentions which prompt an act and the results of this act, the ironic contrast between man's aspirations and his fate—these things are considered more worthy of the tragic art than the trickery of uncertainty and surprise.[47] An action can be interpreted profoundly and definitively only in the light of its outcome.

Profound interpretation of the action was often the main concern of the Greek dramatist, and it would not have long remained so, we may be sure, unless it was as often the main concern of the original audience. The frequent cases of re-use of the same subjects, such as Orestes' slaying his mother, prove that this was so and nicely illustrate the point that foreknowledge is essential to profound interpretation. In the *Electra* of Euripides or Sophocles the plot is merely the framework of the real tableau which the dramatist wishes to present, and the greater our knowledge of the earlier plays the more significant the later plays will be for us. Indeed, we are quite unable to appreciate the author's profounder meaning unless we know the earlier plays.

A catastrophe is far more tragic, furthermore, if it appears inevitable. To achieve great effectiveness, it must be "a thing foreseen and following with a psychological and moral necessity on the action exhibited in the first part of the tragedy."[48] Hence the Greek dramatist usually preferred that the audience should foresee the outcome.

Direct foretelling in the prologue, however, is not always necessary. The *Agamemnon* of Aeschylus, for instance, has no omniscient prologue; but the story of Agamemnon's return and death, repeatedly contrasted with the prospective return of Odysseus in the *Odyssey,* was one of the best-known stories in Greek legend. Even so, the tragic foreboding of Aeschylus' play is so powerful that the intelligent but uninformed modern reader cannot fail to appreciate the bitter irony of Clytemnestra's speeches. In the *Oedipus,* however, Sophocles omits all foretelling and foreboding and frankly assumes a thorough knowledge of this legend, which was probably universally known to theatergoers in his own day. From the first scene, Sophocles exploits the possibilities of dramatic irony, and the modern reader who does not know the legend is likely to miss some of the most powerful effects of the play.

A certain kind of tension, usually called the suspense of anticipation, is frequently maintained even in a play when the outcome is foretold or already known.[49] In the *Electra* of Euripides, the slaying of Aegisthus and Clytemnestra has been made to appear so difficult and hazardous that initial failure seems quite as likely to result as success. Here suspense is maintained over the means by which the foreseen end is to be reached. In the *Oedipus* no audience could fail to be wholly captivated by the process of discovery. We watch Oedipus pursue the disastrous knowledge with the same dreadful fascination with which, as someone has put it, we might watch a distant man walk over a precipice. Essentially the same tension occurs in the *Agamemnon.*

Perhaps the most effective foretelling of all is partial foretelling, like that in the *Bacchae* of Euripides. Here the god Dionysus speaks the prologue, though he does so more as a character of the play than as an omniscient divinity. Almost the whole of his speech is given over to the usual type of exposition, but at the end he declares that if Pentheus calls out the armed forces of Thebes against his worshipers he, the god, will lead his maenads in battle. There is no omniscience here. Pentheus' decision is left entirely to Pentheus. But the fact that Dionysus is a divinity makes inevitable the defeat of Pentheus if he should decide to resort to arms. When Pentheus makes this decision at the climax of the play, therefore, the audience fully realizes that it involves his destruction.

Varying degrees of suspense are maintained in many plays, however, because the outcome is foreseen only vaguely or because the events of minor issues are wholly uncertain. Variations in the legends and the freedom with which the dramatists introduced major changes encouraged such vagueness or uncertainty. In Euripides' *Medea,* for instance, calamity is unmistakably imminent; but precisely what form it will take, on which heads it will fall most heavily, and what precisely will be the cause and manner of the children's deaths—these are all matters of doubt. This doubt is fostered by the human uncertainty of the Nurse speaking the prologue. The fate of Haemon and the punishment of Creon in the *Antigone* of Sophocles also are matters of doubt, for here, too, genuine uncertainty exists in the legend and in the play. Just how much the dramatist will foreshadow or reveal to the audience beforehand, therefore, depends on the particular legend and on the effects which he hopes to achieve.

Complete uncertainty even over the major issue—as complete, at least, as in similar modern plays—is often maintained in the plays having a happy outcome and written about events that were not well known. Here at last suspense may play a major role. In Euripides' *Iphigenia in Tauris* it seems that anything can happen. The recognition is delayed almost interminably; but no sooner has this cause of suspense been removed than another equally grave difficulty, that of escape, arises to continue the excitement. Even after the escape has apparently been successful, an unfavorable gale blows the ship back to the shore obviously in order to heighten the suspense at the very end of the play to the highest possible degree. The same formula is used in the *Helen.*

In order that the irony of the earlier parts of these melodramatic plays may be fully appreciated, the author has cleverly manipulated the developing action so that the audience may have knowledge superior to that of any one character. An omniscient prologue, then, is not necessary in such plays; but in the *Ion,* a similarly melodramatic play, it is indispensable, for the audience must know what no character or group of characters can tell them—that Ion is the son of Creusa. In New Comedy, hidden identities are regularly explained by an omniscient prologue. But it does not follow from the omniscience of the speaker that all the action is foretold.

Incidentally we may note a characteristic subtlety of Euripides which appears in the prologue of the *Ion.* When Hermes has finished his informative speech, he expresses his intention to withdraw to the dells near at hand in order that he may learn how the fulfillment of Ion's destiny is brought about. The god himself is subject to the suspense of anticipation! Naturally the interest of the god stimulates the interest of the audience.

On occasion, the ancient dramatists achieve effects of suspense comparable to those of modern drama. Indeed, individual scenes of great suspense are frequent in the more melodramatic plays, and the excitement of the Greek audience at such scenes is attested by ancient writers. In discussing the most effective tragic incidents Aristotle says: "But the best of all is . . . . what we have in *Cresphontes,* for example, where Merope, on the point of slaying her son, recognizes him in time; in *Iphigenia* [*in Tauris*], where sister and brother are in a like position; and in *Helle,* where the son recognizes his mother, when on the point of giving her up to her enemy."[50] This scene from the *Cresphontes* of Euripides was still famous a half-millennium later. The play told the story of a wicked usurper who had slain a king and all his children except one, Cresphontes, who had been saved by his mother, Merope, and sent to a distant land. The usurper had forced Merope to become his wife and had promised a reward for the slaying of Cresphontes. Years later a man appears to claim the reward. This man in reality is Cresphontes himself, come to take vengeance upon the usurper; but Merope fails to recognize him as her son and believes his claim of having killed Cresphontes. She determines herself to slay this man in revenge after he has fallen asleep (apparently "on stage"). As Merope advances with an ax to slay him, "What a turmoil she creates in the theater," says Plutarch (*Moralia* 998 E), "terrifying the audience with fear, for they are afraid that she may wound the youth before the old man [who doubtless recognizes the youth as Cresphontes] comes up to stop her." A similar motive is found in the *Ion* of Euripides, and it seems to have been used in various other plays. In a famous scene of the *Telephus,*[51] Telephus seized the infant Orestes and rushed to the altar and threatened to slay him. Naturally every spectator knew that Orestes was not slain as a child; and here, as in the *Ion* and probably in the *Cresphontes,* every experienced theatergoer knew that such slaughter was not perpetrated in the Greek theater before the eyes of the audience (if we may judge from extant plays); but the thrilling suspense of such scenes was not spoiled by any such ratiocinations. The audience was too far carried away to reflect upon the impossibility of the tragic deed's actually being committed. The dramatic illusion has a ruggedness that is not easily shattered.

Double motivation.—In the Homeric poems, any inspiration or idea may be attributed to a divinity, which is often little if any more than a personification of a natural force in life, as Aphrodite is a personification of love and desire. Here, in short, divine and human motivation may be one and the same. It is only by a later development, which also appears in the Homeric poems, that divine motivation is separated from human. Artistic considerations make divine motivation very convenient in many situations. When Odysseus is eating away his heart to leave Calypso and return to Ithaca, for instance, no human motivation for Calypso's sending him away willingly can be given if his reputation for being more than acceptable to any nymph—a reputation carefully cultivated by the poet and essential to any hero—is not to be jeopardized. Nor can the dignified Odysseus merely run off like a fugitive slave. A command of the gods seems to be the only solution, and so a command of the gods is used. Thus divine motivation is used where plausible human motivation is lacking. But divine motivation is often used even where ample human motivation is present. Athena advises Telemachus to go to Pylos in search of news of his father though perfectly human considerations are adequate to motivate this journey; here the divinity adds dignity and authority. This use of a divinity to supplement human motivation may conveniently be called double motivation.

As time went on, the best poets came to feel that divine motivation was legitimate only when supplemented by adequate human motivation.[52] This type almost alone is used in Greek tragedy. Most English readers, however, are best acquainted with it from Vergil's epic, the *Aeneid,* in which it is especially obvious. The artistic advantages of such double motivation are many and are best studied in connection with specific plays such as Euripides' *Hippolytus.* But in reading any Greek play one should be constantly aware that divine motivation, too, is primarily an artistic and not a religious phenomenon.

Absence of violent deeds.—In extant tragedy, two suicides occur before the eyes of the audience: that of Ajax in Sophocles' play of the same name, and that of Evadne in Euripides' *Suppliants.* Certain characters who are already ill or wounded, such as Alcestis and Hippolytus, furthermore, actually expire "on stage." But no character ever slays another before the audience. The explanation for the lack of such violence has been much disputed. The present writer believes that this lack is due primarily to the small number of actors employed and to practical limitations of realistic staging and acting, especially in the early period of tragedy when the conventions were being formed.[53]

Economy of roles.—The state furnished the actors for Greek tragedy; and before Sophocles began producing, perhaps in 468 B.C., only two speaking actors were furnished for a given tetralogy. The Athenian audiences were extremely sensitive to the quality of an actor's voice. Much of Greek tragedy was sung, and good lyric voices then, as now, were extremely rare. Still rarer, if we may judge from modern observation, was the combination of a good voice and an ability to act. Since Greek tragedy, in sharp contrast to modern opera, appealed to the intellect as well as to the senses and emotions, it required such a combination. Doubtless few individuals could be found to meet the requirements. Here as elsewhere, furthermore, the Greeks were extremely economical in their use of artistic means.

But doubtless the chief cause of the dramatists' being limited to three speaking actors lies in the requirements of tragedy itself. If the youthful Sophocles could demand and receive a third actor, surely the idolized author of the *Antigone* could have secured a fourth. Aristophanes sometimes used a fourth actor. But Sophocles and Euripides did not need a fourth, for the possibilities of the simple individual play were far from exhausted. In the *Medea,* for instance, the conflict is a duel between Medea herself and the world, represented by a single adversary, now Creon, now Jason, now Aegeus. A large cast here was not only unnecessary; it would have been artistically ruinous. In various other plays the scenic composition of the actors is striking and significant. In the *Electra* of Sophocles, a triangular scenic composition doubtless emphasized the very different reactions of Clytemnestra and Electra to the eloquent speech of the Paedagogus; and the audience, knowing this speech to be false, is able fully to appreciate the irony of both reactions. In the *Trachiniae,* again, the Messenger and Lichas angrily dispute before Deianeira as each attempts to win credence. Essentially the same triangular situation exists in many "debates" in tragedy. A larger number of speaking characters here would merely obscure significant relationships and obstruct the focusing of attention.

Some tragedies, however, could very conveniently have used another actor, and many plays show slight peculiarities of form due to this limitation.[54] At the close of the fifth century, after the possibilities of the simple play had been fully exploited, Sophocles in his *Oedipus at Colonus* is obviously chafing at this restriction. The last play of Euripides, the *Iphigenia at Aulis,* is also on the verge of demanding another actor. If there had been a genius of the first rank to carry on at this point, and if the defeat and bankruptcy of Athens at this particular moment had not prevented it, he would doubtless have employed a fourth actor and developed a more elaborate drama.

Economy of roles was made possible from the very first by the religious inheritance of the use of masks and by the continuous presence of the chorus. The choral lyrics prevented the scene from becoming wholly vacant between the exit and re-entrance of the actor and allowed him time for change of mask and costume.

Masks were made to serve other functions, especially that of revealing something of the identity of the wearer. The characters of tragedy tended to fall into types, such as the old king (Creon in the *Medea*), the spirited young monarch (Oedipus in *Oedipus the King*), the old nurse and confidante (as in the *Medea* or the *Hippolytus*), and many others. The masks and costumes of such typical characters were so conventionalized that the habitual theatergoer would immediately recognize them. A shepherd doubtless would easily be distinguished from a slave of the household, and probably the mask of a messenger bringing bad news would be distinguished from one bringing good news. A writer of the second century A.D. describes twenty-eight masks conventionally used in tragedy.[55] Such means of recognition were convenient, especially because the audience had no handbills and had little if any information about the play.

II

AESCHYLUS

LIFE[1]

Aeschylus was born in 525/4 B.C. His father, Euphorion, was a member of the old Athenian nobility (Eupatrids) and dwelt in the deme of Eleusis. Aeschylus fought with distinction at the battle of Marathon in 490 B.C., and he is said to have taken part also in the battles of Salamis and Plataea. Marathon and Salamis were primarily Athenian victories, and Athens now became the political leader of Greece and the intellectual leader of the world.

Aeschylus seems to have begun writing tragedy at a youthful age, and for some time he appeared himself as an actor in his plays. His plays were not placed first in a contest, however, until he was forty years old (484 B.C.). During his lifetime he is said to have won thirteen such victories and "not a few" after his death; for an exception, unique during the fifth century, was made to allow anyone who wished to reproduce Aeschylus' plays at the regular Athenian festivals. He is said to have written seventy tragedies and various satyr-plays. While this number is uncertain—other figures also are given—we can be sure that he was a very prolific writer. Thirteen victories would presumably require fifty-two plays. It is taken for granted that he produced plays before his first victory, and we know that he was defeated by Sophocles in 468 B.C., when Sophocles won his own first victory. Some of the tragedies of Aeschylus may never have been produced at Athens. For instance, we know that he composed one play to celebrate the foundation and presage a bright future for the city of Aetna, which was founded about the time that Aeschylus first left Athens and went to Sicily to join the court of Hiero, "tyrant" of Syracuse, somewhat as various other Athenian literary men did during this and later periods. While sojourning, apparently a second time, in Sicily, Aeschylus died at Gela in the year 456/5 B.C.

The family of Aeschylus produced many writers of tragedies, including his two sons, Euphorion and Euaeon, and a nephew, Philocles, who won first prize over Sophocles when the *Oedipus the King* was produced. The tradition was carried on by a son and various descendants of Philocles, among whom was Astydamas, one of the most famous writers of tragedy during the first half of the fourth century.

The epitaph which Aeschylus wrote for himself celebrates his bravery at Marathon but says not a word of his literary eminence: "Here lies the Athenian Aeschylus, son of Euphorion, who died in grain-bearing Gela. The plain of Marathon can tell his proven might, and the long-haired Mede who learned of it there."

Though held in the very highest esteem throughout the fifth century, Aeschylus as a dramatist gradually faded out of the practical theater, and during the fourth century, Euripides and Sophocles were far more popular. His dramatic virtues were too simple, and his poetry was too ornate and difficult. Hence in later times, he was always regarded as a great poet but not as a dramatist comparable with his two eminent successors. As in the case of Sophocles, a selection of seven plays was made, probably early in the Christian era, and it is these seven that are preserved. Somewhat later, in Byzantine times, three of these seven, the *Persians,* the *Seven against Thebes,* and the *Prometheus,* were gathered into a smaller group. This group has come down to us in more manuscripts and with a much better text than the other plays.

Especially the *Prometheus,* which is well preserved and is not too difficult linguistically, has exerted very great influence in modern times. But the trilogy on Orestes, which has a very faulty manuscript tradition and is also most difficult, has never until very recently exerted anything like the influence which its intrinsic worth justifies. Contemporary scholars have done much to restore the text of the *Agamemnon;* but that of the *Choephoroe,* especially in the choral passages, is likely to remain unsatisfactory. Critics now, however, universally agree that Aeschylus ranks among the very greatest poets and the most important dramatists.

TRAGEDY UNDER AESCHYLUS

Some ten years before Aeschylus was born, tragedy had been officially recognized at Athens, and Thespis, its "originator," was drawing to the close of his career. Almost nothing is known of Thespis and his creations, but he seems to have made the first step toward converting the dithyramb into choral drama by introducing the first actor. Not much more is known of his immediate successors. The names of only three have survived. Choerilus seems to have had an extremely long and prolific career. Pratinas, a Dorian Greek from Phlius, was noted especially for his satyr-plays. But by far the most important of these early contemporaries of Aeschylus was Phrynichus. He ventured upon historical subjects; he early employed the iambic "prologos" before the entrance of the chorus; he was famous for his choreography;

he is said to have been the first to employ female characters; and, above all, he composed poetry of great beauty.

The author of an ancient *Life of Aeschylus* remarks that if one should compare the plays of Aeschylus with those of his successors, he would think them slight and simple, but that if he should compare them with the plays of Aeschylus' predecessors, he would be amazed at the intellectual power and originality of Aeschylus. This is easily credible, for the development that can be observed even within the seven extant plays is astonishing. But, from the first, Aeschylus has great virtues. To compare Euripides with Aeschylus is to compare the Hermes of Praxiteles with the much earlier Apollo from the pediment at Olympia. The one has the grace and sophistication of a highly cultured humanity, the other, the bold, rugged strength and the dignity of a severe divinity.

In matters of form, various significant changes may be noted in the later plays of Aeschylus: the amount of dialogue is increased and the amount of choral lyric reduced. Perhaps we should say that the proportions of dialogue and lyric are more artistically adapted to the material, and a more dramatic presentation can be achieved when the poet so desires. Thus the first half of the *Agamemnon* is predominantly lyric, the second half predominantly spoken verse. The use of a spoken scene (prologos) before the entry of the chorus has now become the invariable rule. Messenger speeches have become a definite part of the tradition—they may have existed from the very first. The third actor appears, and conversation becomes more elaborate. The third actor, of course, was the innovation of Sophocles; but the second actor, an even more important invention, had been introduced by Aeschylus even before the *Suppliants,* apparently at the very beginning of his career. Aeschylus is credited also with the invention of many details of scenic representation and costume.[2] He may have been the first to write three continuous tragedies on a single legend (trilogy).

Most of the devices of dramatic technique which are customary in Sophocles and Euripides are found already in Aeschylus, although Sophocles had, of course, been producing for ten years before the last plays of Aeschylus were exhibited and the younger poet doubtless influenced the older one as much as he was influenced by him. The use of leitmotifs and tragic foreboding was never more highly developed than in the trilogy on Orestes. Dramatic irony and foreshadowing, also, are used in masterly fashion. But the movements of characters and the complicated manipulation of three actors have not been perfected. This lack of complexity goes hand in hand with extreme simplicity of plot. Recognition and intrigue are employed in the *Choephoroe,* but there the recognition is awkward and the intrigue unrealistically simple. In the other plays of the trilogy, time and place are still handled with archaic informality. But, in general, the technique of Aeschylus is well adapted to his subject matter and physical limitations are frequently turned into artistic advantages.[3]

Although Aeschylus reduced the role of the chorus and centered the interest of his plays in the actors, the relation between the chorus and the actors remains extremely close throughout his plays and this relation is handled with great skill and effectiveness, especially in the *Agamemnon*. Choral lyrics and the dialogue scenes are fused into one essential unity. Even here, furthermore, lyrics assigned to characters may for one reason or another be substituted for choral lyrics. The *Prometheus* and the second half of the *Agamemnon* furnish obvious examples. Occasionally the chorus performs a function in the mechanical development of the plot, as when in the *Choephoroe* they induce the Nurse to change Clytemnestra's message to Aegisthus. In the *Eumenides* the chorus plays an active role, perhaps the leading role, but in a fashion quite different from that of the early *Suppliants*.

The plays of Aeschylus are theatrical and spectacular, owing in part, no doubt, to his experience as actor and director—for he, like the other writers of tragedy, directed his own plays. He dresses his characters in magnificent costumes, which at times, as in the *Persians,* are contrasted with the rent garments of grief.[4] He is fond of men in armor, chariots and cars, trumpets and fanfare of every description. Though his earliest plays seem to have been presented with little or no physical background, in his later plays he apparently employs machines or stage devices to exhibit interior scenes, as in the *Eumenides,* or for various other effects, as in the *Prometheus.*[5] He brings various gods and demons, such as the Furies, upon the scene. He resurrects ghosts and uses graves and altars. Although a heroic dignity is maintained throughout his plays, he is not above effective stage business: Cassandra throws down her staff and wreath, and Orestes exhibits the bloodstained garment in which Agamemnon was ensnared and slain. The importance of these theatrical qualities in this early period can hardly be overestimated. In all probability Aeschylus is chiefly responsible for the essentially realistic nature of European drama—qualities which can be fully appreciated only by making a comparison between Greek tragedy and Sanskrit or Chinese drama. European drama, then, is perhaps more heavily indebted to Aeschylus than to any other individual.

In regard to subject matter the most important contribution made by Aeschylus was the seriousness and dignity which he gave to tragedy.[6] His commanding position in world literature is due mainly to the unsurpassed grandeur of his poetry, the breadth of his cosmic outlook, and the loftiness of his moral and religious conceptions. It was not his nature or the spirit of his age to view life in a trivial or superficial manner. Above all—and this is of tremendous importance for the history of drama—it was not his nature or the spirit of his age to falsify life. Thus a Greek tragedy may end in utter downfall and ruin, as the *Seven against Thebes* (the last play of its trilogy), or in reconciliation and happiness, as the *Eumenides*. The play ends as the action warrants —a basic prerequisite of any great drama.

In Aristophanes' *Frogs* (1043–56) it is intimated that Aeschylus was careful in choosing his subject matter and would not accept the story of Phaedra or Stheneboea as Euripides did, regardless of the historical accuracy of the legend. Whether or not this is true is open to some doubt, but it is clear that Aeschylus interpreted his subject material as of moral, religious, or political significance. The right of sanctuary, the punishment of overweening pride and sacrilege, the replacing of violence by justice and legal process—these are typical themes in the extant plays. Still, as we may see in the Orestes trilogy, he is sometimes vague in his moral causes and unsystematic in his moral solutions. Serious as he may be, he is primarily a poet and dramatist and not a philosopher. Last and most important of all, Athens and her welfare were continuously before the mind of the poet. Etiological subjects, explaining the origin of some social, religious, or political custom, are favorite ones with him. In the *Eumenides*, Orestes and his purification, the proper subject of the play, are overwhelmed by the crescendo of patriotic fervor. The *Persians,* too, is primarily an encomium of Athens, and the *Seven against Thebes,* as Aristophanes says (*Frogs* 1021–22), is certainly a patriotically inspiring play. Small wonder is it that Aeschylus was the universal favorite in Athens of the fifth century or that to Aristophanes he was the symbol of Athens at the height of her glory.

An astonishing development in portrayal of character may be observed within the extant plays of Aeschylus. Pelasgus in the *Suppliants* is no more than the good king of the heroic age, but in the *Agamemnon* even the Watchman is a character of full and lifelike individuality. Portrayal by contrast is deliberately employed in the *Persians*. It is more subtly used in the *Prometheus* and the *Agamemnon*. All the standard devices of character portrayal are combined to bring out the character of Clytemnestra with a vividness that would do credit to any dramatist: direct description by others, subtle allusion especially in the choral lyrics, skillful manipulation of the movements of Clytemnestra, revelation of character by speech and by contrast now with one figure and now with another, and, last and most important of all, demonstration of character in action. Characterization by language, however, though found in the opening scene of the *Prometheus,* is never developed, for considerations of style precluded anything more than slight variation of the language of different characters.

Aeschylus is one of the foremost exemplars of the grand style. His plays, at least in the original Greek, are rich in passages of exquisite beauty. The choral description of the sacrifice of Iphigenia in the *Agamemnon* (205–48) is one of the most famous. His impeccable poetic taste may be illustrated by comparing his beautiful description of the sin of Laius in begetting a son with Euripides' reference to the same event. "Overcome by dear follies," sings the chorus of the *Seven against Thebes* (750–57), "he begat doom for himself, the father-slaying Oedipus, who dared to sow in the pure field of his mother where he was nourished the roots of a line destined to bloodshed. Madness joined insane bride and groom." In Euripides the act of Laius is told with the realism of a medical casebook: "But Laius, surrendering to pleasure and becoming intoxicated, begat a child . . . ." Although the language of Euripides here is not vulgar, and the passage is taken from the spoken prologue of the *Phoenissae* (21–22), whereas the passage from Aeschylus is from a choral lyric, still in Euripides the poetry and beauty is gone and the unpleasant idea of intoxication has been added.

This example brings up another typical characteristic of Aeschylus —his obscurity. The first phrase quoted from the *Seven against Thebes* has sometimes been interpreted as meaning "overcome by the follies of his dear ones," that is, presumably, of his wife. This interpretation occurs even in the ancient commentary, but it is apparently proved wrong by the unmistakable plainness of Euripides. Aeschylus is often thus obscure, and at times even the Greeks of his own day thought him so, if we may judge from Aristophanes (*Frogs* 928–33). The grand style is chiefly characterized by the wealth and boldness of its metaphors, and Aeschylus' diction is filled with rare words and strange coinages. This obscurity caused difficulty in establishing the correct text of Aeschylus in ancient times; and in modern times, with a text further corrupted by long tradition, it causes even more. The misinterpretations of individual phrases, however, have often proved stimulating and important in literature,[7] just as misinterpretations of the basic themes of the plays, especially the *Prometheus,* have made literary history.

The Euripides of Aristophanes' *Frogs* is not entirely unjustified in bringing the charge of bombast against Aeschylus. His taste is not quite impeccable after all. Like other writers of the grand style, Aeschylus sometimes falls into the ridiculous. A case is the notorious metaphor "thirsty dust, twin sister of mud." This phrase from the *Agamemnon* (494–95) is the last, fatal step beyond the imaginative phrase in the *Seven against Thebes* (494), "murky smoke, variegated sister of fire." Aeschylus is also prone to use too many metaphors and to mix them beyond all reason. But these faults are very minor ones when considered along with the heroic vigor and archaic freshness of his poetry.

We shall pass over the metrical and musical development of Aeschylus, as little of this can be appreciated in translations. He is said to have created his own choral dance figures,[8] but we know practically nothing about these. His plays are of great interest even when robbed of their music and choreography, stripped of their dramatic spectacle, and dulled by wholly inadequate translations; but this should not deceive the modern reader into underestimating the importance of music, dance, spectacle, and poetry in the original presentation.

1. *SUPPLIANTS*

(Possibly about 490 B.C.)

The *Suppliants* is probably the earliest of all extant dramas. It seems to have been the first member of a tetralogy of which the other plays may have been those now lost entitled *Egyptians, Daughters of Danaus* (*Danaides*), and *Amymone* (a satyr-play).[9]

Theme.—The interpretation of the *Suppliants* remains uncertain because the subsequent plays of its trilogy have not survived and because the text of the play in crucial passages cannot be determined with certainty. The essential problem of the *Suppliants* as an individual play, however, seems to be the dilemma which is thrust upon King Pelasgus: Is he to honor the right of sanctuary even at the cost of war, or is he to reject his suppliants and see the altars of his gods polluted with their blood? The right and obligation of sanctuary in contrast to a rule of violence is the theme of the *Heracleidae* and the *Suppliants* of Euripides and of Sophocles' *Oedipus at Colonus*. The recognition of this right was an important step in the establishment of law and order.[10]

There is a certain dramatic irony throughout the play, since Danaus, though now a foreigner seeking sanctuary for his daughters, actually is to succeed Pelasgus as king of Argos, and his daughter Hypermnestra is to become the mother of the later Argive kings by a son of Aegyptus. The establishment of this line at Argos, therefore, is in a way the subject of the whole tetralogy.

Precisely why the maidens object to marriage with the sons of Aegyptus is a matter of dispute among critics. It is thought by some that the daughters have an unnatural fear of marriage or an undue devotion to the virgin Artemis.[11] Various passages in the play are cited to support this assumption, but it necessitates the assignment of the choral song in praise of Aphrodite near the end of the play to a chorus of handmaids. It finds support also in a beautiful fragment (frag. 44, Nauck[2]) from the last play of the trilogy, where Aphrodite herself appeared, possibly to defend Hypermnestra,[12] somewhat as Apollo is to defend Orestes in the *Eumenides:* "Chaste Heaven desires to wound the Earth; Desire seizes Earth to receive his love; and the drenching rain of the bridegroom Heaven falls upon Earth. She bears for mortals the pasturage of the flocks and Demeter's livelihood; the yield of orchards too is brought to fruition by his quickening rain. Of these I am a cause." The whole trilogy, according to this interpretation, dealt with the conflict of Artemis and Aphrodite.

Other scholars insist that the main problem of the whole trilogy was that of endogamy and exogamy. Endogamy or marriage within a family group tended to retain property within the family. If an Athenian man died leaving a daughter but no son and no testamentary disposition of his daughter (and property—the two must go together), the nearest agnate male relative might marry her even if divorces were necessary to enable him to do so. If the girl was poor, however, this male relative might prefer to furnish her with a dowry so that she might marry someone else. Thus endogamy might sometimes be to the advantage of the woman; but, in general, endogamy leads to a lower status for women, since by marrying within a family group her natural male protectors become her husband or her husband's friends and she thus has no one to protect her own peculiar interests. Divorce becomes practically impossible for the woman. These scholars think the trilogy explained endogamy and led to the foundation of the Thesmophoria—a woman's festival—as a compensation for the lower status which endogamy entailed.[13]

It seems likely that objection to endogamy is at least one of the reasons why the Danaids are fleeing their cousins (335–41), but the violence of the cousins' efforts to force marriage upon them is repeatedly stressed and must not be underestimated (esp. 226–33, 1031–32). Some scholars think that this violence—effectively illustrated at the climax of the play when the Herald attempts to carry off the maidens by force—has caused their unnatural fear of marriage, and that the final play of the trilogy dramatized not Hypermnestra's defense but the purification of the maidens who had slaughtered their husbands.[14] The beautiful fragment from Aphrodite's speech, then, would be part of her successful effort to restore the maidens to a natural attitude toward love and marriage. The only other fragment of any consequence preserved from the play would fit nicely into this scheme. It seems to direct the foundation of a propitiatory rite in honor of the dead husbands[15]—perhaps an example of the etiological motive that is so frequent in the trilogies of Aeschylus and in the plays of Euripides.

Discussion.—The *Suppliants* is a play of unusual interest in the history of drama because it represents a transitional period midway between the original lyric dithyramb and classical dramatic tragedy. The chorus in this play, as in the dithyramb from which tragedy arose, probably consists of fifty persons, and here the chorus constitutes the chief character of the drama. The play opens with the entrance of the chorus, as in the *Persians* and in the *Rhesus*. The exposition is given in their marching anapests (1–39) and in their lyrics. About half the play consists of choral lyrics, and even in the dialogue scenes their part is very considerable.

The play obviously belongs to the period of two actors, as do perhaps the other extant plays of Aeschylus with the exception of the trilogy on Orestes. Indeed the poet evidently has experienced difficulty in handling even two actors. We might have expected the king to converse directly with Danaus rather than with his daughters, and the long silence of Danaus during this scene is very awkward. When he finally is addressed, he replies with a single speech of only ten lines. The heated dialogue between the king and the Herald of the Egyptians is dramatic and effective but very short. The absence of Danaus in this scene of peril for the maidens is obviously unnatural, and the poet's technical ability is somewhat strained in motivating the exit of Danaus before this scene and his re-entrance afterward (966–72).

Other shortcomings of the play from the dramatic standpoint are obvious. It lacks action; there is too little characterization and too much genealogical and geographical detail. Its lyric diffusiveness marks it as primarily a choral rather than a dramatic production.

But the *Suppliants* has great virtues. The greatest of these is the beauty of its lyrics and the bold grandeur of its language, though both these qualities are obscured or lost in translations. The subject of the play, furthermore, centers about a very dramatic conflict. Pelasgus is forced into a dilemma of great significance for later civilization. A definite feeling of suspense, furthermore, is created during the first of the play. In their lyrics the chorus have declared that they will commit themselves to the god of the underworld if they fail to obtain protection from the gods of Olympus (154–61); and they repeat this determination of suicide to the king, threatening to hang themselves upon the altars and thus create a dreadful pollution (465, cf. 787–91).

Even after the chorus has with great effort won over the king, the final difficult decision of the people must be awaited, and almost immediately after the joyful news of their favorable decision the ship of the Egyptians is sighted. Finally, the threats and warnings of the Herald and the forebodings of the choral lyrics near the end of the play stimulate the interest of the audience in the subsequent plays of the trilogy. Aeschylus has here achieved no mean accomplishment in making the play at once an individual unity and an introduction to the trilogy.

The original presentation of the play must have been spectacular and colorful. There was no "background." A chorus of fifty, possibly with fifty handmaids (954), now danced in the orchestra, now took refuge on the mound.[16] They wore striking Egyptian costumes, finely worked white robes contrasting with their dark masks.[17] Linen veils, perhaps secured by gold bands, covered their heads (120–22). On their first appearance, they carried suppliants' boughs. Danaus wears not the costume of a king but that of a ship's captain. The king Pelasgus, however, enters with royal splendor in a chariot drawn by horses —a favorite spectacle with Aeschylus—and he is doubtless accompanied by a guard with shields and spears and with trumpets which have announced his coming (180–83). The scene wherein the Herald and his henchmen attempt to drag the maidens from their sanctuary and are frustrated by the entrance of the king is extremely dramatic. The vast numbers which take part in the action of the play are more suited to pageantry and spectacle than to ordinary drama, but obviously the author of this play had a magnificent sense of the theatrical and the dramatic. Obviously the importance of these early virtues is incalculable.

2. *PERSIANS*

(472 B.C.)

Aeschylus won first prize with four plays unconnected in subject matter: the *Phineus;* the *Persians;* the *Glaucus Potnieus;* and the *Prometheus (the Fire-Lighter)*, a satyr-play. Pericles, who later became the most famous of all Athenian statesmen, was choregus. The *Persians* is said to have been produced later in Sicily and to have been greatly admired. It alone of the four plays has survived.[18]

Source.—The *Persians*, we are told by an ancient commentator, was modeled after Phrynichus' *Phoenissae,* which was written on the same subject and was produced probably in 476 B.C., when Themistocles, the great hero of Salamis, was the victorious choregus for Phrynichus.

These two plays, along with the *Sack of Miletus* of Phrynichus, were
the only historical tragedies, as far as we now know, written in the
fifth century. It may be significant that the two written on the defeat
of the Persians were both, in all probability, produced with ambitious
politicians as choregi.[19]

Phrynichus' play opened with an iambic prologue spoken by a
eunuch as he made ready the "thrones" for the counselors of the realm.
These counselors possibly constituted a secondary chorus. Phoenician
women whose husbands had gone to the war constituted the main
chorus. This is the first recorded instance of a prologue and a "dust-
ing maid" scene of exposition. The defeat of Xerxes was announced
in this prologue. Aeschylus, though he clings to choral exposition,
shows his superior theatrical genius by postponing the announcement
of Xerxes' defeat and making it one of the best effects of the play.

Theme.—This play is designed primarily as a glorification of the
victory over the Persians at the battle of Salamis, 480 B.C. This victory is here ascribed to the Athenians, and little is said of the other
Greeks who took part. It is historically true, of course, that the Athenians and especially Themistocles were responsible both for the battle
and for the victory, but Aeschylus' attitude in glorifying Athens is
typical of the local patriotism of the period. Still, not a single Greek
is mentioned by name, although scores of Persian names occur and add
local color to the foreign setting. The Dorian Greeks, furthermore,
are given credit for the subsequent victory at Plataea (817).

By presenting the result of the battle of Salamis from the Persian
point of view, Phrynichus and Aeschylus achieve a tragic atmosphere
and avoid an attitude of insolent boastfulness. A fundamental conception of Greek morality is that too great prosperity (*koros*, "satiety")
brings on boastfulness or wanton insolence (*hybris*), which in the end
results in ruin (*ate*). This conception, the most frequent basic theme
of Greek tragedy, occurs repeatedly in the *Persians* and is given compelling emphasis here by having the ghost of Darius blame the defeat
of the Persians on their wanton violence and sacrilege (808–42).

The placing of the action at the Persian court also lends a detachment and dignity somewhat similar to the heroic atmosphere which
envelops themes and characters taken from remote history or mythology.[20] The Athenian point of view, however, breaks through the Persian
setting repeatedly (cf. 213). It is most obvious in the pronouncements
of the ghost of Darius.

Discussion.—The *Persians* is an important historical document,
but Aeschylus has taken great liberty in his presentation of Darius;
for in actual history Darius had suffered major defeats, including two

in his attempted invasions of Greece. Strangely enough, Aeschylus gives only the barest mention (244, 475) to the glorious Athenian victory over the forces of Darius at Marathon in 490 B.C., a battle in which Aeschylus himself took part, as he did also in the battle of Salamis. Darius as a king and general has been greatly idealized in the play for obvious artistic considerations: Aeschylus wishes to emphasize the contrast between Darius and Xerxes—a contrast that is carried out in the physical aspect of the two characters. Darius appears impressively from the top of his funeral mound, probably high above chorus and queen, and he is clad in royal robes of Oriental splendor and is crowned with a royal tiara (659–63). Xerxes, although he enters with his curtained car (1000–1001), has rent his robe (1030) and is doubtless a sorry and pitiful figure. Darius and Xerxes present an early example of character portrayal by contrast, therefore, and this effect is clearly deliberate because it is achieved at the obvious cost of historical accuracy.

The *Persians* is perhaps the least dramatic of all Greek tragedies. There is no basic conflict, although the emotional tone intensifies as the play progresses. The plot is one of tragic discovery rather than tragic decision. The continual shifting of the leading role, furthermore, somewhat tends to disjoint the play. Some technical improvements, however, may be noted.

A distinct advance in handling dialogue has been made. The total amount of dialogue is still only half of the play, and the frequent use of the long trochaic meter is archaic. But the shifts from trochaic to iambic meter and vice versa within a scene are effective in marking a change of tone and tempo.[21] The chorus is no longer an important character in the dialogue when two actors are present. The Messenger, for instance, does first carry on an exchange with the chorus; but after this introduction, his conversation is with the queen, who very naturally is impatient to know the fate of her son, although she cannot in her terror bring herself to ask of him specifically. So the ghost of Darius first addresses the chorus, as is usual for an entering character, but his main dialogue is with the queen, and this shift from chorus to queen is again nicely motivated (703–6). Later he turns again to the chorus, then back to the queen, and then again addresses the chorus with his final words. Another indication of a tendency toward more natural dialogue is found in the less frequent use of choral lyrics interlarded with spoken lines (epirrhematic construction).

The use of a dream and of an omen to foreshadow the development of the tragedy is noteworthy. The dream also prepares for the scene with the ghost of Darius, but the poet could have joined these two scenes more closely by having the queen refer to her dream when she comes on to make the offering to Darius.[22]

The ghost, also, makes his first appearance in extant drama in this play, and a grand and impressive first appearance it is. The manner in which he is exorcised is spectacular and impressive. The time which he may remain, as with all ghosts, is strictly limited. His knowledge, for obvious dramatic reasons, is the reverse of that of the living: he does not know the present calamity of the Persians, although he is able to foretell their future defeat at Plataea. His final words—an exhortation to enjoy life—are not mere idle sententiousness but, like verses 689–90, are designed to remind us of the ghostly character of the speaker.

A phrase in the first line of the play, "those who are gone," contains ominous dramatic irony, and this phrase is frequently repeated.[23] Indeed the foreboding of the first scenes of this play adumbrates the grand effects of foreboding in the early scenes of the *Agamemnon*.

Pomp and circumstance are conspicuous again in this play. Especially noteworthy is the contrast between the first entrance of the queen, royally adorned and in her chariot, and her second entrance, in mourning probably and humbly on foot.

The dramatist obviously has not yet mastered integration of plot. Although the appearance of the ghost of Darius receives skillful preparation (198, 221, 554), motivation and foreshadowing are awkwardly handled. From the queen's lines about her son as she makes her first exit, we should expect Xerxes to appear as the next character.[24] But actually she herself reappears, and then comes the long episode with the ghost of Darius. Darius, furthermore, instructs the queen to meet Xerxes with new raiment, and she expresses her intention of trying to do so; but we hear no more of this, and so we suspect that it is simply an awkward motivation for her exit.[25] Obviously her presence is not desired during the final scene. From the speech of the Messenger, again, we should never know that a large Persian army still remained in Greece.

The most famous passage in the play is the magnificent description of the battle of Salamis (353–432). This is the first long messenger's speech in extant tragedy, and it is perhaps the most thrilling and brilliant of all such speeches.

3. *SEVEN AGAINST THEBES*

(467 B.C.)

Aeschylus was awarded first prize for the Theban tetralogy, the *Laius,* the *Oedipus,* the *Seven against Thebes,* and the *Sphinx* (a satyr-play).²⁶ Of these only the present play has been preserved.

The short scene between Antigone and the Herald at the end of the play is usually considered spurious. If genuine, Antigone's resolve to bury Polyneices in defiance of the command of Creon, the subject of Sophocles' *Antigone* and of Euripides' lost play of the same title, leaves the story unfinished. A similar scene, similarly suspected, occurs in Euripides' *Phoenissae.*

Influence.—In Greek literature and art the Theban cycle of legends was second in importance only to the Trojan cycle. Aeschylus' tetralogy was followed by many other Greek tragedies. Sophocles' masterpiece, *Oedipus the King,* was doubtless influenced by the *Oedipus* of Aeschylus, and Euripides' *Phoenissae* covers essentially the same story as the *Seven against Thebes.* Other extant Greek tragedies dealing with this cycle are the *Antigone* and the *Oedipus at Colonus* of Sophocles, and the *Suppliants* and the *Heracles* of Euripides.

Theme.—The story of the downfall of Laius and his descendants, like that of Atreus and Agamemnon, is a classic example of the truism that the sins of the fathers are visited upon the sons. This theme must have been the basis of the whole trilogy. As an individual play, the *Seven against Thebes* appears to have two subjects. The first of the play is taken up with the fate of Thebes, although the curse of Oedipus is recalled by Eteocles (69–77) and is obviously an important factor in determining the fate of the city. The bitter personal feuds of the various Argive leaders and the presumptious insolence of all except Amphiaraus—who foretells his own fate—have been given such stress that the poet certainly intended thus to foreshadow and at least in part to explain the defeat of the Argives. But after the departure of Eteocles very little is said of Thebes, and only one line tells the fate of the captains who have been described at such length (794) : "Fallen are the mighty men and all their boasts." The second part of the play is primarily concerned with the fate of the house of Laius. Indeed the curse of Oedipus becomes almost an obsession with both chorus and characters. The ruin of the house is considered final and complete, and no hint is given of the war, so famous in legend, which the "Epigoni," or descendants of Eteocles and Polyneices, later waged.

In this play Aeschylus seems little concerned, strangely enough, with the moral dilemma of the two brothers. The play is presented

almost wholly from the point of view of Eteocles and the Thebans.
Nothing is said of a contract between the two brothers. Polyneices has
been banished, and Antigone seems to address the dead Eteocles as the
"primal author of these grievous woes," although this passage is uncertain (998–99). But each of the brothers claims to have justice on
his side. Obviously Aeschylus has refused an opportunity to present a
moral conflict between the two brothers, such as that which forms the
basis of Euripides' *Phoenissae.*

The explanation of this sacrifice of dramatic effect, in the opinion
of the present writer, lies not primarily in the poet's desire to portray
Eteocles as a brave and tragic character. Aeschylus, it seems, is like his
own Amphiaraus, who accuses Polyneices of wickedness and sacrilege
in his attempt to sack his native land (580–86). Aeschylus apparently
cannot entertain the possibility that an attack on one's native city may
be justified. He belonged to that generation which had seen the tyrant
Hippias expelled from Athens and returning with the Persian army at
Marathon. More recently, Themistocles, the savior of Greece at the
battle of Salamis, had been ostracized and forced into exile (probably
471–470 B.C.), and then, possibly before the production of this play, he
had been accused of plotting with the Persians against Greece and condemned. He fled, however, and went over to the Persians. That Persia
was still a menace is shown by the fact that the last great battle, a naval
engagement at Eurymedon in Asia Minor, was fought shortly before
this play was produced. Aeschylus' unqualified condemnation of Polyneices, therefore, and the patriotic fervor of the play may be due to the
contemporary political situation and has almost certainly been influenced by contemporary ideals of patriotism.

Patriotic feeling, furthermore, may account for Aeschylus' failure
to mention the word "Thebes" during the whole play. Thebes had gone
over to the Persians in the recent invasion which ended at Salamis and
Plataea and so was in disgrace with the majority of the Greeks. Here
Aeschylus invariably employs the archaic terms "Cadmeans" or "city
of Cadmus," which are at once more poetic and less offensive to contemporary feelings.

Scholars have been puzzled by the references to the attacking army
as one speaking a foreign tongue (170, cf. 72–73). There are also frequent references to enslavement. These are the results perhaps of a
half-unconscious emergence of the Athenian point of view. For Athenians of that day the siege of a city inevitably suggested the destruction
of Athens in 480 B.C., and the besieging enemy suggested the Persians.[27]

Discussion.—The opening scenes of the *Seven against Thebes* are
among the most natural and effective in Greek tragedy, although the

problem of exposition in this play is perhaps simplified somewhat by the fact that it was the last member of a trilogy.[28] The mention of the curse of Oedipus (69–77), which probably figured prominently in the previous play, is an ominous and foreboding note. The hysterical entrance of the chorus in excited dochmiac meter and probably carrying gifts and crowns for the gods (101) vividly suggests the panic of a city under siege and, by contrast, brings out the cool bravery and unselfish patriotism of Eteocles. His extreme anger when he upbraids the chorus for its fears is well suggested in his language, which is here characterized by the use of hyperbole (197) and the grammatical irregularities of excited speech (250).

This excellent beginning is frustrated, however, by the second entrance of the Messenger (369), who describes each of the seven leaders of the Argives and his shield. Eteocles, probably accompanied by his various captains in their armor, chooses the opposing Theban with regard to the blazon and character of the Argive and says something of each as he sends him forth. Such description is essentially epic, and whereas it might be tolerated in the exposition of a drama it is especially out of place in the very center. It seems to be criticized by Euripides when he presents his Eteocles as protesting that there is no time for describing the warriors when the city is being besieged (*Phoenissae* 751–52). As motivation for this long scene, however, Aeschylus does say that the Argives have halted because the auspices are not favorable (378–79). For a static scene, furthermore, it is magnificently constructed. The descriptions rise to a climax with the figure of Amphiaraus and his denunciation of his own cause. When the Messenger describes Polyneices, Eteocles remains alone, now stripped of all his captains and obviously the one champion to face his brother, who has issued what amounts to a challenge which cannot with honor be refused. The despair of Eteocles and the utter gloom when he departs, like the despair and gloom when Hector departs from Andromache in the *Iliad* (6.529),[29] prepare for the tragic outcome.

The dirge and funeral procession at the end of the play add a solemn pageantry to the action.

Some of the poet's technical difficulties may be mentioned. The foreshadowing of the first entrance of the Messenger is too immediate (36–38). The Messenger on making his exit, however, nicely prepares for his return. The appearance of Eteocles at precisely the same time as the Messenger at verse 372 is convenient (as the chorus remarks!) but should have been more plausibly motivated. The change in the attitude of the chorus during the play is noteworthy. At first panic-stricken, when Eteocles departs for the actual battle and when panic is really in order, they sing not of the battle and their fear for Thebes (except verses 764–65) but of the fall of the house of Laius. Such a change in the attitude of the chorus, however, is not infrequent in tragedy and is characteristic of Old Comedy. Indeed, too immediate foreshadowing and pat unmotivated entrances are also characteristic of Old Comedy. Such technical details were perfected only with time, and Old Comedy cultivated its nonchalance in regard to them.

4. **PROMETHEUS BOUND

Date unknown; possibly earlier than the *Seven against Thebes*. The famous "prediction" of the eruption of Mount Etna contained in verses 363–72 proves that the play is later than this eruption (probably 479/8 B.C.).

The *Prometheus Bound* is usually considered to have been the first member of a trilogy now lost, of which the other plays probably were those entitled *Prometheus Unbound* and *Prometheus the Fire-Bearer*. The satyr-play produced with this trilogy is unknown, but a satyr-play entitled *Prometheus* (*the Fire-Lighter*) was one of the plays produced with the *Persians* in 472 B.C.[30]

Influence.—Two lines of this play are parodied by Aristophanes (*Knights* 759, 836). The *Prometheus Unbound* is cited and quoted frequently by ancient authors. The whole legend was famous in literature and art, but no other Greek play besides the four of Aeschylus is known to have existed. The Roman Accius, however, produced a *Prometheus*.

In modern times the *Prometheus Bound* has had tremendous influence on literature. Conceptions and misconceptions of the play and of individual phrases have inspired an endless number of writers.[31] Christian interpretations of the myth are as old as Tertullian (*ca.* A.D. 155–230). The play exerted important influence on Milton, Goethe, Byron, Shelley (whose poem, *Prometheus Unbound,* is well known), the Brownings, Swinburne, Robert Bridges, and many other poets. Its influence on Thomas Hardy was especially great, as we may observe in the conceptions of his *Dynasts* and in his use of the phrase at the end of his *Tess of the D'Urbervilles,* "the President of the Immortals."

Legend.—The myths concerning Prometheus varied greatly.[32] The most important innovation which appears in this play and which Aeschylus perhaps originated consists of giving to Prometheus the secret of an oracle which threatens the overthrow of Zeus. This oracle was already famous as the explanation of the might of Achilles, whose mother Thetis was the charmer of Zeus and Poseidon until they learned that her son was fated to be mightier than his father. No association of this oracle with Prometheus, however, is known previous to the *Prometheus Bound*. According to the usual version of the myth, the freeing of Prometheus was accomplished by Heracles. Thus Aeschylus has really incorporated two independent solutions of the quarrel between Zeus and Prometheus. The dramatic advantage of this combination is readily seen if the reader tries to imagine the play without one of these two solutions. In a plot of extremely limited possibilities for action, the secret creates a certain suspense and arms Prometheus with a powerful knowledge in his conflict with Zeus. The retention of Heracles, furthermore, lends suspense and interest to the trilogy, for his appearance is repeatedly foreshadowed in the *Prometheus Bound* and, as we know from extant fragments, constituted an important part of the *Prometheus Unbound*. It also justified to some extent the long episode with Io, his ancestress, in the *Prometheus Bound*. Aeschylus was probably the first to join the myth of Io with that of Prometheus. In fact, the wanderings of Io as described in Aeschylus' own *Suppliants* are much shorter or, at least, more briefly told than those described here, and no mention is there made of Prometheus or his desert cliff.

Still another solution is suggested at the end of the play, where Hermes says that Prometheus should not expect an end of his suffering until another god is found who is willing to take his place in Tartarus (1026–29). This condition adds no complication to the present play except that it seems to suggest an impossible solution. Actually, the centaur Cheiron, painfully and incurably wounded by the arrow of Heracles, preferred Tartarus to continued existence.

Staging.—It is usually assumed that Might and Violence and Hephaestus enter at the opening of the play with a wooden figure larger than human size (74, 1023), which they fix to the cliff with chains and a wedge driven through the chest, all doubtless in realistic fashion, for the chorus later declare that they have heard the echo of the clangor in the depths of their caves (133–34).[33] These characters make their exit before Prometheus speaks, and perhaps in actual production the actor taking the role of Hephaestus climbed from below "stage" into the wooden figure of Prometheus, for this play seems to have been presented by two actors. Although the exit of Hephaestus is separated from Prometheus' first speech by only six lines, we should assume that Prometheus is silent for some time before speaking, as he doubtless is again later in the play.[34]

The cliff to which Prometheus is bound seems to have considerable height (142–43). Some scholars assume that Prometheus himself was high above the orchestra; that the wooden figure is brought out from

within the cliff rather than through the orchestra and that the first characters enter from the cliff; that Prometheus' position on the cliff can
be reached only through the air or from within the cliff, as the chorus
reach it in their winged car and as Oceanus reaches it on his winged
steed, doubtless from the side opposite that of the chorus; that the
chorus remain on the cliff near Prometheus during the whole play and
are never in the orchestra; that Io enters in the orchestra, where she
could have ample space for her wild dances; that Hermes, also, enters
in the orchestra; and that, at the end of the play, Prometheus and the
chorus sink down with a part of the cliff out of sight.[35] This last assumption, at least, seems unavoidable, and it would be perverse to deny
the possibility of this effect in the theater of Aeschylus.

Impressive, doubtless, was the sight of Prometheus pinioned against
the rugged cliff, possibly a gigantic, naked figure, wooden and therefore somewhat schematized. This setting and its various spectacular
effects furnished an atmosphere worthy of the Titanic and Olympian
characters of the play.

Theme.—An adequate discussion of the significance of the *Prometheus Bound* is far beyond the scope of this treatment. Intellectually,
it is perhaps the most stimulating of all Greek tragedies, and it has long
been subject to various interpretations. Suffice it here to say that the
basic theme, as often in Greek tragedy, appears to be the conflict between
brute force or violence and intelligence or justice. It seems a mistake,
however, to discover in the play, as some have done, an attack upon
popular religion. Throughout the play, the idea that Zeus is new as
a ruler and that every new ruler is likely to be tyrannical is emphasized
insistently.[36] In fact, it is hard to escape the impression that this is a
fundamental idea of the play and quite possibly of the whole trilogy,
which may have ended with the recognition and adoption of wisdom
and justice by Zeus. Obviously the new and unjust Zeus is not the Zeus
of the *Agamemnon* or the Zeus of Aeschylus' own belief. Attractive
to many critics, therefore, is the assumption that the fundamental theme
of the trilogy was the establishment of Zeus as a god not only all-pow-
erful but also all-just and in the fullness of age and wisdom—a final
and perfect compromise or rather combination of power and justice
(cf. 188–92). The creation of such a god is not accomplished in a day,
and it has been called the noblest work of man. Such a theme would
befit the cosmic profundity of the play.

Some scholars have described the basic theme of the trilogy as the
evolution of man and god. Obviously the tradition of a Golden Age
and of man's gradual decline is reversed in the *Prometheus Bound*,
where primitive man is depicted as a pitiful and helpless brute.

If the third play of the trilogy was *Prometheus the Fire-Bearer,* as seems likely, the trilogy may have ended with the establishment of the torch race and the cult of Prometheus at Athens, for Prometheus was there worshiped as a god and closely associated with Hephaestus. Torch races were held in honor of both gods (among others), and their domains were essentially the same (fire and handicraft). In the *Prometheus Unbound,* we are told by Athenaeus (674 D), Aeschylus said that wreaths were worn on the head in honor of Prometheus and in retribution for his bonds, and we know from a fragment (194, Nauck[2]) that Prometheus there further elaborated his benefits to mankind. So this trilogy, like the Orestes trilogy and other Greek tragedies, may have ended with the establishment of an Athenian institution.

The name Prometheus means "forethinker," and this meaning is so often played upon that an element of allegory is undeniable (86; 442–71, etc.). But any consistent and elaborate system of allegories would be unique in Greek tragedy, and efforts to discover such systems in the *Prometheus* have not been successful.[37] Significant names are not uncommon in tragedy, nor are lines with double meanings. Thus the statement that the acts of the new Zeus are not subject to review (324), like many other passages in this play, reflects Athenian pride in their democracy and hatred of tyranny; but essentially the same statement is applied to Xerxes in the *Persians* (*Persians* 213), and similar passages are extremely common in Greek tragedy. It is not necessary, therefore, to assume any elaborate allegory in the interpretation of the *Prometheus Bound.*

Chorus.—The role of the chorus is markedly reduced in the *Prometheus Bound,* although this reduction and the quiet meters of their songs may be due to peculiar conditions of staging. Choral lyrics constitute about one-seventh of this play, whereas they were approximately half of the *Suppliants.* The chief characters of the *Prometheus Bound,* however, are generously assigned anapests and lyrics, which compensate for the reduced choral lyrics. The number of the chorus is probably twelve; certainly the number is small, for they enter on a machine. The introduction of characters, a usual function, is not here given to the chorus. This would be readily understandable if the chorus was not located in the orchestra, but it may be due to the fact that Prometheus is always present and is omniscient.

Discussion.—The *Prometheus* is a strange and extraordinary play. Action is impossible for the main character, since he is bound upon a cliff. The drama is static, but it is filled with conflict. It falls into episodes according to the secondary character present, and as in the *Agamemnon* no secondary character appears more than once. These

various episodes have no connection with each other; but all, of course,
have a connection with Prometheus, and all serve to bring out his character more vividly.

The *Prometheus* contains the first protatic characters (characters
added to the first of the play for purposes of exposition) in extant
drama, although Phrynichus' lost *Phoenissae* doubtless employed a
protatic character. The prelude scene of the *Prometheus* is nevertheless
a dramatic and very effective one in its contrast of character. Might is
crude and utterly heartless:

> He is as disproportion'd in his manners
> As in his shape.

Might usually speaks of Prometheus in the contemptuous third person,
and he directly addresses the Titan only to taunt him. With a vulgar
curtness that is rare in tragedy he upbraids Hephaestus for his reluctance to bind Prometheus. Indeed, characterization by language is carried perhaps as far in this scene as it ever goes in Attic tragedy. Not
only the diction but the unusual type of conversation line by line (stichomythia) is significant of character, for Hephaestus invariably has
precisely one line and Might precisely two. The comparative shortness
of Hephaestus' speeches emphasizes his reluctance, and reluctance is
the dominant note of his character, although he also appears kind and
compassionate in comparison with the inhumanity of Might. The reluctance of Hephaestus may have been brought out in actual production
also by exaggerating his usual limp as he followed Might and Violence
upon the scene. Since Hephaestus is the smithy god (Vulcan), one
might have expected him to be offended at Prometheus' revelation of
divine fire to mortals. But he is portrayed as distinctly friendly to
Prometheus, perhaps in part because the cults of Prometheus and
Hephaestus were closely associated at Athens.

In the opening scene there is a note of irony in that Hephaestus
must bind the humane Prometheus in this inhuman land. Noteworthy
also is the long delay in mentioning the name of Prometheus and the
effectiveness of the line when Hephaestus finally addresses him (66):
"Alas, Prometheus, for your woes I grieve."

The character of Prometheus, like that of Hephaestus, is brought
out by contrast, mainly by contrast with Oceanus. Oceanus, too, has
taken part in the recent war and discord which have ended so disas-
trously for Prometheus. But Oceanus has escaped all punishment, for
he has followed the old Delphic maxim, "Know thyself." This is the
homely wisdom which he urges upon Prometheus (309), and he means
by it that Prometheus should recognize his own limitations and the

irresistible supremacy of Zeus. In somewhat contemptuously refusing the good offices of the well-disposed Oceanus, Prometheus appears to harden his determination into obstinacy, and his righteous indignation at Zeus' injustice is too much stimulated by an unnatural joy in suffering under persecution. Still, he is hardly a martyr, for he knows that in the end Zeus must release him and compensate for the wrongs done him.

In the final scene, again, Hermes in a quite different tone urges Prometheus to bow before the will of Zeus. Hermes likens him to a newly yoked colt champing the bit and fighting against the reins— Prometheus, like Zeus, is new in his position—and Hermes repeatedly accuses Prometheus of willfulness and obstinacy. The chorus, too, being entirely ordinary and unheroic, except at the very end of the play, urge Prometheus to yield, and they admit the justice of the charge of obstinacy (1037). We cannot fail to admire the truly heroic inflexibility of Prometheus before the tyrannical threats of Hermes, the usual insolent herald of Greek tragedy; but still Prometheus seems willful and obstinate throughout the play. In the prelude, Might confesses that willfulness and obstinacy (*authadia*) are among his own characteristics (79), and he has already used the same Greek word to characterize the unyielding point of the wedge driven through Prometheus' chest (64). So Might is as hard as steel. Later in the play (436–71) Prometheus defends himself against the charge of displaying these same qualities after he has apparently done so to a marked degree in the scene with Oceanus. Prometheus, too, therefore, has the determination of steel.

But if we admit the obstinacy of Prometheus, we must not overlook the tyrannical injustice of the new Zeus, for the chastisement of Prometheus exceeds his offense. The very fact that the conflict will eventually end in a compromise for which both parties will be anxious proves that both parties are at fault. It is obvious from various passages in the play that both Zeus and Prometheus are to undergo change (186–92, 511–13, 980–82). Fragments from the opening of the *Prometheus Unbound,* also, show that later Zeus has softened. He has pardoned the Titans who formed the chorus of that play. These same fragments indicate that Prometheus has suffered greatly and suggest that his obstinacy is gone. Any attempt of modern critics wholly to justify the position of Zeus overlooks the significance of these later changes. The new Zeus of this play is not the Zeus of later times. A bitter contempt for the new Zeus is everywhere obvious in the lines of Prometheus, emphasized by the words for "ruler" that are applied to him. Zeus is nowhere referred to as "king" (the title applied to him in the great chorus in the *Agamemnon,* line 355) or as "Lord" except by Io (584), but everywhere he is "dictator" or "tyrant" (*tyrannos,* 222 and frequently) or "marshal" (*tagos,* 96) or "president of the immortals" (*makaron prytanis,* 169).

In the *Prometheus,* as in the *Seven against Thebes,* the central portion of the play is taken up with a series of long speeches. The Athenian audience, always keenly interested in artistic eloquence, probably took great delight in these speeches. They are skillfully constructed, especially those in the scene with Io, wherein Prometheus' reluctance and the keen interest of the chorus are subtle psychological devices for exciting the interest of the audience. The appeal of these speeches, however, is of an epic rather than a dramatic nature, although in part they constitute further exposition for the trilogy. Indeed, this play, like the *Agamemnon,* has the unusually elaborate exposition which well befits the first play of a trilogy.

Some effort has been made to join together the various phases of the action. Preparation for the entrance of Oceanus is found in the mention of him as father of the chorus (140); but after he appears, strangely enough, no reference is made to the fact that the chorus consists of his daughters. That Prometheus has married a daughter of Oceanus also is here ignored (cf. 555–60). Later Io is reminded that the chorus are the sisters of her father (636). No preparation for her appearance, however, has been given. But she, too, is a victim of the unjust Zeus. Another connection between Io and Prometheus is the fact that one of her descendants (Heracles—not named in the play but widely known as the deliverer of Prometheus) will eventually deliver Prometheus. This descendant, Prometheus tells us, will be the thirteenth generation from Io (774; 871–74; cf. 27). The appearance of Io and the references to Heracles, therefore, obviously prepare for the role of Heracles in the *Prometheus Unbound.* In that play, as the fragments preserved indicate, Prometheus described the wanderings of Heracles in the west as he here describes the wanderings of Io in the east and with a similar wealth of geographical detail. Heracles, also, was a victim of divine injustice. The divinity mainly responsible for the sufferings of both Heracles and Io was Hera, jealous of the many loves of Zeus. She is repeatedly mentioned in this play; but Prometheus blames Zeus for the suffering of Io, for he wishes to stress the injustice of Zeus.

Numerous other references to the freeing of Prometheus doubtless look forward to the *Prometheus Unbound,* as do the threats of Hermes that Prometheus will return from Tartarus to be torn by the eagle of Zeus, "a day-long uninvited banqueter." References to "Earth" or

"Themis," the mother of Prometheus and the important source of his knowledge, prepare for her appearance in a subsequent play of the trilogy.

The severer punishment of Prometheus and his being cast into Tartarus at the end of the *Prometheus Bound* are repeatedly foreshadowed in the earlier scenes, especially by his wish that he had been hurled into Tartarus where his enemies could not see and mock his misfortune (152–59). The boastful threats of Prometheus against Zeus are so plain and stress the possible rather than the actual outcome so insistently that one is inclined to consider them taunts addressed directly to Zeus rather than predictions to Io and the chorus. At least the appearance of Hermes announcing the wrath of Zeus seems the natural result of these boastful threats.

A certain suspense is maintained during the early part of the play. Prometheus mysteriously refers to his secret concerning the possible overthrow of Zeus (169–71; 189), and he does not reveal it to Oceanus. Later he tells the chorus, too, that he will not yet say whether Zeus is to rule forever, because by keeping this secret he will escape his bonds (520–25). This refusal is really as naïve as his refusal to tell his own story to Io simply because he has just finished telling it to Oceanus and the chorus, or his refusal to reveal details concerning Heracles because, he alleges, it would take too long and would profit Io nothing to learn them (875–76). But finally (768) Prometheus does reveal quite frankly the oracle that the son of a certain mother is fated to be mightier than his sire; but he does not, of course, reveal the essential part of the secret—the identity of the mother.[38] The suspense over this secret and that over the outcome of the clash of wills between Zeus and Prometheus constitute the only dramatic interest maintained throughout the play; for here, even more obviously than in the *Persians,* there is no reversal of fortune, and the dramatic structure is unusually simple. But there is a general heightening of tension as the play progresses, especially in the growing wrath and boldness of Prometheus.

The final scene, like the prelude, is highly dramatic. Hermes and Prometheus revile each other in cutting repartee that might appear comic to the modern reader but in reality is spoken in bitter earnestness. At the very end of the play, spectacular stagecraft and the Titanic defiance of Prometheus combine to make a magnificent finale for this "first act" of the trilogy.

5, 6, 7. **TRILOGY ON ORESTES (*ORESTEIA*)
(458 B.C.)

Aeschylus won first place with this, the only complete trilogy of Greek tragedies which has survived. The individual plays are entitled *Agamemnon, Choephoroe,* and *Eumenides.* These three tragedies were originally followed by a satyr-play, now lost, entitled *Proteus.* The first play concerns the murder of Agamemnon, the second the vengeance taken for this murder, the third the results of this vengeance. The title of the second play (Libation-Bearers) suggests the claims of a murdered father, and perhaps the "offerings" made to him (slaughter of his murderers), as the title of the third play (Avenging Furies) suggests the claims of a mother slain by her son.[39] The *Proteus* probably parodied the tale of Menelaus and Proteus as told in the *Odyssey* (4.351–570).

Structure of the trilogy.—This trilogy bears some resemblances, mainly superficial, to a modern drama in three acts. Several years elapse between the first and second plays, some days between the second and third, and during the third play an indefinite time elapses at a change of scene. Although the first two plays have the same background, the palace of Agamemnon, the third play opens before the temple of Apollo at Delphi, then quickly passes, it seems, to an interior scene, and then with a vacant stage shifts to Athens. Both the first and the second play close at a high emotional tension and each obviously looks forward to the succeeding play.

These separate plays differ from the acts of a modern play, however, in that each contains its own problem with sufficient exposition and its own immediate solution, although this solution in the first and second plays is of such a nature that it brings on a new action. Still, the plays could be presented and understood independently. Each play also has its own chorus and for the most part a separate cast of characters. No character appears in all three plays except Clytemnestra—if we are willing to consider her ghost the same personality as the living character. Orestes is doubtless the main character of the trilogy. Though he does not appear in the *Agamemnon,* he is there mentioned several times and his return is ominously foretold.

There is an essential unity in the three plays—all deal with the eventual fate of the house of Agamemnon—but this unity is marred in the *Eumenides* by the emergence of the theme of Athens and her greatness, which eclipses Orestes at the end.

No significant development of character is presented in this trilogy. Clytemnestra seems to break somewhat at the end of the *Agamemnon,* and the modern reader might have expected her to be profoundly affected by the murder during the several years which elapse before the return of Orestes; but she is essentially the same character in the *Choephoroe* that she was in the *Agamemnon*. Perhaps the author deliberately intended that she should be, for change might indicate more humanity and weakness than the author wishes to allow her. Orestes, too, seems to break at the end of the *Choephoroe*; but he is the same individual, convinced of the justice of his cause, in the *Eumenides*.

Legend.—The story of the return and murder of Agamemnon is told in various installments in the *Odyssey*, where his fate is artistically employed as at once a warning and a contrast to that of Odysseus.[40] Aegisthus, according to the Homeric version, invited Agamemnon to a feast at the house of Aegisthus and with the aid of Clytemnestra there murdered him and his company in a wholesale and treacherous slaughter. Cassandra is said to have been slain at Agamemnon's side by Clytemnestra. No mention is made of an earlier delay at Aulis and the sacrifice of Iphigenia. Ambition and lust are presumably the motives in this Homeric version. Various other early poets, especially Stesichorus, treated the theme with certain additions and changes.

In Aeschylus, Agamemnon is slain in his own palace by Clytemnestra with the apparently minor aid of Aegisthus. Hatred conceived at the sacrifice of Iphigenia is suggested by the chorus and is plainly stated by Clytemnestra herself as her motivation. This was not original with Aeschylus.[41] In the *Choephoroe,* however, only one passing reference is made to Iphigenia, and this by Electra (*Choephoroe* 242), whereas the charge is repeatedly made and practically admitted by Clytemnestra that she slew Agamemnon because of her love for Aegisthus (*Choephoroe* 893, 920). Each motivation is successful in its own play, but the second play seems hardly consistent with the first. Aeschylus is stressing the guilt of Agamemnon in the first, that of Clytemnestra in the second.

Influence.—The *Agamemnon* has often been considered the greatest of all Greek tragedies. Its perfection, however, depends primarily on poetic effect and tragic atmosphere—the forte of Aeschylus. Its plot is very simple. For these reasons, and possibly because of its very perfection, it inspired few imitators or adapters. Only one other Greek play is known to have been written with this title (by Ion), although Sophocles apparently wrote a *Clytemnestra* and an *Aegisthus,* the precise subjects of which are unknown.

The *Choephoroe* obviously falls below the *Agamemnon* as drama and in certain ways fails to do justice to the return of Orestes. Both Euripides and Sophocles rewrote this part of the story, and Orestes was one of the most frequently employed characters in Greek tragedy. Although the date of Sophocles' *Electra* is unknown and highly disputed, it is assumed in the present work that Sophocles' interpretation followed that of Euripides, constituting a violent reaction and protest against Euripides' condemnation of Orestes' slaying his mother. We hear of no later Greek play entitled *Electra*.

There is no indication that these plays of Aeschylus were widely read or of great influence in later times.[42] Various scenes from them or from the myth in general, however, are found in vase painting and other art.[43]

Some five tragedies entitled *Orestes* are known to have been written by Greek dramatists.[44] Only that of Euripides survives. The eventual purification of Orestes is the subject also of Euripides' *Iphigenia in Tauris,* as the sacrifice of Iphigenia is the subject of his *Iphigenia at Aulis.*

All these themes were popular among the Roman dramatists, and the extant plays of Seneca include a *Thyestes* and an *Agamemnon.*

The *Electra* of Sophocles and that of Euripides have inspired a great many adaptations among modern writers, including the *Oreste* of Voltaire (1750) and a play of similar title by Alfieri (1786).[45]

The trilogy of Aeschylus was not as influential in Renaissance times and later as one might expect, partly because its language is more difficult and its manuscript tradition has been more imperfect than those of any other Greek tragedy.[46] Considerable progress has been made in these matters, however, and the trilogy has exerted great influence in recent times. Richard Wagner, for instance, was tremendously affected by it; his ideas about the significance of drama and the theater in general were molded by impressions gained from it.[47] Certain dramatists of the present day have been profoundly affected by it. One of the most remarkable modernizations of the story is Eugene O'Neill's *Mourning Becomes Electra.*[48] This trilogy shows striking similarities to the trilogy of Aeschylus in its situations and events, in the use of action in one of the plays significantly parallel to that in another, and in interpreting the plot as an illustration of the principle that one dreadful crime leads inevitably to another. Noteworthy, also, are O'Neill's effective use of the "chorus" as representing "the town as a human background for the drama . . . . ," his repeated description of faces as masks, his very effective use of literal repetition[49] and dramatic irony,[50] and numerous minor details reminiscent of Aeschylus. O'Neill's characters, however, and their motivations and the spirit of his play are very different from those of Aeschylus.

Theme and leading ideas.—The primary theme of the whole trilogy is the curse of a private blood feud inherited from generation to generation and the necessity of its final replacement by public legal process.

Certain ideas pervade the whole trilogy and occur time and time again like leitmotifs. For instance, blood once spilled is, as Aeschylus says, irrevocable, and no really adequate atonement can ever be made.[51] The most memorable expression of this thought occurs in the *Choephoroe* (72–74, Morshead):

> Though in one channel ran Earth's every stream,
> Laving the hand defiled from murder's stain,
> It were in vain.[52]

The "doer must suffer," and one dreadful crime leads to another.[53] Through suffering comes wisdom—this is the main theme of the great opening songs of the *Agamemnon,* with their beautiful description of the sacrifice of Iphigenia.[54]

The fate of Agamemnon himself is interpreted by Aeschylus as an example of the fatal progression from worldly success (*koros*) to overweening pride and insolence, especially against the gods (*hybris*), and its resultant ruin (*ate*). But the chorus insist that it is not mere worldly success but sin—and of course *hybris* is sin—that brings mortals to ruin (*Agamemnon* 750–81).

**AGAMEMNON

Scene.—The scene, as usually in later Greek tragedy, is before a palace, here the palace of Agamemnon. The Watchman appears on the roof of the palace (top of the "skene"). Images of certain gods are visible (513), especially the usual statue of Apollo of the Ways (1081). Agamemnon and Cassandra enter in cars or chariots.

Time.—Double chronology is unusually conspicuous in the *Agamemnon.* Troy is said to have been taken during the night, in which the signals are seen and the action of the play begins (279). Although Agamemnon could not possibly have sailed from Troy to Argos in one day, he nevertheless appears a few hundred lines later.

Theme.—As an individual play, the subject of the *Agamemnon* is the vengeance which Clytemnestra takes upon the king because, she claims, he sacrificed their daughter, Iphigenia, at Aulis ten years previously. The primary theme is the continual destruction, inherited from generation to generation, which a blood feud and crime bring upon a house.

Discussion.—The *Agamemnon* does not contain a great deal of dramatic action. The first half of the play, before the entrance of

Agamemnon, is almost wholly devoted to exposition, preparation, and foreshadowing. The tension, however, rises sharply from the dark hints of the Watchman and the vague foreboding of the first choral songs to the cruel ironies of Clytemnestra, which are all the more alarming because of her outward calm. The real action begins with the dramatic climax—the verbal duel between Clytemnestra and Agamemnon. The surrender of Agamemnon to his wife is the turning point of the play, but the emotional climax comes with the raving prophecies of Cassandra and the death cries of Agamemnon which follow almost immediately. Although the real action is slow in starting, once started there is no delay. The final complete choral song—such songs have a tendency to retard the action, and the first half of this play is unusually rich in them—comes just after Agamemnon's exit. The last six hundred and fifty verses, therefore, are rapid, and their rapidity is matched by their excitement.

From the death of Agamemnon, the action looks both backward to the murders and forward to the events of the succeeding plays. The suspense and excitement are maintained to the end, and the atmosphere remains tense and tragic. Obviously only the immediate problem—the vengeance of Clytemnestra upon Agamemnon—has been solved.

Of the six characters in the *Agamemnon,* five appear or, more properly, have speaking lines only during a single scene each. Clytemnestra is the only character who appears more than once. She dominates the play as she dominates every character in it, with the exception of Cassandra, and the power of the drama comes primarily from this one powerful figure and from the overwhelming tragic atmosphere and pathos which the poet has created. Despite her unquestioned dominance, however, there is not a single colorless or stereotyped character in the whole play. Agamemnon himself approaches the usual type of haughty and overconfident king, but strikingly individual elements may be recognized in his character. He is tired and worn, a disillusioned and almost defeated victor. Although his role as a speaking character is short, the whole play is concerned with his fate and so it is rightly called by his name.

Clytemnestra as portrayed in the *Agamemnon* is one of the most impressive characters in Greek drama. She is described by the Watchman in the opening lines of the play as a woman with the counsel and will of a man. This first reference significantly cites her most striking characteristic. In her first conversation with the chorus she stands out as a self-confident realist. Although she has not neglected to sacrifice at the altars of the city, she scoffs at the idea that her news may depend upon the visions of a slumbering mind or mere rumor.

A technical peculiarity—lack of motivation for entrance and exit—is very effective in the case of Clytemnestra. Whether this is a deliberate artifice on the part of the dramatist may be disputed. One scholar, at least, has seen mere dramatic artlessness in Clytemnestra's unmotivated exit at verse 614.[55] But, since lack of motivation is characteristic of her role throughout the play, it seems reasonable to attribute this feature to the deliberate purpose of the dramatist. It is effective because it adds a certain eeriness to the character of Clytemnestra. She appears and disappears at precisely the proper moment like a baleful apparition endowed with supernatural knowledge.[56]

The *Agamemnon* is one of the few Greek tragedies in which an important intrigue is planned and executed with no explanation beforehand. In the *Medea* of Euripides, for instance, Medea's own foretelling of her plan is essential because the most interesting part of that play is Medea's inner struggle. But that technique could not be employed in the *Agamemnon,* if for no other reason, because Clytemnestra does not and could not—without losing her dramatic stature—waver in her resolve for a single moment. Here we are not even told that Clytemnestra has taken Aegisthus as her paramour. But there have been repeated hints both of this fact and of her murderous desire for revenge, and Aeschylus is obviously taking for granted that the audience knows the story of the return of Agamemnon; many of the lines could not be appreciated without this knowledge. So the *Agamemnon* is not essentially different from the other Greek plays which prefer dramatic irony to surprise; but it is superficially different in that, like the *Oedipus the King* of Sophocles, it takes for granted more foreknowledge than do most Greek tragedies. No play contains more tragic foreboding, however, than does the *Agamemnon.*

Great artistry is employed in the creation of this overwhelming tragic atmosphere of the *Agamemnon.* The first part of the play on the surface announces the Greek victory at Troy and the return of the conquerors. After ten years' struggle and hardship in camp, ten years' anxiety and grief at home, this news would seem to call for great rejoicing. But neither chorus nor characters can rejoice, and each successive phase of the early scenes adds greater tragic gloom and foreboding of disaster.

The gloom sets in immediately with the prologue. Although the Watchman is a protatic character, his speech is one of the most natural and effective monologues in Greek tragedy. Weary of his lonely task, he sings or hums to keep himself awake; but, like the Nurse in Euripides' *Medea,* he soon strikes the note of tragic foreboding, expressing his grief over the fortunes of this house. His dance of joy at sight

of the beacon signal is quickly stifled in the dark thoughts that not all
is well in Argos. The very walls of the house would cry out (at Clytemnestra's unfaithfulness) if they could find a tongue!

The chorus of old men enters with one of the longest series of
marching anapests and choral lyrics found in Greek tragedy (218
lines). They are still in ignorance of the news—a masterly stroke of
the poet here as in the *Persians*—but their songs are very pertinent to
the situation and important both for the exposition and for the emotional tone. Clytemnestra may be present in the background during a
part of these songs, since she is addressed at verse 83 and since her
presence at the altars sacrificing would lend a certain irony to the
moralizing of the chorus that the sinner may not avert the wrath of
heaven by sacrifice (69–71). Here the chorus is speaking with specific
reference to Paris; but their words, as Thomson points out,[57] apply
equally well to Agamemnon, to whose sin such thoughts inevitably lead
the chorus, and to Clytemnestra. Clytemnestra must depart from the
scene, however, before the chorus's description of the sacrifice of Iphigenia. This is a very beautiful and poetic description, approached with
lyric indirectness and viewed with the clear perspective which their
age and the intervening years have given them. The sacrifice of Iphigenia is condemned with a positiveness that strengthens the chorus's
foreboding of revenge and punishment. This story to a certain degree
explains the dark hints of the Watchman and makes possible a proper
interpretation of the ambiguous words and actions of Clytemnestra.
The prophecy of Calchas is repeated with details—doubtless original
with Aeschylus—that foreshadow the action of the play (151–55):
"a sacrifice strange and contrary to our custom, one not followed by a
feast, worker of strife among kin, fearing not the lord of the household; remaining is a dreadful, re-arising, house-ruling, deceptive, un-
forgetting wrath, which will avenge the child." So the chorus sings,
although no translation can reproduce the rugged power and the boldness of the original.

The chorus apostrophizes Zeus in perhaps the loftiest verses in
Aeschylus (160–83), introducing one of the leading ideas of the trilogy, that wisdom is learned through suffering, which Heaven visits
upon man against his will—an attempt to justify the ways of God to
man with specific application to Agamemnon; for Agamemnon, though
warned beforehand by the ominous prophecies of Calchas, nevertheless
sacrificed his daughter. The chorus then returns to their pathetic story,
breaking off at precisely the proper point: "What happened then,
neither did I see nor do I tell . . . ." Like the Watchman, the chorus
has repeatedly foreboded ill and deprecated it by praying in a refrain

for a happy outcome and, finally, by refusing to think of the inevitable events that are to come. At this point Clytemnestra significantly reappears—the embodiment of the family hatred and the exactor of the revenge of which the chorus has sung.

After Clytemnestra has described the taking of Troy as she imagines it, she suggests the possibility that the Greeks with their insolent violence may outrage the gods—as, of course, they did—and that even if they do not commit any such outrage there is still the woe of the dead (337–47).[58] Clytemnestra is here thinking of the dead Iphigenia, but the woe of the dead is a theme that is repeatedly dwelt upon by chorus and Herald in the following scene. At the end of her speech Clytemnestra indulges in a subtle and characteristically Greek device: she picks up and echoes a phrase of the chorus as a good omen (349). The chorus has repeatedly expressed the prayer that the good may win the victory (121, 139); and, more pointedly, as they are about to address Clytemnestra upon her entrance, they pray that "good execution crown all this as our closest, lone-guardian bulwark of the Peloponnesian land desires" (255–57). Clytemnestra is delighted that the chorus here have quite unconsciously prayed for the fulfillment of her vengeance upon Agamemnon, and so she echoes their refrain.

After this episode, the choral song begins as a hymn of thanksgiving to Zeus, who has cast a net of destruction over Troy. Here the audience may shudder at the thought that Clytemnestra is secretly planning to cast such a net of destruction over Agamemnon. But, like the Watchman, the chorus stifles its joy in tragic thoughts, unable to forget the ruin that follows too great prosperity and sin, Paris and Helen, the grief of Menelaus, which is beautifully described, or the sufferings of the homes in Greece to which the god of war, "trafficker in bodies," has returned ashes instead of the men who went away—all for another's sinful wife. The chorus dwell upon the hatred which the people feel toward Agamemnon and Menelaus and the danger of success that is unjust or brought about at the cost of much bloodshed. Thus the chorus interpret Clytemnestra's ambiguous reference to the woe of the dead as a reference to the Greeks slain at Troy, and the final note of their song is one of foreboding of the retribution which this woe will cause and of skepticism over the news of victory.

The Herald brings good news; but, like the Watchman, he shows little joy, and the final effect of his appearance is to aggravate rather than relieve the tragic gloom of the play. From his description of the fall of Troy we surmise that the Greeks have been guilty of excess in their good fortune and of the sacrilege which Clytemnestra ironically deprecated. The very words of the Herald suggest the words which

Clytemnestra has used. One line (527), indeed, states definitely that the altars and sanctuaries of the gods have been destroyed; but the authenticity of this line, almost identical with a line in the *Persians* (811), has been doubted.[59] Even if this line is rejected, the Herald is still much too boastful of the destruction of Troy and the great good fortune and honor of Agamemnon, "most worthy of all living mortals" (531–32). Such boasts, according to ancient belief, invite the envy and wrath of Heaven. Here they serve also to prepare for the appearance of Agamemnon, for they suggest the pride and conceit which are Agamemnon's most striking characteristics.

The Herald elicits from the chorus, whose reluctance to speak is reminiscent of the similar reluctance of the Watchman, that all is not well in Argos. This leads him to recite his depressing report of the toils about Troy that broke the hearts and bodies of the Greeks: "If one should add the tale of the bird-killing winters—how unbearable the snows of Mount Ida made them—or the heat of summer, when the sea lay waveless down to rest upon its stifling noonday couch— Why must we recall such suffering?" Then the Herald refers to those who escaped these toils for the peace of death—the theme of the previous choral song and of Clytemnestra's ambiguous words. He repeatedly breaks off under strong emotion.

Clytemnestra, suddenly appearing, now reminds the chorus of her previous knowledge and of their needless skepticism. Having thus humiliated them, she is in a favorable position to make her false protestations of joy at the return of her husband and of her own loyalty and faithfulness. She maintains her hypocrisy well; but her speeches are interlarded with phrases of double meaning, and at times she yields to her bitterness in lines of bloodcurdling irony (611–12): "I know no joy of another man or shameful rumor any more than I know the dipping of the steel."

After Clytemnestra has withdrawn, the Herald would gladly consider his tale finished, since the good news is told; but the chorus force him to continue with a report of the storm and the fate of Menelaus. Here the impression that sacrilege has been committed by the Greeks is unmistakable, for the storm is attributed to the wrath of the gods (649).

The Herald spends fifteen lines explaining why he should not describe the storm; but this excuse deceived the ancient audience no more than it does the modern reader, for the description of a storm is the favorite tour de force of ancient poets, and a full account of a storm once cited on the horizon in an ancient literary work is absolutely inevitable. Nor can we now resist the temptation to quote three magnificent lines from his description of the deathly calm which followed (658–60) : "When the bright light of the sun came up, before us the Aegean sea blossoms with the corpses of Greek men and the wrecks of ships."

After the Herald departs, the chorus again sings of Paris and Helen and the ruin which they brought upon Troy, where Helen (the sister of Clytemnestra) went as a "maiden-wept Avenging Fury." These thoughts of sin and insolent pride and punishment dominate the verses immediately before Agamemnon enters, and the fate of the house of Agamemnon, as explicitly pointed out in the *Choephoroe* (935–38), is essentially the same as the fate of the house of Priam.

The treachery of Clytemnestra and the conceited pride of Agamemnon are both well portrayed in the scene of their clash. The pride of Agamemnon is of great significance in his character. Already suggested in the Herald's speech, it is now spectacularly symbolized by Agamemnon's triumphant entrance in his chariot with followers and fanfare. He is somewhat grudging in the credit for his success which he allows the gods and his allies (811), and he is too proud of his utter destruction of Troy.[60] His conceit entirely prevents him from properly understanding the veiled warnings of the chorus. From his haughty and contemptuous response to Clytemnestra's hypocrisy, it is obvious that he despises her; but if he has really grasped her ill-concealed innuendoes, he pathetically underestimates his adversary. The essential weakness of his character is only too apparent in this clash with the strong-willed Clytemnestra, and this clash constitutes the dramatic climax of the play. In attempting to make Agamemnon accept her base flattery and walk upon the blood-red tapestry, Clytemnestra is attempting to cause him to commit an act of insolence, it seems, which will evoke the disgust and hatred of men and the vengeance of the gods. Such an act will be a good omen for the success of her murderous designs and will lessen their odiousness. The insolence of the act which Agamemnon does commit is likely to be underestimated by the modern reader. The ordinary ancient Greek house had no rug or carpet upon the floor, and the rich tapestries which are spread for Agamemnon, as he himself says, were proper to the worship of the gods. Some critics, however, think that there is no insolence in Agamemnon's act but that the tapestries are a symbol of Clytemnestra's hypocrisy and that their crimson color symbolizes the coming bloodshed.[61] Certainly the color and action here add to the effectiveness of this magnificent scene.

In order to persuade Agamemnon, Clytemnestra condescends even to using a term of endearment (905), and she prostrates herself in an Oriental manner—a loathsome act of servility in Greek eyes (and later the cause of serious dissension in the army of Alexander the Great). At first Agamemnon brusquely refuses such excesses; but Clytemnestra displays a demonic or, perhaps more properly, feminine cunning. She subtly flatters his pride and makes the issue one of courage—a powerful persuasion when urged by a woman—and of generosity in granting her this desire. As Agamemnon submits with a show of reluctance, he insultingly bids Clytemnestra to receive with kindness the girl, Cassandra, his concubine, whom he has brought with him as his especial prize from Troy.

Throughout this scene there are ironic double meanings in the lines of Clytemnestra. She states that, if Agamemnon had been wounded as often as rumor said, his body would be pierced more than a net (868) —an ill-omened statement. Later we look back upon this and the chorus' earlier reference to a net of destruction with horror. The unhoped-for home to which justice leads Agamemnon, in Clytemnestra's mind, is Hades; and her "care never overcome by sleep," which will justly dispose all else as decreed by Heaven, is her undying hatred and passion for revenge. Near the end of this scene Clytemnestra refers to the crushing of the wine from the unripe grape—the blood of the virgin Iphigenia. One bold word leads to another until, as Agamemnon enters the palace and can no longer hear, she breaks out openly, praying to Zeus to fulfill her prayer.

But there has been one passage in this scene which was charged with an irony that Clytemnestra did not intend—the first mention of her son Orestes.[62]

After the hypocritical and ironic welcome which Clytemnestra tenders Agamemnon, the main theme of the chorus is again dreadful foreboding. The old men have made a feeble and wholly unsuccessful attempt to warn Agamemnon of her hypocrisy, and now they are unable to cast off their fear. A foundering ship may be saved by jettison, they philosophize, and a famine may be averted by a year of plenty; but blood once spilled is irrevocable.

Throughout the duel between man and wife there has been present a third figure—the lie incarnate of their pretended joy and harmony, Cassandra. Now Clytemnestra quickly and unexpectedly returns and commands Cassandra to go within. Nowhere else does Clytemnestra appear so vile a creature as in this scene. She basely attempts to impress upon Cassandra her good fortune in being assigned as a slave to a house of wealth. But here for once Clytemnestra meets her peer, and she can only break out with bloody threats and then leave the stage. The resemblance and the contrast between this scene and the preceding clash of man and wife is most effective.

In extant plays the dramatic exploitation of madness appears first in the scene with Cassandra. Like the first appearance of a messenger's speech in the *Persians,* this has rarely if ever been surpassed. Very effective preparation has been made in the tension built up by Cassandra's stubborn refusal to speak as long as Clytemnestra remains "on stage."

Cassandra's clairvoyance breaks forth in wild and enigmatic lyrics. Her passion and excitement is emphasized by its contrast to the naïve simplicity of the chorus, who undertake to give a pedestrian answer to her exclamation (1087) : "Ah, now whither, Apollo, have you led me!" Later in the calmer mood of spoken iambic lines she describes with dreadful vividness what she has already intimated: the murder of Agamemnon and the murder of herself are soon to take place within the palace. A chorus of Furies, she declares (1186–93), are ever present singing a song of ruin on the roof of this palace. The truth of her relation of the past must be admitted by the old men of the chorus; but, when they are finally made to understand her words concerning the present and the future, they refuse to believe. Then with dramatic sensationalism she throws down her staff and tears the wreath of a prophetess from her head. Amid the consideration of her own death she breaks off to prophesy the coming of the son who will slay his mother to avenge his father's death and will put an end to these destructions (1281; cf. 1104).

As Cassandra is about to enter the palace she recoils at the stench of blood, and the chorus again responds with naïve simplicity. She declares that a woman (Clytemnestra) will die for a woman (Cassandra) and a man (Aegisthus) for a man (Agamemnon). Finally she walks sadly and calmly into the palace with lines in which her own tragedy is generalized into the greater tragedy of the fate of mortals upon the earth. This scene, in which the vengeance for the deed is told before the deed is actually committed, furnishes magnificent preparation for the murder of Agamemnon.

At the death cries of Agamemnon the chorus fall into ineffectual dissension. Indeed each member seems to express his individual opinion, for there are twelve separate speeches. The utter futility of the chorus at such a point would be expected in Greek tragedy, but Aeschylus has carefully prepared for it. At the opening of the play, these old men, "fall'n into the sere, the yellow leaf," have described themselves as "no stronger than a child, a dream of the night lost and wandering in the day" (81–82). Their naïve simplicity in the scene with Cassandra, also, prepares for their weakness and indecision here.

Clytemnestra appears at her greatest superhuman height when she comes forth with the bodies of Agamemnon and Cassandra. She confesses her former deception with no shame or compunction; she describes the slaughter of her husband with amazing sang-froid and heartless irony (1387). When his blood fell upon her, she "rejoiced no less than a field of grain in the labor of the bud rejoices at the fall of rain from heaven" (1390–92). Agamemnon, she declares, filled the mixing bowl of the house with curses, and he himself has drained it. The chorus is amazed at her brazenness; but she is more composed than ever: "Whether you choose to praise or censor me, I care not. This is Agamemnon, my husband, dead and slain by this right hand, a worker of justice. Thus it is."

Her defense is a mother's defense: Agamemnon slew their child. Her jealousy as a wife, also, asserts itself in a bitter, almost revolting passage, and she is proud to have Aegisthus as her defender. Finally, bringing forth the name of Iphigenia for the first time in the play, she pronounces her judgment that the penalty matches the deed.

To the inquiry of the chorus concerning the burial of Agamemnon, Clytemnestra responds that she will bury him, but with no tears, and that his daughter, Iphigenia (the second and last use of the name in the whole trilogy), as is fitting, will welcome her father at the swift-flowing passage of woes, throwing her arms about him and kissing him (1555–59).

Clytemnestra's defense is convincing, for such cold-blooded bitterness is most plausibly interpreted as the result of years of carefully nursed hatred (cf. 912, 1377). The chorus has prepared for this defense in quoting the prediction of Calchas (126–55) and in repeatedly condemning the sacrifice of Iphigenia, calling Agamemnon's consent to the sacrifice sacrilegious, impure, and unholy (219–20). But, strong as Clytemnestra shows herself at the beginning of this scene, the impassioned clash with the chorus is not without its effect on her. At the very last she is broken and admits the truth of the law that the doer must suffer. She bids the curse leave the house, and confesses that she would be content with only a part of the house's wealth if she might free it from its mad slaughter (1567–76). Whether her conscience is awakened is a disputed point. She certainly is fearful of punishment to come.

The *Agamemnon,* like the *Prometheus,* ends in a high pitch of excitement. Such an ending is possible in the first or second play of a trilogy, but single tragedies like those of Sophocles and Euripides almost invariably have an ending of calm finality.

The chorus have been heavily stricken by the death of Agamemnon and amazed at the hard joy of Clytemnestra, but the insolent gloating of the cowardly Aegisthus is more than they can endure. Bitter and contemptuous reviling is exchanged for threats, until finally, with rising excitement, emphasized by a shift to trochaic meter (1649), they decide to resort to arms and draw their swords.[63] Clytemnestra, however, breaking her long silence, takes command of the situation at the crucial moment, and the play ends in a temporary compromise, with the name Orestes repeated and with his return given as the one hope of the chorus.

Preparation for the *Choephoroe* (and *Proteus*??).—Orestes is first mentioned by Clytemnestra (879). Cassandra does not mention him by name, but she clearly foretells his return and the vengeance which he will take. The chorus repeatedly insist that Clytemnestra's deed will bring other distress upon the house and predict that she will pay the penalty for it by citing the law of the talion (1429–30) and by repeating the principle so often enunciated in the play and cited by Clytemnestra herself (1527) in defense of her deed, "the doer must suffer" (1560–66). Near the end of the play, the chorus looks forward to the coming of Orestes (1646, 1667), and their attitude, abhorrence of the deed of Clytemnestra and insistence upon the justice and necessity of punishment, is the attitude of the poet throughout the remainder of the trilogy.

It has been suggested that the passage concerning Menelaus in the Herald's speech prepares for the satyr-play, *Proteus,* which followed this trilogy. This play doubtless told how Menelaus on his voyage from Troy consulted Proteus, the old man of the sea, about his return home. Still, the sinister implications of this passage in the *Agamemnon* are sufficient to justify its inclusion, and some mention of Menelaus seems essential to any account of the return of Agamemnon. Preparation for the *Proteus* may be found in another mention of Menelaus in the *Choephoroe* (1041 b) ; but there the text is uncertain.

CHOEPHOROE ("LIBATION-BEARERS")

The first of the prologue is missing in the manuscripts, but some fragments of it have been preserved in quotations by Aristophanes and ancient commentators. Another textual problem concerns the speech of the first reaction to the news of Orestes' death (691–99), which is given to Clytemnestra in the manuscripts but to Electra by some editors. The text of the lyric parts is often uncertain.

Scene.—The *Choephoroe* shows the same informality in regard to the background as do the *Persians* and the *Eumenides*. This background must have been essentially the same as that of the *Agamemnon,* for the palace is required in both; but the first part of the *Choephoroe* is laid before the tomb of Agamemnon. Even in the first part of the play, however, reference perhaps is made to the statue of Apollo of the Ways (583), which always stood near the entrance of a house, and in the second part the chorus once refers to the tomb (722–25).

At least two entrances to the palace are employed. Clytemnestra probably enters from the women's apartments at verses 668 and 885, as also the Nurse at verse 734. In actual life, of course, such women's apartments would presumably be entered from within the palace.

The chorus withdraw temporarily at verse 874, giving the whole "stage" to the climactic action which follows.

Time.—A considerable length of time, perhaps seven years as in the *Odyssey* (3.304–6), has elapsed between the murder of Agamemnon and the action of the present play; but in the extant text of the play we are nowhere given any precise information on this point (cf. 26; 1012).

The play opens in the early morning, as did the *Agamemnon* and as will the *Eumenides;* but by the time that Orestes comes to the palace night is falling (660).

Legend.—In the *Odyssey* (1.298) Orestes returned from Athens to slay Aegisthus and win renown among all men. Clytemnestra, "his hateful mother," died at the same time, but we are not told in what manner. The version in which Orestes slew his mother and was pursued by her Avenging Furies, however, was certainly well established before the time of Aeschylus, as was Orestes' association with Pylades and the Delphic Apollo. The story of Electra, whose name, meaning "unwed," was reputedly applied to the daughter called Laodice in Homer, belongs to this later version.

Theme.—The theme of the *Choephoroe* as an individual play is again that of revenge, this time the revenge of Orestes upon his mother and Aegisthus for the murder of Agamemnon. Such revenge, according to the law of the blood feud, was the first obligation of Orestes; but here it involves the slaying of his own mother. Aeschylus interprets this deed as necessary but dreadful, and one that must itself be followed by dreadful consequences.

Recognition and intrigue.—The crude implausibilities by which Electra concludes that Orestes has been at Agamemnon's grave are pointed out at length by Euripides in his *Electra* and are best considered in connection with that play. Aristophanes, also, perhaps refers to this scene of Aeschylus (*Clouds* 534–36). But scenes of recognition were not, in all probability, common in early tragedy. This is the first extant tragedy to contain one. Certainly the technique of gracefully managing such scenes was not easy, and it was only gradually developed by the dramatists.

The *Choephoroe* is also the first extant play to contain an intrigue of the type which later became so popular. In this play, as usually later, the intrigue is planned before the audience in order that they may be aware of what is about to take place, although here Orestes does not reveal his intention of announcing his own death—a deception found elsewhere in Greek legend and in Euripides' lost *Cresphontes*. After the plan is revealed, the chorus is here enjoined to silence, as regularly in Sophocles and Euripides (*Choephoroe* 581–82). Incidentally, we may note that Orestes (560–64) says that he and Pylades will imitate the speech of Phocis (the district about Delphi and the home of Pylades); but in the scene with the porter and Clytemnestra no dialect is actually used, although the manner of a lowly traveling merchant is well simulated. The story which Orestes tells is a bare one, however, and has none of the convincing detail of that in Sophocles.

In later tragedy, as had been the case in the *Odyssey*, such intrigues are usually executed with great skill in deception. Here Orestes' plan to go in and slay Aegisthus impresses one as being too unrealistically simple. In fact, he would apparently have failed if chance and the chorus had not come to his aid. Still, there is more complication here than in the corresponding details of Sophocles' play, for here Clytemnestra is skeptical of the report of Orestes' death and summons Aegisthus and his guard. Aegisthus, too, though he fails to receive her message intact, is skeptical. It may be that Aeschylus is making the risks of Orestes great in order to increase the suspense. Certainly there is an element of surprise; for Aegisthus is not discovered within, although there was a well-established tradition, as vase paintings show, that Orestes slew Aegisthus seated on a "throne," and in this play (572) Orestes suggests that he may find Aegisthus on the "thrones" of Agamemnon.[64] There may be an element of suspense in the speech of the old Nurse, also, since rambling and apparently pointless speeches of this sort are effective in increasing the impatience of the audience at an exciting point in the action. Still, the homely garrulousness of the Nurse makes her, like the Watchman in the *Agamemnon,* one of the most vividly portrayed minor characters in Aeschylus. Her realistic description of Orestes as a helpless infant superficially bears a resemblance to comic relief; but, in reality, it subtly prepares for the appeal of Clytemnestra to Orestes to pity the breast which suckled him.[65]

The simple intrigue of Orestes succeeds only because the chorus takes part in the action at this precarious point and directs the Nurse to change the command of Clytemnestra and bid Aegisthus come alone instead of with his guard. A similar important interference of the chorus takes place in Euripides' *Ion* (760–75).

Discussion.—The *Choephoroe* opens significantly with the fervent prayer of Orestes to Hermes and to his dead father. In the section of the prologue now lost he probably revealed the command of Apollo. Certainly he regards the taking of vengeance as an inescapable duty. These are the only facts of importance which he can give; the situation within the palace must be told by the chorus and Electra.

The first words of the chorus sound a depressing, foreboding note. The ominous dream of Clytemnestra is given as the motivation of their entrance; but they are careful not to reveal the details of this dream, which are to be brought in later with great effectiveness. Though the chorus consists of captive maidens, they are more keen in their desire for vengeance and more bitter in their hatred of Clytemnestra than Orestes and Electra themselves.

Electra as depicted in Sophocles and Euripides is the true daughter of the Aeschylean Clytemnestra. By contrast, the Aeschylean Electra, at first glance, appears somewhat weak. True, she does see that to make an offering to the dead Agamemnon on behalf of her mother would be a shameless act; but she appeals to the chorus for instructions, and they must first remind her of Orestes (115). She is uncertain whether it is sacrilege to pray for some god or mortal to come and slay her mother, although when reassured by the chorus she does have the courage to make such a prayer. The manner in which she compares her brother's footprints to her own, furthermore, makes her seem simple. But these evidences of weakness and simplicity are due at least in part to the archaic stiffness of Aeschylus' technique. He must have conversation between Electra and the chorus, and for this he has chosen the unwieldy and formal conversation line by line (stichomythia). The awkwardness of the recognition, too, is due to the poet's own shortcomings.

Electra is not really a weak character. During the long invocation of Agamemnon she flagellates herself into a strong and savage fury. Except for the general atmosphere created, however, this mood finds no proper dramatic effect in the latter half of the play. According to our manuscripts, Electra does not speak after verse 507, although some editors have her re-enter with Clytemnestra when Orestes knocks at the gate and assign her the speech of reaction to the news of Orestes' death (691–99). This is an important speech; but the sentiments expressed are not very different from those which Clytemnestra in her more human moments expresses in the *Agamemnon* (1567–76), and the speech adds greatly to the depth of Clytemnestra's character if the assignment of the manuscripts is retained. Even if these lines should be given to Electra, the dramatic possibilities of her role are still not well exploited, for she does not appear in the final scenes. But she is not strictly pertinent there: Pylades must play the supporting role at the climax in order that Apollo's share in the action may be emphasized; and afterward Orestes is the only important character.

The abuse of Electra is not stressed by Aeschylus as it is by Sophocles and Euripides, but it is nevertheless unmistakable. Electra considers herself a slave (135). The privation and poverty of the rightful heirs is one of Orestes' prime complaints (esp. 246–63). Electra, as her very name indicates, has no hope of marriage unless the usurpers are destroyed (cf. 486–88). When her father was being buried, furthermore, she was shut up, "like a baleful dog," within her chamber (445–50).

As justification for taking vengeance upon his mother, Orestes lists first the command of Apollo, then his grief over his father's death, his own poverty,[66] and the subjection of his countrymen to the rule of two women—for he insists Aegisthus is in spirit a woman (300–305). His prime motivation, therefore, is the command of Apollo; and this leads directly to the following play, where Apollo takes responsibility for his deed, and to the generalizing of Orestes' case into a contest between old divinities and new.

After the recognition has taken place, Orestes, in the strongest terms and with the most optimistic confidence, declares his determination to slay the guilty pair. Instead of translating this into immediate action, however, chorus and characters turn to the tomb of Agamemnon and begin exorcising the spirit of Agamemnon as an aid for the vengeance of his son. This long lyric scene may become tiresome to the modern reader, unacquainted and unsympathetic with such mystic exorcism and finally disappointed, perhaps, that Agamemnon's ghost does not appear as does the ghost of Darius in the *Persians*. Its appearance would nicely parallel that of the ghost of Clytemnestra in the *Eumenides*. Judged from the dramatic standpoint, this scene is undeniably too long. It is conceived perhaps as lasting from dawn till evening. Its length may in part be due to the lack of complication in the plot and the necessity of prolonging the play to the minimum length required of a tragedy. But, in spite of Orestes' determination even before the exorcism, this scene does have its dramatic function. It furnishes the emotional power necessary for the execution of such a horrible deed by creating a frenzy of passion in the participants and, to a less extent, in the audience itself. It stresses the justification of Orestes' act and adds certain details, such as the maiming of Agamemnon's body and the disgrace of Electra. Its music and perhaps its frenzied action, also, probably added greatly to its effectiveness in the theater.[67]

In his first scene with Electra, Orestes has called the murderess of his father a dreadful viper (249)—most aptly and forebodingly, for female vipers were supposed to devour the males and themselves to be devoured by their offspring. Now after the exorcism of the spirit of Agamemnon has been attempted, Orestes inquires of the motive behind the mission of the chorus, and for the first time the details of Clytemnestra's dream are revealed—she dreamed that she had borne a serpent which drew blood from her breast. Orestes is heartened by the coincidence of this dreadful omen. He is ready for the deed.

There is an awful irony in the speech of welcome with which Clytemnestra greets the pretended travelers. One inevitably recalls the welcome given Agamemnon. This house indeed has warm baths and rest from toil for weary travelers!

Aeschylus has not done justice to the cause of Clytemnestra in the *Choephoroe*.[68] He is preparing for the acquittal of Orestes in the *Eumenides,* and apparently he feels that he cannot here give her as strong a defense as she had in the *Agamemnon.* Although she is not here so clearly the woman with a man's will and counsel as she was in the former play, she is still essentially the same. Aeschylus has made no attempt to portray a deterioration of character in her case, though perhaps seven years have passed and though base deeds and base associations normally lead to deterioration of character. Here as in the *Agamemnon* the first reference to Clytemnestra points her chief characterization for the play. She is an ungodly woman (*dystheos*). So say the chorus (46, 525) and Electra (191). She has not lost all motherly feeling for her children, however, if the speech of reaction to the news of Orestes' death is really hers. But unfortunately she is not here given a scene with Electra, which might best be employed, as in Sophocles and Euripides, to bring out her character. Much abuse is heaped upon her by her children, but the most damning evidence against her in the *Choephoroe* is the Nurse's revelation of her secret joy at the news of Orestes' death.

The scene at the climax is a masterpiece. The chorus is temporarily withdrawn in order that all attention may be focused on the action and the characters. The Servant enters frantically calling for Clytemnestra. He has not lost his powers of making objective observations of what is actually going on, but his excitement is intense enough nicely to set off Clytemnestra's unperturbed mastery of the situation. She reads the Servant's riddle when he says that the dead are killing the living—a grand dramatic line. Orestes, the agent, has been thought dead but is actually very much alive; Agamemnon and Cassandra are dead indeed, but they are the true authors of the present slaughter.

Clytemnestra's former strength now becomes apparent. She calls for her "man-slaying" ax—she would clearly slay her son to save her own life. When she is prevented, she bares her breast in her appeal to him. As in the *Agamemnon*,[69] she attempts to lay the blame of her husband's murder in part upon the curse of the house or Fate. But Orestes, in perhaps his most effective line, throws this explanation back at Clytemnestra: Fate, then, is responsible for her own present doom. He charges her with having sold him away into slavery for love of Aegisthus—an idea voiced by Electra near the beginning of the play (132–34). Throughout the play it has been taken for granted, especially in the stasimon recounting the crimes of lustful women (585–651), that lust furnished Clytemnestra her motive for slaying Agamemnon. Even in the *Agamemnon* Clytemnestra has given hints of a real passion for Aegisthus (*Agamemnon* 1434–36; 1654). In the *Choephoroe* her passion is clearly revealed upon the discovery of Aegisthus' corpse. In both plays, furthermore, Clytemnestra insists that, for woman, separation from man is unbearable (*Agamemnon* 861–62; *Choephoroe* 920). Clytemnestra begs Orestes to consider the unfaithfulness of Agamemnon as well as her own; but he insists on the justice of the double standard.

Clytemnestra makes no reference to Iphigenia. Here the author is unfair. Indeed, only one slight reference is made to Iphigenia during the whole play (242). Finally, Clytemnestra, reverting to the riddle of the Servant and playing bitterly on an old proverb, declares that she is pleading with a tomb—Orestes is the spirit of the implacable Agamemnon. Her last words are that she has borne a serpent. Her dream has come true.

Orestes has been a true son of Clytemnestra in this scene. His appeal to Pylades, reminiscent somewhat of the appeal of Electra to the chorus at the opening of the play (122), is dramatically effective in that Pylades, after being silent during the whole play, speaks three lines, citing the authority of Apollo and thus, as it were, placing the stamp of divine approval upon the deed. Still, this appeal would weaken the character of Orestes if it did not seem almost superfluous; for Orestes has been very sure in his purpose all through the play, as sure of it as Clytemnestra was of her purpose in the *Agamemnon*, although Orestes has the direct command of Apollo to support him. For Orestes to falter as Medea does would be sacrilege. His appeal to Pylades, furthermore, comes at the first of his scene with Clytemnestra. If he has shown any real hesitation, it is purely an emotional reaction, for he certainly shows no intellectual misgivings during the subsequent clash. Clytemnestra, however, is never broken as Hamlet's mother is broken.

Orestes is victor, but his superiority is primarily one of physical strength.

The most marked characteristic of Orestes is his bitterness. This is seen from the first of the play, but it comes out most clearly in his final speeches. With sardonic humor he tries to find a name for the bloodstained cloak in which his father was ensnared (973–1006). His lines are charged with the emotion which he so thoroughly suppressed in the scene with Clytemnestra, and these final speeches are strange ones for Greek tragedy. In fact, if we read this speech in a translation which, like Thomson's, is colored by Shakespearean language, we may imagine that we are here reading a newly discovered speech of Hamlet.[70] Again Orestes describes his mother as a deadly serpent whose mere touch would "breed corruption." In these powerful speeches, as in the scene between mother and son, Aeschylus rises to the height of the *Agamemnon*.

Orestes breaks in the final scene as Clytemnestra did in the final scenes of the *Agamemnon*. Orestes' faith in the justice of his cause, however, is never shaken, and the Furies, though not seen by the others present, are external supernatural beings and not merely forces of his own conscience.

Preparation for the *Eumenides*.—The terms "Erinys" and "Erinyes" (Avenging Fury and Furies) occur some nine times in the *Agamemnon,* used with reference to the crime of Paris, to Helen, to the hatred caused by the loss of Greek lives at Troy, and to Agamemnon and his house both because of the sacrifice of Iphigenia (1433) and because of the family blood feud and crimes of Atreus (1580). The same terms are used in the *Choephoroe* in reference to the spirit of Agamemnon demanding vengeance. The most significant of four passages is that in which Orestes describes the Fury of the house as never stinted (577). More definite foreshadowing of Orestes' own punishment is found in the warning of Clytemnestra that Orestes should beware of her curses and her avenging hounds (912, 924). The chorus repeatedly say that blood demands blood and repeatedly stress the difficulty of laying such a curse. These indications may lead us to expect the appearance of the Avenging Furies at the end of this play and the struggle between them and Apollo in the *Eumenides*.

Since Apollo has commanded the deed, however, and since the chorus thoroughly approve and rejoice at the deliverance of the house, we might be led to assume that the curse has been laid once for all. This inconsistency brings out the basic conflict between Apollo, representing Agamemnon and the moral necessity of avenging his foul murder, and the Furies, representing Clytemnestra and the crime against nature of a son's slaying his mother. This conflict, of course, is the central problem of the next play.[71]

At the end of the *Choephoroe,* Orestes says that he will take refuge at the shrine of Apollo in Delphi, and the chorus assure him that Apollo will free him of his woes, although the final note of the chorus is one of bewilderment and uncertainty. This last scene is very similar to the closing scenes of the *Agamemnon:* In each, two bodies are exhibited with their slayer, who attempts to justify the slaughter but is met with opposition, in the *Agamemnon* by the chorus, in the *Choephoroe* by the Furies. In each play, the end obviously has no finality.

EUMENIDES ("KINDLY SPIRITS")

Scene.—The *Eumenides* is one of the few Greek plays in which there is a complete removal of the chorus and a change of scene. The prelude takes place before the temple of Apollo at Delphi. The Priestess, who speaks the prologue, is clearly outside the temple; but Apollo, Orestes, Clytemnestra's Ghost, and the chorus are inside, though actually on a platform (*eccyclema*) or revealed by some other device.[72] When Orestes enters at Athens, he is facing a shrine of Athena; but here the locality is left somewhat vague, for the ensuing trial apparently takes place on the Areopagus (685, "Ares' Hill"), west of the Acropolis. Here again we note the informality of early tragedy in regard to background.

Since almost every Greek temple was built upon a podium of three high steps, there may have been three steps in front of this building, and it has reasonably been assumed that these steps were evident also in the *Agamemnon* and *Choephoroe.* A certain amount of scene-shifting may occur during the play. Possibly a statue of Athena is produced and, later, urns for the voting and perhaps benches for the judges are brought in.

Athena first appears probably in a car or on the machine.

The masks and the appearance of the chorus of Furies were proverbially dreadful. Aristophanes amusingly refers to them in the *Plutus* (422–26). There is an ancient story of very doubtful value to the effect that this chorus of Furies so astounded the audience that children fainted and pregnant women miscarried. (But the presence of women and children in the theater of this period is itself a disputed point.) Certainly the scene wherein the Furies are awakened by Clytemnestra and excited to punish Orestes has an effective eeriness about it. So has their "hypnotizing song" during which they perhaps dance wildly around Orestes clinging to the altar of Athena.

The conversion of the Furies into Kindly Spirits with no change of masks, therefore, somewhat embarrasses the poet; but he has Athena say that she sees great benefit for the citizens coming from these dreadful visages (990–91).

Time.—The action takes place perhaps a few days after that of the *Choephoroe.* An uncertain interval of time passes at the shift of scene.

Legend.—Most of the action of the *Eumenides* seems to have been the invention of Aeschylus, although there was a tradition that Orestes had been tried by the Areopagus with the children of Aegisthus as prosecutors.[73] There was also a tradition, contrary to the version of Aeschylus, that the first trial of the Areopagus was Poseidon's prosecution of Ares for the slaughter of Poseidon's son.[74] That Apollo instigated and purified or protected Orestes was well established in poetry long before Aeschylus.

In popular Greek morality, terms of ill omen were avoided and often replaced by their opposites. Thus the inhabitants of certain areas of the Black Sea, as related in Euripides' *Iphigenia in Tauris,* were accustomed to put strangers to death; accordingly this sea, once the "Inhospitable" (Axine), became the "Hospitable" (Euxine). In like manner, the dread spirits which form the chorus of the present play were properly Furies or Avenging Spirits (*Erinyes*) but by a propitiatory euphemism became the Kindly Spirits (*Eumenides*). Aeschylus in this play, however, explains the change of name as denoting a real change of character. In the earlier part of the play, it may be noted, the term Furies is applied to the chorus by themselves but carefully avoided by others. Near the end, Athena addresses them by this title, but with a complimentary epithet (951). The conception of the Furies as punishing murder only when kindred blood is concerned is not consistently maintained in the previous plays, and it is by no means the invariable conception of them in Greek tragedy.[75]

Theme.—The murder of Agamemnon was a foul deed demanding revenge. Orestes has taken this revenge; but in so doing, in spite of the direct command of Apollo, he has transgressed one of the most basic human laws by slaying his own mother.[76] The liberation of Orestes finally ends the woes of the house of Atreus; but it also offends the Furies, and the last part of this play is concerned with the conversion of these primitive divinities from Furies to Kindly Spirits and with their propitious settlement and the foundation of their cult in Attica. Their conversion symbolizes the abandonment of the law of the talion and the private blood feud in favor of public legal trial. It symbolizes an adoption of justice that is tempered by reason and mercy—equity rather than rigid law, an extremely important advance in the growth of justice. The Athenians proudly considered themselves the originators of laws and legal processes to replace violence. Explanations of Attic customs and institutions, such as here the founding of the Areopagus, were among the most frequent elements of tragedy.

The conversion of the Furies, daughters of Night, constitutes also a reconciliation of the powers of darkness with the powers of light, or the union of the ancient Fates with Zeus (1045–46). This conception of the eventual reconciliation of all divine powers is important in interpreting the prologue and other sections of the play.

At first glance, it may seem unfortunate that the case of Orestes is not honestly argued on the real moral issue: can deliberate homicide, especially the present dreadful case, be justified? But in point of fact, the poet does not attempt anywhere in the trilogy to systematize the moral chaos of this family. The guilt of Agamemnon is never systematically considered, and in the *Choephoroe* the case of Clytemnestra is not argued out in a fair and honest fashion. None of the three plays has a really satisfying moral solution. Obviously Aeschylus here, as perhaps in the *Seven against Thebes,* is not primarily concerned with the moral problem. Indeed he is here deliberately seeking a problem insoluble according to primitive law, for such a problem most clearly sets forth the necessity for a new conception of justice and a new system of legal procedure. This is his primary concern—a political and patriotic and, in a way, religious theme. Since the moral problem of Orestes is a hopeless conundrum, Aeschylus thus made the subject precisely fit his purpose, whereas both Sophocles and Euripides in their own different ways merely broke their heads over the conundrum.

The patriotic and religious themes of this play have overwhelmed the story of Orestes. Like the *Oedipus at Colonus* of Sophocles, the *Eumenides* was written in the poet's old age shortly before his death, and it was obviously designed as a glorious encomium of Athens, "the land most beloved of the gods" (869).

Patriotic and political elements.—One of the main motives of this play is the celebration of the divine foundation of the council of the Areopagus. This council in the time of Aeschylus consisted of former "archons," yearly magistrates chosen by lot from the two uppermost of the four classes of citizens and retaining their position on this council for the remainder of their lives.[77] The Aeropagus held wide juridical, and indirectly, political powers until three years before the presentation of these plays, when it was reduced to a court for homicide cases. This reform was one of the most important steps in the development of the extreme democracy which held sway at Athens during the latter part of the fifth century. Whether or not Aeschylus is criticizing this change is a matter of dispute. Athena commands that the laws be not changed (693)—typical Greek conservatism—and that a mean between anarchy and tyranny be maintained (696), as the Furies have earlier advised (526–37). The council, furthermore, is flatteringly called the savior of the city and the bulwark or garrison of the land (701, 706, 949), phrases which approach the official designation of the Areopagus before its reform as "the guardian of the laws."[78] Still, the council is here founded as a homicide court (682).

Even if we should conclude that Aeschylus is here criticizing the reform of the Areopagus, we cannot accuse him of partisanship, for he certainly praises the alliance with Argos, which had recently been maneuvered by the same party, the extreme democrats. In much the same fashion, Euripides' *Suppliants* celebrates or prepares for the later alliance with Argos in 420 B.C. Even in Homer, Orestes is obligated to Athens, since it is from Athens that he returns to slay Aegisthus. But in Homer, Agamemnon's city is Mycenae, not Argos. The reason for this change in Aeschylus is significant.[79] Mycenae had been destroyed by Argos in 468/7 B.C.; and, by placing the home of Agamemnon at Argos, Aeschylus flatters the Argives as much as he would have insulted them by placing it at Mycenae, and he makes possible the impressive ratification of eternal friendship between Argos and Athens in this play. Preparation for this theme is found in laudatory references to Argos in both the *Agamemnon* (1665) and the *Choephoroe* (302). Orestes solemnly promises faithful alliance to Athena in return for her aid (*Eumenides* 288–91). In his efforts to influence the judges, Apollo, too, promises the faithful alliance of Orestes and his descendants with Athens (669–73). After his acquittal, Orestes declares his everlasting friendship and aid even after death. In the time of Aeschylus the reputation of the Argives needed rehabilitation at Athens because of their doubtful loyalty to the Greek cause during the Persian wars.[80]

Even minor details of the play contain patriotic implications. When Orestes invokes the aid of Athena, he asks her to come "whether she is in the land of Libya . . . . bringing aid to her friends, or watching over the Phlegraean plains . . . ." (292–96). Obviously Aeschylus is here thinking of the large Athenian expedition which was in Egypt when these plays were produced, and of the important Athenian interests in Thrace (Phlegraean plains) and the recently suppressed revolt of Thasos, an island near by. When Athena actually appears to aid Orestes, she says that she has come from the region of the Scamander River (near the site of Troy in Asia Minor), which, Athena continues, was given as a special gift to herself and to the Athenians by the Greek leaders who captured Troy. An ancient commentator tells us that this passage refers to the dispute of Athens and Mytilene over the possession of Sigeum in the Troad.

Athena promises victory among men to her city (913–15), and both she and the chorus repeatedly deprecate civil strife. This deprecation perhaps is not a pointless generality. The friends of the exiled Cimon were contemplating revolt at this time, and the extreme democrats, now in power, were still anxious to avenge the murder of their former leader Ephialtes.[81] But again Aeschylus shows no partisanship. He exhorts the aristocrats against civil war (861–66) and the extreme democrats against exaction of vengeance (979–83).

Discussion.—The *Eumenides* opens with a monologue-prologue in which the Priestess recites mythological history as the author would have it understood for this play. The speaker of the prologue, as in the *Agamemnon,* is a protatic character, and her recitation resembles a prologue from Euripides. The subject matter here is more pertinent than it seems, however, for Orestes' case is being generalized into a clash between old and new gods and old and new conceptions of justice, and this process begins at the very opening of the play.

The action is set in motion with the Priestess' second entrance, terrified at the dreadful sight which she has discovered within the temple. The ensuing rapidly changing scenes are dramatic and spectacular. Orestes is sent forth by his mentor Apollo,[82] and the Furies are awakened for the pursuit by the ghost of Clytemnestra. The appearance of the ghost with her recent wounds and the general goriness of these scenes suggest the horror of Orestes' deed and bind the opening of the new play closely with the ending of the *Choephoroe.* Significantly the name Clytemnestra is withheld in her first speech until the last moment possible (in this meter), and at its sound the Furies are first aroused.

In these prelude scenes the final acquittal of Orestes is foretold by Apollo; but even here it becomes obvious that a momentous clash is developing between the elder Furies and the younger Apollo and Athena. Considerations of great import are at stake: ancient prerogatives, the conception of justice, and the manner of maintaining it among mortals. These momentous subjects gradually emerge and overshadow the personal fate of Orestes as the play progresses. They are the burden of the first stasimon after the chorus has discovered Orestes at Athens (321–96). The attitude of Athena, also, causes these considerations to loom far above the case of Orestes. She refuses to allow such a case to be decided on mere technical grounds—whether or not Orestes actually committed the deed (432)—nor will she in archaic fashion undertake herself to arbitrate the case. She has been placed in a dilemma worse than that of Pelasgus in the *Suppliants*. He had to choose between sacrilege and war; she must choose apparently between two types of sacrilege: rejection of a suppliant or transgression of the Furies' prerogatives with their consequent dread revenge upon her land. Here the more important issue comes to the fore—placating the Furies— for we have been told already that Orestes will be acquitted. Thus the poet prepares for carrying the play beyond the trial of Orestes.

This generalization of Orestes' case is continued in the following stasimon. The chorus predict the collapse of discipline and restraint of crime if he is acquitted—fear of punishment is the foundation of all law and order; crime, therefore, must be followed by punishment.

As this play was designed in part to give divine prestige and sanctity to legal processes in Athens, the trial of Orestes quite naturally has many points of similarity to actual trials there: the preliminary hearing before the case is assigned to a particular court, the clemency shown the accused by allowing him to speak last and by acquitting him if the votes are equal, the repeated exhortations to the jurors to remember their oaths (674–75; 708–10), and various other details. In actual trials on the Areopagus, oaths were taken by the "Venerable Goddesses," another name for the Eumenides, whose sanctuary was the chasm close by the Areopagus to which they are led at the end of this play.[83]

If we care to view the trial unsympathetically, we find still other less admirable similarities to real trials in both ancient and modern times. Orestes indulges in legal trickery by making the chorus admit that they did not persecute Clytemnestra because she was not the blood kin of Agamemnon (605, cf. 212) and then by producing a "professional expert" to testify that a child is the product solely of the father's seed and that the mother is merely a nourisher. This doctrine, doubtless taken from the analogy of sowing seed in the earth, was current among Egyptians and the Pythagoreans. It was accepted or at least used by Euripides (*Orestes* 551–56) and by Sophocles (*Electra* 341–42; cf. Plato, *Timaeus* 50 D). It is found today among certain primitive peoples.[84] Here this explanation has the practical advantage of relieving the Argive descendants of Orestes of any embarrassment at having such an ancestress as Clytemnestra. It is thought that certain of the Athenian nobility, also, traced their descent from Orestes.[85] But worse than this sophistic argument of Apollo—and sound arguments are not altogether neglected (625–39)—is the fact that the presiding judge herself, Athena, is offered as proof of this theory of parentage. She had sprung from the brow of Zeus and was the one known example in all creation of a being without a mother! Apollo also indulges in violent abuse of his opponents in a manner usual in Athenian courts, and he has the effrontery publicly to bribe the judges by offering to make Athens great and Orestes and his descendants faithful allies for all time (668–73). While the jurors are casting their ballots, the chorus and Apollo threaten them and then turn upon each other with mutual insults. The chorus, to whom Apollo symbolizes the younger gods (162) who have dangerously radical ideas concerning the responsibility and punishment of criminals, remind him of another contention which he won by making his opponents, the Fates, drunk!

The presiding officer, Athena, is little better than the advocate; for instead of considering the case on its merits, or voting for acquittal out of clemency, she votes for Orestes because she had no mother and likes men—but not enough to marry one (735–38)!

The serious contention of both Apollo and Athena is that a child owes his first allegiance to his father, and with this doubtless every Athenian would agree. At least the usual Athenian attitude exaggerated the importance of the male.[86] This is the point on which Orestes is acquitted; but it is given no more stress than is necessary to make the acquittal plausible and, even so, half of the judges vote for condemnation. Scholars seem unjustified, therefore, in interpreting the play as primarily an explanation of the patriarchal order or of the Athenian law of inheritance.[87]

The trial is at least a very spirited and dramatic performance. It is the first example of an extended scene with three speaking actors and the chorus all taking important parts. Since the chorus continue their dire threats, the dropping out of Orestes and Apollo does not cause the play to collapse, and the dramatist must be given credit for successfully managing this very difficult transition.

The pageantry at the end of the play, like the opening scenes, would be far more effective in the theater than appears in mere reading. The crowds of supernumeraries, the color, and the music would make a grand spectacle, and the glorification of Athens must have been a moving experience for the original audience.

III

SOPHOCLES

LIFE[1]

Sophocles was born about 495 B.C. and died in 406 B.C., shortly before Aristophanes produced the *Frogs*. He was the son of a wealthy Athenian, Sophillus, and belonged to the deme of Colonus. As a boy he was well educated and was outstanding in both appearance and accomplishments.

The life of Sophocles covered almost the whole of the fifth century during which at Athens the human genius flowered with a brilliance never equaled before or since. Old enough possibly to remember the bringing of the news from Marathon in 490 B.C., Sophocles later led a chorus of youths in celebrating the victory at Salamis (480 B.C.). Athens as a result of these great events became the leading city of Greece, and an enthusiastic national consciousness arose among her citizens. The gradual formation of the Athenian empire and marked economic prosperity followed. Shortly before Pericles emerged as the most influential and imperialistic Athenian statesman, Sophocles came to full manhood and won his first victory (over Aeschylus) in 468 B.C.

The Athenians were tremendously enthusiastic about the plays of Sophocles and insisted upon honoring the author with various political offices. Along with Pericles and others, perhaps in 440 B.C., Sophocles was elected one of the ten generals—the highest elective office of the Athenian state. He is said to have been so chosen in honor of his *Antigone,* a play in which democratic principles and the inalienable rights of the individual are brilliantly championed, and in which Sophistry and its questionable ethics—a movement which was now gaining momentum with alarming rapidity—were, it seems, powerfully indicted. In all, Sophocles wrote more than one hundred twenty plays and won twenty-four victories—more than any other Greek dramatist of whom we know. He was never placed lower than second.

The fifth century at Athens was not, as is sometimes assumed, a period of placid serenity. Athens was engaged almost continuously in external wars and in disturbances attendant on an exploited empire. Political rivalry at home was keen. Exile, ostracism, and even political murders sometimes resulted. Sophocles was not concerned with practical politics; but he did take an active role in the religious life of his times. Here, too, turmoil reigned, with philosophical enlightenment continually attacking the old beliefs. But Sophocles was serenely conservative. He held priesthoods in certain cults and received signal religious honors both during his lifetime and after his death.[2] His religious conservatism is reflected in his plays by their acceptance of the infallibility of the Delphic oracle. They do not, however, show the religious profundity of the plays of Aeschylus. Sophocles' main concern is Man.

Intellectually the period was one of violent upheaval. Euripides was in the very center of this and was closely allied with all phases of the Sophistic Movement. Sophocles himself, regardless of his condemnation of some of its worst phases, was profoundly affected as time went on. Euripides was also more thoroughly involved in the chaotic social and political upheaval of the Peloponnesian War, which began in 431 B.C. and outlasted both poets to end in disaster in 404. Several of the plays of Euripides reveal an obvious intention to influence the course of political events or to affect social conditions or to enlighten the intellectual outlook of his contemporaries. Sophocles maintained a more artistic detachment.

It is a strange but understandable paradox that Sophocles, so artistically aloof, was famous for his sociability, whereas Euripides, so intensely concerned with the contemporary world, was seclusive in the extreme. According to a popular legend Euripides was accustomed to retire from the bustle of Athens to a lonely cave on the island of Salamis overlooking the blue-green Aegean, and there to write his tragedies. In one way, this legend might more aptly have been applied to Sophocles: he more than Euripides was able to detach himself from the political and social chaos of his times and, looking far over the horizon of his contemporaries, to view life stripped of its chronological and geographical bonds and distortions.

Many great figures in the history of literature were the friends and contemporaries of Sophocles. Herodotus, the father of history, was living in Athens at about the time when the *Antigone* was being composed—and when the Parthenon was being constructed. Passages in the *Antigone* and other plays of Sophocles seem to show the influence of Herodotus' writings, and we have a few lines of a poem which Sophocles wrote to Herodotus, perhaps as a farewell when the historian was leaving Athens to become one of the founders of Thurii in southern Italy.[3] Socrates, Thucydides, and the much younger Aristophanes, also, were his contemporaries at Athens. Aeschylus, from whom Sophocles is said to have learned the art of tragedy, himself learned not a little from Sophocles. Euripides, at once more original and more erratic, taught Sophocles much, especially in Sophocles' old age. It was the spirit of the times to give and take with heroic greatness of soul—

or, perhaps we should say, to take and refashion in such a way that the result, though openly acknowledging its indebtedness, became an original work. Sophocles was fundamentally opposed to the intellectual and ethical outlook of Euripides, but he showed that even in extreme old age he honored and appreciated the greatness of his rival by assuming mourning upon the news of Euripides' death. But in the case of these two poets, it is misleading to speak of old age, which usually implies crystallization of outlook and atrophy of intellect. The nonagenarian author of the *Oedipus at Colonus,* like the octogenarian author of the *Bacchae* and the unfinished *Iphigenia at Aulis,* was a Titan of ageless intellect.

Like Euphorion, the son of Aeschylus, Sophocles' legitimate son, Iophon, also wrote tragedies. Though he sometimes competed with his father in the contests, we may infer from a passage in Aristophanes' *Frogs* (73–79) that he leaned very heavily upon his father for literary aid or at times produced plays actually written by his father—a custom followed by Aristophanes' own son and by some other dramatists. Sophocles had at least one son by a woman who was not an Attic citizen and therefore could not be his legal wife. A grandson of this union, named Sophocles, produced the *Oedipus at Colonus* after the great poet's death and himself wrote tragedies.

The plays of Sophocles were frequently reproduced during the fourth century, and throughout antiquity many literary men considered him the greatest of the tragic dramatists. Gradually, however, Euripides became the popular favorite. As with Aeschylus, seven plays of Sophocles were chosen as representative of his work, and these seven have survived. A further selection of three plays in Byzantine times included the *Ajax,* the *Electra,* and the *Oedipus the King.*

At the first dramatic festival following the death of Sophocles, two comic poets honored him. Aristophanes' references are incidental in his *Frogs;* but Phrynichus seems to have dealt with him more in detail, and a beautiful tribute has been preserved from his lost comedy: "Blessed is Sophocles, a happy and fortunate man who died after a long life; author of many beautiful tragedies, he came to a beautiful end and lived to see no evil day."

TRAGEDY UNDER SOPHOCLES

Sophocles, we are told by his ancient biographer, learned the art of writing tragedy from Aeschylus but made many innovations of his own. He broke with the tradition that the poet should act in his own plays; he increased the chorus from twelve members to fifteen; he introduced the third actor; he made certain innovations in costume; and he wrote plays with a view to the actors. Sophocles is also credited by Aristotle (*Poet.* 1449 a) with introducing painted scenery.

These innovations are of varying importance. Whether Sophocles ever acted in his own plays is a disputed point. Certain it is that if he did not act in them, he directed them throughout his career and thus maintained a most intimate connection with the practical theater. The introduction of a third actor, which Aeschylus himself enthusiastically adopted, increased the dramatic possibilities of drama tremendously. Portrayal of character was greatly facilitated by the presence of three speaking actors on scene and the possibility of contrasting reactions.

That Sophocles or his unknown contemporaries made other technical improvements in the conduct of the drama is obvious from his plays. First of all, he seems to have abandoned the form of the trilogy and almost exclusively to have written plays which were self-contained units. Secondly, for exposition he preferred dialogue rather than lengthy and undramatic monologues. Aeschylus himself had sometimes preferred dialogues. Thirdly, he favored dramatic action over narration. Thus in the *Ajax* Sophocles with tremendous effectiveness presents the actual scene of suicide before our eyes, whereas Aeschylus, in a play on the same subject, possibly baffled by problems of staging and dramaturgy, had removed the suicide of Ajax from the scene and had had this event reported by a messenger. No doubt Sophocles here invented the stage trickery which his scene involves. This scene also illustrates another important tendency of Sophocles—his desire to make the action as spectacular and sensational as possible. Changes similar to those made in his presentation of the story of Ajax seem to have been made in other plays now lost.[4] Sophocles also reduced the lyric element of tragedy, but he attempted to keep the chorus intimately attached to the action. Aristotle (*Poet.* 1456 a) prefers Sophocles' practice in this regard to that of Euripides. Finally, Sophocles made great advances in details of dramatic technique such as motivation of entrances and exits.

Since of his more than one hundred twenty plays only seven have survived, Sophocles' development can be followed, if at all, only in outline. He is said himself to have divided his development into three periods, beginning with one in which he imitated the grand style of Aeschylus and ending with one in which he perfected the style most expressive of character.[5] This is the stylistic development which we should expect, and it doubtless corresponded with the development of his dramatic technique; but, since we have no play preserved from the first period and possibly only one, the *Ajax*, that may be assigned to the second or transitional period, this statement is not particularly helpful in appreciating the extant plays. In regard to the characters presented, according to Aristotle (*Poet.* 1460 b), Sophocles aptly remarked that he made men as they ought to be, Euripides as they are.

In handling of plot a development has been traced reaching its climax in *Oedipus the King*. Doubtless this play is constructed as cleverly as Sophocles or anyone else ever constructed a play. But our evidence is too scanty to justify the assumption that Sophocles did not write perfect plays before this one; and we certainly have evidence to show that he wrote some imperfect ones, such as the *Electra* and the *Trachiniae*, afterward. Much more important than petty comparisons, however, is the principle, so often overlooked, that dramatic material varies greatly and that a perfect plot is perfect only for its own subject. A comparison between the *Oedipus the King* and the *Antigone* is likely to obscure more than it reveals, and to compare either of these plays with Euripides' *Trojan Women* is disastrous. Each of these plays constitutes a masterly handling of the material, but the materials themselves and the purposes of the dramatists in handling them are fundamentally different. It is beyond question that Sophocles and Euripides show much greater skill in plot construction than did Aeschylus. But we should view with gravest doubt the frequent assumptions that Sophocles is in general superior to Euripides in this regard and that his seven plays show significant development.

The *Antigone* approaches the pattern of the *Ajax* and the *Trachiniae,* in which the plots follow a closely knit series of cause and consequence but at first glance seem to lack unity because no single character dominates the whole action. This situation is reversed in the *Electra,* where much of the dramatic action has no consequence but the plot seems unified because Electra dominates the scene throughout the play. The *Philoctetes,* a play of elaborate intrigue, has a very different type of plot but one which, in the opinion of the present writer, is strictly unified and perfectly adapted to the material. The *Oedipus at Colonus,* though a still different type, is constructed with equal skill.

Among the distinctive characteristics of Sophocles' dramatic technique may be mentioned his use of oracles or prophecies, which are employed with more or less prominence in every one of the seven extant plays. Traditional oracles or prophecies are freely adapted, and new ones are freely invented in order to foreshadow the coming action. Such foreshadowing nicely facilitates Sophocles' extraordinarily elaborate use of dramatic irony. Thus the use of such predictions, which is not entirely unknown among the other dramatists, is primarily a dramatic device.

Another favorite device of Sophocles is what may be termed distributed exposition. This goes hand in hand with a dialogue opening of the play, which often serves the purpose of characterization as much as it does that of exposition. This is all best illustrated by the *Oedipus the King;* but here of course the plot is one of tragic discovery, which naturally calls for distributed exposition, for the discovery itself is in a way part of the exposition. Here exposition, affecting the dramatic situation, becomes part of the dramatic action. But distributed exposition is very subtly and effectively used in other plays. The relationship between Antigone and Haemon, for instance, is brought out only when the action is well advanced and when this information can most effectively be revealed. In the *Ajax,* also, the arrogant conduct of the hero is told most plainly in the Messenger's speech (762–77) immediately before the death of Ajax.

One use of irony very characteristic of Sophocles is the ringing of a note of joy immediately before the catastrophe. This usually takes the form of a choral song. Thus just before the disillusionment of Oedipus in the *Oedipus the King* the chorus sings a joyful dance song anticipating the long-awaited discovery of the secret of his birth (1086–1109). A joyful choral song before the catastrophe is found also in the *Ajax,* in the *Antigone,* and in the *Trachiniae.* Essentially the same device may be applied to a single character. Thus Aegisthus is brought on very joyful at the news of Orestes' death and at the sight of the dead body just before he is himself about to be slain.

The repetition of this device brings out the dramatic conservatism of Sophocles. He is very economical with his means. Another instance of such repetition is found in the device of having a woman exit without a word when she is about to commit suicide. This is the end of Eurydice in the *Antigone* and of Deianeira in the *Trachiniae,* and the chorus remarks the silence each time. The exit of Jocasta in the *Oedipus the King* is somewhat similar. An entirely different type of repetition is found in the repeated used of the paradoxical antithesis of the dead's slaying the living. This occurs in one form or another repeatedly in the extant tragedies.[6] It may be well for Sophocles' reputation that not all of his more than one hundred twenty plays have been preserved.

Sophocles not only repeats his own motifs; he is prone also to borrow from Euripides. At least his later plays, especially the *Electra,* the *Trachiniae,* and the *Philoctetes,* show the same trends and developments which are conspicuous in Euripides. Since many of these features are those for which Aristophanes so sharply criticizes Euripides, and since they appear in extant plays first in Euripides, it seems reasonable to assume that Euripides himself was largely responsible for them. Among these may be listed the tendency toward the melodramatic, as, for example, the long emotional scene of recognition in Sophocles' *Electra*. This scene is very similar to the famous recognition in Euripides' *Iphigenia in Tauris*. The dates of these plays are uncertain; but the melodramatic scene is obviously more proper to Euripides' play, for that play is frankly melodramatic from beginning to end. The prologue of the *Trachiniae*, also, shows Euripidean influence; and, indeed, the whole play seems a not too successful reworking of the plot of Euripides' *Heracles* with new legendary material. Many musical and metrical effects, also, are similar to those found in Euripides, especially lyrics such as the opening songs of Sophocles' *Electra*. The importance of the chorus is reduced in Sophocles, but perhaps somewhat more skillfully than is the case with Euripides. In the *Philoctetes,* for instance, the chorus tends to become a minor character in the drama rather than an interlude.

All the devices for portrayal of character are exploited by Sophocles. He is especially fond of the use of contrast. Antigone and Ismene, Electra and Chrysothemis, Neoptolemus and Odysseus—these are the more obvious examples; but there is subtle and effective contrast also between Creon and Haemon, Oedipus and Jocasta, Odysseus and Ajax and Agamemnon. Sophocles is also very fond of forcing his characters to extreme limits in order that they may be observed under the most severe conditions possible. The plot of the *Philoctetes* is obviously designed for this purpose, which is carried to such an extreme that the *deus ex machina,* contrary to Sophocles' usual practice, must in the end be employed. The plot of the *Electra* seems to have been considerably distorted in order to raise the stature of the heroine. In both these plays, the consistency of the attitude of the chorus is sacrificed to aid this assaying of character.[7]

Although the profound religion and mysticism of Aeschylus have for the most part been abandoned, the plays of Sophocles are still very serious in tone. A fundamental belief in the conventional religion of his day is maintained without qualification and without inquiry. This is quite different from the endless probings of Euripides. Each subject of Sophocles, furthermore, is interpreted as an illustration of some great moral principle, but etiological explanations of contemporary cults and practices are not as important as in Aeschylus and Euripides. The function of the poet, as Aristophanes has his Euripides say in the *Frogs* (1009), is still very definitely to make men better.

The spirit of Sophocles' plays is severe and heroic. His severity is reminiscent of the iron-gutted Draco, whose laws were said to have been written not in ink but in blood and who, when asked why he made death the punishment for most crimes, responded that he considered the minor crimes deserving of death and that he could think of no greater punishments for the greater crimes.[8] Orestes and Electra seem cruel and unmerciful in the slaughter of their mother; Ajax, by our modern standard, seems cowardly for deserting Tecmessa and their son in order to save his honor; Heracles seems heartless in his disregard of Deianeira; and the old Oedipus seems savage in the curse of his sons. But if the heroic code is severe it is also grand and lofty. No proper appreciation of Sophocles, at least, can be based on any other, and in the final analysis the extremes of modern Romantic sentimentalism seem cheap and tawdry in comparison. The spirit of Sophocles is fundamentally Homeric.[9]

1. *AJAX*

(Perhaps 445–440 B.C.)

The precise date of the *Ajax*, the titles of the other plays produced with it, and the prize awarded are all unknown.

Legend.—The suicide of Ajax as a result of Odysseus' being awarded the arms of Achilles is alluded to in the *Odyssey* (11. 543–67), and the whole subject was treated at length in later epics and in lyric poetry.

Ajax, son of Telamon and second only to Achilles among all the Greek warriors, came from the mountainous island of Salamis just off the coast of Attica. He was the only great man in the expedition to whom the Athenians could lay even an indirect claim, for Athens had been of little importance in Homeric times. Early in the sixth century the Athenians had taken Salamis from their neighbors, the Megarians. Hero cults to both Ajax and his son Eurysaces were maintained among the Athenians, and an annual festival was celebrated on Salamis in honor of Ajax. Ajax, furthermore, was one of the heroes from whom the ten Attic tribes derived their names, and some of the most famous men of Athens, such as Peisistratus, Miltiades, the hero of Marathon, Thucydides, the historian, and Alcibiades, claimed descent from Ajax (but most of them through a son Philaeus who is not mentioned by Sophocles). Ajax had also been invoked for aid before the battle of Salamis, and after the battle captured ships were gratefully dedicated to Poseidon, Athena, and Ajax.[10] Thus Ajax was a great national hero at Athens, and any Athenian audience would naturally view a play concerning him with patriotic fervor.

Source and influence.—Aeschylus had previously written a trilogy on the subject of Ajax and his death. The first of his three plays concerned the judgment by which the arms of Achilles were awarded to Odysseus (*Hoplon Krisis*). This play seems to have contained a debate between Ajax and Odysseus over their respective merits. The second play of Aeschylus concerned the suicide of Ajax, and it was entitled, after its chorus of captive women, the *Thracian Women.* In this play, the suicide of Ajax was not represented before the audience, as in Sophocles, but was related by a messenger. The body of Ajax, according to the legend here accepted, was invulnerable except in one spot, and the sword was reported to have bent like a bow against his body until a divine spirit appeared and showed the hero where he might pierce himself. The third play of the trilogy, called the *Women of Salamis,* probably dealt with the return of Teucer to Salamis and the grief of the father and mother of Ajax. The whole trilogy doubtless ended with the establishment of the cult of Ajax in Salamis, and it was probably designed in part as a further glorification of the hero who was thought to have aided the Greeks in their victory over the Persians.

Sophocles wrote two other plays, entitled *Teucer* and *Eurysaces,* on events subsequent to those of the *Ajax.* The *Teucer* probably dealt, like Aeschylus' *Women of Salamis,* with the return of Teucer to Salamis and with the grief and wrath of Telamon, which forced Teucer to go into exile and found a city, Salamis, on the island of Cyprus. These events are foreshadowed in certain lines spoken by Teucer in the present play (*Ajax* 1006–23). It is possible that these three plays were presented together and formed a trilogy.

The *Ajax* was apparently reproduced frequently, and it was certainly a favorite among late excerpters and commentators.[11] At least three later Greek poets wrote tragedies on the fate of Ajax, and the subject was especially popular among Roman poets.[12] Livius Andronicus, the father of Roman literature, apparently based a play on the *Ajax* of Sophocles.

The argument of Sophocles' play is briefly stated in the first scene (379–81) of the Shakespearean *Titus Andronicus:*

> The Greeks upon advice did bury Ajax,
> That slew himself; and wise Laertes' son
> Did graciously plead for his funerals.

This quotation is remarkable, especially because no English translation of Sophocles existed in the sixteenth century, though Latin versions existed, and reproductions of the originals were not uncommon.[13]

The quarrel over the arms of Achilles and the subsequent suicide of Ajax are favorite themes in ancient art.[14]

Subject and theme.—The subject of the *Ajax* is not the death of Ajax but his disgrace and rehabilitation. This subject bears some resemblance to that of the *Heracles* of Euripides; there, however, the hero is saved from suicide.

The theme of the play may be found in the moral which Athena in the prelude draws from the fate of Ajax (127–33): Let no man wax insolent over superior strength or wealth; a single day suffices to exalt or to overthrow the fortune of any mortal man. This is the old moral that insolence (*hybris*) and pride come before a fall, perhaps the most frequent moral idea in Greek tragedy. Here the moral is illustrated not only by the downfall of Ajax but also by the insolent attitude of Menelaus and Agamemnon, contrasted with the wiser prudence of Odysseus.

The anger of Ajax is here presented as the natural result of the unjust award of the arms of Achilles, but his madness as the result of the intervention of Athena.[15] Athena herself and later Calchas, as reported by the messenger, find the explanation of the downfall of Ajax in his insolent conceit. Though born a mortal he has dared to think more than mortal thoughts (760–61). Here, as frequently in Homer and as in the *Hippolytus* of Euripides, natural motivation is supplemented—or perhaps it would be more proper to say symbolized—by divine motivation. The rationalization of this in the case of Ajax is very simple: Ajax was so conceited that the leaders' preference of Odysseus drove him mad.

Two axiomatic fundamentals of popular Greek morality should be taken into account in any consideration of the motives or character of Ajax. To be laughed at by one's enemies is quite intolerable for a self-respecting person. In the *Medea* of Euripides, also, this is a primary motivation. And Ajax, of course, is far more than a self-respecting person. In his heroic code, honor is everything. To do evil to one's enemies, furthermore, is as natural and commendable as to do good to one's friends. This, of course, was systematically refuted by Plato; but it was long held in popular morality.

That the attitude of Odysseus is both wise and plausible from the Greek point of view is nicely shown by a sentence in Thucydides' brilliant description of the effects of war upon character (3. 84, Jowett): "But, when men are retaliating upon others, they are reckless of the future, and do not hesitate to annul those common laws of humanity to which every individual trusts for his own hope of deliverance should he ever be overtaken by calamity; they forget that in their own hour of need they will look for them in vain." The role of Odysseus in Sophocles' play perhaps is not, however, in accord with his role in that version of the legend which depicted his machinations as the cause of Ajax' disappointment and death. Here the machinations are attributed to the leaders themselves (cf. 1135). Odysseus' generous praise of Ajax (1340–41) might be considered inconsistent with his acceptance of the arms after such a judgment. But these matters are outside the action proper and should not be too closely scrutinized.

Discussion.—From the standpoint of technique the *Ajax* is one of the most extraordinary Greek tragedies. Unusual features are found in the prelude and its presentation of Ajax still in his fit of madness, in the removal of the chorus and the following change of scene,[16] and in the presentation of an act of violence before the eyes of the audience. Unusual, also, is the extended use of a child for emotional effect—a device which became popular with Euripides, as did, also, the heated rhetorical debate. Typical of Sophoclean technique, however, is the deception of the chorus and its song of joy just before the catastrophe.

Sophocles gains tremendously by substituting action for the narration of Aeschylus and presenting the suicide of Ajax before the audience. First of all, Ajax is thus allowed perfect solitude befitting his mood and character.[17] His final words, furthermore, may thus be spoken directly to the audience rather than related by a messenger. The act itself is of great dramatic effect, especially in the Greek theater, where deeds of violence are almost always committed off the scene.[18]

The custom of producing plays with only three actors has a noticeable effect on the action of this play. The roles of Ajax and Teucer were doubtless taken by the same actor. Some other arrangement would have been necessary if Teucer had appeared before the death of Ajax. The role of Tecmessa in the final scenes of the play, furthermore, must have been taken by a mute actor. The shift from speaking actor to mute was made when Tecmessa was sent by Teucer for the child Eurysaces— a clever motivation, adding action and avoiding monotony of setting in the final scenes. Here, as often with a great artist, necessity becomes a virtue.

The exposition of the play, an ancient commentator remarks, could not plausibly have been given to Ajax himself, who would thus speak as if indicting himself, and no one else except a divinity could know precisely what had happened.[19] This ancient commentator has perhaps failed, however, to grasp the more important reasons why Sophocles only here in his seven extant plays employs a divinity in the prologue, as Euripides does so frequently. The joint knowledge of the chorus and of Tecmessa constitutes adequate explanation of Ajax' deeds. But the presentation of the mad Ajax before our eyes and the characterization of Odysseus are of the greatest importance. In Euripides' *Heracles*, the actual rage of the hero is described by a messenger. No effort is there made to exhibit the madness itself. This is as we should expect in Greek tragedy; but Sophocles here, as frequently elsewhere, substitutes dramatic action for narration. The gain in emotional impact is incalculable, for only thus can the eerie atmosphere of madness be effectively created. The bloody scourge which Ajax carries and the terror of Odysseus increase the awfulness of the scene. Indeed, this effect seems the main reason for presenting Odysseus as terrified; for his courage or cowardice, except as a contrast with the courage of Ajax, is not pertinent to this play, though as preparation for his later role, his reverence for the gods and his pity for a fallen enemy must be clearly presented.

This opening scene, furthermore, casts an unmistakably tragic gloom over the coming action, focuses the whole play into an Olympian frame, and points the moral that presumption (*hybris*) is inevitably followed by ruin (*ate*). This scene is distinctly a prelude. The *Eumenides* of Aeschylus offers a close parallel. This prelude in the *Ajax*, again, opens with a "set," as do the *Suppliants* of Euripides and a few other Greek plays. Odysseus is discovered already before the audience by Athena. This in itself is a remarkable feat in the Greek theater, which had no curtain, although a screen, such as that used in the later Graeco-Roman theater,[20] may possibly have been used to serve somewhat as a curtain.

The following scene between the chorus and Tecmessa repeats perhaps too much of the exposition given in the prelude. A certain amount of repetition, of course, is natural and desirable. Such repetition is often found in Euripides, but it usually serves incidental purposes such as that of characterization. In this scene of the *Ajax,* the indirect characterization of Tecmessa and the chorus is of little importance to the plot. Tecmessa does give new details which add pathos to the downfall of *Ajax,* however, and she relates the important events which have taken place since the prelude, especially Ajax' return to sanity and his foreboding dejection. Like Medea in Euripides' play (*Medea* 24–29), Ajax is described as refusing food and drink and wholly inconsolable.

In his first scene with Tecmessa and the chorus, Ajax, though depressed at his failure and disgrace and at the invincibility of Athena, is still the boastful Ajax. He claims that Troy has never seen his equal among the Greeks. He does not except even Achilles. His prayer is still that he might slay Odysseus and the Atreidae and then that he himself might die.

But when Ajax returns to deliver his farewell to Tecmessa and the chorus—possibly the finest speech of the play—his mood has changed. Strong as before, but chastened and resigned, he feels genuine pity for those from whom he is departing, although he must deceive them with dreadful irony in order that they may leave him in peace to accomplish his purpose. The sword of Hector in his hands adds to the irony of his words. He is both sincere and ironical when he says he will learn to yield to the gods and to revere the Atreidae. He sincerely means that he is now prepared to accept the consequences of his deeds—that is, to die. He does not admit error. He still believes in the justice of his cause against the Atreidae, as later in his final speech he shows by calling down divine retribution on them and on the Greeks. But he does admit defeat and resignation to the will of the gods in lines of exquisite beauty (668–77).

From the first it has been clear to all, especially to Ajax, that death is his only course. A noble man must live honorably or honorably die (479–80). Nowhere is there any serious wavering in his resolve. He has no conscience to make a coward of him, and no pale cast of thought paralyzes his action. His men, Tecmessa, and his infant son, and the thought of his mother may arouse his pity; but they cannot touch his resolve, for all that they can urge is quite impertinent to the principle which determines his death. No situation could more effectively bring out the inexorable strength of the mighty Ajax.

The suicide of Ajax, placing the seal of finality upon all his actions, sets the stage for and constitutes the first act of his rehabilitation. Nevertheless, this deed of violence and the disappearance of the hero as a speaking character strain the plot structure. Sophocles, realizing this, has obviously gone to great pains to relieve the strain as much as possible, especially by foreshadowing and preparing for the final quarrel over the disposition of the body of the hero. The denial of burial is earlier suggested when the chorus speak of death by stoning (254), for denial of sepulture would naturally follow this.[21] Ajax himself foresees the effort of the leaders to ruin even his memory. So he prays to Zeus first of all to bring the news to Teucer in order that he may be buried properly. Violation of the corpse might be inferred from the extreme anger of the Greeks, which is repeatedly stressed. Upon discovery of the corpse, furthermore, both the chorus and Tecmessa foresee exultation and laughter from Odysseus and the Atreidae. Teucer, also, immediately thinks of vengeance being taken on the infant son— "for the dead, when they have fallen, all men are wont to mock." The absolute necessity of burial for the rehabilitation of the hero was axiomatic for the ancient spectator, since burial was prerequisite to the proper reception of the departed soul in the underworld.

Elaborate preparation is made for the entrance of those who play the main roles in the final scenes. The return of Teucer is anticipated in various passages, and his role as protector of the infant son and the body of Ajax is clearly foretold (562, 827). The Atreidae and Odysseus again and again have been referred to, especially in the bitter words of Ajax. We have been prepared for Odysseus' role in the final scene by his characterization in the prelude, although this has been somewhat beclouded by the bitter references of Ajax and Tecmessa.

Still other considerations serve to join the final scenes with the earlier part of the play. The physical setting of these is an element of continuity, for the body of Ajax remains before the audience with Tecmessa and the infant son beside it. We should like to think of it as the central point about which the "debaters" are grouped. As in the *Alcestis,* the grim presence of the dead body prevents the quarrel, however bitter, from becoming in the least ludicrous.[22] The reappearance of the chorus and Tecmessa, furthermore, is awaited by the audience, and this, too, serves to aid the continuity.

The two parts of the play are thus bound together. But even for an ancient Athenian, there must have been a considerable difference in tone between the two parts. In the speeches of Ajax, a great soul contemplates death, first with gloomy despair and finally with lofty resignation. The tone of these speeches—and they are among the finest in Greek tragedy—is quite different from the feverish, angry speeches of the debate.

The debate itself is primarily a discussion of the deserts of Ajax, and Teucer's speech to Agamemnon becomes almost a funeral encomium. Not only burial but recognition of the worth of Ajax is essential to his later status as a hero. To say, as one recent critic has done,[23] that Ajax virtually committed an atrocious and silly crime—attempted treason and murder—is to repeat as fact the allegation of Menelaus, with which Sophocles obviously had little or no sympathy, although the idea that Ajax' vengeance would have been silly is entirely modern, of course, and betrays a lack of feeling for the heroic code and for the spirit of the Homeric Age. In his reply to Menelaus, Teucer says that Ajax sailed to Troy as his own master. Although this is disputed by Agamemnon (1234), the Homeric quarrel between Achilles and Agamemnon shows that the organization of the Greeks at Troy was extremely informal. Ajax, like Achilles and Palamedes, had been grossly mistreated (1135), and according to the custom of the Homeric Age any vengeance for such injustice was justified.

It is not necessary to resort to the divinities in order to condone the acts of Ajax. Tecmessa and Teucer do precisely this, although earlier (260–62) Tecmessa has intimated that Ajax has brought these woes upon himself. Thus in the *Iliad,* Agamemnon at one time admits his responsibility (9. 116) and at another he blames the gods (19. 86–144). In modern criminology a similar practice still prevails, and the deities usually blamed are Heredity and Environment. The individual, ancient or modern, has always liked to feel that his future depends upon his own decisions but that the mistakes of his past were thrust upon him. Sophocles certainly intended us to feel that the gods were displeased at the conduct of Ajax, but that Ajax himself was morally responsible for his downfall. The real rehabilitation of his character is found in Teucer's recitation of his virtues and of the wrongs done him, in the generous praise which Odysseus grants him, and in the final words of Teucer.

2. **ANTIGONE

(About 441 B.C.)

The other plays presented with the *Antigone* and the prize awarded are unknown.

Legend.—The legend that Antigone buried her brother contrary to the edict of Creon does not appear to have been a part of the epic or lyric tradition of Polyneices' famous expedition. In extant literature this story is found first at the end of Aeschylus' *Seven against Thebes,* but this passage is often considered spurious. The story may have been a popular Theban tradition long before Aeschylus.[24] It is obviously uncomplimentary to the Thebans, however, and the Thebans were despised at Athens during the fifth century for having proved traitors to the Greek cause in the Persian Wars. They were also notorious for their un-Hellenic propensity to refuse burial to fallen enemies.[25]

Certain features of Sophocles' *Antigone* are thought to be his own innovations. He may have been the first to introduce Teiresias into this part of the story and to play up Ismene as an important foil for Antigone. His most brilliant apparent addition to the story, however, is the role of Haemon. In the epic version Haemon died before Oedipus.[26] Haemon's role in this play adds a carefully restrained romantic interest and binds the fate of Antigone with the fate of Creon. Thus is brought about the dreadful punishment visited upon Creon at the end of the play.

Influence.—Euripides, too, wrote an *Antigone.* This play was perhaps later than that of Sophocles, but little can now be determined concerning its content. In Euripides, Haemon seems to have aided Antigone in the burial of Polyneices. Certainly Haemon and Antigone married, and a son, Maeon, was born to them. Their love obviously played a more important role in the action than it does in Sophocles' play. The "trial" of Haemon and Antigone seems to have taken place, as in Sophocles; and here, too, there was a discussion of government and the necessity for maintaining discipline. Incidentally we may note that Euripides' play opened with a typical Euripidean prologue (frag. 157, Nauck²), explaining the story of Oedipus, and that it may have ended with a *deus ex machina*.

The *Antigone* of Sophocles has always been considered one of his best plays. Its choral lyrics are especially celebrated. It apparently aroused great admiration when first produced, for Sophocles is said to have been elected to a generalship in the Samian War (about 440 B.C.) because of this play. During the fourth century, according to Demosthenes (19. 246), the *Antigone* of Sophocles was frequently produced by the leading actors of the day. The stellar role, incidentally, was that of Antigone herself, while the role of Creon was left to the third actor. In this period a contemporary dramatist, Astydamas, produced an original play on the same subject. The Roman Accius later wrote an *Antigona,* perhaps an adaptation of Sophocles' play. The influence of this play of Sophocles on later art and literature, however, was apparently not great. Modern adaptations, also, are of slight importance, but the music which Mendelssohn composed for a German version is famous.[27]

Theme.—The conflict between secular and divine law is often considered the basic theme of Sophocles' *Antigone.* But this is not an entirely satisfactory statement of the theme, for the decree of Creon is considered invalid by various characters in the play, and probably most of the original Greek audience would have denied this decree the status of law. In the amusing discussion of the definition of law by Pericles and Alcibiades (in Xenophon's *Memorabilia* 1. 2. 40–46), for instance, the decrees of a tyrant, unsanctioned by the people, are denied the status of law. The ultraconservatism of the Greeks and their reverence for established law is well illustrated by the refusal of Socrates to escape from prison and save his life because in so doing he would have been breaking the law.[28] Again, in the Greek town of Thurii in southern Italy, anyone wishing to propose a change in the laws was compelled to do so with a rope around his neck, and he was straightway hanged if the proposed change was not accepted by the majority.[29] Thurii was founded in 444/43 B.C., perhaps about the time the *Antigone* was being written; and the reference to Italy (1119) may well have been suggested by this recent foundation, in which various Athenians and Herodotus, the friend of Sophocles, took part. Their conception of law was probably much the same as Sophocles' own.

The necessity of observing divine law and the invalidity of any human decree which contravenes it are certainly basic concepts in the play. These form the basis of Antigone's defense, and her point of view is championed by Haemon and Teiresias. Creon himself must finally adopt it (1113–14). The blessings of wisdom and its attainment, especially the wisdom of recognizing one's own fallibility and human limitations, form another aspect of the theme here as in the *Ajax* and in the *Oedipus*. The specific application of this concept here is found in the grave obligations of the human ruler and the folly of the unjust judge—a favorite theme in Attic drama, for Athenians were always proud of their democracy and contemptuous of tyrants.[30] "Wisdom is the supreme part of happiness," the chorus declare at the end of the play (Jebb's translation); "and reverence towards the gods must be inviolate. Great words of prideful men are ever punished with great blows, and, in old age, teach the chastened to be wise."

The subject of the *Antigone* bears a resemblance to that of the *Ajax*. Both plays are concerned with a kinsman's burial of a corpse contrary to the decree of the rulers. The primary subject of the *Ajax*, however, is the rehabilitation of the dead hero, whereas in the *Antigone*, no attempt is made to rehabilitate the honor of Polyneices. His very dishonor, in fact, adds to the glory of Antigone's unwavering devotion and applies the most extreme test to her loyalty and to the validity of the law of Heaven. The downfall of Ajax, furthermore, bears no significant resemblance to that of Antigone. It does bear a resemblance to that of Creon, as intimated above; but, otherwise, the similarity between the two plays is only superficial. Many critics have insisted that the structure of the *Antigone*, being the more effective, shows a distinct advance in technique over that of the *Ajax*, and that therefore the *Antigone* must be the later play. This is fallacious reasoning, for the differences in subject rob this comparison of any significance.

Discussion.—A certain amount of suspense is maintained in the *Antigone*. The audience presumably did not know what the outcome would be; for if Euripides in his play could contradict the Sophoclean version (if that preceded) and have Antigone's burial of her brother lead to her marriage rather than to her immediate death, doubtless Sophocles might have arranged some such ending if he had so desired. The suspense is aided by the absence of an expository prologue. The masterly opening scene and the withholding of certain important information are both characteristic of Sophocles' skillful handling of exposition. Preparation for the tragic outcome, however, is found in the fear of Ismene for the fate of her sister (82) and in her conviction that any attempt to bury Polyneices must end in disaster. Antigone herself forebodes disaster. The tone of all the action, furthermore, is tragic except parts of the speeches of the Guard, which approach comic relief. Teiresias, however, at first seems to promise Creon that a change of heart and counsel will save the day. Although his dire prophecy of the death of Haemon is unqualified, the chorus obviously think that Creon's change may still prevent the tragedy, and they joyfully invoke Bacchus to come to the rescue of their city. Such a joyful song immediately before the announcement of the catastrophe is especially pathetic and constitutes a characteristic device of Sophocles for heightening the tragic effect, as may be observed in the *Ajax* (693–718), in the *Oedipus the King* (1086–1109), and in the *Trachiniae* (633–62).

The role of Haemon is handled with consummate skill. Most effective is Ismene's revelation of the betrothal of Antigone to Haemon at the crucial point when Creon is determining the fate of Antigone. Here again the advantage of omitting an expository prologue is seen, for a prologue might naturally have been expected to contain such information. Ismene's revelation serves also as preparation for the entrance of Haemon.

Antigone is not taken off to die immediately after Creon has sentenced her. The play gains tremendously by this delay, which allows time for a change of mood in the heroine, and by the insertion of the quarrel between Haemon and Creon with Haemon's praise of Antigone before she sings her farewell and is led away. Sophocles does not, however, bring Antigone and Haemon on stage at the same time. This is in accordance with his usual classic restraint in treating the soft emotions, and no scene between the lovers could be so profoundly pathetic as the Messenger's brief description of their death.

Some critics have been troubled by the fact that, according to the Messenger, Creon buries Polyneices before attempting to rescue Antigone. This action is really outside the play proper and, therefore, should not be too closely scrutinized. Possibly this order is adopted only for dramatic convenience in order to avoid an anticlimax, but we should note that Teiresias has ordered the burial of Polyneices as the more important act.[31]

The portrayal of the feminine characters is especially noteworthy. A respectable woman in the Athens of Sophocles' own age was restricted almost exclusively to the life of her own home. "To a woman not to show more weakness than is natural to her sex is a great glory," Pericles is represented by Thucydides (2. 45, Jowett) as saying, "and not to be talked about for good or for evil among men." Even in Athens, however, there were exceptional women, such as Pericles' own foreign and therefore illegitimate wife, Aspasia, who had great influence upon the intellectual and political life of her times. The position of women was higher among the contemporary Aeolic and Doric Greeks, as it had been among the Greeks, apparently, during the heroic age; for certainly the position of Penelope and Helen and Arete in the *Odyssey* is a very high one. The heroic type of womanhood, offering vastly superior dramatic possibilities, is usually preferred by the Athenian writers of tragedy. In the *Antigone* these two types of womanhood are effectively contrasted.

From her first words, Ismene is characterized as feminine and helpless. She has heard nothing of the news which has upset Antigone. But she does know her place in life and her own limitations: as a woman she cannot strive with men, and as a subject she must obey her ruler. If she refuses to attempt the burial of her brother, she is not committing sacrilege, because she is not a free agent. Since she cannot defy the ruler of the land successfully, it would be folly to make the attempt. So Ismene reasons and, from the standpoint of practical wisdom, she is right; but she is nevertheless base in her feverish haste to admit her weakness, and Antigone readily so pronounces her. Indeed she is the basest member of the house of Oedipus—and the only one to survive. But if Ismene has the weakness of a woman, she has the strength also. Though declared hateful to Antigone and to the dead, Ismene insists on continuing her love for her sister; and when Antigone is apprehended and brought before Creon, Ismene is willing to die with her in the ecstasy of feminine devotion, which itself is revolting to the deliberate Antigone.

In sharp contrast to Ismene, Antigone stands out as a woman of great will and strength of character. As a tragic role, Antigone ranks with the superhuman Clytemnestra of Aeschylus and the dread Medea of Euripides. But, unlike these other most famous heroines, Antigone, if not wholly good, is at least wholly admirable. She insists that one's first obligation is to those divine laws whose justice is as obvious as it is immutable, and she will admit no exception to this obligation.

If Antigone has a fault it is the admirable fault of Prometheus—the fault of willfulness and stubborn determination to do what appears to her to be right in spite of all opposition and regardless of all consequences. Like Prometheus, Antigone finds her opponent in the figure of a tyrant, though the ideal which she defends is perhaps more definite and more obviously just. As Prometheus is urged to yield before troubles by his well-meaning but not very admirable kinsman, Oceanus, so Antigone is urged to cower before the decree of Creon by her not very admirable sister, Ismene. After Antigone's bitter clash with Creon and her condemnation, the chorus sings that the hope of the last of the house of Oedipus has been brought low "by the blood-stained dust due to the gods infernal, and by folly in speech, and frenzy at the heart" (601–3, Jebb). The opinion of the chorus, then, is clear: Antigone is guilty of folly in speech when she very flagrantly insults Creon. In Euripides' *Phoenissae,* also, Antigone's action is similarly viewed. "A noble spirit you have," remarks Creon there (1680), "but a certain folly, too."

The deliberate defiance of authority by one unjustly accused may be admirable; but, from the worldly point of view, it is certainly folly, and the case of Socrates—for he too insulted his judges—proves that such defiance has never been conducive to longevity. Creon cites Antigone's praise of her deed as adding to her guilt. Willfulness and fury of temper are the faults not only of Antigone but of the whole house of Labdacus. They caused the fatal duel at the crossroads where Oedipus slew his father Laius. They are the most distinctive characteristics of the sons of Oedipus, Eteocles and Polyneices, in Aeschylus' *Seven against Thebes* or in Euripides' *Phoenician Women,* or in Sophocles' *Oedipus at Colonus.* So the chorus in the *Antigone* may well say that the daughter of Oedipus has the fierce spirit of a fierce father, and that she is one who does not know how to yield before troubles.[32]

The character of Antigone is portrayed most vividly by means of contrast with the other characters. Even the Guard serves to bring out the nobility of her action. The Guard is a simple man. He has a simple man's frank cowardice where death is concerned but also a simple man's belief in the inevitability of any misfortune which may befall. Amusingly, the Guard tries to win pardon before telling his tale, and he has a plain man's courage to talk plainly to Creon (323). At first naïvely joyful at having caught Antigone, he later feels some pity for her, but not as much, he simply admits, as he would have felt for himself if he had not apprehended her. Such a figure, with a touch of the comic and something more than a touch of the humorous, is rare in Greek tragedy. He is reminiscent of the garrulous old Nurse in Aeschylus' *Choephoroe,* and he anticipates the Phrygian eunuch in Euripides' *Orestes.* These figures are as near to Shakespeare's simples as the Greek dramatists ever approached. But the function of the Guard here at the opening of the play is obviously not primarily to furnish a touch of comedy but to bring out the heroism of Antigone.

The character of Antigone is brought out also by the description of others. Very effective is the Guard's description of her discovery of the uncovered body of Polyneices: "and she cried aloud with the sharp cry of a bird in its bitterness,—even as when, within the empty nest, it sees the bed stripped of its nestlings" (423–25, Jebb). More important is Haemon's description of the townspeople's praise of Antigone. The scene with this description and the obvious devotion of Haemon prepares for Antigone's farewell scene and adds greatly to its pathos.

In her farewell scene Antigone as before is a strong character, but she has none of the inhuman and dramatically ineffective stoicism of certain characters in Seneca, and none of that fanatic passion for death which characterizes the Christian martyr. She is thoroughly human in her reluctance to die and pitiful in her loneliness—even the gods seem to have deserted her. She is pitiful, too, in her repeated references to death before marriage—obviously she is thinking of Haemon—and in the injustice which decrees her death. The chorus do not relieve her isolation. They had no enthusiasm and only reluctant obedience for Creon's edict concerning Polyneices (211–20), and now they are inclined to think Antigone's act, even if rash and foolish, a righteous one (cf. 505–9). But this is a chorus composed of men, and they are only distantly sympathetic with Antigone. Although Antigone is painfully conscious of her isolation, now that her deed is done and its result is immutable, she need no longer maintain the cold fanatical determination which characterized her in the earlier scenes, and her thorough humanity is now displayed.

One speech of Antigone in this final scene has greatly puzzled critics. She declares that she would not have made an attempt to bury her own child or husband in defiance of the laws of the city but that she did bury her brother because, with parents dead, no other brother could ever again be hers (904–20). These strange lines have been considered spurious by many scholars. They cannot, it seems, be independent of the story which Herodotus (3. 119), the friend and contemporary of Sophocles, tells of the wife of Intaphrenes, and which breathes a very Oriental atmosphere. But Aristotle (*Rhetoric* 3. 16 [1417 a]) quotes two of these lines of Antigone, and there seems no cogent reason for assuming that Sophocles did not write them. In this speech Antigone is thinking of the dear ones who will meet her in the world of the dead, and especially of the brother for whom she has sacrificed her life. It is altogether natural, therefore, that she should here dwell upon the intimate relationship of those who come from the same womb and from the same sire. There is here no real contradiction of her earlier lines (450–60), in which she cites divine law as the motivation for her act; for this divine law devolved primarily on the closest of kin and, as she here points out, she will never again have anyone more closely related to her and therefore more worthy of her sacrifice

(913). It is quite sound psychologically, furthermore, that a character, after reaching a decision primarily through emotional channels and after performing an act, should rationalize and invent all possible intellectual justifications for this act.[33] It is not unreasonable, therefore, to assume that these lines of Antigone are genuine and that Antigone is sincere in speaking them, but that actually she would have performed the same service for child or husband which she has performed for her brother.

Though human and pathetic, Antigone is gloriously defiant to the very end: "Behold me, princes of Thebes, the last daughter of the house of your kings,—see what I suffer, and from whom, because I feared to cast away the fear of heaven!"[34]

Creon is no monster such as Lycus in the *Heracles* of Euripides. Creon's attitude toward government and patriotism are not unlike that of Eteocles in the *Seven against Thebes* of Aeschylus. We may be sure that there was much in his attitude of which Sophocles would approve (cf. 175–90); but times and ideas were changing rapidly in Athens of the fifth century, and Sophocles' patriotism is not the patriotism of Aeschylus. He stands midway between his predecessor and his younger rival, Euripides. Either Sophocles or Euripides might have written Haemon's ringing words (737, Jebb): "That is no city, which belongs to one man." Or again (757, Jebb): "Thou wouldest speak, and then hear no reply?" As Hippolytus accuses Theseus in the later play of Euripides (*Hipp.* 1056), Haemon here accuses Creon of being an unjust judge—a weighty crime in one whose judgment is subject to no appeal, and often a crime of fatal consequences. The simple Guard has already indirectly accused Creon on this score (323), and Antigone, of course, repeats the charge. Especially offensive to an Athenian audience would be Creon's contention that the ruler of a city must be obeyed "in small things and in just things and in the opposite" (667). The sophistic wording here adds to the statement's offensiveness. Ruler and judge are one in the city of a tyrant, and in a way the charge of being an unjust judge embraces all the other charges against Creon.

The charge of impiety is denied by Creon. He angrily rejects the suggestion of the chorus that a god may have buried Polyneices—a suggestion made plausible by the fact that no beast or dog has maimed the corpse. Creon insists that the gods can have no concern for the body of a man who came to burn their shrines (280–89). This contention is not wholly without specious justification.

Proper burial of the dead, according to Greek religious thought, was prerequisite to the soul's immediate entrance into its permanent abode in the underworld. Proper burial, therefore, was of the greatest importance and devolved as a prime duty upon the closest surviving relative. Denial of such burial was sacrilege. In Attic law, furthermore, anyone passing an unburied corpse was required to cast earth upon it.[35] Certain exceptions to these rules, however, were commonly recognized. Temple robbers and some other types of criminals were normally denied burial.[36] In the *Electra* of Sophocles (1487–88) Electra insists that the corpse of Aegisthus be cast forth to dogs and carrion birds; in Euripides' *Electra* (896–98), also, Orestes intimates that Aegisthus has been slain in circumstances which justify the denial of burial. The Dioscuri at the end of Euripides' play, however, command the burial of both Aegisthus and Clytemnestra; and this was in accord with popular legend; for centuries later, as Pausanias (2. 16. 7) records, the grave of Aegisthus was still pointed out. In another play of Euripides, the *Heracleidae* (1050–51), a character makes a command similar to that of the Sophoclean Electra. The denial of burial in extreme cases, therefore, is not without precedent in Greek law or in Greek tragedy.

But Creon's assumption that Polyneices should be treated as one who has desecrated the temples of the gods is not borne out by the facts, and his whole case against Polyneices is founded upon very sophistic reasoning. He repeatedly insists that the wicked should not have equal honor with the good even in death. He seems possibly to intimate that the burial of Polyneices is an impious act (301). Later, Creon is himself obviously guilty of impiety when he declares that he will not allow the burial of Polyneices even though eagles defile the throne of Zeus himself (1039–43; cf. 780). Sophistically he attempts to justify these words by claiming that no mortal can defile a god.[37]

Sophistry, of course, has always existed; but those professional teachers and rhetoricians known as the Sophists were just beginning to play an important role in Athenian life when the *Antigone* was produced, and some scholars think that Sophocles by means of the figure of Creon is here attacking their methods and their ethics.[38] Especially shocking to many Athenians, as we may readily observe in Aristophanes, was the brazenness of the Sophists in indulging in all sorts of devices and practices with no consideration for moral implications, and their bold claim that, in any given case, they could make the better side appear the worse or the worse appear the better. So Creon here not only attempts to justify his sacrilegious decree but possibly intimates that disobedience to his decree would be sacrilege.

Before Antigone is apprehended, Creon seems to have a legitimate excuse for his severity. A state of emergency exists at Thebes, and

SOPHOCLES: *OEDIPUS THE KING* 111

certain factions seem to be dissatisfied with him—he is a comparatively new ruler. This is the implication of his first speech to the chorus, and he later tells us that certain people have muttered against
him (289–92). The fact that Antigone is so closely related to him
and a member of his household adds to the inhumanity of his judgment, however, when he discovers that actually the breaking of his
edict has no political implications. But, instead of realizing this, Creon
perversely insists that the close kinship of Antigone aggravates her
crime of disobedience. Creon adopts much the same attitude toward
his son; and his injustice here is made to appear in an even worse
light because of the extreme tact with which Haemon approaches his
father. It is typical Sophoclean irony that in the end Creon himself
must do that which he has gone to such lengths to prevent others from
doing.[39]

Creon has one characteristic in common with Antigone: he is very
headstrong. Indeed, both Creon and Antigone are repeatedly charged
with folly. Haemon, for instance, uses practically the same argument
—that stubbornness is a dangerous vice—against Creon (712–18)
that Creon earlier used against Antigone (473–83). Creon and Antigone charge each other with folly (470, 562), and the chorus sooner
or later agrees with both (383, 1348–53). But there is a vast difference. Creon's perverse maintenance of his error, as Teiresias bluntly
points out, is a fatal vice, whereas the steadfastness of Antigone, if
not wise, is at least admirable.

Some critics have maintained that Creon and not Antigone is the
main character of the play.[40] In the dramatization of an ethical problem there naturally arises an opposition between the character who
takes the better point of view and the other who takes the worse. Naturally the fate of Creon, who has taken the worse point of view, is
much more dreadful than that of Antigone, and the last of the play
is concerned with Creon's tragedy. The introduction of Eurydice and
her suicide concerns Creon alone. But Creon's tragedy is dwelt upon
at such length not because Creon is the main character of the play—
he is vastly overshadowed by Antigone—but because the dreadfulness
of his fate is the final justification of Antigone.

3. **OEDIPUS THE KING*

(Perhaps about 430 B.C.)

The date of this play is highly disputed. Athens was the victim of
a devastating plague in 430–427 B.C., soon after the Peloponnesian War
began. Some scholars think the description of the plague in this play

was suggested by the plague at Athens; others, recalling the unfortunate experience of Phrynichus (who was fined for presenting a play which reminded the Athenians of the misfortunes of their allies, the Milesians), think this play must have been produced before the plague. The *Iliad,* of course, opens with a description of a plague.

The titles of the other two tragedies produced along with the *Oedipus* are unknown, but an ancient commentator tells us that Sophocles was second in the contest, being defeated by Philocles, a nephew of Aeschylus.[41]

In order to appreciate the irony of the play, the modern reader must know, as the ancient spectator certainly did, that Oedipus has slain his own father, Laius, and is now married to his mother.

From the time of Aristotle, the *Oedipus the King* has frequently been taken as the perfect model of Greek tragedy. But this does not mean that the *Oedipus* is a typical Greek tragedy. No one play, indeed, could be called typical of all Greek tragedy, for the plays vary greatly in type; but if we were forced to choose one play as most representative, we should probably choose the *Bacchae* of Euripides. Nor is the *Oedipus* superior to other Greek tragedies in all respects. The *Agamemnon* of Aeschylus, for instance, is superior to the *Oedipus* in the grandeur of its poetry. Indeed, it is unfortunate that the *Oedipus* is so often taken as the model of Greek tragedy, for it is unusual in various important respects. The plot is unusual, for it does not concern any fatal error which occurs during the action of the play; this plot, like many of the plots of Ibsen, deals with the mere discovery of former errors and events. Here, the discovery of the identity of Oedipus constitutes and coincides with his reversal of fortune. Such coincidence, as Aristotle points out, is dramatically very effective; but it is not common in Greek tragedy, though mere recognition of identity, such as Electra's recognition of her brother Orestes, is frequent. In the *Oedipus* there is also greater dependence on the audience' previous knowledge of the story than in most tragedies. The exposition, as one would expect in this type of plot, is very slight and is diffused throughout the play.[42]

The Greek conception of fate, furthermore, is likely to be misinterpreted by anyone who is familiar only with this play. The *Prometheus* and, in a different way, the *Ajax* are more enlightening in this regard.

Another reason why the play can hardly be called typical is because it has almost no etiological significance—no Greek custom or institution is explained.

The *Oedipus* does not, however, wholly lack typical features. It exhibits strict unity of subject, effective use of dramatic irony, and characters who are thoroughly human. Its great reputation as a masterpiece is fully deserved; for in dramatizing this legend as a powerful illustration of the irony of Fate, Sophocles has come very close to perfection.

Legend.—The story of Oedipus and his sons was the central part of the Theban cycle of legends, which was second only to the Trojan cycle as a theme for Greek epic poetry. None of the early epics on the Theban cycle, however, have survived, and our present knowledge of them is slight. According to the brief account given in the *Odyssey* (11. 271–80, Butcher and Lang), where Odysseus sees the mother and wife of "Oedipodes" in the underworld, Oedipus had slain his father and married his mother, and then "straightway the gods made these things known to men." Oedipus remained the ruler of Thebes and, we may assume, did not blind himself. But Jocasta hanged herself; "for him she left pains behind full many, even all that the Avengers of a mother bring to pass." In a passage in the lyric poet Pindar (*Olympian Ode 2.* 42–46), a contemporary of Aeschylus, the sons of Oedipus are slain by the Avenging Fury of Laius.

In certain versions of the story the four children of Oedipus are born not from Jocasta but from another wife. This relieved of embarrassment those famous houses which claimed descent from Oedipus. The Attic writers, so far as we know, first presented the version wherein these children are born of Jocasta.[43] The existence of such children, of course, greatly increases the dramatic potentialities of the story.

Source and influence.—The story of Oedipus, according to our present knowledge, was dramatized more often than any other legend. Some thirteen different Greek authors, including Aeschylus, Sophocles, and Euripides, are known to have written plays on this subject.

Of the trilogy which Aeschylus wrote on this subject, the last play, the *Seven against Thebes,* is extant. This play concerns the fate of the sons of Oedipus, but from it we glean a few facts concerning the second play of the trilogy on the fate of Oedipus himself. Here Oedipus blinded himself and cursed his sons. The primary motivating force throughout the trilogy, as in the Orestes trilogy, was the curse and Avenging Fury of the house descending from generation to generation. In Aeschylus, furthermore, Laius was said to have been slain at a junction of roads, not in Phocis as Sophocles relates, but in Boeotia near a place sacred to the goddesses of the underworld and to the Avenging Furies. It may be that Aeschylus, like certain other writers, also gave the "original" home of Oedipus not as Corinth but as Sicyon, another place associated with the worship of the Avenging Furies. Sophocles, obviously wishing to change the interpretation of the story, has carefully eliminated all associations with the Avenging Furies.[44]

Of Euripides' *Oedipus* almost nothing is known except that in his version Oedipus was apparently blinded not by himself but by the servants of Laius. Little is known of the later versions, but it is obvious that Sophocles' play did not discourage later dramatists from attempting the subject.

Other extant Greek tragedies dealing with the story of Oedipus and his children are the *Antigone* and the *Oedipus at Colonus* of Sophocles, and the *Phoenissae* of Euripides.

The early Roman dramatists apparently neglected the story of Oedipus, but Julius Caesar as a youth tried his hand at a tragedy on this subject in the fashion of the day, doubtless with much more success than Cicero's brother had when he wrote four tragedies in sixteen days, or than Augustus had with his *Ajax* (his *Ajax* was forced to commit suicide!).[45] The *Oedipus* of Seneca is extant (see below).

The *Oedipus* of Sophocles was one of the most famous Greek tragedies in later classical, Byzantine, and medieval times. It seems to have been in the popular repertoire of Polus, one of the most famous actors of the fourth century B.C., and, later, the Roman emperor Nero is said to have played, among other roles, Canace in labor, Orestes the matricide, the blinded Oedipus, and the mad Heracles.[46] The *Oedipus* was the favorite Sophoclean tragedy of the humanists of the sixteenth century, and it has been imitated and adapted by various dramatists. For Racine it was the ideal tragedy.[47] It has frequently been produced in the original and in translation both in this country and abroad, including a production by Max Reinhardt and a presentation in Paris by the famous actor Mounet-Sully.[48]

Modern adaptations.—A comparison of Sophocles' play with the modern adaptations of various authors is profitable and enlightening. The most striking difference, perhaps, is the sharp contrast between the severe classicism of the Greek and the extreme romanticism of the French versions. The length of a Greek tragedy, furthermore, is obviously not sufficient for a modern presentation, especially after the choral songs have been omitted. Every modern adapter, therefore, must add to the plot.

The Oedipe *of Corneille* (*1659*).—Perhaps the best criticism of Corneille's play is that which is made in the brilliant preface to the *Oedipus* of Dryden and Lee:

In our own age, Corneille has attempted it, and, it appears by his preface, with great success. But a judicious reader will easily observe how much the copy is inferior to the original. He tells you himself, that he owes a great part of his success to the happy episode of Theseus and Dirce; which is the same thing as if we should acknowledge that we were indebted for our good fortune to the under-plot of Adrastus, Eurydice, and Creon. The truth is, he miserably failed in the character of his hero: If he desired that Oedipus should be pitied, he should have made him a better man. He forgot that Sophocles had taken care to show him, in his first entrance, a just, a merciful, a successful, a religious prince, and, in short, a father of his country. Instead of these, he has drawn him suspicious, designing, more anxious of keeping the Theban crown than solicitous for the safety of his people; hectored by Theseus, condemned by Dirce, and scarce maintaining a second part in his own tragedy.

The Oedipus *of Dryden and Lee* (*1679*).—The play of John Dryden and Nathaniel Lee very clearly illustrates the vast difference between a Greek tragedy and an English tragedy of the long and elaborate Elizabethan type, although this play is obviously an inferior specimen of the type. It fails primarily for the same reasons which the authors so brilliantly pointed out as the causes for the failures of Seneca and Corneille; for here, too, there is too much pompous rant, and the hero is almost lost in the complicated and endless business of the minor plot. The melodramatic sensationalism of the play is its most striking characteristic. This begins with the first stage direction: "The Curtain rises to a plaintive tune, representing the present condition of Thebes; dead Bodies appear at a distance in the Streets; some faintly go over the Stage, others drop." Before our eyes, Oedipus must walk in his sleep and describe his terrifying dreams. The ghost of Laius, who was merely described by Creon in Seneca's play, is here brought on stage twice, and he calls out at numerous other times. He is first seen standing armed in his chariot as when he was slain by Oedipus. At the end of the play, the stage flows with blood in the general butchery.

Not only these incidents but the characters themselves are melodramatic, especially the villainous hunchback Creon. He is in love with Eurydice, an invented daughter of Laius and Jocasta, and is continually plotting to possess her against her will by fair means or foul and to overthrow Oedipus. Eurydice loves Adrastus, a captured prince of Argos. The scenes of love-making, though not especially crude, transgress the bounds set in Greek tragedy. Worst of all in this respect, but effective in its crude irony, is the scene between Oedipus in his nightshirt and Jocasta in her gown, wherein Oedipus, in order to allay his terrifying dreams of parricide and incest, insists that he must immediately exercise his marital prerogatives.

The tone of the play varies greatly. It descends to low comedy when Eurydice in the first act revilingly describes the deformed Creon to his face.

Some brilliant strokes, however, are found in the play. The best of these, perhaps, are the ill omen of Jocasta's speeches upon her first entrance and the motivation of Oedipus' ignorance of the circumstances of Laius' death (end of Act I) :

> a confused report
> Passed through my ears, when first I took the crown;
> But full of hurry, like a morning dream,
> It vanished in the business of the day.

In Dryden and Lee, as in Seneca, the story of Oedipus is a tragedy of fate; but the English authors are obviously unconcerned with moral interpretations.

The Oedipe *of Voltaire (1718).*—Voltaire's play is perhaps the best of the more famous modern versions. To provide a minor plot he has invented a frustrated love affair between Jocasta and Philoctetes. This exalts the virtuous character of Jocasta and creates a minor climax after Philoctetes is accused of the murder of Laius. This climax is reached in the third act and is relieved when the process of Oedipus' discovery of his real identity begins. From this point on, the minor plot almost wholly disappears, although Oedipus near the end of the play (V, i) recommends that Philoctetes succeed him as king of Thebes.

Oedipus and Jocasta both are here very admirable characters, and Voltaire interprets their downfall as exhibiting the injustice of fate and the cruelty of the gods. "Impitoyable dieux, mes crimes sont les vôtres," cries Oedipus (V, iv). The last line of the play by Jocasta is very similar, and the chorus, of which Voltaire has retained a vestige, voice the same sentiment.

Of the changes made in the Sophoclean material itself perhaps the final scenes, which have been influenced by Seneca, are the most successful. Here Oedipus is forced himself to reveal his identity to Jocasta, and at the very end Jocasta commits suicide on stage.

The unquestioned popularity of Voltaire's play in Paris may have been due in part to certain scandals concerning incest in contemporary court circles.[49]

Aristotle's criticism.—It is easy to understand why such a skillfully articulated play should appeal to the systematic Aristotle. In the *Poetics,* the *Oedipus* is cited more frequently and praised more highly than any other play.

The best type of plot, Aristotle maintains (*Poetics* 1452 b), is one which is complex, that is, one containing a sudden reversal of fortune (peripety) or a discovery of identity or both, arising as a necessary or probable consequence of the antecedents. The plot is especially neat, in his opinion (1452 a), when the discovery constitutes the reversal, as in the *Oedipus;* and the tragic effect in this play is very powerful in that the messenger who comes from Corinth thinks that he is bringing good news for Oedipus but actually reveals the dreadful secret of his birth. The fortunes of the main character, Aristotle continues (1453 a), citing Oedipus and Thyestes, should change from happiness to misery (that is, the ending should be tragic rather than happy) ; and the cause of this change must not be extreme depravity of character but rather some great error on the part of a man who is outstanding in reputation and prosperity.[50]

There are various devices by which a discovery of identity may be made. The clumsiness of Aeschylus in managing the recognition of Orestes in the *Choephoroe,* most modern critics assume, was criticized by Euripides. Now the best of all discoveries, according to Aristotle (1455 a, Bywater), is that "arising from the incidents themselves, when the great surprise comes about through a probable incident, like that in the *Oedipus* of Sophocles . . . ."

Tragic fear and pity, Aristotle points out (1453 b), may be aroused not only by the spectacle but also—and this, he says, is more effective— by the very structure and incidents of the play, as in the *Oedipus,* because the mere recital of this story would have such an effect upon one. This fear and pity are strongest when the tragic deed is done within the family. Aristotle is here referring to the fact that Oedipus has slain his own father.

Further, Aristotle states, there should be nothing improbable about the incidents of the play; but if improbabilities are unavoidable, they should be outside the action proper of the play as in the *Oedipus* (1454 b). A later reference (1460 a) shows that Aristotle here is thinking especially of the lack of plausibility in the assumption that Oedipus should have remained ignorant of the circumstances of Laius' death during all the years with Jocasta.

The *Oedipus* is cited also in connection with Aristotle's contention that tragedy is superior to epic poetry (1462 b).

Subject and theme.—The subject of the play is Oedipus' discovery of his identity and his consequent realization that he has slain his father and married his mother. In the course of the play, he does not, like Antigone or Medea or Pentheus, commit any act which results in his downfall. "Oedipus, by Zeus, never enjoyed good fortune," Aristophanes makes his "Aeschylus" say in the *Frogs* (1183–85), "but he was unfortunate in his very being; for before his birth Apollo had said that he would slay his sire . . . ." Such a conception of one's fate as unalterably determined before birth is not typical of Greek popular thought. Fate is something that is usually spoken of in the past tense; where the future is concerned, there is usually an alternative or an uncertainty. This is clearly seen in the *Prometheus,* and it was almost invariably the case in the oracles given at Delphi. Without such duplicity, this institution of Apollo would never have lasted for more than a thousand years. Sophocles places no emphasis upon determinism in this play, but he does stress the infallibility of the oracle of Apollo. This is obvious in the second stasimon and in the speech of the conservative Creon to Oedipus near the end of the play (1445, Jebb): "Aye, for thou thyself wilt now surely put faith in the god." The oracle at Delphi needed rehabilitation in Sophocles' day, for it was widely recognized to have been bribed in certain famous cases. Even the pious Herodotus reports this (5. 63; 6. 66), and he also shows that it had done considerable damage to the Greek cause in the Persian Wars by anticipating a Greek defeat (7. 148 and 169). The Delphic oracle predicted a Spartan victory in the Peloponnesian War, as Thucydides reports (1. 118); but Sophocles may have produced the *Oedipus* before this prediction was made. How Aeschylus and Sophocles could believe in the infallibility of such an institution is difficult to comprehend. We must not, however, assume that oracles and predictions have such an important role in the tragedies of Sophocles primarily because of the author's own religious convictions. Like ghosts and witches in Shakespeare, oracles and prophecies are employed primarily for purposes of foreshadowing, for dramatic irony, and for creating tragic atmosphere.[51] Oracles not in the legendary tradition are freely invented by the dramatist.

The basic theme of the *Oedipus* is the irony of fate. No mortal man, however powerful and wealthy, can be pronounced happy until after he is dead; for no man, however wise, knows what the morrow will bring. This is the burden of the last complete choral song and of the last lines of the play (which are sometimes considered spurious). This was a basic conception in Greek popular thought, best illustrated by the story of Solon and Croesus as told by Herodotus. Croesus, the fabulously wealthy king of Lydia, thought that his power and fortune made him the happiest of all men, but Solon refused to pronounce him or any other man happy before the full course of his life had been run successfully. Herodotus closes his version of this story with the following remark (I. 34, Rawlinson): "After Solon had gone away a dreadful vengeance, sent of God, came upon Croesus, to punish him, it is likely, for deeming himself the happiest of men." Such belief in the envy of the gods is not found in the *Oedipus*. Although it is typical of Greek popular belief, it contradicts determinism; for if one's future were really unalterably fixed, nothing that he or anyone else might say could change it.

The moral guilt or innocence of Oedipus has troubled many critics. Aeschylus interpreted his downfall as due to the sin of his father and the family curse. Sophocles has eliminated this and apparently has substituted no other moral justification. But, since the story is interpreted primarily as an illustration of the irony of fate, we should not expect any other justification than the portrayal of Oedipus as a character who might conceivably have committed his fatal errors even though the gods had not determined them in advance. The character of Oedipus is not ideal or perfect, and he does not appear an entirely innocent victim of circumstance. He has inherited the pride and uncontrollable temper of his father. His insolence, according to Euripides in the *Phoenissae* (41), was responsible for his clash with Laius at the junction of roads. Oedipus' anger and high spirit are cited as the cause of his misfortunes in the *Oedipus at Colonus* (855, 1195–98). In the present play Oedipus confesses that he slew the men at the crossroads in anger (807), and his excessive spirit is brought out in his clashes with Teiresias and Creon. Since the dramatist is not here exhibiting the fatal acts which Oedipus long ago committed, he cannot portray the particular emotional disturbances which led to these acts. But he can portray the inveterate moral faults or emotional weaknesses which were at least in part responsible for these fatal acts, and he must portray these unless the tragedy is to be governed by mere fate or by a malign demon. This is a principle of "dramatic justice" which critics often overlook. In the action of the play not only the pride and temper of Oedipus are exhibited but also his injustice as a ruler and his unorthodox attitude toward seers and oracles. Oedipus does not, therefore, appear to be a man pre-eminently virtuous and just.

Still, many critics insist that Oedipus is entirely guiltless and that the gods of Sophocles merely represent the universe as it actually is and that accordingly they are not subject to blame for the misfortunes of men.[52] Greek gods, it is true, often seem only personifications of natural forces; but certainly prophecy presumes intelligence. This interpretation of the gods, therefore, does not seem wholly acceptable for the *Oedipus*. Nor can it be successfully maintained that the actions of Oedipus in the play are entirely just and proper.

When Oedipus first considers the possibility that he has slain Laius, and before he has the slightest suspicion of any kinship with Laius or Jocasta, he declares (828–29, Jebb): "Then would not he speak aright of Oedipus, who judged these things sent by some cruel power above man?" But after the catastrophe, though his fate turns out to be far more dreadful than this, and though he does cite Apollo as the author of his misfortunes, he does not charge the god with cruelty or injustice (1329). His deeds, though unintentional, are so dreadful and his pollution so black that further opposition to Apollo is unthinkable, and he can only confess his utter ruin. His situation closely resembles that of Ajax, and the moral of the play resembles the moral which Odysseus draws from the downfall of Ajax: even the greatest of men and the greatest good fortune is but an unsubstantial shadow (*Ajax* 121–26).

It is possible—but most scholars do not think it likely—that the *Oedipus* was presented during the plague at Athens and constituted an indirect political attack upon Pericles. Pericles was the most powerful man in Athenian politics until his death in 429 B.C., a victim of the plague; and he had strongly advocated the war against Sparta. Just before serious hostilities were begun, the Spartans, wishing to avoid war and knowing that Pericles was its chief advocate, sent an embassy to Athens asking that they drive out "the curse of the goddess." The curse to which they referred was attached to the descendants of certain men who had committed acts of sacrilege some two hundred years previously.[53] Pericles was one of these descendants, and after the plague broke out his situation bore an obvious and striking resemblance to that of Oedipus in the play of Sophocles.

Dramatic irony.—Dramatic irony, as we should expect if the theme of the play is the irony of fate, is perhaps the most important element of the play. It begins with the first appearance of Oedipus in his kingly robes and with his first words, "I myself have come hither, Oedipus, famous among all men." Almost every speech in these first scenes is charged with irony, as every situation is charged with it. The pitiful townspeople have appealed for aid to the one who in reality is the cause of their woe. Teiresias is the blind man who sees, Oedipus the seeing man who is blind.

With pity the enlightened spectator witnesses Oedipus' welcome of the information which Creon has brought from Delphi. With pity we view his optimism and his zeal to carry out all the commands of Apollo and punish the murderer of Laius. Oedipus fears that this same murderer may wish to slay him! But at the beginning of the next episode it is with horror that the spectator hears Oedipus curse the murderer of Laius and say (258–65):

"But now, since it has been my lot to possess the powers which he once held and to possess his bed and the wife who has received the seed of both of us [*homosporon*], and since children kindred and common to both of us

had been born of the same mother if offspring had not fared ill for him—
But, as it is, fortune has struck him down. I shall be his champion, therefore, as though he were my father . . . ."

Such irony is truly dreadful. Oedipus has begotten children that are
all too much his own kindred, and he thinks that Laius has had no offspring; but his words are frightfully ambiguous. In the next scene,
Teiresias casts at Oedipus words which recall the irony of this passage,
especially the phrase, "sower of seed where your father sowed" (*homo-
sporos*, 460). Later in the play, when Oedipus begins to suspect that
he is himself the murderer of Laius, to describe his possible fate he
uses in part the same words that he previously used in pronouncing
the interdiction of the murderer (817–19; cf. 238–41).

Discussion.—The chief virtues of the plot structure of the *Oedipus*
are the rapidity and the inevitability of its progression. Nothing can
be omitted; nothing really pertinent could be added. Each incident, with
the one exception of the entirely plausible arrival of the messenger
from Corinth, follows naturally from what precedes and leads inevitably to what follows.

The play is marked off into six sections by five choral songs. These
sections vary in length from seventy-six lines to three hundred and
fifty. This unevenness in length is characteristic of the episodes in
Greek tragedy, and is a much more natural type of division than the
modern convention of having three acts of about equal length. Characteristic also is the adaptation of the number of sections—the other
Greek tragedies have from four to seven sections—and of the function
of each section in the individual play. There is no regularity such as
the rule of five divisions or acts, which is usually observed in Seneca.
In the *Oedipus,* as frequently, it is obvious that great artistry has been
employed in constructing each section as a unit and in placing the choral
songs at precisely the proper points. The choral songs themselves are
strictly pertinent to the subject of the dramatic action, and they are
important in reflecting or modulating the tone of the play. The meter,
also, is skillfully adapted to the content of these songs. So were the
dance movements which accompanied them.

The opening scene of the *Oedipus* (prologos, 150 lines) plunges
into the midst of things—to use the famous phrase of Horace—and the
small amount of exposition given is wholly incidental. The appeal of
the townspeople to Oedipus really begins the action of the play, and the
complication starts with the entrance of Creon and his report. This
entrance, however, is somewhat abrupt, for it takes place almost immediately after Oedipus has informed the townspeople that he has sent

Creon to Delphi and that he is troubled over the long delay. Naturalness has here been sacrificed to rapidity. Characterization of Oedipus, also, is an important function of this scene. Sophocles has taken care, as Dryden and Lee remark in the preface to their *Oedipus,* to show Oedipus "in his first entrance, a just, a merciful, a successful, a religious prince, and, in short, a father of his country." The pride of Oedipus, also, is evident from his first lines. After the report of Creon, Oedipus expresses his suspicions that bribery from Thebes emboldened the thieves who slew Laius, and he suspects the same party would like to put him out of the way in similar fashion. These suspicions prepare for the later erroneous conviction of Oedipus that an intrigue exists between Creon and Teiresias. The first section of the play ends with Oedipus' resolve to search out and punish the murderer, and with his command that the Thebans be summoned before him—a nice motivation for the appearance of the chorus.

The chorus of Theban elders, loyally devoted to Oedipus, now enter (parodos, 65 lines). In solemn tones they first express their trepidation at the message from the oracle, and then they invoke various gods to come to their aid. Turning to the plague, and in somewhat more spirited measure, they describe the endless woes of suffering and death which it brings, and again they pray for succor. Then in still more excited measure they ask that the god of death be driven out and destroyed by Zeus, lastly invoking Apollo, Artemis, and Dionysus to fight in their behalf "against the god who has no honor among gods." These opening choral songs furnish what might be called the emotional exposition of the play.

The next section (first episode, 247 lines) opens with Oedipus reassuring the chorus somewhat too confidently, as if he could answer their prayers now as he did when he rescued them from the Sphinx. Exhorting them to aid him in the search for the murderer of Laius, he proclaims his curse upon the murderer with dreadful irony, interdicts him from concourse with Thebans, and emphasizes his own zeal in this cause. The chorus insist that they are without a clue, but they suggest that Teiresias be consulted. To this suggestion Oedipus replies that he has already sent for Teiresias on the instigation of Creon—an important bit of information, for the fact that Creon first offers this suggestion later makes Oedipus, already suspicious of political intrigue, surmise that Creon is the plotter, and this prepares for Creon's re-entrance.

Oedipus marvels that Teiresias has not already appeared, and the seer enters almost immediately. This is a precise repetition of the awkward technique previously used for introducing Creon. Another slight blemish is found in the fact that Teiresias already knows of the inter-diction of the murderer which Oedipus has just pronounced—for we can hardly assume that Teiresias is omniscient.[54]

Just before Teiresias enters, the chorus praise his infallibility. This character preparation adds to his dignity and, by assuring us that Teiresias speaks the truth, emphasizes the irony of Oedipus' skepticism and suspicions of treachery. The bitter quarrel which follows has various important effects. It brings out certain unattractive features in the character of Oedipus, his wrath and his unjust haste to condemn without evidence. The portrayal of these features is of the utmost importance, for they perhaps explain in part his slaughter of Laius, and they certainly furnish some moral justification for the downfall of Oedipus. The quarrel serves also to recall Creon into the action, who, in turn, naturally brings in Jocasta, his sister and the wife of Oedipus; and it furnishes the motivation for Jocasta's all-important story of the death of Laius. Most significant of all, perhaps, the dire predictions of Teiresias first name Oedipus himself as the slayer and prepare Oedipus to be thoroughly shaken when he hears that Laius was slain where three roads meet.

It has been suggested that Sophocles may have intended this scene between Teiresias and Oedipus to level the differences of knowledge of the story among the spectators;[55] but since the most powerful dramatic irony of the play precedes this scene, we must assume that the dramatist takes for granted a full knowledge of the story from the very beginning of the play.

One of the main problems which the dramatist faced in this play was the difficulty of maintaining Oedipus' ignorance of his identity with plausibility. The suspicions of Oedipus concerning political intrigue, false but not implausible, constitute one of the devices for maintaining his ignorance and motivating his disregard for the pronouncements of Teiresias. Another is found in the circumstances of the quarrel itself. Oedipus loses all patience and without the slightest shred of evidence accuses Teiresias of the murder. Teiresias responds by immediately accusing Oedipus. His accusation, therefore, seems not a seer's prophecy but the mere return of Oedipus' angry abuse. So the chorus at this point interpret the accusations of both Oedipus and Teiresias (404–5).

The episode ends with Teiresias pronouncing his prophecy—though for Oedipus this is essentially a repetition of the oracle given him long ago at Delphi—now for the third time, in language as ominous as it is plain and unmistakable. Thus the emphasis of the whole episode is placed upon its most significant content.

The chorus now sing their first song after completing their entrance (first stasimon, 50 lines). In spirited measure they wonder who the murderer may really be and poetically imagine his futile efforts to escape the inevitable vengeance of Apollo. In more passionate strain, they confess that they are dreadfully troubled by the words of Teiresias but know of nothing that confirms the charge; the gods have true knowledge, but there is no certain evidence that seers know more than other men; and they will never condemn Oedipus without proof, for he has formerly been the savior of the state.

The second episode (350 lines) begins with the quarrel between Oedipus and Creon. Here Oedipus expresses a very tyrannical and offensive theory of autocratic rule. His words remind us of those of Menelaus in the *Ajax* and those of Creon in the *Antigone*. (Creon there, though "historically" the same person, is an entirely different character from Creon in the *Oedipus*.) The injustice of Oedipus here is very different from the calm and pious justice of Creon in the final scene of the play. This characterization of Oedipus continues that of the former scene; and although this quarrel seems to threaten a complication extraneous to the basic plot, it really advances the plot, for Jocasta very naturally comes in as an arbiter between her brother and her husband.

The scenes of the quarrel differ in tone and subject from the revelations of Jocasta, but all three scenes are properly included in one section of the play. If they had been divided by a choral song, the smooth transition from the quarrel to the more pertinent story of Jocasta would have been disrupted, and the plot movement would have been retarded here where rapidity of action is highly desirable. Choral interruption would also have given an improper emphasis to the quarrel and Creon. Still, a break in the rhythmic monotony of the iambic lines is desirable, and this is obtained in two ways. First, iambic lines are divided between two speakers (*antilabe*). This division indicates extreme excitement, and here it marks the climax of the quarrel. It is at this point that Jocasta enters. The monotony of the iambic lines is again broken by agitated lyric exchanges (*kommos*), in which the chorus entreat Oedipus most earnestly not to condemn Creon on an unproved charge, and they swear that they are not devising Oedipus' overthrow. After Oedipus has somewhat grudgingly acquiesced, there is another interchange, corresponding precisely in meter and division of lines, except that Jocasta now takes part. The chorus urge her to take Oedipus within, but she insists on hearing an explanation. Oedipus angrily protests the intercession of the chorus on behalf of Creon, and they respond with another assurance of loyalty and gratitude.

Jocasta's intervention leads to Oedipus' reviewing his case against Creon, especially the declaration of Teiresias that Oedipus is the murderer of Laius. It is noteworthy, incidentally, that the other prophecies are not related. They might more quickly suggest the true identity of Oedipus to Jocasta. Mention of Teiresias' prophecy leads to Jocasta's ironic effort to prove that prophecies and oracles are all untrustworthy by citing the oracle given to Laius. In her story Jocasta mentions one fact which strikes Oedipus most forcefully: Laius was murdered where three highways meet. Oedipus' optimism has been checked by the quarrels with Teiresias and Creon; but now, though Jocasta's story was designed to allay all these fears, he conceives his first real apprehension. Now he realizes that he is within the toils, and the remainder of the play is taken up with the frantic and pitiful efforts of Jocasta and himself to free him. But with growing horror the audience realizes that every move, though it may seem to promise release, really binds the victims all the more tightly. If Jocasta had not long ago resolved to put no faith in oracles and if Oedipus had not been so prejudiced and infuriated at the pronouncements of Teiresias, one or both must have seen that the oracle which Oedipus now relates supplements the oracle given Laius. It also agrees with the prophecy of Teiresias; but this fact might have caused Oedipus to be even more skeptical of Teiresias—as if the seer were repeating an old oracle to embarrass him. Now, however, Oedipus has begun to suspect that he is the murderer of Laius: the place, the time, and the appearance of Laius and his followers all coincide, but Oedipus was traveling alone and thought that he slew every man of the party, whereas Laius was said to have been slain by a band of robbers or wayfarers (cf. 292) and one member of the party escaped. Even the language in which Creon has first reported the oracle suggests that more than one man was responsible for the murder (107). We must not forget, furthermore, that Oedipus still believes himself the son of Polybus and Merope of Corinth. Oedipus, thoroughly shaken, anticipates his own wretchedness if the man whom he slew was "akin to Laius." His anxiety naturally leads to the summoning of the one surviving witness. Jocasta, however, insists that the man's story, known to all, cannot now be changed; and, instead of recognizing the whole truth, she here sees further proof of the untrustworthiness of oracles—for Apollo said that Laius must die by the hand of his own child! Here, on a note of false and ironic optimism, and as we await the story of the witness of Laius' death, the second episode ends with fine dramatic effect.

In reflective mood, the chorus now pray that they may ever keep the divine and deathless laws of heaven (second stasimon, 48 lines).

Insolence begets the tyrant, but at the very moment of its triumph insolence is hurled to utter destruction. Here the chorus is reflecting upon the insolent manner in which Oedipus has brought his unfounded charges against Creon, upon the unorthodox attitude of Jocasta toward oracles and prophecy, and upon the discussion of the pollutions of blood guilt and incest. In their second strophe and antistrophe, which continue in the same meter and tone, they curse those who show no reverence for the gods. Where such a person dwells, who can be safe from the avenging wrath of Heaven? Zeus must not allow the oracle concerning Laius to go unfulfilled, for faith in the gods would thus be destroyed!

Jocasta's orthodox prayer to Apollo, which begins the third episode (175 lines), shows that she has faith in the gods themselves and adds a necessary corrective after the extreme criticism of the chorus. The joyful messenger from Corinth appears immediately, as if in answer to these prayers. Some preparation for his appearance has been made in the repeated mention of Polybus and of Corinth and in the story which Oedipus related of his early life. Jocasta is elated at the news of the death of Polybus, "father" of Oedipus and king of Corinth, for she interprets this news as releasing Oedipus from his predicted fate and as further proof that all oracles are false. Now for the third time Jocasta has cited such "proof," and with each repetition the irony of her words has become more apparent and more dreadful. But Oedipus is convinced that she is right, though he still fears wedlock with his mother. Jocasta again attempts to reassure him by pointing out that many men in dreams have lain with their mothers, but that such dreams and thoughts are best disregarded and forgotten (981–82).[56] This is the only hint of an "Oedipus complex" in the play, and the adoption of this ugly phrase by modern psychology is unfortunate and misleading.

The joy at the news of the death of Polybus is stifled when the Messenger, like Jocasta earlier and with similarly ironical result, attempts to reassure Oedipus and to remove his fears concerning his mother. Oedipus was not the son of Polybus and Merope. He was exposed by a servant of Laius on Mount Cithaeron with his ankles pierced. ("Swellfoot," as Shelley translated it, is the real meaning of the name Oedipus.) The effect which these words have on Oedipus stands out in strong contrast with that which they produce on Jocasta, since this information constitutes full recognition for her, and she rushes into the palace with ominous words. Such an exit was a favorite device with Sophocles. So Eurydice withdraws in the *Antigone* just before her suicide, and Deianeira in the *Trachiniae*.

For the moment, Oedipus is saved by his pride. Curiosity about his birth has been a primary motive in his life. It caused him to leave Corinth; it made him for an instant forget his wrath at Teiresias (437); and now, in his turmoil of spirit, it prevents him from recalling Jocasta's story of Laius' child and its exposure on a "lonely mountain" with its ankles pierced. The episode ends with Oedipus rejecting the ominous warning of Jocasta and expressing his determination to solve the riddle of his birth.

Thus the subject of Oedipus' inquiry has shifted from the identity of the murderer of Laius to his own identity. But the audience hardly realize this, for they know that the answer to both questions is the same. The change is almost imperceptible, furthermore, because the preparation for it has been so subtle. Reference has been made to the birth of Oedipus by Teiresias. Then, too, Oedipus himself has related his history. But, most important of all, the dramatist has facilitated this shift by making the servant who exposed the infant identical with the surviving attendant who witnessed the death of Laius. Thus the resolving character of both inquiries is the same person, and both inquiries are solved at the same time, so that an earlier and unnecessary discovery, as in Seneca's *Oedipus,* is avoided and the plot is more neatly unified. Sophocles has also made the shepherd who gave the infant Oedipus to Polybus identical with the messenger from Corinth. This could be rationalized by assuming that the man who originally found Oedipus would be most interested in his future welfare and in bringing the good news to him. Still, we must admit that the dramatist in making use of both these combinations has employed the long arm of coincidence to facilitate ease and rapidity of plot progression. Simplification of minor details adds greater emphasis to major ones.

The following choral song is very short (third stasimon, 24 lines), since Oedipus remains on stage, tensely awaiting the arrival of the shepherd who exposed him at his birth and who witnessed the death of Laius. To a gay and lively measure, the chorus dances and sings of Mount Cithaeron as the nurse of Oedipus, and then they speculate on which of the gods was his sire and who was his mother. An ironically joyful song just before the catastrophe, such as this, is a favorite device of Sophocles.

The fourth episode is the shortest section of the play (76 lines). Jocasta is gone, and Oedipus faces his cruel destiny alone—a magnificent climax to the play. The tortured reluctance of the herdsman— nicely contrasted with the eagerness of the messenger from Corinth— is finally overcome. Again at the climax the iambic lines are divided between speakers, and most skillfully divided. Of the first divided line,

Oedipus is given two-thirds and the reluctant slave only two words; the next two lines are divided approximately into halves; but of the following line the horrified Oedipus has only a single word, while the slave completes the recognition with the rest of the line. Oedipus winces in this scene, but nowhere is his masculine honesty more clearly portrayed. Unlike Jocasta in her final words, Oedipus is determined to have the whole truth, however disastrous it may be. His recognition of his identity constitutes the reversal of his fortune (peripety). From his final lines, in which he prays now for the last time to look upon the light of day, we might expect his suicide if we had not heard the prophecy of Teiresias.

The chorus begins the lament for the fate of Oedipus in unusually weighty and solemn measure (fourth stasimon, 37 lines). As frequently in Greek tragedy, the fate of the hero is generalized into the fate of all mankind. No human lot can be counted surely blessed if such a one as Oedipus, after achieving the pinnacle of worldly good fortune and saving the state, is thus destroyed. The second part of the song is a dirge over the dreadful fate of Oedipus, ending in the wish that they had never laid eyes upon him; for, though he once saved them, he has now brought them to grief.

The final section (exodos, 308 lines) is essentially an epilogue to the main plot, for the tragedy is practically complete with Oedipus' discovery of his identity. The Messenger reveals that the house is polluted with such ills that not even the great rivers of the Danube and the Rion (Phasis) could wash it clean—a simile that flows through Seneca to *Macbeth* (II. ii. 60).[57] This report prepares for the shocking sight of the blinded Oedipus.

Here again a lengthy section includes several scenes. Rapidity is highly desirable after the catastrophe. But again the rhythmic monotony of the iambic lines is broken by a lyric exchange between Oedipus and the chorus. A more important result of employing lyrics here, however, is the raising of the tone to suit the wild grief of Oedipus, and the meters here, as elsewhere, are most subtly adapted. At the first horrifying appearance of the blinded Oedipus, the chorus breaks out into a lament in simple anapestic meter. The woeful cries of Oedipus begin in the same meter—primarily a marching meter and well suited to accompany an entrance. The chorus now drops back into the simplest subdued iambic meter, whereas Oedipus, in sharp contrast, laments in a most passionate measure (dochmiac). Verbal gemination adds to the pathos of the meter.

At one point Oedipus predicts to Creon the strange manner of his death: ". . . . neither sickness nor aught else can destroy me; for never had I been snatched from death, but in reserve for some strange doom."[58] These lines suggest the supernatural death of Oedipus at Colonus, a tradition dear to Sophocles, since he was born in the district of Colonus. This death is the subject of the *Oedipus at Colonus,* which was written in the last years of Sophocles' long life. The unity of the play is not disturbed, however, by any mention of the famous quarrel of the sons of Oedipus or of the heroism of Antigone in burying her brother.

At the very end of the play, Creon and Oedipus break into animated trochaic measure. The same shift in meter is made near the end of the *Philoctetes,* when Neoptolemus finally agrees to take Philoctetes home.[59]

These final scenes are designed primarily to impress upon us the full import of the tragedy. They suggest the miserable future of Oedipus and his children. The young girls add pathos to his downfall by their very presence and by bringing out the more kindly aspects of his character. Thus after the catastrophe Sophocles here, like Euripides in the *Bacchae* and elsewhere, presents his main character in the most favorable light.

4. *TRACHINIAE* ("MAIDENS OF TRACHIS")

(Possibly about 413 B.C.)

The *Trachiniae* appears to be an inferior play. Euripides' *Heracles* probably preceded and inspired it. Both plays concern the final return and suffering of Heracles; but Euripides boldly invents, whereas Sophocles reverts to the established legend. It has been suggested that Sophocles may here be "correcting" Euripides.[60] All the characters except Heracles himself are entirely different in the two plays, and there is also wide divergence in the characterization of the hero.

The events of the *Trachiniae* are the subject of Seneca's extant *Hercules on Oeta.*

Discussion.—The theme of the play is perhaps the irony of the inglorious death of Heracles, the great warrior and benefactor of Greece. The theme has sometimes been taken to be the destructive power of love, and certainly Heracles is destroyed by the women whose captive he has become; but this is not emphasized or generalized at the end of the play as we might expect if the author intended it as the theme.

The most difficult problem which the play presents, however, is the problem of its structure. Many critics have felt that the play presents

two tragedies, that of Deianeira and that of Heracles. Some have gone
so far as to insist that Deianeira's tragedy alone is effective. It is true
that Deianeira dominates the scene during most of the play; but the
author possibly intended her dominance, like that of Amphitryon and
Megara during the earlier part of Euripides' *Heracles,* to be physical
only. The main concern of Deianeira and of everyone else is the fate
of Heracles. The oracle that is several times repeated during the first
scenes concerns Heracles and stresses the fact that the crisis of Heracles' life has come. The danger is his, and the foreboding concerns him
first of all, although it is made obvious that the fate of his family is
involved (85). After the entrance of Lichas, furthermore, the arrival
of Heracles is awaited. There is no hint of any physical danger to
Deianeira before she has discovered the ominous potency of the oint-
ment used on the robe. This foreboding comes late in the play (720)
and is not maintained for long, for her suicide is reported shortly
afterward. In this interval the misfortune of Heracles is described at
length and his imminent arrival announced by Hyllus. Thus the death
of Deianeira is treated as incidental. Still, it must be admitted that her
tragedy has greatly detracted from the tragedy of Heracles.

The differences between this play and the *Heracles* of Euripides
are noteworthy, for the plots have basic similarities; but Euripides
has not allowed any minor character to overshadow Heracles. In his
play, two characters rather than one dominate the scene before the
arrival of Heracles. Both these characters are passive sufferers and
comparatively colorless. Their immediate safety depends upon the early
arrival of Heracles. Megara, the wife of Heracles, is later slain by
her husband in his madness; but she is an entirely innocent victim, she
has been maintained as a distinctly minor character, and, even in the
account of her death, interest is centered upon Heracles. In Sophocles,
however, Deianeira has been made the most active character, whereas
Heracles himself is passive. She alone dominates the scene during most
of the play. Lastly, she has been made a very appealing character. A
conservative critic has said that by general consent she has been recognized "as one of the most delicately beautiful creations in literature."[61]

But here as elsewhere in classical literature, the modern reader
must guard against being prejudiced by romantic sentimentalism. Deianeira is devoted to her husband, kind to the captives brought into her
house, sympathetic with all human suffering. But she is no paragon
of virtue, no perfectly innocent character brought low by fate. Her
intentions are good from her own selfish point of view, but she is
lacking in foresight. She employs deception, furthermore, when she
inveigles Lichas into confessing the truth. That this deception is de-

liberate is shown by her previous and by her subsequent speeches, in which there is no hint of vacillation or sincere change of purpose. Deianeira assures Lichas that she will not offer any opposition to Heracles' latest fancy, and Lichas compliments her for "thinking mortal thoughts." The audience, however, knows that she is not thinking mortal thoughts but only saying them, and she strikes a very ominous note when she intimates that she would be vainly struggling against the gods if she did not accept her husband's unfaithfulness with resignation.

Deianeira's experiment, furthermore, is not as innocent as the modern reader may assume. The use of magic and witchcraft, though common among certain classes, was dangerous. It was always suspect and publicly condemned.[62] Deianeira knows that her attempt is a bold one (582–87), and she seems actually base when she enjoins the chorus to silence and adds that even if one does disgraceful things one will never be disgraced provided they are kept secret (596–97).[63] Still, she intends no evil. She later sums up her action very correctly when she realizes that out of fair hope she may have done a great wrong (667; cf. 1136). Deianeira is essentially a good and admirable woman, but she is ruined by a fatal error.

Heracles himself is a pitiful but not very appealing character. Indeed, as critics have pointed out, Heracles is not a character who lends himself to effective tragedy. Though the *Trachiniae* is written about his fate, he is on scene only during the last quarter of the play. Even before he enters, the catastrophe is practically complete; and there is no dramatic action after he is brought on. This final scene is largely etiological. It explains the circumstances of Heracles' death and the marriage of Hyllus to Iole. Mount Oeta was an important site in the later cult of Heracles;[64] it has been mentioned repeatedly in the earlier part of the play,[65] and we are now told of the pyre that is to be built there.

The play has its technical weaknesses. There are too many long narrative speeches, and there is too much talk of oracles and prophecies. The exposition is awkwardly managed. It is patently implausible that Hyllus should have so much news of his father which he has never told Deianeira. Hyllus' entrance at this point also is too mechanical, and later his movements are confused—he should enter from the house at verse 971, but, if he does so, his appearance again seems too pat.

Various indications of Euripidean influence upon Sophocles are noteworthy. Besides the play's general indebtedness to the *Heracles,* certain motifs seem to have been taken from that play,[66] and one line which Heracles speaks is almost the same in both plays.[67] Another line in Sophocles' play perhaps was taken from Euripides' *Suppliants.*[68] The prologue, however, is the play's most obvious Euripidean feature. It is very similar to the prologue of the *Heracleidae.* There too the character begins with a proverbial commonplace followed by a personal application. There too the speech is essentially an expository monologue, though other characters are on the scene. Various other features have been considered Euripidean,[69] including the tone of the final lines. These lines of protest against Zeus have a bitterness that does resemble the bitterness of the protests of Amphitryon and Heracles in Euripides. In neither play, however, can these protests be fairly interpreted as serious indictments of the gods by the poets themselves. The characters speaking them are humanly blind, as Hyllus himself points out (1270), and they do not see the whole scheme of things. The audience knows that through his suffering Heracles rose to the level of the gods themselves.

5. *ELECTRA*

(Possibly about 410 b.c.)

This play dramatizes the same events as those of Aeschylus' *Choephoroe* and Euripides' *Electra.* For various reasons, to be presented below, the present writer assumes that Euripides' production preceded that of Sophocles.[70] Several scenes of Sophocles' play, especially those between Electra and Orestes and those with Aegisthus, are masterpieces; but the play as a whole is an inferior work.

Source.—Sophocles' *Electra* follows the main lines of Aeschylus' *Choephoroe.* In the play of Aeschylus, however, Orestes is the chief figure, and the role of Electra is comparatively a minor one; Orestes' nurse appears, and there is no Chrysothemis or Paedagogus; the scene of recognition and reunion is very brief; the dream of Clytemnestra is somewhat different, and it is differently exploited by the dramatist; a considerable portion of Aeschylus' play is taken up in invoking the spirit of Agamemnon, whose grave is represented before the audience; Orestes' report of his own death, very casual and brief, arouses the suspicions of Clytemnestra, which threaten the success of the plan; Aegisthus is the first to be slain; Orestes then faces his mother in a powerful scene in which Pylades speaks; and after her slaughter Orestes is profoundly shaken. Aeschylus, furthermore, views the slaughter of Clytemnestra by Orestes as an evil deed which must be done, and which is inevitably followed by retribution. Examining the plays either from the logical or from the moral and psychological point of view, we can hardly avoid the conclusion that the changes of Sophocles, with the possible exception of his removal of the grave of Agamemnon from the scene, are not improvements. Aeschylus' play, however, appears somewhat archaic because of the simplicity of its action and a certain clumsiness in handling its characters. In these technical matters, of course, Sophocles shows great improvement.

Sophocles' *Electra* exhibits many striking similarities to the *Electra* of Euripides, but these should be viewed without prejudice before one undertakes to decide which poet is following the other.

Considerable influence of Homeric and later epic, also, is observable in the play of Sophocles. Homeric is the detail of Agamemnon's having been slain at a banquet (203), also the contention of Electra and the chorus that Clytemnestra's main motivation for slaying Agamemnon was lust and the persuasion of Aegisthus (197). Electra's insistence that the body of Aegisthus be cast out unburied has a Homeric ring (*Odyssey* 3. 258). Homeric, too, is the moral interpretation of Orestes' deed as praiseworthy and followed by no punishment or suffering, although the manner of Clytemnestra's death is not told in Homer—she may possibly have committed suicide. From later epic is taken the assumption that Agamemnon had four daughters, and perhaps the story of Agamemnon's offending Artemis by slaying a stag in her grove and boasting about it. The role of the old man, also, occurs in previous versions, although he was sometimes identified as the herald of Agamemnon rather than as a *paedagogus*.

Sophocles' one important change in these previous events is noteworthy: Electra was responsible for Orestes' being saved from the murderers (12).[71] Thus begins Sophocles' glorification of Electra.

Influence.—The Latin dramatist Atilius made an adaptation of Sophocles' *Electra*. Cicero's brother, a literary dilettante, wrote a play on this subject—one of four written in sixteen days. Many modern and contemporary versions have been attempted with varying success.[72]

Theme.—Throughout the play the vengeance which Orestes takes upon the murderers of his father is considered an obligation as just as it is inescapable. Apollo has commanded it, and his wisdom is beyond question (1425). Even the ax with which Agamemnon was slain longs for vengeance.[73] Sophocles, himself, therefore, interpreted the act of Orestes as an entirely admirable one.[74] In so doing, he clashes with Aeschylus, who viewed the deed as necessary but dreadful; he clashes even more violently with Euripides, who considered the act an evil one which should not have been committed.

Generalizing at the end of the play, Orestes insists that summary execution should be meted out to all who transgress the laws, in order that others may be deterred from crime. Electra has earlier made essentially the same contention (1382).

Recognition and intrigue.—Electra's speech over what she believes to be the ashes of her brother is undeniably a masterpiece. Naturally this scene, and indeed the whole role of Electra, were favorites with great actors. Polus, the most famous actor of the later fourth century, is said to have done this scene with an urn containing the ashes of his own dead son![75]

The recognition which follows arises from this probable incident. It belongs, therefore, to that category of recognitions which was considered the most natural and effective by Aristotle (*Poetics* 1455 a).

The deception by which Orestes gains entrance to the palace is here essentially the same as in Aeschylus and involves the assumption that Clytemnestra does not recognize her own son. The device of announcing one's own death was employed in Euripides' lost *Cresphontes,* also, and elsewhere in Greek legend. In Sophocles' play, the plan is explained to the audience beforehand, and the Paedagogus is sent ahead to make the first announcement. That Clytemnestra should not recognize the Paedagogus is extremely improbable, though a weak effort is made to excuse this (42–43). The story which the Paedagogus tells, furthermore, was criticized as improbable by Aristotle (*Poetics* 1460 a), perhaps because the Pythian games did not exist in the time of Orestes or more probably because it was extremely unlikely that such a falsehood could successfully be told about a public event.[76]

This false tale does not excite the least suspicion in Clytemnestra or in Aegisthus, and no complication threatens the success of the intrigue. In Aeschylus' play, the suspicions of both are aroused; but there, it is true, the account is much simpler and is casually reported by Orestes himself. No urn is produced. In Sophocles' play, furthermore, Clytemnestra may reasonably be supposed to accept the news with no misgivings, for the Paedagogus enters immediately after her prayer to Apollo, as if in answer to it, and her dream has been much less ominous than it was in Aeschylus.[77]

Discussion.—The *Electra* of Sophocles opens with a scene in which Orestes explains to his Paedagogus and the supernumerary Pylades the deception to be employed against Aegisthus and Clytemnestra. Instead of executing their plan immediately, however, Orestes and Pylades go off to the tomb of Agamemnon and do not reappear until two-thirds of the play is completed. During much of this interval, all action essential to the plot is suspended.

The cries of Electra have been heard by Orestes before he hastily leaves the scene, and thus Sophocles avoids the awkward vacant stage which occurs at this point in the very similar opening of Euripides' play. Electra enters with slow marching anapests. These and her following lyric exchange with the chorus are devoted mainly to an exposition of her grief and misfortune and to her desire for vengeance. The general form of this entrance and duet, though not precisely that of Euripides' *Electra,* is typically Euripidean, as one may see from the *Trojan Women.*

The first episode continues on this expository theme and introduces Chrysothemis, who plays the foil for Electra as did Ismene for Antigone. Especially reminiscent of Ismene is Chrysothemis' insistence that she is subject to superior force and hence that she will be forgiven if she makes no futile attempt to avenge Agamemnon's murder (400; *Antigone* 65). Here the contrast between the two sisters is exaggerated by dress and appearance. But Electra is not wholly unsuccessful in her pleas to her weaker sister, and at the end of the episode Chrysothemis agrees to cast aside the funeral offerings of Clytemnestra and to take instead those of Electra and herself to the grave of Agamemnon. We naturally expect her to meet Orestes there or at least to see his offerings.

After a choral song in which the punishment of Clytemnestra and Aegisthus is anticipated, Clytemnestra enters. Her clash with Electra is a pertinent scene if her murder is to be justified. At the end of the scene, Clytemnestra fulfills the original purpose of her coming forth by offering a prayer to Apollo, the very god, as the audience realizes, who has sent Orestes. Immediately afterward, as if in answer to this ambiguous prayer, the old Paedagogus enters and recites his false story of Orestes' death. His brilliant description seems to be elaborated partly for its own sake—the Athenian audience was tremendously enthusiastic about such speeches. Two minor points may be noted: the old man does not give a false oath, as Orestes directed (47), and in his fictional chariot race, an Athenian is the winner! The important effect of this scene is found in its contrast between the reactions of Clytemnestra and those of Electra and in the irony of both series of reactions. Clytemnestra is further condemned, for she obviously wishes Electra as well as Orestes dead.

The scenes which follow are not strictly pertinent to the revenge of Orestes except in that thoughts of vengeance are still dominant; for Electra, as the audience knows, is laboring under a false grief, and her laments and actions have no effect upon the plot as a whole. Her grief is sharply contrasted with the joy of Chrysothemis, who now enters with what she considers very happy tidings. An ironic and melodramatic clash between the two sisters ensues, in which Electra to no avail urges Chrysothemis to undertake the murder of Aegisthus with her. This scene is very similar to the opening scene in the *Antigone,* even in details such as the strong sister's spitefully bidding the weak to betray her secret (1033; *Antigone* 86). The episode ends, as in the *Antigone,* with the warnings of the weaker sister and with the stronger sister determined to act alone. But in the *Antigone* this determination is immediately translated into action, whereas here neither Electra's resolve nor the ominous warnings of Chrysothemis have any consequence. The minimum change necessary to make them pertinent to the plot would have been definitely to state or imply that Orestes himself could not accomplish the murders without great danger. But this is not done. The warnings of Chrysothemis in their context are hardly sufficient for this (cf. 1001–2), and in the subsequent action there is very little emphasis upon the danger of the undertaking. This scene, however, does increase the dramatic height of Electra; and Sophocles, as we may observe most clearly in the *Philoctetes,* likes very much to force his characters to the extreme limit. The true explanation of this scene, therefore, may be that Sophocles, deceived by a specious similarity between Electra and Antigone and lured by the theatrical effectiveness of a powerful heroine, has more or less unconsciously followed his earlier masterpiece too closely.

The next episode opens with the entrance of Orestes. Electra's speech over the urn and their recognition follow. This whole episode has the pathos and seriousness of tragedy; but it has the sudden shifts in emotional tone characteristic of melodrama, and it is drawn out to a length which in such a dangerous situation is proper only to melodrama. It shows marked similarities to the recognition scene in Euripides' *Iphigenia in Tauris,* where the melodrama is quite in place. The excitement at the climax of the *Electra* is heightened by the entrance of the nervous and worried Paedagogus, at whose insistence Orestes and Pylades resolutely march into the palace to slay Clytemnestra—but only after another melodramatic scene in which Electra takes the hands of the old man and doubtless kisses them in gratitude for his services. The efforts of the old man to cut the episode short, like the earlier efforts of Orestes, increase the tension and suspense.

Sophocles makes short shrift of the murder of Clytemnestra. Electra follows Orestes and Pylades into the palace but returns almost immediately to punctuate the cries of her dying mother with the most bloodthirsty encouragement to the slayers. Orestes reappears, only to retire within a few lines when Aegisthus is seen approaching.

The scene with Aegisthus is one of the most dramatic of the play, but it has the implausibilities and technical weaknesses characteristic of melodrama. Sophocles has not explained how the news of the Phocian strangers could have reached Aegisthus. Although the absence of Aegisthus has been mentioned repeatedly and his return has been anticipated throughout the play, still his entrance at precisely the most convenient moment appears too pat, "like the catastrophe of the old comedy." It is obviously implausible, furthermore, that Electra without prearrangement and without exciting suspicion should lead Aegisthus to believe that the body of Orestes is within. It was not the Greek practice to transport corpses great distances, and the Paedagogus in giving the news to Clytemnestra clearly stated that the body of Orestes had been burned (757). But the coincidence of Aegisthus' pat entrance is hardly noted in the excitement of the scene, and the implausibility of pretending that Orestes' body is present can be forgiven because of the dramatic and powerful scene which it makes possible. The body is revealed, and Aegisthus utters an ironic boast over it. It has not fallen "save by the doom of jealous Heaven" (1466–67, Jebb). He then uncovers the eyes to find those of Clytemnestra.[78]

The problem of the *Electras*.—Our consideration of the structure of Sophocles' play reveals several astonishing features. Like the plays of Aeschylus and Euripides, this play seems to be constructed to lead to the death of Clytemnestra as its climax. The process of blackening her character is carried far beyond the limits set by the other dramatists. The woes and complaints of Electra, which directly forward this process, constitute a large part of the play. Any blackening of Aegisthus, of course, is wholly superfluous. From the Greek point of view, his death needs no justification; it is without question a commendable act in the view of every writer who treated the subject. Electra speaks only of slaying Aegisthus, it is true, when she is making her resolve to avenge the murder of her father (956–57). For her the slaying of the man, of course, would loom as the more difficult task. Earlier she has intimated that she would like to see her mother slain (583), and the chorus certainly assume that both are now included in her plan (1080–81). The action of the play, also, is concerned much more with Clytemnestra than with Aegisthus.

The play of Sophocles, therefore, is constructed to lead to the slaying of Clytemnestra as its climax. The reason for the actual subordination of her slaughter to that of Aegisthus, in the opinion of the present writer, lies in Sophocles' adoption of incompatible elements in the play. He has taken certain features from Aeschylus and perhaps some from Euripides which are not really compatible with his Homeric interpretation of Orestes' deed as a thoroughly commendable one. In the *Odyssey* the climax of the return of Orestes is the slaughter of Aegisthus; but there the vengeance of Orestes seems to involve only the physical difficulties of a lone exile's slaying a king. Sophocles, too, might have presented the matter in this way; but he has not. In his play there is no emphasis placed upon the physical difficulties or dangers of Orestes' slaying Aegisthus. Indeed, this slaughter seems unrealistically simple in plan and execution. Simple as it is, the slaughter of Clytemnestra is even simpler, apparently because Sophocles wishes to give the impression that the justice of her death is unquestioned and unquestionable. Thus her death is passed over here almost as nonchalantly as in the *Odyssey,* although here this is not consistent with the great pains which have been taken in describing and portraying her in the earlier scenes of the play.

Sophocles' acceptance of the Homeric interpretation of Orestes' deed as wholly commendable involves another serious difficulty. Sophocles doubtless thought that Orestes was presumed to have slain his mother in the Homeric version, and he may have been correct in so thinking. But in the Homeric version, greed and lust are the motivations of Aegisthus; lust and jealousy over Cassandra are the equally obvious motivations of Clytemnestra. Homer says nothing of a delay or human sacrifice at Aulis or of a daughter of Agamemnon named Iphigenia.[79] The introduction of this sacrifice into the story inevitably brings with it a motivation for Clytemnestra which cannot be dismissed as lightly as Sophocles has dismissed it. It still may not wholly justify the murder of Agamemnon; but, as we see in Euripides' *Iphigenia at Aulis* (1146–1208), it can be made a defense of tremendous power. Certainly the sacrifice of Iphigenia, fairly viewed, makes the Homeric interpretation no longer valid according to either the Homeric or the later Athenian moral code. Sophocles has not, therefore, been successful in his effort to combine the antecedent data of Aeschylus and perhaps that of Euripides—Iphigenia was now, of course, an indispensable element of the legend—with the Homeric interpretation.

Equally strange are other aspects of the structure of Sophocles' play. Although Electra herself dominates the scene throughout the play, entering before the chorus and remaining on stage continuously except during one short choral song, yet she performs no important function in the machinery of the plot. She does not devise the deception. Orestes needs no urging to slay his mother, and surely he stands in no great need of Electra's bitter plea that Aegisthus be slain and cast forth unburied. Orestes, though on stage for only one-third of the play, performs all the important action practically unaided except for the important role of the Paedagogus.

Why should Electra become the central figure in a plot which concerns the return and vengeance of Orestes? She is not such in the play of Aeschylus, although her importance there might readily have been increased, especially by giving her the role of Pylades at the climax. In the play of Euripides, however, Pylades has lost his importance as the representative of Apollo, and Electra has quite properly become the central figure because there she devises the deception by which Clytemnestra is lured into the hut and slain; there Orestes by his own admission needs her aid from the very first. At the climax he falters and is overwhelmed with revulsion at the thought of slaying his own mother; but Electra repairs his resolution and actually grasps his sword at the crucial moment. Afterward, Electra takes the main responsibility for the act. It is only by making the slaughter of Clytemnestra a dreadfully difficult task—a feature essential to Euripides' interpretation of the murder as a dreadful act which should not have been committed— that the author can present Orestes as sorely needing his sister's aid and encouragement and thus can play up Electra into the main role of the drama. The *Electra* of Euripides not only utilizes all the power and force built into the figure of his Electra; his play, because of its interpretation of the slaughter, demands such a figure. A play such as Sophocles' *Electra,* which interprets the slaughter of Clytemnestra as an easy and noble deed, does not demand such a figure and cannot, it seems, be made properly to include such a figure.

Some critics are of the opinion that Electra's strange dominance of the scene can be explained only by assuming that Sophocles, in his fondness for his Antigone, wished to insert such a type into the present legend. To make Electra's resolution to slay Aegisthus plausible to an Athenian audience, these critics contend, Sophocles has increased her pious regard for her father and her hatred of her mother to the highest possible degree. Sophocles, they necessarily conclude, was interested primarily in the character of Electra.[80]

The character of Electra is indeed a memorable one. Sophocles doubtless intended it to be an admirable one as well, but few modern readers are able to admire her. The comparison with Antigone was made inevitable by the author himself, but this comparison is all to the advantage of Antigone. Electra's personality has been distorted by years of mental suffering and an obsession for vengeance. Antigone, in contrast, acts from a resolve as spontaneous as it is determined. The purpose of Antigone, furthermore, is one which all must consider righteous and glorious. Electra's purpose is so considered by the chorus (1095–97) but with doubtful justification. Quite different from Antigone (*Antigone* 523), Electra seems to have been born to hate rather than to love. She admits that she is ashamed of her behavior toward her mother, but she insists that such behavior has been forced upon her (616–21). She is capable of genuine tenderness toward Orestes, although even in the scenes in which she weeps over his death she weeps for the loss of an avenger as much as for the loss of a brother (808– 12); and she lacks that pathetic humanity which Antigone so beautifully portrays in her contemplation of death. Worst of all is Electra's callous delight at the death of her mother. Her hatred of Aegisthus pursues him beyond the grave. This Electra is truly the daughter of the Aeschylean Clytemnestra.

Other considerations make Electra's dominance of the play dramatically effective. The dreadful tragedy of this house can be portrayed most powerfully through her figure.[81] She was a sensitive girl old enough to appreciate what was happening when Clytemnestra first began her affair with Aegisthus. Electra has been forced all her life to live in this house of crime with these loathsome creatures. Because of the torture to which she is being subjected, especially the imminent threat of imprisonment in a dungeon (381), a major interest tends to develop about her own rescue and delivery. This theme is repeatedly stressed, and it must be allowed considerable importance.[82] In Sophocles' play, therefore, Orestes is playing not only the proper role of Orestes but the role of Perseus as well. In 412 B.C. Euripides created a tremendous sensation at Athens by producing a brilliant romantic melodrama on Perseus' rescue of Andromeda, and it is not impossible that Sophocles is adapting the motive of that play to the story of Orestes. Electra moping at the gates is not so very different from Andromeda chained to the cliff.

We have already observed how Sophocles, deceived by a specious similarity between Electra and Antigone, distorted his plot for the effective second clash between Electra and Chrysothemis. Theatrical effect, to be sure, is a prime consideration of Sophocles, and although the relative merits of the three plays on the vengeance of Orestes may be endlessly debated, there is no question as to which play a great actor would choose for the display of his talents. Few if any figures in extant Greek tragedy remain so continuously on stage and traverse the whole gamut of the emotions as does the Electra of this play. Sophocles certainly had his better eye on the theater in composing it. We are reminded of Aristotle's remark: "I call a Plot episodic when there is neither probability nor necessity in the sequence of its episodes. Actions of this sort bad poets construct through their own fault, and good ones on account of the players."[83]

Still, we cannot accept the contention that Sophocles was interested only in theatrically effective individual scenes and cared little or nothing for moral interpretation.[84] Although this play has many of the features of melodrama, the opening and closing scenes make it undeniable that Sophocles, like Aeschylus and Euripides, was greatly concerned with the moral interpretation of the vengeance. Piety for the father and hatred of the mother who murdered him are stressed throughout the play and are strictly pertinent to this moral interpretation. Nowhere else in Sophocles, furthermore, do we find great care and attention expended upon a character who does not materially affect the development of the action. Sophocles is not a photographer but a portrait painter: every line in his other compositions has an artistic meaning and result. Critics may claim that in the *Trachiniae,* Deianeira overshadows Heracles and spoils the unity of the play. There are some grounds for denying this; but, even if it is admitted, the second half of the play obviously follows as a consequence of the first, and the first is determined by the actions of Deianeira. The *Trachiniae* and the *Ajax* in reality have a logical unity but do not appear unified because no one character dominates the scene during the whole play. The *Electra* is not strictly unified but seems so because one character does dominate. In the theater this semblance is doubtless more important than the fact.

But there is another more plausible explanation of Electra's dominance in Sophocles' play, if we assume that the play of Euripides preceded it. This is essentially the same type of explanation as that given for the extended second clash between Electra and Chrysothemis. Just as Sophocles there followed his own *Antigone* too closely, so perhaps in the dominance of Electra, again deceived by a specious similarity and lured by the theatrical effectiveness of a powerful heroine, he has followed the *Electra* of Euripides too closely. Such dependence, as already pointed out, would also explain the anomaly of the climax of Sophocles' play. General Euripidean influence is obvious in the opening duet and in the sentimental and melodramatic elements of the play. Euripides and not Sophocles, we should like to assume, was the creator of an Electra who appears with shorn head, half-starved, and miserably clad.[85] It seems unlikely, furthermore, that Sophocles would have been driven to his extreme moral interpretation—inconsistent with the data and structure of his play—by the interpretation of Aeschylus; but it seems altogether likely that the bold interpretation of Euripides would have elicited such a reaction. That Sophocles should follow in the wake of Euripides need occasion no surprise. In his *Philoctetes,* he rewrote and reinterpreted a story dramatized by both Aeschylus and Euripides.[86] Lastly, it seems incredible that such an elaborate character as Electra should have originally been designed for any plot except that into which she fits so perfectly and effectively—the plot of Euripides.

6. *PHILOCTETES

(409 B.C.)

Sophocles was awarded first prize. The titles of the other plays which he produced at this festival are unknown.

Staging.—It is obvious from the first lines spoken by Neoptolemus that the cave of Philoctetes was located above the level of the orchestra. This is a clear example of a raised position (but not a stage) being used during the fifth century. We may assume that scenery was employed to suggest a wild and rugged cliff. The scene is reminiscent of the *Prometheus Bound.*

Legend.—The story of Philoctetes is briefly sketched in the *Iliad* (2. 721–25), and it was told at greater length in various epics now lost. In these epic versions, Diomedes, not Odysseus, was sent to bring Philoctetes to Troy; Lemnos was always known as an inhabited island; and, at least in one late account, many of the fellow country-men of Philoctetes were left with him as attendants when he was abandoned.[87]

Philoctetes was the intimate friend of Heracles; and when Hyllus refused to light the pyre of his suffering father, as foretold in Sopho-cles' *Trachiniae* (1193–1216), Philoctetes performed this service. As a reward he received the famous bow and arrows with which Heracles had once taken Troy. So the prophecy that these weapons could again take Troy seemed a very natural one.

Source.—The story of Philoctetes was one of the most popular subjects of Greek tragedy. Besides this extant play, Sophocles himself wrote a *Philoctetes at Troy,* the situation of which is suggested by the speech of Heracles at the end of the present play. We hear of plays entitled *Philoctetes* by five or six other dramatists, including Aeschylus and Euripides. The play of Euripides was produced along with his extant *Medea* in 431 B.C. Besides a few fragments of these plays by Aeschylus and Euripides, we very fortunately have preserved two es-says by an ancient rhetorician, Dio Chrysostomus, one of which is a comparison of the three plays on Philoctetes by Aeschylus, Euripides, and Sophocles, and the other is a paraphrase of the opening scenes of the play of Euripides. Dio thought each of the plays admirable in its way: that of Aeschylus for its simplicity, its heroic greatness of soul, and the boldness of its thought and language; that of Euripides for its keen rhetoric, its subtlety, and its choral exhortation to virtuous deeds; and that of Sophocles for its dignity and plausibility.[88]

Aeschylus was the first writer, as far as we know, to have Odysseus rather than Diomedes go to Lemnos for Philoctetes. Since Odysseus was the most hated enemy of Philoctetes and the most crafty of all the Greeks, this change obviously made a complex and dramatic situation out of a comparatively simple one. But it also introduced the improbability of Odysseus' facing Philoctetes without being recognized. Aeschylus seems to have ignored this improbability, although Dio thinks that it might have been excused by assuming that the memory of Philoctetes had been impaired by the years of solitude and by his long suffering. Euripides resorted to having Odysseus disguised by the divine aid of Athena—a device used in the *Odyssey* and to a very minor extent in Sophocles' *Ajax*. At first glance this may seem a lame device; but of course Odysseus was famous for his cleverness in disguising himself, and perhaps Euripides meant little more than that Odysseus used this gifted cleverness.

In Aeschylus' play, it seems, Philoctetes was overcome by a paroxysm of suffering, as he is in Sophocles and in a later play, now lost, by Theodectes.[89] In Euripides, however, the diseased heel of Philoctetes had greatly improved with time. From the scientific point of view this improvement may be more plausible, but from the dramatic it is certainly less effective.

Euripides fused the Aeschylean with the epic version by having both Odysseus and Diomedes come for Philoctetes. Philoctetes was miserably clad in the skins of animals which he had slain, for his clothes had long since worn out! This realistic touch may be an indirect criticism of Aeschylus,[90] as the remarks on clothes certainly are in Euripides' *Electra* (539–44); but such meticulous attention to petty details was despised by the more conservative Greeks, and the costume of Euripides' Philoctetes is satirized by Aristophanes in the *Acharnians* (424). Still, Sophocles, we may note, is careful to explain why his Philoctetes wears ordinary clothes—occasional unwilling visitors to the cliff have given him food and clothes (308–9). The Roman Accius in his *Philocteta* (frag. 543, Warmington) had the hero dressed in the feathers of birds which he had shot!

Euripides began his play with a typical Euripidean monologue-prologue by Odysseus, in which the whole situation was explained and stress was placed upon the precariousness and the importance of the mission. The most significant innovation of Euripides, however, was the introduction of a rival embassy from the Trojans, who wished to secure the famous archer for their own forces. The main part of Euripides' play seems to have consisted of a brilliant debate between Odysseus and the Trojan ambassadors when each side attempted to win over Philoctetes. The disguised Odysseus pretended that even though he

had been wronged by the Greeks he was unable to stand silently by
while the Trojans urged Philoctetes to join their forces against the
Greeks. Patriotism, therefore, seems to have been the theme of Euripides' play—a very timely theme, since his play was produced in the first
year of the great Peloponnesian War.

In the plays of Aeschylus and Euripides, the chorus consisted of
inhabitants of Lemnos. This introduced the improbability that Philoctetes should have been neglected so long by the Lemnians. Again Aeschylus ignored the improbability, and Euripides tried to improve upon
Aeschylus by having his chorus, immediately upon its entrance, make
apology for their long neglect. Euripides also introduced a certain
Lemnian who had been a friend and visitor of Philoctetes. These lame
devices, however, instead of explaining and removing the improbability,
really called attention to it and made the situation of Philoctetes less
forlorn and pitiful. Another improbability inherent in a chorus of
Lemnians consisted of Philoctetes' reciting his woes to them as if they
had never heard of him before, although, as Dio remarks, it is the character of those who suffer from a chronic illness to dwell upon their
troubles even to people already well acquainted with them.

In Sophocles, Odysseus does not face Philoctetes until the bow has
been stolen, and the chorus consists of followers of Neoptolemus. Thus
the main improbabilities of Aeschylus and Euripides are eliminated;
but a new minor one has crept in, for the island of Lemnos is spoken
of as utterly deserted and harborless, although the audience knew that
Lemnos, or at least parts of it, had always been inhabited since epic
times and was well supplied with good harbors. Granting the poet
some indulgence, however, we may assume that the desolate cliff of
Philoctetes has been approached only by sailing vessels in distress and
that Philoctetes, because of the pain which made even a few steps ex-
cruciating torture for him (285–99), was unable to reach the inhabited parts of the island. The great innovation of Sophocles, however,
is unquestionably the substitution of Neoptolemus for the comparatively colorless Diomedes.

Theme.—Dio remarks the loftiness and nobility of the characters
in Sophocles' play.[91] It seems clear from the development of the play
and from the changes which Sophocles has made in the story that his
Philoctetes is designed primarily as a character study of Neoptolemus
and Philoctetes. Nowhere in Greek tragedy is a moral dilemma more
clearly pointed or more honestly decided than is that of Neoptolemus.
The whole action of the play progresses on his moral choices. Philoctetes, however, is the most tragic figure of the play, and his own moral
dilemma of willingly going to Troy or stubbornly refusing to do so

even at the cost of his life becomes one of the main interests of the play after Neoptolemus has revealed the intrigue. The immediate point of the outcome of the play is not only the fate of Philoctetes but also the fate of Neoptolemus and the Greeks at Troy. Since the story of Philoctetes was so famous, naturally the play must bear his name; and from the actor's point of view his role clearly offers the greatest possibilities.

The theme of the play may perhaps be stated as the principle that to be just is better than to be worldly wise (1246), and that true nobility of soul must triumph over baseness. Another moral lesson of the play is found in the words of Heracles that virtue is achieved through labor (*per aspera ad astra!*).

Some critics have discovered a political allegory in the *Philoctetes*. When it was presented in 409 B.C., Athens was in desperate straits in her long war with Sparta. A revolution had taken place two years previously. The oligarchical party had seized power in the city of Athens, but the main fleet and expeditionary force had remained loyal to the democracy. The leaders of these forces had recalled Alcibiades, the brilliant and erratic nephew of Pericles and probably the one living man who might have won the war for Athens. Formerly he had been under sentence of death and exile. In 409 B.C., after the democracy had been re-established in the city, Alcibiades was anxious to return to Athens.

While Sophocles may have had this contemporary political situation in mind when he composed the play, and although he may have intended to suggest that the internal quarrels of Athens should be forgotten for the common good, no elaborate allegory seems to be intended—Alcibiades in character had not the slightest resemblance to Philoctetes but was as unscrupulous as Odysseus himself. Although Agamemnon and Menelaus, and to a lesser extent Odysseus also, suggested and symbolized the Doric enemies of the Athenians, still Sophocles is not here primarily concerned with patriotism as was Euripides and perhaps Aeschylus.

Discussion.—Sophocles, as we should expect, begins his play not with a monologue, as did Euripides, but with a very natural dialogue between Odysseus and Neoptolemus. Thus he distributes the exposition and—a result which is even more important—allows Philoctetes himself to relate his own pitiful history.

The first scene and the first chorus furnish unusually elaborate preparation for the entrance of Philoctetes.

The intrigue, or at least part of it, including the appearance of the Merchant, is carefully explained to the audience before it is put into execution. This is the normal procedure in all classical drama. The intrigue is entirely plausible. In fact, Dio remarks that Sophocles' arrangement of the details of his play is the best and most plausible.[92] But we should not be misled, as some critics have been, into thinking that the whole intrigue is explained by Odysseus in the first scene. Here, as in various other plays, enough information is given so that the audience can understand the development and appreciate the dramatic irony. The real intention of Odysseus is apparently first to gain possession of the bow and then to persuade or force Philoctetes to accompany them to Troy.[93] Some critics have complained that the episode with the Merchant is impertinent to the plot and that there are inconsistencies in the play, especially in regard to the prophecy of Helenus. But these complaints are due to a failure to understand the intrigue. The prophecy of Helenus stated, as the Merchant says (612–13) and as we know from Dio's account of Euripides' play, that Philoctetes himself must be brought to Troy. In the opening scene of Sophocles' play, it is true, Odysseus seems to suggest that the weapons alone are necessary. Odysseus here, however, is intentionally vague, for he does not care to risk offending the honest and intractable Neoptolemus even more by revealing the whole disgraceful procedure. This procedure as Odysseus has planned it becomes clear later when Odysseus falsely declares to Philoctetes that the weapons alone are sufficient. Odysseus has surmised that the promise of health and fame will be sufficient to win over Philoctetes, especially when the alternative is loss of the bow to the hated Odysseus and slow, self-willed death. Odysseus' reasoning fails, and perhaps its baseness contributes to Neoptolemus' final decision to return the bow; but this reasoning is nevertheless powerful, and to an Odysseus it would naturally seem irresistible. That Odysseus is dissembling when he says the weapons alone are necessary should be obvious and would doubtless be made more so by a skillful actor. If the weapons alone were necessary, Odysseus would not order his men to prevent Philoctetes from committing suicide (1003).

The episode of the Merchant is designed by Odysseus to prepare Philoctetes for the future development of the intrigue. According to the Merchant's story, both Neoptolemus and Philoctetes are being pursued by a Greek embassy. Thus both are placed in the same precarious situation and would naturally be inclined to unite against their foes. So Neoptolemus is given another opportunity—he has already agreed to Philoctetes' request to be taken home—to appear as the friend and champion of Philoctetes. Because of his own helplessness, Philoctetes now throws himself wholly upon the protection of Neoptolemus. The Merchant's story has other desirable effects. It is essential to the final persuasion of Philoctetes to go to Troy that Philoctetes should learn of the prophecy that he is fated to play an important part in taking the city. This prophecy is genuine; but, in order that Philoctetes may believe it, he should hear it from an apparently disinterested party such as the Merchant. Lastly, the information of the Merchant adds a compelling urgency to Philoctetes' situation and prepares for the appearance of Odysseus. Just when this appearance was to take place according to Odysseus' plan is uncertain, but he must have anticipated such an appearance sometime after the bow was in the possession of Neoptolemus. Thus if Neoptolemus had played his part well, the Merchant's information might have enabled Odysseus and Neoptolemus to conceal the whole amazingly clever intrigue from Philoctetes.

In the latter part of the play Odysseus twice makes very sudden and sensational entrances at crucial points (974 and 1293). These are not unnatural in a play of intrigue, where Odysseus may be conceived as always lurking in the background, and where the scenery may have facilitated such action.

In such plots of intrigue it is usually necessary to delay the solution by introducing various minor complications. This naturally results in the maintenance of a certain amount of suspense. The intrigue of the *Philoctetes,* furthermore, demands certain delaying action and complication in its own development. Unforeseen complications are produced by the paroxysm of pain which overcomes Philoctetes and by the moral vacillation of Neoptolemus after he has the bow in his possession. Philoctetes himself wavers in similar fashion when Neoptolemus makes a final appeal for him to come to Troy of his own free will. Suspense and uncertainty over the moral solution of the plot is maintained until the very end.

The dialogue of the *Philoctetes* is perhaps as close to actual conversation as any found in Greek tragedy. The language is simple, and the iambic lines are very frequently divided between speakers. Indeed a single line is sometimes divided into three or even four parts (753, 810). In Philoctetes' most agonized moments his cries of pain interrupt the iambic meter. The dialogue line by line (stichomythia), as normally in Sophocles, is handled in a very natural fashion, since there is no monotonous regularity of distribution. One of the sudden entrances of Odysseus occurs in the middle of an iambic line (974), as does a sudden entrance in the *Iphigenia at Aulis* (414), where the interruption is even more abrupt. At the final climax of the *Philoctetes,* precisely when Neoptolemus agrees to take Philoctetes home, there is a shift to the excited trochaic meter (1402). This meter occurs with some frequency in early tragedy and in the late plays of Euripides, but in the extant plays of Sophocles it is used only here and at the end of the *Oedipus the King*. The metrical structure of the iambic lines, also, is very free in the *Philoctetes* and is similar to that of the later plays of Euripides.

The importance of the chorus is sharply reduced in this play. As the retinue of Neoptolemus it naturally tends to become a minor character, and the rapid and complex intrigue make interruption highly inadvisable. There is only one formal choral song (stasimon) after the parodos. This song comes when Neoptolemus has successfully deceived Philoctetes; and, somewhat like the parabasis of an Aristophanic comedy, it divides the play into two parts. Other lyric passages, however, relieve the monotony of the iambic meter without breaking the continuity of the action. In the first long scene between Neoptolemus and Philoctetes, corresponding lyrics are interlarded in the dialogue and become integral parts of it (epirrhematic construction). In the second half of the play there are lyric exchanges (*kommoi*) between Neoptolemus and the chorus and especially between Philoctetes and the chorus.

The inconsistency of the attitude of the chorus toward Philoctetes has troubled some critics. But such inconsistency is a frequent phenomenon. The chorus in Sophocles' *Electra* acts in similar fashion (1015–16 and 1058–97). There at one point the chorus urges Electra to follow the baser course, as here the chorus urges Neoptolemus. Thus the moral strength of the main character is brought out.

Neoptolemus, although physically the mightiest warrior of all the Greeks, is very young and inexperienced. He is addressed as "my son" (*teknon* or *pai*) throughout the play. In disposition, he closely resembles his father, whose regular characterization in drama Horace (*Ars Poetica* 120–22) describes as follows: "Let Achilles be a man of action, quick to wrath, inexorable, and fierce; let him declare that laws were not made for him, and let him have recourse to arms to settle every dispute." So Neoptolemus in this play is a man of action. He is quite ready to use force against Philoctetes, but he has only contempt for the mental and moral gymnastics at which Odysseus is so expert.[94] Nor is this honesty of Neoptolemus caused by a mental simplicity which would prevent him from being clever in dishonesty, for when he once is won over to the intrigue by Odysseus he carries through the deception in its initial stages with skill and tact. Indeed, he never quite fully confesses all his deception to Philoctetes; for near the end of the play, when Philoctetes brings up again the false story of Neoptolemus' being robbed of his father's armor, the young man is not so simple as to disillusion his friend at this crucial point (cf. 1364–67), since he still hopes to persuade Philoctetes to go willingly to Troy. But we can readily believe Neoptolemus when he tells Odysseus that he prefers to act justly and fail rather than to act basely and succeed (94–95). Odysseus tries to dismiss this as merely the idealism of youth, claiming—but not convincingly—that he, too, was such a one when he was young. In the very act of persuading Neoptolemus, Odysseus offends him. Very offensive is the word for thief or thieving, which is used several times (55, 57, 77, cf. 968). Unfortunate, too, are the words "baseness" (80) and "shamelessness" (83). Most offensive of all, perhaps, is the brazen assumption of Odysseus that virtue, as if it were a cloak, can be doffed or donned as the occasion requires: "We shall show ourselves as just men some other time," he tells Neoptolemus.[95] To all this Neoptolemus fittingly responds that he shudders to hear such words and loathes the thought of indulging in such deeds. Odysseus urges the patriotic argument that Neoptolemus' refusal will cause the Greeks much pain, but the really convincing argument is the assurance that thus and only thus will Neoptolemus obtain the glory of being the conqueror of Troy. Ambition to be known as a great warrior, the true successor of Achilles, the father whom he never saw alive and whose memory he worships (350–51), is obviously the most important weakness of his character.

The motivation of Odysseus more nearly approaches patriotism; but Odysseus is so lacking in any moral or religious consciousness that he can hardly represent the true patriot. Even in Sophocles' own day, furthermore, there was little unity among the various city states, and Panhellenic patriotism did not flourish. Never has rugged individualism been carried to such an extreme as among the Greeks, and never have its results been at once more glorious and more disastrous. The two great heroes of the victories over the Persians, Pausanias of Sparta and Themistocles of Athens, "the two most famous Hellenes of their day,"[96] were both accused of high treason and died in disgrace; Pausanias was starved to death in a temple at Sparta in which he had taken sanctuary, and Themistocles died at the court of the greatest enemy of Greece, the king of Persia!

For Philoctetes, likewise, patriotism is not a prime consideration. When Neoptolemus makes his final appeal near the end of the play, his strongest arguments are fame and restoration of health for Philoctetes. Loyalty to the Greek cause, though perhaps the winning argument in the plays of Aeschylus and Euripides, is not given any emphasis. We must not forget, of course, that Philoctetes had been foully mistreated by the Greeks and that his most outstanding characteristic is an obsession of hatred for the Greek leaders who caused this mistreatment.

The character of Neoptolemus is brought out more clearly by the contrast with that of Odysseus. In the first scene of the play this contrast points up the utter duplicity of the one and the essential honesty of the other. Once Neoptolemus has resolved to undertake the deception, the play becomes a study of how he succeeds with Philoctetes but fails with his own conscience. The characters of both are nicely designed to supplement each other and to make this development of the plot seem inevitable. The character of Neoptolemus inspires confidence in Philoctetes, and that of Philoctetes appeals to the sympathy of Neoptolemus. Neoptolemus, of course, was not a member of the original Greek expedition; he is unknown to Philoctetes, therefore, and free of any possible implication in the original injustice done. Achilles, his father, was the bitter enemy of subterfuge and device. The son is himself a young and mighty warrior. All these qualities recommend him to the confidence of Philoctetes. To increase the appeal of Philoctetes to Neoptolemus, on the other hand, Lemnos has been made, at least for Philoctetes, a deserted island, so that he may be utterly desolate and forlorn. Philoctetes is allowed to recite his own pitiful story. He moans at the news of the death of Achilles and equates Achilles with the god Apollo (336). Up to this point, Neoptolemus has been hard and calculating, but here he is obviously moved. Philoctetes then learns of the death of Ajax, and he bitterly contrasts the loss of these good men with the preservation of the evil Diomedes and Odysseus. The justice of this Neoptolemus is forced to admit, remarking that war ever likes to take away the good man and spare the evil (436–37), and he doubtless is again reminded of the evil character of his associate Odysseus. Philoctetes' abject plea to be rescued drives further into the compassion of the younger man. But still stronger appeals are to come: the confidence of Philoctetes and his willingness to let Neoptolemus alone of all men handle the bow—we should note the pathetic and profound gratitude of Philoctetes at this point. Then comes his paroxysm of pain, perhaps the strongest appeal of all to Neoptolemus. When Philoctetes revives, his gratitude to Neoptolemus is boundless. Last of all, his pitiful pleas—his life depends on the bow—and his disillusioned revilings after Neoptolemus has confessed his treachery would affect anyone except an Odysseus. Philoctetes strengthens his appeal also by citing Neoptolemus' promise and by mentioning the name of Achilles.[97] At this point, the resolve of Neoptolemus to go through with the intrigue is utterly broken, but he cannot bring himself to take the last irrevocable step of returning the bow. Odysseus enters, and, far from restoring the resolve of Neoptolemus, makes the return of the bow inevitable; for Neoptolemus, who stands silent throughout the bitter clash between Philoctetes and Odysseus, cannot fail to see the cruel injustice and baseness of the one contrasted with the nobility of the other—the character of Odysseus is again used to bring out the character of another by contrast—or fail to admit the irony and injustice of the good fortune of Odysseus and the misery of Philoctetes (cf. 1019–28). The scene ends with an ambiguous speech of Neoptolemus, who still hopes somehow, it seems, to reconcile honor with expediency and cannot yet bring himself to reveal the duplicity of Odysseus.

After Neoptolemus has decided to return the bow, the clash between him and Odysseus brings out in action the same qualities of character which were revealed in their words during the first scene. We can hardly call Odysseus' refusal to fight the son of Achilles cowardice; his original challenge of the younger and mightier man was mere duplicity.

The influence of long suffering upon the character of Philoctetes is depicted with remarkable psychological acumen. Typical of one with a chronic and offensive illness is his fear that strangers will shun him (225–31), as, of course, he actually has been shunned in the past. He is disillusioned, and his pessimism extends to bitter condemnation of the gods (446–52). When Neoptolemus urges him to go willingly to Troy, he seems to take a spiteful child's delight in refusing fame and restoration to health because with these would inevitably come the triumph of Odysseus and the Greeks (cf. 1316–20). But in reality his hatred of those who have caused his long suffering has become an obsession which overwhelms his reason. Still, we can hardly fail to admire his steadfastness of purpose and his stubborn unwillingness to give way before misfortune, as we admire the same characteristics in Antigone and Prometheus,[98] although Philoctetes is defending a cause less admirable than theirs.

The *Philoctetes* reminds one somewhat of the *Iphigenia in Tauris* in its use of the *deus ex machina.* Near the end of the play Neoptolemus presents very strong arguments why Philoctetes should go with him to Troy, and Philoctetes is on the point of deciding to do so. Indeed, a final weakening of Philoctetes, while morally perhaps somewhat disappointing, might have been made plausible. Such a decision was the solution of the plays of Aeschylus and Euripides, in which it was doubtless made entirely plausible. A willing decision to lay aside personal hatred for the common welfare was obviously the only satisfactory solution in a play where patriotism was the primary theme. Sophocles, however, chooses a different solution, for the theme of his play is not patriotism but nobility of character. By making Philoctetes remain steadfast and Neoptolemus choose justice rather than apparent expediency, and then by employing the *deus ex machina* to end the play as legend demanded that it end, Sophocles is enabled to present both Philoctetes and Neoptolemus as stronger and more admirable characters. Neoptolemus, in choosing to fulfill his promise and take Philoctetes home, forfeits his hope of becoming the glorious conqueror of Troy—obviously the greatest of all his ambitions. This choice is the final triumph of justice in his character. If Sophocles had presented Philoctetes as weakening and going to Troy of his own accord, Neoptolemus never would have been forced to make this final moral choice. Thus the *deus ex machina* in this play seems to be employed primarily to perfect the characterization of these two men.

7. *OEDIPUS AT COLONUS (OEDIPUS COLONEUS)*

(401 B.C.)

Sophocles died in 406 B.C., and the *Oedipus at Colonus* was produced after his death by his grandson and namesake, who was himself a writer of tragedies. First prize was awarded this play and those produced with it.[99]

Deeply concerned, perhaps, over the desperate situation of Athens when this play was being written, Sophocles here is apparently attempting to revive the confidence of the Athenians in themselves and to restore their belief in the destiny of their city.[100] The poet's concern with contemporary Athens, which naturally has discouraged ancient or modern adaptations of this play, and his religious mysticism may somewhat repel the modern reader. The play is nevertheless an artistic work of universal significance and beauty—a dramatic and poetic masterpiece.

The *Oedipus at Colonus* does not form a connected and wholly consistent story with the much earlier plays of Sophocles dealing with these same characters. In general, however, the action of this play is supposed to follow that of the *Oedipus the King* and to precede that of the *Antigone*. The action of the *Antigone* is here adumbrated repeatedly by Antigone's championship of the cause of Polyneices, by Polyneices' plea for burial rites if he is slain, and by the sisters' return to Thebes at the end of the play.

Legend.—The location of the grave of Oedipus was a much-disputed point in ancient times. Euripides in the *Phoenissae* (1703–9), a play produced only a few years before the *Oedipus at Colonus,* is the first author definitely to place his death at Colonus.[101] Euripides, however, gives no hint that Oedipus found refuge in a grove of the Eumenides or that his death was accompanied by supernatural phenomena. Graves of heroes were often considered protective influences for the land in ancient times. Near Colonus in 407 B.C. the Athenians had actually defeated a Boeotian detachment in a skirmish. This defeat of the Thebans, of course, is the benefit which Oedipus in Sophocles' play repeatedly promises Theseus and Athens. The reference of Euripides and this actual battle may have inspired Sophocles to write the play.

One minor but dramatically significant change in the legend may be noticed: Sophocles makes the exiled Polyneices the older son. Since this is contrary to the versions of Aeschylus and Euripides, the point is made repeatedly and very clearly. The obvious purpose of this change is to strengthen the appeal of Polyneices and his cause.

Discussion.—Written when Sophocles was almost ninety years old, the *Oedipus at Colonus* in a way sums up the work of his whole life. Like the *Triptolemus*,[102] which was perhaps one of the plays produced for his first victory in 468 B.C., the *Oedipus at Colonus* is primarily an etiological explanation of an Athenian religious belief and a glorious tribute to Athens and Colonus, the district of Sophocles' own home. In this play, furthermore, reappear those two characters which were probably the greatest creations of his career: Oedipus and Antigone.

The figure of Oedipus is one of extraordinary impressiveness. He retains the heroic grandeur which Sophocles originally gave him. He continually insists upon his moral innocence, but he still exhibits his great weaknesses—high spirit and passionate wrath—and these are pointed out as the curse of his life.[103] They are most evident in the appalling scene with Polyneices. Still, the nobility with which Oedipus has weathered the most dreadful calamities and years of suffering makes him, though obviously cruel in cursing his sons, at once a more appealing and a more impressive character than he was in the *Oedipus the King*. He rises to his greatest height in the mystic finale of the play. "Magnificent, are the images which Sophocles has conceived of the death of Oedipus," says "Longinus" (15.7, Rhys Roberts[104]), "who makes ready his burial amid the portents of the sky."

The figure of Antigone also is a memorable one. She is clearly the more spirited of the two daughters, but there is no suggestion that Ismene lacks courage or devotion. Antigone here appears somewhat more feminine than in the earlier play. The portrayal of her distracted grief in the final scenes is profoundly moving and deserves the highest praise.

The unity of the play has sometimes been impugned, but adverse criticisms on this point are unjustified.[105] The subject of the play is Oedipus' search for peace in a befitting death. Although the oracle

(87–90) assures his eventual success, three main obstacles arise: threatened expulsion from Attica, the efforts of the present Theban government to gain control of him, and the efforts of the opposition under Polyneices to do the same. The second obstacle and, by implication, the third (392, 417) are skillfully announced before the first has been overcome. If Oedipus had been expelled from Attica, furthermore, he would obviously have fallen victim to one of the two contending parties at Thebes, who are not beyond the use of force. The action of the play is closely knit, therefore, as well as rapid and dramatic. The play is some two hundred fifty lines longer than any other extant play of Sophocles and is filled with spirited action. Indeed it can be presented by three speaking actors only with great difficulty. Oedipus himself, like Sophocles' Electra, remains on the scene almost continuously and dominates the action throughout.

The continuous presence of Oedipus, the desire for rapidity, and the high pitch of the emotional tone are well served by the unusually large number of lyric exchanges between characters and chorus (*kommoi*). At the exciting climax when Antigone is being dragged away by the henchmen of Creon, such lyrics are employed with iambic lines separating strophe and antistrophe (epirrhematic construction). As Theseus here rushes in to the rescue, his first lines are in the excited trochaic measure. The final scenes after the Messenger's speech, also, are wholly in anapestic or lyric measures. Such metrical fluidity, to a certain extent characteristic of this period, adds to the theatrical effectiveness of the presentation, and the lyrics thus allowed add to the poetic qualities of the play.

The poetry of the *Oedipus at Colonus* is unsurpassed in Sophocles. The choral lyric in praise of Athens (668–719) ranks with the speech of Pericles in Thucydides (2. 35–46) and with the choral lyric in Euripides' *Medea* (824–45) as one of the most glorious tributes ever made to the most deserving of all cities. The lyric on old age, also, is noteworthy (1211–48). Depressing in its profound pessimism, this poem is very different from Euripides' enthusiastic verses written on his sixtieth birthday, so to speak, in the *Heracles* (637–700). Euripides, however, was writing when Athens despite some ten years of war was still a powerful city, Sophocles when Athens was face to face with defeat and ruin. Euripides' zest for life was still that of a youth ready to live life over again; Sophocles was an old man ready to die. But perhaps it is unfair to attribute the sentiments of this lyric in any part to Sophocles himself; certainly this lyric is closely knit with its dramatic context and effectively prepares for the coming death of Oedipus.

Like the other late plays of Sophocles, the *Oedipus at Colonus* is heavily indebted to Euripides. Besides being inspired perhaps by the *Phoenissae,* the poet owes much to plays like the *Suppliants* for the figure of Theseus and the theme of Athens as the refuge of the persecuted and oppressed, although Euripides himself found this theme in Aeschylus. Indebtedness might be pointed out in metrical and various other aspects, but these obligations are of trivial importance in this instance; for the *Oedipus at Colonus* has been so heavily charged with Sophocles' own genius that essentially it is an entirely original and harmonious production.

IV

EURIPIDES

LIFE[1]

Euripides, son of Mnesarchides of the deme Phlya, was born about 480 B.C. on the island of Salamis. One tradition says that he was born on the very day of the great battle. From the first he seems to have been a problem. His father, deceived by an oracle which said that his son would be a victor in contests, insisted on training him as an athlete in wrestling and boxing—severe sports in ancient times, as one may recall from the *Iliad* (23. 653–739). Indeed Euripides is said to have been a victor in the local athletic games. But the legend that his father was responsible for all this is thoroughly plausible. At least Euripides later despised athletics as much as he despised oracles.[2] He tried his hand at painting. At the age of eighteen, according to Gellius (15. 20. 4), he began writing tragedy; but he did not succeed in producing until several years later, in 455 B.C.

Euripides' first production was rated third and last. This is typical of the reception which his plays received at Athens during his whole career. In spirit he belonged not to the generation of Sophocles and Herodotus (and Aristophanes!) but to that of Anaxagoras, Socrates, and Thucydides. Profoundly involved in the intellectual revolutions then in progress, he wrote for the revolutionaries and for the generations of the future. With a self-confidence amazing in a dramatist, for fifty years he remained contemptuous of mere popular acclaim and, except for an occasional bolt of annihilation,[3] oblivious to the ugly jibes of the comic poets. No other writer of theatrical drama has been so long impervious to the theatrical public, and perhaps no other has succeeded so well in finally forcing both public and rival dramatists to his point of view. In all, Euripides wrote at least eighty-eight plays, producing at some twenty-two festivals; but he was awarded only five victories (one posthumously). The bulk of his work roughly corresponded to that of Shakespeare's plays, but Euripides' period of activity was much longer than Shakespeare's.

Euripides is said to have attended the lectures of Anaxagoras, Prodicus, and Protagoras—the leading philosophers and Sophists of his early manhood in Athens. He is said to have been a student of Socrates also, and Aristophanes repeatedly claimed that Socrates was the real author of Euripides' corrupting ideas. But Euripides was thinking for himself when Socrates was only a child, as fragments of his earliest play, the *Daughters of Pelias* (*Peliades*), reveal.[4] Euripides doubtless learned much from these men; he almost certainly taught them at least something.

Like Socrates and like many honest men of every generation, Euripides was personally unpopular with his fellow citizens. He was too serious and thoughtful, too fond of his own company, and too much disgusted with that of most of his fellow citizens. Unlike Socrates, Euripides was a recluse. He is said to have retired to a cave on Salamis to write his tragedies, and Aristophanes repeatedly sneers at his large collection of books. Still, Euripides was much more keenly aware of contemporary problems than was the ever amiable and sociable Sophocles. Unlike Socrates, again, Euripides finally left Athens in the last chaotic years of the Peloponnesian War and went to the court of Archelaus, king of Macedon, where some of the most promising geniuses of Greece, especially Agathon and the painter Zeuxis, were gathering. It was there, apparently, that he wrote his splendid last plays, the *Bacchae* and the *Iphigenia at Aulis*. Probably in 407 B.C., he was killed, perhaps by the hunting dogs of Archelaus. He was buried there, but a cenotaph was raised to him at Athens. Of the three sons who survived him, one was an actor and another produced his father's last plays at Athens.

In the eyes of the Greek world in general, if not of the Athenians, Euripides was the foremost literary figure of the times even before his death. The Greeks of Sicily, bitter political enemies of Athens, almost worshiped him. Some of the Athenians captured there in 413 B.C. are said to have saved their lives and re-won their freedom by reciting his verse.[5] After his death, Dionysius of Syracuse is said to have purchased his lyre and writing instruments at a high price and to have dedicated them to the Muses. "If the dead really had perception, gentlemen, as some believe," runs a fragment of Philemon (130, Kock), the poet of New Comedy, "I should have hanged myself to see Euripides."

During the fourth century the plays of both Sophocles and Euripides were greatly admired and frequently reproduced; but as time went on, though Aristotle much preferred Sophocles, Euripides became more and more the most popular of all dramatists. The survival of a comparatively large number of his plays is doubtless a result of this popularity, which was especially great among rhetoricians and scholars interested in skillful argumentation. As selections of seven plays of Aeschylus and seven of Sophocles were made, so a selection of perhaps ten plays of Euripides was made, including the *Alcestis,* the *Medea,* the *Hippolytus,* the *Andromache,* the *Hecuba,* the *Trojan Women,* the

Phoenissae, the *Orestes,* the *Rhesus* (the extant play is probably spurious), and perhaps the *Bacchae.* The later Byzantine selection of three plays chose the *Hecuba,* the *Phoenissae,* and the *Orestes*—all plays filled with debate. Fortunately eight other tragedies and one satyr-play not in the earlier selection of ten plays have also been preserved.

In modern times Euripides' reputation has varied greatly. During recent centuries he has been held in contempt too often because the critic did not have the historical knowledge requisite to the proper interpretation of his plays or because the criteria employed were too narrow. The *Trojan Women* is an outstanding case in point. Critics and scholars now, however, usually do him full justice, and in drama of the present day Euripides and Aeschylus are perhaps more influential than Sophocles.

TRAGEDY UNDER EURIPIDES

It has been said that in speculation Euripides was a critic and a free lance, whereas in artistic form he was intensely traditional.[6] Perhaps this statement is true in the sense in which it was intended, but it is likely to mislead the unwary. Euripides made no important innovations in such external matters as the number of the actors or the chorus. Some of these matters, of course, were fixed beyond his powers to change them. But Euripides showed little respect for traditional artistic forms merely because they were traditional. Even the use of the chorus, though forced upon him, was permanently affected by his genius. In certain other respects, Euripides gives the impression of being conservative because he reverts to an apparently archaic form; yet he does this, not out of slavish respect for the conventional, but from deliberate artistic choice. Indeed in his very reversion to an archaic form Euripides exhibits the same bold originality that he does in matters of speculation.

We might more accurately state Euripides' paradoxical tendencies as a dramatist by saying that he shows a marked inclination toward both realism and formalism. His realism is obvious in many ways and most of all in his portrayal of character. Sophocles was on the whole correct when he said that he portrayed men as they should be, Euripides men as they are.[7] Such realism was probably characteristic of Euripides from the very first, certainly from the time of the *Telephus,* which was produced in 438 B.C. along with the *Alcestis.* This humanization of characters was a progressive process which eventually led to the reduction of heroic figures to the level of our everyday world. Agamemnon in the *Iphigenia at Aulis* may be taken as an example of the extreme development. When tragedy treated such thoroughly human characters it was ready for plots taken from everyday life; but unfortunately there was no great dramatist to carry on at this point.

Realism in portrayal of character entailed other important developments. Problems that might formerly have been considered too indelicate and characters that might have been considered too depraved now became proper material for drama. Phaedra, the faithless wife and indirectly the murderess of Hippolytus, was a character who, according to the Aeschylus of Aristophanes' *Frogs* (1053–54), should have been passed over in discreet silence. Euripides would have no part in this stupid prudery which Aristophanes recommended. He did not believe that human problems could be solved by ignoring them or that any character was so depraved as not to deserve unbiased study and analysis. Thus Euripides seems to take delight in rehabilitating characters apparently beyond the pale of rehabilitation. To make such characters wholly credible and even worthy of sympathy was a feat requiring the most profound understanding of human actions, and such understanding did not come without study and labor—or without important results for ethics and science.

The morbid and the abnormal fascinated Euripides. He "is most assiduous in giving the utmost tragic effect to these two emotions—fits of love and madness," says "Longinus." "Herein he succeeds more, perhaps, than in any other respect, although he is daring enough to invade all the other regions of the imagination."[8] Phaedra again is one of the best examples. Orestes in the play named after him is another. But these are extreme cases.

More significant for the history of drama, perhaps, is Euripides' approach to the sentimental. The reunion of Orestes and Iphigenia in the *Iphigenia in Tauris* is deliberately exploited for sentimental effect. The appeal of Iphigenia to Agamemnon in the *Iphigenia at Aulis* is pathetic in the extreme. She doubtless takes the infant Orestes in her arms and asks him to intercede in her behalf. Effective use of children and infants, though found in the *Ajax* of Sophocles, is another aspect of this development. Exploitation of the sentimental and of the melodramatic is a marked characteristic of Euripides' later plays and perhaps the one most important development in drama during this period.

Realism in portrayal of character was accompanied by realism in costume and details of dramatic technique. Indeed this external realism stimulated internal realism and may in no small part have been responsible for it. At least as early as the *Telephus,* heroic characters who were in pretended or genuine distress were brought on the scene in rags and tatters. This was an innovation which Aristophanes never ceased to satirize, and in the *Acharnians* an appalling number of plays containing such characters is cited. But here as in all other matters Euripides was quite impervious to unjustified criticism. He persevered, and his innovation became the rule. Sophocles later could bring on the long-marooned Philoctetes dressed in ordinary costume but not without offering an explanation for it.[9]

In his meticulous attention to details such as motivation and the movements of his characters, also, Euripides attempts to give the illusion of reality. Thus two characters may enter in conversation with each other, as in the *Suppliants* (381) and the *Iphigenia at Aulis* (303); or a hurrying messenger may rush on and interrupt a conversation, as in the *Iphigenia at Aulis* (414). Such realism, once introduced, soon became the rule. Sometimes an explicit motivation serves more to call attention to unusual or awkward action than to excuse it; but in the great majority of instances Euripides has been eminently successful in plausibly motivating the action of his plays, and his attention to such details is a distinct advance in dramatic technique.

The tendency toward naturalism is very noticeable also in the style of Euripides. "Notwithstanding that he is by nature anything but elevated," says "Longinus" (15. 3, Rhys Roberts), "he forces his own genius, in many passages, to tragic heights . . . . " In his dialogue, it is true, Euripides does seem prosaic when compared to Aeschylus or even to Sophocles. Only a conversational style would be compatible with the other realistic developments of Euripides. In his lyrics, however, especially when he has a subject that is truly tragic and wholly congenial to him, such as that of the second stasimon of the *Trojan Women* or of the *Heracles,* the sublimity of his poetry is natural and unforced.

If Euripides lost something in elevation in his dialogue scenes, he gained something in forensic eloquence. Here he has only one rival in the field of drama—his ardent follower, Menander. The Roman critic Quintilian (10. 1. 67–68) ranks Euripides as almost the equal of the philosophers in his conceptions and the equal of the greatest of the orators in pleading and debate—admirable in his handling of all the emotions, but easily the most eminent in arousing pity.

This forensic eloquence in no small degree accounts for the tremendous popularity of Euripides in the fourth and subsequent centuries, and for the survival of so many of his plays in modern times. There are not many of the extant plays which do not have a more or less clearly defined debate, and persuasive speeches are extremely common. To make a good rhetorical point, Euripides will forfeit consistency of character, as when Hecuba is made to talk of "foreigners" as if she herself were a Greek.[10] Indeed, Euripides will even change the legend if rhetorical effectiveness seems to advise it, as when he changes the story that the disguised Odysseus was discovered by Helen alone in order that Hecuba may have a more powerful appeal for the mercy of Odysseus.[11]

Euripides' rhetorical eloquence, of course, is a direct result of his vital interests in ethical and philosophical questions and in contemporary events. His heavy sincerity sometimes breaks through dramatic characterization and cannot wholly be thrown off even in his satyr-plays. His characters all tend to be philosophically inclined Athenians. In general this makes for more interesting and more significant drama; but Euripides at times went too far and spoiled his dramatic effect.[12]

Formalism is perhaps most obvious in Euripides' prologues. The prologue of the *Medea* shows that when the poet so desired, he could dramatize the exposition of a play with great skill. Almost invariably, however, Euripides preferred a staid, comparatively undramatic prologue. Sometimes, as in the *Bacchae,* a monologue is probably the most effective introductory scene possible for a given play. But usually Euripides chose this type merely because it furnished the simplest and most direct method of presenting the background.[13] Some compensation for the formalism of the prologue, however, is found in the great variety and freedom which he showed in managing the entrance of the chorus (parodos).

Formalism is very noticeable also in Euripides' use of conversation line by line (stichomythia). This is one of the most striking examples of his boldness in adopting and exaggerating an Aeschylean usage; and, strangely enough, it is most extensively used in his realistic later plays. In such dialogue a certain amount of artificiality is inevitable, since each speech must be precisely one complete iambic line.

Another type of formalism is found in the precise balancing of long speeches. This is a natural tendency in formal debates, however, and its artificiality is doubtless much more obvious to the reader, who may stop to count the lines, than it was to an audience. In the *Medea,* for instance, Medea and Jason each have main speeches of precisely fifty-four lines (if verse 468 is omitted here; it occurs also as verse 1324). So in the *Hecuba,* Polymestor and Hecuba are given speeches of fifty-one lines each. Less precisely balanced speeches are common.

The use of the *deus ex machina* furnishes another striking example of Euripidean formality. Here the same basic considerations which led Euripides to formality led him also to the use of the supernatural. Both are artificial and external and both facilitate the drama as he wrote it. The various advantages of the *deus ex machina* have been discussed elsewhere; but we may here observe that this device is regularly combined with Euripidean realism, for the speeches of the *deus ex machina* regularly make a connection between the action of the play and the customs of Euripides' own day. Such references often sound a patriotic note, as in the *Iphigenia in Tauris;* and—perhaps more important, since customs that are not Attic are frequently cited— they add plausibility and significance to the action of the play. Finally, such references connect one legend with another and tend to develop a cosmic whole. Especially noteworthy are Euripides' frequent references to the subjects of other plays which he has written or intends to write; thus in the *Electra* (1282–83), the Dioscuri refer to the story that a mere wraith of Helen was sent to Troy. Nor are such references by any means limited to these final speeches; they may occur anywhere in the play.

The reduction of the importance of the chorus is a noteworthy innovation of Euripides. His method here tends toward making the chorus an interlude entertainment. Thus again he anticipates the later development, though his method in this regard is not as artistic as that which Sophocles employs in the *Philoctetes,* where the chorus tends to become a minor character. Even so, this tendency is a more artistic one in Euripides' own plays than critics usually allow. One might find the beginnings of this in the *Medea,* where the chorus in its early songs views the action from a certain detachment and perspective but at the climax is drawn wholly into the excitement of the moment—certainly a skillful and effective arrangement. The same technique is used in the *Phoenissae.* Again, when pure interludes first occur they are used at the most exciting climax of the melodramatic plays, *Iphigenia in Tauris* and *Helen,* apparently in order that the suspense may not be jeopardized by either word or tone. The development of lyric monodies or duets by the actors, furthermore, is equally skillful and is designed to increase the importance of the actors and allow them to hold the center of attention without interruption. The best example of this perhaps is found in the *Iphigenia at Aulis.* Various innovations in the field of meter and music, entirely lost in translations, accompanied this important advance in dramatic technique.

As Euripides reduces the role of the chorus and brings the actors into greater prominence, so, especially in his later plays, he develops a more complicated dramatic action. In the *Phoenissae,* the longest of his plays, this is accompanied by the skillful insertion of a minor plot; in the *Iphigenia at Aulis,* by adding complications to the main plot.

In plot structure, the best tragedies of Euripides are in no way inferior to the best of Sophocles, although Euripides was bolder in introducing changes in the accepted legends. The melodramatic plays of Euripides also are well constructed. They tend to have four responsive choral songs dividing the play into five sections and thus anticipating the later practice of having five acts.

Euripides has been most severely criticized perhaps for constructing plots wherein the various events do not follow in the relationship of cause and result, plots like those of the *Andromache* and the *Trojan Women.* These plays are undeniably weak if one judges them by the conventional standards of unity. The form of a play, however, is determined by the subject matter and the purpose of the author, and we may well doubt if any set of standards should be applied to all plays. The purpose of Euripides in writing these plays of unusual form must be taken into consideration. It is hard to imagine any play constituting a more effective attack upon Spartans and the Delphic oracle than Euripides' *Andromache.* To assume that such an effective and consistent attack is the result of artistic gaucherie would be preposterous. Euripides here was fully aware of what he was doing, and he deliberately sacrificed conventional unity of incident for a unity of tone and effect. Every incident, almost every line of the play, makes its point against the enemies of Athens. The theorist may claim that a great artist will combine his material and purpose with excellence of form. But such a claim would seem to involve the very doubtful assumption that a great artist chooses his material and his purpose with a view to his form. Many who have been considered great artists have refused to limit their choice of material or purpose and have at times sacrificed form to purpose. Aeschylus did so in the *Eumenides;* Shakespeare did so in *Henry the Eighth,* if he was responsible for the structure of that play. Most modern critics, furthermore, consider the *Trojan Women* a masterpiece. The form of Euripides' plays, we must conclude, is skillfully adapted to the subject material and to the author's purpose.

1. **ALCESTIS**

(438 B.C.)

At this competition Sophocles won first prize; Euripides won second with the *Cretan Women* (*Kressai*), the *Alcmaeon at Psophis,* the *Telephus* (a play repeatedly satirized by Aristophanes), and the

Alcestis. Only the last of the four has survived. It took the place of the frolicking satyr-play which usually came after the three tragedies.

The presentation of the *Alcestis* probably required only two actors.

Legend.—According to an old tradition, it seems, Admetus was about to die on his wedding day when his bride Alcestis offered to sacrifice herself for him. She died; but, perhaps by the favor of Persephone, she returned to life.[14] In the play of Euripides, however, her death has significantly been placed long after her original decision, and to increase its pathos Euripides has included two small children. The supernatural elements of the story have here been minimized. In some versions Apollo aided Admetus in yoking lions and wild boars to the marriage wagon—a task prerequisite to the marriage. Again, Admetus was said to have incurred the wrath of Artemis by neglecting to sacrifice to her and therefore to have found a tangle of snakes in his bridal bed as an omen threatening his death.[15]

In every extant version of the legend Alcestis is brought back to life. This may possibly not have been the case in the original version, but such resurrection was essential to apotheosis. Euripides may refer to a cult in Alcestis' honor at Sparta and Athens (445–54, a disputed passage; 995–1005). It is often assumed that Alcestis and Admetus were originally Thessalian chthonic deities.

Source and influence.—The story of Alcestis had been the subject of a play by Phrynichus, the older contemporary of Aeschylus. Only one fragment and one important reference to this earlier play have been preserved. From these we may conjecture that Heracles appeared in the play, and we know that Death did so. The subject was not, we are told, treated by either Aeschylus or Sophocles; and no record of any other ancient tragedy with this title has been preserved except the *Alcestis* of the Roman dramatist Accius.[16] Several comedies on the subject, however, are known to have been written, one by an obscure Aristomenes, which was produced in competition with Aristophanes' *Plutus* (388 B.C., entitled *Admetus*), another by the contemporary comic writer Theopompus (not the famous later historian). Still another comedy, an *Alcestis,* was produced by Antiphanes, one of the leading writers of Middle Comedy (roughly about 350 B.C.).

The Roman satirist Juvenal (6. 652–53) refers to the presentation of an *Alcestis* in his own day, and a pantomime on this subject is mentioned by Lucian (*On Dancing* 52). Both these writers lived in the second century A.D.

In modern times the *Alcestis* of Euripides has inspired a vast number of adaptations and imitations.[17] Trissino's *Sofonisba* (1515), the first modern attempt at tragedy in the ancient style, was strongly influenced by it. Of the many later plays, special mention may be made of those of Alexandre Hardy (lived 1570–1631), Wieland (1773), Herder (1803), and Alfieri (1799). Operas have been written by Händel (1727) and Gluck (1767). James Thomson's poem, *Edward and Eleonora,* was influenced by Euripides' play.[18] Perhaps the best adaptation is found in Robert Browning's *Balaustion's Adventure.*

The subject of Alcestis was a favorite one in ancient art and is not unknown in modern art. In the Boston Museum of Fine Arts is a bronze statuette by Rodin entitled "The Death of Alcestis."

Theme.—Most modern adapters and critics have failed to realize how nicely articulated is the plot of Euripides' play and how thoroughgoing is the dependence of its action upon the characterization of the leading roles. This dependence will become clear in the subsequent consideration of the various characters, and a sound interpretation of the play can be made only on this basis.

Primarily, the weaknesses of the characters prove their salvation; and so the *Alcestis,* like many a Greek tragedy, illustrates the irony of fate. Since it is the softhearted kindness of Admetus to his slaves that has won him the favor of Apollo, and since it is his excessive hospitality that wins him the favor of Heracles, the virtue of these particular vices might be called the theme of the play. Perhaps the poet was more keenly interested, however, in the characterizations themselves and in studying the effect of Alcestis' sacrifice upon Admetus.

Discussion.—During the eerie scene with Death, Apollo foretells the coming of Heracles and the resurrection of Alcestis. Doubtless most if not all the audience knew that her resurrection was an essential feature of the myth, and knew also that the play must presumably have a happy solution, since it came after three tragedies and was substituted for the usual satyr-play. This foreknowledge removes any hint of surprise at the event, and it therefore removes any possible objection to a solution which inevitably contained this element of the supernatural. Foreknowledge also makes possible dramatic irony throughout the play. For the audience, the scene of farewell does not have the same tragic finality which it has for Alcestis and Admetus. Although this scene is full of the eternal sadness of human life, the poignancy of its sadness has been removed by the feeling that we are viewing a romantic reverie. The same is true of the later scenes depicting the grief and remorse of Admetus. In the scene with Pheres, however, dramatic irony is of little consequence. It regains its importance in the following scenes with Heracles, where ambiguity facilitates Admetus' deception of Heracles. For the audience, the mood and effect of the whole play are determined by their foreknowledge of the ending. This is an important point; many critics, overlooking it, have claimed that the play disconcertingly varies from the tragic to the comic.

Undeniable comic elements, however, are found in the play, especially in the swaggering figure of Heracles. With his boisterous exuberance he stands out in sharp contrast from the other characters. Though found in genuine tragedy, Heracles was a favorite character in satyr-plays and comedies, where he was famous not only for his strength and violence but also for his appetite. His propensity toward feasting and carousing is brought out in the *Alcestis,* and the grossness of his other natural desires is suggested.

The irony of the final scene, also, is essentially comic: Heracles obviously enjoys deceiving Admetus and testing his faithfulness to Alcestis; but it is not an altogether fair return, for Admetus' earlier deception of Heracles in welcoming him was a pathetic deception.

The comic elements of this play are strictly pertinent to the plot and are proper to a play which took the place of a satyr-play—though comic elements, not wholly unknown in Greek tragedy,[19] should not offend a modern audience accustomed to the practice of Shakespeare. But the prevailing tone is heavy with the prolonged contemplation of death. This is especially true of the choral songs and should be a warning to those who search for the comic throughout or for the diabolical laugh of the iconoclast.[20] The final note of Heracles himself is serious: he must be off to his unending labors.

The chorus furnish the social background for the action and nicely reflect the attitude of the common man toward Alcestis and her death. They very appropriately become the funeral procession and leave the stage, although such withdrawal is rare in Greek tragedy. The following scene between Heracles and the Servant, of course, is much more effective without their presence.

Metrical effects, though lost in translation, are skillfully employed in the original. The funeral song after the death of Alcestis is thought to have echoed well-known ritual melodies.[21] The return of the chorus and Admetus from the grave, furthermore, is solemn and impressive. After they have reached the palace, Admetus cannot bring himself to enter; and perhaps the continuing anapestic meter indicates that he paces up and down distracted with grief. Some have thought that the last complete choral song on "Necessity" as the supreme deity expresses the philosophy of the poet himself.[22]

Certain ideas recur in the manner of a leitmotif throughout the play. One, which adds pathos to Alcestis' sacrifice, is the fact that it is more natural and fitting for the old (the parents of Admetus) to die than for the young, and this conception has sometimes been considered the main theme of the play.[23] Again, the phrase, "you have lost a goodly wife," is spoken by the chorus (418; cf. 200), echoed by Pheres (615–16), and repeated verbatim by Heracles in the final scene (1083). Thus all join in the same generous praise of Alcestis. Other less striking repetitions occur.

There is also a delicate play upon words in the scene wherein Admetus deceives Heracles into accepting his hospitality. The ordinary Greek word for "wife" is the same as that for "woman," as in French, although in Greek the wordplay is more effective than it could be in French because of the naturalness of the omission of any pronominal adjective or indefinite article. Thus this deception, essential to the plot of the play, is much more subtle and ironic in Greek than in English; and this same ambiguity is used by Heracles in the final scene where he deceives Admetus just as Admetus has earlier deceived him.

Other subleties usually lost in translation are the use of assonance to lend a tone of unpleasant insistence to a passage (722–24; 782–85), and the division of a single iambic verse between two speakers. Such a division (*antilabe*) occurs only four times in this play, and its effect is to jolt the hearer and emphasize the importance of the interruption. It is used for the last weak words of the dying Alcestis (390–91) and for Heracles' final loss of all patience with the evasions of his host and the servants (819). It is used again at the climax of the final scene where Admetus receives Alcestis into his hands (1119).

The reason for the silence of Alcestis in the final scene has long been a subject for discussion. The prevailing opinion seems to be that any words which she might speak would inevitably be anticlimactic and spoil the effect of the scene.[24]

The most appealing character of the play is Alcestis herself.[25] Still, there is no unnatural heroism attributed to her. She sees very clearly that by her sacrifice the best interests of both her children and her husband are served. Once her decision is made—and of course we assume that, once made, it is irrevocable—she does not regret it, and she does not blame Admetus for accepting her sacrifice. If the best interests of her family obligated her to offer herself, she may have reasoned, then these same considerations obligate Admetus to accept her sacrifice. She acts of her own free will, conscious and proud of her virtue in doing so (324). Like Hippolytus, perhaps she has the assured conceit proper to a divinity. But she expects a sacrifice from Admetus in return, namely, that he, too, place the best interests of their family before all else and not jeopardize the happiness of their children by marrying again.[26] This demand is not motivated by mere feminine jealousy; for the crimes of stepmothers against children by a former wife, especially in royal families, were notorious in both legend and history.

Alcestis is not motivated by the thought that she is a mere woman and that any wife should sacrifice herself for her husband. This may have been a motive in the primitive legend (compare lines 180–81), in which, apparently, fate was to overtake Admetus on his wedding day. But in the play of Euripides, Alcestis and Admetus have lived together many years; they have had two children; and Alcestis has made her decision, based on calm and well-pondered reasoning, long before the fatal day arrives (524). By placing this decision in the past, Euripides obviously gave up that part of the myth which might at first glance seem to offer the greatest dramatic possibilities—the inner struggle of Alcestis over the decision. He gave up, also, the opportunity of making Alcestis the leading role throughout the play and attaining a character with the dramatic stature of an Antigone. Indeed, the play is not primarily concerned with the character of Alcestis, who, though essentially human, does not have the fatal weakness necessary for the most effective tragic character. There is only one character of the play who conforms to Aristotle's pattern (*Poetics* 1453 a), Admetus; and the real theme of the play appears to be the effect of Alcestis' magnanimous sacrifice upon Admetus. If the play bears the name of the wife, perhaps it is because of her unusual experience,[27] or possibly because the name Admetus seemed less appropriate to a tragedy, or merely because the play of Phrynichus was called the *Alcestis*. The chorus, we may note, is composed of men and is designed primarily as a background for Admetus.

The characterization of Admetus is the most difficult artistic problem which the material presents. Various modern dramatists and poets have attempted to draw him on more heroic lines by having Alcestis offer herself unasked and even without the knowledge of her husband.[28] These plays, however, usually fall deep into sentimentalism and substitute saccharine perfection for the pathos and simple humanity of the characters as drawn by Euripides. Nor can the issue of the characterization of Admetus be avoided by the device of Goethe, who contended that Euripides' Admetus was altogether admirable in his acceptance of the sacrifice of Alcestis because he was acting according to nature.[29] Admetus' own father certainly did not think that he was so acting. The indecent quarrel between Pheres and Admetus, also, has been eliminated by some modern adaptors. Likewise modern scholars are unfortunate in their efforts to prove Admetus an entirely admirable and noble character who does not change within the play.[30]

The more thoroughly the play is studied and compared with modern efforts on the same theme, the more obvious the skill of Euripides becomes: If Alcestis had not taken pride in her devotion to her husband, she would not have offered to sacrifice herself. If Heracles had not been callous and crude, he would not have entered a house of mourning. If Admetus had not been selfish and unimaginative, he would not have accepted his wife's sacrifice; if he had not been weak, he might not have received Heracles, and he certainly would not have finally agreed to take the woman whom Heracles forces upon him at the end of the play.[31] Euripides' characterization of Admetus, in short, is essentially the only satisfactory one possible. So Browning wrote:

> When King Admetos went his rounds, poor soul,
> A-begging somebody to be so brave
> As die for one afraid to die himself. . . .

Just as the original decision of Alcestis does not take place within the play, so there is no consideration of Admetus' original acceptance of her sacrifice. Indeed, Admetus here seems to sympathize more with himself than with her. Similarly the chorus repeatedly, the servants, and the children appear to pour out more sympathy upon Admetus and themselves than upon the dying queen. Alcestis herself sympathizes with them (295–97). Since Admetus is practically causing her death, some critics have found his laments ambiguous and repulsive. Especially repulsive to many is Admetus' declaration that he will have a statue of Alcestis made to take her place when she is gone. But here perhaps Admetus is really promising to establish a cult of Alcestis in his house to do the greatest honor to her memory.[32] Certain it is that the grief of Admetus is very sincere. Even before his wife's death he insists that her death is worse than any death to him, and finally he begs Alcestis to take him with her to the underworld.

It is in regard to his parents that the character of Admetus appears in its worst light. Alcestis herself first condemns them (290–98), and so convincingly that one cannot fail to see that she is justified. In her condemnation, however, there is none of the bitterness which we find in the words of Admetus (338–39), and he has much less moral right to condemn others for refusing to die.

In the scene with Pheres, Admetus is seen to be an ungrateful son and a selfish and unimaginative man. It is apparent that he has always assumed that, just as his power is over all men, so his happiness and welfare are the supreme considerations before which all must yield. Pheres is precisely the same type of character, though age has taken away his power. (Here, as in the *Hippolytus,* we may observe Euripides' keen perception of the influence of heredity upon character.) This scene is of primary importance in the structure of the play, for it brings out a side of Admetus which we see only here, and it determines the subsequent development of his character. To omit this quarrel between father and son would be to change the whole import of the play. Although the immediate cause of the quarrel is a part of the romantic reverie, the quarrel itself is very real. It is symbolic of the basic hostility between the parental and the marital ties: the contrast of their obligations, the antagonism of their loyalties and affections. Here, where compromise would be loathsome, the outcome is stark and tragic and irremediable. Heracles and Apollo can resurrect the dead, but they can never restore the affection between father and son. There is no comic element in this scene. The bitter earnestness of the antagonists makes it one of awful seriousness, as does also the presence of the dead Alcestis.[33]

The motives of Alcestis' sacrifice have previously been explained so simply and so plausibly that her willingness to die has seemed entirely natural and justified. But these motives are based upon such intimate unselfishness that others could hardly be expected to appreciate them, and, in fact, Admetus himself never brings them to his own defense. Heracles seems to assume that Admetus' acceptance of the sacrifice of his wife is entirely natural (524), but Heracles is no person to draw fine distinctions or weigh nice moral problems. The attitude of Pheres, however, is quite different. Having been compelled to face the dilemma himself and still, no doubt, mindful of his fearful reluctance at choosing either alternative, he stands in humble admiration of Alcestis; but toward his son he feels a hatred born of fear and humiliation. This hatred, so far repressed, now at the taunts of his son breaks forth with bitter ferocity. For the first time, Admetus is plainly told that his action has been base and cowardly. Admetus replies to his father by accusing him of precisely the same disgraceful weakness—an altogether natural reaction but, in point of fact, a desperate evasion rather than a defense. The charges of both father and son are essentially true.[34]

Admetus' realization of the manner in which others will view his acceptance of Alcestis' sacrifice—the result intended in the scene with Pheres—is largely responsible for the change which comes over him in the last scenes of the play. Most of the emotions which Admetus here reveals, it is true, are evident also in the earlier scenes. From the first he appreciates the sacrifice which Alcestis is making, and his reluctance to survive her is found throughout the play.[35] His effort to commit suicide (897–99), therefore, and his longing for death do not come as a surprise. But in these final scenes he regrets his acceptance of Alcestis' sacrifice with profound remorse; and the realization that she has chosen the better alternative and that his own hateful life will now be worse than death, although suggested in the earlier sections of the play,[36] comes upon Admetus with all its poignant force only after the burial.

The modern romanticist is offended by the fact that Heracles finally persuades Admetus to accept the veiled woman before she has been recognized as Alcestis. It must be admitted that Admetus here again betrays a weakness of character in his reluctance to offend Heracles, but this is the same weakness which caused Admetus to receive Heracles into his house. It is a noble rather than a base weakness, however, for it is due to the exaggeration of a virtue, the hospitality and generous friendship of Admetus, those very qualities which Heracles has already cited as the cause of his undertaking to rescue Alcestis; and, as his parting injunction to Admetus, Heracles bids Admetus practice justice in future time and show reverence to his guest-friends. That this characteristic of Admetus, at once his weakness and his salvation, is one of the moral motivations of the play seems undeniable, and it can be minimized only at the cost of misinterpreting this final scene.[37]

Such is Admetus in the final scene of the play. A certain critic has said that Admetus as we see him here would not accept the sacrifice of Alcestis a second time.[38] If this is true, then the character of Admetus has changed for the better, and we may assume that the chief concern of Euripides in writing this play was to portray the ennobling effect which the sacrifice of Alcestis had upon Admetus.

2. **MEDEA

(431 B.C.)

The *Medea* was the first of the usual series of four plays. The other three, no longer extant, were the *Philoctetes* (compare the extant play of Sophocles, produced in 409), the *Dictys* (the protector of Danaë and her child Perseus), and a satyr-play, the *Reapers* (*Theristai;* subject unknown). The plays of Euphorion, the son of Aeschylus, were awarded first prize in this contest, those of Sophocles second, and those of Euripides third and last.

The play was produced in the first year of the Peloponnesian War. Since a bitter hatred existed between Corinth and Athens and since Corinth played a major role in the events which led to the opening of hostilities, this was an auspicious time to present any enemy of Corinth, such as Medea, in a favorable light. The main theme of the *Philoctetes,* furthermore, seems to have been that of patriotism.

Legend.[39]—There were many variations in the stories told about the later history of Jason and Medea at Corinth. In all versions, however, one point is certain: their children died at Corinth. A cult in honor of them was practiced there in the sacred precinct of Hera Acraea during the time of Euripides and later. The audience, therefore, doubtless expected the death of the children and their burial at Corinth. But the manner and cause of their death was a matter of great uncertainty. There is some evidence which seems to indicate that Euripides was the first to represent Medea as deliberately murdering them.[40] If this is true, then Euripides created the most important element of the plot. The rest of his play consists of details either chosen from the several and often contradictory versions of the story or created by the poet.

Source and influence.—Euripides wrote at least two other plays concerning Medea: the *Daughters of Pelias* (his first play, 455 B.C., third prize), and the *Aegeus*. The subject of the present play was treated by neither Aeschylus nor Sophocles. It was the opinion of certain ancient critics that Euripides was appropriating the treatment of an obscure dramatist named Neophron. The few fragments of this play of Neophron indicate similarity of treatment, but for various reasons it seems likely that Neophron followed rather than preceded Euripides. One of these reasons is interesting as a matter of dramatic technique. Euripides' introduction of Aegeus was criticized as extraneous by Aristotle (*Poetics* 1461 b). It probably had been criticized before, and it certainly has been since then.[41] Neophron, however, motivated the appearance of Aegeus very cleverly, for he had Aegeus come to Medea to consult her on the interpretation of the obscure oracle which he had received. Thus it appears that Neophron was improving upon Euripides.[42]

The *Medea* of Euripides has always been one of the most famous Greek tragedies. The story exerted tremendous influence on both literature and art, and it was one of the most popular in Athenian drama. Some six other Greek plays and a similar number of Latin plays with this title are cited.[43] Among these Latin plays, the extant tragedy of Seneca is obviously based directly or indirectly upon the play of Euripides. Several Greek comedies, also, are cited by the title *Medea.*

There are many modern adaptations, including those of Corneille in French (1634), Grillparzer in German (1822), and Glover in English.[44] The theme is treated also in *The Life and Death of Jason* by William Morris (1867).

Several Italiote Greek vases depict scenes connected with the theme of this play. Similar scenes are found in bas-reliefs on sarcophagi, in statuary, and on funerary urns, terra cottas, and gems.[45] Julius Caesar paid a vast sum for two pictures by a famous contemporary painter, one of Medea and the other of Ajax (compare the extant play of Sophocles), in order to dedicate them in the temple of Venus Genetrix which he built in his forum in Rome.[46] Wall paintings of Medea have been found in both Herculaneum and Pompeii.

Theme.—The theme of the *Medea* seems to be that passion may so overwhelm reason as to lead one to a course of action inhumanly cruel and disastrous. In later writers Medea's wrath and jealousy become proverbial.[47]

The essential nature of the problem of the play has not always been grasped. No less a critic than Aristotle himself (*Poetics* 1454 b) apparently failed to grasp it, for he cites the *Medea* as an example of a play wherein the solution is brought about by the machine. Likewise, the most recent editor of the play says that the poet does not attempt to solve the problem which Medea and Jason propound, and that the "fantastic conclusion of his play—child-murder, dragon-chariot—is an end and not an answer."[48] But the problem of the play, of course, is not the unsolvable one of desertion or marital compatibility, although family obligations are interestingly discussed during the play. The problem of the *Medea* is the same as that of so many other great tragedies: revenge. This revenge must be of such a nature that it is final and complete; the price which Medea is willing to pay for such revenge may be great; but it must be freely paid and not exacted by her enemies, and she must survive her enemies. Such revenge is her purpose and her achievement. The most intense drama of the play is the titanic struggle within Medea's own soul. When she has steeled herself to murder her children and to destroy her happiness, and when the deed is actually committed, the main complication of the play is solved, since the other difficulties, an asylum and a device for killing Creon and his daughter, have already been overcome. Medea has never considered mere physical escape a problem. Though it might have been a problem in real life, there is no slavish realism in Greek drama which requires the poet to concern himself overmuch with mechanical details. But there must be a semblance of realism, and in order to have the final scene between Medea and Jason the magic chariot is introduced. The end of the play would have been anticlimactic if Medea after slaying her children had run out the back door and off to Athens, as she would have done in real life, just as it would have distinctly weakened the dramatic structure of the play if Jason had died, as he did in some versions of the story, along with Creon and his bride. If Medea faces Jason—and the dramatic desirability of her doing so is obvious—then she must have a means of escape, although it is true that even with the magic chariot, her children must still be buried in the sacred precinct of Hera Acraea. This is historically necessary. It is dramatically necessary—in order to maintain the characterization of Medea—that she bury them herself and not allow Jason to touch them. Thus, even granting the magic chariot, we cannot consider her escape a realistic one. An element of magic, furthermore, is not out of place here just as it is not objectionable in connection with the death of Creon and the bride; for, in both instances, this element of magic is entirely external and in keeping with Medea's reputation as a sorceress. In fact, there is scarcely an instance of the use of the machine in Greek tragedy that is more justified. Here it makes possible the final encounter between Medea and Jason, which in turn allows Medea like a *deus ex machina* to prophesy the mean death of Jason, and it furnishes a marvelous and spectacular finale.

The play is essentially a duel between Medea and the world. Her adversary is now Creon, now Jason, now Aegeus. Indeed not more than two speaking characters are on scene at any one time, and this of course is due not to the comparatively early date of the play but to deliberate artistic design. A third party on scene would confuse the stark simplicity of the composition.[49]

Discussion.—The *Medea* contains the most skillful and effective scenes of exposition found in the extant plays of Euripides. The Nurse, as she later explains (56–58), has been overwhelmed by an irresistible longing to come forth and cry the misfortunes of Medea to heaven and earth. Such vocal expression of strong emotions is common in Greek literature, beginning with Homer, and it was not unnatural for the ancient peoples of the Mediterranean basin.[50]

The story of the Argonauts was well known. A few words suffice to relate it and to remind the audience that Jason and the Corinthians were deeply obligated to Medea. The present situation of Jason and Medea at Corinth, however, receives much more careful explanation. The Nurse's emotions are no less important than her information. Her regret concerning Medea's wild career, her resentment of Jason's treachery, and her forebodings of violence to come—all are charged with profound significance.

The Nurse is a human being, and so her speech has no omniscient revelations and does not jeopardize suspense or surprise. In very natural fashion, furthermore, the Nurse suggests not only those events which actually take place during the play but also possibilities which do not materialize. The picture which she presents of the rage and grief of Medea, for instance, suggests the likelihood of suicide: she lies without food, abandoning herself to grief, and wastes away from continuous weeping; she refuses to lift up her eyes and is as deaf as stone to the pleas of her friends; she loathes the sight of her children. Then the Nurse explicitly voices the fear that Medea will commit suicide or slay Creon and Jason.[51]

No less ominous than these forebodings is the reluctance of the Paedagogus to reveal the new misfortune of exile. Indeed there is a subtle irony in the first appearance of Medea; for her wrath, however great it may now be, will be far greater when she learns the news which the audience knows to be in store for her. Meanwhile, the forebodings of the prologue become more definite and ominously recur like leitmotifs in the ensuing scenes.

The entrance of Medea is perhaps as effective as that of any character in Greek tragedy. In general, this scene dramatizes what the Nurse has described. Medea curses her children (112–14), whose appearance here at the beginning of the play has effectively emphasized their peril and the importance of their fate. She also invokes her father and her native land and recalls the foul murder of her brother with bitter remorse, galled by the realization that her base deeds are not appreciated or rewarded even by the man who caused them and profited by them. When she learns of her final disgrace and exile in the subsequent scene with Creon, however, all other considerations are lost in the crescendo of her desire for revenge.

The scene with Aegeus has been criticized as unmotivated and abrupt from the time of Neophron and Aristotle.[52] It is easy to assume that the scene was inserted mainly for its connection with Athens, especially because of the beautiful ode to Athens which follows the departure of Aegeus. But this ode, as an ancient commentator remarks (on line 824), is designed to deter Medea from her dreadful purpose by pointing out that if she persists, she will be wholly unworthy to be received in such a city. The praise of Athens, therefore, is strictly pertinent to the dramatic action. Another possible external reason for the scene may lie in a desire to connect the action of the *Medea* with that of a play entitled the *Aegeus,* which Euripides had written or was to write concerning Medea after she had come to Athens and married Aegeus. (Thus she fulfilled her promise to cause him to beget children!) References to the subjects of .his other plays are common in Euripides. But this scene with Aegeus, though its introduction is undeniably abrupt,[53] has an importance and an effectiveness in the *Medea* itself which are quite sufficient to justify its presence.

The desperate loneliness of Medea has been stressed from the opening lines of the play, and if her triumph over her enemies is to be complete she must make them suffer in such a way that they cannot themselves be revenged upon her.[54] Thus a secure refuge after she has destroyed her enemies is absolutely essential. This is the thought of Medea before the appearance of Aegeus (386–92); after his departure she cites the refuge which he has offered as the solution of her greatest difficulty (769). Medea has been careful to bind Aegeus with an inviolable oath in order that he may not be able to refuse her asylum, regardless of the crimes which she may commit before leaving Corinth.[55] To provide such a refuge, therefore, is the primary purpose of introducing Aegeus.

But the poet has a secondary purpose as keen and subtle in its psychology as any effect in Greek tragedy: Aegeus is a childless king. He is an object of special pity; for sterility of earth or of living creature was always considered a curse, and the higher the station of the one afflicted the more pitiful his misfortune. Throughout the scene, Aegeus' desire for offspring is stressed. He grants Medea's request, first, because it is his sacred duty to do so and, secondly, because she has promised, somewhat ambiguously, to cause him to beget children.

Immediately after Aegeus departs, Medea delivers a speech resembling a prologue for the second half of the play. Here she forms her plan to slay the bride by sending the children to her with poisoned gifts. This plan, Medea realizes, will necessitate the slaying of her children by her own hand to save them from the vengeance of Creon's kinsmen. But, with their slaughter, she will confound the whole house of Jason; for he will never again see his children alive, nor will he have his bride to bear him others. Thus will he suffer most (817). Like Aegeus he will be childless and miserable.

The presence of the chorus is most embarrassing in a drama of intrigue where a murderous plot must be conceived and executed with their connivance. In this play, to be sure, the chorus are women favorably disposed toward Medea, and a promise of silence has been exacted from them according to the usual convention (259–68); but the damage to verisimilitude is inevitable. In general, however, the chorus of the *Medea* is well handled. In the first three stasima the opening verses are devoted to contemplative generalizations on some theme having a bearing on the action of the play; the final verses are addressed to Medea and point the specific application of the generalizations expressed. It is especially effective, therefore, that the fourth stasimon (976–1001), though of similar metrical structure, is wholly concerned with the immediate action at the climactic point. Medea has just sent her children with the fatal gifts, thus dooming them to certain destruction. The chorus can no longer think in generalizations, but break forth in a song bemoaning the fate of the children and anticipating the death that will soon overtake the bride. In the following stanzas, they condemn Jason and sympathize with Medea. Thus the chorus, having lost their previous detachment and calm and being wholly overcome by the pathos of Medea's fatal action, heighten the excitement at the climax of the play.

Later, when Medea enters the palace to slay her children (1250), the chorus in very excited measure (dochmiacs) deprecate her purpose. When the shouts of the children are heard from within, the chorus beat at the doors; but, like the chorus in the *Agamemnon*, they are futile and helpless. After the fatal deed has been done, they sing that they have heard of only one other mother's "raising her hand against her dear children"—Ino, who had been driven mad by Heaven. Since actually similar cases were well known in Greek legend, Ino alone may be named because the poet perhaps wished to suggest that Medea, like Ino, has committed her deed in madness. Still, these two women were conventionally represented as entirely different types, and Medea, unlike Ino, does not commit suicide.[56]

One of the chief difficulties which Euripides faced in writing this play was in the humanization of Medea, for the Medea of popular legend was both the most famous witch of antiquity and the cold perpetrator of barbaric murders. A fair picture of this Medea may be found in the play of Seneca. Indeed a comparison with that play illustrates most clearly the genius with which Euripides achieved his purpose of making Medea entirely human. The excessive grief of Medea, her hatred of her children, and her dreadful cleverness in taking revenge upon her enemies are directly described by the Nurse in the prologue. Indirectly these same qualities are portrayed in the speeches of Medea herself,[57] and her character is even more effectively brought out in the scenes where she is contrasted with her several adversaries. We cannot but admire the astuteness with which she contrives to win her request from the naïve Creon. Especially clever is her denunciation of Creon's distrust of her cleverness, in which just enough truth is mixed with the false to make the whole credible. With an ironic smile, we are quite ready at the end of the scene to agree with Creon. "My will," he says (348–51), "has never been in the least like that of a tyrant, and in respecting others I have often made mistakes. Even now I see that I am wholly erring, woman, and yet I grant you this request."

In her first scene with Jason, Medea, despite all her shortcomings, is revealed as a character commanding some respect and admiration, whereas Jason appears utterly contemptible. He is insultingly abrupt and dins the hateful idea of exile into the ears of Medea. Then comes the "debate," which is almost as formal in its structure as the debate characteristic of Old Comedy.[58] The speech of Jason, especially, is filled with the sophistic cleverness which was so highly esteemed in this period and for which Euripides was famous for centuries. From the dramatic standpoint, however, there can be no objection to the use of such sophistry here, for it splendidly characterizes Jason. In his conceited haste to deny that he owes his success to a woman, he is all too glib in his answer to the charges of broken faith and lack of gratitude. He intimates that Medea saved his life only to satisfy her own lust. Granted that he has a debt of gratitude, he has more than repaid it by bringing her from an uncivilized land to Hellas and fame. As for his recent marriage, he boldly contends that here he has been wise, modest, and proper, and, finally, a great benefactor to Medea and their children. At this point (550) Medea restrains herself with difficulty. Under the pretext of such admirable virtues, Jason proceeds to reveal his fatal and most damning vice: desire for wealth and power. He is "a man entirely set upon building up a great career," says Murray,[59] "to whom love and all its works . . . . are for the most part only irrational and disturbing elements in a world which he can otherwise mould to his will." Jason reaches his lowest depth with the words (600–602) : "Do you know how you should change your prayer in order to appear wiser? Pray that wealth may never seem grievous to you and that if you possess a fortune, you may never think yourself unfortunate." In sharp contrast to this cupidity is Medea's reply to Jason's condescending offer to give her money for her exile. "The gifts of a base man," she replies (618), "bring no gain." In an adieu which strikes the final ominous note of the scene Medea taunts Jason with his lust for his newly won bride,[60] but one feels that Jason's is a lust of a different sort. Sincere amorous passion is ennobling ; but Jason's love is all for gold and power.

The second scene between Medea and Jason resembles the scene with Creon, for Medea shows the same cleverness in pretending to yield, subtly repeating Jason's own sophistic arguments. Little is added here to the character of Jason. His base niggardliness is brought out again when he protests the richness of the gifts which Medea has prepared for the bride. Though he prays that his sons may grow to manhood— the irony is effective—he shows no tenderness for them as Medea does.

The obvious tenderness which Medea feels for her children is one of the chief means which the poet employs to prevent her from becoming a monster. Seneca has Jason show more affection for the children and Medea less, thus increasing the pity which the audience feels for Jason at the expense of the humanity of Medea. In Euripides, Medea has been presented in the first part of the play, it is true, as hating her children. Externally, so to speak, this foreshadows their death ; but, internally, it does so only in part. As a characterization of Medea, the hatred for her children, like her desire to die, portrays the desperateness of her grief and not any clearly defined intention of violence. When she first determines upon slaying her children, it is not primarily because she hates them. Her prime motivation is desire for revenge upon her enemies. Medea herself must slay her children in order to anticipate the partisans of her enemies and their revenge. This is her reasoning when she first determines to slay them (774–93); but there immediately follows the thought that thus Jason will be made utterly childless and forlorn. In the second scene with Jason she weeps as she sees her children in the arms of their father and as she darkly and distractedly hints at their destruction.[61]

The departure of the children with the fatal gifts dooms them irrevocably; but the real struggle in Medea's soul is yet to come. In the first half of the play, the gradual steps which lead up to Medea's mad desire for revenge seem quite natural. Her determination to exact this revenge even at the price of her children's life, however deplorable, is humanly understandable in the light of her mad fury. It is only when her revenge upon Creon and the bride is complete and when she takes her farewell of the children that this fury departs and she fully realizes the awfulness of her course. She falters and thinks of taking her children with her into exile. Then in a confusion of emotions between an angry desire to punish Jason and a wild fear of her children's falling into the hands of her enemies, she again resolves to slay them; for her wrath, as she confesses (1079), has overcome her better judgment. From her first thought of slaying the children, there has continually recurred the realization that such an act will make her the most miserable of mortals (818, 1036–37, 1245), and her last words before committing the deed give, as her final motivation, the desire to keep them from falling into the hands of her enemies: "In truth, even if you slay them, yet were they dear—and I a woman cursed of heaven."

Jason, like Pentheus in the *Bacchae,* is presented in a more sympathetic light in the final scene of the play. With effective dramatic irony, he says that he has come to save his children from the vindictive wrath of the kinsmen of Creon. When he learns of their death at Medea's hand, his first thought is to punish her. At this point Medea appears in her magic chariot on the "machine." It is a spectacular scene: Medea's appearance high above and far out of the reach of Jason emphasizes the futility and helplessness of his position. Jason vents his wrath upon her in a brilliant speech, but he perceives that what he says has little effect upon her—all that he can charge her with, murdering her own children, betraying her fatherland, and killing her brother, she has long since confessed. As the scene progresses, almost degenerating into an indecent marital quarrel, Jason gradually realizes his utter ruin. Medea remains adamant and refuses Jason's last request that he be allowed to bury his children. The scene closes with Jason's bitter wish that he had never begotten these children for her to destroy. Pitiful as Jason and cold as Medea may appear in this final scene, we cannot forget Jason's infidelity and baseness. Our contempt for Jason may have changed to pity, and our sympathy for Medea may have vanished; but we must still regard her, perhaps with a somewhat awful admiration, as the one great character of the play.

3. **HIPPOLYTUS

(428 B.C.)

Euripides was awarded first prize, an honor which his plays received only five times. Sophocles did not compete, but his son Iophon (see Aristophanes, *Frogs* 78–79) was second; and Ion of Chios was third. The titles of the other plays produced at this time are not known.

Legend.—Hippolytus was worshiped as a god and hero in Troezen. This town, the scene of the play, is situated in the Peloponnesus across the Saronic Gulf from Athens, and in legendary times it was ruled by Pittheus, father of Aethra, the mother of Theseus. Here a temple and sacred precinct were dedicated to Hippolytus; yearly offerings were made to him; and every bride, as Artemis directs at the end of Euripides' play (1423–30), dedicated a lock of hair to him.[62] A stadium, also, was built in honor of Hippolytus, and a gymnasium, according to an inscription, was called the "Hippolyteion."[63] In this play, Hippolytus is characterized as being keenly interested in athletics (1016). At Athens and Sparta, as well as at Troezen, Hippolytus was honored as a hero. According to certain versions of the myth, Hippolytus was brought back to life by Asclepius.[64] Some such resurrection would be prerequisite, of course, to apotheosis.

The mother of Hippolytus was an Amazon, named either Antiope or Hippolyte, whose union with Theseus, according to some versions, was one of violence. The name Hippolytus was usually interpreted by the ancients to mean "he who was destroyed (or torn limb from limb) by his horses."[65] The love of Phaedra for Hippolytus and the character of Hippolytus remain essentially the same in all versions, and it is obvious from what Aristophanes makes his Aeschylus say in the *Frogs* (1052–53) that the legend was accepted as essentially true.

Source.—An ancient commentator informs us that this play was the second *Hippolytus* which Euripides wrote and that it was called the

Hippolytus Crowned, to distinguish it from the earlier play, which was known as the *Hippolytus Veiled.* All that was unseemly and worthy of censure, he continues, has been corrected in the present play. He adds that this play is one of the first rank.

The same events constituted the subject of both these plays; but important differences in detail occurred, and there was doubtless little or no literal repetition. In the earlier play, Phaedra resorted to magic rites in an effort to secure the love of Hippolytus;[66] Phaedra claimed that she had fallen in love with Hippolytus because of the faithlessness of Theseus;[67] Theseus probably was thought to be in the underworld and, as in Seneca, he returned in the course of the play (frag. 440, Nauck[2]); Hippolytus, as in Euripides' extant play, appeared before his angry father and tried in vain to defend himself (frag. 439, 441); Phaedra may possibly have confessed to Theseus directly, as in Seneca, and then have committed suicide; and it is probable that at the end of the play Artemis appeared and commanded the foundation of the cult of Hippolytus as a late but good reward of his virtue and piety (frag. 446; cf. *Hippolytus* 1419–25). It is often assumed, also, that Phaedra declared her love to Hippolytus in person, as in Seneca, where the scene is so brilliantly conceived and written that one would like to attribute it to the genius of Euripides. Such a scene, from the moral point of view, may have constituted the most objectionable feature of the play. Aristophanes never tired of satirizing the Phaedra of Euripides, and it is assumed that this was the objectionable Phaedra of the earlier, lost play.[68]

Sophocles, also, wrote a tragedy on these events, entitled *Phaedra;* but its date and the details of his treatment are unknown. It is certain, however, that Theseus returned from his expedition to the underworld in the course of the action, and that Sophocles' chorus consisted of women and were enjoined to silence as in Euripides (*Hippolytus* 713–14).[69]

Influence.—Throughout antiquity this extant play of Euripides was famous, and it exerted important influence on literature and art. Only one later Greek tragedy on this subject, however, is mentioned. A comic writer of the fourth century is known to have parodied the legend. Euripides' earlier treatment seems to have been the main source for Ovid, who wrote a charming letter of Phaedra to Hippolytus (*Heroides* 4), and for Seneca, whose tragedy *Phaedra* is still extant.[70]

In his masterpiece *Phèdre* (1677), Racine skillfully combines the treatment of Euripides' extant play with that of Seneca. Certain original elements, especially a love affair between Hippolytus and a character named Aricie, are added. This makes a more complex and theatrical play, but it also robs the story of the moral significance with which Euripides endowed it.

Various other modern adaptations have been made, including one by Gabriel d'Annunzio (*Fedra,* 1909).[71]

Theme.—This story is an example of that plot of which the most widely known version is the story of Potiphar's wife in Genesis (chap. 39). Somewhat the same plot was employed by Euripides in his dramatization of the story of Bellerophon and Stheneboea (two plays, before 425 and 423 B.C.) and in his *Phoenix* (before 425 B.C.).

Although critics still debate the relative importance of Phaedra and Hippolytus in this play, there can be no real doubt that the center of interest is Hippolytus. At the precise middle of the play Phaedra dies, and Hippolytus, who has been an important character in the first half of the play, is the main concern of the second half. The fate of Hippolytus is almost the exclusive concern of both Aphrodite in the prologue and Artemis in the finale. The etiological explanation of his cult, furthermore, is an important element of the play (1423–30). Debate concerning Euripides' earlier play and the extant play of Seneca is justified, but there can be no doubt concerning the present play.

This play, like many other Greek tragedies, seems primarily designed to illustrate the wisdom of "Nothing too much." "Mortals who flee Aphrodite too much," runs a fragment of Euripides' earlier play (frag. 428), "suffer a malady no less than those who too much pursue her." The folly and injustice of Theseus, too, are important moral elements in the play.

Character of Hippolytus.—Hippolytus is a young man, somewhat beyond the age at which young men normally become interested in women; but he is still perhaps an adolescent (118) and is idealistic to the point of being a fanatic. Though proud and imperious (1086–87), he seems to feel the disgrace of illegitimacy keenly (1082–83). It would be easy to assume that this cold son of a cold Amazon mother has an aversion to women because of the stain of his birth and because the union of Theseus with his mother was perhaps one of violence;[72] but such an explanation is not explicitly given by Euripides.

In the prologue Aphrodite describes Hippolytus briefly as the only citizen of Troezen who says that she is the basest of divinities, who refuses wedlock, and who considers Artemis the noblest of divinities. With Artemis and his swift hounds he prefers hunting wild beasts to association with human beings. There follows a colorful scene designed primarily to illustrate and emphasize this direct description by indirect dramatic portrayal. Hippolytus enters with a supplementary chorus of hunting attendants and doubtless with his hounds and hunting equipment. His words to Artemis reveal his love of virtue, his conceited opinion of his own attainment of virtue, and his wish to finish his life as he has begun it.

But the most important incident of this scene is Hippolytus' impetuous and haughty refusal to follow the old servant's advice to pay some regard to Aphrodite: "I keep my distance—since I am pure—when I greet her!" (102) And as he leaves the scene his farewell to Aphrodite is so contemptuous that it is almost a curse: "I bid a long farewell to that Cypris of yours!"[73] This is one of the most important lines of the play. Hippolytus here exhibits such an insolent contempt for a divinity, or, perhaps more properly, for an elemental force of the natural world, that his downfall now from the Greek point of view seems not only justified and natural but almost inevitable. This impression is strengthened by the old servant's foreboding prayer to Aphrodite.

From the modern point of view Hippolytus appears at his worst in the scene in which he bursts from the house and denounces Phaedra. Although his denunciation is too violent—and of course the author has designed it to appear too violent and possibly a little ridiculous, as might be expected in a pretentious adolescent—still, we should not overlook the enormity of the crime that has been suggested. This is sufficient motivation for almost any anger, however excessive, especially in a pure youth so conscious and proud of his frigid virtue; but his anger and haughtiness lend Phaedra some excuse for her terror and her false indictment.

That a youth so pure should be the victim of such a foul intrigue is indeed tragic and ironic (cf. 1034–35); but all too often in life, as the Nurse points out (443–46), he who refuses to recognize the elemental forces of nature is in the end overwhelmed by a fate that is unnaturally severe. However excessive some of these lines of Hippolytus' denunciation may appear, there is no hint of sexual perversion anywhere in the play or in the legend. In fact, many passages prohibit such an interpretation, and to assume such would be to miss the point of the whole play. Since the Greek dramatists did not shrink from speaking frankly about perversion,[74] and since both natural and unnatural passion fell within the province of Aphrodite,[75] such an interpretation would never have suggested itself to a Greek audience. Hippolytus is a youthful hater of women, like the young Melanion who is described by Aristophanes in the *Lysistrata* (781–96).

In the scene between Hippolytus and his father our sympathies are all with the youth, although we realize that Theseus, returning from a pilgrimage with a garland upon his head and in a joyful mood, has been driven almost mad by his sudden grief. But Theseus is by no means an innocent victim of circumstances (cf. 1316–27). Before seeing his son, Theseus has cursed him with a fatal curse. The chorus begs the father to rescind this curse, assuring him that he will discover that he is in error. The chorus would make the best witness to prove Hippolytus' innocence, but the chorus has given an oath of silence (713–14) and has already lied to Theseus concerning its previous whereabouts. It is precisely in such a situation as this that the presence of the chorus is most embarrassing to the dramatist. But here the protest of the chorus and Theseus' refusal to regard it are used to incriminate Theseus. When the son appears, he is accused of utter baseness by his father, charged with being an Orphic fanatic and a vegetarian[76] and one who becomes intoxicated on the shadowy writings of a mystic cult. All this haughty religious fervor, according to Theseus, is merely a shield for wickedness, and he advises all men to beware of such people.

Hippolytus' defense is artificial and sophistic. Since we should expect him to be carried away with emotion far beyond the point of indulging in commonplaces and rhetorical argument, we may assume that Euripides is here deliberately characterizing the pretentious seriousness and adolescent awkwardness of this strange young man. Hippolytus insists that no man is more virtuous than he in the sight of god and man, that he knows not love and has no desire to know it, that the charge against him is unlikely because, he intimates, Phaedra was not the most beautiful of women and he had no desire by union with her to acquire the rule of the land.[77] Finally, he solemnly swears that he has not violated his father's bed, and he curses himself if he is not telling the truth. His father returns this very curse, rejecting his son's plea for a fair trial or for the consultation of seers with the same contemptuous phrase which Hippolytus used at the first of the play to reject the worship of Aphrodite (113, 1059). For the Greek audience the repetition of these impious words sounds a fatal knell for Theseus: Like father, like son. Theseus will be punished for his insolent disregard of justice as Hippolytus is already being punished for his insolent disregard of Aphrodite.[78] Elsewhere both Theseus (831–33) and Hippolytus (1379–84) bemoan the visitation of the sins of the fathers upon the sons, and although these lines are pertinent in their obvious meaning, they are designed to carry a deeper ironic and tragic meaning. Hippolytus has all too surely inherited his father's vice of holding the established laws in contempt.

Hippolytus debates with himself the advisability of breaking the oath which he has been deceived into giving. The breaking of an oath exacted under false pretenses would seem justified in modern morality. It was justified by certain ancient philosophers; but in conventional Greek thought a very strict formality was maintained. By the mere suggestion of breaking such an oath the enlightened Euripides is here, as often in his plays, calling into question a basic tenet of Greek morality, and this caused him to be criticized severely by Aristophanes. But Hippolytus does not actually break his oath; he sees that in any event he would not succeed in convincing his father.[79]

Theseus, like the old servant in the first scene, is galled by the pretentious righteousness of his son. This, perhaps, is the very thing which prevents Theseus from believing Hippolytus; for just as those who fanatically oppose natural forces are often overtaken by an unnatural fate, so we are prone to attribute to such people unnatural crimes, and the man who is ever dour and solemn in his self-righteousness, when faced with such a charge, finds himself at a greater disadvantage than the man of lighter character. Solemnity is more impressive when it stands out in sharp contrast to one's normal attitude. But Hippolytus is at least consistent, and in his last lines of the scene he again attests his own virtue.

In the powerful final scene, also, the character of Hippolytus remains the same. He calls upon Zeus to witness that he, the righteous worshiper of Deity, surpassing all men in virtue, now dies, and that his life of piety has been in vain (1363–69). With admirable generosity, he grieves more for his father than for himself, as Alcestis grieves for Admetus. But the last note of his character, like the first, is one of self-righteousness. Such conceit is proper to the semidivinity which he has now become. The whole characterization of Hippolytus, indeed, has been designed to be compatible with his eventual status as a god or hero.

Character of Phaedra.—The story of Phaedra is essentially a sordid tale. In the *Phaedra* of Seneca and the *Phèdre* of Racine her love is the main concern of the play and Phaedra is the main character. It was doubtless more important in Euripides' earlier, severely criticized, version of the story. But in the present play the tragedy of Phaedra is subordinated to that of Hippolytus, and Euripides has deliberately attempted to remove those features which proved most objectionable in the original play. He has been eminently successful in here presenting Phaedra as a character worthy of sympathy. This remarkable feat is accomplished by various devices. First of all he hedges her about with divine approval; Aphrodite is introduced and reveals the coming fate of Hippolytus and Phaedra with a definiteness that is rare even in the divine prologues. This foretelling is designed primarily not to facilitate irony but to intimate that Phaedra is the innocent means by which Aphrodite will take revenge upon Hippolytus (47–50). Again, near the end of the play, Artemis excuses Phaedra on the grounds that she was stung by the poison of Aphrodite; trying to recover herself by means of reason, she was brought to ruin against her will by the deceptions of the Nurse; she wrote the false letter in fear of being herself charged with her guilt.

Whether such divine indulgence can really constitute justification might be questioned, especially since in this same play the sins of Hippolytus and Theseus seem, from the modern point of view, mere peccadillos compared with those of Phaedra, yet these sins are punished with the most heartless severity by the gods. In point of fact, however, these divinities are essentially personifications of basic forces of nature. This is repeatedly brought out where Aphrodite is concerned. She feels no envy at the happiness of Artemis and Hippolytus (20), but Hippolytus must still pay the penalty for his sins. Aphrodite, therefore, is not subject to petty human emotions, but punishment follows violation of her law as inevitably as it does naturally. Such punishment often involves innocent victims. To call Aphrodite here or Dionysus in the *Bacchae* cruel and heartless is simply to rage against the immutable forces of nature. Euripides' interpretation of this divinity, which resembles that of Aeschylus (frag. 44) and many another before him, is brought out most plainly in the beautiful lines of the Nurse (447–50): "Cypris goes to and fro in the heavens; she is upon the wave of the deep; and from her all things arise. She it is who sows and scatters love, whose children all we upon the earth confess ourselves to be."

This interpretation of Aphrodite makes it possible for Euripides to view Phaedra's love in a light quite different from that of ordinary morality. Phaedra is not guilty of deliberate sin; overwhelmed by an irresistible natural force, she struggles against it in vain and is destroyed. She is in a way the innocent victim, therefore, by which Hippolytus' sin against nature is punished. Here as elsewhere, however, Euripides uses this divine motivation as a means of profoundly interpreting human action and not as a substitute for psychologically sound, human motivation; for Phaedra's passion, like the actions of Hippolytus, has been made thoroughly plausible from the purely human point of view.

A sympathetic and extremely skillful characterization constitutes the second device by which Euripides presents Phaedra in as favorable a light as possible. At the opening of the play, the Nurse is not, as in Seneca, acquainted with Phaedra's passion. For three days Phaedra has taken no food, wishing to die rather than confess her desires, and her body is weak and wasted (274–75). As she is brought on stage, however, her first lines reveal her feminine vanity, her conscious admiration for her lovely arms and hands, and her care to have her locks tossed most becomingly over her shoulders. Then in her wild delirium, she expresses the longing to visit those haunts and indulge in those pursuits which, as the audience knows, are the favorite haunts and pursuits of the one with whom she is in love.

When Phaedra has returned to normal consciousness and realizes the implications of her words, she is covered with shame and confusion. The concealment of her dreadful passion is her primary concern— though in a way, of course, she secretly wishes to confess it. Brief references to her heredity make this passion more plausible. Her mother, Pasiphaë, conceived an unnatural desire for the white bull presented to Minos by Poseidon (338); and her sister, Ariadne, aided Theseus in slaying the Minotaur only to be deserted by him on the island of Naxos, where the god Dionysus came to comfort her (339).[80] The Nurse with the greatest effort finally succeeds in discovering the malady of Phaedra. The Nurse, not Phaedra, must first speak the name Hippolytus.[81] This whole scene is a masterpiece. Phaedra's pathetic speech of defense further softens her character: "We know and recognize the good, but we are unable to achieve it . . . . " (380–81). Most ingratiating with the Athenian audience, moreover, must have been the virtuous sentiments which Phaedra here expresses, especially her desire to die rather than betray her husband and disgrace her children (419–21).

The Nurse serves as an effective foil for Phaedra in the portrayal of her passion, and the role of the Nurse is another device by which Euripides has rehabilitated the character of Phaedra. A servant may well be depicted as prosaic and practical and somewhat crude. At the first of their scene together on stage, Phaedra consistently uses highly poetic Doric Greek forms, whereas the Nurse uses familiar Attic, although even the Nurse's lines are poetic and in similar anapestic meter. When Phaedra in her ravings longs to quaff the pure waters of a cold woodland fount, the Nurse unimaginatively points out that near the palace there is a cold unfailing stream from which she may have drink! The Nurse, furthermore, must here bear much of the onus for the tragic events which probably fell on Phaedra in the earlier version of the play as in the play of Seneca. The one immoral speech of the present play is that in which the Nurse answers the very virtuous sentiments of her mistress. The Nurse's reasoning is very seductive; and the chorus admit that her suggestions are practical, but they cannot approve of them. Phaedra herself severely condemns them. But the Nurse, with strongly contrasting crudity, remonstrates at Phaedra's pretentious words and reminds her that she is in need not of specious words but of the man (491).

The Nurse finally wins Phaedra over by telling her that she knows of love charms which will cure her malady, and without harm or disgrace, if Phaedra will have courage. She then suggests that she will work a magic spell upon Hippolytus. Phaedra falters, makes timid inquiries, and expresses fears lest she be played false by the Nurse, and especially lest the Nurse inform Hippolytus. The Nurse reassures her and, since belief in the efficacy of such magic spells was popularly held in ancient times,[82] it seems most reasonable to assume that Phaedra is genuinely deceived by the Nurse (cf. 1305).

Phaedra's false indictment of Hippolytus is her basest act, nor is it here condoned by the thought that the father will deal leniently with his son. Still, there are extenuating circumstances. She does not have the brazenness to face Theseus, as in Seneca, and indict Hippolytus in person. Although Phaedra and the Nurse have no real justification for thinking that Hippolytus will break his oath of silence, Phaedra insists that he will inform against her (689–92). Her desire to save the honor of her children and to avoid disgrace herself—her primary concerns in the earlier scene (419–21)—motivates her suicide. She finds justification for her false indictment, first conceived in these last lines, in her desire to forestall Hippolytus' gloating over her death and to avenge herself upon him for his haughty contempt. Under such circumstances, and especially since she is in a frenzy of despair and is taking her life, her false indictment is at least humanly understandable, and she herself appears more a victim of circumstances than a deliberately evil perpetrator of crime.

4. HERACLEIDAE ("CHILDREN OF HERACLES")

(Possibly about 427 B.C.)

The *Heracleidae* is probably the earliest of Euripides' extant political plays. It is an inferior production, and its influence has been negligible. Some scholars assume that our present text of the play is faulty and that lacunae occur at the end of the play and at various other points. There is no certain evidence, however, that any extended passages are missing.

Discussion.—Aeschylus wrote a play entitled *Heracleidae,* and though very little is known of his treatment it is altogether probable that Euripides is here following the main lines of that play.[83] The legend of Eurystheus' persecuting even the descendants of Heracles was an old one, but the role of Athens in this legend is presumed to be an innovation of the fifth century.[84] The Athenians were very proud of this role, however, and the subject matter of both the *Heracleidae* and the *Suppliants* is found in a single passage of Herodotus (9. 27) wherein an Athenian is pointing with pride to the great deeds of Athens in early times. The precise date of the publication of Herodotus' work is a matter of uncertainty; but his account of the present events, we may be sure, was subsequent to the play of Aeschylus.

The chief purpose of the *Heracleidae* seems to be to remind the descendants of Heracles of their obligations to Athens,[85] or perhaps more properly to remind Athenians that Theseus, their great king, was the kinsman and friend of the Dorian Heracles, that the Heracleidae were indebted to Athens, and that an invasion of Attica by their decendants was contrary to justice and accursed. The play is also a flattering encomium of Athens, and more than any other extant play of Euripides it glorifies the martial spirit. If Aristophanes had wished to be fair to Euripides in the *Frogs* (1021), he might have cited at least this play of Euripides, for it is as "full of Ares" and possibly as efficacious in instilling the spirit of Marathon as any of the plays of Aeschylus. Praise of Athens as the refuge of the oppressed and the home of justice, furthermore, was politically very desirable at this time, for Athens was now known as the tyrant city and was feared and hated by almost all the Greeks. So Thucydides (2. 8) relates, and about this time Aristophanes was boldly attacking the exploitation of the allies.

Certain scenes are especially effective in achieving the purpose of the play. Very impressive, for instance, is the scene when Iolaus has the children of Heracles join hands with the Athenians and solemnly directs them forever to remain grateful friends of Athens. The noble self-sacrifice of Macaria, furthermore, is symbolic of that sacrifice which men and women are called upon to make in any state if battles are to be won; and it must have deeply affected the citizens of Athens in the midst of a very costly war.[86] The irrepressible lust for battle which even the ancient Iolaus feels is another tribute to the martial spirit. Even Eurystheus, though depicted as cowardly in refusing to face Hyllus in single combat, is ready to die without flinching. The Argive forces are treated with even greater respect. There is no vilification of the enemy here except by those who are obviously prejudiced in their judgments.

An interesting incidental feature of the play is found in the comic touch of the scene wherein Iolaus arms for battle. Coming after the self-sacrifice of Macaria, this might fairly be called comic relief—one of the very few cases of such relief in Greek tragedy.[87]

As a whole, however, the *Heracleidae* is dramatically weak. Like the *Suppliants,* it contains a series of minor complications which are immediately followed by their solutions and none of which is built up to the height of a powerful climax. The final scene, furthermore, somewhat disrupts the specious unity of the play. Iolaus, who has been the leading figure up to this point and who has been perhaps the hero of the battle, is now dropped with a lame excuse (936–37). Alcmene is a much less effective figure—to say nothing of the disconcerting shift of the center of interest—and she now becomes persecutor rather than the persecuted and pitiful suppliant of the former scenes. This shift in mood also is disconcerting. From the ancient point of view, there is nothing inhuman or especially cruel in her desire for vengeance; but certainly by the time she tries to circumvent the decree of Athens, and Eurystheus has revealed the oracle of his dead spirit's becoming a benefactor and protector of Attica,[88] the sympathy of the audience tends to shift from Alcmene to Eurystheus.

5. *ANDROMACHE*

(Possibly about 426 B.C.)

An ancient commentator (on verse 445) says that this play was not produced at Athens. Some scholars think that it was produced at Athens but by another person (though the authenticity of the play is not doubted), some that the play was produced at Argos, and some that it was produced at the court of the king of the Molossians, who traced his ancestry back to Achilles by way of Andromache's son and whose favor Athens now had reason to court.[89]

The *Andromache* certainly belongs to the series of Euripides' political plays. For the modern reader it is perhaps one of his least interesting productions, unless the reader is primarily concerned with examining the basic material from which Racine constructed his *Andromaque* (1667), a very free adaptation, in which Neoptolemus (Pyrrhus) is made a central figure in an exciting, close-knit drama. Euripides' own play was produced at the Comédie Française in 1917.[90]

Discussion.—The author's chief purpose in the *Andromache* seems to be to vilify Sparta and the Spartans, among whom, one might almost say, is included the Delphic Apollo—regularly termed Loxias or Phoebus in this play. At the beginning of the Peloponnesian War the Spartans had consulted the Delphic oracle and had been told that they would win the war if they fought well, and that the god himself would be their ally.[91] This prejudice of the oracle, of course, infuriated the Athenians, who already had more than one just cause for recognizing the corruption of this institution and for hating it.[92] The *Andromache* is the one play of Euripides wherein a deliberate and sustained attack is made upon Phoebus with no subsequent mitigation of the charge.

Achilles and the Thessalians, as ordinarily in Greek tragedy, are viewed from an entirely sympathetic standpoint. Thessaly was at times an ally of Athens, and "the common people of Thessaly were always well disposed towards the Athenians."[93] Peleus in this play declares that he will raise the son of Andromache as a great enemy of the Spartans, but perhaps this should be referred to the Molossians rather than to the Thessalians (724; cf. 634–36). The city of Argos, whose favor the Athenians were courting when this play was written, is thought by some scholars to be the city to which Menelaus refers as formerly friendly to Sparta but now hostile (734–36).

The play has been severely criticized for its lack of unity. In the early scenes, the action is primarily concerned with the fate of Andromache and her son. After Peleus has come to their rescue, however, Hermione usurps the stage and in turn is rescued by Orestes. Finally Peleus returns and becomes the central figure. These incidents follow one another partially in the relation of cause and effect. The hysteria of Hermione, whose danger is foreshadowed in the lines of Peleus (709–10), follows as the result of her failure to do away with Andromache. Hermione's problem is solved by Orestes, who is also responsible for the death of Neoptolemus. The structure here would be improved very considerably if jealousy and resentment over Hermione's present circumstances were the sole motivation for Orestes' slaying Neoptolemus and if Phoebus and his resentment, like that of "an evil mortal," were eliminated. The choral song on the grief which Phoebus brought Troy and the Greeks, however, forms a very nice transition from Orestes and Hermione to the murder of Neoptolemus at Delphi and the subsequent vilification of Phoebus.

In all the episodes of the play, furthermore, Neoptolemus and his fate have been important considerations. Andromache in the prologue says that Neoptolemus has gone to Delphi "to make atonement for his folly"—an ominous phrase—in taking Phoebus to task for the slaughter of Achilles (51–55). This is echoed by Orestes when he suggests that Neoptolemus is about to be slain at Delphi (1002–4), and later by the Messenger in reporting the words of Neoptolemus himself (1106–8). The play as a whole relates the destruction of the house of Achilles, the man who sacrificed so much in winning the war, by the son of Agamemnon and the daughter of Menelaus and Helen, those who caused and benefited most by the war.[94] Still the figure of Neoptolemus is too shadowy to give the play any effective unity.

One consistent and emphatic theme runs through the play, however, and all the action contributes to it—the vilification of Sparta, Spartans, and Phoebus. That the play well fulfills this purpose cannot be denied, and a close examination of the play seems to indicate that Euripides deliberately sacrificed dramatic unity to his desire to make his indictment as damning as possible. So Neoptolemus' death is not made the result of Orestes' desire to rescue Hermione, for to make it so would eliminate the worst charge against Phoebus. This would constitute a change in the legend also; but in other details Euripides has introduced changes where they enable him to paint the Spartans and Phoebus in blacker colors. Thus, according to one version of the legend, Tyndareos, Hermione's grandfather, made the engagement between Hermione and Orestes while Menelaus at Troy made the contradictory promise of Hermione to Neoptolemus. But, in Euripides, Menelaus treacherously made both promises (967)—somewhat implausibly, perhaps, since Hermione and Orestes were infants when Menelaus went to Troy and he doubtless did not anticipate being away for seventeen years. Again, Neoptolemus was commonly thought to have been killed at Delphi, but for various reasons none of which concerned Orestes. Euripides first, so far as we know, presents him as slain in a most foul, cowardly manner by Orestes and his confederates, among whom is Phoebus (1147–49).[95]

The most eloquent indictment of Sparta is contained in Andromache's words when Menelaus brazenly confesses his treachery (445–53). Almost endless minor details could be cited to show the great care which has been taken to vilify the Spartans and Phoebus at every opportunity. Orestes, for instance, is usually called the son of Agamemnon, as we should expect; but he first introduces himself as the son of Agamemnon and Clytemnestra (884), and later the Messenger once calls him merely the son of Clytemnestra (1115), obviously to remind the spectator of his matricide. Orestes more than once is made to refer to the slaughter of his mother, furthermore, and to dwell upon the disgrace which he has suffered because of this act (971–81; 999). The chorus are horrified at the thought of a divinity's commanding matricide (1027–36). This subject is especially effective for the purpose of the play, since it vilifies both Orestes and Phoebus.[96]

The marital difficulties of Neoptolemus' household are exploited primarily as a means of attacking Menelaus, Hermione, Helen, and Spartan morals in general. This attack is carried out with some subtlety. When the distracted Hermione appears, for instance, it is with garments loose and revealing charms that should be decorously hidden (832)—an illustration of the Spartan custom which Peleus has previously condemned (598), though her state of mind may furnish some excuse here. Perhaps Hermione's willingness to go away with Orestes, who is in love with her and with whom she has perhaps been corresponding,[97] is intended as an illustration of what Peleus has said about her mother Helen and about girls being similar to their mothers. The play cannot be considered a serious handling of the question of bigamy; for Andromache, the character which the author wishes to present sympathetically, is on the wrong side of this question, and here the chorus must support the side of Hermione though they despise her as an individual (464–93).

No other play of Euripides is so severe in its criticism of women. Hermione, somewhat out of character perhaps, advocates their harem-like seclusion (943–53). This suggestion, which approaches Athenian practice, sounds strange coming from the author of the *Medea;* but the political purpose of the *Andromache* demands criticism of the emancipated women of Sparta and unqualified praise of Attic conservatism.[98] These pronouncements, therefore, can hardly be taken as the frank and honest expression of Euripides' own ideas. The whole play has been directed toward one goal, and not only unity but even free opinion—always dearer to Euripides—has been sacrificed to this end. But we can accept as sincere and sound doctrine at least the fulminations of Peleus against marriage with the daughter of an evil woman regardless of the dowry which she may bring with her (619–23; cf. 1186–93). The repetition of this idea as the last spoken lines of the play gives it such emphasis that one must conclude that it is seriously intended as one generalization of the tragedy. The actions of Hermione also, like those of Helen before her, have forcefully illustrated this truth.

6. *HECUBA*

(Possibly about 425 B.C.)

The *Hecuba* attempts to combine tragic suffering with a somewhat melodramatic plot of revenge. It is not a very successful play.

Discussion.—Euripides himself is perhaps the best critic of the *Hecuba,* for in his *Trojan Women* he has taken essentially the same situation and has made a much more powerful play. He has there corrected the weaknesses of the *Hecuba,* or at least he has better exploited its latent possibilities. Indeed the *Trojan Women* could almost be called the revised edition of the *Hecuba.*[99]

The formal structure of the *Hecuba* has been worked out with care and shows a considerable degree of unity. The ghost of Polydorus speaks the prologue—the importance of proper burial from the ancient point of view nicely motivates his appearance. He foretells the coming sacrifice of Polyxena and Hecuba's discovery of his own corpse. This foretelling along with Hecuba's ominous dream lends some feeling of inevitability to these two episodes, and their external juxtaposition from the very beginning of the play obscures and excuses the lack of causal connection between them. Indeed this juxtaposition is skillfully maintained throughout the first part of the play. Polyxena refers to her brother with pathetic optimism, and the slave who finds his corpse has been sent for water with which to wash the body of Polyxena. Still, the unity of these incidents is only a specious one. But the discovery of the corpse is the direct cause of Hecuba's plot for revenge.

This later development of the play comes as a startling surprise. Since there was no legendary tradition to jeopardize this effect—the whole story of Polydorus and Polymestor seems to be the invention of Euripides[100]—the poet is allowed free rein, and he takes full advantage of this. The omniscient prologue has given absolutely no hint of any such development, though it has introduced the name of Polymestor and the general background. When Hecuba explains her plan for vengeance, furthermore, she does so only in vague terms. Indeed we are repeatedly led to expect the death of Polymestor himself. Agamemnon assumes that this is to be the vengeance (877), and Hecuba seems to intimate as much both to Agamemnon (886–87) and to those who know her purpose when she is addressing Polymestor himself with her cruel irony (1006). The chorus too assume as much after Polymestor has been lured within the tent (1024–32). Such false foreshadowing is almost unique in Greek tragedy.[101]

The *Hecuba* fails to achieve great tragic pathos, however, for various reasons. It has an unduly large number of persuasive speeches and debates.[102] At times these are awkwardly introduced, though they are brilliantly executed compositions and filled with quotable epigrammatic sententiae. Most famous are the lines in which Persuasion is described as the Queen of mortals (814–19). These very characteristics made the *Hecuba* a favorite play with later rhetoricians. It was one of the three plays chosen in Byzantine times to represent Euripides, along with the *Phoenissae* and the *Orestes,* and it was then one of the most frequently read Greek tragedies. Its popularity extended into the Renaissance.[103] But this intellectuality weighs heavily upon the play and does not allow the emotions the full sweep that they deserve.[104]

The various episodes of the *Trojan Women* are in themselves much more effective than those of the *Hecuba.* Polyxena is a colorless figure compared to Cassandra. The union of Cassandra and Agamemnon becomes almost sordid in the *Hecuba,* whereas it is dreadfully tragic in the *Trojan Women.* Cassandra's prediction of the death of Agamemnon, furthermore, is more natural and far more impressive than the very crude pronouncements of Polymestor.[105] The purposes of tragic irony, also, are much better served by having this prediction come near the beginning of the play rather than in the last lines.[106]

The child Astyanax and his mother Andromache have a far greater appeal than Polydorus, and the inclusion of Astyanax' execution within the action of the play creates more pathos than the mere discovery of the corpse of Polydorus. The appearance of Helen, too, is an improvement in the later play. The various maledictions pronounced against her in the *Hecuba* are not very effective. Vilification of Helen was always a favorite topic with Euripides, but as a subject it deserved the serious treatment that it received in the trilogy of which the *Trojan Women* was the final play. Helen there becomes the antagonist of Hecuba, and their clash is far more significant in the tragedy of the fallen Trojan queen than the clash of Hecuba with the essentially extraneous Polymestor in the present play. The final scene of the *Hecuba,* also, is immeasurably weaker than the impressive finale of the *Trojan Women.*

Most important of all—but closely connected with the role of Helen—is Euripides' interpretation of the action. In the *Hecuba* no profound interpretation of the war or perhaps of anything else is offered. The play opens on the note, "How are the mighty fallen!" But at the precise mid-point of the play, Polydorus' body is brought in, and now the theme becomes that of vengeance. The spectacular action which follows is not consonant with the spirit of profound and hopeless grief which has characterized the first part of the play and which is maintained so successfully throughout the *Trojan Women.* Some critics see a causal connection here—grief drives Hecuba to an inhumanly cruel vengeance. But this is at least doubtful, and there is nothing especially barbaric about her vengeance. Almost any number of parallels could be cited from Greek legend: Ajax' attempted vengeance on the Greeks at Troy, Creusa's on Ion, not to mention the far more barbaric vengeance of Atreus on Thyestes or the horrors of civil strife which actually occurred at Corcyra and at Athens during Euripides' own lifetime. Hecuba's act is comparable to Medea's vengeance on Creon and his daughter, but not at all to Medea's slaughter of her own children. The "law" of vengeance was extremely severe in ancient times even among the Greeks.

The success of Hecuba's vengeance, furthermore, gives the end of the play a note of triumph for the Trojan queen. The play approaches the spirit of heroic comedy. This is not the spirit to which the figure of Hecuba most naturally lends itself. Her tragedy is stark and terrible; and it should be, as in the *Trojan Women,* unrelieved.

7. *CYCLOPS.* A SATYR-PLAY

(Possibly about 423 B.C.)

Since there is no information concerning the original production of this play, and since this is the only complete satyr-play preserved, no very reliable criteria exist for dating it.[107] Its comments on the Trojan War and Helen are similar to those in such plays as the *Trojan Women.*

The satyr-play.—During the fifth century at Athens, a tragic poet was usually required to present a series of three tragedies followed by one satyr-play. The chorus of such a play always consisted of sportive satyrs. These with their "father," the drunken old Silenus, obviously connected the play with the god Dionysus, as did their gay revels and their very frankly and indecently expressed delight in the joys of wine and love. The custom of following tragedies by such a play may have arisen after tragedies had become wholly serious and after a need had begun to be felt for re-establishing a close connection in subject matter and in tone between drama and the god in whose honor dramatic festivals were given.[108] The production of such a play also offered variety and relief, which were doubtless very welcome to the spectator after some five hours of serious and often depressing tragedy. The variety was probably welcome also to the poet. At least, the addition of the satyr-play gives a completeness to Greek tragedy and its poets which is typical of Greek art and literature and of the Greek way of life. No one can wholly appreciate the profundity of Aeschylus or the dignity of Sophocles or the thoughtfulness of Euripides until he has smiled at the playful fantasy and laughed at the indecency of their satyr-plays.

The satyr-play exhibits some resemblance to Aristophanic comedy. Both delight in gay revels, frank indecencies, and comic goriness (cf. *Cyclops* 234–40). Both show their connection with Dionysiac fertility rites by the use of the phallus, worn by Silenus (*Cyclops* 169) and by the chorus in the satyr-play but only by the actors in Old Comedy. Both types of plays have little regard for plausibility and move with careless rapid progression. The language of Euripides' *Cyclops* is essentially the diction of tragedy but contains colloquialisms and slang such as frequently occur in Old Comedy. The case is very much the same with the meter. Satire is a main feature in both genres. An extant fragment of a satyr-play of Euripides attacks the excessive emphasis on athletics in Greece with the directness of a parabasis of Aristophanes;[109] but the covert satire of men and their ways found in the *Cyclops* more closely resembles that of later comedy, such as the thoughtful skepticism of Onesimus in the last scene of Menander's *Arbitration.* In subject matter, of course, satyr-plays differ radically from the political comedies of Aristophanes. But there were other types of comedy, we must remember. Mythological travesty was a favorite subject with the Sicilian Epicharmus, the "father of comedy," and it was used at least occasionally by the contemporaries of Euripides and Aristophanes. It may be that the satyr-play bore other resemblances to the comedies of Epicharmus and to later mythological travesties. In atmosphere, satyr-plays are more bucolic than Old Comedy, since satyrs are naturally rustic creatures. But the greatest difference between the satyr-play and Old Comedy is the very basic difference in structure.

Structure.—In form the *Cyclops* shows no resemblance to Old Comedy. It is basically the same as tragedy, but its choral odes are much less elaborate and usually lack the responsion so characteristic of tragedy.[110] Four choral songs, such as they are, divide the play into five sections. The length of the whole (709 lines) is much less than that of any extant Greek comedy or tragedy. The play opens with a brief monologue-prologue in the usual Euripidean style. This is followed by the entrance of the chorus with a responsive song (parodos). The first episode quickly introduces Odysseus, and the dramatic action begins. Complications set in when the Cyclops surprises Silenus and Odysseus trafficking in his goods. Here the amusing lies of Silenus lead to a "trial" scene like those in many of Euripides' tragedies. The episode closes with the condemnation of Odysseus and his foreboding prayer to Athena and Zeus. A choral song follows which is usually considered not to have responsion.[111]

The second episode, if it may be called such, opens with Odysseus' report on the slaughter and consumption of two of his companions. He also divulges his plan for vengeance—making the Cyclops drunk and blinding him. A series of choral anapests are now followed by an exchange of verses with the tipsy Cyclops.[112] The Cyclops has been brought on stage here merely for illustration and amusement, since the scene has no effect on the dramatic action except to dissuade the Cyclops from calling on his friends—a threatened complication that has received some notice earlier (445–46). When this simple difficulty has been resolved—extreme simplicity characterizes the play throughout—Silenus and the Cyclops recline on the greensward and continue their drinking bout. Finally the Cyclops becomes amorously inclined toward his cup-bearer, the hideous and drunken old Silenus, whom he has mistaken for Ganymede, the beautiful young cupbearer of Zeus. The episode ends with their retirement and the prayer of Odysseus for success in his intrigue. After a choral song that has no responsion, Odysseus returns and tries to persuade the satyrs to fulfill their promise of helping him in his dangerous task. But they are of the opinion that discretion is much better than valor, and Odysseus is forced to make shift without them. His absence within is covered by a lyric so short that it could hardly be regarded as constituting another division of the action. The blinded Cyclops now comes on for the amusing scene of head-bumping as Odysseus and the satyrs make their escape. In his final lines, the Cyclops, like a *deus ex machina,* foretells the future wanderings of Odysseus.

Discussion.—The *Cyclops* is a travesty of the tale of Odysseus and Polyphemus as told in the *Odyssey* (9. 105–566). This subject had been introduced into drama by Epicharmus, and it is probable that the satyr-play of Aristias and a comedy, *Odysseuses,* by Cratinus also preceded the *Cyclops* of Euripides. Various changes have been made in the story by Euripides or these predecessors. Silenus and the satyrs have been added. The action has been condensed into a single day instead of extending over several days, and consequently only two of Odysseus' companions are devoured. The huge stone used to block the mouth of the cave in the story in the *Odyssey,* furthermore, has been omitted, and the escape from the cave is not made underneath the sheep. These last details have been changed doubtless to facilitate dramatic presentation, and also because Odysseus' escape hanging beneath a ram would have done injury to the dignity of his character as here portrayed. True to the precept of Horace (*Ars Poetica* 225–33), Odysseus in this play, like an ancient "matron ordered to dance at a religious festival," very distinctly retains his dignity even in this rude company. The satyrs and Silenus may indulge in various indecent jests, and the Cyclops may make an utter fool of himself in more ways than one; but Odysseus refuses to play the coward and invariably retains something of the heroic in language as well as actions.

In regard to the incidents, we may note also that Polyphemus in the *Odyssey* is blinded because the huge stone blocks the exit of the cave and Odysseus and his men could never get out if the Cyclops were slain. In this play, however, there is no reason for not slaying the Cyclops, but the blinding is retained because it was the tradition and because it makes possible the very amusing scene of head-bumping at the end of the play.

The *Cyclops* is a delightful little play. It is rich in quiet humor punctuated occasionally by boisterous laughter. (Both humor and laughter are sadly clouded in some translations.) Its spirit throughout is one of delicate travesty. But just as Odysseus still remains the Homeric hero in spite of his undignified surroundings, so the poet still remains Euripides. The play is not all light fancy. Even the barbarian Cyclops is made to scoff at a war waged over one indecent woman and to hold forth against the gods (and indirectly against men and their materialism) like a skeptic philosopher. Odysseus, furthermore, describes the devastating effects of the war upon the conquering Greeks in lines that might well have been inserted in the *Trojan Women* (*Cyclops* 304–7). The hand that strikes so hard in that tragedy cannot resist the temptation of at least a filip in this satyr-play.

8. *HERACLES*

(Perhaps about 422 B.C.)

Like the *Heracleidae* and the *Suppliants,* the *Heracles* is a play with a political purpose. Euripides is depicting the kinship (1154), mutual obligations, and noble friendship of the Attic Theseus and the Doric Heracles. Since the tone of the play with respect to Thebes is so favorable (1281–82), it may be that this play was written in an atmosphere of reconciliation before the possibility of an alliance of Argos and Thebes had become evident and perhaps before the Thebans had treacherously destroyed Panactum, thus enraging the Athenians. But the *Heracles* is also a study of distress and courage with universal significance, and its poetry at times rises to sublime heights.

Lycus' mortal threat to the family of Heracles and the bringing of Heracles to Athens near the end of his life are both fictions of Euripides. It may be that Sophocles' *Trachiniae* was designed in part to correct Euripides' novel version and to reassert the established legend concerning the death of Heracles.[113]

The extant *Mad Heracles* of Seneca follows the main lines of Euripides' play, but the theme of the glorification of Theseus has been excised. Robert Browning translated Euripides' play, "the perfect piece," in his *Aristophanes' Apology.*

Discussion.—The dramatic structure of the *Heracles* is an unusual one. It has frequently been criticized as lacking unity, but such criticism obscures more than it reveals. The appropriateness of the material chosen and of the poet's purpose may be questioned, but the skill shown in dramatizing the material is beyond doubt. The play does consist of two parts: Heracles' rescue of his family from the tyrant Lycus, and Theseus' rescue of Heracles after his madness and destruction of his wife and children. But the contrast of these two parts and the emotional variation are themselves the heart of the drama. Euripides' primary purpose is to present Heracles' being rescued *de profundis* by the loyal Theseus, just as Theseus himself had been rescued from the less appalling depths of the underworld by Heracles. To emphasize the profound distress of Heracles most effectively, he must be presented first in the glory of success and victory. Only thus can the great pathos and irony of his fall be appreciated.

Heracles, according to the legendary tradition, was an innocent victim of the wrath of Hera. His great success led Hera to destroy him. This motivation, though divine and external, befits Euripides' purpose; for the most annihilating discouragement is the conviction that one has been ruined through no fault of his own but by the injustice of Heaven. A wholly innocent victim, however, can normally be effective in tragedy only as a powerful indictment against this world and the divinities who are supposed to direct it.[114] But such an interpretation here would detract too much from Euripides' purpose; for this, if for no other reason, it is rejected in the lofty passage near the end of the play where Heracles renounces the legendary tales of the sins of the gods (1340-46). Though an innocent victim of the most appalling punishment, Heracles is made to have the courage to face adversity through the friendship of Theseus and through his own nobility.

Euripides has taken great pains to knit the play as closely as possible without compromising his basic purpose. The inestimable value of friendship is the last note of Amphitryon's prologue, and the need for courage in adversity, his last note before the entrance of the chorus. Courage in adversity is also the theme of Megara when she determines to die willingly and nobly. These moral themes are maintained throughout the play.

Preparation for the entrances of Heracles and Theseus, the main characters, is carried as far as it plausibly can be. For Heracles, this is wholly adequate. His return is the prayer and only hope of the suppliants from the very first. It is most pathetically pictured in the winsome lines of Megara describing the anxiety of his children (71-79). The choral song celebrating his great deeds like those of a cult hero, furthermore, furnishes the most magnificent emotional preparation. For the entrance of Theseus, however, no such elaborate preparation is possible. Heracles briefly relates the rescue of Theseus, who, he adds, has gone home to Athens, joyful in his escape from the underworld. But at least Theseus has been given excellent motivation for his entrance when he does appear: he has come with armed force to support Heracles against Lycus.

The consideration of the children's fate during the first scenes of the play, though failing to suggest the manner of their eventual death, is still pertinent to this death, and the pathos built up over their fate is not lost. Those of the audience acquainted with the legend may well have expected the children to be slain by Heracles, for this was an established item in the tradition.[115] Even to spectators unacquainted with this part of the legend, the second appearance of the children, now dressed and wreathed as victims for death, was doubtless too ill an omen to be dismissed by their immediate rescue: these children were consecrated to death.

The pathos of the scene of rescue can be appreciated fully only if the scene is visualized. Weeping and trembling, Megara and her children cling to the garments of Heracles as, with pathetic dramatic irony, he says that his homecoming is fairer to them than his departure and that he will draw those clinging to his robes like a ship towing skiffs, for all men alike have this in common, that they love their children! This whole scene, of course, is in a way preparation for Heracles' slaughter of his children.

The ensuing choral lyric on youth and age is one of the most beautiful in Euripides and artistically one of his most perfect poems.[116] The chorus have repeatedly complained of their helpless old age (the previous stasimon ended on this theme, 440–41); and now they are rejoicing at the rescue effected by the youthful might of Heracles. All this subtly adds pathos to the coming action. But there is a deeper meaning to this lyric, perhaps, which emerges in the second strophe. Euripides himself "on his sixtieth birthday," so to speak, and now, as he thinks, an old man, professes his zest and his faith in a life devoted to the Graces and to the Muses—to enlightenment and to poetry and the theater—a life which, he intimates with obvious truth, he would be allowed to repeat if the gods were wise.[117]

The shift from joy to sorrow at the climax of the play is a violent one, but the action here is continuous. The appearance of Iris and Lyssa should be viewed not as a second prologue but as a very unusual and dramatic means of reporting to chorus and audience the all-important action that is taking place off the scene.[118] The use of divinities is wholly warranted, because Heracles is being presented as the innocent victim of Hera and because madness in ancient times was conceived of as the visitation of Heaven. Iris explains this visitation as the consequence of Heracles' superhuman success, and in the external structure of the play—a point that the play's critics usually overlook—the madness and its sequel are presented as the catastrophe of the previous action. The last stasimon of the play is the joyful celebration of the death of Lycus, ending with the ironic implication that Justice still reigns in Heaven. The scene of Iris and Lyssa and all that follows is technically a single section, the exodos, of the play. Though incidental lyrics occur three times in this section, the action is very rapid and no pause is allowed for a complete choral song. Somewhat similar is the structure of Aeschylus' *Agamemnon,* where the final stasimon occurs just after Agamemnon has entered the palace and the last six hundred thirty-five lines constitute the final section of the play. Thus the madness is the reversal of fortune which overwhelms Heracles at the height of his glory.

9. *SUPPLIANTS*

(Perhaps 421 B.C.)

The *Suppliants* seems to be designed to remind Argos of her obligations to Athens and of her ancient enmity toward Thebes. The play's bitter criticism of Thebes and somewhat sharp tone toward Argos suggest that it may have been written during those months of 421 B.C. when an alliance between Argos and Boeotia, Athens' bitterest enemy, seemed a distinct possibility.[119] The play is also an encomium of Athens as champion of the oppressed. Although these purposes are well served, the play is an inferior production.

Discussion.—These same events were dramatized by Aeschylus in his *Eleusinians.* The use of such material, the play's tendency to become a threnody over the dead, its elaborate pageantry, and its effusive praise of Athens all suggest that Euripides is closely following Aeschylus. We are told that in Aeschylus, however, Theseus secured the bodies not by a successful battle but by parley and persuasion.[120] The events are related also in Herodotus, who has an Athenian say (9. 27, Rawlinson) : "Again, when the Argives led their troops with Polyneices against Thebes, and were slain and refused burial, it is our boast that we went out against the Cadmeians, recovered the bodies, and buried them at Eleusis in our own territory." Here too a battle is assumed, and the work of Herodotus was probably published before the *Suppliants* was produced. This old legend had taken on new meaning in 424 B.C., when the Thebans, winning a battle over the Athenians at Delium, had at first refused to allow them to bury their dead.[121]

Throughout the *Suppliants,* the poet seems to vacillate between enlightenment and prejudiced enthusiasm. Theseus at first analyzes the cause of Adrastus with searching and passionless logic. He all too convincingly concludes that Adrastus made a great mistake in undertaking an expedition against Thebes contrary to the will of the gods, that the young men associated with him were motivated by ambition and greed, and that now there is no adequate reason for Athens to undertake a war in behalf of the Argives. But when his mother Aethra makes a passionate appeal with the age-old phrases about religion, honor, justice, and the preservation of the Hellenic way of life, Theseus, though he still recognizes the correctness of his logic, can no longer resist. He has earlier pointed out that Adrastus gave way to emotion rather than to logic (161), and now he does the same himself. This, it is true, is man as he is and not as he ought to be; but the inconsistency seems to detract from the dramatic effectiveness. In defense of the poet it may be stated that the political purpose of the play requires that Theseus undertake the cause of the Argives primarily out of gracious generosity and that religion and the age-old phrases be taken very seriously.

Another inconsistency is found in the attitude toward young leaders. Theseus himself is praised as a young and goodly leader (190–91). Some scholars think that Euripides in the figure of Theseus is indirectly praising Alcibiades, who was now rapidly rising to power.[122] And yet Theseus' own fulminations against rash young men who are interested in self-aggrandizement and personal gain read very much like Thucydides' subsequent description of the motives of Alcibiades in undertaking the Sicilian expedition.[123] Near the end of the play, furthermore, Theseus seems to be not unfavorably disposed toward these same rash young leaders of the expedition (929), or at least he allows Adrastus to praise them for modesty and altruism.

The attitude of the poet toward war also seems to be confused. The decision of Theseus, which has already been discussed, is pertinent here; but much more important are the speeches of Adrastus in which the folly of resorting to war and the wisdom of arbitration to settle international disputes are stressed.[124] These pronouncements may be vaguely directed toward the Athenians as a plea to make and keep a permanent peace. But the primary purpose of the play cannot be the advocacy of pacifism; for, if this were so, Sparta (187) and Thebes would not be vilified, and persuasion, not force, would be used by Theseus to recover the bodies. At the end of the play, furthermore, the sons of the fallen chiefs along with the son of Adrastus look forward to vengeance. Their plan is given divine approval by Athena, as we might expect, because this second Argive expedition was very famous in legend and was wholly successful. The political purpose of the play made it advisable after dwelling so long on an Argive defeat also to flatter the Argives by reminding them of their final victory over Thebes.

The lengthy discussion of democracy by Theseus and the Herald from Thebes is not surprising in Euripides. It not only flatters the Athenian audience; it makes a very important contribution to the political message to Argos, for it calls attention to the basic hostility between the forms of government of Argos and Thebes and the basic compatibility between those of Argos and Athens. Incidentally, this discussion also furnishes a good opportunity for abusing Thebes; indeed the very occurrence of the discussion is cleverly laid to the impudent talkativeness of the Herald (456–62).

Several minor technical features of the play are noteworthy. The opening tableau of suppliants must have appeared somewhat trite to Euripides' audience, as he uses it also in the *Heracleidae* and the *Heracles,* not to mention the single suppliant of the *Andromache* and the later *Helen.* In the *Suppliants,* however, the whole chorus is on the scene and must have presented an arresting spectacle. The second entrance of Theseus in abrupt conversation with his herald is extraordinarily natural and effective (381). This technique is repeated later in the play (837), but it is so unusual for Greek tragedy that some scholars have suggested emendations to soften the abruptness.

The episode of Evadne and Iphis has often been criticized as extraneous or at least abrupt. It might be considered a minor plot, but it seems strictly pertinent to the theme of the suffering of the Argives. The chorus represent the mothers of the slain; Evadne and Iphis, the wives and fathers. The appearance of Evadne is admittedly abrupt, though it has been given as much preparation as plausibly possible by repeated references to Capaneus. This most notoriously wicked of all the seven, furthermore, has been rehabilitated into an ideal gentleman and citizen.[125]

The portrayal of the grief of the chorus is wholly compatible with the genius of Euripides and is doubtless the best feature of the play. The character of Theseus, however, is not tragic in any sense of the word. Again we note the spiritual dichotomy of the play. But this dichotomy and the various inconsistencies pointed out are after all not very conspicuous. Indeed, the inconsistencies are no greater than men "as they are" actually show in regard to war; but the poet's idealization of Theseus and his praise of Athens make it unlikely that he is deliberately depicting men "as they are." He has simply fallen into the same inconsistencies himself, inconsistencies inherent in idealizations and glorifications. Euripides was too enlightened and too honest to write a play successfully for any purpose beyond exhibiting the truths inherent in the material. It is unfortunate that he undertook an ulterior motive in writing the *Suppliants*.

10. *ION*

(Possibly about 417 B.C.)

This melodramatic play, like the *Iphigenia in Tauris* and the *Helen*, should be read without any previous knowledge of the story, for the events covered were vague or unknown to the original audience, and suspense and surprise are important elements of the drama. The plot is one of intrigue and discovery of identity.

Discussion.—The story of this play is designed to establish Ion, the founder of the Ionian Greeks according to late legend, as the son of Apollo, who was the patron god of the Ionian Greeks. The story is designed also to account for the fact that no such divine ancestry was commonly attributed to Ion. Further, the play indicates that Dorus and Achaeus, the titular founders of the other Greeks, were mere mortals and that all were originally Athenians! This genealogy, though obviously false, was intended to stress the close kinship of the Attic and Ionian Greeks and to justify the Athenian claims of empire over the Ionians (cf. *Ion* 1584–85).

No indication of the divine ancestry of Ion is found in any previous writer. Indeed, in Euripides' lost *Melanippe the Wise*, Ion was considered the son of Xuthus.[126] Sophocles wrote a *Creusa* and perhaps an *Ion*, but the dates and stories of these plays are unknown. Even if the divine origin of Ion is not original with Euripides, the incidents of the present play probably are original.

This particular task of glorification was not compatible with Euripides' enlightenment. He himself had frequently made sport of legends of divine ancestry,[127] and even now when he wishes to use one he cannot treat it with the ethical naïveté which is proper to such stories and the periods when they thrive. He must consider the moral implications. These, of course, are all against the divinity and involve Euripides in a curious medley of naïve myth and enlightened criticism. His skepticism becomes embarrassing and almost comic at the end of the play, where Ion, in a plainly marked aside to Creusa, is very humanly inclined to think that Creusa's talk of Apollo is only a pretty tale to cover a maiden's sin. (But Ion's skepticism also furnishes a good motivation for the *deus ex machina*.) Many critics have mistaken Euripides' own confusion in this play for a subtle attack upon popular religion. But the *Ion* is obviously not a polemical play; it is rather an exciting piece for the theater and a patriotic glorification of early Athenian history.[128]

The great beauty of the opening songs of Ion, like that of the following choral lyrics, must have had a powerful and somewhat nostalgic effect upon those members of the original audience who had made a pilgrimage to Delphi, as it has upon those modern readers who have done so; for Delphi is one of the most majestic sites in the world, with the crags of Parnassus and the eagles of Zeus—still there—standing out above, and the olive groves stretching down the precipitous sides of the mountain below. The genuine local color contained in these songs is extraordinary, for the setting of almost all Greek tragedies is vaguely generalized.[129] Critics who think this play a serious attack upon Apollo—or anything else—must be strangely impervious to the mood and poetic beauty of these early scenes.

Romantic and sentimental pathos dominates the play throughout. This is seen especially in the tale of Creusa, told four or five times in the course of the play, and in the wistful longing of Ion to know his mother. His most pathetic musings are those in the final section of the play when the Priestess has given him the cradle. This sentimental romanticism accounts in part for the very high esteem in which many modern critics hold the play. Ion has been called the most appealing youth of Athenian poetry and has been compared to the inimitable youths of Greek art.[130]

The most interesting technical feature of the play is its suspense. The prologue must be spoken by a divinity, since the true identity of Ion as Creusa's child must be revealed so that the audience may appreciate the very elaborate ironies which characterize almost every scene. The manner in which Ion's recognition by Creusa is to be accomplished, however, remains wholly uncertain; no hint is given of the exciting complications that are to develop. Indeed, one line of the prologue indicates that Ion is not to be recognized by Creusa until he has come to Athens (71). This is the divine plan (1566–67), and the intentions of Xuthus seem to coincide with it (657–60). These lines of the prologue seem designed deliberately to mislead the audience—an almost unique instance of such technique in Greek tragedy. Even the experienced playgoer, who would naturally infer from the remainder of the prologue that the play is to be one of recognition, must have been puzzled. Euripides apparently wishes to give the impression that the course of the action, though largely directed by Apollo, is not unalterably determined beforehand, and that the interference of the chorus when they reveal Xuthus' secret to Creusa changes everything and upsets the plans of the god.

There is nothing misleading or incorrect, however, about the statement in the prologue that the relationship of Ion to Creusa and Apollo is to be kept secret. Although Athena at the end of the play reveals this relationship before the chorus, it is never to become known to Xuthus and the world in general. The presence of the chorus here is admittedly embarrassing, but it is unavoidable. Besides, the chorus is thoroughly devoted to Creusa and her cause. That this relationship should be kept secret is required for an entirely happy solution of the play. It is required also as an explanation of history's failure to record that Ion, the founder of the Ionian Greeks, was the son of Apollo.

At the end of his prologue Hermes expresses his intention of retiring to the grove near by in order to see the fulfillment of Ion's destiny—the god himself is subject to the suspense of anticipation!

Suspense is deftly maintained after Ion has been recognized by Xuthus. First of all, the youth is reluctant to leave his present happy life, although some preparation for his eventual willingness to go to Athens has been made in his earlier thought of a change in fortune (153) and in his praise of Athens and his interest in Athenian history (262–98). After he has finally been won over, the suspense is given a new impetus by his great anxiety over the identity of his mother (563–65). Creusa has previously been introduced. The audience is presumably more interested in her than in Xuthus and is looking forward to the solution of her problem. Concern over Creusa's reaction to Xuthus' recognition of Ion is expressed by the chorus, by Ion—who even suggests the possibility of being slaughtered or poisoned by her devices—and, finally, by Xuthus himself (567–660). These thoughts all foreshadow further serious complication. But the episode of this first recognition very properly ends on Ion's conjectures concerning his mother and on his hope that she may be an Athenian.

The choral song which follows is wholly devoted to the misfortune which Xuthus' discovery of a son has brought upon Creusa. The chorus determine to reveal the secret to their mistress even though they have been enjoined to silence with a threat of death (666–67).[131] They curse Xuthus and pray for the death of Ion.

The plan for slaying Ion adds greatly to the tension of the play. Like the various intrigues in the other melodramatic plays of Euripides, it is conceived by the woman involved. This situation, wherein one unwittingly plots against a close kinsman, is a favorite motive with Euripides and is declared by Aristotle to be the most effective tragic situation.[132] It should here be noted especially that Creusa has not only a lethal potion of the Gorgon's blood but a curative one as well (1005). This is according to the legend of the Gorgon's blood,[133] but the inclusion of the curative potion here seems to be designed to suggest that Creusa would be able to bring Ion back to life even after he had drunk the poison—conceivably another instance of false foreshadowing in the play. At least, complete uncertainty as to the development of the plot is maintained.

The possibility of Creusa's committing suicide, also, has been suggested (763); and the chorus now declare that she will slay herself rather than be ruled by a foreigner—she is a true Athenian! All this adds to the danger, the uncertainty, and the chaotic excitement at the climax, which is one of the most thrilling and melodramatic in extant Greek tragedy.

Various aspects of the *Ion* are suggestive of New Comedy. Intrigue and recognition by trinkets are there stock incidents, although comic intrigue is not so serious as the intrigue in the *Ion.* Indeed the whole story of this play comes very close in its essential features to that of the *Arbitration* of Menander, in which the illegitimate child of the wife is finally recognized as the child of the husband also. In Euripides' play, Ion first surmises that this, or something approaching this, is the solution of his own ancestry (1468–69). The sentimental irony of the *Ion,* also, resembles that of the *Arbitration.* The tone of the *Ion,* though more serious than that of a comedy, never perhaps reaches that of genuine tragedy. Some scenes verge on the comic, as when Xuthus attempts to embrace Ion. Lastly, the end of the play is written in the lively trochaic meter. So, as a rule, are the final lines of the comedies of Plautus and Terence.[134] The *Ion,* therefore, definitely foreshadows the developments in drama during the subsequent century.

11. *TROJAN WOMEN (TROADES)*

(415 B.C.)

An obscure poet named Xenocles won first prize with three tragedies, *Oedipus, Lycaon, Bacchae,* and a satyric drama, *Athamas.* Euripides placed second with his *Alexander, Palamedes, Trojan Women,* and a satyric drama, *Sisyphus.* These plays of Euripides were definitely connected in subject matter and doubtless constituted a type of tetralogy. Although the *Trojan Women* alone has been preserved, the other tragedies can be reconstructed to a certain extent. Indeed a knowledge of these other tragedies is essential to any sound interpretation of the *Trojan Women,* and critics have frequently gone astray through neglect of them.

The subject matter of the *Trojan Women* is very similar to that of the *Hecuba,* and incidents from both plays are combined in Seneca's extant *Trojan Women.*

Alexander.—When the child Alexander (Paris) was born to Hecuba and Priam, he was exposed on Mount Ida to die because of an ominous dream of his mother. But shepherds saved and reared the child. Years later he returned to Troy, and in athletic contests dedicated to the "dead" Alexander he vanquished even Hector and Deiphobus, the foremost princes of Troy and really his brothers. Deiphobus in his anger wished to slay Alexander. Perhaps his sister Cassandra, the prophetess doomed never to be believed, also wished to slay him, for she knew that he would cause the Trojan War and the ruin of Troy. But he was recognized and accepted as a son by Priam despite her dire warnings.[135]

Palamedes.—Palamedes, the wise son of Nauplius, had revealed that the madness of Odysseus just before the Trojan War was only feigned in an effort to escape joining the expedition. Odysseus in revenge planted an amount of gold in Palamedes' tent and forged a letter ostensibly from Priam. Palamedes attempted to defend himself in a trial scene, in which Agamemnon perhaps did not distinguish himself as a judge. Palamedes was then stoned to death by the army as a traitor. The chorus of this play, like that of the *Trojan Women,* may have consisted of Trojan captives.[136] Certainly the action was interpreted from a point of view sympathetic to Palamedes and inimical to Odysseus and the Peloponnesian leaders of the Greeks.

Sisyphus.—The precise subject of this satyric drama is unknown, but Odysseus—the "villain" of the *Palamedes* and of the *Trojan Women*—was frequently considered the bastard of Sisyphus.

Discussion.—The *Trojan Women* is a stark and unrelieved tragic spectacle of tremendous power, a play in which choral drama and the poetic gift of Euripides are seen at their best. Few literary works so devastate the martial spirit; few have so effectively shown the futility of war and its annihilation of victor and vanquished alike. Although the play is not without elements of patriotism, it is truly remarkable that such a play was produced by the Athenian state in the midst of a bitter war. The Athenians had just finished the siege and barbarically cruel destruction of Melos, and now they were soon to send out their great but ill-fated expedition to Sicily. The whole trilogy has an obvious bearing on this contemporary situation, but precisely how much if any allegory is intended is a matter of dispute.[137]

The *Trojan Women* would be termed a play of simple plot according to the Aristotelian classification, for it has no reversal of fortune or recognition but, like the *Prometheus,* moves directly from the tragic to the more tragic. According to modern terminology, it is a play without plot. When read, it may appear somewhat disjointed and episodic, for the various incidents do not regularly follow in the relation of cause and effect. In its original context as the third play of a trilogy, however, the various incidents must certainly have seemed pertinent.

Even as an individual play, the *Trojan Women* exhibits a certain unity, and from the technical point of view the devices used to achieve this specious unity are among the play's most interesting features. First of these are the continuous presence of Hecuba throughout the action and the repeated appearances of Talthybius. The bracketing of the scene with Menelaus and Helen by the two scenes dealing with Astyanax also tends somewhat to knit the action together. Meticulous preparation, furthermore, is made for each episode, and the tone and the spirit of the action and especially of the choral songs are consistent throughout. If the subject of the play is considered to be the miseries of Hecuba and the horrors of war, every scene is distinctly pertinent.

The prologue, like that of the *Alcestis,* casts a certain irony over the whole action of the play, for it foretells the eventual punishment of the barbaric cruelty (764) and sacrilege of the triumphant Greeks. This prelude was important also for the preceding *Palamedes,* since the wreck of the Greek fleet off Euboea was presumed to have been caused in part by Nauplius, who took vengeance for the foul murder of his son by setting false beacons, as mentioned in Euripides' *Helen* (767), to lure the fleet to the Euboean reefs.[138]

Cassandra, like Hecuba, had appeared in the *Alexander.* In the *Trojan Women* preparation for her entrance is found in Poseidon's mention of her future enforced and sacrilegious union with Agamemnon (41–44) and in the reference to the sacrilegious violation of her by Ajax, son of Oïleus (70). Hecuba, furthermore, deprecates Cassandra's coming forth from the tents; and when Talthybius appears Hecuba inquires first of Cassandra's fate. The dramatic effectiveness of Cassandra's entrance and the following eerie scene, which recalls the scene with Cassandra in Aeschylus' *Agamemnon,* can hardly be overestimated. The irony created by the revelations of the prologue is here continued. The flaming torch which Cassandra bears is ostensibly the symbol of marriage; but the torch is also the symbol of death and the symbol of frenzy. Her joy is real, though none of the other characters can appreciate it, since they do not believe her prophecies of the ruin of Agamemnon's house. Indeed, Cassandra's mad joy is so sane and reasonable that this scene might tend to relieve the stark tragedy of Hecuba, and we can easily imagine that a modern playwright would place this scene last of all and end the play on the note of poetic justice and "heroic comedy." But Euripides does not wish Hecuba's tragedy to be relieved, and hence he is careful to place this episode early in the play and not allow it to terminate with the triumphant departure of Cassandra. The second episode closes with the departure of Andromache and Astyanax and the third with the departure of Helen and Menelaus, but this first episode must continue for fifty lines after the departure of Cassandra in order that the tone of the play may swing back to Hecuba's leitmotif: "How are the mighty fallen!"

The preparation for the scene with Andromache and Astyanax is less elaborate than that for Cassandra. Andromache's fate has been told by Talthybius (273), where the disposition of Astyanax has been left in ominous silence. Hector, too, has been mentioned by Cassandra (394) and by Hecuba (493). Andromache's magnificent review of her past life and her declaration that she would prefer the fate of the dead Polyxena to the future before her are only less appealing than her pathetic farewell to her infant son.

The scene with Helen, which might at first glance seem impertinent to the sufferings of Hecuba and inconsistent with the tragic tone of the play, receives the most careful preparation and, of course, harks back to the *Alexander*. In the prologue (35) we have been told that Helen is within and that she is regarded as a prisoner. Helen is repeatedly declared to be the cause of the war,[139] though Paris is sometimes burdened with the main responsibility (597). Again and again she is damned and called a disgrace to Greece. When Menelaus enters he insists that he came to war against Troy not for a woman who deserves death but to take revenge on the man who betrayed his hospitality and stole his wife. Helen is brought forth and, in the following debate, Hecuba succeeds in condemning her as personally responsible. Menelaus now admits that Helen must have gone with Paris willingly, thus apparently placed the main guilt on her rather than on Paris. In a way this scene is the climax of the whole trilogy, therefore, and proves that one shameless woman has caused the war and all its tragedy.[140]

It is clear to the chorus (1105–9) and doubtless to Hecuba also that Menelaus will never punish Helen. Perhaps it is not too much to assume that the actor impersonating him interprets the scene so as to suggest that version of the legend according to which Menelaus actually drew his sword to slay Helen but threw it away at sight of her breasts.[141] Indeed Menelaus' admission of Helen's guilt followed by the indication that he will be too base ever to punish her damns his character more effectively than all the vituperation of the *Andromache* or the *Orestes*. This scene with Helen does not, therefore, give Hecuba even an appearance of satisfaction for her wrongs.

The final scene with the funeral of the child Astyanax and the burning of Troy sums up this tragedy of grief and annihilation with magnificent effectiveness.

12. *ELECTRA*

(Probably 413 B.C.)

This play dramatizes the same events as those of Aeschylus' *Choephoroe* and Sophocles' *Electra*. Euripides is obviously "improving" upon Aeschylus. Some modern scholars think that Sophocles' play also preceded that of Euripides. Perhaps it is more likely that Sophocles was following Euripides' general treatment of the material but was feverishly attempting to correct his moral interpretation.

Although the play of Euripides is not wholly satisfying from the moral and religious point of view, it is a powerful drama. In theatrical scenes it is not much inferior to the *Electra* of Sophocles, and in structure of plot it is superior to that play. Some critics, however, are offended by the realism of Euripides and the ordinary humanity of his characters.[142]

Source.—In rewriting the material treated by Aeschylus, Euripides doubtless had two ends in view: he wished to interpret the matricide of Orestes from his own moral point of view, and to make the characters more realistic and the action more plausible. To serve these ends he made an innovation which, though somewhat bizarre, is as melodramatic as his innovation of the secret marriage in his *Antigone* or that of the Trojan embassy in his *Philoctetes*. He here presents Electra as formally but not actually married to a poor farmer and living in a desolate spot on the borders of Argive territory. Both the marriage and the location have very important effects upon the story, and it is impossible to determine which constituted the germ of this innovation. The primary effect of the marriage is that it brings out in dramatic fashion the abuse of Electra and makes her more realistically human. She, like Orestes, has been made an exile and robbed of her patrimony. She is practically a slave (1004–10). The primary effect of the location is to make Orestes' return appear far more cautious and the whole plan of slaying the guilty pair more plausible and realistic.

In accordance with these changes, the character of the farmer, the husband of Electra, is introduced, but he retains his active role for less than one-half the play. The Old Man in a way takes the role of the Nurse in Aeschylus. Pylades is here reduced to a supernumerary, and Aegisthus is eliminated as a speaking character. Most important of all, Electra is played up into the main role of the drama. Euripides reverts to the Homeric story for certain details. Aegisthus is given more importance in the actual slaughter of Agamemnon, and the superhuman stature of the Aeschylean Clytemnestra is correspondingly reduced. Menelaus and Helen, furthermore, are said to have returned on the day of Clytemnestra's death (1278–79).

Theme.—The Dioscuri at the end of the play seem to express the interpretation of the poet when they declare that Clytemnestra deserved her punishment but Orestes should not have been her slayer. Here, as occasionally elsewhere, Euripides in viewing legendary material from the standpoint of his own enlightenment falls into difficulty; for if Aegisthus and Clytemnestra were to be punished, and if Menelaus was not present to punish them, then presumably Orestes was the only person to do so. In heroic times, there was no public machinery for the punishment of criminals. The contention of Tyndareos in the *Orestes* (500) that Clytemnestra should have been prosecuted by legal process is a bold anachronism. From the historical point of view, therefore, Euripides' solution of this problem is not satisfactory.

There are references to Orestes' matricide in various others plays of Euripides. In the *Andromache* (1036) the chorus protests against Apollo's oracle. In the *Iphigenia in Tauris,* Iphigenia calls it an ill but righteous deed (559, Potter's translation), and King Thoas protests that not even a barbarian would have done such a deed (1174).

Recognition and intrigue.—When Electra openly criticizes the devices by which Orestes is recognized in the *Choephoroe* of Aeschylus, it seems that Euripides is calling attention to the inadequacy of the means of recognition in Aeschylus. The technique of recognition in general was not easy, and its perfection required time and practice. Euripides is unquestionably much superior to the older poet in such matters, but perhaps he criticizes these details at too great length (518–46). Criticisms that are similar though less conspicuous are found in various other plays of Euripides,[143] and it may be that in this same play he again criticizes Aeschylus when the Old Man warns Orestes that he cannot simply go within the city and slay Aegisthus.

The plan for slaying Aegisthus and Clytemnestra is indeed simple in both Aeschylus and Sophocles. In Aeschylus, there is at least some subsequent complication, for the success of the plan seems threatened when the old Nurse is sent for Aegisthus and his bodyguard. In Sophocles there is no such complication, but the report of Orestes'

death has been subtly elaborated. In Euripides separate plans are
formed for the two slayings, and both are more involved and more
plausible.

The scene of reunion between Orestes and Electra is extremely
brief in Euripides as in Aeschylus. The joy of brother and sister
is sternly suppressed in order that the great task before them may be
taken up without delay. This stands out in sharp contrast to the
lengthy scene in Sophocles. Although the situation of Orestes when
the recognition takes place is there much more critical, the soft emotions
are given full play.

Discussion.—The character of Electra in Euripides is not unlike
that of Electra in Sophocles. Her whole life has been cankered with
hatred of her mother and with loathing of her persecutor, Aegisthus.
She takes an unhealthy delight in dwelling upon her unfortunate condition and displaying it to the gods. In actual production, of course,
her filthy dress, her unwashed body, her torn cheeks, and her shaven
head would accentuate her misery (146–48; 1107, etc.).

Her "marriage" to the farmer, like the rejected invitation of the
chorus to join them in a joyful celebration, obviously makes her state
more pitiable. A real marriage would have been contrary to the accepted legend in which Electra married Pylades. It would also have
been incompatible with that part of heroic dignity which the characters
of Euripides still possess. Although Orestes in a very democratic speech
(367–72) insists that nobility is entirely an individual matter and not
the result of birth, Euripides does not go all the way in breaking down
the nobility of birth.[144] The real marriage of Electra to a farmer,
even for Euripides, is inconceivable.

Electra is a much stronger character than her brother. Upon
Orestes' first entrance, he states that he is seeking his sister's aid,
and for her part she is more than willing to help in accomplishing the
death of Clytemnestra. She plans the device for the entrapment, and
she never falters in her resolve. When Orestes himself falters, she
is ready to add strength and resolution to his vacillation in a passage
that is one of the most pathetic and perhaps the most honest statement
of Orestes' dreadful task in any of the three dramatists (962–87).
Orestes cries, "Alas! How am I to slay her who bore and nourished
me?" Electra responds, "Just as she killed your father and mine."
This line of Electra is almost the same as an earlier one in which Electra
congratulates Orestes for slaying Aegisthus, "who killed your father
and mine" (885). By this repetition she effectively implies that Clytemnestra must be considered in the same category as Aegisthus.[145]
Orestes inveighs against Apollo and the thought of slaying his own

mother. Like Hamlet, Orestes wonders if it can be a fiend instead of a god who has commanded such a vengeance.[146] Electra still reassures him.

With such a scene as this in the play, there is no need of a foil like Chrysothemis in Sophocles' play to bring out the strength of Electra, nor does such a strong Electra allow any real place for Pylades in the action. Euripides' technique is at once more economical and more effective than that of Sophocles; for, after all, Sophocles' Chrysothemis is basically an extraneous character. But Euripides' technique is made possible by the weakness of his Orestes. Pylades is not needed in either Sophocles or Euripides, because he serves as the representative of Apollo and neither poet gives Apollo's command the significance which it has in Aeschylus. In some respects Sophocles' Electra appears stronger than Euripides' Electra. In Sophocles she resolves herself to slay the guilty pair if Orestes is dead, whereas, in Euripides, Electra resolves to commit suicide if Orestes is unsuccessful in his attempt against Aegisthus; but these two resolutions can hardly be compared, because the situations which elicit them are very different. In Euripides, again, Electra thinks of Orestes as a man of heroic stature and courage. She assures the Old Man that he is mistaken in thinking that Orestes returns by stealth through fear of Aegisthus.[147] A similar nice bit of characterization is found in Sophocles (1220–21), where Electra thinks of Orestes as far more a man than the youth who confronts her in the recognition scene.

At the climax of Euripides' play, Electra stands out cold and heartless. She has been quite unmoved by all that Clytemnestra has said, as is amply revealed by the diabolical irony of her own words and actions. "You will indeed sacrifice to the gods the sacrifice which you should make to them," she says as Clytemnestra goes within; "the ritual basket is at hand, and the sacrificial knife is whetted . . . ." Then, since Clytemnestra is no longer able to hear, Electra drops her ghastly irony and plainly foretells her mother's death. This passage vividly recalls the similar scene in the *Agamemnon* of Aeschylus, where Clytemnestra has enticed her husband into the palace with a similarly ironical welcome. A daughter worthy of her mother! The pictorial similarities and contrasts of these two scenes also, at least for those who had seen a production of the *Agamemnon,* must have been extremely effective.

In the actual slaying Electra grasps her brother's sword, and after the deed she takes full responsibility. But she is overwhelmed by the dreadfulness of it and suffers a complete moral collapse. Here she shows a weakness and humanity that is entirely lacking in the Sophoclean Electra; but her ordeal has been a more harrowing one, for Clytemnestra herself is here a more piteous character and Electra has taken a more intimate part in her slaughter. Even for the audience, indeed, though somewhat inured to horror after the scene wherein Orestes enters with the head of Aegisthus, the very appearance of brother and sister bespattered with their mother's blood must have been harrowing.

These characters of Euripides lack the heroic stature of those of Aeschylus or Sophocles; but they are not, as critics have often insisted, base or contemptible. Orestes returns with the intention of slaying both Aegisthus and Clytemnestra, and there is nothing unheroic about the extreme caution which he shows in the execution of his plans. True, he is so cautious that he does not reveal his identity even to the sympathetic Electra; but this merely adds plausibility and suspense to the action.[148] In Homer, Odysseus is no less cautious when he returns to his home. Orestes slays Aegisthus manfully, and his courage there is effectively contrasted with his reactions when Clytemnestra is seen approaching. Here he falters much more seriously than does Orestes in Aeschylus, and his collapse after the murder is even more complete than that of his sister. At this point he appears in his most unheroic light but not as unheroic as some translations make him— for the assignment of lines in this lyric scene is confused. The bitter reproach addressed to Electra which manuscripts and some translations assign to Orestes should, according to Murray and others, be given to the chorus (1201–5). This correction—and the responsion of the passage shows that some correction is necessary—improves the character of Orestes considerably. Euripides' play approaches melodrama at times, but there is nothing in it so melodramatic as the Sophoclean Electra's resolve herself to slay the guilty pair. If the characters of Euripides are weak, they are also human.

In Euripides' play the one character who is most strikingly different from the corresponding character in Aeschylus is Clytemnestra. She is no woman with a man's will, no figure of superhuman stature, but a very human sister of Helen of Troy. Her guilt, though never denied, is made less odious in various ways. First of all, Clytemnestra here, as in Homer, has been merely the accomplice of Aegisthus in the actual murder of Agamemnon.[149] Aegisthus, furthermore, has wished to slay Electra; but Clytemnestra, though cruel, has saved her daughter from him (25–28). Both of her children hate her intensely, and the Old Man is very anxious to see her slain (663); still, she will come to Electra when she hears of the birth of the child, although she doubtless took a selfish delight in the birth, as Electra intimates (658), because it would reduce Electra to the status of the peasant class and practically eliminate her and her child as potential avengers.[150]

The scene between Clytemnestra and Electra is a masterpiece, effective in its pictorial as well as in its verbal aspects. Clytemnestra enters upon her chariot, dressed in queenly attire and attended by a throng of captive Trojan maidens—"a poor though pretty consolation" for the daughter whom she has lost. These captives are themselves gorgeously bedecked with Oriental robes and gold finery (317–18). Small wonder, then, that in the presence of these, Electra—another daughter whom Clytemnestra has "lost"—should come forward and confess herself a slave, ready to perform the servile task of aiding the queen to step down from her chariot. Clytemnestra is nicely characterized as a grand lady condescending to do a service for her unfortunate daughter, but at the mention of the word "father" by Electra she launches into a defense of her actions. Her first words upon entering have already intimated that the sacrifice of Iphigenia will be her main defense. She does not deny that such a sacrifice might have been justified if it had been made to save the city or the other children; but Helen did not deserve such a sacrifice, and the subterfuge of Agamemnon in claiming that Iphigenia was going forth to wed Achilles was base.

This defense of Clytemnestra might have been made even stronger, as Euripides himself has shown in his *Iphigenia at Aulis* (1146–1208). Only there in all Greek drama are the full possibilities of this defense exploited. But there Clytemnestra is a different woman. Incidentally, if Sophocles' *Electra,* in which Clytemnestra's guilt is made more odious in every possible way, preceded that of Euripides, we should expect Euripides, in reaction to an interpretation which must have been offensive to him, to give Clytemnestra here as strong a defense and perhaps as respectable a character as possible. But here in his *Electra* Euripides portrays Clytemnestra as the vain and licentious sister of Helen of Troy, and his purpose is obviously to give her not the strongest possible defense but only the defense which such a character deserved. Thus he has Clytemnestra confess that she would not have slain Agamemnon if he had not come home bringing a concubine with him— a strange confession, for Clytemnestra had presumably long before begun an intrigue with Aegisthus and her choice upon Agamemnon's return was doubtless to slay or to be slain.[151] Still, one often rationalizes after an event and in perfectly good faith gives not only the actual motivation for his action but every conceivable motivation. Perhaps, however, the poet intends this as a patent instance of bad faith.

More plausible is Clytemnestra's contention that she was forced to turn to Agamemnon's enemies if she wished to take vengeance on him. But Electra insists that her mother was playing the wanton even before the sacrifice of Iphigenia—a contention made only in Euripides. Electra cites Clytemnestra's cruel treatment of her children and rightfully concludes, as in Sophocles, that if Clytemnestra was justified in murdering Agamemnon, then Orestes and Electra are justified in murdering her.

Finally, real remorse is shown by Clytemnestra. In Sophocles (*Electra* 549–50), Clytemnestra insists that she has no regrets over what has taken place; but in Euripides, she is "not so very happy" about what she has done, and she sighs with regret at her present course of persecuting her children, although she has perhaps been somewhat softened by the ironic thought that Electra and her baseborn child are now no longer potential avengers. This Clytemnestra has often been compared to the mother of Hamlet, and her humanization fits well into Euripides' general plan for making the deed of Orestes and Electra a more appalling one.

Deus ex machina.—This play nicely illustrates the justifiable use of the *deus ex machina*. Euripides, like Aeschylus, wishes to interpret the slaughter of Clytemnestra by her son as a dreadful deed which is followed by dreadful consequences. But, since Euripides is writing a single play rather than a trilogy, it is technically impossible to present a dramatic solution of the state of turmoil in which the characters find themselves near the end of the play. Hence the *deus ex machina* is introduced to relate the eventual solution, which somewhat resembles that of the *Eumenides* of Aeschylus (though Orestes is not sent to Delphi). An admirable dignity and finality, also, is thus given to the close of the play. The author's own opinion of Orestes' act, furthermore, is here stated with more authority than a pronouncement of the chorus could carry.

Several incidental points are noteworthy in the speech of the Dioscuri. They command proper burial for both corpses, thus contradicting Orestes' earlier intention of throwing the corpse of Aegisthus to beasts and birds (cf. 896–98). The legend of the real Helen's having been taken away to Egypt and never having been at Troy is confirmed—apparently in preparation for the *Helen,* which was produced in 412 B.C., perhaps one year later than the present play. The peasant "husband" is not forgotten in the disposition of happiness. As in comedies and melodramas, everyone must be remembered. In their last lines, finally, the Dioscuri reveal that they must hasten away to aid the great Sicilian expedition which the Athenians had sent out in 415 B.C. and which was annihilated in 413 B.C. This reference serves to date the play. The most competent leader of this expedition and probably the one Athenian who could have made it successful, Alcibiades, had been forced into exile soon after the expedition sailed. It is just possible that Orestes' repeated references to the ills and misfortunes of an exile may be covert allusions to the situation of Alcibiades, although such lines on exile are a commonplace in Euripides. In all three dramatists, furthermore, the fact that Orestes has been robbed of his patrimony and made an exile is a motivation for his action. There is no certain evidence, therefore, that any political allusion is intended.

13. *IPHIGENIA IN TAURIS*

(Perhaps 414–412 B.C.)

Either this play or the *Iphigenia at Aulis* was reproduced at Athens, 341 B.C.

This play shows striking similarities to the *Ion* and especially to the *Helen* (412 B.C.), but it is impossible to determine the chronological order of these three plays with certainty. They all resemble melodrama in that their actions depend primarily on romantic and sensational incidents rather than on forces of character, and in that conventional sentiments tend to be exaggerated.

The *Iphigenia in Tauris* seems to have been highly esteemed by Aristotle. No play except the *Oedipus* is favorably noticed more frequently in the *Poetics*.

Legend.—"The Tauri have the following customs," writes Herodotus.[152] "They offer in sacrifice to the Virgin all shipwrecked persons, and all Greeks compelled to put into their ports by stress of weather. . . . . The goddess to whom these sacrifices are offered the Tauri themselves declare to be Iphigenia the daughter of Agamemnon."

Human sacrifice was practiced in prehistoric Greece, as in other ancient and modern primitive societies. The legend of Iphigenia's being herself saved from sacrifice at Aulis is an etiological myth, like the story of the sacrifice of Isaac in Genesis (chap. 22), designed to explain the cessation of human sacrifice. The various legends about the sacrifice at Aulis and even the name Iphigenia are not mentioned in the Homeric poems. There the daughters of Agamemnon are named Chrysothemis, Laodice, and Iphianassa (*Iliad* 9. 145). The name Iphigenia ("Strong-Birth") was originally and properly the name of a goddess of childbirth, later identified with Artemis. A statue of Artemis "Tauropolos" in her temple at Halae in Attica was supposed to have been brought from the Taurians by Iphigenia. This part of the legend, obviously, is due to popular but false etymology. The epithet "Tauropolos" has no real connection with the name Tauri; but, in addition to the verbal similarity, two coincidences aided this popular conception. The Taurians actually indulged in human sacrifice, and there were vestiges of human sacrifice, explained by Athena at the end of this play, in the worship of Artemis Tauropolos.[153]

From these various confusions, which are typical of early religions, one may easily conjecture how the story of the exile of Iphigenia arose. The story of Orestes' rescuing her and bringing her back to Greece, however, may be the innovation of Euripides or of Sophocles in his lost *Chryses* (before 414 B.C.). The majority of the original audience probably knew the tradition, reported in Herodotus (1. 67), that Orestes died in Greece, and so they might expect him to return safely at the end of the play.

It need occasion no surprise that these legends are wholly ignored in all the plays concerning Electra and the vengeance of Orestes. Those plays are grim and serious tragedy, far removed from the realm of fantasy, and there the assumption that Iphigenia was not actually sacrificed at Aulis would introduce a confusing complication.

Influence.—The *Iphigenia in Tauris* seems to have been one of the most popular of Euripides' plays. It resembles the *Electra* of Sophocles in that Iphigenia assumes that her brother is dead and mourns for him and in that the recognition scene is extended to melodramatic length and the softer emotions are allowed melodramatic freedom. The dates of these two plays are unknown; but since these characteristics seem more proper to the melodrama of Euripides than to the tragedy of Sophocles, it may well be that Sophocles in this instance has imitated his younger rival. This recognition scene probably influenced still other plays, as the contest in generosity between Orestes and Pylades almost certainly did.[154]

We hear of two other Greek dramatizations of this story and a Latin version by Naevius. The story was also burlesqued. Euripides' play had tremendous influence on ancient art, and many temples of Artemis from Asia Minor to Sicily claimed to possess the true Taurian statue of the goddess.[155]

Among modern adaptations of the play may be mentioned a sketch for a first act by Racine and plays by Lagrange (1699), de La Touche (1757), and J. E. Schlegel (1742). Goethe's famous version appeared in 1779, and in the same year the opera by Gluck, with a text based on the tragedy of de La Touche.[156]

Theme.—Plays such as the *Iphigenia* seem to be designed almost wholly for entertainment, and it would be a mistake to insist upon finding any great moral or political significance in them. The tendency to write such plays during this period is due at least in part to a natural desire of both playwright and audience for a romantic escape from the depressing chaos at Athens during the last years of the long Peloponnesian War. This is the period when Aristophanes' comedy of escape, the *Birds*, was produced (414 B.C.). Sophocles, too, was influenced by this trend, as is shown by what we know of his lost *Chryses* (before 414 B.C.) and by his *Philoctetes* (409 B.C.), although our knowledge of the dates of plays is not sufficient to indicate precisely how far this trend went with him. Euripides seems to have been the leader in this movement. Along with the *Helen* in 412 B.C., just after the devastating catastrophe of the Athenian defeat in Sicily, he produced his *Andromeda*, which seems to have been the most romantic and the most brilliantly successful of all these plays of escape. The *Iphigenia in Tauris* itself appears very romantic and melodramatic when compared to most Greek tragedies; but it is still far—how far can best be appreciated by a comparison with Goethe's *Iphigenie auf Tauris*—from modern romanticism.

The *Iphigenia in Tauris*, like many Greek tragedies, is designed incidentally to explain and glorify Attic religious customs, especially the festival "Tauropolia" and the cults of Artemis at Halae Araphenides and Brauron in Attica. Certain practices at the festival of the "Pitchers," also, are explained (958–60). Iphigenia's insistence upon the essential goodness of the gods (391) is similar to the Platonic Socrates' contention that God is wholly good and cannot, therefore, be the cause of evil (*Republic* 379 C). Orestes' inveighing against Apollo, furthermore, should not be considered an attack upon religion, because Orestes is here laboring under presumptions which are proved false in the course of the play.

Discussion.—The opening scenes of the *Iphigenia in Tauris*, which resemble those of Euripides' *Electra,* are unusually awkward and, according to dramatic standards, exemplify the Euripidean prologue at its worst. The relation of the dream of Iphigenia should come first of all, for it was the custom, as we may observe in Sophocles' *Electra* (424, on which see the ancient commentator), to describe one's dream to the morning sun in order to avert any evil consequence. Psychologically, too, this should be Iphigenia's first concern. Some of the information which precedes the relation of the dream is superfluous and must have been known to every person in the audience. Even so, it is repeated with desirable incidental effects in later scenes (cf. 214–35). What is not superfluous could have been inserted unobtrusively in the relation of the dream, perhaps, although Iphigenia's escape from Aulis must be explained fully and unmistakably. Awkward also is the "vacant stage," like that in Euripides' *Electra* and *Phoenissae,* which follows Iphigenia's speech. The second prologue by Orestes and Pylades does not improve things.

In plays of genuinely tragic outcome the most ominous foreboding often has a note of ironic optimism, a pathetic hope that all will turn out well in the end. Thus Oedipus is confident that with the aid of Apollo he can free Thebes of its plague, and Teiresias in the *Bacchae* of Euripides prays that Pentheus and his city may come to no harm. This ironic optimism may continue up to the climax of the play, and it makes the reversal of fortune all the more tragic. In melodrama, however, the process is usually reversed. The play opens on a note of ironic pessimism. The dramatist makes every effort to create pity and fear, which become more intense as the action progresses, and to maintain suspense by delaying as long as possible the happy ending. This is the scheme followed in the *Iphigenia in Tauris.*

The prologue of Iphigenia, though exciting pity and fear, does not give the impression of imminent doom. Iphigenia obviously makes a too pessimistic interpretation of her dream, and Orestes appears immediately afterwards. Although the oracle seems to promise Orestes' safe return, the extreme danger of the two young men is stressed upon their first entrance, as it has been indirectly suggested by Iphigenia's description of the grim rites of human sacrifice and of her ominous dream. This danger is made even more obvious at the first encounter between brother and sister; for both, as in the first encounter of Creusa and Ion in the *Ion,* have a distinctly hostile attitude, though they are secretly attracted to each other.[157] Iphigenia, offended by her father's attempted sacrifice of herself and embittered by the conviction that her brother no longer lives, is now more than willing to sacrifice Greek strangers. Orestes, for his part, is offended by Iphigenia's sentimental pity for his home and family and by her apparently impertinent curiosity. Hence Orestes sullenly refuses to reveal his name, and the suspense is effectively maintained.

Serious dramatic irony, with which both the words of brother and sister and their situation are heavily fraught, increases the effectiveness of this scene. Iphigenia in her ignorance seems to be on the point of officiating at the sacrifice of her own brother. One later writer, as Aristotle (*Poetics* 1455 a, Bywater) points out, brought about the recognition by having Orestes declare: "My sister was sacrificed, and I am to be sacrificed like her." Such a situation, wherein one unknowingly jeopardizes the life of a kinsman, is most powerful in arousing pity and fear, in the opinion of Aristotle (*Poetics* 1453 b), and these situations were a favorite device with Euripides.[158]

Actual recognition of brother and sister is postponed as long as possible. Meanwhile Pylades tries to allay the wonder of Orestes over the identity of the priestess. Then the two young men indulge in their contest of sentimental generosity, which makes it appear for a time as if neither will make any effort to escape. That an ancient audience was as enthusiastic about such a melodramatic scene as a modern one could be is proved by comments which Cicero makes about a Roman play with a scene apparently modeled on this one:

What applause arises from the throng and even from those of no education in the theater when these famous words are spoken, "I am Orestes," and the other contradicts him, "No, I am really Orestes, I tell you!" And again when a solution is offered by both together to the confused and puzzled king, "We both, then, ask to be slain at the same time." Does this scene ever fail to arouse the greatest admiration when it is acted?[159]

The best of all types of recognition is that which naturally arises out of the incidents themselves, as Aristotle (*Poetics* 1455 a) says, citing the *Oedipus* and the *Iphigenia;* for it is not improbable, he continues, that Iphigenia should wish to send a letter home. Nor is the process by which Iphigenia is brought to read the letter improbable; an oath was absolutely binding according to ancient thought, and it is natural that Pylades should insist upon being relieved of his oath in case of shipwreck and loss of the letter. The impatience of Iphigenia at Orestes' interruptions while she is reading the letter and, after he has declared himself, her skepticism over his identity lengthen out the excited expectation of the audience. Except in depth of pathos this scene rivals the scene with the urn in Sophocles' *Electra.*

Despite the precariousness of the situation, Iphigenia and Orestes must express their joy of reunion, Iphigenia must ask about Electra and the family, and Orestes must explain his past at length. Then their attention is turned to the desperateness of their situation. Iphigenia's first thought is for bold and concerted action; but she immediately loses heart, and a second contest in melodramatic generosity, this time between Iphigenia and her brother, threatens to stifle action. In casting about for a plan, the crude suggestions of Orestes are rejected; but Iphigenia's skill in device—a typical characteristic of women in ancient tragedy and comedy—is demonstrated by her discovery of a plan for deceiving the king which has something of Oriental subtlety and boldness.

According to theatrical convention the chorus must be sworn to silence after the formation of the intrigue; but instead of employing this device in the usual stereotyped manner, which really calls the attention of the audience to the implausibility of forming an intrigue before so many witnesses, Euripides has here elaborated this conventional notice of the chorus into such a long and pathetic appeal by Iphigenia that the audience, far from remarking any implausibility, cannot fail to be impressed with the extreme precariousness of the situation.[160]

The excitement remains at a high pitch during the scene with Thoas. The elaborate deception practiced upon him by Iphigenia seems more proper to melodrama or comedy than to tragedy and is reminiscent of Euripides' satyr-play, the *Cyclops*.[161] One is tempted to laugh when Thoas naïvely compliments Iphigenia, saying that Greece has made her wise, and when Iphigenia warns him that Greeks know no faith. Comic irony is contained also in Iphigenia's request that Thoas assign some of his own bodyguard to go with her, in Thoas' pleased assent to her command that all citizens remain within their homes, and in his joining Iphigenia in her prayerful wish that the purification may succeed "as she desires." The growing tenseness of the scene is emphasized by a sudden shift to the fast trochaic meter with very short and rapid exchanges between the king and Iphigenia. The ironic prayer to Artemis forms a fitting conclusion to this scene of deception.

When Iphigenia and her kinsmen leave the scene, the chorus sing an interlude song that has no immediate connection with the present tense situation although it is concerned with Apollo, who is the ultimate author of all this action. This type of interlude was condemned by Aristotle (*Poetics* 1456 a). It is possible, however, that the poet designedly inserted an interlude at this point, believing that the extreme emotional tension here would be jeopardized less by an interlude, like an entr'acte in the modern theater, than by any effort of the chorus to heighten or maintain the tension.

The Messenger enters, mauled and disheveled. The chorus attempt to deceive him, but this results only in their becoming implicated in the plot and themselves incurring mortal peril. The ship is being washed back upon the shore, and Thoas seems to be on the point of destroying Iphigenia and her kinsmen—a climax worthy of any melodrama—when Athena appears as the *deus ex machina*.

Deus ex machina.—The *Iphigenia in Tauris* shows most plainly that the *deus ex machina* in Greek tragedy is not necessarily a device employed to solve an otherwise unsolvable complication, for here a natural solution is deliberately avoided by the poet. Since the ship of Orestes could easily and plausibly have escaped safely, it is obvious that the storm and these last reverses, like so much of the remainder of the play, are designed to maintain suspense and excitement to the very end and to necessitate the spectacular finale of a *deus ex machina*. A divinity may also best put an end to all thought of pursuit or revenge on the part of Thoas—perhaps a mere device for immediately announcing the eventual result of the action. By introducing Athena, furthermore, Athens may be praised and the divine origins of certain Athenian customs may be explained. The future of Iphigenia and of Orestes also may be foretold—information which could not be imparted without divine aid—and the chorus may be rescued, so that Iphigenia's earlier promise to them does not go entirely unfulfilled (cf. 1068). Lastly, the action may be brought to a close with a finality that is as satisfying as it is absolute.

Character of Iphigenia.—The willingness of Iphigenia to invent and execute the deception of the king has sometimes been criticized as a blemish upon her character. In the *Iphigenie auf Tauris* of Goethe, for instance, it is Pylades and not Iphigenie who invents the deception, and although Iphigenie at first makes an attempt to carry out the plan, in the end she finds that she cannot bring herself to practice such dishonesty. She frankly reveals the whole plan to the king, therefore, and throws herself and her kinsmen upon his mercy. The king is thereupon discovered to be almost as noble as she, for he can only send her and her kinsmen away with his blessing. Such romantic falsification or, at best, idealization of human character—we must not forget that Thoas was a barbarian practicing human sacrifice—would in the Greek theater have been considered proper only to the fantasy of comedy, which is wholly unconcerned with plausibility.

The attitude of the Athenian dramatists toward deception is much the same as that of Homer. An ability to deceive is an indication of superior intelligence and an admirable and very desirable trait if the deception is practiced only against enemies and only where open combat could not possibly be successful. In the *Philoctetes* of Sophocles we may see a higher moral code, but the deception which Neoptolemus is there asked to practice obviously becomes base and despicable and cannot in any important respect be compared to the deception by which Iphigenia saves the life of her brother. In this deception, according to ancient standards, there is nothing despicable or unheroic.

14. *HELEN*

(412 B.C.)

Along with the *Helen,* Euripides produced the *Andromeda,* which told of Andromeda's being chained to a cliff in "Ethiopia" as a sacrifice to a sea monster and of her being rescued by Perseus, the flying Greek hero. This romantic tale of a maiden in distress was one of the most popular melodramas of Euripides. (By the irony of fate the brilliant *Andromeda* has been lost and the very mediocre *Helen* preserved.) The satirist Lucian amusingly relates that after the people of Abdera, a town in Thrace, had seen a production of the *Andromeda,* they became so mad with enthusiasm over it that they all turned pale and went about the streets declaiming passages from the play.[162]

Legend.—The legend that a mere wraith of Helen accompanied Paris to Troy doubtless originated in an effort to exonerate the deified Helen. This was a natural movement at a time when the rising ethical consciousness was beginning to subject early legends and divinities to critical re-examination. The Dorian poet Stesichorus (seventh and sixth centuries B.C.) was reputedly the originator of this version of the legend of Helen, whose cult was of course important mostly among the Dorians; but Stesichorus, so far as we know, made no connection between this story of the wraith and Egypt.[163]

Herodotus (2. 113–20) was told by Egyptian priests that Helen and the treasures taken by Paris from Sparta never went to Troy but were retained in Egypt when the king, Proteus, learned how they had all been stolen. The Greeks, they continued, mistakenly sailed to Troy and only after the city was captured did they finally believe the Trojans, who had from the first insisted that Helen and the treasures had been taken from Paris and held in Egypt. Traveling thither, Menelaus was received with the kindest hospitality. Helen and his treasures were restored to him. But he returned evil for good by seizing two Egyptian children and sacrificing them to secure a favorable wind.

Euripides has combined these two legends, and the result is a story very similar to that of the *Iphigenia in Tauris.* We need not, with some scholars, interpret the *Helen* as itself designed to rehabilitate that heroine whom Euripides had so often vilified in his earlier plays. He was to vilify her even more in his subsequent plays. But a plot naturally favorable to Helen has been accepted for two reasons: it constitutes excellent material for a melodrama, and it allows Euripides again to interpret the Trojan War—and by implication perhaps all war—as a wholly mistaken cause. He had made this point in the profound tragedy of the *Trojan Women,* and he now repeats it in a play of entirely different tone and spirit. Although Euripides was mainly concerned, no doubt, with the dramatic effectiveness of the material, this second point is given such emphasis that it must have been seriously intended.[164]

Discussion.—The *Helen,* like the *Andromeda,* is apparently a romantic play of escape. Escape from tragic reality seems to have been Euripides' primary reaction to the appalling disaster which had just befallen Athens with the destruction of the Sicilian expedition in 413 B.C. But beneath the surface of the *Helen* there are a seriousness of purpose and a profound despair which are not found in the *Iphigenia in Tauris*. In the *Helen* (744–57), for instance, the Messenger denounces divination and oracles in a speech which resembles a parabasis of Aristophanes addressed directly to the Athenians. The chorus echo his skepticism. Such skepticism is obviously out of place in this play, where Theonoe and her omniscience have an important bearing. But it was especially appropriate to the Athenians after the failure of the Sicilian expedition, for various oracles had been cited in favor of this rash venture.[165] Again, Menelaus (1441–50) prays to Zeus for deliverance from their misfortunes in lines which every Athenian might well have repeated after him.

The *Helen* is essentially the same play as the *Iphigenia in Tauris*. A list of their common features will reveal the formula upon which they are written—still an excellent one and with slight changes still used. Both plays are laid in a foreign and exotic land; both open with the heroine's monologue, which is filled with despair, and soon continue with the heroine's lamentation over the supposed death of the hero. The hero on entering delivers what amounts to a second prologue. He is actually in great danger, for Greeks are put to death by the king of the land. Ironic hostility marks the first encounter of hero and heroine, but the recognition finally is accomplished. The suspense, however, now increases instead of disappearing, since the situation is fraught with danger and apparent hopelessness. In a contest in generosity hero and heroine pledge their faith to live or die together. The hero fumbles about for a plan of escape and clumsily suggests slaying the king. The heroine comes to his rescue, however, and with typically feminine cunning and deceit devises a dangerous but hopeful plan. The chorus, composed of Greek women favorably disposed, are enjoined or sworn to silence. Their own rescue is held out as a reward. The barbarian king now appears and is deceived by the clever Greeks in a scene filled with comic irony; indeed, he is made a ridiculous dupe by being inveigled into furnishing the means of escape or very materially aiding the escape. At this climactic point the chorus sing a lyric having nothing to do with the immediate action. Thus they maintain the suspense by giving no hint in word or tone of the outcome. Escape is now made by sea, although various unforeseen complications have arisen to threaten its success. The king is informed of the escape by a messenger and is about to take violent action when a *deus ex machina* appears to end all efforts of pursuit or revenge.

Such is the formula which Euripides uses in both plays. The *Iphi-*

genia in Tauris appears to fit the formula more precisely, however, and to exploit its possibilities more effectively, especially at the beginning of the play. The belief that Orestes is dead makes a very important contribution to the first half of the play, whereas in the *Helen* the belief that Menelaus is dead becomes merely an excuse for melodramatic laments. Indeed, the whole scene with Teucer seems clumsy and basically impertinent. Theonoe's threats to reveal Menelaus to her brother, also, seem patently designed to introduce a melodramatic situation and an inferior example of that persuasive oratory of which Euripides was so fond. The simple pathos which is so effective in the *Iphigenia in Tauris* has been entirely lost in the *Helen*. We should like to assume, therefore, that the *Iphigenia in Tauris* is the original play.

Some scholars, however, have contended that the latter part of the formula was designed for the *Helen* and that the *Helen,* therefore, is probably the original play.[166] But such a view seems to be based on the assumption that this deft intrigue of deception and escape was original with Euripides, whereas it was probably a formula hoary with age when Euripides was a child. Briefly stated, its main features are these: someone, usually a husband or lover, is persuaded to send away a girl with another man; he is duped into furnishing their means of escape or into materially aiding their escape and possibly into giving large gifts in addition. The deception is usually planned by the girl, and its success is threatened by exciting complications. But in the end all comes out well, and pursuit or revenge is prevented by some device. This plot is found in a comedy of Plautus, *The Braggart Warrior* (*Miles Gloriosus*), and in various Oriental and European stories.[167]

The elements of this deception and escape are so simple and their effects are so obviously desirable that it may possibly have been independently invented many times. Still, Euripides may have taken it from story or legend. Once discovered, it was the almost inevitable solution of a romantic plot of escape. One must not, therefore, contend that, in the *Iphigenia in Tauris,* Orestes and Iphigenia, already having a ship, might escape secretly or more easily than they actually do.

The deception practiced in these endings is essentially comic; but the deception of Theoclymenus is not the only comic element in the *Helen*. The Old Woman who answers Menelaus' knocking at the gates is a lowly character, and this scene is not very different from a stock scene in New Comedy in which an ill-humored slave answers one knocking at the door. The scene in which the hero, by a reversal of nature, resists the advances of the heroine, also is amusing (567). The Old Man who brings the news of the wraith's disappearance to Menelaus is serious enough on the whole, but his tirade on the good and evil slave

(726–33) is a commonplace of New Comedy. Many comic elements, therefore, are found in the *Helen,* and indeed such plays of Euripides as this became the model for later comedy.

15. *PHOENISSAE* ("PHOENICIAN WOMEN")

(Possibly 409 B.C.)

Euripides won second place. His other tragedies may have been his *Oenomaus* and his *Chrysippus,* and these three plays are sometimes termed a trilogy; but the connection, it seems, could not have been close.[168] Events of the legend before and after those of the *Phoenissae* formed the subject of his lost *Oedipus* and *Antigone* and of his extant *Suppliants.*

Influence.—The *Phoenissae* was one of Euripides' most popular plays, often reproduced, apparently, and widely read, especially in the Byzantine period. The Roman Accius wrote a *Phoenissae,* which seems to have been an adaptation of this play. Two or three scenes for such a play are preserved from Seneca. The Roman Papinius Statius wrote an epic poem, the *Thebaid,* the story of which is thought by some to have been taken primarily from Euripides. In modern times the play has exerted important influence on Rotrou, *Antigone* (1638), Racine, *La Thébaïde ou les Frères Ennemis* (1664), and Schiller, *Die Braut von Messina* (1803).[169]

Discussion.—Euripides in this single play has attempted to cover the whole story of the downfall of the house of Oedipus. Every important character of the generation of Oedipus appears in the play—one of the largest casts of any Greek tragedy—and great skill is shown in handling them. Jocasta and Antigone, who are portrayed with keen psychological insight, are introduced at the opening of the play. (Antigone is apparently included in the *Seven against Thebes* of Aeschylus but only at the very end of the play.) The use of a stereotyped Euripidean prologue, however, results in a somewhat clumsy opening with two unconnected expositional scenes. Antigone's scene of observation from the palace roof is much more picturesque and could doubtless have been made to serve all the purposes of exposition.[170] This scene is reminiscent of the famous scene in the third book of the *Iliad* where Helen points out the Greek warriors to Priam from the walls of Troy. But the audience must clearly understand that Jocasta is still alive and Oedipus within the palace, since these facts contradict the accepted legendary tradition. The two opening scenes, then, aid in presenting the broad background of the action and prepare for the subsequent roles of Jocasta, Antigone, and Oedipus. The mere mention that such an important personage as Oedipus is within the palace, of course, unmistakably foreshadows his appearance. Reference is made to him again and again, and his very existence haunts the whole play. A certain amount of deliberate suspense, also, characterizes these opening scenes. Some lines might be interpreted as foreshadowing the defeat of Thebes, as when the Paedagogus stresses the justice of the cause of Polyneices and fears that the gods will view it with favor (154–55).

The *Phoenissae* is much concerned with matters of state and patriotism. Indeed few if any debates in Euripides are more interesting and more dramatically effective than the debate of Polyneices and Eteocles before their mother. It was justly famous in ancient times. Julius Caesar like Marius before him, Cicero implies, took as a motto the infamous defense of Eteocles: "If it is necessary to do wrong, to do wrong to achieve the power of a ruler is best; but in other matters one should be just."[171] This is similar to the contemptible sophistry of Odysseus in the *Philoctetes* of Sophocles. That play was produced in 409 b.c., as the *Phoenissae* may well have been, shortly after the collapse of the tyrannical and bloody revolution of 411 b.c., when civil strife was frequent at Athens and many citizens were unjustly forced into exile. Euripides, unlike Aeschylus, had lived to see the time when tyrants had seized the city and an attack by exiles or political opponents would obviously have been justified.

The *Phoenissae* is one of the longest Greek tragedies and one of the very few which contain a well-defined minor plot. Its structure, accordingly, is unusually elaborate. The quarrel and death of Eteocles and Polyneices is the subject of Aeschylus' extant *Seven against Thebes*. This earlier play is extremely simple. Its scene is located within the city of Thebes; Eteocles is the only important actor; the justice of the cause of Eteocles is accepted without question, and his cause is identified with that of Thebes. The enlightened Euripides, as Aristophanes (*Frogs* 958) derisively points out, must question all things, and he is obviously improving upon Aeschylus when he makes the moral dilemma of the two brothers a main theme of the play. His introduction of Polyneices and the debate of the two brothers before their mother Jocasta is a master stroke. The portrayal of the duel scene itself very unfortunately has been omitted, possibly because limitations of staging and the very small number of actors available for a Greek dramatist seemed to preclude such a scene. Euripides' dissociation of the cause of Eteocles from that of Thebes also allows the plausible introduction of Creon and Menoeceus and the minor plot. This Menoeceus and the whole incident concerning his sacrifice seem to be the invention of Euripides.[172] Its artistic purpose, no doubt, is to contrast the glorious patriotism of Menoeceus with the mad selfishness of the two brothers.[173]

The minor plot is articulated with the quarrel of the two brothers with consummate artistry. Incidentally, its introduction immediately after the departure of Eteocles prolongs the suspense concerning the fate of the brothers. It is Eteocles who first directs that Teiresias be consulted and who first mentions Menoeceus. This consultation with Teiresias involves the fate of Oedipus and of his sons as well as that of Thebes and Menoeceus. Very subtle is the foreshadowing of the death of Menoeceus contained in the early lines of Teiresias. Here he relates that he has just returned with his crown of victory from Athens, whose citizens by his aid have won a victory over their enemies. Creon accepts this news as a good omen—somewhat ironically, for Athens has been saved only by the sacrifice of a daughter of the king,[174] just as Thebes is to be saved by the sacrifice of a son of Creon. Tragic irony again produces its effect just before Teiresias announces the necessity of this sacrifice, when Creon says that Menoeceus would rejoice to hear the means of safety. After the death of Menoeceus the minor plot is joined closely with the major one when the messenger reports this patriotic sacrifice to Jocasta, who is primarily concerned with the fate of Eteocles and Polyneices, and at the same time reports the progress of the battle and finally with reluctance the resolve of the brothers to decide the issue by single combat.

But Euripides is not satisfied with these artful sutures immediately preceding and following the incident. The final section of the play opens with Creon's bringing on the corpse of his son in order that Jocasta—ironically enough, for she is now dead—may prepare it for burial. The cause of Thebes, furthermore, is a major concern throughout the action, and this cause is saved by the sacrifice of Menoeceus.

The problem of joining the final scenes to the earlier action also was a difficult one, and the degree of success which Euripides has here achieved is a matter of dispute. Creon plays an important role here just as he serves to articulate the minor plot with the major. The chorus, though often criticized for its loose relation to the action of the play, continually reminds us of the wider historical background of the action—its exotic costumes add to this effect—and thus prepares us for the final scene and the author's interpretation of the subject of his play as the downfall of the house of Oedipus and not merely the tragedy of the two brothers.

Antigone's resolve to bury her brother even at the cost of her life seems, if we may trust the textual tradition, to be a part of the endings of both the *Seven against Thebes* and the *Phoenissae*. Significant

preparation for this outcome in the *Phoenissae* may be found in Antigone's words at the first of the play when she expresses the impetuous
wish to fly with the wind and embrace "the pitiful exile" (156–67).
In Euripides, furthermore, it is Eteocles who first issues the order that
the body of Polyneices shall be refused burial and that anyone, even
a friend, who may bury him shall be put to death (775–77). Since
this decree originates in the blind hatred of Eteocles, Antigone is more
obviously justified in her insistence that the body be given burial, and
her motivation is strengthened by the dying request of Polyneices to be
buried in his native land (1447–50). The sympathetic portrayal of
Polyneices and the insistence on the justice of his cause, also, increase
the importance of his proper burial.

Still, this resolution of Antigone suggests a new action and causes
the play to lack that utter finality which is the rule in Greek tragedy. In
the ending as it stands, furthermore, Antigone resolves also to accompany the blind Oedipus to Attica. Both ancient and modern critics have
considered these two resolutions contradictory, and parts of this ending
are frequently considered spurious. These two resolutions would certainly be contradictory if we accepted Sophocles' version of the subsequent events as given in his *Antigone;* but Euripides' *Antigone* gave a
very different ending to the story, wherein the heroine married Haemon.
These two resolutions, therefore, might both be possible in Euripides'
very free adaptation of the legend.[175]

In its number of deaths and calamities, the *Phoenissae* far surpasses
any other extant Greek tragedy. This number is excessive in the opinion of an ancient critic,[176] and certainly it would do honor to an Elizabethan tragedy.

16. *ORESTES*

(408 B.C. Reproduced at Athens, 340 B.C.)

"This play belongs to that class of plays which is effective in the
theater," says the ancient critic Aristophanes of Byzantium; "but it is
very poor in its characters, for they with the exception of Pylades are
all mean."

Although the proper names of the *Orestes* are taken from legend,
the main incidents are wholly fictional. Even Homeric tradition is
violated in various important respects.

The *Orestes* did not lack a certain popularity in ancient times. Its
original presentation, however, was marred by the leading actor's slip
in reciting verse 279. Here the deranged Orestes, slowly returning
to his senses, says that he discerns a calm returning over his troubled

sea. The Greek word for "calm" as here used differs from the word for "weasel" only by having a sharply rising accent instead of a rising and falling accent. The actor Hegelochus gave the wrong accent with disastrous results which Aristophanes (*Frogs* 304) and the other writers of comedy never forgot.

The *Orestes* not only was reproduced in the fourth century but later was among the nine or ten plays chosen as representative of Euripides and also among the three selected from this group in Byzantine times. The play is crowded with excited dramatic action, but this late popularity is due primarily to the very skillfully written debates in the play. The modern reader, however, is likely to be repelled by these, as when Orestes, for instance (591–95), reasons that Apollo ordered him to slay Clytemnestra; if this act was a crime, he concludes, Tyndareos and the Argives should consider Apollo the criminal and slay him! Such sophistry foreshadows the plays of Seneca.

Discussion.—The plot of the *Orestes* is not well constructed. The first half of the play is concerned with the appeal of Orestes to Menelaus. The failure of this appeal and Orestes' consequent failure to obtain mercy from the Argives lead to the intrigue for murdering Helen and seizing Hermione. Both the appeal to Menelaus and in part this later intrigue, furthermore, are designed to save Orestes and Electra, and both concern primarily the same characters. But the spirit and the action of the two parts vary so greatly that the feeling of unity has been disrupted. The plan for taking vengeance on Menelaus by murdering Helen is not really pertinent to the main problem of escape; indeed, it seems to contravene this main objective, for obviously a stronger appeal could be made to Menelaus if both wife and daughter were seized as hostages. The vilification of Helen in the early part of the play repeats a theme obviously dear to the heart of Euripides and nicely prepares for this later plan to slay her. But the effectiveness of this vilification is wholly vitiated by her miraculous escape and by Apollo's pronouncement that the gods are responsible.

The ending of the play is unsatisfactory for other reasons. The whole complex entanglement is solved by the *deus ex machina*. Nor is it easy to understand how, even at the command of a god, Orestes and Menelaus are now to forget, the one his contempt, the other his jealousy and hatred; or how Hermione is to love and cherish the man who lately held his sword at her throat. The guilt of matricide and the torment of madness, furthermore, are merely waved away by the divine hand. At this, of course, Orestes' repeated denunciations of Apollo lose all force; for here, as in the *Iphigenia in Tauris*, these denunciations are in the end discovered to be mistaken and due to human failure to foresee the outcome. Such a mechanical and external solution solves none of the interesting moral problems presented in the play. Indeed, this ending, as an ancient critic remarks,[177] is more proper to a comedy.

What is the explanation of this failure of Euripides to meet the conventional requirements of plausibility? We might assume that he was here interested primarily in presenting an exciting melodramatic spectacle, or, with one recent critic, that Euripides here set out to dramatize a situation and that "it got the better of him."[178] But in view of Euripides' usually serious intentions and of his usually competent dramaturgy these assumptions are not attractive. It seems more likely that Euripides here, like Seneca later, is primarily interested in making a study of characters under the most violent stresses of emotion. The action of the play, if this assumption is correct, has been artificially manipulated in order to observe the responses of the characters under almost inhumanly severe situations. In the *Alcestis,* one may recall, the legend itself presented a series of events that was impossible in actuality but highly desirable as a dramatic and psychological situation. Perhaps in the *Orestes* Euripides has deliberately created such a series of events.

As a drama, however, the *Orestes* has various other shortcomings. It employs too many motives that are not well adapted to the present play or that have here been too obviously exaggerated for effect. The character of Menelaus in the *Orestes,* as in the *Andromache,* approaches that of the villain of modern melodrama and is all too certainly colored by war prejudice.[179] Aristotle (*Poetics* 1454 a, 1461 b) rightly protested against this unnecessary debasement. Pylades suffers from the opposite tendency. His contest in generosity with Orestes and his resolve to live or die with him are too closely modeled on his role in the *Iphigenia in Tauris,* where these noble sentiments are perhaps more plausibly motivated. Reminiscent of that play also are the mortal danger of the characters, the farewell of Orestes and Electra when they think they are about to die, the excitement and suspense, and the thrilling climax with the *deus ex machina.* The final scene of the play where Menelaus below helplessly pleads with Orestes on the roof of the palace is apparently taken from the final scene of the *Medea.*

But Euripides has not limited himself to imitating his own former successes. The *Electra* of Sophocles seems to have inspired the scene in which Electra stands before the palace and cries out bloodthirsty encouragement to Orestes and Pylades while they are attempting to murder Helen within. Indeed, the *Orestes* is often considered a reply to Sophocles' *Electra* by those who think that Sophocles' play was designed to answer the condemnation of Orestes' matricide in the *Electra* of Euripides. Certain it is that Euripides in the *Orestes* repeatedly insists that Orestes' act was a dreadful crime (538–39, etc.), though the *deus ex machina* somewhat nullifies this insistence along with all the other contentions of the play. Euripides retains the view that Clytemnestra's adulterous love was her motive in slaying Agamemnon (26–27; 917–42). He thus meets Sophocles on his own ground and does not give Clytemnestra the very strong defense which she has in his later *Iphigenia at Aulis*. Even so, Euripides twice, with subtle indirectness, makes the point—made more effectively and doubtless originally in the *Iphigenia in Tauris* (1174)—that the act of Orestes was that of a barbarian or even worse (485; 1424). The contention of Tyndareos that Clytemnestra should have been punished by legal process, however, really begs the whole question. No such process existed in Homeric times, and if such a course had been open to Orestes he never would have been faced with his appalling choice.

Other less obvious adaptations in the *Orestes* are the opening scene and the spectacular use of torches—these items perhaps from the *Trojan Women*. The seizure of a child as hostage was made famous in the lost *Telephus* of Euripides. The unwashed, unkempt, somewhat repulsive appearance of the main characters is reminiscent of the *Telephus,* the *Philoctetes,* and many another play of Euripides. If all the tragedies of Sophocles and Euripides were preserved, it would doubtless be found that such motives and devices were repeated more frequently than the few preserved plays indicate. Still, the *Orestes* is too largely a cento of previous plays. This may account for its failure to generate any deep pathos.

The *Orestes* is not, however, wholly without original features. Its portrayal of madness is widely admired,[180] and here Euripides has made a distinct improvement over the *Iphigenia in Tauris* by presenting Orestes' seizure "on stage." The figure of Helen, also, has rightly been called a "triumph of characterization."[181] The scene between Electra and her is a masterpiece. It is of prime importance in bringing out the ironic and pathetic contrast between the ruin of the house of Agamemnon, who won the war, and the prosperity of the house of Menelaus and Helen, who caused it—a significant theme throughout the play.[182] The scene with the Phrygian eunuch, also, is startlingly original. This character nicely emphasizes as background the harem-like atmosphere surrounding Helen and even further alienates all sympathy for her,[183] at the same time allowing author and audience to exercise their contempt for the effete East. The frantic excitement of the eunuch requires lyric meter for this messenger's speech—the one example in Greek tragedy. It is also one of the rare scenes with distinctly comic aspects.

17. **BACCHAE ("THE DEVOTEES OF BACCHUS")

(About 405 B.C.)

After the death of Euripides, his son produced at Athens the *Iphigenia at Aulis,* the *Alcmaeon at Corinth,* and the *Bacchae.* A first prize was awarded Euripides after his death, and it seems plausible to assume that these were the plays which won it. The *Bacchae* was probably written after Euripides left Athens (about 408 B.C.) and went to the court of King Archelaus in Macedonia.[184]

The *Bacchae* is unsurpassed for stark tragedy and theatrical effectiveness. It may well be taken as the most representative play of all Greek tragedy. The structure of the *Bacchae* is not inferior to that of *Oedipus the King,* for its action progresses with equal rapidity and inevitability. Its plot is one of tragic decision, whereas that of the *Oedipus* is one of tragic discovery—a less frequent and perhaps less interesting type. The third episode of the *Bacchae* with its eloquent messenger's speech and its fascinating contest between Pentheus and Dionysus is one of the finest scenes in drama; but it is surpassed by the second messenger's speech and the scene where Agave enters with the head of her son thinking it the head of a mountain lion.

Legend.—The coming of the god Dionysus or Bacchus to Greece was a frequent theme in poetry and art. Opposition to this new religion was offered especially by the Thracian Lycurgus (not to be confused with the Spartan lawgiver or the Athenian orator of the same name) and the Theban Pentheus. The fate of Lycurgus is told in the *Iliad* (6. 129–40). Pentheus met his doom, according to some versions of the legend, in open combat with Dionysus and his Maenads. This version is mentioned by Aeschylus in the *Eumenides* (25–26). In the *Bacchae* (51, 780–809) it first appears that open conflict may be the outcome. Pentheus' more dreadful fate of being torn apart by his mother and her sisters may have been the invention of Euripides.[185]

Source and influence.—Perhaps no theme is older in Greek tragedy than the story of Pentheus and Dionysus. Thespis, the "originator" of tragedy, is said to have written a *Pentheus* (but this, like almost everything said of Thespis, is of very doubtful authority). Aeschylus wrote on the same subject and also produced a tetralogy on the legend of Lycurgus. In 415 B.C. an obscure Xenocles, with a set of plays including a *Bacchae,* defeated Euripides' *Trojan Women* and other plays. (It is noteworthy that both Xenocles and Euripides placed their *Bacchae* last in the series of three tragedies produced. This subject, like a satyric drama, was dedicated to the god of the theater.) Iophon, the son of Sophocles, also wrote a *Bacchae* or a *Pentheus*. Various other dramatists treated the legend of Pentheus.[186]

Among the Romans, both Pacuvius and Accius were attracted to this subject and wrote plays which in the main, it seems, followed the treatment of Euripides.

The *Bacchae* had a wide influence on later literature. In classical Latin literature it is one of the most influential Greek tragedies. Catullus reveals an intimate acquaintance with it. One passage (*Bacchae* 918–19) is quoted by Vergil (*Aeneid* 4. 469–70). It seems to have been the favorite tragedy of Horace if we may judge from the number and importance of his quotations and references.[187] That the *Bacchae* was widely popular during the period is shown by the story concerning Hyrodes the Parthian and Artavasdes the Armenian in Plutarch. These two rulers were giving each other entertainments at which Greek compositions were frequently introduced.

Now when the head of Crassus was brought to the king's door, the tables had been removed, and a tragic actor, Jason by name, of Tralles, was singing that part of the "Bacchae" of Euripides where Agave is about to appear. . . . . Jason handed his costume of Pentheus to one of the chorus, seized the head of Crassus, and assuming the role of the frenzied Agave, sang these verses through as if inspired . . . .[188]

The *Bacchae* exerted an important influence also on early Christian writers. Though greatly admired in modern times, its peculiarly pagan subject has not encouraged adaptation. This story is a favorite one in ancient art, especially the scene of the rending of Pentheus and that of the mad Agave with the head of her son.[189]

Theme.—The *Bacchae* is one of the most interesting of all Greek tragedies in part because its interpretation is so provocative and baffling. This magnificently vigorous swan song of Euripides has sometimes been taken as a recantation of his skepticism and a return to orthodoxy. While criticizing the "almost childish incompetence" of this view, Gilbert Murray is convinced that we here have "a heartfelt glorification of 'Dionysus' "; but he interprets Dionysus in a broad and somewhat mystical fashion.[190] Other critics have taken a diametrically opposed view and have seen in the play another indictment of popular religion.

It is undeniable that there is a certain "orthodoxy" about the play, but there is none that does not seem entirely proper in its context and dramatically desirable. The chorus consists of the ardent worshipers of Dionysus. Thus Pentheus is isolated, and the choral lyrics in honor of Dionysus and the joys of life add greatly to the poetic qualities of

the play. The chorus' reiterated praise of an orthodox religious attitude and of simplicity, however, need not be interpreted as indicating
that Euripides himself is actually renouncing his enlightenment. This
praise is designed to emphasize the folly of the pretensions to wisdom
and virtue of a man like Pentheus, who in the end is discovered to be
less wise and less virtuous than the average person of no pretensions
whatever. Essentially the same explanation may be offered for the
orthodox sentiments of the messengers. Simple folk, furthermore, are
always prone to superstition and are so depicted in both tragedy and
comedy. The religious enthusiasm of Teiresias and Cadmus, also, forms
an effective foil for the cold skepticism of Pentheus. At the end of the
play Cadmus admits that Pentheus sinned and cites his fate as a warning to those who disdain the gods (1325–26); but he also inveighs
against the severity of the god, precisely as we should expect Euripidean
characters to do under similar circumstances. "It becomes gods," says
Cadmus, "not to imitate the wrathful acts of mortals." And Dionysus,
as cold as a marble statue, answers (1349): "My father Zeus long ago
ordained these things." The words of Dionysus may be taken to mean
that violation of natural law is followed by punishment according to
the law of Necessity; perhaps it is more reasonable, however, to take
them as a statement of mere determinism. In the prologue, Dionysus has
seemed to intimate that the course of events is not determined; but we
have observed elsewhere that Greeks and moderns alike tend to view
the future as undetermined but the catastrophes of the past as inevitable
and fixed from the beginning.[191] An especially strong condemnation
of Dionysus is pronounced by Agave (1374–76): "Dreadfully, in
truth, has Lord Dionysus wrought this outrage against your house."
Here Dionysus responds by citing the dishonor which he has suffered.
Greek morality was characterized by a rigid severity, but certainly the
punishment here does seem too severe and the tragedy too overwhelming
for the play to be a glorification of Dionysus in any sense or to create
in the spectator any affection for such a divinity. That Euripides' version of the story did not present the god in a favorable light seems to
have been the opinion of certain later authors who modified this version
in order to make the sin of Pentheus more deserving of his punishment.[192] We cannot, therefore, interpret the *Bacchae* as a glorification
of Dionysus.

Equally untenable, however, is the view that Euripides is writing a
condemnation of Dionysus. If the poet had wished to emphasize the
fate of Pentheus as unjust, we might have expected the chorus to change
its allegiance and denounce the punishment, or perhaps some other god
to appear and condemn Dionysus. The defense which Dionysus makes

is curt and formal, but we cannot overlook the fact that Pentheus has been quick to wrath and has betrayed his trust as the chief justice of the land. He has been guilty of insolence—always a serious crime in Greek morality—toward the divinity and his worshipers, especially toward the innocent Teiresias. Pentheus' charge of immorality in the worship, however plausible, is shown to be unfounded. Pentheus himself beneath his apparent constraint and continence has revealed an unhealthy viciousness. Even if his acts were predestined, plausible human motivation has been given him. Obviously he must be held responsible for his moral choice. His guilt, therefore, is sufficient to nullify any attempt to interpret the play as primarily an attack upon the divinity.

The *Bacchae* seems most naturally interpreted as essentially similar to the *Hippolytus*. Dionysus in certain aspects is the male counterpart and supplement of Aphrodite.[193] Such divinities in the Athens of this period were little more than poetic abstractions. Genuine religious fervor was centered in the worship of the mysteries at Eleusis and similar cults. Indeed, we may well doubt whether a serious iconoclast would have expended his efforts on worship as purely formal as that of Dionysus. In the *Bacchae,* Dionysus is the spirit of physical enjoyment in life and is opposed by the intellectual, abstemious, and somewhat unnatural Pentheus. Such a divinity, in reality hardly more than a personification of a basic force of man's nature, is quite incapable of mercy or pity or any other human emotion.[194] He is utterly inexorable. Punishment follows transgression of his law as inevitably as it does that of any other natural law. Such a divinity is wholly beyond the realm of human ethics, beyond good and evil—beyond belief and disbelief, also, for his existence and power theist and atheist alike must admit.

Discussion.—Dionysus himself speaks the prologue (63 lines). He mentions, but with no appearance of wrath, the opposition of Pentheus. Distinctly ominous is his description of this opposition as contending against divinity—a phrase that occurs again and again as a leitmotif throughout the play. Dionysus also declares that if the city takes up arms against his devotees he will lead his Maenads against its forces in battle; but he appears to lack clairvoyance and to leave the decision entirely to Pentheus. Such partial foretelling is dramatically the most effective, for now the audience knows that Pentheus' decision involves his fate.

The entrance song of the Bacchic chorus is one of the longest series of lyrics in Euripides (parodos, 106 lines). With mystic enthusiasm the chorus sing a gay and excited encomium of Dionysus and his worship, suggestive of the choral dithyramb from which tragedy is said to have originated. They exhort Thebes to join in the worship of its own Dionysus.

As if in answer to the exhortation of the chorus, Teiresias now enters and very skillfully introduces himself and Cadmus (first episode, 200 lines). These old men present a somewhat ridiculous (line 250) appearance each with his fawn skin and thyrsus (staff with a pine cone affixed to the end, a symbol sacred to Dionysus). Their gray heads are crowned with ivy, and perhaps they are tipsy under the influence of this god of wine. But they have chosen to take no chances of incurring the wrath of a new god.[195] Cadmus is further influenced by the fact that Dionysus is his grandson and any honor to him is an honor to his family, whereas a denial of his divinity would constitute an admission that Semele had given birth to an illegitimate child.

Pentheus first enters in a state of great excitement. His bold condemnation of the new worship stands out in sharp contrast to the sly caution of Cadmus and Teiresias. His first lines reveal the obsession which never leaves him and which is his main reason for opposing the worship of Bacchus: he believes that the women have gone off on a drunken revel in order to indulge in sexual immoralities. He pronounces the same slander of Semele (245) which Dionysus has cited in the prologue (31) as his justification for maddening the women of Thebes. The ill omen of this pronouncement is made unmistakable in the original by the literal repetition of a half-line. Sighting the two old men, Pentheus upbraids his grandfather Cadmus and accuses Teiresias of promoting the worship for his own selfish ends. The refutation which Teiresias attempts begins with a poetic description of the two great blessings of human existence: the grain of Demeter and the liquid of the grape cluster, discovered by the child of Semele, "which relieves suffering mortals of their grief, whenever they are filled with the flow of the vine, and gives a sleep that knows not the misfortunes of the day; nor is there any other sedative of woes." Eloquent this, especially in a land where bread and wine were and still are the staples of ordinary existence. But the old seer proceeds to sophistic rationalizing which leaves us cold indeed.[196] Cadmus, also, attempts to win over Pentheus, urging the honor of the family again and ominously reminding Pentheus of the fate of his impious cousin Actaeon.[197]

In answer to their invitation to join them in worshiping the god, Pentheus orders the seat of augury of Teiresias to be destroyed utterly and the effeminate stranger to be apprehended. The anger of Teiresias now breaks out, and he denounces Pentheus as a persistent fool[198] and prays that the wrath of the god may not be aroused against Pentheus or the city. The vagueness of this warning and the deprecation of Pentheus' coming to grief are here noteworthy, since the most effective foreboding tends to have a certain ironic optimism. On this significantly ominous warning the first episode comes to an end, having dramatized the situation described in the prologue and having portrayed Pentheus in a specific insolent act against established religion.

The chorus now echo the ominous words of Teiresias by calling the goddess of Sanctity to witness the insolence of Pentheus and by suggesting the evil fate that awaits Pentheus and the folly of unwise wisdom and of too great an ambition (first stasimon, 64 lines). The second part of the choral song celebrates Dionysus as the natural companion of Aphrodite, the Graces, and Desire (402–15); he loves Peace, the bringer of wealth and nourisher of children. The final note returns to the folly of too much wisdom and the desirability of accepting the ways and thoughts of the common man.

The mysterious stranger (Dionysus), whose apprehension was ordered at the close of the previous episode, is now brought on (second episode, 85 lines). The guard recounts the disconcerting gentleness of the prisoner and the miraculous escape of the imprisoned Maenads. But Pentheus is unimpressed and proceeds to insult the god and to reveal his own unhealthy curiosity concerning the rites of worship. The imperturbable dignity of the god emphasizes the angry insolence of Pentheus. As the god is finally led off to prison, he warns Pentheus in vain. For the second time Pentheus has refused to recognize evidence of godhead or to recant.

The chorus now protest at Thebes' opposition to her own god and invoke Dionysus to come and destroy Pentheus, who dares to contend against the gods (second stasimon, 57 lines). The voice of Dionysus is heard; the earth quakes; the entablature of the porch is rent (a few stones probably fall by some stage device); the fire on the tomb of Semele flashes. The chorus fall to earth before these divine manifestations.[199]

Dionysus, who announced at the end of the previous episode that the god would release him when he willed (498), now appears, again in his disguise as "the stranger," and reassures the chorus in trochaic meter—which is presumably suited to the excitement of the chorus rather than to the mood of Dionysus himself, for he maintains an Olympian calm in effective contrast with the rage and futile busyness of Pentheus (third episode, 286 lines). The young king is quite blind to the significance of the miracles which he has observed. He is equally blind to the report of the messenger, who now arrives in mid-episode[200] again to refute the charges of immorality and drunkenness upon which Pentheus has insisted. Further evidence of miracle and divinity is presented. Finally the messenger makes his own appeal (769–74) : "Then receive into your city this divinity, whoever he may be, my master, for he is great in respect to these other marvels and especially so in this: he it was, they say, who gave the care-releasing vine to mortals and, were there no wine, Love would no longer exist nor any other joy among men."

But here, as each time before, instead of assuming a calm and unbiased attitude and reaching a decision based on the evidence, Pentheus persists in his blind prejudice. Though chief justice of the land and presuming to represent the cause of reason against orgiastic superstition, he is anything but reasonable or just. As Theseus in the *Hippolytus* casts his son out of the land without allowing him a fair trial, so Pentheus repeatedly refuses to recognize the most unmistakable evidence of the presence of divinity. He clearly is guilty of insolence (*hybris*), and his punishment follows inevitably.

The climax of the play is pointed with unusual distinctness. Pentheus orders out his troops against the women—an action which Dionysus in the prologue (50–52) has cited almost casually as justification for the marshaling of his own forces. He now warns Pentheus that the god will not tolerate this, and he even offers to bring the women back of his own accord. But Pentheus calls for his armor, and Dionysus acts (810). Before "most gentle to men," Dionysus now becomes "most dreadful" (860–61).

The first line which Dionysus speaks when he begins to intoxicate Pentheus is of the greatest significance for his method: "Would you care to see the women sitting together on the mountain heights?" Dionysus has perceived the weakest spot in the character of Pentheus, a weakness which was observable on close scrutiny earlier in the play, especially in the first scene between Pentheus and Dionysus, and which might be accentuated by a skillful actor. Though presuming to be the champion of virtue and high morals, Pentheus under the spell of the god of wine reveals his prurient desires, emerging distorted and unlovely because of the suppression that has formerly inhibited them.

With keen psychological insight Euripides presents Pentheus, now drunk, as resisting Dionysus not on the main moral issue, the lecherous spying upon the women, but on a secondary act, the assuming of the dress of a woman. Still this itself is disgraceful, and the issue here, though secondary, consists of a single definite choice and so stands out with unmistakable clearness. The dramatic irony of many of the lines of this scene is noteworthy, as when Pentheus says that the sight of the drunken women would be painful to him (814). He is still vacillating when he retires into the palace, but Dionysus knows what the choice of

Pentheus will be and foretells his fate in a speech that is substantially a prologue to the latter part of the play.

After Pentheus and Dionysus have retired into the palace, the chorus sing of joyous escape (from the threats of Pentheus) and of reveling (third stasimon, 50 lines). In a refrain typically pagan in feeling, they express the joy of revenge upon an enemy. They celebrate the sure vengeance of the gods and again the happiness of the simple conventional life.

When the little remaining moral compunction of Pentheus has been dissipated on the secondary issue of clothing himself in the dress of a woman, he has lost all shame and is wholly in the power of the god (fourth episode, 65 lines). Now disgustingly drunk, he allows his costume to receive its final touches on stage as though he were a woman being tended by her maid. He descends to his lowest depths, however, when he says that the women must not be overcome by force, and when he fancies seeing them in the woods caught like birds in the sweetest snares of their beds of love (957–58). Here for a moment we suspect that Pentheus not even yet expresses his most intimate desires, that he really wishes to join in the immoralities of the women with the utmost abandon. The scene closes with a fearfully ironic exchange between Pentheus and Dionysus and with the god's again foretelling the fate of Pentheus.

In highly excited meter, the chorus envisage the fate of Pentheus out on Cithaeron (fourth stasimon, 47 lines). They pray for justice and vengeance upon "the godless, lawless, unjust" Pentheus with a refrain similar to that in the previous choral song. Again wisdom is renounced and the orthodox life is praised.

The final scenes open with another brilliant messenger's speech (exodos, 369 lines). After the innocence of the pursuits of the Maenads has again been stressed, we hear the dreadful story of the death of Pentheus and finally how Agave regards the head of her son as that of a lion. This prepares us, as the chorus have previously done (985–90), for the ensuing scene.

After a very short lyric, without responsion, in which the chorus rejoice, the mad Agave enters with her ghastly trophy. She is followed by other revelers, and she joins the chorus in an excited lyric exchange. Her exultation forms perhaps the most powerful scene of dramatic irony in all tragedy.

Such scenes with intoxicated or insane characters have an eeriness and effectiveness all their own.[201] One need recall only the scenes of the mad Ophelia in *Hamlet*. Euripides was especially skillful in depicting them. Here in the *Bacchae* the effect of the scene with Agave is overwhelming. The emotional tension has been magnificently built up by the divine manifestations of earthquake and lightning and by the scenes of the gradual intoxication of Pentheus.

Pitiful beyond words is the figure of the mad Agave. Even the chorus, though they have greeted the news of the death of Pentheus with merciless joy, must show some pity for her. She thinks of her son Pentheus and repeatedly wishes that he might come and rejoice with her (1212; 1252). She regrets that he is not a good huntsman like herself and that he is able to contend only with gods. The mad joy of his daughter embitters the grief of old Cadmus, who has now entered with the mutilated body of Pentheus, as if in answer to Agave's wish that her father and her son come and nail up on the front of the palace as a trophy the head which she bears. Agave madly insists on the appropriateness of a feast to which she invites the women of the chorus, and commands Cadmus, also, to invite his friends. Although the old man realizes that his daughters would be happier if they could remain mad always, he gradually brings Agave back to her senses by questioning her on those facts which she should know best of all. Cadmus admits the justice of the anger of the god, but he complains of the severity of the punishment and bemoans the ruin of his house, now without male issue.[202] He ends on the note on which the Messenger previously ended —the necessity of worshiping the gods.

At this point a considerable number of lines have been lost from the play. (Our one manuscript for this part of the play dates from the fourteenth century.) For modern tastes, however, it may be well that the lines have been lost, for we are told by a certain rhetorician that Agave "taking each of the members of Pentheus in her hands, laments them one by one."[203] We may be sure that for the Greek audience, however, Euripides so managed the scene that pathos did not degenerate into the revolting or the ridiculous.

Finally Dionysus appears as the god and foretells the future for these characters. But he in no way mitigates the ending of this most tragic of all Greek tragedies.

Character of Pentheus.—The technique used in the portrayal of Pentheus is noteworthy. It consists of a gradual unfolding, and only in the final scene is this process completed. On his first entrance his mask would have revealed him to be a very young king (cf. 1185–87). His actions show him to be quick to wrath, high-spirited, and too imperious—faults which later the first messenger with servile bluntness attributes to him. But Pentheus has the virtues as well as the faults of youthful nobility. He is idealistic and resentful of the introduction of demoralizing influences. He is also skeptical of the unreasonable and the implausible, contemptuous of seers and miracles and mysticism. In his first clash with Dionysus a hint of another of his faults is given, for here he shows an unhealthy curiosity concerning the rites of the new worship and a contempt that is not all contempt for the beauty of the stranger. With this revelation his insistence on the immorality of the devotees begins to take on a new light.

At first this suspicion of immorality has seemed plausible enough. Insistence upon the demoralizing influence of too much wine is common in Greek thought, including Euripides himself (cf. *Ion* 550–53). In very early Rome this conviction resulted in the severe ruling that a matron might even be put to death for drinking wine. Orgiastic cults appealing to women met opposition in both Athens and Rome.[204] However reasonable such a conviction may seem in the present play, the substantiation of it would, of course, justify the position of Pentheus to such an extent that the present outcome of the play would be unbearable. Euripides is primarily not a rationalist or a psychologist or an iconoclast, but a dramatist, and in the *Bacchae* these repeated charges of immorality are repeatedly refuted.[205] It is undeniable, furthermore, that wine and the joys of life need not lead to bestiality. Indeed it is only the unhealthy who associate these things with bestiality. The charges of Pentheus, therefore, are doubtless intended in part to reveal the unhealthy pruriency of his own mind. Certain it is that this pruriency makes it impossible for Pentheus to give credence to the refutation offered even by his own representatives. It is this pruriency, then, that is his tragic fault.

The pruriency of Pentheus' mind is brought out most clearly in his last scene when all inhibitions have been removed by intoxication. He is still pitiful rather than contemptible, however, for his vice is not such a very unnatural or unforgivable one in a spirited youth whose idealism has hardened into bigotry. Pentheus, then, is enough like ourselves to arouse our own fear of similar error, and his misfortune is not so thoroughly deserved but that it evokes our profound pity. He is the most effective type of tragic character.[206]

The admirable virtues of Pentheus, however, are well brought out only after his death—when the information is most tragic. Cadmus describes him as the affectionate and zealous guardian of his old age, and in the original text Agave also doubtless extolled his good qualities.

Some critics have maintained that Dionysus and not Pentheus is the main character of the play. Some also feel a "bewildering shift of sympathy" away from Dionysus to Pentheus as the play progresses.[207] But it is Pentheus who makes the tragic decision and suffers the reversal of fortune. The actor Jason of Tralles in the story from Plutarch already quoted chose to play the roles of Pentheus and Agave rather than the single role of Dionysus. Surely any actor would do the same. It seems likely, furthermore, that Euripides intended the audience to be sympathetic with Pentheus from the outset. Dionysus is so perfect, so utterly self-sufficient and untouched by human weakness, that a human being can hardly have the slightest community of feeling with him. Certainly Dionysus needs no pity and excites none. Pentheus, it is true, stands isolated from sympathy and support throughout most of the play.[208] But this is no indication that the poet does not wish the audience to feel sympathy with him. Indeed, the poet, by displaying absolutely no pity himself for Pentheus, obtains the greatest pity for him from the audience.

18. *IPHIGENIA AT AULIS

(About 405 b.c.)

The *Iphigenia at Aulis* was produced along with the *Bacchae*. The *Bacchae* seems to have been finished before the death of Euripides, but the *Iphigenia at Aulis* was apparently left unfinished. In comparison with the texts of the other plays, at least, the faulty text of the *Iphigenia at Aulis* resembles that of a production copy.

This play, which might be termed a melodramatic heroic comedy, is one of the most emotionally stirring of all Greek tragedies and perhaps the one most romantic and modern in its atmosphere. Its brilliantly developed plot has more complication and more dramatic action than is usual in Greek tragedy. Indeed, few if any Greek tragedies surpass it in this respect. Its appeal to the modern reader is correspondingly strong. Many noteworthy innovations—including innovations in degree—account for these effects. Although these effects may be very desirable, they are in part incompatible with the form and spirit of classical Greek tragedy. Dramatic complication and romantic excitement are achieved somewhat at the cost of classic simplicity and profundity.

Source and influence.—Aeschylus and Sophocles both wrote plays on the sacrifice of Iphigenia. A tragedy by the Roman (Oscan) Ennius on this subject seems to have been based primarily on Euripides' play. Among modern adaptations may be mentioned the *Iphigénie* of Racine (1674), the opera by Gluck (1774), and a contemporary production, *Daughters of Atreus,* by Robert Turney.

The sacrifice of Iphigenia was a favorite subject in ancient art. A famous picture of Timanthes, a contemporary of Euripides, is described by Cicero (*Orator* 74) and by Pliny the Elder (35. 73). Timanthes, we are told, had exhausted every means of depicting sadness in the faces of those standing about; so he covered the face of Agamemnon, whose grief he was unable adequately to depict. But doubtless the artist so portrayed Agamemnon because the father would naturally not wish to look upon the slaughter of his child.[209]

Discussion.—The opening dialogue in anapestic meter is one of the play's most noteworthy innovations. It may have been designed by some adapter to replace the monologue by Agamemnon, which may possibly have been the genuine Euripidean prologue.[210] This monologue constitutes an unusually dull prologue, for it insists upon reciting at length the story of Helen, which must have been known to every person in the audience. The alternative dialogue, however, is dramatic from the beginning and in a more spirited meter. This dialogue also contains very subtle preparation for the Old Man's revealing Agamemnon's secret to Clytemnestra (46–48), and for the wrath of Achilles when he learns of the low use to which his name has been put (124–27; 133–35). Aristophanes in his *Frogs* (1206 ff.), which was produced at about the same time as this play, severely criticizes the monotonous prologues of Euripides. Obviously a movement for a more dramatic opening scene is under way.

Alternate final scenes have not been preserved; but all scholars agree in rejecting the extreme end of the present play as spurious, and most scholars think that in the original ending Artemis appeared as the *deus ex machina.* A fragment of such a speech, describing the substitution of the hind, has been preserved, though its authenticity is sometimes questioned. Some lines spoken by Iphigenia in her final scene (1440–42), furthermore, obviously foreshadow her rescue and later apotheosis. It seems fairly certain, therefore, that the original ending included the supernatural rescue of Iphigenia despite the fact that such a rescue somewhat vitiates the very strong case which Clytemnestra has here been given against Agamemnon. This version of the sacrifice of Iphigenia reminds one of the story of the sacrifice of Isaac in Genesis (chap. 22). Such myths are designed to explain and justify the abandonment of human sacrifice. The main change made by the substitution of the extant final scene for the original one seems to be the introduction of a messenger's speech instead of the appearance of Artemis. It is possible that this change was undertaken to eliminate another favorite device of Euripides, the appearance of a divinity.[211]

Certain metrical practices of the play are noteworthy. Several shifts from the ordinary iambic trimeter to the excited trochaic tetrameter occur, usually with the entrance of a character. The lyrics show the peculiarities characteristic of Euripides' late lyrics—peculiarities satirized by Aristophanes in the *Frogs*. The tendency for long solo arias to replace choral songs is very marked, especially near the end of the play where the dramatist wishes rapidity of movement and desires to maintain Iphigenia as the center of interest.

Minor technical advances toward realism are noteworthy. Menelaus and the Old Man enter with lines that suggest they are continuing a conversation already in progress. Later in the same episode, a messenger enters and interrupts Menelaus in the middle of a line (414).[212] Very naturally these innovations were adopted by later dramatists.

In the *Iphigenia at Aulis* Euripides employs melodramatic devices to a remarkable extent. Intense pathos characterizes many scenes. Though at times genuinely tragic, as when Iphigenia greets her father, this pathos goes far beyond the limits usual in Greek tragedy. Indeed it often borders on sentimentality. Thus Iphigenia begs the infant Orestes to intercede in her behalf (1241–48), and later she pronounces a very pathetic farewell to the infant.[213] Suspense, also, plays a very important role in the play. But suspense and surprise, of course, tend to preclude that inevitability which characterizes most serious Greek tragedy. Again, spectacular scenes and events crowd the action of the play.

Still, the characters of the *Iphigenia at Aulis*, far from being the stereotyped puppets of melodrama, are vividly depicted individuals. They are drawn with a degree of homely realism that is uncommon even in the later plays of Euripides. Agamemnon, for instance, is a contemptible weakling. He vacillates helplessly and finally becomes the victim of circumstances which he should presumably command. His frantic efforts at base deception are as pitiful as they are futile. Menelaus has somewhat more determination but even less probity. Achilles, if proud and conceited, is at least brave and, to a degree, honest; but his cautious deliberateness differentiates him from that Achilles who is wrathful and inexorable and fierce, who recognizes no law as applicable to himself but refers all things to arms.[214] In Euripides' play the Homeric hero has been transformed into the more or less ideal, law-abiding citizen of Athens in the fifth century.

These characters are unheroically weak and ruled by external events. But this is not, as in true melodrama, the result of the poet's becoming primarily interested in these external events. Euripides wishes deliberately to expose the very ordinary humanity of these men and to contrast their weakness with the moral strength of Iphigenia. He wishes to dramatize what is perhaps the most pathetic paradox in all human life: ordinarily human beings are mean and contemptible, but at times one may rise to the most glorious heights of generosity and self-sacrifice.

The most melodramatic feature of these characters is found in their startling reversals of attitude. Agamemnon no sooner realizes that he is caught inextricably in events and must, after all, sacrifice his daughter than Menelaus himself shifts his position—or pretends to do so[215]— and begs his brother's pardon and admits that the sacrifice should not take place. Achilles enters complaining of the delay, but when he discovers that his name has been basely used—in an effort, of course, to put an end to the delay—he is willing to die in opposing the very factions which he at first represented.[216] But the most startling reversal of all is that of Iphigenia. The same intimate and trivial realism of portrayal of character which reduces Agamemnon and Menelaus to the unheroic now creates a very appealing Iphigenia. As an affectionate girl of timid modesty, she greets her father and later makes her tearful appeal to him. But after she has come to realize his helpless dilemma and to appreciate the gallant if rash bravery of Achilles, she suddenly becomes a courageous heroine. This reversal of attitude is criticized by Aristotle (*Poetics* 1454 a). We may assume perhaps that Aristotle was acquainted with a reluctant Iphigenia of Aeschylus and Sophocles. He was perhaps more surprised by this change, therefore, than the modern reader is likely to be. The effect of Iphigenia's reversal may indeed be melodramatic, but it is undeniably powerful. After the spineless vacillation of Agamemnon, after the frantic terror of Clytemnestra and the futile busyness of Achilles, emphasized by their nervous exchange of half-lines immediately before this climax, Iphigenia finally speaks out and announces her glorious resolve. She is unwilling to endanger family and fatherland, to block the united effort of Hellas, to see Achilles risk his life in contention with his own army, or to oppose Artemis. Helen has caused battle and death; Iphigenia will become the savior of Hellas.

This contrast between Helen and Iphigenia is an important theme of the play. Careful preparation has been made for it. Every choral lyric except that dealing with Achilles and Iphigenia has sooner or later come around to the theme of Helen and Paris. The chorus and almost every character of the play have insisted that Helen and her wicked passion have caused the war. Iphigenia now redeems Hellenic womanhood in saving the Greeks from internecine strife.

This stress upon Helen as the cause of the war may seem to spoil the contention of Iphigenia that the war is being waged for the honor of Hellas. Certainly the argument which Agamemnon uses with her (1259–75) is not consistent with all that has been said in his first clash with Menelaus. But consistency has never characterized such discussions in times of war. The original cause of war may well be greed of belly, groin, or back; but when war is once undertaken, honor and life itself are at stake for everyone. Iphigenia's contention that her sacrifice will save Greece and the men of Greece is not, therefore, wholly an illusion. Glorious self-immolation, furthermore, has been a favorite theme with Euripides from his first preserved tragedy, the *Alcestis,* and sacrifice for the fatherland has repeatedly been celebrated—Macaria in the *Heracleidae* and Menoeceus in the *Phoenissae* will be recalled. The patriotism of Iphigenia has a message for Athens in the last desperate phases of the Peloponnesian War. If Iphigenia is proud and conscious of her greatness, we must view her, like Hippolytus, in the light of her subsequent apotheosis.

The one character of the play having full tragic stature, however, is Clytemnestra. She is never reconciled to the sacrifice, despite the pleas of Iphigenia (1369–70; 1454), and she darkly hints of revenge upon Agamemnon when he returns home (1187, 1455). Indeed this play, like the *Trojan Women,* must be interpreted in the light of subsequent events.[217] Only in the *Iphigenia at Aulis,* furthermore, is Clytemnestra's case against Agamemnon stated with the full power which it obviously possesses. Here is Euripides' final word on the injustice of the vengeance of Orestes, and his final word utterly devastates the cold interpretation of Sophocles.

19. *RHESUS*

(Authorship and date uncertain)

Euripides seems to have written a play entitled *Rhesus,* but the genuineness of the present play was questioned even in ancient times. Some modern scholars, following an ancient critic, think that this play is a youthful work of Euripides; others with perhaps more justification believe that it was written by an unknown dramatist of the fourth century B.C.[218] It is probably the poorest of all extant Greek tragedies.

Discussion.—The *Rhesus* is a dramatic adaptation of the tenth book of the *Iliad.* Two major changes in the material may be noted. The Homeric version deals primarily with the Greeks, whereas the play is written from the Trojan point of view. This is obviously a necessary change if the play is to have anything of tragedy in it.[219] The other change, however, is a dramatic blunder which destroys the close connection between Dolon and the murder of Rhesus. In the Homeric version, Odysseus and Diomedes, having captured Dolon, inquire the whereabouts of Hector and the guards. Dolon in his craven efforts to save his life answers all their questions but gives an especially glowing account of the steeds and rich armor of the newly arrived Rhesus. Odysseus and Diomedes then dismiss any thought of attempting to find Hector and go straight to the camp of Rhesus. Athena appears only at the end of their depredations and warns them to flee. In short, the Homeric version is closely knit and uses divinities only for poetic effects. The playwright has made Athena give information affecting the immediate dramatic action—a device unparalleled in Greek tragedy—and the substitution of Athena's information for that of Dolon destroys the close connection between Dolon and Rhesus or, in short, the unity of the action. This blunder seems to betray an inferior dramatist.

In certain respects, the *Rhesus* shows striking similarities to other Greek tragedies. The final scene of the Muse with the body of her son may have been modeled on a similar scene of Eos (the Dawn) with the body of Memnon in the lost *Psychostasia* of Aeschylus.[220] The similarity of the subject matter here is also noteworthy: Memnon, like Rhesus, was an ally of the Trojans. Reminiscent of the words of Artemis at the end of Euripides' *Hippolytus,* furthermore, is the contention of the Muse that Athena is responsible for the death of Rhesus and that Achilles too must die.[221] But in the *Hippolytus* the quarrel of the divinities has profound significance; here it seems pointless. Again, some modern critics have thought that the scene of Diomedes, Odysseus, and Athena is modeled on the opening scene of Sophocles' *Ajax.* This may be so, but the dramatic function of the divinity in Sophocles' play is merely to allow this very spectacular scene of exposition, for Odysseus' own cleverness is equal to the task of discovering the guilt of Ajax. Similarly in Euripides' lost *Philoctetes,* Odysseus was disguised by Athena, but perhaps this was hardly more than a manner of saying that Odysseus showed inspired artistry in disguising himself. In the *Rhesus* Athena's interference is of a much more tangible nature.

The dramatic irony and certain other effects of the play are crude and heavy. Dolon promises to bring back the head of Odysseus or Diomedes—the very men who are to slay him. Rhesus is greeted by Messenger and chorus as the one man to slay Achilles. The chorus consider him Zeus or Ares and the deliverer of Troy. The boasts of Rhesus himself are no less extravagant. He will destroy the Greeks in a single day even without the help of Hector and his forces. This cannot be interpreted as mere braggadocio, since Athena herself later confirms it (600–604). It must be intended as dramatic irony and perhaps as serious glorification of Rhesus. As either it is overdone. To Rhesus' request that he be allowed to face Achilles, Hector responds by reminding him that there are other Greeks equally formidable—Ajax, Diomedes, and Odysseus. The crafty Odysseus, he continues, has done the land more harm than anyone else. He has entered Troy as a disguised spy and has stolen the statue of Athena and slain the guards. Rhesus is only contemptuous of such ignoble craft and promises to impale Odysseus as a temple robber! Even cruder are the words of the Charioteer near the end of the play, who in charging Hector himself with the murder intimates that no enemy could have discovered Rhesus unless some god had revealed him. Such irony is really comic.

Some good dramatic qualities, however, are found in the *Rhesus*. The opening scene is excellent. The entrance of the chorus at the very beginning of the play, however, is unique in Greek drama after Aeschylus and is thought by some critics to constitute deliberate archaizing. Ancient commentators reveal that two alternative opening scenes in iambic verse were known to them. One of these, attributed to actors, consisted of a scene between Hera and Athena.[222] The appearance of opposing divinities in prologue and epilogue is again reminiscent of the *Hippolytus*. Such hurry and excitement of the chorus as they enter in the *Rhesus,* furthermore, is more characteristic of Old Comedy than of tragedy. But no serious fault can be found here. Previous exposition is quite unnecessary, and the present opening gives a realistically effective impression of the disorder and confusion of the night camp.

The atmosphere of night is well simulated and maintained throughout the play—no small achievement, since the play was to be acted in the intense light of the open Greek theater. The entrance of Rhesus also is well managed. The Messenger's speech presents a splendid first description of Rhesus, and the second stasimon furnishes a spirited fanfare. The chorus are deftly involved in the action and play the role of a minor character. Their lyrics contain very little poetry—it takes more than one nightingale (550) to make a poetic drama. The departure and re-entrance of the chorus are plausibly motivated and effectively allow a vacant "stage" for the very melodramatic scene with Odysseus and Diomedes.

An excellent theatrical effect is achieved when the two Greeks enter with the wolf skin of Dolon. Thus the audience immediately realizes that the Trojan spy has been slain. This effect, of course, is not found in the Homeric version.[223] It is aided by the immediately preceding foreboding of Hector and the chorus. Odysseus' clever use of the watchword at the end of the scene is also the dramatist's own. The later scene with the wounded Charioteer is good theater, and the grief of the Muse is not without pathos.

As a whole, however, the play fails to create anything but the most superficial tragic effect. It lacks a tragic character. Hector is well portrayed in the early scenes, but unfortunately he has little to do with forwarding the dramatic action. Nor is the impact of the events of the play brought to bear upon him in an effective fashion. He well represents the Trojans, and the two tragic events of this night could have been interpreted as making the final ruin of Troy inevitable. If Hector had been made less confident in the opening scenes, the loss of Rhesus would have affected him more profoundly. The much less important loss of Dolon might have contributed something to this effect upon Hector. As it is, though the fate of Dolon is revealed to the audience, Hector only surmises it, and hence there is no occasion to depict any profound emotional reaction. Hector as presented is not a tragic character.

Nor does the play reveal any profound significance. The dramatist toys with the theme of divine Nemesis when the chorus hail Rhesus as a god and when Rhesus himself makes his extravagant boasts. But we hear no more of this theme. The anger of Hector at Rhesus' late arrival lends plausibility to the Charioteer's suspicions of treachery, but all this too is without significance. In short, the author has not been equal to the task of making this material into great tragedy. Indeed, he appears to have attempted only a loosely connected sequence of exciting action.

Part Two

OLD COMEDY

V

INTRODUCTION TO
OLD COMEDY

Comedy was first officially recognized at Athens in 486 B.C.[1] From this time it was produced at the City Dionysia, but it was more at home at the less formal Lenaea. Three comic poets, each with a single play, competed; and the comedies seem to have come in the afternoon after a series of three tragedies, beginning in the early morning, and usually a satyr-play also. Comedy of the fifth century was very different from the types which later developed, and it is termed Old Comedy. It had run a long course before Aristophanes produced his first play in 427 B.C.; but the only extant examples of Old Comedy are the first nine of his eleven extant plays.

Old Comedy is one of the "sports" of literature. Fantastic from the very beginning, if we may judge from the costumes of the *komos*-chorus, it deliberately cultivated its perversity. Tragedy, having developed earlier and remaining the more important dramatic presentation at each festival, naturally exerted constant influence upon comedy; but during the period of Old Comedy this influence was largely of a negative type—the one thing absolutely forbidden comedy was seriously to resemble tragedy. Formality in all its aspects and plausibility were the governing forces in the development of tragedy; hence informality and fantasy rule Old Comedy. Here as almost nowhere else in Greek literature the imagination runs riot, pure fiction is esteemed, and no idea can be too extravagant.

After the defeat and financial ruin of Athens in 404 B.C. there developed a type of comedy much less political and much less poetic, in which the chorus became almost wholly an interlude chorus, having little or no connection with the action. The favorite type of subject matter was now mythological travesty, including travesty of romantic and erotic adventure. The comedy of this period is called Middle Comedy; but except for the last two plays of Aristophanes no complete Greek play has been preserved from this period.

During the fourth century the romantic or erotic adventures of typical young Athenian gentlemen gradually became the dominant subject. The setting was now that of everyday life among the upper middle class at Athens. This type of comedy is called New Comedy. From this period have been preserved several fragmentary Greek originals of Menander, discovered during the last fifty years, and the twenty-six modified Latin translations of Plautus and Terence.

Details of these developments are best taken up in considering the transitional last plays of Aristophanes and New Comedy.

ORIGIN

Aristotle (*Poetics* 1449 a) says that comedy originated in the improvisations of the leaders of the phallic rites.[2] An example of these ceremonies, designed to assure the fertility of field and herd and human being, is found in the *Acharnians* (237–79), where Dicaeopolis marshals his family to celebrate the Rural Dionysia. Such ceremonies are described by other writers, also; but it is far from obvious just how comedy originated from them. Indeed, Aristotle himself (*Poetics* 1449 b) confesses that comparatively little was known about the early history of comedy even in his own day. It is often assumed, however, that the comic chorus of twenty-four members originated in Attica from the drunken revel (*komos*) in connection with the worship of Dionysus—basically a fertility divinity—whereas the actors were taken from the chorusless comedy that existed among the Doric Greeks long before Old Comedy came into being at Athens. Epicharmus, a comic poet among the Doric Greeks of Sicily, had gained a great reputation by the beginning of the fifth century B.C. His comedy related or dramatized amusing situations and sometimes, it seems, contained debates.

Doric comedy, also, had a close and obvious connection with phallic worship, for the actors were costumed in a lascivious manner and wore the phallic symbol.[3] Very similar was the costume of the actors in Attic Old Comedy—very different from the dignified costume of tragedy. These facts tend to substantiate the theory that the actors of Attic comedy were derived from the earlier Doric. The chorus of Attic comedy, however, was dressed differently, for the chorus did not wear the phallus—it is not worn but is carried on a pole in the ceremony in the *Acharnians*—and the chorus often appeared in fantastic disguises such as those of birds, flies, or horses with riders. Masks, of course, were universally worn, and Doric masks were not so very different from the masks of the actors in Old Comedy.[4]

STRUCTURE OF OLD COMEDY

The typical plot of an Aristophanic comedy is constructed very differently from that of a tragedy or a later comedy. Normally the leading character conceives a happy idea, ridiculous in its very extravagance and impracticality. So Dicaeopolis in the *Acharnians* conceives the idea of making a private peace with the Spartans. This idea normally meets with violent opposition—in the *Acharnians* from the old charcoal burners—but this opposition is overcome in a debate or "agon." The idea is now ready for the test of actual practice. But at this point the actors retire and the chorus come forward to address the audience in the "parabasis." After this purely choral section is completed, the actors return to the scene. The happy idea is now in practice, and the results are dramatized in a series of scenes between the main character and various typical figures who have been affected. These scenes have little or no connection with each other and there is no dramatic development, but emotionally they tend to rise to a climax. Normally, feasting and wenching gradually become the main concern of the chief character, as might be expected in a comedy which originated in the *komos*-revel and which was presented at the festival of Dionysus.

The structure of Old Comedy is ideally suited to polemics: the first half of the play is devoted to a statement and debate of the question, the second half to demonstration. The "plot" of the comedy is an idea, which is set forth in part by the dramatic action, in part by direct verbal appeal. Failure of the critic to realize this leads to endless confusion.

The comedies invariably open with a scene in simple iambic meter. In Aristophanes these scenes are usually very striking ones—old Dicaeopolis sitting alone on the Pnyx ruminating on the war and gazing longingly at his beloved countryside. The technique of giving the exposition shows an interesting development. A monologue suffices in the *Acharnians,* and this monologue is followed by a series of scenes which in general dramatize the situation already described. Essentially the same technique is used in the *Clouds.* The *Knights,* however, opens with a dialogue; but, instead of bringing out all the exposition in this most natural fashion, the author merely whets the interest of the audience, and then one of the speakers steps forward and gives the exposition in a frankly informatory address to the audience. This technique is repeated in the *Wasps,* the *Peace,* and the *Birds.* Real dramatic exposition has been achieved in the *Lysistrata,* the *Thesmophoriazusae,* and the *Frogs.* The final two plays, the *Ecclesiazusae* and the *Plutus,* tend to give up the ground won and revert to a monologue-prologue of the Euripidean type, which became the rule in later comedy.

The happy idea is normally revealed and the action proper begun in this opening iambic section of the play or "prologos." This section closes with the entrance of the chorus or "parodos," but the action here is usually rapid and continuous. The parodos in turn normally leads up to the agon. This agon has a very elaborate and carefully balanced form with interlarded lyrics (epirrhematic construction).[5] It begins with a lyric sung by one half-chorus (*strophe*); the coryphaeus or leader then encourages the first speaker in two lines of spirited recitative (*katakeleusmos*). The antagonist, who is sure to be the loser, then presents his case. A monotonously long harangue is avoided by having his opponent frequently interrupt with questions or amusing comments (speech or *epirrhema*); the first speaker ends his case with a more rapid final appeal spoken perhaps in one very long breath (choker or *pnigos*). The process now begins anew. The second half-chorus sing a precisely corresponding lyric (*antistrophe*), and their leader encourages the second speaker (*antikatakeleusmos*). He presents his successful case; the speech is again interrupted by the remarks of his opponent (*antepirrhema*), and is again concluded with a final rapid appeal (*antipnigos*). The chorus now give their decision in favor of the second speaker (seal or *sphragis*). Normally the adversary also accepts the happy idea, and it is ready to be put into practice.

Such is the perfect form of the agon. This occurs in the *Wasps* (526–727) and elsewhere; but more frequently, as in the *Acharnians* (490–625), the clash or debate is adapted to a somewhat less formal pattern.

The parabasis is even more obviously formulaic than the agon.[6] It it is a choral part and wholly undramatic; but it, too, is a type of interlarded lyric construction. The parabasis normally begins with the chorus' exhorting themselves to cast aside their cloaks and speak the anapests. The coryphaeus steps forward and usually in the beautiful eight-foot anapestic verse, for which Aristophanes has always been famous, addresses the audience. A fair impression of the original Greek meter may be gained from Roger's translation of the *Birds* (685–86):

Ye men who are dimly existing below, who perish and fade as the leaf,
Pale, woebegone, shadowlike, spiritless folk, life feeble and wingless and
        brief, ...

Except in the *Clouds,* a play never produced in its present form, the coryphaeus normally speaks this address in his own person and normally on a subject intimately connected with the theme of the play, such as, in the *Acharnians,* Aristophanes' boldness in attacking the monster Cleon. Indeed, the function of the anapests is to state the theme of the play or a plea closely bound up with this theme in unmistakably plain language. But the coryphaeus often refers to other plays of Aristophanes, insists upon the inferiority of the rival poets, and sometimes breaks out in the first person as if he were himself the poet. The anapests end with a more rapid final address (*pnigos*). At this point the coryphaeus steps back among the chorus. The first half-chorus then sing a strophe in which they normally invoke various divinities. The leader of the first half-chorus then recites a series of trochaic verses (usually sixteen). He normally speaks from the point of view proper to the chorus and on some serious subject. The second half-chorus then sing the corresponding antistrophe, and their leader recites a corresponding series of trochaic verses.

Both the agon and the parabasis are elaborate forms, and some scholars, assuming that such forms require historical explanations, have thought that these were ultimately derived from religious rituals. Such theories are very tenuous, however, and there is no evidence that any such religious rituals ever existed. But these elaborate theories cannot here be given a fair discussion. Suffice it to say that unsubstantiated theories have invited and excused a careless acceptance of these forms without any adequate analysis or understanding of their theatrical use and effectiveness. Such an analysis, in the opinion of the present writer, so clearly justifies and explains these forms that they no longer seem to call for any historical explanation more remote than early tragedy. The construction of interlarded lyrics is frequent in early tragedy. Indeed, it has been plausibly surmised that this construction is the earliest form of dramatic dialogue: the chorus sings, the actor responds in spoken verse.[7]

The short and incomplete lyrics of the interlarded construction, as clearly shown in tragedy,[8] join together, whereas the long complete lyrics of the episodic construction sever. Interlarded lyrics also tend to hasten the pace and create an obvious balance. Since the choral lyrics must correspond perfectly, there is a natural tendency for the spoken lines which the lyrics bracket to correspond. Interlarded lyrics, therefore, are naturally well adapted to a debate, where balance is almost inevitable and where, in the absence of dramatic action, it is especially important that the pace be made as rapid as possible. Nothing is more important in comedy, as Aristophanes himself intimates,[9] than rapidity. Even in tragedy, debates tend to become balanced and somewhat formalized; but the dignity of tragedy would not allow the development of fixed formulae and artificial schematic structure, whereas the informality of comedy invites such development. Still, the earliest extant tragedy, the *Suppliants* of Aeschylus (348–417), contains a formalized debate between the chorus and a character. This is constructed with interlarded lyrics and perfectly balanced speeches. There is an approach to such a form also in the last play of Aeschylus (*Eumenides* 778–915), but in both these cases the chorus is playing a major role. Debates are very frequent in the tragedies of Euripides. Here interlarded lyrics are not used—they are almost unknown in the tragedy of this period—but the speeches of the disputants tend to become balanced, and the chorus often encourages a speaker and gives its decision at the end.[10] From these various considerations it appears that the formal agon of comedy is simpler and more naturally adapted to its function than might appear at first glance, and that it may easily have developed from the less formal debates of tragedy.

It has been assumed by some recent scholars that comedy took the construction with interlarded lyrics from tragedy at a very early date, and this seems a likely assumption.[11] It also seems likely that this construction in comedy was first and most naturally adapted to the debate or agon. Certainly we need assume no ritualistic origin for the chorus' exhorting each of the speakers at the beginning of the debate and for its delivering a decision at the end. The only thing that remains to be explained, therefore, is the choker or *pnigos*. The theorists may derive this from religious formula if they choose; but let us not overlook its amusing effectiveness both in the agon and in the parabasis. Similar breath-taking rapidity is common in the light opera of Gilbert and Sullivan.

As for the parabasis, the delivery of the anapests by the coryphaeus is certainly striking.[12] To one with modern prejudices it seems that this direct address to the audience should come either before the play or after it. But obviously it could not possibly come before or after an Aristophanic comedy. The chorus is not on stage at the beginning of the play; their entrance is often spectacular and thoroughly in character. The typical ending of an Old Comedy, furthermore, is the revel-rout or *komos*, wherein nothing serious could be tolerated. The simple formula for the plot in Old Comedy naturally causes the play to break into two parts, and the pause between these is the only suitable place for such an address.

It need occasion no surprise that the coryphaeus in the anapests breaks the dramatic illusion by referring to their poet, his rivals, and similar literary or political matters, or that he even speaks as if he were the poet himself. The dramatic illusion is flouted at every opportunity in Old Comedy. An actor or the chorus elsewhere than in the parabasis may speak as the poet himself.[13]

The remainder of the parabasis is again mere interlarded lyrics. The subject matter—invocations to divinities, serious appeals, and sometimes personal abuse—is not peculiar to the parabasis. There seems to be no compelling reason, therefore, why we should assume that the parabasis is a vestige of undramatic ritual. But, whatever the origins of these forms, the student of literature should be concerned primarily with their functions.

The first half of the comedy including the parabasis is constructed with interlarded lyrics. Similar construction may be used in part after the parabasis, also, if the dramatic material warrants it; but here the episodic construction, typical of tragedy, dominates. In the episodic construction, a given scene or set of scenes is preceded and followed by choral lyrics consisting of strophe and antistrophe delivered as a unit without any interruption (stasimon). True episodes seem never to occur before the parabasis. These facts, also, have attracted the theorists. They have surmised that the first half of comedy with its interlarded lyrics may come from the Attic *komos* and may originally have ended with the parabasis, and that the second half with its episodic construction may come from the chorusless Doric comedy. It seems inconceivable to the present writer, however, that the *komos*-revel ever ended in the formal and dignified parabasis or in anything other than an ecstatic *komos*-revel.

Certainly the different constructions of the two parts of comedy can be adequately explained by functional considerations. In regard to subject matter, the first half is closely knit, and events follow in the relationship of cause and consequence. The section between the entrance of the chorus and the parabasis is normally taken up with the debate. The chorus here is intimately concerned with the action—more intimately than is normal in tragedy. Interlarded lyrics, therefore, are eminently suited to this section of the play, for they naturally lend themselves to continuity, to balanced speeches, and to binding the chorus more closely with the actors. The second half of the comedy is normally quite different in subject matter. A series of independent scenes illustrate the happy idea in practice. These scenes very naturally become independent episodes.[14] The individuality and the importance of the chorus here fade very markedly—their function as antagonists has been fulfilled. Even in tragedy the importance of the chorus often fades in the final scenes. But if a debate occurs in this part of a comedy, of course it will normally be constructed with interlarded lyrics. In short, the structure of Old Comedy, though strange at first glance, can be explained in terms of the material and of the effects to be achieved. Comedy's traditional informality and its resultant tendency toward schematization were important contributing factors.

VI

ARISTOPHANES

LIFE[1]

Aristophanes was an Athenian of the deme Cydathenaeon and the tribe Pandionis. The son of Philip and Zenodora, he was born perhaps about 445 B.C. His first comedy was certainly produced in 427 when he was very young. The *Plutus*, the last extant comedy, was produced in 388, but he is known to have written two comedies after this. All together he is said to have written forty plays—an average of one each year during his productive life. Of these, only eleven have survived; but these are well chosen and represent every period of his productivity.

Aristophanes is said to have acted the role of Cleon in the *Knights*, and modern scholars have often assumed that he took the role of Dicaeopolis in the *Acharnians*. He does not, however, seem to have been favorably disposed toward producing his own plays and often handed this task over to another. The reason for his doing so is disputed; but it is known that other writers of comedy indulged in the same practice, and the task of producing an Old Comedy was doubtless a laborious and exacting one.[2]

Aristophanes had three sons. One of these, Araros, produced comedies of his father and of his own, winning a victory in 387 B.C., possibly with a play of his father entitled *Cocalus*. Little is known of the other details of Aristophanes' life except what can be gleaned from the plays themselves. Included in this information is the fact that he was bald even when the *Peace* (771) was written. An interesting picture of Aristophanes is given in the *Symposium,* and a charming compliment is paid him in an epigram of Plato (Roger's translation):

> The Graces sought a heavenly shrine which ne'er
>   Shall come to nought,
> And in thy soul, Immortal Poet, found
>   The shrine they sought.

COMEDY UNDER ARISTOPHANES

One of the strangest and yet most characteristic features of Aristophanic comedy is its intermingling of serious political appeal, uproarious low-comedy farce, and beautiful lyric poetry. Some of the finest Greek lyrics—and that is to say some of the finest lyrics produced by the human genius—are found in his plays. Such is the Epops' invocation to his mate the Nightingale in the *Birds* (209–59). The parodos of the *Frogs,* also, has some beautiful poetry—and some most indecent personal abuse.

No element is more indigenous to Attic comedy than indecent personal abuse. Such abuse was one of the most important features of the old phallic ceremonies—ritualistic abuse, designed originally to drive out the evil spirit of sterility. From the beginning it was directed toward specific individuals and was outrageously frank and obscene.[3] The literary development of comedy had subordinated such abuse to the dramatic plot,[4] but the poets still. clung tenaciously to this privilege. Thanks to it, they had made comedy an important influence upon contemporary life.

The chief immediate predecessors of Aristophanes had turned their powerful streams of personal abuse upon the political and intellectual leaders of their day. Pericles especially was bitterly and repeatedly attacked, and attempts to suppress this license had failed.[5] Thus Old Comedy had become primarily political and social satire, and it was in this vital type that Aristophanes found his favorite subject matter. The political leaders of his day, far inferior to Pericles, cried out for such satire; and Aristophanes answered this call with masterly effectiveness. It is a mistake, however, to view Aristophanes as partisan in the narrow sense of that word. Wistfully looking back to the glories and simple prosperity of Athens after Marathon and Salamis, Aristophanes saw that the Peloponnesian War was a senseless contest of annihilation. He saw this more clearly perhaps than did any contemporary figure except Thucydides, for with this one exception the historical sagacity of Aristophanes was unequaled. Indeed, his criticisms of democracy are still practical and significant.

Aristophanes' loathing of the age in which he lived, however, went deeper than mere external political events. He hated the intellectual demagogues as bitterly as he hated the political ones—the Sophists for their ridiculous pretentiousness, Socrates for his disturbing and apparently destructive intellectual curiosity, and Euripides for these same qualities and for his emphasis on skillfully written and ingeniously produced drama rather than on great poetry.[6]

These hatreds of Aristophanes were keen and unequivocal; they knew no charity; they felt no obligation to be fair. Like many satirists, motivated by a high moral purpose, Aristophanes was himself often immoral in his refusal to present his arguments fairly; and at times, no doubt, he did more harm than good in his attacks, especially in the cases of Socrates and Euripides. Without his strong prejudices and hatreds, however, Aristophanes' passion would have been less intense, his wit less keen, his pathos less profound. As it was, this natural bent of his genius toward satire was happily fostered and stimulated by Old Comedy's traditional license of speech. The result was the world's greatest writer of poetic satirical comedy.

The purpose of an Aristophanic comedy, therefore, is almost invariably serious. Beneath its wild fantasy, it often reveals an allegory. But, true to the informality of Old Comedy, this allegory is thinly disguised and only carelessly maintained. Thus in the *Knights* the Paphlagonian at one time speaks of kneading a cake in Pylos, at another of capturing Spartans there.[7]

However serious, furthermore, Aristophanic comedy directs its appeal primarily to the emotions rather than to the intellect. An emotional appeal is at once more effective and more dramatic. It is also a more natural appeal for a type of literature originating in the bibulous glorification of Dionysus. The advantages of peace, for instance, may be the subject of debate in various plays. But more vivid in our memories than these arguments are certain scenes—those scenes of Dicaeopolis preparing his eels and thrushes for a glorious banquet in the *Acharnians,* or his gayly dancing about the orchestra with the flush of Dionysus on his face and a luscious girl on either arm.

Just how much influence the comic poets actually exerted upon public opinion is a matter of some uncertainty and dispute. Aristophanes did not succeed in stopping the Peloponnesian War. Indeed, his bitterest attacks upon Cleon did not prevent that gentleman from basking in the fairest favor at Athens. Still, the comedies may have had some part in causing Cleon to take the field in 422/21 B.C. or in bringing about the Peace of Nicias. Doubtless Aristophanes' attacks were most effective when his cause was most obviously just, as it was in these cases. Again, Hyperbolus may well have been driven from Athens in 417 B.C. partly by the incessant attacks of Aristophanes and his fellow poets, although the main cause of the ostracism of Hyperbolus was a coalition of the factions of Nicias and Alcibiades.[8] The career of Alcibiades, also, may have been affected by the attacks of Eupolis in his *Dippers* (*Baptai*) and of Aristophanes in his *Triphales.* If so, this is doubtless a case where the comic poets dealt a body blow to their state and contributed to her downfall. That the state tolerated bitter criticism of public policy and public leaders during the Peloponnesian War is a tribute to the enlightenment of Athenian democracy and possibly, we must reluctantly admit, an indication of its impracticality.

The custom of taking subjects from public affairs often led more

than one poet to write on the same subject at the same time. Both Aristophanes and Ameipsias attacked philosophers in 423 B.C. Aristophanes
and Phrynichus both produced comedies dealing with the great tragic
poets at the Lenaean festival in 405 B.C. As their subject matter tended
to be the same, so did their attitude, which was regularly negative. They
were all highly critical of their own day and "praisers of the times gone
by." Like dramatists of all periods, they were an imitative lot. Aristophanes' attack on Cleon led to the attack of Eupolis and others on
Hyperbolus—and to Aristophanes' loud cry of plagiarism (*Clouds*
545–59). But this charge is of little importance. In this same passage
Aristophanes condemns Eupolis for imitating Phrynichus in bringing
on a drunken old woman doing an indecent dance. But in the *Wasps*
Aristophanes himself brought on a drunken old man in such a dance.
So Aristophanes criticizes the other cheap jokes and devices of his contemporaries, and then uses them himself![9] Nor are we to take seriously
his contention that his own comedies are lofty compositions and those
of his rivals mere farcical trash.

Aristophanes frequently plunders his own plays—in spite of his
early disclaimer (*Clouds* 546). His parody of the *Telephus* in the
Acharnians was very effective; hence he uses essentially the same
scene again in the *Thesmophoriazusae*. He never tires of satirizing
Hippolytus' threat to renounce his oath, and the eternal remarks about
Euripides' mother must have become most boring to the spectators.
Repetition of motives within a given play, also, is common. The
Knights furnishes an especially glaring example.

As a result of its emphasis on political and social satire, Aristophanic comedy was written for a day and an hour. It is topical
rather than universal, and the modern reader may often be unable to
appreciate a quip or a scene or a whole play because he does not know
the person or event or situation to which the poet is making reference.
Another result of writing topical comedy is found in the use of generalized characters. Dicaeopolis is "Mr. Good Athenian," and his name,
specially coined by the author, declares that;[10] accordingly, he is not
given any personality that marks him out as an individual. In short,
the characters of Aristophanes are generalized, and the situations are
topical and specific.

A result of Aristophanic comedy's disregard of plausibility and its
contempt for realistic psychology is its frequent glaring inconsistencies.
In the *Birds*, for instance, Pisthetaerus leaves Athens to escape from
its litigiousness, its imperialistic war and chaos; but he soon institutes
a scheme of superimperialism for gaining control of the universe. In
the *Ecclesiazusae*, women are praised for their conservatism, but when

they gain control of the government they introduce communism. In the *Knights,* the Sausage-Seller begins by being worse than Cleon but ends by restoring Demos to his glorious former self. Various considerations may explain these inconsistencies. At one time the author is playful, at another serious. Like all good writers of comedy, he will say anything to raise a laugh. Sometimes it is difficult to determine whether he is playful or serious, for his wit is a hard brilliant gem of endless facets, and it often takes a diabolical turn that deceives the unwary. Thus at the end of the *Wasps,* when the chorus congratulate Bdelycleon on the success of his reforming his father and later say that never before has a chorus left the orchestra dancing, the wit is probably found in the falsity of both statements. Minor inconsistencies are so very numerous that they need no explanation, and except in the *Clouds,* perhaps, they should never be used to support any analysis of the plays into original and revised compositions. All the comedies, it seems, were dashed off in the rosy flush of genius and with a single bottle of wine— but a large one.

The minor phases of dramatic technique are characterized by the same careless informality. The scene of the play may shift with bewildering rapidity and nonchalance. The *Acharnians* opens on the Pnyx, but no sooner is the assembly dismissed than Dicaeopolis seems to find himself before his home in the country, and a few hundred lines later he is knocking at the house of Euripides on an ordinary street in Athens. The unity of time is handled with similar freedom. In the same play, Amphitheus is sent off to Sparta and returns from his negotiations and journey of some three hundred miles less than fifty lines later.

The dramatic illusion, a much more hardy illusion than critics sometimes realize, is greatly abused. Old Comedy laughs at everything, including itself and its audience. Trygaeus in the *Peace* is flying to heaven on his winged beetle when he suddenly addresses the audience and warns them not to attract his beetle by indulging in certain natural processes for the next three days; and he has soared aloft only a few more feet when he calls down to the stagehand to be careful with the flying contraption! In the *Acharnians,* Dicaeopolis usually speaks as an Attic farmer; but now he becomes the poet Aristophanes (377–82; 502–7), though a few minutes later, it is the coryphaeus who is speaking as the poet (659–64).[11]

Stage movements, also, are on occasion hardly more than schematic. Thus Lysistrata (*Lysistrata* 199) calls for a jar of wine to be brought out, and it immediately appears. Not a single line is said in the meantime, and we should probably assume no interval. Old Comedy utterly disregards mechanical plausibility or realism. Again in the *Lysistrata* the Lacedaemonian Herald appears from one wing (line 980) and the Athenian Magistrate practically at the same time from the other. No explanation is given for this pat coincidence. In similar fashion foreshadowing and preparation—details worked out with great care and admirable skill by the great tragic poets—are almost wholly neglected.

The last notable feature of Old Comedy, like the first, is its perversity. Though we analyze and generalize, the one universally true generalization is that no universally true generalization can be made concerning Old Comedy. A formula can be extracted from the various plays, but no play fits it precisely. The formula is varied with Protean metamorphoses; the versatility of Aristophanes is astounding.

The death of Old Comedy was made inevitable by the loss of real political independence at Athens. The very versatility of its poets, also, brought on change and development. The influence of tragedy, too, in the end proved irresistible, for the Gargantuan efforts of comedy to be unlike tragedy gradually were enervated. But tragedy itself, of course, was undergoing changes. It had descended from the Olympian heights of Aeschylus until in the later plays of Euripides it had almost reached the level of the ordinary Athenian street.

Mythological travesty had furnished subject matter as early as Epicharmus, and it had never been totally eclipsed even in the days of Aristophanes' early career. Something approaching a comedy of manners, also, had occasionally appeared during this period.[12] Perhaps the early development of this type was prevented by comedy's role as the foil of tragedy. In Aristophanes' extant works, romantic themes appear first in parodies of single scenes from romantic "tragedy," as in the *Thesmophoriazusae*. Later he may have written sustained parodies of whole plays. His *Cocalus*,[13] at least, dramatized events which may have been included in Sophocles' *Kamikoi*. What began as parody ended as romantic comedy: witness Plautus' *Amphitryon*. Thus a new world was opening up: a new type of comedy was springing from the ashes of the old.

It was most fortunate for this development that the great master of Old Comedy placed the stamp of his approval upon the most important steps: the elimination of the chorus as an integral part of the action, and the shift to homely subject matter. In his last preserved play, the *Plutus*, both of these steps have been taken. Thus comedy survived as a vital literary form. If a tragic poet of similar importance and originality had lived to make similar changes, tragedy too might have survived.

1. *ACHARNIANS

(Lenaea, 425 B.C.)

The *Acharnians* was produced not by Aristophanes himself but by Callistratus, and it won first prize. Cratinus won second with his *Storm-Tossed Men* (*Cheimazomenoi*) and Eupolis third with his *New Moons* (*Noumeniai*). Nothing is known of either of these lost plays, but it is noteworthy that the three competitors were the three most eminent poets of Old Comedy and that they are here ranked as they were later by ancient critics. It is often assumed that the role of Dicaeopolis in the *Acharnians* was played by Aristophanes and that the audience knew this.[14]

The *Acharnians* is a brilliant production. Any one of several scenes—the parody of the *Telephus,* the scene with the Megarian selling his starving daughters, or the final scenes with Lamachus—would make a comic poet's reputation secure for life. A vast array of incidental characters appears in the play, and the poet repeatedly rushes over change of scene and passage of time with bewildering rapidity and nonchalance. The variety of incidents, also, is amazing. In the first half of the play each incident follows naturally from what precedes, and the chorus plays an important role. In the second half of the play the chorus loses almost all its characterization and importance. The episodes here are practically unconnected, but all clearly show the advantages of peace.

Historical note.—Since the geography of Greece made communication difficult and defense easy, the country naturally developed many small independent units. Independence was fostered also by slight differences in language and race and by petty jealousies. Some degree of Panhellenism had been achieved under the stress of the Persian invasions, but this was superficial and brief. Afterward Greece tended to divide into two groups, neither very harmonious, under the leaderships of Sparta and Athens.

Sparta was a land power, governed as a socialistic oligarchy. Spartan citizens were vastly outnumbered by their dissatisfied serfs and slaves. This basic instability added to their conservatism. Sparta had no ambition to expand her power or increase her commercial activity. Her citizen army required no pay, and money was of little value in the very simple life of her citizens. Sparta's chief concern was in maintaining the *status quo*. The states which recognized her leadership, therefore, were not required to pay any tribute; but democratic governments were distrusted and oligarchies governing in the Spartan interests were supported on occasion by the use of force.[15]

Athens was a sea power, the natural leader of the islands and Ionian cities during the crisis with Persia. All these contributed to the maintenance of a fleet—much more expensive than an army. At first only the smallest states contributed money rather than men and ships; but later payments in money became obligatory, and the treasurers were Athenians. This was a definite step toward the formation of an empire from a league of presumably independent states.

The second administrative step came with the discontinuance of league assemblies at Delos, the religious center of the Ionian Greeks, and with the transference of the treasury from Delos to Athens (454/53 B.C.). The third step was the appropriation of the league's funds by Athens. Pericles argued that the members of the league had nothing to say about the disposition of the money as long as they were protected by Athens (about 443 B.C.).[16]

Simultaneous with these administrative developments was an ominous hardening of attitude toward states within the league's sphere which were not members and toward states which chose to secede. Force was used in both cases as early as about 470 B.C. Such use of force was extremely distasteful to the Greeks, who were most jealous of any encroachment upon rugged individualism; and Athens gradually came to be considered the tyrant of Greece.

Various factors encouraged Athens in her imperial designs. Attica was naturally a poor country, and prosperity came only with foreign trade and mastery of the sea. Pericles, furthermore, had discovered and was systematically exploiting the great weakness of democracy— the corruption of the electorate by the use of public funds. He had come into power by this method about 461 B.C., and by it he maintained control of the government for the remainder of his life.

At Athens public funds came largely from levies on trade and imperial tribute. It was natural, therefore, that Pericles should maintain a policy of ardent imperialism. Vast schemes of expansion were conceived. Expeditions were sent to Egypt with results only less disastrous than the results of the later expeditions to Sicily. Vast programs of public works were undertaken at home. These had the most glorious results for art—the Parthenon and the sculptures of Pheidias. But for the city this policy in the end was ruinous. The limitless ambitions of Pericles and Athens under his leadership finally led to a serious clash with Sparta in 431 B.C. Pericles deliberately chose to fight at this time; and, since he was an able commander, he might well have prosecuted the war to a successful finish if the unforeseen, as happens so frequently in war, had not occurred.

The Spartans and their allies invaded Attica, as Pericles had expected, for they were much superior on land. They camped in the neighborhood of Acharnae and hoped that the Acharnians, now within the walls of Athens and themselves a considerable part of the Athenian state, would be impatient at the destruction of their property and would communicate a desire to fight to the whole Athenian people.[17] But Pericles succeeded in restraining them. This was excellent strategy but perhaps unfortunate; for the next year, when the invasion recurred, a dreadful plague broke out in the overcrowded city, and vast numbers of fighting men and other citizens died. Pericles himself fell a victim in 429 B.C. A minor epidemic broke out again in 427. Meanwhile Athens had her share of successes in the field; but these did not begin to offset the dreadful ravages of the plague.

The main successor of Pericles was Cleon. Like his predecessor, Cleon was a master of political device; but, unlike Pericles, Cleon was small and mean and cowardly. Suffice it here to say that in 427 Cleon induced the Athenians to order the death of all male citizens of Mytilene, which had recently revolted, and the enslavement of all the women and children. This decree was fortunately revoked before it was executed, but the day was soon coming when Athens passed such decrees and did not revoke them.

At this crucial period of Athenian history—and during the fifth century Athenian history almost alone constitutes the cultural history of Western civilization—the precocious Aristophanes produced his first comedy. That a young genius should be attracted to comedy at such a time seems strange only to one unfamiliar with the seriousness and vigor of Athenian comedy during the fifth century. In point of fact, it is inconceivable that such a man as Aristophanes, at once a fiery patriot and a literary genius, should have been attracted to any other type of expression at this time.

Aristophanes' first production was awarded the second prize in 427 B.C. Called the *Banqueters* (*Daitales*) and produced by Callistratus, it was a social satire of Sophistry and the newer education. It was a very timely piece, for in this year the Sicilian Sophist Gorgias was to create a sensation at Athens with his novel and affected oratory.

At the City Dionysia in 426, Aristophanes' *Babylonians* was produced by the same Callistratus. This play was a very bold attack upon the imperialistic policy of Cleon and Athens, the cruelty of which had clearly been shown in the recent proposed treatment of Mytilene. It has been conjectured that the play took its name from a chorus of cities being worked by Cleon as Babylonian slaves. This called down the wrath of Cleon as related in the *Acharnians,* and Aristophanes was launched on his great career.

Happy idea and theme.—When Dicaeopolis finds that not even the god Amphitheus ("Divine-on-both-sides") can advocate peace in the assembly without being manhandled by the police, he decides to have this deity negotiate a private peace for him. As a consequence, the Acharnians accuse Dicaeopolis of treason, and he must attempt to defend his actions even before these hard-bitten old charcoal burners. The second half of the play shows Dicaeopolis' private peace in action. The Dionysiac delights of feasting, drinking, and wenching are described with such sustained vividness and such youthful exuberance that even the most martial spectators must finally have been overcome with a nostalgic longing for the gay abandon of peaceful celebration. This emotional appeal for peace is the main purpose and the main effect of the play.[18]

The intellectual appeal for peace is comparatively weak. This consists first of the defense of Dicaeopolis. Perhaps in parody of the story of Helen and the Trojan War, he explains the whole Peloponnesian War as originating over three hussies, and lays the blame for it (496–556) upon Pericles and the Athenians, where, of course, the blame actually belonged. The short scene with Lamachus which follows harks back to the theme of envoys and political corruption. The parabasis carries on these same topics in much the same vein. The anapests (626–58) are a defense of the poet, it seems, against the charge of treasonable sentiments, just as the agon has been a defense of Dicaeopolis against this charge. Indeed, Dicaeopolis, with the loose informality of Old Comedy, has identified himself with the poet in the earlier part of the play (377–82) and in his defense proper (502–7; cf. 595) in order to lash out fiercely at Cleon, who has been repeatedly attacked from the first lines of the play. Now the coryphaeus identifies himself with the poet for the same purpose ("choker" or *pnigos,* 659–64).[19] The mention of the Lacedaemonian proposals for peace, of course, is strictly pertinent to the main theme of the play.

Parody of tragedy.—Criticism of Euripides and parody of scenes from his tragedies are already favorite devices of Aristophanes in this the earliest of the extant comedies. Here, at least, this parody is not mere fun or mere literary criticism. Euripides in this period was supporting the national effort with plays glorifying the martial spirit, like the *Heracleidae,* and with plays bitterly attacking the Spartans and Delphi, like the *Andromache.* To discredit Euripides, then, is to forward the cause of Aristophanes.

Here, as later, the *Telephus* of Euripides is Aristophanes' favorite victim. Dicaeopolis' seizure of the charcoal basket as hostage and his threat of slaughtering it is a brilliant travesty of Telephus' seizure of the child Orestes in order to gain a hearing from the Greek chiefs.[20] All this nicely prepares for the following scene, introduced by mock tragic lyrics, in which Dicaeopolis appeals to Euripides for the rags and paraphernalia of a suppliant. Incidentally the tragic device for showing an interior scene is satirized by having Euripides appear upon the *eccyclema*. An amazingly long list of ragged heroes is recited before Euripides comes to the miserable Telephus. But Dicaeopolis is not satisfied with the mere rags; he continues his detailed requests for equipment until Euripides, as the experienced spectator might anticipate, complains that he is being stripped of his whole tragic art. Thus Aristophanes intimates that the art of Euripides consists wholly of external trappings.

The more formal defense of Dicaeopolis before the chorus, also, is a parody of the defense of Telephus, and perhaps the sudden entrance of the panoplied Lamachus when half the chorus has been convinced is reminiscent of the entrance of Achilles when Telephus had almost persuaded Agamemnon.[21]

Parody plays an important role also in the later part of the comedy. Dicaeopolis greets the Copaic eel like a long-lost child recognized in a Euripidean melodrama.[22] The chorus announces the messenger who comes to summon Lamachus in such a way that the mask may be identified as that of the tragic messenger bringing news of calamity (1069–70). The servant who reports the fate of Lamachus also delivers a speech that is reminiscent of tragedy.

2. *KNIGHTS (HIPPES, EQUITES)*[23]

(Lenaea, 424 B.C.)

The *Knights* was produced by Aristophanes himself and won first prize; Cratinus won second with his *Satyrs,* Aristomenes third with his *Wood-Carriers (Hylophoroi).* Eupolis in his *Dippers (Baptai,* 415 B.C.) claimed that he collaborated with Aristophanes in writing the *Knights,* and ancient commentators attribute the later part of the second parabasis (1264–1315) to Eupolis.[24]

The *Knights* is one of the least interesting plays of Aristophanes for the modern reader. It is wordy and lacking in progressive action. Four contests are dramatized and a fifth is reported. In these contests the various charges against Cleon are repeated over and over again. The point that he stole the victory at Pylos is made no less than four times (56, 745, 778, 1201). In spite of these faults, however, the play doubtless made a strong appeal to the original audience owing to Aristophanes' boldness in so attacking Cleon at the height of his glory. The general conception and the comedy of the opening scenes, furthermore, are brilliant. Aristophanes' political analysis and also his kindly satire of Demos are most apt.

Historical note.[25]—During the summer following the presentation of the *Acharnians,* the Athenians carried out one of their most successful campaigns during the whole war. As a fleet of forty ships was being made ready to sail to Sicily, Demosthenes, perhaps the best Athenian general at this time (not to be confused with the great orator of the next century), gained permission to use the fleet as he chose when it was coasting along the Peloponnesus. He had secretly conceived the brilliant idea of establishing a garrison at Pylos, a strong position on the coast some fifty miles west of Sparta. This was to be held by Messenians, who had been the original inhabitants of the country before being driven out by the Spartans, and who spoke the same dialect as the Spartans and could therefore disguise themselves and very effectively make incursions into Spartan territory. When the Athenian fleet actually reached Pylos, Demosthenes made known his plan; but he was unable to convince the commanders or the men of the wisdom of such a bold venture, and they would have refused to put in despite Demosthenes' official commission if bad weather had not suddenly forced them to take shelter at this point.

When the weather continued adverse, the men as a mere pastime began the fortification for which Demosthenes was pleading. They worked six days with the stone and natural timber at hand. Then good weather returned and the fleet sailed on, leaving five ships with Demosthenes and his folly.

The Spartans were more amused than frightened at the first news of this; but on second thought they began to take the matter more seriously. Their army had already invaded Attica; but, after only fifteen days of ravaging, it was withdrawn to be sent against Pylos. The Spartan fleet, an encounter with which was the immediate objective of the Athenian fleet, eluded the Athenians and also came to Pylos. The temporary garrison under Demosthenes was attacked by these vastly superior forces but not before two ships had been sent to summon the Athenian fleet, which returned to surprise and defeat the Spartan ships. This event left four hundred twenty Spartan heavy infantry stranded near by on a wooded island, Sphacteria, and now at the mercy of the Athenians.

When officials from Sparta perceived the desperateness of the situation they asked for a truce, and envoys were sent to Athens. Their suit for peace was rejected, mainly at the instance of Cleon (*Knights* 794–96), an enemy of peace "because he fancied that in quiet times his rogueries would be more transparent and his slanders less credible."[26]

Hostilities were resumed after the Athenians had treacherously re-fused to return sixty ships which the Spartans had given over as a guaranty for maintaining the truce.

Weeks passed. The Athenians did not dare attack the Spartans on the rough and dense island. Great ingenuity was shown in getting sup-plies to the Spartans despite the constant watch of the Athenian ships. As time passed, the Athenians at home became fearful that winter would overtake the siege and allow the Spartans to escape; they became incensed at Cleon for causing them to reject the Spartan overtures. Cleon laid all the blame on the command; and pointing at Nicias, the leading general still at Athens, he said that it would be easy, if the generals were real men, to sail against the island and take the Spartans, and that he would do just this if he were general. To Cleon's surprise Nicias was quite ready to allow him to take this command. Cleon was forced to do so, therefore, and boasted that within twenty days he would kill or capture the men on the island. At this, "the wiser sort of men were pleased," says Thucydides (4. 28, Jowett), "when they reflected that of two good things they could not fail to obtain one—either there would be an end of Cleon, which they would have greatly preferred, or, if they were disappointed, he would put the Lacedaemonians into their hands."

By a happy accident a fire had swept over the island and denuded it, and Demosthenes was preparing an attack when Cleon arrived. The attack was successfully carried out as Demosthenes had planned, and "the mad promise of Cleon was fulfilled."

On his return to Athens, Cleon was rewarded with a golden crown, with the privilege of dining in the Prytaneum along with the descend-ants of great national heroes—the greatest honor in the Athenian state and one never enjoyed even by Pericles (*Knights* 283). Cleon was also given a seat of honor in the theater at all public festivals (702); but at the very next festival Aristophanes presented his *Knights!*

Meanwhile Nicias had sailed across the Saronic Gulf with an Athenian force including two hundred cavalry. Mainly by the aid of this cavalry he scored a minor success against the Corinthians. A reference is made to this expedition in the *Knights* (595–610).

Happy idea and theme.—At the opening of the play, Nicias is racking his brain for some clever Euripidean plot for the overthrow of Cleon, and with the aid of the prophecies he and Demosthenes hit upon the idea of finding a greater rogue than Cleon to supplant him. The idea is itself a satire of the tendency of democracy, once having begun a course of basic corruption, to fall victim to more and more depraved leaders. Pericles, though personally incorruptible and magnanimous, had begun the corrupt practice of maintaining his power by the use of public funds. After his death, various demagogues, including Cleon, exploited these same devices in the most shamelessly corrupt fashion. Cleon was fated to be succeeded by Hyperbolus, an even more depraved scoundrel, who is ominously looming upon the horizon even in the *Acharnians* (846) and whose fantastic scheme for an expedition against Carthage is attacked in the *Knights* (1300–1315).

The *Knights* is a merciless satire of the contemptible practices of these demagogues. It also shakes a paternal finger at the Athenians for being taken in by such practices. But the thought that Athens was inevitably going from bad to worse, however sound, is not a happy one, and Aristophanes refuses to maintain it throughout the play. Agoracritus does beat down Cleon by shouting louder and by stealing more cleverly; but long before Demos actually renounces Cleon, there is a change in Agoracritus' attitude toward Demos; indeed, Agoracritus is gradually metamorphosed into Aristophanes. Thus when Demos first enters, Agoracritus upbraids him for his rejection of the "good and fair" gentlemen in favor of lamp-sellers (Hyperbolus), hide-stitchers, cobblers, and leather dealers (Cleon). This repeats the criticism of Athens' rejection of educated leaders voiced by Demosthenes (*Knights* 191–93) and by the chorus in the early part of the play (334; cf. 986). At the end of the play, furthermore, Demos does not remain under the control of rogues but is rejuvenated and restored to his condition under Aristeides and Miltiades. The serious plea of the *Knights,* therefore, is much the same as that of the *Frogs*—the return to the limited democracy of the period of the Persian wars.

Only minor references are made to peace in the course of the play; but in the end Aristophanes repeats the sensual appeal of the *Acharnians* for a thirty years' truce with Sparta.

Structure.—The *Knights* is somewhat peculiar in form. In an amusingly frank address to the audience, the action of the play is more thoroughly anticipated than usual in Aristophanes.[27] Here all the main charges against Cleon are listed, and the ensuing action consists largely of dramatic illustration of the points here made. The happy idea, furthermore, leads only to interminable abuse and to one contest after another. The first extended clash between Cleon and Agoracritus becomes a formal agon (303–460), which ends in Cleon's taking his adversary, as he had once taken Aristophanes (*Acharnians* 379), before the Council. After the parabasis, Agoracritus delivers a long speech, modeled on such reports in tragedy, in which the results of the contest before the Council are made known. Cleon then enters and insists on carrying his case to Demos himself.[28] A second formal agon is the result (756–941). This ends with a demonstration of the baseness of Cleon's motives and with Demos' dismissal of Cleon as his steward.

There is now a shift from the construction with interlarded lyrics, which characterizes a formal agon (epirrhematic), to the episodic structure. This change is made not because the coming scenes are any less eristic but because both Cleon and Agoracritus must retire before each episode for the preparation of their equipment and doubtless because the poet wishes to avoid monotony.

The contest in oracles satirizes the gross abuse of popular superstition which had become so common during the war.[29] This contest, too, ends in favor of Agoracritus. After a lyric interlude, another episode follows. This time, food is the bait for gaining the favor of Demos. The climax of this scene, and indeed of the whole play, comes when Agoracritus steals the hare which Cleon is about to give Demos and presents it as his own, just as Cleon stole the victory at Pylos.[30] But the final test of the rivals is an examination of their baskets. Cleon's is found loaded with good things which he is holding back for himself.

The short closing scene showing the rejuvenated Demos is the only one which exhibits the result of the contests, the function to which, as a rule, the whole second half of an Aristophanic comedy is devoted.

The cast of the *Knights* has only five roles—the smallest of all ancient comedies preserved—and of these five Demosthenes and Nicias are essentially protatic characters used for purposes of exposition. Even so, we may note incidentally, these two figures are very nicely characterized with their historically correct individualities, Demosthenes as bold and resourceful and fond of conviviality, Nicias as cautious—but personally courageous—devout, and a water-drinker. In production, the actor taking the role of Nicias obviously played that of Cleon also,[31] while the actor of Demosthenes took the role of Demos.

Although the whole play is concerned with Cleon, his actual name occurs only once (976).

3. *CLOUDS (NEPHELAI, NUBES)*

(City Dionysia, 423 B.C.)

Cratinus won first prize with his *Flask* (*Pytine*), Ameipsias second with his *Connus,* and Aristophanes third with the *Clouds.*[32] This defeat very much galled Aristophanes, who in the *Knights* (526–36) had intimated that Cratinus was now practically dead and should be "buried" with the greatest respect. A revision of the *Clouds* was undertaken and published some time between 421 (production of Eupolis' *Maricas; Clouds* 553) and 417 (the ostracism of Hyperbolus). This revision is carelessly thrown together and was never produced.[33] Both versions perhaps were current in later antiquity, and we are told that the changes made affected practically every part of the play. Cited as belonging specifically to the revised edition are the present parabasis, in which the Athenians are taken to task for not appreciating such a good play, the speech of the Just Argument against the Unjust, and the end of the play in which the school of Socrates is burned.[34]

In all periods, the *Clouds* has been one of the most widely read comedies of Aristophanes. It has been highly esteemed by many critics —including Aristophanes himself! From the historical point of view it is certainly one of the most important ancient plays. In the development of comedy, also, it is extremely interesting, for it furnishes the first example of a well-developed plot and a tendency toward higher comedy. Still, it is carelessly constructed. The judges were doubtless correct according to the standards of Old Comedy. It is lacking in low-comic effects—Aristophanes boasts of its higher plane (518–62). At times it is too intellectual for a comedy, but it is never intellectual enough for philosophical criticism.[35] The play ends, at least in our extant version, on a sour and moralizing note that is most inappropriate to the spirit of Old Comedy. Perhaps such a direct attack on the spirit of intellectual investigation, furthermore, was not likely to be popular with Athenians of the fifth century.

Socrates and the *Clouds*.—The relation of the true Socrates to the Socrates of the *Clouds* and to Aristophanes personally has been the subject of endless discussion.[36] It seems clear, however, that the Socrates of the *Clouds* is a composite figure made up from the various Sophists of the day. Thus the theory that the form of the universe resembles that of a half-spherical oven was held by Meton, as Aristophanes knew very well (*Birds* 1000–1001), and by various others; the theory of the supreme importance of air was that of Diogenes of Apollonia;[37] a keen interest in natural phenomena was characteristic of Anaxagoras; Prodicus and many others were greatly concerned with astronomy.[38] The practice of making extravagant claims to secure pupils at very high fees was characteristic of most of the Sophists but was entirely foreign to Socrates—as his poverty most eloquently testifies. Specifically, an ability to make the worse argument appear the better was the promise of Protagoras,[39] and this was the most offensive and immoral aspect of Sophistry.

The manner in which these characteristics of typical Sophists have been foisted upon Socrates is subtle and effective. Aristophanes has given him the physical peculiarities which everyone knew the true Socrates to possess: he wears no sandals (*Clouds* 103), he always needs a haircut (836), and he is definitely opposed to hot baths (837). His habitual gait and manner are well described and doubtless were well imitated by the actor taking the role.[40] Since these known characteristics were faithfully reproduced, it was natural—but illogical and false—to assume that all his characteristics were faithfully reproduced. His intimate friends would recognize the falsity of the Aristophanic characterization; but *hoi polloi,* understanding little philosophy at best, would probably accept the portrait as painted.

Plato has represented Socrates on trial for his life in 399 B.C. as protesting the long-standing prejudice against him and as citing the play of Aristophanes in which "a character called Socrates is swung about saying that he is treading on air and ranting a great deal of other nonsense—things of which I understand nothing whatever."[41] Socrates had been attacked by other comic poets, especially Eupolis, and he was probably a character in the *Connus* of Ameipsias. But only Aristophanes' attack is here specifically noticed, and the charges which Socrates here lists as the most important ones brought against him can all be found in the *Clouds:* he acts unjustly, he wastes his time investigating natural phenomena, he makes the worse cause seem the better, he teaches others to do these same things, he corrupts the youth (cf. *Clouds* 916–19), and he does not believe in the gods in which the city believes. Obviously Socrates as Plato portrays him felt that Aristophanes' play had been very influential and had done him great harm.[42]

Theme.—Like the *Banqueters* (*Daitales*), the first production of Aristophanes, the *Clouds* is a satire of the new Sophistic education and of the scientific method. Its purveyors are attacked under the figure of Socrates, who was by no means a typical Sophist but who lent himself readily to comic caricature because of his personal peculiarities. There was an even more important reason, however, for singling out Socrates rather than any other individual. Just as Aristophanes considers the minor tragic poets almost beneath his contempt and attacks Euripides himself because Euripides was by far the most important writer of "New" tragedy, so he chooses Socrates because Socrates was by far the most profound of the new teachers. Aristophanes makes no attempt seriously to represent the true teachings of Socrates, just as he makes no attempt to do justice to the plays of Euripides. But we must again give the comic poet credit at least for unerringly perceiving the most significant forces in a confused and complex situation and for courageously attacking the most important personality.

Like the attack upon Euripides, the attack upon Socrates, though unfair and in a way mean and small, has a certain justification. Aristophanes, like many men in our own day, was profoundly disturbed by the observation that the increase in learning and the advancement of science bring no real improvement in human relations, national or international. Indeed, they seem to bring corruption and chaos. In Aristophanes' day, as in our own, the bases of social morality were being undermined.[43] Sounder doctrine was actually being quarried out and substituted by Socrates and later by Plato, but this process was slow and esoteric; meanwhile the social structure was suffering undeniable harm. Aristophanes' plea in this situation was a foolish one: he advocated the restoration of the beliefs and customs of the past. In reality, these, once exposed to the light, had disintegrated forever. But Aristophanes was justified in insisting that the trends of his age were decadent and would lead to ruin.

Discussion.—The financial predicament of Strepsiades, which gives rise to all the action of the play, is dramatized most amusingly in the brilliant opening scenes. Here are mentioned the names of his creditors, who are to appear later in the play when the "twenties" of the month have come, and it is time to arrange for payment. Here too Strepsiades conceives the not so happy idea of sending his son to Socrates' university. But this idea is not subjected to formal debate. Father and son dispute it briefly until Pheidippides walks out in disgust.[44] This temporary frustration leads to Strepsiades' going himself to Socrates. Structurally, this part of the play has no consequence, but it furnishes an opportunity for much foolery—in a play where light comedy is scarce—and for some satire of Socrates. In the course of this scene the chorus of clouds is incidentally summoned by Socrates, but no choral break in the action occurs until Strepsiades retires with his teacher. Here the parabasis occurs (510–626); but it does not divide the play into two structural units. Like a stasimon in tragedy, its function is merely to provide an interlude while Strepsiades is being put to the test.

Strepsiades, after being rejected by Socrates as an utter moron, reverts to his original plan and persuades Pheidippides, who is still very reluctant, to take his place at the university. Father and son now hear the debate between the Just and the Unjust Argument (agon 949–1104).[45] This debate, also, is mere decoration from the structural point of view, for Strepsiades is already firmly convinced that he wants his son to learn the Unjust Argument, and his opinion is not in the least affected by the debate.

While Pheidippides is being taught, the chorus again fill the interval by delivering an address to the judges (usually called the second parabasis, 1115–30). Some days are now supposed to have elapsed. We are well along in the "twenties" of the month, the period to which

Strepsiades was looking forward with dread at the first of the play (17). Pheidippides is returned to his father, now such a master of sophistry that by the aid of a few points which he makes Strepsiades himself is able to rout his creditors for the time being, confident that his son can never be worsted in court. All this occurs in a sequence unbroken by choral lyrics (1131–1302.) A stasimon follows, constituting the third major break in the action. In mock-tragic fashion, the chorus foresee the downfall of Strepsiades.

These forebodings are immediately translated into action with the violent quarrel between father and son (second agon, 1345–1451). Pheidippides has not taken any part in the routing of the creditors, as we might have expected him to do; by a surprising turn of events such as Aristophanes employs so frequently, his new learning is all spent in abusing his father and in threatening to abuse his mother. Though Strepsiades realizes all too clearly that he is responsible for his fate (1338), his son and the chorus insist upon reminding him of this unpleasant fact (1403; 1454–55; cf. 865). All his machinations have gone awry, and he himself has become their victim. He bewails his immoral folly and decides to take a quick vengeance upon Socrates by burning down his "Think-Shop."[46]

The plot of the *Clouds* is obviously modeled on tragedy and is poorly adapted to the usual formula of Old Comedy. The action does not fall into two parts separated by the parabasis, like that of the *Acharnians,* but into four sections separated by various types of choral interlude. By an irregular progression the action rises to a climax at the end of the third section and the main character suffers a reversal of fortune at the opening of the fourth and final section. The play is then brought quickly to a close. Except for marking the passage of time and covering vacant stages, the chorus is little more than an encumbrance. Indeed, a purely interlude performance by the chorus, according to the manuscripts, occurs before line 889.[47] In its form as well as in its dependence upon higher comedy, therefore, the *Clouds* foreshadows Middle and New Comedy. The seriousness of its purpose, however, is typically Aristophanic, and its characters are still the wooden puppets of Old Comedy.[48]

4. *WASPS (SPHEKES, VESPAE)*

(Lenaea, 422 B.C.)

The data concerning the production of the *Wasps* are uncertain. Perhaps it was produced by Philonides and won second prize. Perhaps Philonides produced Aristophanes' *Preview (Proagon)*, also, for first prize.[49] It is certain that Leucon was third and last with his *Ambassadors* (*Presbeis*).

The *Wasps* is a very amusing play, but it deals with a contemporary political problem which has little interest for the modern reader. Consideration of this problem is practically confined to the earlier section of the play (1–1008). The episodes after the parabasis, low comedy at its uproarious best, illustrate Bdelycleon's contention that Athenian citizens might be indulging in one continuous round of pleasures if they once threw off the tyranny of the dishonest demagogues like Cleon (698–712).

Happy idea and theme.—Bdelycleon has perceived that the dicasts are not really the powerful figures which they think themselves to be but are pitiful slaves of an unworthy master. He is determined, therefore, to enlighten his father and cure him of his morbid fondness for the law courts.

Despite Aristophanes' disclaimer (62–63), the *Wasps* is essentially another attack upon Cleon. This time Cleon's main source of power—his virtual control of the jurors—is exposed and denounced. By increasing their pay, most scholars believe, Cleon had definitely won the staunch support of the six thousand jurors,[50] and such a large organized group went far toward controlling the popular assembly, especially in time of war when many of the younger citizens were off on campaigns. The support of the jurors in the courts, furthermore, was itself an inestimable service to a demagogue, especially since political prosecutions were extremely common at Athens.[51] Bdelycleon loudly protests that Cleon is receiving credit for benefits which the Athenians have in reality themselves won by their own hard labors (682–95), and he insists that Cleon is profiting from human misery and wishes the Athenians to be paupers dependent upon the demagogues for public support (703–4). Athenian citizens, Bdelycleon contends, might be rolling in wealth and living a life of gay dissipation if it were not for the evil demagogues.

The unholy alliance between Cleon and the jurors is the main concern of the play. But Cleon is attacked on other scores. The cry of "thief," still echoing from its incessant repetition in the *Knights,* is heard in the prologue (*Wasps* 35) and recurs throughout the play. There is another cry: Cleon stays at home and talks while the other public leaders are doing their best—which in the immediate past has been very poor—with the Athenian forces in the field. This cry seems to be the serious point of the trial of "Labes." Aristophanes does not seem to attack Laches, and he certainly does not defend him from the charge of theft. In the *antepirrhema,* also, the drones who stay at home and accomplish nothing are denounced. All this seems designed to shame Cleon into again taking the field, doubtless in the hope that he will have the good fortune of another Pylos or some catastrophe that will put an end to his popular favor. Either as a result of this subtle criticism or possibly by mere coincidence, Cleon was chosen general at the following annual elections and actually went to Thrace to take command of the Athenian forces there. He had apparently deceived even himself into thinking that he had some military ability. Soon afterward he died a coward's death in a defeat brought about by his own blunders.[52]

Athenian litigiousness and legal processes, which were all too often vitiated by rhetoric and improper procedure, are severely satirized in the *Wasps*. Service upon the juries is specifically condemned (esp. 505). The shockingly raw prejudices of the jurors have been noticed in the *Knights* (1359–60), and they are here more specifically attacked. The propensity of the jurors to find treason everywhere and the severity of their judgments receive even more attention and furnish much of the banter in the *Wasps*.

The criticism of the jurymen themselves, however, is of a benign variety—advisedly so, for to attack the jurymen unconditionally would be to alienate the largest organized political body in Athens. The picture of the old men assembling with their lanterns and young sons as guides is a charming genre painting. Few passages in Aristophanes— or any other author—are more pathetic than that wherein the little boy, just chastised because he allowed the lamp to burn too prosperously, appeals for some figs. The old father's anger merely conceals his grief at being so poverty-stricken that he can hardly procure the barest necessities of existence. Aristophanes here is not indulging in idle sentimentality; with thorough understanding and sympathy he is explaining the basic economic problem which gave rise to the abuses which the *Wasps* is designed to correct. Incidentally he is suggesting the blessings of peace, for Attica produced an abundance of olive oil and figs under normal conditions. During the war Attica had repeatedly been invaded; the olive and fig trees had been cut by the enemy and the grapevines as well. Athenian citizens normally supported by the produce of their small farms must have suffered intensely, and now the very existence of many, no doubt, was dependent upon their small jury fees.

But the most winsome picture of all is Philocleon's description of his evening welcome, when his daughter lovingly wheedles away his three obols and his wife brings him his supper (605–15). Instead of being an additional burden to his family, the old man is its one breadwinner and the darling of the household, for here Philocleon is the typical Athenian juror and not the father of the very affluent Bdelycleon. The kindliness of Aristophanes toward the jurors as individuals is shown also by the flattery of the parabasis. The final scenes of revelry, too, are designed to cast glory upon them; for the fantastic exuberance of Philocleon intimates that the men of Marathon, even in old age, are still far superior to the present gilded generation, superior—if they care to set their hands to the task—even in gilding themselves!

Structure.[53]—The structure of the *Wasps* is typical of the Aristophanic formula. The exposition, as in the *Knights,* is frankly delivered to the audience by one of the slaves. The remainder of the first section is devoted to dramatizing this same expository material (prologos, 1–229). Incidentally, but significantly, Philocleon reveals that his life will be blasted if a defendant ever escapes him (158–60). The action proper begins with the entrance of the chorus (parodos, 230–315). The issue is defined at some length (scene with interlarded lyrics, 316–525), and the formal debate between Philocleon and Bdelycleon ensues (agon, 526–727). The chorus is thoroughly won over by Bdelycleon's arguments. Philocleon, too, is intellectually convinced; but in his heart he still longs to play judge and juror. A domestic trial, therefore, is devised for him—a dramatization of the procedures previously satirized and a further attack upon Cleon (scenes with interlarded lyrics, 728–1008). But, structurally, the result of this trial is to have Philocleon unintentionally acquit a defendant and so be cured of his malady. In the closing lines Bdelycleon foretells the action of the later sections of the play—that Philocleon will now accompany him in his continuous round of pleasures.

After the parabasis Philocleon is given his first lesson on behavior in polite society—a scene of foolery and mild satire (episode, 1122–1264). Philocleon's warning of the dangers of drinking foreshadows his own outrageous conduct as depicted in the final scenes. There follow the personal abuse and the reference to Aristophanes' feud with Cleon in the second parabasis (1265–91). During this, considerable time is supposed to elapse. In the next scene the drunken Philocleon returns and indulges in much very low and very amusing comedy (episode, 1292–1449). In the ensuing stasimon, the chorus enviously contemplate the change in Philocleon's character and compliment the wisdom of his son (1450–73). These sentiments are not, as many scholars have thought, out of place in the manuscripts; they are spoken with diabolical irony. In the exodos (1474–1537), Philocleon comes on to dance extravagantly in parody of Euripides' *Cyclops,* it seems, and of the rhythms which the sons of Carcinus used in their inferior tragedies.

5. *PEACE (EIRENE, PAX)*

(City Dionysia, 421 B.C.)

Eupolis won first prize with his *Toadies* (*Kolakes*), Aristophanes second, and Leucon third with his *Clansmen* (*Phratores*).[54] An actor named Apollodorus took the leading role in Aristophanes' play.

The *Peace* is characterized by several very spirited scenes; but it is seriously lacking in dramatic conflict. After the recovery of Peace in the opening scenes the play becomes a somewhat obvious encomium. An advance from the artlessness of the *Acharnians* may be observed; for the change of scene is here managed with care, and the final episodes are anticipated in the earlier part of the play.

Historical note.—The Athenians were unduly elated, as the Spartans were unduly discouraged, by the capture of Pylos and Sphacteria in 425 B.C. Other minor Athenian successes followed; but their expedition to Sicily, made by the naval force which began the whole affair at Pylos, was a total failure. At one time the Athenians seemed to have won a major success at Megara (424 B.C.), but this was nullified by the sudden appearance of the Spartan Brasidas with a large force. Later Brasidas proceeded to Chalcidice to protect and foster the movement of defection which was already under way there among the allies of Athens. He quickly made a reputation for justice and moderation, and under the cry of freedom for all Hellenes he met with very notable success. At about this time the main army of Athens suffered a serious defeat at the hands of the Boeotians (Delium, 424 B.C.), and a truce was made for one year (423 B.C.). This truce was violated by Brasidas —with some justification—and in 422 B.C. Cleon sailed to Chalcidice and took up a position before Amphipolis, which was held by Brasidas with small forces. When Cleon blundered in maneuvering, Brasidas attacked for a signal victory. But the rash personal bravery which had long distinguished Brasidas lured him to his death. His continued leadership might have won the war for Sparta. A second stroke of good fortune for the Athenians was the death of Cleon, who was cut down as he fled like the coward that Aristophanes had so long insisted him to be.[55]

Thus both the Athenians and the Spartans were disappointed in their hopes and, now reaching a stalemate, they both desired peace. Indeed the Athenians now regretted not having made peace after Pylos. The Spartans were anxious to cease hostilities before their truce with Argos expired and to recover the men whom the Athenians had taken at Pylos. Negotiations were instituted, and the treaty was finally concluded immediately after the City Dionysia, 421 B.C.[56]

Happy idea and theme.—Trygaeus has the happy idea of going directly to Zeus in order to secure peace and save all Hellas. There is not a drop of money with which to buy bread in his house; but if he succeeds in his mission, he tells the little daughters who plead with him not to make such a dangerous attempt, there will be plenty (114–23). In the final lines of the play, also, when Peace has been recovered and Trygaeus is taking Harvest-Home as his bride to the country, he promises that all who come with him will eat cake.

Produced at the very crucial time when Brasidas and Cleon, War's two pestles, had recently been slain and when a treaty was under negotiation, the play is a fervent appeal to the Athenians for peace. As in the *Acharnians,* the appeal is primarily a sensuous one. At times, especially in the second parabasis, this appeal becomes one of charming poetic beauty. Panhellenic harmony, also, is a major concern throughout the play (esp. 993–98). This theme was very appropriate to the City Dionysia, when many visitors, doubtless including the Spartan ambassadors, were present in the theater.

Structure.—The exposition of the *Peace* closely resembles that of the *Knights* and the *Wasps.* Action proper begins with Trygaeus' flying up to heaven—a parody of Euripides' *Bellerophon* and the use of machines in tragedy. Trygaeus discovers that Peace has been imprisoned and that War intends completely to destroy the cities of Greece (prologos, 1–300).

With the entrance of the chorus (parodos, 301–45) all hands set about to recover Peace.[57] These efforts lead to incidental satire of the various interests opposed to peace, especially the militarists and the makers of armament.[58] Various Greek states which would like to see the war continued also are satirized. When Peace has been recovered, the play becomes an encomium of her blessings (scenes with interlarded lyrics, 346–600). In a speech resembling that of an agon (601–56). Hermes offers a novel explanation of the origin of the war and then interprets the various grievances which Peace holds against the Athenians. But Peace and her interpreter are finally placated; Trygaeus is given Harvest-Home (Opora) to wife and asked to conduct Festival (Theoria) to the Athenian senate.[59] Finally, the beetle is not forgotten (scene, 657–728).

The parabasis sings the praises of Aristophanes. Repeated references have been made to Cleon in the earlier parts of the play, and now Aristophanes quotes several lines from the *Wasps* as if to remind the audience that he dared to use the severest language against Cleon when the monster was still alive and at the height of his power (parabasis, 729–818).[60]

As Trygaeus returns to earth, the change of scene is clearly noted with an effective joke upon the audience. The disposition of the two beautiful maidens is accompanied with *double entente* suggestive of the joys of peaceful festivity. A second scene prepares for the sacrificial feast and contains a prayer for harmony among the Greeks (scenes with interlarded lyrics, 819–921, 922–1038). Both scenes end with praise of Trygaeus, who now has almost become Aristophanes himself.

A soothsayer interrupts the sacrifice and is beaten off (quasi-episode, 1039–1126).[61] The second parabasis follows, beginning as a beautiful if homely idyll in praise of rural peace and plenty and ending by comparing this life with that of war (1127–90). The following scene contrasts the reaction of the makers of farm implements with those of the makers of armament—a theme anticipated earlier in the play (447, 545). A second contrast, also anticipated, is made between the son of Lamachus, the general, and the son of the coward Cleonymus (quasi-episode, 1191–1304). The exodos is a glorious revel celebrating Trygaeus' marriage to Harvest-Home.

6. *BIRDS (ORNITHES, AVES)*

(City Dionysia, 414 B.C.)

The *Birds* was produced by Callistratus and won second prize. Ameipsias won first with his *Revelers* (*Komastai*), Phrynichus third with his *Hermit* (*Monotropos*).[62]

The *Birds* contains some of the most charming of all Greek poetry; it is filled with winsome and capricious fantasy—a product of human imaginativeness at its most brilliant height. It is often considered Aristophanes' best comedy. The care with which the plot is worked out, the consistency of the characterization of the chorus, and the comparative absence of low comedy mark distinct advancements.

Happy idea and theme.—Pisthetaerus and Euelpides have become disgusted with the mad litigiousness (42) and the political officiousness of Athens (121, 147). Taking refuge in the land of the birds—a Utopia[63]—Pisthetaerus conceives the happy idea of building a city and blockading the gods from all traffic with human beings in order to secure the sovereignty which, he claims, originally belonged to the birds.

Many critics consider the *Birds* a fantasy of escape in which references to contemporary persons or events are wholly incidental. This interpretation may be correct. Certain it is that much of the play is obvious, innocent fantasy and will bear no allegorical interpretation of any kind. But a complete lack of serious purpose is hard to reconcile with the hitherto invariably serious intent of Aristophanes' comedies and with some apparently serious passages in the *Birds*.

Some critics think that Aristophanes is giving comic representation to the many high and ambitious schemes which were in the air at Athens when the Sicilian expedition was sent forth. But if we recall the bitter criticism of Hyperbolus' dream of an expedition against Carthage in the *Knights* (1300–1315), we shall hardly conclude that the gloriously successful Pisthetaerus is supposed to be the father of any such scheme.

An ancient commentator insists that Aristophanes is covertly advocating a change of government and, if need be, a change in the whole nature and scheme of things.[64] The idea of a serious political intent must not be dismissed too abruptly. Athens was in desperate straits in 414 B.C. She had dangerously weakened herself by sending out the huge Sicilian expedition; and, when Alcibiades had been forced to quit the leadership of this expedition and go into exile, Aristophanes with his keen political sagacity must have abandoned all real hope of the venture's success. His indirect references to the expedition suggest as much,[65] and his silences are even more eloquent (1369). Satire of oracle-mongers at this particular time, furthermore, almost amounted to denunciation of the expedition; for vast arrays of oracles had been brought forth in favor of it. To advocate anything resembling a revolution at such a time, however, would be worth a man's life.[66] If Aristophanes is doing so, he must of necessity conceal the fact from a very intelligent audience; indeed, he must advocate it so vaguely that if he should be called into court and accused, he could prove that he is not doing so. We may be sure, therefore, that even if the *Birds* advocates a change in government, no ancient sycophant or modern scholar could prove the point. This very fact makes any dogmatically certain interpretation of the *Birds* utterly hopeless.

At times in the *Birds* a seriously conceived Utopia seems to be developing, as when the absence of money is approved (157–58) and possibly the abolition of private property envisioned (995–1020). But the play as a whole does not put forward any Utopia. Pisthetaerus begins with a search for a quiet, peaceful city; but no sooner is his new foundation made than he institutes a blockade, breaks off diplomatic relations with gods and men, and ends with a policy of superimperialism.[67] Besides, Aristophanes' sense of humor was too keen to allow him to view any Utopia seriously, and yet Pisthetaerus and his ambitious schemes are sympathetically presented.

At times the city which Pisthetaerus has founded seems to represent

Athens, and the Olympian gods seem to be the Doric Greeks. The talk of blockade and embargoes suggests this, as does part of the scene where the embassy sues for peace (especially 1596–1602). But the demands which Pisthetaerus makes as a price for peace are far too ambitious to represent Aristophanes' suggestion for a settlement of the Peloponnesian War.

Again, it seems as if the Olympian gods may represent the popular leaders now in control of Athens. Prometheus' description of Basileia as the stewardess of all good things, including the juries' pay, though obviously humorous, seems an excellent description of the sovereign power at Athens. Pisthetaerus could easily be conceived to represent Aristophanes' ideal Athenian citizen. The restoration of sovereignty to its original possessors would then mean the restoration of the old limited democracy which was always Aristophanes' ideal. Such an interpretation, also, is consistent with Pisthetaerus' original purpose of finding a city free from sycophancy and officious politics. The figure of the Triballian fits very nicely into this picture; for he is openly likened to Laispodias, a popular leader of the day. The Triballian's costume, as the ancient commentator points out, and doubtless also his mask, are those of Laispodias, and the democracy is satirized for electing such a man to represent it (1567–71), as it has earlier been satirized for electing Dieitrephes (798–800, cf. 1442). But the early sections of the play do not suggest any such interpretation, and even these final scenes have much in them that is inconsistent with or contradictory to such an interpretation—although we should never expect allegory to be consistently maintained in Aristophanes.

Still another interpretation is that recently presented by Van Daele.[68] After the departure of the Sicilian expedition, he points out, Athens became a very unpleasant place for honest men because of the reckless persecutions that followed certain acts of sacrilege.[69] These persecutions are doubtless being satirized in the Birds by the references to litigiousness and sycophants. If Athens were free of such processes, free of duped juries, corrupting Sophists, impostors, and sycophants, then Athens would present a picture of perfect felicity of which the Olympian gods themselves would be jealous! This interpretation is a very attractive one.

Structure.—The exposition is managed very much as in the Knights and similar plays, but here the speakers are the chief character of the play and his foil rather than unimportant protatic characters (prologos, 1–208). Such a foil, we may note incidentally, is here used more effectively and elaborately than in any previous extant comedy. For the usual entrance songs of the chorus Aristophanes has substituted the charming lyrics of the Epops (parodos, 209–450 ?). The chorus excitedly clash with the old men, and Pisthetaerus' formal presentation of his case follows. He succeeds in convincing the chorus of their rights of sovereignty, and after they have heard his clever plan of campaign they turn over the direction of affairs to him and promise themselves to furnish the "man power" (agon, 451–638). A short scene at this point gracefully introduces the Nightingale and gives the actors plausible motivation for retiring (scene, 639–75).

The beautiful parabasis follows and is delivered wholly in character by the chorus of birds. It is as pertinent to the subject of the play as are many other speeches and lyrics. This is an advance in artistic formality over the first five plays (parabasis, 676–800).

Pisthetaerus and Euelpides reappear with wings and proceed to the business of founding the city. Euelpides is sent out to see to the walls and does not reappear—his role as foil has been sufficiently exploited, and the actor is needed for other parts. In rapid succession the poet now satirizes the pretentious parasites who prey upon civilization for their own selfish ends: the priest, the popular poet, the oracle-monger, the civil engineer and expert in city planning, and—in a single scene—the commissioner of colonial affairs and the professional lawmaker (scenes with interlarded lyrics, 801–1057).

In charmingly sportive verses, the chorus sing of the benefits of birds and of their delights. An edict is issued against a birdcatcher, and the judges of the comedies are cajoled and threatened (second parabasis, 1058–1117).

The plot proper is now resumed with the entrance of a messenger, somewhat awkwardly introduced,[70] who announces the completion of the walls. The embargo against the gods is thus instituted, and Iris, the first offender, is threatened with dire consequences for having crossed the border without a visa! Finally, the imminent arrival of men who wish to acquire wings is announced (scenes with interlarded lyrics, 1118–1312).

Wings are made ready as the chorus praise their city for being the seat of Wisdom, Love, Culture, and gentle Ease (quasi-stasimon, 1313–34).

The various undesirables now appear and apply to Pisthetaerus (episode, 1335–1469). These scenes, like those with the previous series of individuals, are not pertinent to the contest for sovereignty, but they seem to grow rather naturally out of the action.

The chorus now begin an interrupted series of satirical verses. The first two stanzas attack the eternal butt, Cleonymus, and the contemporary gangster, Orestes (stasimon, 1470–93).

The plot is definitely resumed with the entrance of Prometheus, who sneaks in to inform Pisthetaerus of the plight of the gods and to advise his demanding Basileia as his wife—a new and exciting complication. On his departure the chorus continue their satire with a stanza on Socrates and the coward Peisander. The embassy, whose imminent arrival has been foretold by Prometheus, now appears. This scene constitutes the well-marked climax of the play. As with many an Athenian embassy, bribery is cleverly used and Pisthetaerus makes peace on his own terms. The chorus continue their satire with a bitter attack on sycophants and Sophists, specifically Gorgias (scenes with interlarded lyrics, 1494–1705). The play ends with the gay marriage of Pisthetaerus to Basileia.

7. *LYSISTRATA

(411 B.C.)

The *Lysistrata* was produced by Callistratus, possibly at the Lenaean festival, but detailed information is lacking.

The *Lysistrata* is excellently constructed and is crowded with scenes of uproarious low comedy and brilliant wit based with frank directness on perhaps the most amusing of all situations. It is the first extant comedy in which women play major roles. At times this comedy has been somewhat neglected because of its unusual frankness; but critics of the present day, free from the prejudice of both prudery and prurience, have come to regard it as one of Aristophanes' best plays. Though written for a day and an hour, it can be understood and appreciated by the modern audience more readily perhaps than any other play of Aristophanes, and it has been successfully reproduced by the commercial theater both in Europe and in America.[71]

Happy idea and theme.—Lysistrata has the happy idea of instituting a sex-strike among all Greek women in order to force the men to make peace. Despite the extravagance of this reversal of nature and the droll low comedy of much of the action, the play makes a powerful appeal for renovating the national texture and for establishing Panhellenic peace and unity. The author has been courageously fair to the Spartan point of view without in the least jeopardizing his loyalty to Athens. It is a tribute to his city, however, that fairness would be tolerated in the midst of a bitter war.

Structure.—The *Lysistrata* is more artistically constructed than any of the earlier comedies. As in the *Birds,* the happy idea involves an intrigue which becomes a well-defined dramatic plot. Various difficulties arise to threaten its success and to heighten the general tension. By an interrupted progression, therefore, the action rises to a climax, after which the play is brought quickly to a close. The whole is very tightly constructed: even the low comedy seems inevitably to develop out of the dramatic situation, almost nothing impertinent is included, no motive is repeated, and the action moves with sustained dynamic rapidity.

The exposition is more naturally brought out in the *Lysistrata* than in any of the previous comedies. A minor climax is built up when Lysistrata thoroughly arouses the curiosity of her companions before revealing her happy idea—if it can be called such. Incidentally these first scenes furnish a splendid opportunity for satirizing the foibles of women, and extraordinary care has been taken to characterize the minor figures. While Lysistrata is trying to explain much more serious matters to her, Cleonice prattles on about what she will wear to detract the male from martial pursuits. Lampito is nicely characterized by her healthy Spartan figure and her broad dialect. Her first words refer to the gymnastic training of Spartan girls—always a scandal to the more cautious Athenians.[72] Later Lampito makes references to Spartan geography (117) and mythology (155–56). Her realistic portrait is completed by an uncomplimentary reference to the Athenian democracy (170–71). These nicely drawn characterizations add color to the background of the action; but unfortunately they are not made to have any definite effect upon it. Perhaps a modern dramatist would at least have given Cleonice's picturesque role to Myrrhina, for Myrrhina does have some slight importance in the later scenes. Lysistrata herself, furthermore, is hardly more than the feminine counterpart of Dicaeopolis or Pisthetaerus. But we should expect most of the characters to be generalized, for they are designed as representatives of their class rather than as individuals.

The opening scenes conclude with the women's seizing the Acropolis (prologos, 1–253). This motivates the entrances of the two half-choruses of old men and old women. Their age nicely contrasts with the blossoming youthfulness of the main characters, and their clash symbolizes the dramatic struggle of the play. The division of the chorus, therefore, is eminently suited to the action, and their various antics furnish some of the best low comedy in Aristophanes (parodos, 254–386).

The Magistrate—one of the extraordinary officials appointed after the disaster in Sicily—is a typical conservative Athenian. His low opinion of women's place in life is amusingly ironic in view of his utter inability to master the present situation. Following his physical humiliation comes the formal debate of the play, in which Lysistrata's frank castigation of the Athenians is made palatable, as we should expect in Aristophanes, first by the obvious sanity of the criticisms, then by the interspersed comic foolery and by a dash of pathos. Lysistrata recites the hardships of women in wartime: the loss of their sons, their loneliness, and the sterile wasting away of the younger generation (scene, 387–466; agon, 467–613).

The homely advice of Lysistrata for fulling the state as the women full their wool has approached the revolutionary;[73] and, after the retirement of the actors, the old men of the chorus now raise the cry of "tyranny," while the old women defend their right to advise the ill-conducted state. Low comedy again characterizes the clash of the two choruses and adds to the unusual features of this unique parabasis (614–705).

After the supposed lapse of some days (cf. 881), Lysistrata appears and announces that their revolt is threatened with internal collapse. A short scene dramatizes this situation, and with some difficulty Lysistrata succeeds in repressing her weaker sisters (episode, 706–80).

The two half-choruses express their mutual hatred—and they do not limit themselves to mere words (stasimon, 781–828).

The distressing situation of the males, already suggested (763–65), is now dramatized with Cinesias and his wife Myrrhina in the main roles.[74] For the pit this scene must have been the high point not only of the play but of several seasons! When Cinesias makes his reluctant exit, the Herald of the Spartans enters to announce—and to illustrate—that the Spartans are suffering from the same malady.[75] A meeting of plenipotentiaries is quickly arranged (quasi-episode, 829–1013).

The hostile choruses now at last are reunited in a scene of touching sentiment (choral interlude, 1014–42). As if to celebrate their harmony, they sing a lyric outrageously teasing the audience. The climax of the play follows with the entrance of the plenipotentiaries of Sparta and Athens. Lysistrata as the center of a spectacular tableau now makes the most serious appeal of the play. For once Aristophanes writes a speech in tragic style that is almost too serious to be parody. Whole lines are taken from Euripides, especially from the *Erechtheus,* a splendidly patriotic tragedy which had appeared possibly some ten years before. This speech of Lysistrata is a noble appeal for Panhellenism: Spartans are reminded of their obligations to Athens and Athenians of their obligations to Sparta, and reconciliation is finally effected. With another lyric, the chorus continues teasing the audience (scene with interlarded lyrics, 1043–1246).

The play ends in revelry and in songs of great beauty which are reminiscent of Alcman, the great Spartan poet of days long past.[76]

8. *THESMOPHORIAZUSAE*[77]

(411 B.C.)[78]

This play is a very amusing but basically serious attack upon Euripides and his satellite Agathon. Aristophanes' criticism of Euripides, seriously begun in the *Acharnians,* was continued in various lost plays both before and after this one, and given its final form in the *Frogs.*

Theme. Parody of tragedy.—The *Thesmophoriazusae* resembles the *Clouds* in that the "idea" turns out to be not very happy but furnishes much low comedy and becomes the framework for the serious theme of the play. This theme is more important than it might seem at first glance, for Aristophanes manages directly or indirectly to criticize almost every phase of Euripidean tragedy—most phases are criticized again and again.

The first lines of the play single out the characteristic for which Euripides was forever best known: the sophistic niceties of his language and his preoccupation with philosophical concepts—Euripides the Wise and Euripides the Philosopher of the Theater. The clever novelty of Euripides' ideas is illustrated by his plan to send a secret advocate to the women's assembly and later by his inexhaustible resourcefulness in thinking up devices to rescue this advocate. The criticism of Agathon—his use of stage machinery, his effeminacy, the affected prettiness of his language, and the seductiveness of his music—all this is something more than incidental fun, for in the end Euripides is made to confess that he was just such a one when he was young (173–74). In refusing Euripides' request, furthermore, Agathon, like Dionysus later (*Frogs* 1471), uses one of Euripides' own lines, implying that Euripides should run his own risks (194).

The assembly of the women is a brilliant device for furnishing a very amusing scene at the expense of Athenian women and also for airing one of the most characteristic features of Euripidean tragedy. It is part of the comedy that the women do not protest the truth of the revelations which Euripides has made; they merely deplore the harm done them and resolve to punish the person responsible. Here the serious concern is with Euripides' subject matter. This, as Aristophanes never tired of insisting, was far below the standard of dignity set by Aeschylus and Sophocles, a standard proper, in Aristophanes' opinion, to all tragedy. Euripides is here being indicted for his almost morbid interest in feminine psychology and for the intimate domesticity of his plots. He delights in exhibiting love-sick women and in portraying other indecent scenes on stage; adultery and deception, according to the charge, are stock-in-trade with him; so are girls with illegitimate

children and wives buying infants to conceal their sterility. A young
wife is shown to be a tyrant over an old husband, and wives in general
are proved wholly untrustworthy.

Aristophanes' indictment of Euripides is in general sound. Euripides was the first to present profound and intimate studies of women
in the Athenian theater, studies which were not circumscribed as to subject matter and which were very frank. The implication that this type
of subject matter is beneath the dignity of great tragedy also has some
specious justification. At least, this is the very type of subject matter
(with the exception of a woman's adultery) which became common in
later comedy. The claim that Euripides exhibits Phaedras and Mela-
nippes but no Penelope, however, is patently false (546–48). The heroine of the *Helen* herself is a model of fidelity, not to speak of the noble
Alcestis or the daughters of Erechtheus.

Another woman adds to the charge that Euripides has convinced
men that there are no gods—and so interfered with her trade in gar-
lands!

In reply to these complaints, Mnesilochus insists that the women
have been fortunate to be let off so easily, and he proceeds to list a vast
array of feminine vices which are too sordid even for a Euripidean
tragedy. From Aristophanes' point of view, this defense of Euripides
has the double advantage of being most amusing and no real defense
whatever.

The scenes in which Mnesilochus casts about for a device of escape
are mainly clever parodies of scenes from Euripides' plays and further
satire of Euripides' inexhaustible ingenuity. The first play called upon
for a contribution is the *Telephus*. This was now a somewhat ancient
production (438 B.C.); it had furnished much of the material for the
Acharnians. There the "child" seized as hostage was a charcoal basket;
here it turns out to be a wineskin disguised as a baby with little white
slippers. The next play called upon is the *Palamedes* (415 B.C.), wherein another very clever device is discovered. But this scene is mostly
foolery—and a good excuse for Mnesilochus later to intimate that his
device fails because Euripides was ashamed to acknowledge his frigid
Palamedes (848).

Mnesilochus now shifts to the very latest plays of Euripides, first
to the *Helen*. This procedure is effective, for these plays would be most
vivid in the minds of the audience, and it obviously seems fairer to
parody Euripides' latest plays rather than to select from a large number
of previous ones. The melodramatic distress of Helen fits Mnesilochus'
situation almost perfectly, and the parody is played at some length.
Euripides doubtless enters as Menelaus dressed in rags and tatters—

another slap at realism and at appeals to sentiment through mechanical effects. Very amusing comedy is added to this scene by the interruptions of one of the women and also by occasional lapses in character. The *Andromeda,* however, furnishes the best show of the play. If Aristophanes is repeating the motive of a maiden in distress, so did Euripides; for both the *Helen* and the *Andromeda* were presented at the same festival. The *Andromeda* was famous in ancient times as one of Euripides' most beautiful plays;[79] but it invited comic parody, for a maiden chained like Prometheus to a cliff is the extreme of romantic melodrama and Echo mocking the heroine's sad laments is the boldest theatrical novelty. All this, however, is not enough: the play opens beneath the starry night;[80] the hero enters, in all probability, gliding through the air on the "machine." The *Helen* and possibly the *Andromeda,* furthermore, dealt with a clever Greek's getting the better of a somewhat stupid barbarian, and the final scenes of the *Thesmophoriazusae* outrageously parody this melodramatic plot of intrigue and escape.

Such attacks as this may in part have caused Agathon and also Euripides to leave Athens and go to Macedonia. Agathon was the only young tragic poet of great promise in Athens; and Aristophanes lived to regret, or at least publicly to renounce, this bitter attack upon him.[81]

Structure.—Like the *Clouds,* the *Thesmophoriazusae* is a comedy of unsuccessful intrigue. The first attempt at instituting the "idea" is a total failure. A later attempt for a while seems successful, but it brings on various complications which lead to a climax near the end of the play. All the action is designed with a view to the satire which constitutes the poet's main interest. The *Thesmophoriazusae,* however, is much more neatly constructed than the *Clouds.* Indicative of Aristophanes' growing concern with minor technical details is the subtle preparation for the appearance of Cleisthenes by an earlier thrust at him (235). The "child" also is specifically noted some time before the scene in which it plays a major role (cf. 608–9). There are no irrelevant or loosely attached scenes. The basic action of the play, however, is very slight, and the ending is distinctly flat for an Old Comedy.

The exposition is deftly brought out in the opening dialogue along with various indirect criticisms of Euripides. The action proper begins when Mnesilochus decides himself to undertake Euripides' defense.[82] Euripides is forced to swear that he will come to Mnesilochus' aid in case of distress, thus anticipating the later action (prologos, 1–294).

Some mechanical shift in the background, if we may believe a stage direction in the best manuscript, is now made (276). The women formally assemble and undertake the judgment of Euripides (parodos, 295–379). The indictments of the women and the response of Mnesilochus follow (quasi-agon, 380–530). This leads to a heated clash between the women and Mnesilochus, whose identity is finally disclosed with the aid of Cleisthenes (scene, 531–654).

In lyric measure the chorus search about their council seat for other possible interlopers whom they threaten with dire punishment. Realizing his danger, Mnesilochus seizes a woman's "child" as hostage and flees to the altar. He demands his own release in exchange for the "child's" life, but the "child" turns out to be only a skin of wine. In despair, Mnesilochus now resorts to the device used in the *Palamedes* in order to inform Euripides of his predicament (scene with interlarded lyrics, 655–784).

While Mnesilochus is waiting patiently, the chorus deliver a lengthy defense of women. This parabasis, sharply curtailed in form, is unique in the extant comedies in that characters remain "on stage" during it. Nor does it constitute any sharp break in the action (785–845).

Finding himself still forsaken, Mnesilochus undertakes to play Helen in distress, and Euripides, true to his word, assumes the role of Menelaus the rescuer; but the entrance of a magistrate and Scythian policeman at the crucial point causes this intrigue to miscarry (episode, 846–946).

The chorus now sing a series of lyrics which reflect the dancing and singing characteristic of the true Thesmophoria.[88] These lyrics are of unusual interest because the dance movements which accompany them are described. First the twenty-four members of the chorus join hands to form a circle about the altar in the center of the orchestra and swing about rapidly as they sing three identical stanzas. Then perhaps they stop and break. Next they seem perhaps to come forward toward the audience with a strophe and to reverse this movement with the antistrophe. For the subsequent lyrics the choral figures are changed, but they cannot be followed in detail. As to content, all these songs are invocations to various Olympian deities (introduction and stasimon, 947–1000).

Euripides now assumes the role of Perseus, and Mnesilochus that of Andromeda chained to the cliff. This furnishes a nice opportunity to parody the lyrics of Euripides as those of Agathon have already been parodied. Before Euripides actually enters he plays the role of Echo to the maiden's complaints and to the low-comedy barbarisms of the Scythian. Euripides then attempts the rescue, but he finds that all his cleverness is wasted on the utterly stupid Scythian (episode, 1001–1135). The chorus now continue their invocations and dances (stasimon, 1136–59). The play ends with the rescue of Mnesilochus while the Scythian is being seduced and in the end confounded.

9. **FROGS (BATRACHOI, RANAE)**

(Lenaea, 405 B.C.)

Aristophanes won first prize, Phrynichus[84] second with his *Muses* (which apparently dealt with Euripides and Sophocles), and Plato "Comicus" (not the philosopher) third with his *Cleophon*. The *Frogs* was produced by Philonides; it was so admired because of its parabasis, Dicaearchus an ancient critic records, that it was presented a second time, and Aristophanes was signally honored for his civic virtue by being given a wreath made from Athena's sacred olive tree on the Acropolis.[85]

The *Frogs* has often been considered Aristophanes' most brilliant comedy, but any appreciation of it requires some knowledge of Aeschylus and Euripides.

The motive of going to the underworld for the advice of great men, found in the *Odyssey* (10. 492), had been used by Eupolis in his *Demes* after the death of Pericles, perhaps also in his *Generals* (*Taxiarchoi*), and by other comic poets including Aristophanes himself. Dionysus the coward, furthermore, like Zeus the adulterer and Heracles the glutton and bully, was a stock figure in comedy.[86]

Historical note.[87]—Control of the government at Athens was seized by the Four Hundred Oligarchs in 411 B.C.; but the Athenian fleet based at Samos, among whom this revolutionary movement had started, remained faithful to the democracy and set itself up as the true Athenian government. Under the leadership of Thrasybulus they recalled Alcibiades, who had been in exile since 415 B.C., voted him full restoration of rights, and made him one of their generals. Alcibiades retained his position when the democracy was restored at Athens, but he did not dare return to Athens until 407 B.C. after various successes with the Athenian fleet. The populace was sharply divided over his return, but he won the day and was elected commander-in-chief. After four months and the collection of a considerably larger force, he sailed off again to the islands with Aristocrates and Adeimantus (*Frogs* 1513) as generals of his land forces.

At about this time a remarkable man was sent out from Sparta to command the Peloponnesian fleet, Lysander, who shortly won a minor victory over the Athenian fleet while Alcibiades was absent. The engagement had been invited by the Athenians contrary to Alcibiades' express command. The Athenians at home, however, were furious with Alcibiades and replaced him—a fatal mistake, for only he was able to cope with the brilliant Lysander. Alcibiades returned to a private fortress on the Hellespont. Fortunately the Spartans, too, made a mistake. They recalled Lysander. One of the new Athenian commanders with a considerable number of ships fell into extreme peril and was blockaded at Mytilene. Athens made a desperate effort and succeeded in assembling another expedition for rescue. On this, slaves were accepted with a promise of their freedom and slightly limited citizenship as a reward for fighting (*Frogs* 191). This new expedition met the body of the Spartan fleet at Arginusae. The result was a decisive Athenian victory, but the Athenian commanders did not pick up the survivors from their own wrecked ships because of a storm and possibly because of a desire to surprise the remaining Spartan ships at the siege of Mytilene.

Again the people at Athens were furious and deposed the responsible generals, replacing them with Adeimantus and Philocles. Two of the deposed generals foresaw trouble and went into voluntary exile. The other six involved returned, and in a chaos of dishonest political manipulation and unconstitutional procedure they were condemned and executed. One of the leaders in their prosecution was Archedemus (*Frogs* 417, 588), a popular leader in charge of the "two-obol fund" (*Frogs* 141) for the relief of distress.[88] Another prosecutor was Theramenes (*Frogs* 541, 967). According to the commanders he had been one of the officers placed in charge of picking up the survivors. Later the Athenians repented their unjust action and started prosecution of some of the underlings of Theramenes, but these escaped in the midst of a factional disturbance in which Cleophon (*Frogs* 679, 1504, 1532) lost his life. Cleophon had repeatedly prevented the Athenians from accepting the favorable terms which Sparta offered even as late as this time.

Lysander now returned to command the Spartan forces, and both fleets moved to the Hellespont, through which the Athenians imported much of their food supply. Alcibiades, living there in exile, came to the Athenian fleet and urged the commanders to choose a more favorable base than the very disadvantageous one which they had taken up; but they stupidly refused to listen, and within a few days Lysander by clever strategy attacked and practically annihilated their fleet (405 B.C.).

Facts only too eloquently prove that Aristophanes was right in saying that Athens was being ruled by its worst elements and that these worst were scoundrels of the blackest sort. It was not wholly without justice that Lysander soon tore down the walls of Athens to the tune of flutes. Perhaps no Greek or Roman state ever committed so many publicly deliberated atrocities as did the Athenians from 427 to 399 B.C. The history of Athens during the fifth century, like a tragedy of Aeschylus, is a fatal progression from prosperity (*koros*) to insolence (*hybris*) and finally to ruin (*ate*).

Happy idea and theme.—Dionysus, passing the time before the battle of Arginusae by reading the *Andromeda*,[89] has suddenly been struck with an irresistible longing for Euripides, and so he has decided to recall him from the underworld.

The recent deaths of both Euripides and Sophocles suggest a final appreciation of the three great tragic poets—Phrynichus, also, had the idea—and the recalling of a first-class poet symbolizes the urgent need of Athens to restore the rights of disfranchised citizens and to recall its political exiles, specifically Alcibiades. These literary and political motives are elaborately combined. Careful preparation for the serious political appeal begins in the parodos. The man who does nothing to banish civil strife but stirs it up for private gain is asked to withdraw from the sacred chorus.[90] The battle of Arginusae and the enfranchisement of the slaves who fought there have already been mentioned several times (33, 50, 191); Archedemus and Theramenes, the prosecutors of the commanders at that battle, have been fiercely attacked.[91]

One subtle connection between the action of the play and its political theme has sometimes been overlooked. The entrance songs of the chorus are closely modeled after the ritual celebration of the Eleusinian festival (end of September) when the statue of Iacchus (Dionysus) was carried from Athens to Eleusis with great pomp and festivity. During the latter part of the war, however, the Spartans controlled the land even this close to Athens, and the celebrants, therefore, had been forced to make the short trip from Athens to Eleusis by boat without much of the pomp and festivity and certain of the customary rites. But when Alcibiades had returned to Athens in 407 B.C. he had taken all his soldiers and conducted this procession again by land.[92] This was some sixteen months before the *Frogs* appeared and doubtless stood out in sharp contrast with the succeeding dampened celebration four months before when Alcibiades was absent and again in disfavor. Just as the scene of phallic celebration in the *Acharnians* suggests the joys of peace, so this scene in the *Frogs* suggests the joys to be had if Alcibiades is again recalled and placed at the head of the Athenian forces.

The main political appeal of the *Frogs,* of course, is made in the parabasis. The epirrhema pleads for a general amnesty, contrasting the disfranchisement of many good citizens with the acceptance of slaves who fought in a single battle. The antepirrhema pleads for using the men of pristine virtue, who have been neglected in favor of the baser men just as the older and better coinage has been driven out by the newer and debased.

The literary debate itself is closely bound up with the political theme.

Significantly the criterion for judging the virtues of the two poets is their efficacy in improving the citizens (1009–10). It is here repeated that the present citizens are a very bad set, and Aeschylus spends much of his defense in describing the Athenians of "the good old days." Arginusae and Theramenes, furthermore, are not forgotten in the latter part of the play (967–70; 1195–96).

The serious political theme becomes even more obvious at the climax of the play, where Dionysus, unable to decide on artistic grounds, falls back on the criterion of civic usefulness. He has come, he now says, to carry back a poet in order that the city may be saved and have its choruses. Asked for civic advice, Aeschylus intimates that Alcibiades should be recalled; Euripides pleads for a change of administration and the use of those now neglected. This advice, heartily welcomed by Dionysus, repeats the exhortation of the antepirrhema of the parabasis, while the advice of Aeschylus has given a specific example of the general course advocated in the epirrhema. Most important of all, the choice of Aeschylus at the end of the play combines in an inoffensively allegorical manner the political theme with the literary contest: Aeschylus is the first and foremost of the old school which, if allowed to return to power, will restore Athens to her pristine glory.

Criticism of Euripides and Aeschylus.—Surprise is the device which Aristophanes most frequently uses for comic effect. The experienced spectator, therefore, might well conjecture, even at the beginning of the play, that in the end Dionysus will not bring Euripides back to Athens. The tenor of the opening remarks about the dead Euripides, furthermore, is unmistakably that which Aristophanes had long been maintaining about the living Euripides. Indeed, the phrases which Dionysus here cites contain the most serious indictments of Euripides—baseness of style, sophistry, and immorality. These indictments are repeated time and time again throughout the play; but their most elaborate presentation is in the agon (895–1098) and the series of scenes which follow, dealing first with the prologues, next with the lyrics, and finally with the weighing of the lines.

The charge that Euripides writes in a comparatively prosaic style, of course, has no little justification. But Euripides' style is not so bad as Aristophanes has tried to make it. "Ether, the apartment of Zeus" is not precisely Euripides' phrase, and no great fault is found in "the foot of time" (100); it may be bold, but Shakespeare seems to have liked it well enough. Aeschylus, too, made mistakes in these matters. His "thirsty dust, twin sister of mud," which Aristophanes is too prejudiced to cite, is ridiculous bombast (*Agamemnon* 494–95).

The weighing of the lines near the end of the play is mostly foolishness, but here again Aristophanes has been unfair. Euripides' line about "throwing two aces and a four" is so atrocious that we are almost willing to agree with Aristophanes on all points. But, when a beautiful line of Aeschylus is cited from his description of Death and Persuasion, "For of all gods Death only loves not gifts," fairness would demand a few lines from the beautiful choral lyric in the *Alcestis* (962–82) on Necessity and Persuasion.[93] The poetry of Euripides here rivals that of Aeschylus.

The charge of immorality is introduced at the beginning of the play when Dionysus (101–2) refers to the famous line from the *Hippolytus* renouncing an oath exacted under false pretenses.[94] Heracles terms this line immoral sophistry. At the end of the play Dionysus again uses this same line from the *Hippolytus* in renouncing his intention to bring Euripides back to earth (1471). At the beginning of the play (80), Euripides is called a bold "stop-at-nothing" in contrast to Sophocles the "serene."[95] Later Aeschylus repeatedly attacks Euripides for his exhibition of immoral love affairs and for his psychological studies of passion. Finally he calls Euripides a "stop-at-nothing, a liar, and a coarse fellow" (1520–21). Impudent boldness, furthermore, is perhaps the outstanding characteristic of Euripides as he is dramatically portrayed in the *Frogs*. The charge of immorality, along with that of talkative sophistry, is the most insistent charge against Euripides; and these two counts damn him at the end of the play. Here, as long before in the original edition of the *Clouds,* it is intimated that Euripides has been too much under the influence of Socrates.[96] These are the charges, of course, which serve to equate Euripides with the wicked politicians whom Aristophanes is attacking and to unite the literary theme of the play with the political.

Euripides' plays are undeniably sophistic; debate is often dragged in to the detriment of proper balance between discussion and dramatic action. But the charge of immorality as here made is false, unless it is immoral to face any question frankly and to refuse to pass over in silence, as Aeschylus here advises (1053), certain serious human problems. Still, an essential justification, unfortunately, exists for Aristophanes' hatred of Euripides. Truth and enlightenment, the ideals which Euripides served so unflinchingly, do not feed the belly, clothe the back, or satisfy the groin; liberal education does not fit one to be a warrior. The older Athenian sailors, Aeschylus says (1070–73), did not know enough to argue and dispute, and doubtless their ignorance was an advantage. Pericles insisted that enlightenment did not dull Athenian courage or stifle Athenian competency for efficient action;[97] but, if he was mistaken, then Euripides, in part responsible for Athenian enlightenment, was in part responsible for the decadence and downfall of Athens.

Other serious charges, however, are brought against Euripides. He is a beggar-maker and rag-stitcher (842); he introduces kings clothed in tatters for sentimental effects (1063–64). He is an atheist, it is implied, or at best an agnostic; his loyalty to Athenian democracy is brought into question (952–53). The charges against the realistic tendencies of Euripides' plays could be answered with some justification, but of course no serious attempt is made to answer them. The defense given Euripides is really an additional indictment. There is an answer also for the question of Euripides' loyalty to Athens. His *Orestes* (902–30) is usually cited in this connection, but here his praise of sturdy yeomanry is essentially the same as that of Aristophanes' himself in several of his comedies. Euripides had presumably fought in many Athenian battles; during the first fifteen years of the Peloponnesian War he had written enthusiastic and inspiring plays of patriotism in spite of Cleon and Hyperbolus and the gross blunders and cruel atrocities of the government. He saw the Athenians go from bad to worse—much worse in the final years of the war, when no honest and enlightened man could approve of their organized cruelty and folly. He saw Aristophanes and the other comic poets attack himself and attack Alcibiades, the one man who probably could have won the war for Athens. Athens was now only a mockery of the great city of Euripides' former days, and he went off to Macedonia. He was an honest man more than he was an Athenian.

Euripides is not given a fair defense, but Aeschylus is by no means allowed to escape all criticism. The long silences of his characters— essentially a lack of dramatic action—is satirized along with his interminable choral odes; when the characters did speak, it was in sesquipedalian crested words that the audience could not understand (930). This charge of using pompous and difficult compounds is repeated indirectly in the speeches of Aeschylus himself and in the comments of Dionysus and the chorus. Indeed, it is the most obvious feature of the style of the real Aeschylus. Euripides boasts that he took over this tragedy swollen with bombast and conceit and reduced "her" with his clever learning to his own neat model, where everything, beginning with the prologue, is plain and direct, and where everyone has a share in the action—the slave, and even the tender virgin (who, according to the more conservative Athenian conventions, should be neither seen nor heard). Euripides introduced nice arguments, subtle reasoning, and universal skepticism. He brought tragedy down to the level of ordinary domesticity.

To this point in the agon, Aristophanes is essentially accurate; but he now takes a tack which is eminently unfair, although it is pertinent to his serious political theme. Euripides is made to cite his "pupils" and to contrast them with the pupils of Aeschylus. Of course neither dramatist had such pupils. Aristophanes is merely saying indirectly that the Athenians should favor old-fashioned men and discard the too modern Cleitophon and Theramenes. The whole idea of pupils is false and impertinent, but it is brought in here as a graceful transition to the coming arguments of Aeschylus and the serious theme of the play. To aid the argument of Aeschylus, furthermore, Euripides is made to admit that the one criterion for poetry is improvement of its audience. This passage has frequently been cited to illustrate the naïveté of Greek literary criticism. In point of fact, this criterion is valid; it is also pertinent to the present discussion; but, like the other arguments of this play, it is used unfairly, and the prominence given it here is due to its connection with the serious theme of the play and not to any naïveté or distortion of Aristophanes' own literary theories. Later Dionysus himself tacitly admits the criterion of pleasure derived from literature as a prime consideration (1413; cf. 1468).

Aeschylus opens his defense by begging the question.[98] Citing his *Seven against Thebes* as a play of valor and manliness, he takes credit for making the Athenians of his own day what they were, when in point of fact, as chronology proves, he was the result and not the cause of the great deeds of his time. Euripides might in turn have been allowed to cite his *Heracleidae,* his lost *Erechtheus,* or his very recent *Phoenissae*; for all these plays breathe a spirit which, though somewhat more enlightened, is no less fervent and patriotic than that of the *Seven against Thebes.* Aristophanes, however, directs his argument not as fairness but as his purpose and prejudice demand.

For his lofty style Aeschylus is given a sound and irrefutable defense: it is justified because great deeds must be clothed in great language (1058–60). Euripides obviously should have been allowed to justify his own style with the corresponding defense: realistic deeds must be clothed in realistic language. The two poets were writing different sorts of drama, and each chose an appropriate style. Still, Aristophanes insists that the subject matter of Euripides is beneath the dignity of great tragedy.

The agon has been indecisive. The chorus, therefore, exhort the poets to greater effort, and an iambic scene ensues in which Aristophanes has great sport with Euripides' prologues. The examples are nicely arranged, starting with those in which the ridiculous tag, "lost his little bottle of oil," can be attached to the third line, proceeding to those where it will fit the second, and ending with one example where it can be attached to both the first and the second lines. This last example, however, is unfairly chosen; for these lines were not, the ancient commentator informs us, the opening lines of the play. The main point of serious criticism here is that Euripides' prologues are monotonously formulaic. The only defense for this is the plea of simplicity and directness. A previous remark of Euripides, which nicely prepares for this scene, has already intimated that these are the guiding principles of his prologues (946). It must be admitted, however, that if such openings began all four plays of a series, they would surely seem stilted and artificial.[99] Little information concerning such series is available, but we do know that the prologue of the *Telephus* differed somewhat from that of the *Alcestis* and the prologue of the *Medea* from that of the *Philoctetes*. The anapestic opening of the *Andromeda,* also, stood out in sharp contrast to the typical prologue of the *Helen*.

Proceeding to Aeschylus' choral odes, Euripides finds the ring of the dactylic hexameter monotonously frequent.[100] But Aeschylus is at no loss to discover faults in Euripides' lyrics, especially his monodies. Aeschylus' first thrust is his most effective one. He calls for castanets, and indeed Euripides had actually presented Hypsipyle as singing to her infant ward with castanets—a scene recently discovered in papyrus fragments.[101] Euripides is accused of prostituting the art of music for novel effects, which include the use of "immoral" meters,[102] the holding of a syllable for more than one note (a musical shake, extremely common in modern music), repetition (gemination) of words, and triviality of content. Innovations in music have always been offensive to most contemporaries;[103] and, except for the charge of triviality, these criticisms only show the narrow-mindedness of their author.

Aristophanes, we must conclude, keenly appreciated the essential qualities of the great dramatists, though he was narrow and prejudiced in his judgments. There was no naïveté or serious lacuna in his literary theory. His presentation of the contest, however, has been distorted for various reasons. First of all, he was compelled to be amusing, and it was the natural bent of his genius to exaggerate and to distort and to scoff. Secondly, distortion served to emphasize his serious political purpose in writing the play. Finally, Aristophanes had always been the enemy of Euripides. He did not have the slightest intention or desire to be fair to Euripides, nor did he feel any moral obligation to be so. He accepted the ancient code of doing good to friends and evil to enemies; and, besides, his purpose of inspiring the Athenians would doubtless have seemed to him justification for any amount of such unfairness.

10. *ECCLESIAZUSAE*[104]

(392 or 391 B.C.)

The *Ecclesiazusae* was apparently produced first among the comedies at this festival, since the chorus at the end of the play beseech the judges not to be like wicked courtesans and remember only the "latest." The other comedies and the results of the contest are unknown. Produced perhaps thirty-five years after Aristophanes' first comedy (427 B.C.) and thirteen years after the *Frogs,* the *Ecclesiazusae* lacks the brilliance, vigor, and inexhaustible resourcefulness of the earlier plays. Aristophanes' life was not, like that of Sophocles or Euripides, one of eternal youth. Still, he has not forgotten the old formulae, and he can still run the gamut of comic devices.

Happy idea and theme.—Praxagora has conceived the happy idea of disguising the women as men and thus pre-empting the seats of the public assembly and voting the control of the state into their own hands. By a surprising development all this turns out to be only a preliminary to the establishment of communism.

Perhaps the basic theme of the play is its somewhat tame satire of the Athenian passion for ceaseless innovation.[105] The relation of Aristophanes' satire of communism to Plato's serious study in the *Republic* has long been a problem. Since this work of Plato presumably appeared some years after the play, it is now usually assumed that speculation on socialism, communism, and other political theory was rife during this whole period.[106] It is not especially remarkable, therefore, if Aristophanes seems to satirize or anticipate some of the doctrines of Plato on this subject.

Structure.—Essentially the *Ecclesiazusae* is still Old Comedy. Its plot is that of the extravagant idea put into practice; the leading politicians of the day, especially Agyrrhius, are satirized; and dishonesty of officials and misgovernment, especially political raiding of the treasury, are deprecated; gross indecency still plays a major role; the comedy is little concerned with plausibility; unmotivated entrances are too pat; the houses of the background are now those of Blepyrus and his neighbors, now those of courtesans; jokes are made upon the audience; and the action is loosely thrown together, for there is no inevitability in the progression of events, although each scene does have some connection with the whole. Worst of all, the leading role shifts with almost every scene.

Significant developments, however, may be discerned. Three-fourths of the play is written in iambic trimeter—a proportion similar to that of late tragedy. The chorus has no entrance song; they leave the scene

for a considerable interval, and after they re-enter their role is almost
wholly limited, as in New Comedy, to furnishing interlude amusement.
With the exception of what may be termed a half-agon the play externally is constructed on the episodic model of tragedy and falls into
five "acts." Even the names of the characters are changing: Praxagora
("holder of an assembly") is a coined name of Old Comedy, but the
everyday names Chremes and Parmeno, frequent in New Comedy, here
make their first appearance in the extant work of Aristophanes. The
background—a street with private houses—is the usual one for later
comedy.

The play opens with Praxagora's addressing the lamp in a monologue that mildly parodies a tragic prologue addressed to the sun and,
perhaps, a lover's elegiac apostrophe to the lamp. The information here
revealed is very slight—merely the plan of the women to disguise themselves and seize control of the assembly. In the ensuing scene, which is
reminiscent of the *Lysistrata,* the women practice parliamentary conduct. This gives a good opportunity for satirizing Athenian democracy
and various individual demagogues. Praxagora's speeches here are the
most serious appeals of the play, but compared to the appeals of the
earlier plays they are the weak and hopeless protests of a discouraged
old man. Worthy of the former Aristophanes, however, is the inconsistency with which women's conservatism is praised and then communism is instituted by them.[107] The women who have gathered as individuals and small groups for the most part constitute the chorus, but
their first lyric is not sung until they hasten off to the assembly (prologos, 1–284; introduction and stasimon, 285–310).

After the withdrawal of the chorus—a unique event in the extant
comedies—Blepyrus appears for an episode of very low comedy. Only
now is it clearly revealed, at least to the modern reader, by what device
the women have made sure that their husbands would never get to the
assembly. Later Chremes appears and gives a report of the assembly—
a report markedly unlike the messenger speech of a tragedy. Blepyrus'
first reaction to the news of feminine domination is the revolting
thought that he may now be forced to make love to his wife. This erotic
motif, touched upon in the prologue, is to come to the fore in the later
action (episode, 311–477).

The chorus of women now return, anxious to get back and doff their
disguises before they are discovered. Praxagora, having taken command of the situation, faces her husband in an amusing little scene
which is more domestic than anything hitherto found in Aristophanes.
For a moment we feel as if we were witnessing a comedy of a later
period; but we are suddenly brought back to Aristophanes with Prax-

agora's declaring that unlimited blessings will come from the system of government to be instituted by the women (epiparodos, 478–503; preliminary to the agon, 504–70). After receiving encouragement from the chorus, Praxagora briefly propounds communism to Blepyrus, whose queries and objections for the most part merely facilitate her exposition and furnish comic effect. As if by accident, this discussion of community of all property swings around to the community of wives and children. This leads to the Platonic contention that if children did not know their parents all the younger generation would respect all the older (641–43). The discussion ends with Praxagora's description of the gay banqueting and amorous dalliance which will characterize her communistic state (half-agon, 571–729).

After an interlude of choral dancing—no choral song is given in the manuscripts—we are shown a scene in which the difficulties of instituting the community of property are illustrated. The optimistic Chremes marshals his petty belongings; but a more skeptical neighbor has no intention of giving over his property, though he is ready enough to do his share of receiving when the banquet is announced (episode, 730–876).

After another interlude by the chorus, a scene dramatizes the difficulties involved in the community of women and in Praxagora's novel ideas for controlling supply and demand in this unstable field where quality and personal taste play so disturbingly important a role (scene, 877–1111).[108]

The comedy ends in festivity and song as Blepyrus[109] and his children are called to the state banquet (exodos, 1112–83).

11. *PLUTUS*[110]

(388 B.C.)

The festival at which this play was produced and the prize awarded are unknown. At the same time, however, Nicochares produced the *Laconians,* Aristomenes an *Admetus,* Nicophon an *Adonis,* and Alcaeus a *Pasiphae.* Five comedies, it will be noted, were now produced at each festival. The preoccupation of these poets with mythological travesty, obvious from the titles here given, is characteristic of Middle Comedy.

This was the last play which Aristophanes produced under his own name. He wrote two later comedies, however, to be brought out by his son Araros. One of these, entitled *Cocalus* (Cocalus was a Sicilian prince to whom Daedalus fled), was a mythological travesty which is said to have been the forerunner of New Comedy, for it contained "seduction and recognition and all those other things which Menander affected."[111]

No play of Aristophanes was so widely read in late antiquity, medieval times, and the Renaissance as the *Plutus*. This popularity was no doubt due to the comparative simplicity of its language, the rarity of topical allusion in it, and the universal application which its satire suggests.

Happy idea and theme.—Chremylus has the happy idea of restoring the eyesight of Plutus, who then, he is convinced, will become the most powerful of all deities.

Like the *Ecclesiazusae* and various earlier plays, the *Plutus* is a fantasy which dreams of a better and more prosperous life, especially for the old-fashioned Athenian whose honesty in the turbulent age of Aristophanes seemed only a handicap. Aristophanes wished to satirize the Athenians for their injustices and sycophancy, says an unknown commentator,[112] and for becoming rich by these means. But the case is so generalized that the commentator might almost have said not "the Athenians" but "mankind in general."

In the *Plutus,* political and temporary elements have almost disappeared, and the satire itself, compared to that of the earlier plays, is benign and innocent.

Structure.—Like the *Ecclesiazusae,* the *Plutus,* though essentially an Old Comedy, shows various developments significant of later comedy. The *Plutus* is the first extant comedy in which a slave plays a major role, and this slave is the impudent confidential Athenian servant introduced to us in the *Frogs* and destined to become one of the most important figures in New Comedy. Owing in part to this character, most of the action of the play has that household intimacy and triviality which is typical of later comedy. The importance of the chorus, also, has been still further reduced. Only one choral song occurs in the manuscripts, and the coryphaeus with the exception of introducing the agon (487–88) is allowed to take part in the conversation only as a last resort when a single actor is on stage and a monologue would otherwise result.[113] Even so, one monologue very similar to the monologues of New Comedy is employed.[114] The function of the chorus has been reduced almost wholly to interlude dancing. Perhaps six such interludes occur, thus dividing the play like a tragedy into episodes. Finally, the frequency of extended conversations of three characters is noteworthy, and the language itself reminds one of the language of Plautus.[115]

The *Plutus* opens with a monologue-prologue; but other speaking characters are already on stage and, after a few important facts have been made known, a dialogue is developed in which the remainder of the exposition is brought out and the action proper is started. The discovery of the identity of the blind man leads to Chremylus' immediate resolve to restore his sight. At the end of the scene, Cario is sent off to summon the fellow farmers of Chremylus, and Plutus is taken into the house (prologos, 1–252).

Cario now enters with the chorus in extravagantly sportive mood (parodos, 253–321). After their verses, Cario retires on a weak excuse (in order that his actor may assume the role of Blepsidemus). There follows a very amusing scene in which Blepsidemus, an old friend, tries to discover by what dishonest method Chremylus has suddenly acquired his wealth. In order that he may keep it without risking his life, Blepsidemus offers to undertake the commission of buying off the politicians. The truth is finally revealed, and the two men are about to take Plutus to the sanitarium of Asclepius when Poverty suddenly and dramatically appears to assert her rights. A debate follows over the relative merits of Poverty and Wealth, but Chremylus absolutely refuses to be convinced that Poverty is superior no matter what the arguments may be (600). Poverty is finally driven off,[116] and Plutus is taken to Asclepius (first episode, including quasi-agon, 322–626).

After a choral interlude during which a night is supposed to have elapsed, Cario appears, and like a messenger in tragedy—except that his mood is more sportive than ever—he relates to Chremylus' wife that "the operation has been a success." Very amusing is his description of Dr. Asclepius making his rounds with two feminine assistants, Iaso (Healing) and Panacea (Cure-all). Finally Cario goes off to meet his returning master and Plutus—so he says—but this, perhaps, is merely an excuse for his exit in order that his actor may now take the role of Plutus (second episode, 627–770).

Another choral interlude follows, and the restored Plutus is joyously welcomed to the house of Chremylus (third episode, 771–801).

A later comedy might have ended at this point, for the plot is now really complete—or, more properly, no later comedy would have attempted to manage with such an extremely simple plot. Aristophanes, however, in his usual fashion fills out his play by adding a series of scenes in which the effects of the happy idea in practice are observed. Such a procedure had real point in a play like the *Acharnians,* where the author's main purpose was to drive home his thesis with as powerful an emotional appeal as possible. But here the formula does not really fit the subject; the scenes are amusing and add to the satire; but they are obviously inorganic, and the ending is flat.

Cario and Chremylus alternately take the leading role in these scenes. After another interlude, Cario is the first to appear, describing the new luxuries of the house in a long monologue. A Just Man is welcomed. He and Cario disconcert and finally drive off a sycophant who has come to protest at the loss of his livelihood (fourth episode, 802–958).

Another interlude follows, and Chremylus faces a faded lady whose wealth has formerly been the source of her satisfaction in life. But now, with the new order, she has lost her admirer, who himself comes on to pay his respects to Plutus (fifth episode, 959–1096).

The chorus dance again. The god Hermes, patron of thieves, now appears. He is half-starved and begs Cario for a bit to eat—a scene reminiscent of the *Birds*. Being refused, the god asks that he be adopted as a fellow slave; but, since he is primarily the patron of thievery and deceit, his usefulness in the new order is a matter of grave doubt to Cario until the god, in telling off his various attributes, finally recalls that he is also the patron of sports. He is hereupon accepted, and he and Cario go into the house. A priest of Zeus now appears and is handled in much the same fashion by Chremylus, who reports that Zeus himself, as predicted at the first of the play (123–26; compare the *Birds*), has found his importance greatly reduced and has now actually joined the court of the mighty god of wealth. As a finale, Plutus is conducted to the state treasury—which no doubt was badly in need of him (sixth episode and exodos, 1097–1209).

Part Three

NEW COMEDY

VII
INTRODUCTION TO
NEW COMEDY

During the fourth century the Athenian theater belonged primarily to comedy. The superior vitality of comedy is shown by the early increase of the number of comedies presented at each festival from three to five. The number of newly written tragedies was at times reduced, and the innovation of reproducing an old tragedy at each festival was instituted.[1] Tragedy had ceased to evolve with the death of Euripides; but comedy had only begun to evolve, and as the living Euripides had been the chief force in the development of tragedy, so the dead Euripides perhaps more than any living dramatist governed the development of comedy—though it is misleading to class among the dead a poet who held the boards as continuously as Euripides did during the fourth century.

The early development of Middle Comedy, as it is called, has already been noticed in connection with its only extant examples, the *Ecclesiazusae* and the *Plutus* of Aristophanes. In these transitional plays the peculiar form of Old Comedy—suited only to polemics—has already been replaced by the form of tragedy and the satyr-play—suited to a narrative plot. Political controversy has given way to mythological travesty as the main source of material, personal satire has practically disappeared, and the organic choral lyrics are rapidly being replaced by interlude choruses. Gradually the chorus became wholly or almost wholly an interlude, and plots from everyday life came in. These were very naturally introduced by similar plots from mythology and tragedy: the situation in the *Ion,* for instance, is easily reduced from the heroic, as Menander has reduced it in his *Arbitration.* So can that of the *Amphitryon* be reduced to ordinary life. Alcmene is easily converted into a Glycera and her affair with Zeus into merely suspected infidelity with a Moschion, as in Menander's fragmentary *Shearing of Glycera* (*Perikeiromene*).

The dramatic tradition is continuous; but from about the time of Alexander's coming to power (336 B.C.) the comedy written is called New Comedy.

STRUCTURE OF NEW COMEDY

The interlude choruses, it has been assumed, often numbered four in New Comedy, thus dividing the play into five "acts."[2] Menander's partly extant *Arbitration,* at least, seems to have been so divided and to have had these acts artistically constructed as units—a natural development of the usage of tragedy, where the episodes are so constructed. It will be recalled that Euripides' melodramatic plays of intrigue and escape, the *Iphigenia in Tauris* and the *Helen,* have four complete choral songs. One should not, however, assume that the originals of all the plays of Plautus and Terence had five acts or that any such division was being slavishly followed by the Greek dramatists of the fourth century.

The omniscient prologue was almost indispensable in plays which exploited dramatic irony based on hidden identities. Hence the Euripidean prologue became the rule with dramatists using this type of material, especially Diphilus and Menander. Menander, however, was fond of opening his plays with a dramatic prelude and inserting the prologue within the action. This was especially effective in plays which required elaborate exposition from two different points of view: one is displayed before and the other after the prologue. The use of a divinity for omniscient prologues was still popular. Just as Hermes speaks the prologue in Euripides' *Ion,* so the goddess Ignorance—really the patron divinity of much of New Comedy—speaks the prologue in the *Shearing of Glycera* and the star Arcturus in the Plautine *Rope,* to say nothing of Mercury in the *Amphitryon.* Sometimes, however, a mere prologue-speaker serves as a more obvious emissary of the poet. When the matter to be explained does not require omniscience, a character of the play may be employed, though such a character in Plautus may reveal the name of the Greek original or may impart knowledge which later as a character in the action he does not possess.

Though the incidents of New Comedy are often highly improbable, the plots themselves are usually simple. Terence, it is true, had a definite formula for main and minor plot. He developed this in his first play, the *Woman of Andros,* by adding a character. In four other plays he may have found it ready-made in the Greek originals. Two young men are in love, one with a virtuous girl and the other usually with an ordinary courtesan. The problem of one is solved by recognition of the girl as an Attic citizen of good birth, that of the other by securing money through an intrigue. The two actions are closely knit and nicely complicate each other. Such a plot furnishes an ample amount of dramatic business. Other types of double plots are found, such as that of

Plautus' *Pot of Gold,* where Euclio and his gold are the main concern of the play, but the future of his daughter and her lover is an important and closely associated secondary interest. Usually, however, only one young man is concerned, and his problem is solved either by recognition or by securing money. Such a plot tends to be too slight. Padding of low comedy is inserted, and sometimes, as in Plautus' *Braggart Warrior,* a minor action is clumsily suspended within the major without really contributing anything to it.

The solution of a play of New Comedy must be a happy one; often it is saccharinely happy, though sometimes it has a touch of tartness, as in Terence's *Brothers* or Plautus' *Twin Menaechmi.* Not infrequently this solution leans heavily upon the long arm of coincidence, such as the arrival of Crito in Terence's *Woman of Andros;* and sometimes the resolving character very much resembles an improperly used *deus ex machina,* as Callidamates does in Plautus' *Haunted House.*

SUBJECT MATTER

The subject matter of New Comedy was taken almost exclusively from the everyday life of the upper middle class at Athens. Contemporary historical background for the most part is superficial or wholly lacking, and so these plays made excellent material for Roman and later adaptation. The contrast here with Old Comedy, written for the day and hour, is most striking. New Comedy is much more generalized in subject and in appeal. Its sons and its fathers are very much like sons and fathers of any age, and its milieu of family life is perhaps the richest mine of comic material to be found. The general social background of Athens during the Hellenistic Age, though based on slavery, was a highly enlightened one—a brilliant backdrop for light comedy. Still, this generalization of the material and abstraction from the historical background leads to a monotonous repetition of the same plots and the same situations. Perhaps the custom of tragedy's re-using the same legends lent a specious justification for this. Certainly the heartiest reader of New Comedy becomes surfeited with the son's need of money for his sweetheart and with the machinations of the clever slave to secure this money from the father. Eventually tiring, also, is the recognition of long-lost daughters and the violation of maidens by tipsy young gentlemen. Not a single one of Menander's plays, we are told by Ovid,[3] lacked its love affair; yet he wrote more than a hundred. Indeed the length to which even the best poets went in reworking the same plot is almost incredible. That a young man should unknowingly marry the very girl whom he has previously violated, for instance, would seem an extravagant improbability to be used once perhaps in light comedy; but Menander employed it repeatedly. Again, Menander's *Andria,* we are told by Terence himself, was practically the same play as his *Perinthia.* Diphilus seems to have used plots that closely resemble each other in the originals of the Plautine *Rope* and of the fragmentary *Tale of a Traveling Bag* (*Vidularia*). All this is not in the least surprising, however, when we consider the vast number of plays turned out by these writers. Mass production necessitates systematization.

As these comedies were similar in large things, so they were in small. The characters of the best plays, especially those of Menander, are vitalized and filled out to the status of complete individuals. But usually the characters tend toward the typical: the unresourceful young lover, the testy old father, the indulgent mother, the worried moneylender. Some of the most frequent types, furthermore, are specifically Athenian: the parasite, the impudent slave, the braggart soldier, the boasting caterer. Minor motives too are somewhat stereotyped: the running slave who has good news, the porter infuriated at the knocking on the door, the master ordering a house cleaning, the parasite looking for a meal.

The results of studied analysis, however, should not be allowed to dominate one's first impression of the plays. This is often not unfavorable, for an endless variation of minor details makes the better plays appear fresh and original. The dramatists themselves were not always blind to their shortcomings; and some, such as the author of the *Captives,* made distinct efforts to work into new material. Occasionally, too, a dramatist, disgusted with the superficial, will press his plowshare deeper into the old ground and turn up something really remarkable, such as the Plautine *Truculentus.* Still, the Athens of this period was a far more colorful city than we should judge from New Comedy, and the dramatists did not fully exploit the possibilities of their contemporary world.

The moral code of New Comedy, though not obvious to the modern reader, is a strict one. It frankly accepts the double standard. A husband's infidelities are often depicted, as in the *Twin Menaechmi,* but usually such a husband is made utterly ridiculous. This is certain to be the case if a father becomes the rival of his son. But a wife's deliberate infidelities, though the subject of incidental jests in Old Comedy, are here stringently excluded. Indeed, even unwilling infidelity, such as that of Alcmene, is admitted only when it is a well-established legendary tradition. No man ever marries a girl who has been intimate with another man, though virtuous girls who have been held as slaves are often married. In such cases, however, their virtue is made unmistakably plain, and stress upon this foreshadows recognition. There are many cases where maidens of good family have been violated, but invariably the young man is made to take the onus of this and the maiden's character is saved by the assurance that force was employed. One might well be skeptical if force was so often necessary in real life. Indeed in tragedy, which is allowed more frankness in this regard, the frailty of woman is readily admitted.[4] The indulgent attitude toward a young man in such cases may shock the modern reader. "To the Greeks," it has been most aptly said, "a baby without a wedding was a better guarantee of love and union than a wedding without a baby."[5]

That no ordinary courtship in the modern sense of that term is found in New Comedy is not the fault of the dramatist. It simply did not exist in the society of contemporary Athens. Girls of good family were held in the strictest surveillance, which they were apparently unable to elude except at the great festivals. Such festivals, incidentally, are quite beyond the imagination of a modern English or American reader unless he has seen a Latin Mardi gras or unless he has been a visitor in Athens for a Greek Easter or a feast of St. George. Marriage in ancient Athenian life was arranged by the parents, and the principals had often scarcely seen one another before the ceremony. The haste of the arrangements in comedy, however, should be attributed to dramatic exigencies.

The language of New Comedy is designed to give the impression of being that of everyday speech; but actually it is a highly artistic development, strongly influenced by Euripides' dialogue. It is simple and natural, especially in the hands of the master stylist, Menander, but the extremes of colloquialism are carefully avoided. The meter, too, is extremely simple.[6]

Greek New Comedy employed conventional costumes and masks. These devices allowed an actor to take more than one role and thus reduced the expense of production. They also aided the audience, not provided with handbills, in readily identifying characters. Thus one might tell at a glance whether a young man was a naïve country youth or a dissipated cosmopolitan, whether a slave girl was a hardened courtesan or a virtuous young lady eligible for recognition as a citizen and for marriage. The use of significant names also contributed to the identification of characters.[7] Thus the name Smicrines ("small") denoted an ill-humored old man too careful with his money, Pamphila ("all-lovable") normally a young lady, and Habrotonon ("pretty thing") a courtesan. Many of the names used, such as Laches or Pheidias, are such common ones in actual Athenian life that their etymological meaning had long since faded; but even these are used with conventional limitations in comedy—Laches is an old man, Pheidias a young one. The greatest shortcoming of New Comedy's theater, however, is its inability to portray an interior scene—a marked handicap for comedies of ordinary family life. One must not, therefore, be too severe in his criticism of the dramatists if entrances and exits are occasionally awkward; for even the most intimate scenes must somehow be brought out in front of the house on the street.

These various limitations and the narrowness of its outlook, along with the ancient audience's demand that comedy amuse and delight, all had a paralyzing effect on the genre. Indeed New Comedy never gave any real promise of developing into serious drama. It is clever and amusing and delightful. We should expect no more of it.

LEADING PLAYWRIGHTS[8]

There were scores of writers of New Comedy; but only three attained real eminence: Menander, Diphilus, and Philemon. Menander (about 342–292 B.C.), in the opinion of later critics, was incomparably the best of these. His great fame in later times, however, was due in no slight degree to his mastery of language and argumentation. He was an Athenian of high social and economic status. What little we know of him does not furnish us with the slightest justification for thinking that he was a type interested in serious revolt of any sort, intellectual or otherwise. Sophisticated and urbane he certainly was, and as cosmopolitan as anyone could be who, in the justified conceit that his city was the intellectual capital of the world, spent his whole life in one city and refused to live in any other even at the invitation of kings. He had a warm and all-pervading humor, a marvelous deftness in depicting characters, and an impeccable taste and discrimination where sentiment was concerned. These were his virtues, the virtues of a genial and brilliant *bon vivant* living an aristocratic life in an affluent but basically decadent age, and we need not be astonished if we do not find in his face the profoundly thoughtful brow or the tragic mouth of Euripides.

Though Menander's dramatic activity extended only some thirty years, he is said to have written slightly more than one hundred comedies. Of these only the recently discovered *Arbitration* is preserved for somewhat more than half the play, although lengthy fragments of other plays also have been found. Roman adaptations of his plays are extant in three plays of Plautus, the *Two Bacchides,* the *Casket,* and the *Stichus,* possibly also the *Pot of Gold* and the *Carthaginian,* and in four plays of Terence, the *Woman of Andros,* the *Self-Tormentor,* the *Eunuch,* and the *Brothers.*

Diphilus was born not at Athens but at Sinope on the Black Sea. He was a contemporary and rival of Menander. He is said to have written one hundred plays. Taken from originals by him are Plautus' *Casina* and *Rope*, not to mention the fragmentary *Tale of a Traveling Bag* (*Vidularia*) and the lost *Suicide Pact* (*Commorientes*).

Philemon also was not a true Athenian, coming from Soli in Cilicia or from Syracuse—the tradition varies—though he was later given Athenian citizenship. He was some twenty years older than Menander and lived some thirty years after Menander's death. He is said to have been active as a comic poet to the very end of his hundred years and, according to one account, to have died from excessive laughter! The number of his comedies is placed at ninety-seven. The Plautine *Merchant* and *Three Bob Day* are taken from his plays, perhaps also the *Haunted House*.

VIII

MENANDER

*ARBITRATION (EPITREPONTES)

(Possibly about 300 B.C.)

Many critics consider the *Arbitration* the best extant play of New Comedy. Certainly the scene of arbitration is brilliantly written, and the charm of Menander's style is unsurpassed. Distinct virtues also are the almost total absence of low comedy and, above all, the depth of character of Charisius and his frank consideration of the moral problems involved.

The major portion of this play and fragments of various others were recovered from papyri discovered in Egypt in 1905.

The *Arbitration* was famous in ancient times as one of the masterpieces of Menander. That this play inspired at least one imitation is shown by an extant play of Terence, the *Mother-in-Law,* the original of which was written by a successor of Menander, Apollodorus of Carystus. The similarity of these plays was remarked in ancient times.

Influence of tragedy. — No extant play shows so clearly New Comedy's indebtedness to tragedy and especially to the melodramatic "tragedy" of Euripides. Besides the restrained iambic dialogue and the general structure, most of the characters of the *Arbitration* are individualized with a care and treated with a seriousness that is unusual in comedy. The play's elaborate exploitation of dramatic irony, also, closely approaches Euripidean technique as displayed in a drama like the *Ion.* Each important character has his own version of the situation, and each, of course, acts in accordance with his own particular error. The tone of the play, too, except the beginning and the end, resembles that of the *Ion.* A sentimental spectator might easily find excuse for tears in the tender scene where the gruff old Smicrines metes out justice to his own grandchild, or that where the forlorn and miserable Pamphila is informed by Habrotonon that Charisius is the father of her child, or that where the remorseful Charisius is given the same information. The incidents themselves, though common in Greek legend and to some extent doubtless in Greek life, are typical of melodramatic tragedy. Euripides' *Ion* is built about the violation of a maiden, concealed childbirth, and recognition. Indeed certain lines of the *Ion* perhaps suggested the highly improbable coincidence of a child's being recognized as the result of a wife's violation before marriage by an unknown man who is later discovered to be her present husband (*Ion* 1468–69).

In the *Arbitration,* however, the indebtedness goes beyond these generalities. The scene of arbitration itself is reminiscent of a play of Euripides now lost, the *Alope.* In that play, it seems, a beautiful princess Alope had borne a son to the god Poseidon. The child had been wrapped in royal vestments and exposed. Instead of dying it was nourished by a mare—Poseidon was the patron god of horses as well as god of the sea. Finally the child was taken up by one shepherd and given to another. But the first shepherd retained the rich garments of the child, and when the second shepherd demanded them a quarrel arose which was finally taken to the king for arbitration. The king recognized the garments as torn from the dress of his daughter.[1]

In the pleadings in the *Arbitration,* furthermore, Syriscus makes a reference—more apt than he suspects—to the tragedians and to the story of Neleus and Pelias. This legend was the subject of several tragedies entitled *Tyro* after the name of the children's mother. But a *Tyro* of Sophocles was famous, especially for its scene of recognition. The way in which Syriscus takes the baby in his hands and has it appeal to Davus, furthermore, is very similar to the scene in Euripides' *Iphigenia at Aulis* (1241–48), wherein Iphigenia asks the infant Orestes to appeal to Agamemnon to save her life.

Scenes of debate, though characteristic of all ancient drama, were especially frequent in Euripides. Indeed he owed much of his tremendous popularity in later times to his oratorical skill. According to Quintilian (10. 1. 68) he may be compared to any of the great orators. Menander admired and followed Euripides, Quintilian continues, and proved himself a true orator in debates such as those in his *Arbitration.* Certainly the whole speech of Syriscus is a masterpiece of argumentation and subtle emotional appeal.[2] His case is not an easy one, for the letter of the law is against him and he has to rely upon equity. Besides his many sound points, furthermore, this clever Syrian indulges in sophistry such as that for which Euripides was so mercilessly satirized by Aristophanes. Thus Syriscus claims that he did not at first ask for the trinkets because then, not having come into possession of the child, he had no right to speak in its behalf.

There are also several quotations from Euripides in the *Arbitration.* The important soliloquy of Charisius adapts a line from the *Orestes* (922). In the last scene preserved, Onesimus' reasoning about the gods is strongly Epicurean (and Stoic!), but it also is reminiscent of a passage from a lost play of Euripides (frag. 506, Nauck[2]). When Smicrines asks the old Nurse if his daughter has had an illegitimate child, she answers with two famous lines of Euripides from the *Auge*: "Nature willed it so, and Nature cares nothing for human laws; woman was made for this very purpose." The old Nurse then threatens to recite the whole passage!

Significant names.—The names Carion (Caria), Syriscus (Syria), and Davus (Dacia) are taken from the names of foreign countries, doubtless the countries from which these slaves or their ancestors are presumed to have come. Smicrines (*smikros,* "small") is a regular name in New Comedy for a petty, ill-humored, miserly old man; Onesimus ("useful") is a name of a slave; Charisius (*charis,* "charm") and Chaerestratus ("delighting in the army") are names of young gentlemen; Pamphila ("all-lovable") is normally the name of a young lady, and Habrotonon (*habros,* "pretty," "luxurious") the name of a courtesan.

Plot.—A man's suspicions of infidelity on the part of his wife or mistress, his first violent reactions, his later remorse, his final discovery of her innocence, and their reconciliation—this sequence constituted a favorite plot for Menander. This is the plot used with variation of details and characters in every one of the three plays that are best preserved. In the *Girl from Samos,* however, it was not the main plot but a major complication; and here, as in the *Shearing of Glycera* (*Perikeiromene*), the girl concerned appears to be of low birth but was doubtless recognized as an Attic citizen in the end. In the *Arbitration,* however, the girl is of good family and legally married. The outcome of this plot in all the plays, as the audience well knew, was inevitably fixed by convention; for it was unthinkable in New Comedy that a wife should be guilty of deliberate infidelity.

The means employed for arousing these suspicions and for the final discovery of the truth vary in the three plays; but in each case hidden identity and recognition play an important part. In the *Girl from Samos,* the man suspects that his mistress is the mother of his (adopted) son's child. In reality the child's mother is a girl of respectable family whom the son has seduced and is about to marry. The mistress has very generously undertaken to pass this child off as the father's and her own temporarily in order to save the young couple embarrassment. In the *Shearing of Glycera* the young man in whose arms the girl has been surprised by her lover is really, as the girl knows, her brother. Such concealed identity, while less natural than that in the *Girl from Samos,* is not too unlikely. But that a man should unknowingly marry a girl whom he has formerly violated is extremely improbable. This situation occurs not only in the *Arbitration,* however, but also in the fragmentary

Heros, and apparently it occurred in still other plays.[3] Such an unlikely coincidence, of course, is proper only to light comedy and melodrama.[4]

The plot of the *Arbitration,* therefore, labors under several artistic disadvantages. Still, a fresh arrangement of details and characters prevents the plot from appearing trite, and the virtues of the play are impressive.

Structure.—The *Arbitration* seems to have been written in five acts. The intervals were taken up with an interlude chorus. At the end of the first series of scenes, Chaerestratus says: "Let us be going, as some crowd of tipsy youths are coming this way, and I think it advisable that we should not bother them." There follows a space in the papyrus labeled "chorus's." Obviously this introduces the chorus of revelers regularly found in Greek New Comedy. This label occurs again after Onesimus has secured the ring from Syriscus. It is reasonably assumed to have occurred also after Smicrines enters the house of Charisius, where the text has not been preserved, and again after Charisius has learned the truth, where there is a vacant space in the papyrus.

The play opened, our fragmentary evidence seems to indicate, with a "maid-and-butler scene" of exposition between the cook, Carion, and Onesimus. The cook, like the parasite in the *Captives* of Plautus, is the one thoroughly comic character of the play; and his jokes, incidentally cited by Athenaeus (659 B), doubtless elated the audience and made it favorably disposed toward the play. In all probability there followed a long interior prologue spoken by some divinity in which the true identity of the child was made known, for the audience must be in a position to appreciate the pathetic irony of Smicrines' deciding the fate of his grandson without knowing it. After this prologue, the important action of the play begins with the entrance of Smicrines and his determination to take some action for the protection of his daughter and her dowry.

The second act is devoted primarily to the brilliant scene of arbitration and to Onesimus' securing the ring of his master from Syriscus. These are two major developments in the process of the recognition.

The third act seems to have fallen into two parts with no vacant stage between. The first concerns the plan of Habrotonon and Onesimus to reveal the ring to Charisius—an unusual type of intrigue that is intimately bound up with the recognition. After Habrotonon has left, Onesimus makes his exit in order to avoid Smicrines. The second part is very fragmentary, but it opened with a monologue of Smicrines brooding over his troubles. The cook is present again; but he makes his exit when Chaerestratus and Simias, companions of Charisius, enter and converse with Smicrines. Thus the old man learns the situation of Charisius and Habrotonon, and he determines to recover his daughter and her dowry.

The fourth act begins with a scene between Pamphila and her father. His departure leaves Pamphila miserably depressed. This is the crisis of the play. The peripety of Pamphila's fortunes takes place with the entrance of Habrotonon and her recognition of Pamphila as the mother of the child, since Charisius has already admitted being its father. These two women withdraw when they hear Onesimus opening the door—thus again avoiding a vacant stage. After some amusing lines of Onesimus, Charisius himself enters—apparently his first entrance in the whole play. In a very serious soliloquy he roundly condemns himself and is thus prepared for his reconciliation with Pamphila. In the following scene with Onesimus and Habrotonon, Charisius learns the whole truth, and the serious difficulties of the play are solved.

In the final act Habrotonon was doubtless rewarded fittingly. The very amusing scene preserved presents Onesimus, apparently a student —but not a very good one—of his contemporary, Epicurus, making great sport of Smicrines.[5]

These acts are obviously constructed as artistic units. The development is rapid, and the whole is closely knit. A deliberate effort has been made to avoid a vacant stage between scenes. The movements of the characters are plausibly motivated. An entering character, Onesimus, after the scene of arbitration, begins speaking in the middle of a line, as occasionally in the last plays of Euripides and Sophocles and as frequently in Terence.

Discussion.—Although the character portrayal in the scene of arbitration is perhaps the most skillful in New Comedy, the character of Charisius interests the modern reader even more. There is nothing priggish about Charisius, and his first reaction to the misfortune of his young wife is precisely what we should expect of any young gentleman of ancient or modern Athens, where the moral code of feminine virtue was and remains extremely severe. But with typical Menandrean irony and pathos, Charisius, no matter how much money he squanders on wine and women, still must be painfully sober and painfully in love with his wife. His change of heart when he learns of her loyalty is first described by his confidential slave, Onesimus, who thinks that his master has gone mad. He reports that Charisius is calling himself a barbarian, a heartless creature, and is raging with bloodshot eyes. The slave is dreadfully frightened at the master's approach; but when Charisius actually comes on, he is too much engrossed in his own remorse to notice anything of his surroundings. He condemns his own stupid narrow-mindedness and marvels at the generosity and loyalty of his wife, as he well may; for he has discovered that he himself is in precisely the same moral situation as his wife except that he is a guilty perpetrator and she an innocent victim. There is another difference between them: upon his discovery of Pamphila's misfortune Charisius considered himself outraged and would have nothing more to do with her; but when she discovers the misdeed of Charisius she is quite willing to forgive him and even to defend him against her father. This throws such a revealing light upon his double standard of morals that he can no longer uphold it, and he is overcome with remorse. The tone of this soliloquy is very serious, and its diction approaches that of tragedy. From the modern point of view, however, it is most unfortunate that Charisius' earlier discovery of Pamphila's misfortune and his first reactions have not been presented dramatically.

Charisius' indictment of the double standard is a compelling one. He is clearly convinced that his wife's misfortune is far less reprehensible than his own misdeeds, and he is determined to keep her as his wife even before he has learned that he himself is really the father of the child. Thus the complication of the play is solved not merely by a mechanical and external discovery but by a profound change in the attitude of Charisius. Still, Pamphila's child does turn out in the end to be his own, and since the audience from the beginning doubtless knew that the child was his, the play is robbed of any profound significance as satire or criticism of the superficial moral standards of the day. Indeed, because of this highly improbable coincidence, the play remains essentially a comedy of errors, and the comedy of errors is essentially a farce. Certainly this is not the type of material from which great drama can be made. The minimum change necessary to raise the play above the level of light comedy would be to have the father of Pamphila's child remain unknown—an intolerable outcome for a comedy of this period. The *Arbitration,* then, is New Comedy at its best, but it remains New Comedy.

Part Four
ROMAN COMEDY

IX

INTRODUCTION TO
ROMAN COMEDY[1]

Formal dramatic composition began at Rome with Livius Andronicus, who was a Greek brought from Tarentum with the conquest of southern Italy. In 240 B.C., he produced a tragedy and a comedy at the Roman Games. These plays were both Latin versions of earlier Greek originals. His innovation was a success, and his literary activity continued through 207 B.C. The practice of adapting Greek plays was quickly taken up by his contemporaries.

One among these was Gnaeus Naevius (died 201 B.C.), apparently a Campanian, who showed great originality in his activity as dramatist. He perhaps attempted to convert comedy again into a political weapon such as it had been in the days of Aristophanes; but, unfortunately for Roman literature and perhaps for Roman politics as well, this experiment ended with the poet's being thrown into prison. Plautus makes a sympathetic—but not too sympathetic—reference to this contemporary event in the *Braggart Warrior* (209–12). Another Aristophanic tendency of Naevius was his use of gross indecency, far surpassing, it seems, the bounds usually respected by Plautus.[2] Remarkable also was the wide range of Naevius' subject matter. One of his adaptations dealt somehow with manslaughter,[3] and another with horse racing.[4] Incidentally noteworthy is his praise of his own plays[5] and possibly the use of literary prologues somewhat like the later ones of Terence.[6] Naevius practiced contamination or the free combination of more than one Greek original, and in general he was doubtless very free in adapting his plays to Roman audiences.[7] Indeed he wrote original plays on purely Roman subjects.

Although the practice of writing plays on original Roman subjects survived, comedy during the next half-century dealt almost exclusively with versions of Greek plays. All the extant comedies, twenty of Plautus and six of Terence, belong to this period and are adaptations of Greek comedies, none of which has survived.

Certain changes were generally or invariably made by Roman dramatists in adapting Greek comedies for production at Rome. The interlude chorus which was the rule in Greek New Comedy, a clumsy and inartistic interruption of the play, seems invariably or at least usually to have been eliminated, and certain minor changes seem to have been

331

made in order to facilitate continuous portrayal. There are usually no "acts," therefore, in a Roman comedy, and the division into five acts found in the modern texts dates from Renaissance editions. It is sometimes demonstrable that this modern division does not reflect the original Greek division or the possible Roman division. These modern divisions should be subordinated or omitted in translations, and they are wholly ignored in the present work, where reference is invariably made to the line number. The division of the comedies into scenes, though perhaps not going back to the Greek authors or to the Roman adapters, is ancient and useful.[8]

The meter of Greek New Comedy, if we may judge from the extensive fragments preserved, was almost invariably the simple six-foot iambic. Trochaic meter of seven and one-half feet occasionally is used as a dialogue meter in Menander and elsewhere. Any other verse, however, is extremely rare.[9] The Roman dramatists abandoned primitive Italic verse for Greek meters, but naturally the exigencies of the Latin language called for certain changes. The six-foot iambic, somewhat changed, remains the standard verse in Roman comedy and tragedy. The trochaic meter, however, is really much better adapted to the Latin language, and it becomes extremely common. Indeed in Plautus the trochaic line of seven and one-half feet is slightly more frequent than the six-foot iambic. But a vast array of other meters, basically Greek but employed in new ways, comes in. Thus the Greek plays, in which the monotony of the staid dialogue was relieved by choral interludes, now in Latin apparently lose their choral lyrics and develop into musical comedies or operette.[10] The Romans were obviously very fond of elaborate cantica and a good voice; solos, duets, and trios abound in the later works of Plautus and were common in other writers of comedy and also in Roman tragedy. Terence, however, is very sparing in their use. Unfortunately the lyricism and amazing metrical variety of Plautus' plays are usually lost in English translations.

The changes made in the manner of staging must have been considerable. Roman actors, of course, stood upon the long stage, which was not over five feet high so that the senators in the orchestra might have a good view. The chorus, if used, as in Roman tragedy, stood upon the stage. Masks, we are told—though the matter is disputed—were not used during the period of Plautus and Terence but were introduced in the first century B.C.[11]

X

PLAUTUS

LIFE[1]

Titus Maccius Plautus, born in the Umbrian city of Sarsina, perhaps about 254 B.C., came to Rome as a young man, and worked, it is said, in connection with theatrical productions, perhaps as an actor or producer. After having saved some money in this pursuit, the tradition continues, he went on a trading journey to seek his fortune. Luckily, however, he lost everything. Upon his return to Rome he was forced by poverty to take the servile task of grinding at the mill of a baker. In this situation he wrote three comedies and finally gained success. He was the first important man of letters at Rome to follow the Greek custom of confining his activity to a single genre.

Although this tradition may well be apocryphal, it explains the very noteworthy fact that Plautus did not begin writing plays until late in his life, also that he, like Livius Andronicus and Terence, belonged to the distinctly lower classes at Rome. The *Braggart Warrior,* apparently his earliest extant play, dates from about 205 B.C., and he was obviously a prolific writer from that time until his death in 184. Whether he ever acted in his own plays is uncertain. But he must have been in close touch with the actual theater. Certainly he had gained a good sense of theatrical effectiveness. It is equally sure that he delighted the audiences of his own day and those of Cicero's day also. "After Plautus has met his death," he is said to have written as his epitaph,[2] "Comedy goes into mourning, the theater is deserted; then Laughter, Sport and Jest, and Immeasurable Measures with one accord have burst into tears."

A large number of comedies were attributed to Plautus in later times, but only twenty-one were admitted by all ancient scholars to be genuine. It is presumably this group which has survived, although the final play has come down in very fragmentary form and is usually ignored in translations.

The comedies of Plautus were frequently reproduced, it seems, beginning about the time of the death of Terence and extending for a century or more through the time of Cicero. Like other remains of Early Latin, they enjoyed great popularity among the educated reading public in the second century A.D. In the Middle Ages, his plays were little known. In the Renaissance they returned to popularity, and they have exerted great influence upon modern comedy.

333

COMEDY UNDER PLAUTUS

The twenty extant plays of Plautus constitute an astonishingly varied collection of good, bad, and indifferent comedies. Even the worst, however, usually have one or more effective scenes, and most of the indifferent ones doubtless were successful in his theater. For modern dramatists, good and bad alike have served as a continually plundered storehouse of interesting comic characters and amusing situations. The structure of the *Amphitryon*, for instance, is not well proportioned, to say the least; but the play's situation is so infallibly amusing that it has attracted innumerable adapters. Nor have imitators been frightened away from the *Twin Menaechmi* merely because its basic situation is fantastically improbable. The *Braggart Warrior* is very poorly constructed, but its title character remains eternally popular. The widely adapted *Pot of Gold*, however, calls for no apology on any score, for it is a masterpiece. These four plays, the most influential ones, well illustrate the variety of Plautus' work.

It is obviously difficult to determine the personal contributions of a dramatist all of whose plays are adaptations of Greek plays now lost. Still this can be done for Terence with comparative clarity, for his literary prologues and the ancient commentaries give much detailed information. Besides, his plays themselves are remarkably consistent in subject matter, structure, and various other features of dramatic technique, some of which are known not to have been characteristic of Greek comedy. But for Plautus the situation is quite different. He has no literary prologues, and no commentaries have been preserved. We are thrown back, therefore, upon the plays themselves; and, except in style, these show great variation.

In meter the variation is great but consistent and significant: Plautus began his career using little or no lyric measure and gradually increased its use as time went on. The *Braggart Warrior*, for instance, is dated by its reference to the imprisonment of Naevius (lines 209–12) about 205 B.C. It has no elaborate lyric and, except for a single passage in anapests, it is confined to iambic and trochaic lines of six or seven and one-half feet. This is the simplest metrical structure of any Plautine play. The *Stichus*, produced in 200 B.C., opens with an elaborate lyric, has two passages in anapests, and one passage in lyric iambic measure of eight feet, as well as a few lyric lines at the end of the play. The *Pseudolus*, dated 191 B.C., is literally filled with lyric and anapestic measures. These are the only plays which can be dated with certainty,[3] and with these three as a framework modern scholars have arranged the other plays in the order of their metrical elaborateness and have assumed that this was more or less the order of their composition. This assumption must not be pressed too closely, however, for presumably a serious comedy of character like the *Pot of Gold* admits fewer true lyrics and requires more restrained dialogue than an extravagant farce like the *Casina.* It is hardly necessary to add that in Plautine comedy, as in Greek tragedy and Aristophanes, the meters are skillfully adapted to the subject matter. Changes in meter emphasize changes in tone and are especially effective in a melodramatic play like the *Rope.*[4]

In subject matter, Plautus seems to run the gamut of New Comedy and perhaps to reach into that of Middle Comedy; nor has any clear and significant development in this regard been observed.[5] The mythological travesty of the *Amphitryon* is certainly the oldest material, but the elaborate meter of this play places it in the period of Plautus' maturity. The *Captives,* usually assigned to this same period, is an extraordinary play concerning the exchange of prisoners of war. The majority of Plautus' plays, however, like most of those of New Comedy, concern the gay life of the gilded youth of Athens, their eternal need of money with which to purchase sweethearts, and the frequent recognition of these sweethearts as Attic citizens.

The dramatist's attitude toward his material shows equal variety. Thus the *Pot of Gold* is a serious comedy of character, the *Haunted House* a farce, and the *Two Bacchides* a comedy of character and intrigue. These are all from the mature or late periods, and Plautus seems to have undergone no development in this regard, although comedies of intrigue are the most frequent from the beginning of his career to the end. Thus the *Comedy of Asses* presumably comes near the beginning and the *Pseudolus* near the end; the intrigue of the one is very similar to that of the other, although the *Pseudolus* is in every way vastly superior.

In dramatic structure, also, the plays vary tremendously. The *Braggart Warrior,* the *Comedy of Asses,* and the *Merchant,* all having simple metrical structure, are usually classed together as the earliest plays. But of these three, the *Merchant* is constructed excellently, the other two miserably. The *Stichus,* slightly later, has practically no plot at all— not, of course, necessarily a fault. Among the later plays, however, it is not so easy to point to such indisputable contrasts, and' it may be that Plautus improved somewhat in this regard. Still, certain of the late plays, such as the *Persian,* are surely not distinguished in structure or in their general technique.

Another item of remarkable variation is found in the total length of the different comedies. The longest are the early *Braggart Warrior* (1,437 lines), the *Carthaginian* (1,422), and the middle or late *Rope*

(1,423) and *Pseudolus* (1,334). The shortest are the *Curculio* (729), the *Epidicus* (733), the *Stichus* (775), and the *Persian* (858). These plays are from the early, middle, and late periods.

This astonishing variation of the plays, in the opinion of the present writer, seems to indicate that Plautus took his plays without much critical discrimination from a wide variety of authors and that these authors are responsible for the main features of the plays. It is conceivable, of course, that the actual manuscripts available to Plautus at Rome may have been limited. If he used any criterion consistently, it was that of theatrical effectiveness. Horace was not wholly unjustified in saying that Plautus rushed over the stage in loose "socks" and cared only for popular success.[6] Many modern critics, however, assume that Plautus so mauled the original Greek comedies that he himself is responsible for most of the faults of his plays. Perhaps these critics would have a higher opinion of Plautus' intellect if they set their hands to translating the delightfully delicate ironies and the brilliant wit of the *Amphitryon*. Certainly all but the very keenest modern translators have fallen far short of Plautus' attainment.

That Plautus had no slavish respect for the Greek originals is obvious from the plays themselves. As he changes the meters to suit himself, so he introduces various Roman allusions. References to Greek places or customs or events that would be obscure to a Roman audience are usually eliminated. Greek gods are changed to Roman. This, of course, is mere expert translation, and even Terence regularly followed this practice. But Plautus has the habit of mixing Greek and Roman in a way offensive to the modern reader, though it doubtless seemed natural enough to his original audience. It is now disconcerting, for instance, to have the Greek atmosphere broken by a reference to the Praetor. Even more disconcerting is a reference to a particular place in the city of Rome or—for comic effect—to the country town Praeneste or Plautus' own Sarsina. Terence was careful to avoid all such confusion.

Plautus sometimes combined two Greek plays into one Roman or omitted a scene from the original, and in general he adapted with considerable freedom. So says Terence in defense of his own practice.[7] Modern scholars have expended a huge amount of energy in attempting to analyze the comedies and determine the innovations of Plautus; but most of these studies have been made without sufficient literary background and consist, as someone has said, of a comparison of the known with the unknown. To assume that the very prolific Greek writers of New Comedy made no blunders or allowed no inconsistencies to creep in is obviously fallacious. In short, a detailed reconstruction of the original plays from the plays of Plautus is quite impossible. In matters of style, the personality of Plautus, greatly influenced by the conventions of his day, is observable throughout his works. His dialogue is vigorous and rapid and filled with delightful humor. In general, however, his style, like that of his contemporaries, is far more exuberant than the chaste elegance of Greek New Comedy. Plautus' Latin abounds in alliteration, redundancy, puns, and word play. This exuberance is seen in its most extreme manifestation in his anapestic and lyric passages, an English prose translation of which often sounds utterly ridiculous. Such passages should, of course, be translated into the idiom of modern popular songs. Ancient critics such as Cicero give Plautus credit for an admirable mastery of colloquial Latin.[8] He is very bold in his word coinages, which are often made for comic effect, such as in the awkward "loan translation" of a Greek compound, *turpilucricupidus* ("filthy-lucre-grabber"). Occasionally a bit of Greek or local dialect is admitted for the same effect. But very few cases of merely bad translation are found.

In certain respects Plautus distantly resembles Aristophanes. Certainly his sense of humor is robust and all-inclusive. He is fond of comedy based on physical effects, such as the pouring of slops on Amphitryon near the end of that play, the vomiting of Labrax in the *Rope,* and the drunken belching of Pseudolus. He likes indecent jests; but these usually seem a little prim in comparison with those of Aristophanes or those of Naevius. His language and his meters are similarly exuberant. His use of interminable lists, as in the *Pot of Gold* (508–19), and his employment of a dinning repetition line after line, as in the *Rope* (1212–24), also strike Aristophanic notes. He is similarly informal. So the property manager in the *Curculio* interrupts the play to give a discourse on the various quarters of Rome. More frequently, the dramatic illusion is broken by direct address to the audience or by directly insulting the audience. So Euclio in the *Pot of Gold* (718) declares that many of those in the audience, as he well knows, are thieves. We need not assume that any of these characteristics of Old Comedy had wholly died out in the Greek tradition, but possibly they are somewhat more frequent in Plautus than in his originals. The contrast with the dignified and formal Terence, at least, is again most striking. Nor need we assume that Plautus is consciously following the Aristophanic tradition—it is merely that he has a strain of the immortal comic spirit.

1. *AMPHITRYON*

Though constructed with something of the careless nonchalance of Old Comedy, the *Amphitryon* is so filled with delightful irony and irrepressible low comedy and tells such an immortal story that it is one of the most interesting plays of Plautus.

About three hundred verses, it is usually assumed, are missing from the text after line 1034.

Legend.—The legend concerning the twin birth of Heracles and Iphicles, like that of the triple birth of Helen, Castor, and Pollux, finds its eventual origin in the old popular superstition which attributed multiple births to supernatural causes. Thus the strong twin, Heracles, was thought to be the son of a divinity and only the weaker Iphicles the true son of the mortal Amphitryon.

The most striking features of the legend of Heracles' birth were the disguise of Jupiter, the long night which was necessary for the conception of this mighty child, the divine manifestations at his birth, and the miracles wrought by him in infancy. Obviously there should be at least seven months between the long night and the birth, and some months more between the birth and the miracles.[9] But if Aristophanes in the *Acharnians* could have Amphitheus go to Sparta, arrange truces there, and return to Athens all within the space of fifty lines, his contemporaries, if they so chose, could doubtless combine the long night—transformed, as in Plautus' play, perhaps from the night of generation to a night of incidental dalliance—the birth, and the miracles all into one comedy.[10]

Source.—No subject material has held the boards so long and successfully as the story of Alcmena and Amphitryon. Only the story of Oedipus and possibly that of Medea and a few others were more frequently dramatized by the Greek poets. Aeschylus wrote an *Alcmene*. So did Euripides and each of at least three minor poets of the fifth and fourth centuries. Other plays entitled *Amphitryon*, which may have dealt with entirely different phases of the story, were written by Sophocles, an Alexandrine poet, and the Roman Accius.

This subject would seem naturally to lend itself readily to parody; and the comic writers, as usual, doubtless centered their attention on the version of Euripides. A reference at the opening of Plautus' *Rope* (86) amusingly recalls the realistic stage effects which were employed at the climax of Euripides' play. Two contemporaries of Aristophanes essayed the subject—one, Archippus, calling his play the *Amphitryon;* the other, Plato "Comicus," calling his the *Long Night (Nux Makra)*. Philemon also wrote a *Night,* and Rhinthon, a Greek of southern Italy writing burlesque, was the author of an *Amphitryon*. Almost nothing is known of these plays.

It is usually assumed that the immediate original of the Latin play was a comedy of the Middle or New period.[11] This may be correct. But the *Amphitryon*, though in some ways typical of New Comedy, exhibits more technical characteristics of early comedy than any other play of Plautus. One can hardly doubt that such writers as Archippus and Plato "Comicus," perhaps Rhinthon also, have left their marks upon the play. Informality is its most striking feature. The scene at one time seems to be laid before the house of Amphitryon, at another somewhere near the harbor. Such variation was not unnatural on the long Roman stage, however, and less striking examples are found in other plays.[12] The very fact that Thebes is placed near the sea is a bold distortion, like the coast of Bohemia in Shakespeare. The utter contempt for the dramatic illusion, also, is reminiscent of Old Comedy. So are the various effects of low comedy: the beating of Sosia and Mercury's pouring ashes and slops down on Amphitryon. Time is boldly telescoped. There is something too of the inimitable spirit and verve of Old Comedy.

Influence.—There are vast numbers of modern adaptations of Plautus' *Amphitryon*. One of the most famous of these is Molière's *Amphitryon* (1668), which has been translated into many languages and frequently reproduced. Especially noteworthy in his version is the introduction of Sosia's wife. Sosia's "girl friend" is given only a brief reference in the play of Plautus (659).[13] Well known also are the version of Rotrou (*Les Sosies,* 1638), which had considerable influence on Molière, that of John Dryden (1690), and that of von Kleist (1807). In the *Comedy of Errors* Shakespeare adopted certain motives from the *Amphitryon*.[14]

Most interesting of all, however, is the brilliant contemporary production of Jean Giraudoux, *Amphitryon 38*. This is an astonishingly original reworking of material so often dramatized before, and it has very little in common with the play of Plautus. Indeed the story has been made into delightfully high comedy. In a bedroom scene filled with subtle irony Jupiter praises the night just past in the most effusive terms, but for his every adjective Alcmène insists upon recalling a night (with Amphitryon, of course) that was much superior.[15] Thus the comedy is mainly at the expense not of Amphitryon but of the god himself! Alcmène also pays her generous share, for she mistakes the real Amphitryon for the god and, thinking that she is playing a clever deception upon him, sends him in to the bed of Jupiter's former playfellow, Leda. The comedy closes with a gift of forgetfulness—a faint reminiscence perhaps of Molière's ending. An English adaptation of this play was produced in America with great success.

Discussion.—Except for the *Plutus* of Aristophanes, the *Amphitryon* is the only example of mythological travesty that has been preserved. This genre, though occasionally written at Athens during the fifth century, came into great popularity duing the first half of the fourth century and to some extent prepared the way for the development of intimate social comedy.

The basic plot of the *Amphitryon,* a wife's adultery and the duping of a husband, was one which convention usually forbade comedy. The cruel irony of the situation, difficult for any husband to enjoy wholly without misgivings, is well exploited, however, even in the *Iliad* (3. 369–454), where Menelaus still toils on the field of battle while Paris, rescued from him by Aphrodite, has taken Helen to bed. The situation is softened in the comedy of Plautus because a well-known myth is being parodied and because Alcmena is morally innocent. Here the duping of the husband is played up into a comedy of errors and, to make confusion worse confounded, Mercury is introduced in the disguise of Sosia.

The opening of the *Amphitryon* is remarkably recitational and farcical. Here is the best example of the proverbially long-winded god of the prologue. Almost a hundred lines of clever foolery have gone by before Mercury finally begins with the argument of the play. Another fifty lines are used for explaining the situation. Since this is a comedy of errors, the poet is careful here and throughout the play to instruct the audience with painful explicitness before every new development. Incidentally Mercury reminds us that some Roman actors, being slaves, might be whipped for a poor performance, and he makes interesting revelations concerning *claqueurs* in the ancient theater.

The entrance of Sosia does not begin the action but leads to another prologue! Now we hear in detail the story of Amphitryon's campaign, and the mortal is no more concise—and no less clever—than the immortal has been. Practically nothing in this long monody, occasionally punctuated by a remark of Mercury, has any structural significance except the reference to the gold cup of Pterela (260). No normal dramatic conversation develops until almost three hundred fifty verses have been spoken in these two prologues. Still, this opening, though static, is far from dull.

After the amusing low comedy between Sosia and Mercury, the slave departs, and the god speaks another prologue! We are now told the complications that are about to take place, and even precisely how everything will be made right in the end.

The two scenes between Jupiter and Alcmena are among the best of the play and prove that, after all, ancient dramatists could write scenes of sentimental dalliance. The exchanges here, of course, are pervaded by a delicate irony.[16] Alcmena can well say, "Gracious me! I am discovering how much regard you have for your wife (508)." And Mercury can be quite sure that he is telling the truth when he says to Alcmena: ". . . . I don't believe there's a mortal man alive loves his own wife (*glancing slyly at Jupiter*) so madly as the mad way he dotes on you."[17] Incidentally in this scene Jupiter gives Alcmena the gold cup which, as we have heard before (260, 419–21), Amphitryon has received as his special reward, and which is to play such an important role in the subsequent action.

The comedy of errors now continues with the introduction of Amphitryon; and the structural function of the earlier mystification of the slave, it now appears, is to furnish the first step in the gradual mystification and maddening of the master. The second step quickly follows with the strangely cold reception which Amphitryon receives from Alcmena. Her production of the gold cup adds a third. Meanwhile the irony continues, but it is not always as delicate as it is in the very proper oath of Alcmena (831–34): "By the realm of our Ruler above and by Juno, mother and wife, whom I should most reverence and fear, I swear that no mortal man save you alone has touched my body with his to take my shame away."

When Amphitryon, convinced of his wife's infidelity, has rushed off to find her kinsman, Jupiter returns for another session of dalliance and to set the stage for the supreme humiliation of Amphitryon. He also foretells the coming action and solution, repeating in part what Mercury has said previously. Later Mercury reappears as the "running slave," and carefully explains how he will mock Amphitryon.

Failure to locate the kinsman of Alcmena aggravates Amphitryon's ill humor, and when he returns to find the house closed to him his frustration knows no bounds. But this is only the beginning of his grief. He must be taunted unmercifully by the divine lackey and finally have ashes dumped upon him and slops poured over him—a scene which doubtless brought down the house, be it Greek or Roman. All this time Jupiter is taking his pleasure of Alcmena inside. Finally Jupiter himself comes forth and tows the conquering hero Amphitryon about the stage by the nape of his neck. There is not a scene even in Aristophanes that carries low comedy quite so far as this.

When Amphitryon finally regains his feet, now stark mad, he resolves to rush into the house and slay everyone whom he meets. But at this crucial moment come thunder and lightning, and he is struck down before his house. There can be no vacant stage here, and doubtless Bromia quickly enters, though her subsequent account reveals that a great deal of time is supposed to have elapsed. Amphitryon, recognizing the unmistakable signs of divinity, is thoroughly placated. He considers it an honor to have had his wife adulterated by Jupiter. Nevertheless, the play must end in true tragic fashion with an appearance of Jupiter as the god from the machine. The last line of all, reminiscent of the humor of Mercury in the prologue, is perhaps the best of the play (Nixon's translation): "Now, spectators, for the sake of Jove almighty, give us some loud applause."

2. COMEDY OF ASSES (ASINARIA)

The *Comedy of Asses* is one of the least interesting of Plautus' plays. Its characters are typical and lack individuality. Its plot, a simple intrigue to secure money for a desperate lover before a rival anticipates him, does not furnish enough dramatic action, and so most of the play is taken up with merely incidental talk and buffoonery. The structure, simple though it be, is awkwardly managed; but it is somewhat improved by the assumption of Havet that the young man who appears with Cleareta near the opening of the play is the rival Diabolus rather than Argyrippus.[18] If Diabolus is introduced here, his entrance near the end of the play is less abrupt and his function less like that of a *deus ex machina*. In the simplicity of the meters used, the *Comedy of Asses* resembles the *Braggart Warrior* and is therefore usually considered one of Plautus' earliest plays.

The *Comedy of Asses* is not, however, wholly without its virtues. The contract which Diabolus has drawn up is a very amusing document.[19] The final scene, furthermore, is excellent drama as well as excellent amusement. The shrewish wife, with her "Get up, lover, and go home," doubtless saved the play in actual production.

3. *POT OF GOLD (AULULARIA)

The *Pot of Gold* is a delightful comedy of character with an abundance of dramatic action. Unfortunately the final scene has been lost, but fragments and the arguments of the play indicate the main features of the solution.

It is thought that Menander was the author of the original—a very attractive but unproved assumption. The miser was a favorite type with Menander, as may be seen in his *Arbitration,* where also a cook is used for a scene of low comedy.

Significant names.—The name Staphyla ("bunch of grapes") suggests that this character, like so many of the old women of comedy, is addicted to winebibbing, and certain of her lines confirm this (354–55). The cooks, too, are picturesquely named Congrio (*gongros,* "eel") and Anthrax ("a coal"). From the point of view of American slang, however, the most aptly named character is that of the young man who has violated Euclio's daughter—Lyconides ("wolfling").

Influence.—The *Pot of Gold* has been a very influential play.[20] Ben Jonson's *The Case Is Altered* is an adaptation of this and of the *Captives.* But by far the most famous adaptation is Molière's *L'Avare* (1668), which itself inspired various imitations, including comedies entitled *The Miser* by Shadwell (1672) and by Fielding (1732).

A comparison of the play of Molière with that of Plautus is a profitable study; but only a few points can here be noted. Molière, like Plautus, employs significant names. Among these Harpagon ("grappling hook," "snatcher") is a Greek-Latin formation and was doubtless suggested by the cognate verb which occurs in the *Pot of Gold* (201), or by the name Harpax in the *Pseudolus* (esp. 654). Molière has enriched the plot by adding a son and his love affair, in which Harpagon himself is involved. Several passages closely follow Plautus. Harpagon rages at the loss of his gold much as Euclio does and even descends to making similar remarks directly to the audience (IV, vii). The scene where Valère confesses to Harpagon also follows Plautus very closely in its elaborate irony. The Menandrean humanity of Euclio, however, has been wholly lost in the grossly exaggerated Harpagon.

Discussion.—The main plot of the *Pot of Gold* is an unusual one. A miser, Euclio, through excess of caution, is made to lose his recently discovered treasure. By the good offices of a young man who has violated his daughter, however, he recovers the treasure. Meanwhile he has learned a lesson; and so he apparently gives the money to his daughter as a dowry and is happy to be relieved of the task of guarding it. Thus this comedy, like the *Brothers* of Terence, has a serious theme. The minor plot concerning the daughter and her violation is trite, but skill is shown in combining it very closely with the main plot. Indeed it is employed almost wholly to bring out the character of Euclio and facilitate the main action.

The play opens with an omniscient prologue by the patron divinity of the household. Noteworthy here is the explanation that the proposal of the old man, Megadorus, is merely a device of the divinity for uniting the girl to the father of her child. Surely a modern playwright would have preferred to dispense with the prologue altogether and to reserve Megadorus' proposal for an exciting complication. But the ancient dramatist has some justification for rejecting this method. He is anxious in no way to detract from the emphasis on Euclio's character. Even in the prologue, the primary concern is to show that the miserliness of Euclio has been inherited for generations. Indeed the proposal of Megadorus itself is primarily designed to bring out the point, essential to the plot, that the present Euclio will not even give a dowry to his daughter though she must inevitably lose social status if she marries a wealthy man without one. So the very liberal character of Megadorus is designed by contrast to display the niggardliness of Euclio.

The scenes between Euclio and Staphyla, also, serve to illustrate the character of the miser. Incidentally, preparation for his subsequent distrust of the very bland Megadorus is contained in his complaint that all his fellow citizens, seeming to know that he has found a treasure, now greet him more cordially.

Eunomia and Megadorus are introduced with an elaborate duet in which it is brought out that an old brother is being forced to do his duty to society by an old sister who has already done hers. Since Eunomia must have a role later in the play, the dramatist has done well to introduce her here, and she is very nicely drawn. Her slightly archaic Latin perhaps suggests that she belongs to that class of staid matrons whom attention to the home has caused to lose contact with the latest developments of a changing world—a type of old-fashioned womanhood well known and admired by Cicero.[21]

The cooks furnish low comic relief in this very serious play but are also necessary in the machinery of the plot. Significantly emphatic are the repeated references to the notorious thievery of cooks, especially the slave's monologue devoted exclusively to this subject immediately before the re-entrance of Euclio (363–70). The distinctly lower atmosphere of these menials is subtly suggested also by a few indecent jests.

So Euclio is brought to the fatal mistake of removing his hoarded gold and burying it elsewhere. Megadorus' genial threat to make him drunk merely adds to his uneasiness, though he has been pleased with Megadorus' disgust of rich wives and their extravagance.[22]

The action which leads the slave of Lyconides to steal Euclio's treasure is well motivated; but the technique of eavesdropping is awkward in the extreme, for misers, however old or fond of talking to themselves, are careful not to talk of their treasures aloud. To present their thoughts in soliloquies may be permissible, but to have another discover the secret by overhearing such a soliloquy violates all probability.

The best scene of the play, perhaps, is that in which Lyconides confesses one sin but Euclio thinks that he is confessing another. The ambiguity here is more easily maintained in Latin or French than in

English. Highly amusing, too, is the later effort of Lyconides' slave to withdraw his confession of having stolen the treasure.

Doubtless little of importance has been lost at the end except Euclio's final speech of reformation.

4. *TWO BACCHIDES* (*BACCHIDES*)

(Date unknown, but later than the *Stichus* [200 B.C.] or the *Epidicus*.[23])

The *Two Bacchides,* somewhat like the *Self-Tormentor* of Terence, opens as a splendid Menandrean comedy of character but soon hastens off into the usual stereotyped play of intrigue. Noteworthy is the rapid shift in the fortunes of the various individuals.[24] Mnesilochus now has an abundance of money, now none, and soon an abundance again. The fortunes of his father change even more rapidly and, of course, end at a humiliatingly low level.

An undetermined number of verses have been lost from the opening, but the play is essentially intact.

Source.—The source of Plautus' play is revealed by verses 816–17, which translate one of Menander's most famous lines, "Whom the gods love dies young." Menander's play was called the *Double Deceiver* (*Dis Exapaton*). From the title it is obvious that Menander's play also centered about the intrigue to secure money. Some modern scholars, however, have insisted that Plautus has added one deception—the second letter. Chrysalus does cite three deceptions (953–78). That later Nicobulus (1090) and one of the sisters (1128) count only two has been taken to indicate that Plautus here reverts to the original text of Menander. But it is ridiculous for modern scholars to assume that Plautus could become confused on such a simple score. The inconsistency is only apparent. Indeed, Bacchis clearly says that Nicobulus has been "trimmed" twice; and this certainly, as presumably the earlier phrase of Nicobulus and the Greek title, can only refer to actual financial losses. In short, there is no evidence that Plautus has changed the plot, though we can feel certain that he has greatly elaborated the simple meters of the original.

Influence.—More important than the few adaptations in modern times has been the influence of certain of the play's many types of characters, especially the strait-laced pedagogue and the deceiving servant. Chrysalus' wild tale of the sloop (279–305) eventually, perhaps, turns up in Molière's *Les Fourberies de Scapin* (1671; II, xi)[25] after appearing in various intermediary plays, including Cyrano de Bergerac's *Le Pédant Joué* (possibly 1654).

Discussion.—The *Two Bacchides* exhibits an embryonic double plot, for it contains two young men and their difficulties in love. The best of the play is doubtless found in the opening scenes between the naïvely innocent Pistoclerus and the more than competent Bacchis. Both are delightfully characterized, and Bacchis shows great skill in ensnaring him as she and her sister are later to ensnare the fathers of both young men. Very amusing is the reaction of Pistoclerus' pedagogue, Lydus, who cannot realize that his ward is no longer a child and whose moral code, in comparison with that of his masters, is ridiculously high.

From the first, Pistoclerus has been acting as the agent of Mnesilochus, and with the return of this second young man, the need of money to save his love from the soldier becomes the chief concern of the action. Pistoclerus practically disappears after he has caused the minor complication of Mnesilochus' returning all the money brought from Ephesus to his father. Part of this money must now be recovered through the usual type of intrigue engineered by the usual clever slave. The victim is forewarned repeatedly, as in the *Pseudolus,* and yet repeatedly deceived. As in the *Pseudolus,* also, return of part of the money is promised to the victim at the end of the play. The intrigue itself and especially the elaborate comparison which Chrysalus draws between himself and Ulysses are clever and amusing, though of course the whole depends upon the mechanically pat entrance of the soldier. As a comic character, however, Chrysalus falls far below the level of the colorful Pseudolus.

In general the portrayal of characters is masterly. But contrast of characters, except for the indirect contrast between the strait-laced Lydus and the unscrupulous Chrysalus, is not here employed as effectively as in the *Brothers* of Terence and in other Menandrean plays. This shortcoming is all the more striking because the cast includes two young men, two old men, and two courtesans.

The final scene wherein the sister courtesans take in the old men has often been criticized on moral grounds. Though amusing, it is undeniably crude. Satire is often so. There is not the slightest ground, however, for thinking that either crudity or satire is not Menandrean. The Greeks saw life whole and honestly recorded what they saw.

5. *CAPTIVES

The *Captives* is a quiet comedy of delightful humor and somewhat melodramatic pathos. Lessing considered it the finest comedy ever produced because, in his opinion, it best fulfills the purpose of comedy and because it is richly endowed with other good qualities.[26] The opinion of Lessing, however, was attacked in his own day, and the merit of the *Captives* is still a matter of debate and violent disagreement. This arises in part from differences of opinion concerning the purpose of comedy and from attempts to compare incomparables. Various types of comedy naturally have various appeals, and the *Captives* is admittedly lacking in the robust gaiety and occasional frank indecencies of the *Pseudolus* as it is lacking also in the verve and activity and romance of the *Rope*. It is nevertheless a very successful play.

Nothing is known concerning the Greek original.

Influence.—Among comedies indebted to the *Captives* may be mentioned the following: Ariosto's *I Suppositi* (about 1502, adapted into English by George Gascoigne [1566]), Ben Jonson's *The Case Is Altered* (about 1598, combining the *Captives* and the *Pot of Gold*), and Rotrou's *Les Captifs* (1638).[27]

Significant names. — The significance of the name Ergasilus ("working for a living," but here, as elsewhere, with the connotation of "courtesan") is explained by the parasite himself in his opening lines. The name Hegio ("leading citizen") obviously suggests a gentleman. The names Philocrates ("lover of mastery"), Aristophontes ("best-slayer"), and Philopolemus ("lover of war") all suggest mighty warriors, and there is more than a shade of irony in the fact that all these men have been captured in war. Stalagmus ("drop") is a derisive name applied to a slave of diminutive stature. The name Tyndarus is apparently taken from the legendary Tyndareos, father of Helen, and is obviously a slave's name.

Structure.—The *Captives*, like most of the plays of Plautus, was probably presented without intermission or interlude; but the traditional "acts," which date from the Renaissance, here divide the play into well-defined chapters of action. It is not unlikely, therefore, that these divisions are the same as those of the original Greek play, which probably had five sections marked off by four choral interludes.

The first section (126 lines) is designed to put the audience into a pleasant mood, characterize Hegio, and repeat the essential facts of the exposition (for the play is a unit practically independent of the prologue). The second section (266 lines) again explains the confusion of identity and successfully launches the intrigue by which Hegio is made to send away the gentleman, Philocrates, rather than the servant, Tyndarus. The third section (307 lines) presents Hegio's discovery of the ruse and the downfall of Tyndarus. The fourth (154 lines) announces the return of Hegio's captive son and is mainly concerned with the foolery of the parasite Ergasilus. The fifth (107 lines) contains the actual arrival of Philocrates, Philopolemus, and the wicked slave

Stalagmus.[28] Most important of all, Tyndarus is here recognized as the long-lost son of Hegio.

Discussion.—An intrigue by which two enslaved captives cheat their purchaser furnishes subject matter refreshingly different from that of most later Greek comedies. But the *Captives* still has many conventional features. The parasite is the usual stereotyped character, and to eliminate him would be to sacrifice the most amusing character of the play. Stock incidents, too, are found in the confusion of identities and in the use of intrigue and recognition. The appearance of Stalagmus, also, is too happy a coincidence for serious drama. No proper explanation is given for his return, although some preparation for this and for the recognition is made by Hegio's account of his earlier loss of a son (760). Nor is it true, as the speaker of the prologue alleges, that the play contains no indecent lines, although moral purity has contributed more than its share to the popularity of this play in modern times. In order to be fair to the poet, however, we must admit that even the conventional features are handled with unusual skill and freshness. The indecent jests are few and are employed almost exclusively to emphasize Ergasilus' irrepressible exuberance when he is bringing the good news to Hegio (867, 888). The confusion of identities is here entirely credible—although this has been disputed—and bears no resemblance to the implausibly maintained confusion in the *Twin Menaechmi*. The actors may well commend this play, therefore, for its effort to break away from the stereotyped characters and the stock incidents of New Comedy.

Unique in New Comedy is the appearance of two actors along with the speaker of the prologue in order that the audience may understand the true identity of Philocrates and Tyndarus beyond all doubt. The prologue also reveals that Tyndarus is the son of Hegio, although Tyndarus and Philocrates do not know this during the subsequent scenes. This inconsistency should hardly be considered a fault, for it is here assumed that the play has not yet begun.

Although most of the information given in the prologue is as usual repeated in the following scenes, a prologue was absolutely essential in this play, for without the knowledge that Tyndarus is Hegio's son the audience would fail to appreciate much of the dramatic irony which pervades the whole action and constitutes perhaps the chief virtue of the play.

Dramatic irony and suspense tend to be mutually exclusive, since the one often depends upon the superior knowledge of the audience and the other upon its ignorance; yet the *Captives* combines both to a remarkable extent and with unusual subtlety. The suspense concerns the return of Philocrates, of course, and it is built up primarily by means of the irony of Philocrates' lines and the earnest anxiety of Tyndarus in their scene of farewell.

The dramatic irony of the play begins when Hegio first addresses his two captives. Philocrates plays the role of the confidential slave with consummate skill especially in his assured self-reliance and in his impudent boldness, whereas Tyndarus assumes the modest restraint of a gentleman. Many of these speeches obviously have one meaning for Hegio but another, truer, meaning for the captives and the audience. This humorous irony is very materially aided in Latin by the usual omission of articles and pronouns. Thus when Tyndarus, posing as the gentleman, speaks of sending the "slave" Philocrates *"ad patrem,"* the reference is amusingly ambiguous.

The dramatic irony reaches its greatest height, however, in the scene of farewell. When the supposed master recites at great length the virtues of the slave, he is really praising himself; and when the supposed slave recites the virtues of the master, he, too, is really praising himself. But the poor naïve Hegio is so taken in by the deception that he is greatly impressed with what he thinks to be the sincere mutual praise of master and slave (418–21). The effect here is primarily comic; but there is real pathos in the true Tyndarus' fear of being abandoned, a fear which Hegio cannot understand but which the audience fully appreciates. The high point of this aspect of the dramatic irony comes when the "slave" who is being sent home gives an oath to Hegio and to his former "master" that he will never be false to Philocrates. Such an oath reassures Hegio, but it can only disquiet the true Tyndarus.

The most serious and pathetic irony in these scenes, however, is contained in those speeches in which the truth can be appreciated only by the audience. The true Tyndarus in his first conversation with Hegio, for instance, says that he was formerly just as much a free man as Hegio's own son and that his father misses him just as much as Hegio misses his own son. Whereas Tyndarus here intends to lie and Hegio thinks that Tyndarus is Philocrates and is telling the truth, the audience know that Tyndarus is really saying what is true because he is the son of Hegio.

Another scene of pathetic irony is that in which Hegio undertakes to punish Tyndarus, really his own son. When Tyndarus boldly insists that his action has been commendable and proper, Hegio himself is forced to admit that he would have been very grateful indeed if a slave had performed such an action for a son of his. This is precisely what Tyndarus has done, for by securing the release of Philocrates he has really made possible the return of his own brother, the captured son of Hegio.

Indirectly, of course, Tyndarus has also made his own recognition possible. Yet Hegio thinks that this action of Tyndarus has made him lose his second and last son. Although this scene is not without its touches of humor, the tone is on the whole very serious, and the solemn simplicity of the iambic meter here, as Lindsay points out,[29] is reminiscent of tragedy and offers a very strong contrast with the bustling comedy of the preceding scene.

Hegio is not the stupid old man characteristic of comedy, although his figure has its amusing aspects; nor is he the stereotyped kindly old gentleman. He is thoroughly an individual. Before his entrance he is described briefly by Ergasilus as a man of the old school whose present business of trading in captives is most alien to his character. Thus we are prepared for Hegio's being taken in by the clever ruse of the captives. Undeniably amusing is his meticulous but naïve and wholly ineffectual caution in handling the captives. This caution is brought out both in his directions to the Guard and in his first conversation with the "slave" Philocrates. Amusing also is the manner in which Tyndarus and Philocrates talk to each other in their scene of farewell with an irony which wholly deceives the old man.

Sudden changes in the emotional tone of the play are emphasized by the figure of Ergasilus. Besides enlivening this unusually serious play with the usual low comedy, Ergasilus serves as an emotional foil for Hegio. At the beginning of the play both Hegio and Ergasilus are worried and not too optimistic. But as the play progresses and arrangements are made for sending the "slave" to Elis, Hegio becomes elated at the prospect of securing the return of his captured son. Just at this point, Ergasilus appears and, in strong contrast to Hegio's elation, pours forth his woeful tale of hopeless failure to discover a patron in the forum or even to raise a laugh. He would gladly dig the eyes out of this day that has made him so hateful to everyone. Immediately after this depressing monologue and the exit of Ergasilus, Hegio reappears in a state of elation greater than before, relating how he has been congratulated by everyone for successfully arranging the return of his son. The irony of his situation again presents the old man in a somewhat humorous light.

After the deception of the captives has been discovered, Hegio himself falls into a dreadfully depressed state and presents a figure of almost tragic pathos. But Ergasilus now appears in a state of ecstatic elation over the good news which he has for Hegio. The day which before was so hateful to him he now recognizes as his greatest benefactor. Ergasilus has time for only a few lines, however, before Hegio reappears. In a brief song, very different in tone from his earlier song of self-congratulation, Hegio now bitterly complains of his disappointment and chagrin, anticipating the scorn of everyone when they learn of the way in which he has been taken in. Here the irony of Hegio's depressed state fuses the pathos and the humor of his figure to make him the most appealing character of the play. A final brief song by Hegio, in the same meter, opens the last section of the play and expresses Hegio's solemn gratitude for the return of his captive son.

Tyndarus and Philocrates, like Hegio, are entirely admirable characters, and their virtues are fittingly rewarded as we should expect in a comedy. Still, they do not become saccharine in their goodness. Tyndarus is more than willing, for instance, to see Stalagmus punished. Sentimentality, which might have run rampant in the final scene,[30] has been avoided by maintaining the usual classic restraint and honesty.

6. *CASINA*

(Perhaps 185 B.C.[31])

Like much of Aristophanes, this spirited musical farce is grossly indecent and irresistibly amusing. Its popularity is well attested in the prologue, part of which, at least, was written for a reproduction some time after Plautus' death. The text in the broad scenes near the end of the play is only partially preserved. The play as a whole is the most lyric of Plautus' comedies, and many a delightfully extravagant line of the original falls very flat in translation.

The *Casina* has had some unimportant modern adaptations, but the resemblance of its plot to the *Mariage de Figaro* of Beaumarchais is thought to be fortuitous.[32]

The original Greek version of this play, like that of the *Rope,* was written by Diphilus, who called his comedy the *Lot-Drawers* (*Kleroumenoi*). Modern scholars often assume that Plautus has revamped the whole play and introduced much of its grossness. Diphilus, however, was distinguished among the poets of New Comedy for his frankness,[33] and it is not easy to imagine how this material could be handled very differently from the way in which Plautus has handled it.[34] It is obvious from Diphilus' title that his play too centered about a contest, and it is likely that this contest was the rivalry of two slaves, reflecting, as in Plautus, the rivalry of father and son. Certainly if the father was involved, the subject was a scandalous one and fitted only for broad farce.

If Plautus is responsible for the suppression of the nauseatingly frequent motive of recognition, he is to be heartily congratulated; but there is no trustworthy evidence on this point. Certainly the play is skillfully constructed, and the tone is consistent throughout. Quite in keeping with this tone is the burlesque of tragedy when Pardalisca first comes rushing upon the stage in pretended mortal terror (621).[35] Similar is Palaestra's song of more genuine terror in the *Rope* (664). But to discuss at length a play which makes its simple point—uproarious laughter—so obviously and so adequately would be mere pedantry.

7. CASKET (CISTELLARIA)

(Not later than 202 b.c.[36])

The text of this comedy is so badly mutilated that no very accurate opinion of its virtues can be obtained. (The complete play ran to some twelve hundred lines.) The Greek original was Menander's *Women at Luncheon (Synaristosai)*.[37] A mosaic at Pompeii is thought by some to illustrate the scene which gave the Greek play its name—the name sometimes cited also as that of Plautus' version.[38]

This play is said to have influenced Molière's *Les Femmes Savantes*.[39]

The stereotyped plot is that of a young man, Alcesimarchus, in love with the virtuous but lowly Selenium while his father is trying to force him to marry another girl. He is saved, of course, by the recognition of Selenium. Thus the basic situation is similar to that in Terence's *Woman of Andros*. The process of recognition in the *Casket*, however, is unusually elaborate, though based on the trite and highly improbable coincidence of a man's unknowingly marrying the girl whom he has earlier violated.

The opening scene is an excellent one of dramatic exposition, including a revealing contrast between the virtuous Selenium and the hardened Gymnasium. But after this scene the expository material is clumsily elaborated by a monologue of the Procuress and an omniscient prologue. The information of the prologue, furthermore, appears superfluous. At least the play as it now stands does not exploit dramatic irony to an extent which would justify this foretelling. The interior position of the prologue, employed in plays of Aristophanes such as the *Knights*, was a favorite one with Menander. It is used also in Plautus' *Braggart Warrior*. It has the advantage of allowing the play to open with a dramatic scene, and it serves to break the monotony of introducing two different sets of characters when these two sets cannot be fused into a single scene until late in the play.

Alcesimarchus is the most violent lover of New Comedy. Perhaps he would be the most romantic and the most interesting one, if several of the scenes in which he played an important role had not been mutilated or lost. Incidentally noteworthy is the parody of tragic conversation line by line (stichomythia) in which his slave abuses him for neglect of his sweetheart (241–48). Alcesimarchus' efforts to soothe the ruffled Selenium, if we may judge from the fragments, constituted a delightful scene of love-making. One of the very few hysterical episodes of New Comedy occurs near the end of the play when Alcesimarchus appears about to commit suicide, and then abducts Selenium instead. The scenes of actual solution, however, are extraordinarily ineffective.

8. *CURCULIO*

The *Curculio* is one of the least interesting plays of Plautus. Its scene is laid, not at Athens, but at Epidaurus, a city famous for its curative cult of Asclepius and, incidentally, the site of the best-preserved ancient Greek theater.

The play's trite plot is that of a young lover, Phaedromus, who is in need of money in order to save his sweetheart. A parasite, Curculio, sent to procure the necessary funds, returns without them but with the stolen ring of a soldier who has contracted to buy this very girl. Slave dealer and banker are deceived into delivering the girl into the hands of the disguised Curculio. Serious complications at the appearance of the soldier are avoided by the girl's recognizing him as her brother.

In the usual manner this recognition is foreshadowed from the beginning of the play by the insistence upon the girl's chastity and virtue. The deception closely resembles that of the *Pseudolus,* but it is much simpler. Indeed, dramatic action is sadly lacking. Despite obvious padding of the scenes with mere foolery, this play, along with the *Epidicus,* is the shortest of Plautus' comedies. Its metrical structure, too, is unusually simple. Noteworthy in the one lyric passage, however, is the lover's sentimental address to the closed door of his sweetheart (esp. 147–54)—a parody of a frequent motive in ancient sentimental verse.[40] Indeed the whole opening of the play is very picturesque and amusing, and the enticement of the porteress is imitated in Massinger's *A Very Woman, or the Prince of Tarent.*[41]

In the middle of the play, a curious address by the property manager has been introduced to cover what would otherwise be a very awkward vacant stage (462–86). The various places in Rome where men and women of different classes congregate are described at length. This passage furnishes one of the most interesting literary records of early Rome.[42]

9. *EPIDICUS*

(Date unknown, but earlier than the *Two Bacchides*.[43])

The *Epidicus* is another play of intrigue and recognition. Though not as gay and spirited as the *Pseudolus,* it is interesting from several points of view. The intrigue is extraordinarily complicated, although the action as a whole, lacking any elaboration of the love affair or of the involved past of Periphanes, is too slight. This play and the *Curculio* are the shortest ancient comedies.

The crafty slave Epidicus, who dominates the action from the beginning to the end, has played an important role in the formation of modern counterparts such as Scapin, Scaramouche, and Figaro.[44]

The plot begins as the usual one of a young man in love and desperately needing money to secure his sweetheart. The situation here, however, is somewhat complicated; for Epidicus has previously secured a slave girl, Acropolistis, of whom the young Stratippocles has until recently been enamored. This girl is already within the house at the opening of the play, and the father is convinced that she is his natural daughter. But now Stratippocles returns from the wars with his newer sweetheart, who is hardly his own until he pays the banker her purchase price. The stress placed upon the virtue of this second girl foreshadows her recognition, but we may well be astounded when by this recognition the girl turns out to be Stratippocles' half-sister. Nowhere in New Comedy, perhaps, is there a more startling surprise. This has been made possible by the absence of an omniscient prologue and—even more strikingly—by the failure to elaborate the story of Periphanes' illegitimate daughter, references to whom are enigmatically brief, though the matter is subtly maintained before the minds of the audience by Periphanes' references to his past indiscretions (382–92, 431–32).

Many scholars think that Plautus is responsible for the omission of a prologue.[45] If so, it would seem that he is deliberately striving for suspense and surprise and is thus anticipating the regular practice of Terence. Similar to Terentian technique also is the excellent scene of dramatic exposition and the employment of a protatic character to facilitate it. But the original existence of a prologue is at least doubtful. Though it is customary to inform the audience in plays where recognition occurs, the *Epidicus* gives no opportunity for effective dramatic irony on this score. It should be noted also that the whole emphasis of the piece is upon the machinations of Epidicus and not upon the love of Stratippocles. Indeed it is obvious that this infatuation is only a few days old. Its frustration in the end, therefore, is a matter of little consequence, especially since his former sweetheart, as Epidicus himself points out (653), has already been secured for him. The play has been criticized, also, for the nature of its ending, which leaves various incidental matters unsettled. But perhaps the playwright is superior to his critics here again; for Epidicus must remain the center of attention, and his affairs certainly are beautifully concluded in the amusing final scene. He is savèd by a highly improbable coincidence—Stratippocles' buying his own sister—but this, of course, is typical of New Comedy.

The comic ironies are noteworthy. Epidicus feigns great modesty before the old men, and they praise the cleverness of his scheme. With less truth but with equal comic effectiveness Epidicus praises the shrewdness of Apoecides. Epidicus convinces the old men that he has bought the flute player, who is actually only hired; he also convinces them that the girl herself has been deceived into thinking she is only hired. Thus, when the ruse is discovered, the girl proves to be hired as she has claimed to be from the start.[46] This phase of the humor reaches its high point when Apoecides says that he too pretended that the girl was only hired and assumed an expression of dullness and stupidity. Then he proceeds to illustrate this expression for Periphanes and the audience; in production, we can be sure, his actor did not make the slightest change in his expression to illustrate dullness and stupidity on the face of Apoecides (420).

10. *TWIN MENAECHMI (MENAECHMI)*

This skillfully constructed farce is very spirited and amusing. It has fared unusually well at the hands of English translators,[47] furthermore, and it is said to be the Latin comedy most frequently reproduced in American schools and colleges.

Nothing is known of the Greek original, although Athenaeus (658 F), an ancient scholar who had read more than eight hundred plays of Middle Comedy alone (336 D) and whose interest was centered in cooks and foods, says that slave cooks can be found only in the plays of Poseidippus. Cylindrus in this play, of course, is a household slave. Except for the elaboration of monologues into cantica, the Latin version presumably follows the Greek original.

Significant names.—Especially noteworthy among the names used in the play is that of the parasite, whose Latin name, Peniculus, means "Sponge," perhaps the most apt name for a parasite that occurs in Plautus.[48] Erotium, "Lovey," is an effective but not uncommon name for a courtesan, and her cook is well named Cylindrus, "Roller."

Influence.—Along with the *Amphitryon,* the *Pot of Gold,* and the *Braggart Warrior,* the *Twin Menaechmi* has been one of the most influential plays of Plautus.[49] Various adaptations have appeared, including those of Trissino (1547, *I Simillimi*), Rotrou (1636), Regnard (1705), and Goldoni (*I Due Gemelli Veneziani*). But Shakespeare's adaptation (1594 or earlier), of course, is by far the most famous.

The Comedy of Errors takes certain motives from the *Amphitryon,* especially the twin slaves and the exclusion of Antipholus from his own house while his twin is inside; but it is primarily an elaboration of the *Twin Menaechmi.* Here we may observe Shakespeare at work and may analyze that fusion of the classical and romantic traditions which characterized Elizabethan drama. From the romantic come its abundance of incident and its utter disregard of plausibility, its plethora of youthful emotional appeal, its insistence upon a romantic love affair, its melodramatic suspense, its vacillation between the comic and the tragic—both sentimentalized—and its grand finale where almost everyone shares in the general happiness. From the classic tradition come its elaborate plot, its observation of the essential unities, and its fundamentally realistic dramatic outlook.

Discussion.—Basically the plot of the *Twin Menaechmi* is one of recognition. A great deal of complication, however, is built up about the somewhat involved personal relations of the Epidamnian Menaechmus. The similarity of the appearance of the twins naturally leads to a comedy of errors. This was a favorite motive, and no less than eight Greek comedies are known to have been given the title or subtitle "Twins." Indeed this motive plays an important role in several other comedies of Plautus himself, including the *Amphitryon,* the *Two Bacchides,* and the *Braggart Warrior.*

In a comedy of errors, the ancient playwright thinks it essential to explain the real situation very carefully beforehand to the audience, and the *Twin Menaechmi* opens with a long omniscient prologue.[50] This is followed by another long monologue when Sponge enters. Two such speeches make for a slow opening. But with the amusing song of the Epidamnian Menaechmus the play assumes that rapid pace which is necessary for successful farce.

The scene between this sporty gentleman and Erotium finishes in the details of the setting and with the theft of the wife's mantle initiates the dramatic action. As gentleman, parasite, and courtesan withdraw, the Syracusan Menaechmus, accompanied by his slave Messenio, steps into the situation which has been nicely elaborated for them.

The weary Messenio warns his master that here in Epidamnus the world finds its greatest voluptuaries and drinkers; it is full of sycophants and flattering parasites; the courtesans are the most seductive on earth, and the city is so named because almost no one stops here without his purse's suffering damnation. The amusing reaction of his master is to demand the purse in order to avoid at least one risk in Epidamnus! The cook Cylindrus immediately appears and seems to prove the accuracy of Messenio's description beyond all question. Indeed, Messenio is taken in by his own cleverness, as we should expect in a comedy of errors; and, instead of realizing at once that his master is being mistaken for his lost twin brother, Messenio feels certain that they are being attacked by the pirate courtesans of this Barbary coast. His worst fears seem quite justified when the seductive Erotium appears. Thus the dramatist creates a very amusing situation while he is furnishing some plausibility for the long continuation of the comedy of errors.

There now follows a series of scenes wherein one person after another mistakes the Syracusan for the Epidamnian.[51] After Cylindrus and Erotium comes Sponge, and then a servant of Erotium. In these episodes the twins are shown to resemble each other as closely in their dishonesty as in their appearance. The Syracusan is also mistaken by the wife of the Epidamnian Menaechmus and finally by the father-in-law as well. All the complications which these errors involve are skillfully manipulated. Especially noteworthy is the way in which the parasite, usually an unessential figure, is worked into the mechanism of the plot to become the link between the double lives which the Epidamnian Menaechmus is living.

The best of the episodes of error, however, is that with the physician. Of all the galaxy of comic characters none perhaps surpasses the medical quack in age. He is listed in accounts of early Greek improvisations.[52] Though this passage is the only one in Roman comedy where he has survived, he must have been a stock figure. His most striking characteristics in any age are here well brought out—his technical jargon, his endless number of impertinent questions, his extravagant claims, and of course his utterly incorrect diagnosis. Characteristic too of quack or expert in all ages is his prescription of the most expensive treatment possible.

Only near the end of the play does Messenio meet the Epidamnian Menaechmus and mistake him for his master. This error quickly leads to the climax, where no one except the slave, apparently, has enough sense to bring about the solution. If the gentlemen had been given more, the play could not have continued so long!

Very different is the ending of Plautus from that of Shakespeare. Far from arranging a reconciliation between the Epidamnian Menaechmus and his wife—to say nothing of Sponge—the cold cynicism of the author remains to the last lines, where along with the other chattel to be offered at auction is included the wife—if anyone is so foolish as to wish to buy her.

11. *MERCHANT* (*MERCATOR*)

The *Merchant* is a delightful comedy-farce. Though almost wholly lacking in significant portrayal of character, its plot is distinctive, its simple structure neat, its action vigorous and rapid. Since the metrical structure is very simple, the play is usually considered one of the earliest of Plautus' comedies.

The original Greek comedy bore the same title (*Emporos*), and like the *Three Bob Day* (*Trinummus*) was written by Philemon.

The *Merchant* has not played an important role in influencing modern drama. But the motive of rivalry between father and son, found also in the *Casina* and the *Comedy of Asses* (not to mention the *Two Bacchides*), is introduced in Molière's *L'Avare*.

The plot is that of a young man, Charinus, who through fear of confessing his love affair almost loses his sweetheart to his own father. The situation is nicely complicated by the introduction of the family next door, whose father, Lysimachus, undertakes to conceal the girl during the absence of his wife and whose son, Eutychus, is most anxious to recover the girl for Charinus. The wife, of course, must turn up at the most inopportune moment and take the girl to be her husband's mistress.

The play opens somewhat clumsily with Charinus' long prologue, which in part is within the dramatic illusion and in part without. Incidentally he recites a quaint idyl of his father's laborious youth in days gone by. With the entrance of the slave and the news of Demipho's infatuation, the action is under way.

Demipho himself first enters with a long monologue recounting his dream.[53] This parody of a frequent tragic motive is amusing in itself and in its immediate application of the monkey to friend Lysimachus. Lysimachus' first lines about the old buck, also, are amusingly obvious in their application to Demipho. As frequently in tragedy, the dream also forecasts the future developments of the play.

Perhaps the best scene, however, is that in which father and son lock horns over the disposal of the girl. They can both readily agree not to give her to "mother." Here Demipho recites a delightful description of the annoying attentions that strange men would inevitably pay to such an attractive slave girl (405–9). Even more amusing is the way in which father and son bid against each other to obtain the girl for a "client." Their various lies, like those of Trachalio and Gripus in the *Rope,* shift with amazing rapidity and inconsistency. Finally, the old merchant, so careful of his son's professional honor when honor seconds his own interests and otherwise so contemptuous of it, shows that his long experience in business has not been wholly futile and easily wins the day over his less-practiced son.

Several of the later scenes too are excellent. The girl Pasicompsa ("elegant in every respect") is enticingly depicted. Lysimachus makes a most ridiculous figure when he becomes involved with wife and caterer, where the comedy, though obvious and even inevitable, is still very effective. Incidentally the wife's old slave delivers an interesting protest against the double standard (817–29).

Excitement runs high at the climax between the despairing Charinus and the overjoyed Eutychus. Charinus opens the scene with an extravagant farewell to home and fatherland that has a distinctly tragic ring. His mad dashing about as Eutychus tries to stop him is followed by his hallucinatory journey into exile. This would doubtless seem puerile were it not another parody of tragedy—this time of a great messenger's speech in Euripides' *Heracles* (943–71), where the mad Heracles is described as imagining that he was driving from Thebes to Mycenae.[54]

The final scene, as in the *Casina* and the *Comedy of Asses,* is reserved for the thorough humiliation of the old man who has been so rash as dare to fall in love and become the rival of his son.

12. *BRAGGART WARRIOR (MILES GLORIOSUS)*

(About 205 B.C.)

The *Braggart Warrior,* usually assumed to be one of the earliest extant plays of Plautus, is interesting for several reasons. Of all ancient comedies it presents the most complete portrait of the immortal braggart soldier, and it has therefore been very influential. The two plots of the play, also, are immortal. Its characters are vividly drawn, and the final scenes are uproariously funny. But the whole play is very crude farce, and the deception of Sceledrus in the opening sections has little to do with the later entrapment of the soldier.

Significant names.—Pyrgopolinices is an elaborate Greek compound meaning "victor of fortresses and cities." The name Artotrogus signifies "bread-chewer," Acroteleutium "tip-top," Philocomasium "fond of drinking bouts," Sceledrus "dirt," and Palaestrio "wrestler," or "trickster."[55]

Source.—The title of the Greek play is given in the internal prologue, the *Braggart* (*Alazon*); but nothing is known of the Greek author. Most scholars assume that two plays have here been combined by Plautus; and this may well be so, but any Greek dramatist who would stoop to the crudity of such farce might also fail to appreciate the niceties of plot construction.

The literary motive of the secret passageway is very old. In an age when lack of transportation and the need of protection necessitated extreme conservation of space within cities, common walls between houses were the rule, and secret passageways must not have been such very rare exceptions.

The second plot also is a very ancient one. A man, usually husband or lover, is persuaded to send away a girl with another man and even to give them gifts or the means of escape. The deception is threatened by various complications in its final stages; but all comes out well, and pursuit or revenge is prevented by some device. This plot is used by Euripides in the *Iphigenia in Tauris* and especially in the *Helen*. The scene of departure in the *Helen* is notably similar to that in the *Braggart Warrior;* comic irony plays a major role in both. Palaestrio's grief in this comedy, furthermore, shows more than a tinge of Oriental deception, resembling the grief of an Egyptian prince taking leave of Caesar during his Alexandrine campaign.[56]

The motive of the secret passageway is found combined with this second plot of deception not only in Plautus. In a fascinating Albanian tale, a priest is duped into marrying his own pretty wife to a merchant next door. At the ensuing wedding banquet, the priest is made drunk, his beard is shaved off, and he is disguised as a robber and left by the side of the road. When he awakes in the morning he actually joins a band of robbers. But here, although the secret passageway is used precisely as in Plautus, the person deceived by it is the main character, and the two plots are closely and effectively joined.[57]

Influence.—The professional soldier of fortune was a very common figure on the streets of Athens during the period of New Comedy, and nowhere was he more popular than on the comic stage. This is evidenced by many plays of New Comedy, including Menander's *Shearing of Glycera (Perikeiromene)*, Terence's *Eunuch,* and various other plays of Plautus, especially the *Two Bacchides,* the *Carthaginian,* and the *Truculentus.* This type is exploited in innumerable modern plays and finally results in such masterpieces as Falstaff. Indeed, Pyrgopolinices' boast that his children live for a thousand years (1079), as has been pointed out, is a gross understatement.

Many comedies have been directly influenced by the *Braggart Warrior.* Among the most notable may be mentioned Nicholas Udall's *Ralph Roister Doister* (before 1553; indebted also to the *Eunuch* of

Terence), Dolce's *Il Capitano* (published 1560), Baïf's *Le Brave* (1567), Mareschal's *Le Capitan Fanfaron* (published 1640), and Holberg's *Jacob von Tyboe*.[58]

Discussion.—The *Braggart Warrior* is very clumsily constructed, for only a feeble effort has been made to connect its two actions. The soldier, the main character of the second action, is well characterized and his propensity for the fairer sex is given significant emphasis at the opening of the play. Thus the minor plot, which follows immediately, is suspended within the major. Several incidental references are made to the twin sister, an important element of the first action, during the latter part of the play. Sceledrus, too, is there mentioned and may reappear at the very end. Both actions, furthermore, are engineered by Palaestrio, and both are crude and farcical. But the first makes no real contribution to the second. The long episode with the genial old Periplectomenus has little to do with either. Incidentally annoying are the innumerable asides used to elaborate obvious jests. At times Palaestrio's handling of the soldier, however, shows real cleverness.

13. HAUNTED HOUSE (*MOSTELLARIA*)

Like the *Three Bob Day* (*Trinummus*), the *Haunted House* begins with a series of excellent scenes presenting situation and characters but soon hastens off into the most obvious farce. Here, however, the farce is as good as farce can be.

The Greek original seems to have been entitled the *Ghost* (*Phasma*). Records of three such comedies have been preserved, and it is usually assumed that the original of this play was the one written by Philemon. This assumption, even though no sound evidence for it exists, is attractive because of the play's structural similarity to the *Three Bob Day,* which was certainly written by Philemon. The tendency of high comedy to degenerate into farce, however, is observable in other plays such as the *Two Bacchides.*

The *Haunted House* has been very influential.[59] Among adaptations may be mentioned Thomas Heywood's *The English Traveller* (printed 1633), Regnard's *Le Retour Imprévu* (1700) and its adaptation by Fielding, *The Intriguing Chambermaid* (1733), and Holberg's *Huus-Spögelse* or *Abracadabra.* The names Tranio and Grumio, furthermore, are used for servants in *The Taming of the Shrew,* in which perhaps certain motives also are taken from Plautus.[60]

The *Haunted House* has very little plot. A young Athenian gentleman, Philolaches, has been living a gay life in the absence of his father. Upon the father's unexpected return, Philolaches is surprised in a very embarrassing daytime carousal. The clever slave Tranio, therefore, undertakes to prevent the father from entering the house until the members of the party have sobered and dispersed. Constantly threatened with exposure, Tranio constantly becomes involved in more and more elaborate deceptions.[61] Finally, after his ruses are all discovered, he is rescued by the boon companion of Philolaches, who smoothes things over with the ease of a *deus ex machina*.[62] All the activity of Tranio, of course, has really been much ado about nothing, for at best he could hope to deceive the old man for only a few hours. The initial pretext, however, is not implausible at first glance, and the rapidity of the action allows us no time for cogitation.

Although the whole play is amusing, the opening scenes are by far the best. Their primary function, of course, is to create the atmosphere of gay living. Various characters also are brilliantly presented here. But both creation of atmosphere and portrayal of character are carried Obviously the dramatist intends these scenes to be enjoyed for their intrinsic charm. far beyond the length justified by their importance in the main action.

In all New Comedy, no better scene of exposition is found than that of Grumio and Tranio. Not only is the situation most vividly presented but an effective warning of a day of reckoning is sounded, and the brazen Tranio is thoroughly individualized by contrast with the honest Grumio. The one fault of the scene is that Grumio, who is characterized even more interestingly than Tranio, does not reappear in the play.

The scenes presenting Philolaches and his companions also are delightful. The humor of Philolaches' remarks as he watches his love Philematium ("Little Kiss") complete her toilet and the masterly portrait of this delightfully naïve girl more than justify the theatrical awkwardness of the staging. The carousal too is skillfully presented. The drunken man, of course, is almost infallible low comedy; but Callidamates, with all the seriousness and moral callousness of inebriation, plays the role so entertainingly that we forget the triteness of the motive. Indeed this whole group of characters is so interesting that we, somewhat like Philolaches, may well regret the return of father Theopropides; for he is merely the stereotyped old man of comedy, conservative to—and beyond—the point of stupidity, so cautious where there is no need of caution and elsewhere so rash. He forms the perfect dupe for the wily Tranio, and these two monopolize the stage for the remainder of the play.

14. *PERSIAN (PERSA)*

(After 196 B.C.[63])

The *Persian* is a thin but amusing little farce of "high life below stairs." It is unique, however, in certain respects. The original Greek play is thought by some scholars to have been written before the conquests of Alexander (line 506, very doubtful evidence) and therefore to have belonged to Middle Comedy. A free girl who is a virgin takes an active role in the play; and the whole seems more closely to approach comic opera than any other play of Plautus.

The simple plot concerns the intrigue of a slave, Toxilus, who in the absence of his master is living the life of a king (31), which of course includes being in love with a strumpet and keeping a parasite. Toxilus, like any young gentleman, wishes to free his sweetheart. With the aid of a friend and of the parasite's daughter he succeeds in doing so and in thoroughly humiliating the slave dealer. Perhaps it is unfortunate that this material has not been more effectively employed as a burlesque of the life of Athenian gilded youth.

The comic opera elements are many, of which lyricism is the first and most important. External formalism also is noteworthy. The first lines between Toxilus and Sagaristio constitute the only certain case of metrical responsion in Plautus. Balanced speeches are the rule throughout this first scene and frequently occur elsewhere in the play, especially in the scene of pert repartee between Sophoclidisca and Paegnium. The very admission of such a scene is suggestive of comic opera, for it is obviously inserted merely for its quaint buffoonery. Below the ordinary level of New Comedy, furthermore, is much of the stage action, especially the "planting" of the girl and Sagaristio to come in just at the right moment, and later the similar "planting" of Saturio. The extravagant implausibility of the intrigue, the use of disguises, and the way in which the intrigue is made a mere joke in the final scene—these, too, are proper to comic opera or burlesque. The saucy Paegnium ("plaything"), though far from the harmless innocent of the modern stage, belongs to this same sphere. Perhaps the daughter of the parasite might here be included. The reversal of nature by which daughter lectures father on honesty and reputation is ridiculously incongruous with the girl's lowly position in life, as with her unenviable role in the intrigue— incongruous, indeed, with the whole atmosphere of this comedy of low life. Last of all may be mentioned the exotic costumes and the carefully identified dances in the very gay final scene.[64] While some of these features may well be due to Plautine originality, they would not be unnatural developments of the lyricism and extravagance of Old Comedy. Certainly the Persian's four-line name (702–5) and the drunken revel (*komos*) of the final scene are reminiscent of Aristophanes.

15. *CARTHAGINIAN (POENULUS)*

The *Carthaginian* is miserably constructed and is a poor play in every respect. It has often been assumed that the faults of the play are due to contamination (the fusion of two Greek originals), but here as elsewhere no dependable evidence exists. The prologue states that the title of the Greek original was the same (*Karchedonios*), a title which is recorded for Menander and also for Alexis, a leading poet of Middle Comedy. Incidentally this interminable prologue gives an unsurpassed description of a Roman audience.

Noteworthy are the use of Semitic in certain passages—the only examples of the Carthaginian language preserved—and the occurrence of various alternate versions in the text.[65] Obviously the play was adapted in reproduction. Written by Plautus during or soon after a very bitter war between Rome and Carthage, the play reveals no prejudice except a brief reference to "Punic faith" (113).

Somewhat like the *Braggart Warrior,* the *Carthaginian* has two successive plots that are only superficially connected. A young gentleman Agorastocles is in love with Adelphasium, a virtuous girl who, like her sister, is in the possession of a slave dealer. To secure her, Agorastocles and his slave plan an elaborate intrigue, based, as in the *Persian,* upon a certain law. This intrigue is successful; but it is made unnecessary by the recognition of the girls and of Agorastocles himself as Carthaginian citizens of good birth. Apparently the dramatist was determined to have this multiple recognition, based on a tortuous and implausible series of events; but he could not make a whole play of it, and so he filled in the first section with a typical sequence of intrigue. Even so, the scenes with Hanno leading to the recognition are somewhat tedious. Like the *Pseudolus* and the *Persian,* the *Carthaginian* ends with the utter ruin of the slave dealer.

16. *PSEUDOLUS*

(191 B.C.)

The *Pseudolus* is a very amusing light comedy and one of the best plays of intrigue. Its plot is the usual one of a young man in love and desperately in need of money to save his sweetheart from the clutches of another. Stereotyped motives, too, are employed, such as the abuse of the slave dealer, the braggadocio of the cooks, and the theme of the conscientious slave (Harpax). Reminiscent of other comedies is also the amusing way in which the victims are forewarned and yet taken in. But from the first scene to the last, the action of the *Pseudolus* is rapid and intense, and the wit has an extraordinary keenness and exuberance. Pseudolus himself is one of the most delightful characters of New Comedy, especially in his happy nonchalance and his assured self-confidence.[66]

Among modern adaptations of the play may be mentioned Holberg's *Diderich Menschen-Shräk.*

The first and last scenes are perhaps the best of the play. Phoenicium's love letter is as unforgettable as are the jokes which Pseudolus makes over it—jokes best appreciated by one who has tried to decipher a lover's scrawl at Pompeii or an ancient letter on papyrus. Ballio's marshaling of his household, also, is a good if somewhat crude scene. Later, the comic irony of Ballio's mistaking the real Harpax for the minion of Pseudolus is most amusing. But the final uproarious scenes with the drunken Pseudolus must have surpassed all the rest—an appropriately low ending for this frankly low comedy.

Nothing is known of the Greek original of the *Pseudolus,* but it is often assumed that Plautus has here indulged in contamination. Inconsistencies concerning the twenty minae are pointed out. But the undeniably bewildering financial confusion of the play seems only another aspect of its humor. Again, in the opinion of many critics Callipho should reappear after he expresses his delight in watching the sport of Pseudolus and promises to devote the rest of the day to this (551–60). It does seem unfortunate that the dramatist has not combined the roles of Callipho and Charinus. But expressions of interest in the action such as Callipho makes are deliberately designed to stimulate the interest of the audience, and they cannot be taken as sound evidence of contamination.[67] Besides, the *Pseudolus* moves too rapidly to allow the spectator time for reflection on minor inconsistencies.[68]

17. *ROPE (RUDENS)*

The *Rope* more nearly approaches the spirit of romantic comedy than any other ancient play. It contains more important characters and more dramatic action than almost any other, and it is among the longest (1,423 lines). It is noteworthy not only for its romantic atmosphere but also for its unsurpassed vivacity, its irrepressible and sometimes sardonic humor, its dramatic irony, and its melodramatic pulsation of emotions.

Source and influence.—The god of the prologue intimates that the author of the Greek original was Diphilus, but the name of that play is not given. It has been argued that Plautus made many important alterations in the play, but these arguments seem unconvincing.[69]

Among adaptations, which have not been numerous, may be mentioned Thomas Heywood's *The Captives* (1624).

Discussion.—The *Rope* is primarily a play of discovery in which, somewhat as in Menander's *Arbitration,* a father unwittingly adjudicates the fate of his own lost daughter. Various exciting complications are furnished by the daughter's shipwreck, the quarrel between her lover and the slave dealer who is attempting to recover her, and the contest of the two slaves over the trunk. That honesty is the best policy is the obvious moral to be drawn from the action.

The locale of this comedy is as picturesque and striking as it is unusual: the desolate seashore near the North African city of Cyrene, an ancient Brighton or Deauville.[70]

Since the play is to contain concealed identities and a recognition, the author has considered an omniscient prologue essential in order that the irony of the action may be fully appreciated. Perhaps such a prologue is also the simplest method of revealing the complicated exposition of the play—the soundest justification for the Euripidean prologue, which seems to have been used regularly by Diphilus.[71] Not much of the coming action, however, is here foreshadowed in the prologue.

Very unusual is the scene in which Sceparnio pretends to look off and sight the shipwrecked men and the two girls in a lifeboat. Action that could not be presented "on stage" frequently occurs in tragedy, where it is usually described in a messenger's speech. In comedy, such action is rare, and the method of describing it here employed, though informal, is very effective.

As soon as the stage is cleared—the exit of Daemones is dramatically necessary but surely somewhat forced and implausible—Palaestra, like a tragic heroine, appears singing her monody of complaint against Heaven and her cruel fate. The pathos of this is more significant for the audience, since they know that she is actually standing very close to the house of her long-lost parents. After Ampelisca has entered with a few plaintive lines we have a charming duet with the tragic cretic meter beautifully adapted to the scene (esp. lines 235–37). Indeed, this whole episode is one of the most charming in Plautus. As poetry, however, it is hardly superior to the "chorus" of fishermen who appear soon afterward. Here we have a passage of real beauty such as is common in Aristophanes but rare in New Comedy and apparently unknown in Menander. This chorus is usually considered a vestige of the old comic chorus, and their introduction here is certainly very felicitous. With their reed poles and, doubtless, fishermen's hats, they add a delightful bit of local color—obviously an artistic addition rather than an interruption like the ordinary interlude chorus. Their quaint humor forms a winsomely comic relief for the tragic tone of the two girls in distress.

Lovers' dalliance on stage is rare in ancient comedy, but slaves are allowed more liberty of action in certain situations than ladies and gentlemen, and we find an amusing if somewhat risqué example of love-making in the scene between the slaves, Ampelisca and Sceparnio.[72] We may assume that Ampelisca starts this flirtation by ogling Sceparnio and caressing her words in a manner most likely to win over a stranger from whom she wishes to ask a favor. Sceparnio, however, is won over even more effectively than she wished, and it is all the girl can do to keep the situation in hand. With the aid of feminine tact and deceit, however, she succeeds in gaining her request by mere promises. While Sceparnio is gone to fetch the water, she is put to flight by the approach of the slave dealer. When Sceparnio returns with his high hopes of an easy conquest, he presents a figure whose ridiculousness can hardly be appreciated without actually seeing him as he carries the jug and searches eagerly about the stage for the vanished girl. His fear now of being caught as a thief and, finally, his utter disgust at having done some real work for nothing form a very amusing contrast with his high spirits at the opening of the scene.

Various scenes of low comedy occur throughout the play which set off and relieve the more serious episodes. Amusing is the scene wherein the slave dealer Labrax and his friend Charmides first emerge from their shipwreck. They come on stage with their garments drenched, shivering and, as the meter apparently indicates, chattering from cold. They curse their fortune and each other. They run the gamut of low comedy from miserable puns to vomiting.

The influence of melodramatic tragedy is evident in many scenes of the *Rope,* but most of all in the scene where the girls flee from the temple of Venus to the altar. Palaestra's monody here is remarkably similar to a fragmentary monody. from a tragedy of Plautus' contemporary, Ennius, wherein a woman, Andromache, is seeking refuge.[73] Both songs are in part written in cretic meter, characterized by elaborate alliteration and assonance, the use of synonyms and various artificialities of high style. The grouping about the altar, furthermore, is remarkably similar to that of a scene from an unknown tragedy represented on a Greek vase.[74] The whole scene here, then, may be a parody of a definite tragedy.[75]

The amusing Sceparnio does not appear in the second half of the play; but a counterpart for him is found in the fisherman, Gripus, the slave of Daemones, who is not mentioned in the prologue and of whom we hear nothing until Daemones comes on stage to deliver a short monologue and then returns into the house (892–905). Obviously this somewhat awkward speech is designed solely to introduce Gripus, who enters immediately after Daemones makes his exit. The emotions of Gripus, like those of Sceparnio, shift very rapidly: he enters in the greatest elation over his discovery of the wicker trunk, and in an amusing monody he daydreams aloud on becoming a millionaire, a tycoon in the world of trade, and on founding a city to commemorate his fame. The humorous irony of these lines may easily be overlooked in reading the play; but it could not be lost in the theater, for we may be sure that during his monody, as he walks slowly toward the center of the stage, his spying adversary, Trachalio, is already on stage behind him.

One of the most delightful scenes of the play is the ensuing one between Gripus and Trachalio with their mock juristic arguments. It is easy to understand why Plautus chose to name the play after this scene and the tug of war of the two slaves over the trunk. Especially delightful is the naïve way in which the slaves, when their casuistry runs short, resort to barefaced lies and elaborate threats of violence which reveal that each is actually very much afraid of the other.

The scene in which both slaves appeal to Daemones is a continuation of this argument, in which Gripus is at least more consistent than Trachalio, who at one time renounces all personal claims (1077) and at another demands half of the booty (1123). The zeal of Gripus increases as the apparent justice of his case fades away, and he does not fail to anticipate every possible device of his opponents.

Comedies usually come to a close very shortly after the solution of the plot, but the *Rope* continues for some time after the main complication has been solved with Palaestra's restoration to her parents. Still, there are minor threads of the plot that must be neatly finished off. The play does not, therefore, appear to be unduly extended, especially since the final scenes are so gay and amusing; throughout this comedy, gaiety and amusement are more important than the progression of the plot.

The romantic pulsation of emotions, already noted in the earlier parts of the play, continues to the very end and is nicely emphasized by appropriate metrical variation. Trachalio and Daemones are in high spirits, Trachalio and Plesidippus in even higher spirits—especially Plesidippus, who is ecstatic over the good fortune of Palaestra and their coming marriage. These scenes, of course, are in the gay trochaic meter which was probably accompanied by music. But between these scenes with Trachalio, wherein the author runs riot in word play in a manner more characteristic of Aristophanes or Rabelais than of New Comedy, the ill-humored Gripus in prosaic iambics continues his haggling argument with his master over the ownership of the trunk. This ill-humor is even more amusing, of course, than the gaiety of the other characters.

The ironic humor, also, with an occasional thrust of real satire, is maintained to the last line, where the audience, if they will applaud loudly, are invited to a drinking party—all, that is, under sixteen years of age.[76] Sixteen was the usual age for the assumption of a man's dress and status at Rome, and from this passage it has been concluded that minors were not allowed in the Roman theater.

18. *STICHUS*

(Plebeian Games, 200 B.C.)

The *Stichus* is a thin little piece but a very merry one, especially in the final scenes, which, like those of the *Persian,* depict the gaiety and enviable freedom of slaves. Plautine contamination or originality is often blamed for the formlessness of the play, but it is hard to discover the germ of a conventional dramatic plot in any phase of the material.

According to the record of the first production,[77] the Greek original was the *Brothers* of Menander.[78]

The *Stichus* has less plot than any other Roman comedy. Its center of interest shifts from one set of characters to another and then to still another. There is some slight connection between these, to be sure, and the author is careful, before he has finished with one set, to introduce the next. The play opens with what appears to be a dramatic situation: the two sisters, wives as faithful as Penelope, are being urged by their father, Antipho, to renounce their long-absent husbands. But the wives and even the father himself assure us that he will not compel them, thus destroying any dramatic tension almost before it has been created. Gelasimus and his problem of food are now introduced on a very weak pretext. With the announcement of the return of the husbands and their great wealth, the problem of the wives is settled; and after Panegyris has heard this news and dealt Gelasimus his first disappointment, these wives do not reappear even to welcome home their dearly beloved husbands. Panegyris' husband, Epignomus, now comes on with Stichus and announces his reconciliation with father Antipho. Hereupon Stichus' problem of an appropriate celebration is introduced, only to give way immediately to the problem of Gelasimus. This parasite, after an unsuccessful clash with Epignomus, retires again disappointed. Antipho appears with the second husband and gives an illustration of restored family harmony. Antipho, too, has a personal problem, which the somewhat casual gift of a slave girl by one of his sons-in-law promises to solve. Incidentally noteworthy is the characterization of the old man here and in his earlier scene by the use of language resembling riddles— a unique motive. Gelasimus reappears and is finally rejected. His complete disappointment adds a tartness much needed in this almost too pleasant comedy and perhaps intimates that the brothers have grown wiser and will not again dissipate their fortunes for the likes of Gelasimus. Last of all, Stichus, Sagarinus, and their mutual sweetheart take over the final scenes for a typical revel ending (*komos*)—and a very gay revel it is, where even the musician is induced to become drunk.[79]

19. *THREE BOB DAY* (*TRINUMMUS*)

(A festival in honor of Cybele; not before 194 B.C.[80])

Lessing considered this play second only to the *Captives* among Plautus' comedies, but such a high rating seems hardly justified.[81] There are certainly some excellent scenes of high comedy, especially in the first part of the play; but the climax falls off disappointingly into obvious farce.

The Greek original, as we are plainly told, was the *Treasure* of Philemon (*Thesauros*). Probably some monologues of the original have been elaborated into monodies, but otherwise perhaps few if any changes have been made.[82]

No female role is found in the *Three Bob Day*. This feature, so entirely natural in a play like the *Captives,* is here somewhat unfortunate from the modern point of view, in that this unusual plot seems ideally suited for intimate romantic comedy. Such development, however, was left for a Frenchman, Néricault Destouches, whose adaptation, *Le Trésor Caché,* brought to life the two girls that are to be married to the young men at the end of Plautus' play.[83] Another adaptation, Lessing's *Der Schatz* (1750), is well known.

Discussion.—Precisely to define the plot of the *Three Bob Day* is difficult, and this very fact marks the play out as extraordinary in New Comedy, where the plots are usually all too stereotyped. The main problem, however, concerns the honor of Lesbonicus, a young man who in the absence of his father has so dissipated his property that he finds himself greatly embarrassed over the prospect of his sister's being forced to marry without a dowry. The modern reader may easily underestimate the seriousness of this situation. According to the Athenian moral code, this young man's first duty in life was to look to the honor and decent marriage of his sister. For her to marry without a dowry and thus to sacrifice all social prestige naturally meant utter disgrace for him. A minor problem of the play is centered about the honor of Callicles, an old friend whom the father of Lesbonicus has charged with something of the family interests during his absence. Both these problems are excellent dramatic material.

After a quaint prelude which well strikes the moral tone of the play and also serves as a literary prologue, the play opens with a very delightful scene between Callicles and a friend, Megaronides, who has come to castigate him for his apparent breach of faith. Both are nicely characterized as old men by their jests on wives and marriage, their use of proverbs, and their complaints of the moral degeneration of the times. Their main function, of course, is to give the exposition; and this they succeed in doing in a most natural fashion. Megaronides is not, as we might expect, a protatic character but has been skillfully worked into the subsequent action. One fault, however, may be found with this scene: no immediate dramatic action or complication is suggested. The mention of Lesbonicus' sister has been too brief, and nothing has been said that might suggest her marrying in the near future.

When this episode is ended, Lysiteles, a young man of whom we have heard nothing, appears with a charming monody, the length of which, if nothing else, indicates the importance of the speaker.[84] His problem is a serious one: to be or not to be—in love. Seeing only too clearly that love is a waster of property and a corrupter of good morals, this strange young man decides that he will not be. He wishes, as we later discover, to marry instead!

When Lysiteles has reached this very virtuous decision, his father, Philto, opportunely comes on, and the ensuing scene is even more delightful high comedy than that between Callicles and Megaronides. Philto lectures his son in a moral fashion that qualifies him to rank as an ancestor of Polonius. But Lysiteles is somewhat cleverer than Laertes. He actually encourages his father; indeed he anticipates Philto in reaching the extreme limit of virtue and suggests a definite virtuous action—marrying a girl without a dowry. Any translation of virtuous words into action would doubtless have been disconcerting enough for Philto; and this particular action carries virtue far beyond the limits which he had envisaged even in his most abstract cogitations. But the receptiveness and docility of Lysiteles have been so great that the father is now embarrassed to refuse. Never in New Comedy is a father thrown for a neater and less-expected fall than this. The whole scene is a masterpiece.

Philto agrees to his son's marrying the sister of Lesbonicus without a dowry. This initiates the dramatic action at last, and it also sets the stage for the entrance of Lesbonicus, whose efforts to trace down the rapid flight of his funds are very amusing. Philto, as if he had not learned his lesson, continues with philosophizing, and his subsequent interview with Lesbonicus nicely points up the dilemma of this young man. Indeed, Lesbonicus becomes so desperate that he actually longs for the return of his father! Stasimus, his impudent slave, furnishes the low comedy of the scene. This reduces the level of the play's humor somewhat, although, in his not very successful efforts to deceive Philto, Stasimus is made the butt rather than the author of the humor.

Lesbonicus has been unable to settle the problem of the dowry with Philto, and so goes off to find Lysiteles. Meanwhile Callicles reappears and makes known his intention of somehow providing for the dowry. Lesbonicus knows nothing of this, however, and he is still desperate when he returns with Lysiteles and they debate the matter at great length. This scene might be called the climax of the play, for here the complication reaches its point of highest tension.

The play now degenerates rapidly. Megaronides' plan to provide the dowry from the secret treasure of Charmides is too much the usual comic intrigue. With the timely arrival of Charmides, furthermore, the working out of this plan becomes obvious farce. The stage technique, also, especially the continual use of asides, is somewhat awkward.

The farce in these later sections of the play can hardly be said to strike an inharmonious note, for the tone of the play has been charmingly light throughout. But it seems unfortunate that the serious moral dilemma of the young men is not exploited in a more satisfactory manner. The solution adopted, of course, is purely external. Another fault of the play is its failure at an early point to focus upon a single character and to maintain him as the center of interest. Unfortunate also is the continual harping on the moral degeneration of the times.[85] This theme, a commonplace in New Comedy, is put to real service where Philto is concerned, and possibly the play as a whole would have been more effective if it had been reserved for him alone.

20. *TRUCULENTUS*

The *Truculentus* is a remarkable but not an amusing play. Like the novel *Sapho* of Alphonse Daudet, it is written for the enlightenment of a young man on youth's eternal problem. Vice would flourish less, says Diniarchus in his "prologue" (57–63), if the experience of one generation could be passed on to the next. The play, then, is very serious. We might be tempted to call its outcome tragic. Certainly few tragedies are so depressing. But Aristotle (*Poetics* 1452 b) says that the spectacle of the evil prospering is the most untragic of all. Phronesium is certainly evil, and she certainly prospers. An amazing detachment is maintained by the dramatist throughout, and he coldly refuses to display the slightest sympathy with his characters. Indeed, this play is one of the most remarkable pieces of stark realism in classical drama. Its ending is similar to that of the *Two Bacchides* and the *Eunuchus;* but those plays seem very light and gay compared to this.

The *Truculentus* ha's been somewhat neglected by modern scholars because the text tradition is deplorably bad—the worst of all the plays of Plautus, though there are no lengthy lacunae.

The author of the Greek original is unknown.

Discussion.—The play has almost no plot. It is merely the spectacle of a very real Circe turning men into swine. Four men are chosen for purposes of illustration. They are all typical, and properly so, for the author wishes to include all mankind; but they are treated in a far from typical manner. The various episodes dealing with these four are adeptly interwoven, though there is no artificial complexity about the play. The young Athenian gentleman, Diniarchus, is the first to be taken up and the only one whose case history is given in some detail. He has long since been a lover of courtesan and of courtesan's maid alike and, now bankrupt, he still is their lover. After he has been introduced and retires into Phronesium's house, the truculent slave comes on. He is the most picturesque character of the play. From his first line he is most aptly characterized as a bumpkin. His metaphors are rustic, and he swears by the hoe. Such referential swearing, though common in Aristophanes, is not frequent in Roman comedy. He is also characterized by his quaint perversity in the use of language, something like Antipho's use of riddles in the *Stichus.* Though this slave shows some signs of human frailty to the courtesan's maid, we naturally expect him to remain truculent throughout the play; and when he leaves the stage with the declaration that he will inform his old master of the young master's goings on, we anticipate the appearance of the old man. Such action would recall that of Lydus in the *Two Bacchides.*

Diniarchus now returns to the stage, and after the splendid fanfare of the early scenes, Phronesium makes her entrance and works her magic spell upon him. Much of this scene is concerned incidentally with the story of the soldier and the supposititious child, thus anticipating the appearance of the next victim and preparing for the discovery of the child's true identity. When Diniarchus has gone off to scrape up gifts, the stage is carefully set and the preparations perhaps include a seductive negligee. As the soldier enters he informs the audience by direct address not to expect the usual foolery of the braggart soldier from him; and indeed this soldier does not strut in the ordinary comic fashion, though a few mild jokes are admitted. The theme of Diniarchus is now fused with that of the soldier upon the entrance of the young gentleman's slaves bearing his gifts to Phronesium under the very eyes of the soldier. Nothing could better portray the soldier's enslavement; and after this scene has passed, we put little faith in his wrathful decision to remain aloof for a few days in order to bring Phronesium to her knees. At this point Strabax, the rustic young master of the truculent slave, comes on with money which he has purloined from his father for the woman whom he loves more than his mother (662). He is taken in with little ado, and immediately his slave reappears, no longer truculent and not with his old master, as we expected, but actually with his savings and a determination to take a fling at the type of life which is so attractive to his betters. Thus free and servile, weak and strong, all are here enslaved.

Diniarchus returns in the greatest elation over Phronesium's reception of his gifts and her invitation to rejoin her. The unexpected appearance of Strabax with far more money, however, has already changed Phronesium's situation and given her an actor for the role of the soldier's rival. So the maid keeps Diniarchus outside the house and regales him with a description of Strabax' enjoying the provisions which Diniarchus himself has lately furnished. Diniarchus is bitterly disillusioned. His futile protests before the house are interrupted by the episode with Callicles. No hint of Diniarchus' violation of Callicles' daughter has been given previously. But the dramatist here, as in the sudden change of the truculent slave, is not striving for surprise; he merely wishes to repress the minor phases of the play and maintain an effective unity.[86] This incident with Callicles is designed merely to illustrate the utter ruin of Diniarchus. After he learns that his lack of restraint has cost him so dearly, he is still unable to master his passions and to demand the child—discovered to be that of Callicles' daughter and himself—from Phronesium, who now comes on mildly intoxicated but still having far more self-mastery than her lovers, drunk or sober. With a view to securing her favors after his marriage, Diniarchus weakly allows her temporarily to retain the child in order to swindle the soldier. After this moral nihilism, the baseness of the soldier and Strabax in their final agreement to share Phronesium seems almost an anticlimax.

XI

TERENCE

LIFE[1]

Publius Terentius Afer, as he was later called, was born at Carthage, possibly in 195 B.C., and was perhaps a Berber. He was brought to Rome as a slave of the Roman senator, Terentius Lucanus, who not only educated him in a manner befitting a free man, since he was intelligent and handsome, but also soon freed him from slavery. The freedman, as was customary, took the name of his former master with the addition of a cognomen indicating the country of his origin.

Terence is said to have lived on intimate terms with many of the Roman nobility, especially Scipio Africanus the Younger (born 185 B.C., really the son of Aemilius Paullus) and Gaius Laelius. Indeed there were rumors that Terence was aided in his literary productions by these men; and Terence himself did nothing to stifle such compliments, as we may observe from the prologue of the *Brothers* (15–21).[2]

Terence produced six comedies, all of them translations or close adaptations of Greek plays. When the first of these, the *Woman of Andros,* was offered to the officials in charge of games and theatrical entertainments, Terence is said to have been ordered to read the work to Caecilius, an established and famous writer of comedies.[3] As the young dramatist, poorly dressed, came into the presence of Caecilius at dinner, he was relegated to a low (servile) bench; but after he had read a few verses Caecilius invited him to recline on the dining couch and have dinner with him, after which Terence ran through the rest of the play to the great admiration of Caecilius.

Although it is obvious from the prologues that Terence's literary career was a somewhat stormy one, his plays, with the single exception of the *Mother-in-Law,* seem to have been well received in his own day. Certainly the *Eunuch* was an outstanding popular success.

After producing the six comedies that have been preserved, Terence left Rome and went to Greece. This journey was probably planned as a *Studienreise*—the earliest known example[4] of what later became so popular with young Romans—and perhaps Terence wished to collect more plays of Menander and see Athens. From this journey he never returned. Some said that he perished at sea as he was returning with new plays translated from Menander, others that he died in Greece in

159 B.C. either from disease or from grief and worry over the loss of his baggage containing new plays which he had written.

Terence is said to have left an estate of certain small gardens on the Appian Way just outside the Porta San Sebastiano.[5] He was survived by one daughter, who afterward, it is said, married a Roman of the upper middle class (*eques*).

All of Terence's plays were originally produced by the same actor and manager, Lucius Ambivius Turpio, and the music for all of them was composed by the same slave, one Flaccus. Reproduction of the plays, especially during the decades 150–130 B.C., seems to have been frequent. By the time of Cicero, Terence had become a classic of Latin literature, and he has remained so ever since. He was highly esteemed during the Middle Ages, and his influence on Renaissance and modern comedy, though not as great as that of Plautus, has been very considerable.[6]

An interesting feature of the manuscripts of Terence is their illustration. Many scenes are quaintly pictured, and these representations are presumed by certain scholars, such as Bieber, to be based ultimately on ancient ones and to reveal something of the costumes, gestures, and groupings on the stage. According to other scholars, including Jones and Morey, these pictures originated in the fifth century of our era and have no important connection with the ancient theater.[7]

COMEDY UNDER TERENCE

Like Caecilius, Terence was a devoted follower of Menander. Four of his six comedies are primarily translations of plays by this Greek master of New Comedy, and the other two are taken from Apollodorus of Carystus, who himself was strongly influenced by Menander. It is quite natural, then, that Terence held the first place among Roman writers of comedy for portrayal of character.[8] That was clearly his main interest. Accordingly his plays are marked by quiet humor rather than boisterous laughter. Effects of low comedy are occasionally found. A scene of the "running slave," as stereotyped an incident as anything in New Comedy, is used even in the *Brothers* (299–320), Terence's most serious play. The *Brothers* also contains a very obscene jest (215), and this example is by no means unique in his plays. In general, however, Terence shows a distinct preference for high comedy.

Choice of subject matter in Terence as in Menander shows an extremely limited range. The plots of five of his six comedies are based primarily upon an uncertain liaison or marriage which in the end is stabilized. In four of these plays the solution is brought about by the recognition of the girl as an Attic citizen of good family. Terence's use of such well-worn though highly improbable events and his dependence upon the long arm of coincidence were not, of course, really compatible with his tendency toward high comedy. His plays accordingly do not rise far above the ordinary mediocrity of New Comedy.

Some slight changes were made by Terence in the subject matter of the Greek originals. Most striking is the addition of a minor plot in the *Woman of Andros* based on a young man's desire to marry a girl of good family and of unquestioned virtue. It is unfortunate that this faltering step did not lead to a serious development of respectable courtship and love as a new mine of subject material. In making this addition, furthermore, Terence succeeds remarkably well in individualizing his new characters. Several other times, especially in the *Brothers,* we find him making minor changes in the originals for the purpose of pointing the individuality of his characters with greater clarity. Still, his portrayal of character lacks something of the subtlety and charm of Menander.

Most of the changes and innovations which Terence made, however, are technical ones and are designed to make the plays more dramatic. The plots of New Comedy were all too often pitifully thin and trite. His addition of the love of Charinus in the *Woman of Andros* is precisely the type of elaboration which is added by modern dramatists when they take over such plots. Thus Shakespeare in *The Comedy of Errors* added Luciana and her romance with Antipholus of Syracuse, Molière in *L'Avare* added both Mariane and Cléante, and Steele in *The Conscious Lovers* added Phillis and her romance with Tom (Davus). In Steele's play this addition constitutes a tertiary plot, and it is by far the best element of the play. By means of such additions, dramatic action is increased, the complication is made more serious, the climax is heightened, and general romantic felicity is made to reign at the end of the play.

The comedy which Terence wrote second but did not succeed in presenting until several years after the first attempt, the *Mother-in-Law,* retained its original simple plot without addition. Strange to say, Terence apparently made no effort to revise it despite its lack of success; but he learned a lesson from this, and in all subsequent plays he used a double plot. He doubtless chose his Greek originals in part, at least, upon this criterion, for in these later plays the minor phase of the plot is well fused with the major into an essential unity which seems to be the work of the Greek author. Normally the two phases complicate each other, and the solution of the one may heighten the other's climax.

The minor phase is not, as in the *Braggart Warrior* of Plautus, merely juxtaposed or suspended within the major.

In general there are more movements on and off the stage in the comedies of Terence than in those of Plautus. Indeed the number of scenes is consistently high in four of his six plays.[9] Still his plays are extremely short, averaging about one thousand lines with remarkable regularity. The even shorter *Mother-in-Law* is the one exception. These facts might be taken as indicating that Terence has reduced the extent of the original plays but increased—or at least not reduced—the amount of dramatic movement.[10]

Terence did not use the omniscient expository prologue which was so frequently employed in New Comedy. His consequent achievement of suspense and surprise has been considered his greatest contribution to plot construction.[11] Not all the original Greek comedies had omniscient prologues; but those whose plots were built about concealed identities, it is usually assumed, invariably did so. Such plays among the extant works of Plautus usually have omniscient prologues. There are exceptions; but that Terence's practice was a distinct innovation in his day is obvious from his literary prologues and from other information.[12] Five of his plays contain concealed identities and probably had omniscient prologues in their original form. The original of the *Brothers,* also, may have had such a prologue.

Several factors probably contributed to Terence's elimination of omniscient prologues. They would have been very awkward if they had been combined with or made to follow his literary prologues. They would have required the use of divinities or a prologue-speaker or, as in the *Braggart Warrior* of Plautus, a deplorable lapse in the dramatic illusion. All of these were clumsy devices and contravened Terence's desire for naturalness and plausibility.[13] Especially offensive, no doubt, was the use of a divinity. Seneca, too, though fond of the supernatural, was to have a strong aversion to the use of a divinity as *deus ex machina.* Indeed, no single step brought Terence closer to modern feeling than his rejection of the mechanism of divinities.

To what extent Terence adapted his plays for presentation without omniscient prologues is a matter of uncertainty. Perhaps little or no adaptation was necessary in many cases, for it was the Greek convention to construct the plays as unities almost independent of the prologue; and, where recognition was to take place, preparation and foreshadowing seem invariably to have occurred within the body of the play itself. The beauty and virtue of a girl, for instance, may be praised, and talk of her being an Athenian citizen may occur. Indeed, these indications do occur so frequently that the experienced playgoer must inevitably have grasped their significance. The main function of the omniscient prologue, then, was not to foretell the recognition but to explain the secret identities in order to facilitate dramatic irony. Often in the plays of Terence, especially in the *Woman of Andros* and the *Mother-in-Law*, this irony has been lost with the omission of the prologue. The ineffectiveness of the *Mother-in-Law* is due in large part to this loss; for it is almost exclusively a play not of action or decision but of discovery, and in plays of discovery, as best shown by Sophocles' *Oedipus the King*, dramatic irony normally plays a major role. The *Phormio* too has lost some effective irony—Demipho tries to eject from his house the very girl to whom, if her identity were known, he would wish his son married. But in general the *Phormio* employs suspense and surprise with remarkable success.

Substitution of dramatic dialogue for monologue is another technical improvement which Terence has made over his originals. This occurs in the expositional scene of the *Woman of Andros* and in the *Eunuch* where Chaerea relates his conquest. Terence has apparently supplemented narration by action in the *Brothers* where the scene of abduction has been added. Plautus, in adapting the play from which this scene is taken, perhaps had substituted narration for action.[14] Once in the *Mother-in-Law* Terence too may have substituted monologue for dialogue;[15] but usually Terence has shown an excellent sense of theater in such matters.

Terence has made several distinct advances in the use of dialogue. His style is closely modeled upon the beautifully simple style of Menander, which itself follows that of Euripides; and it is ideally adapted to drama of everyday life. Whereas the language of Plautus is more spirited and in general more colloquial, Terence more closely approaches natural speech in certain important respects, such as in his use of interjections.[16]

Consonant with this simplicity of style is the simple metrical structure of Terence's plays. He uses far less lyric meter and far less recitative than Plautus. This reduction, it appears from our scanty evidence, was characteristic of the other dramatists of his day, at least to some extent. Terence still uses more lyric and recitative, no doubt, than did the Greek dramatists.

Asides, which were very rare in Greek tragedy, were frequently employed in Greek comedy. Indeed they were very natural in the vast Greek theater or on the very long Roman stage when a chorus was not present. Terence uses them especially to reveal whether or not one character is supposed to overhear what is being said elsewhere on stage. Asides are also used for irony and humor, and Terence is given the credit for perfecting this type of aside by using it to express one's inner thoughts punctuating the continued speech of another.[17]

Somewhat similar is the beginning of a scene in the middle of a line. This bit of naturalism, used most effectively by Euripides near the end of his career, was well established in the Greek tradition by the time of Menander; but it had been abandoned by Plautus.[18]

Finally Terence made a great advance in dramatic realism by eliminating direct address to the audience.[19] Though he still allows monologues patently designed to impart information, most of his long monologues are true soliloquies. This is especially clear in the *Brothers,* where each of the three principal characters at one time or another seriously meditates his situation. Direct address is found in the last lines of the *Woman of Andros,* as frequently at the very end of a Plautine comedy; but in all the later plays of Terence the actors' lines are completed without breaking the illusion, and the musician, as convention allowed, asks the audience to applaud.

From this discussion it is clear that Terence handled the Greek originals with some freedom. Such practice, it appears from his prologues, was not the fashion of his day, and it brought down no little criticism upon his head. He staunchly maintained his point of view, however, and even in his last play, the *Brothers,* he inserted a scene from a different Greek author into Menander's play. Such a combination of two Greek originals—contamination as it was called—was the special object of attack; but Terence insisted that the practice of Naevius, Plautus, and Ennius, his greatest predecessors in the field, furnished him sufficient justification. In most respects, however, Terence clings more closely to the Greek originals than do these earlier writers, and thus he adheres to the fashion of his own times. He avoids Roman allusions of almost every sort. Some concessions, however, are made. In the opening scene of the *Self-Tormentor* (63), for instance, he has substituted a vague phrase for a specific Attic place name which would have been quite unknown to the Roman audience. Again, in the original of the *Phormio* (91), we are told by an ancient commentator, the young men learned of the maiden in distress from the barber who had cut the girl's hair as a sign of mourning. Terence changes this, for it was not the custom at Rome to cut the hair in mourning.[20] But these minor changes merely show Terence's expertness in translation.

That Terence made various technical improvements does not mean that his plays were superior to their Greek originals. Very few translations have ever been superior to the original works. The practice of contamination, though introducing some desirable features, entailed difficulties which Terence did not always solve satisfactorily. Since none of the Greek plays has been preserved, comparison in detail is impossible. But Julius Caesar, apparently an excellent literary critic, considered Terence lacking in a certain force and verve. The fact that Terence has toned down Menander is attested also by Cicero.[21] Finally, the Greek fragments preserved reveal some losses.[22] But Caesar and Cicero still hold Terence in high regard.

To consider one who never wrote an original play a great dramatist would of course be a mistake. But Terence made these important advances in dramatic technique at a time when originality was and long had been extremely rare. Indeed, Terence shows more technical originality than any other figure in New Comedy, including Menander himself, and to deny him generous credit for his improvements would be grudging indeed. If he did not invent these himself, he at least recognized them; and the early recognition of an improvement is hardly less important than the invention. Certainly his plays and their dramatic technique have exerted important influence upon Renaissance and modern drama.

1. *WOMAN OF ANDROS (ANDRIA)*

(Festival in honor of Cybele, 166 B.C.)

The *Woman of Andros* tells a charming story and was doubtless successful,[23] but it lacks the technical finish of Terence's later plays.

Interesting adaptations are found in Steele's *The Conscious Lovers* (1722), and in Bellamy's *The Perjured Devotee* (1739). Thornton Wilder's contemporary novel, *The Woman of Andros,* is a sentimental and romantic idealization of the story, especially revealing to the student of literature who wishes to understand the essential difference between ancient classicism and modern romanticism.

Sources and originality.—The *Woman of Andros* is primarily a translation of a play of Menander of the same name (*Andria*), but Terence confesses that he has taken certain features from Menander's very similar *Woman of Perinthos* (*Perinthia*).

In the *Andria* of Menander, as the ancient commentator (on line 14) explains, the old man told his story in a monologue, while in the *Perinthia* he conversed with his wife. Terence has used dialogue instead of monologue, doubtless to make the scene more dramatic. For the wife, however, a freedman, Sosia, has been substituted. This involves one or two minor difficulties. It seems surprising that a household servant should not know the manner of Pamphilus' life better than Simo himself. Again, in the final lines of the scene Sosia is told to frighten Davus and observe Pamphilus. Although these lines are doubtless designed to stimulate the interest of the audience in the coming events,[24] they seem to look forward to Sosia's subsequent appearance, whereas he is actually a protatic character.

Much more important is Terence's addition of a minor plot. The characters Charinus and Byrria were not in Menander, according to the ancient commentator (on line 301), who adds that they were introduced by Terence so that Philumena might not be left pathetically without a husband when Pamphilus marries Glycerium. The romantic tendency to secure an entirely happy ending is observable elsewhere in Terence, as in the *Eunuch,* and in other plays of New Comedy. Especially noteworthy from the modern point of view is the nature of the love affair of Charinus and Philumena: Charinus has sincerely fallen in love with a girl of good family whose virtue is still intact. This is an almost unique example of such a love affair in New Comedy, and it here appears to be a distinctly Roman touch.[25]

But in adding these characters Terence no doubt was chiefly motivated by a desire to enrich the dramatic action. Significantly the minor plot is made to heighten the suspense and interest of the major plot. Still the fusion of these two elements is not as skillfully carried out as in the later plays of Terence. The exit of Byrria at verse 337 seems abrupt. So does his reappearance soon afterward when he eavesdrops and overhears Pamphilus agree to the marriage—an awkward scene somewhat similar to a passage in the *Phormio* (606–81). The entrance of Charinus near the end of the play also seems poorly motivated. In the final analysis, both Charinus and Byrria appear to be external appendages.

More than any other characters in the play, however, Charinus and Byrria are colorfully individualized, and it is possible that Terence originated these characterizations. Byrria is depicted as a crude, mundane, and skeptically realistic person, thus standing out in sharp contrast to Charinus, who is a romantic and idealistic young gentleman. When Charinus debates with sensitive modesty the advisability of approaching Pamphilus, Byrria shows no hesitation and crudely suggests that if Charinus accomplishes nothing else at least he can give the impression that he will become the bride's paramour if Pamphilus dares marry her. A few lines later, his master breaks down and is quite unable to tell Pamphilus of his love; but Byrria is ready to do so with brutal directness. Later, when Byrria overhears Pamphilus promise to marry, he immediately concludes that Pamphilus has betrayed Charinus, and from his wisdom of the world and its ways, he fully understands, as he thinks, the whole situation: the girl is a very pretty person and of course Pamphilus would prefer himself to spend nights with her rather than see Charinus have the privilege of doing so.[26]

Discussion.—The *Woman of Andros* has a plot that is essentially single. A young man is in love with a "foreign" girl, but his father is forcing him to contract an advantageous marriage with an Athenian citizen. Recognition of the "foreign" girl as herself an Athenian of good family brings about the solution. To this situation, all too frequent in New Comedy,[27] Terence has happily conceived the idea of adding a second young man.

The opening scene is a masterpiece of exposition in beautifully limpid verse.[28] Simo's description of Glycerium as a young lady of unusual beauty and modesty prepares for her recognition later in the play. Incidentally Pamphilus is here well characterized as the typical weak and somewhat colorless young man of New Comedy, Davus as the equally typical clever and unscrupulous slave. Simo reveals also that the marriage is a fictitious one but that if his son consents to it, he will attempt to make it genuine. The audience, therefore, later realizes the irony of the situation when Davus is elated to discover that no preparations are actually being made and when he succeeds in inducing Pamphilus to consent to the marriage for this reason.

The scene with Davus and Simo serves mainly to emphasize the comic fear of the slave, which is to increase as the action progresses and which nicely motivates the soliloquy after Simo has departed. In this soliloquy the exposition is continued by giving a picture of the love affair from Pamphilus' point of view. A child is about to be born, Davus relates, and they have madly decided to raise it. They have made up a fiction, he continues, that Glycerium is an Attic citizen. In New Comedy the merest mention of citizenship where such a girl is concerned invariably foreshadows her recognition. The skepticism of Davus over this story, far from blurring the foreshadowing here, makes it unusually deft and effective.

Pamphilus is now introduced, astounded at the news of his immediate marriage. His scene with Mysis is important not so much because it passes on the information of the childbirth to him as because it forces him in person to promise that he will remain faithful to Glycerium. Incidental to this, he relates the story of Chrysis' death—a beautiful and pathetic description.[29]

Since Charinus is so deeply in love with Chremes' daughter and so anxious to marry her, his introduction at this time seems to offer a possible solution to Pamphilus' difficulties. But the discovery of Davus that no real preparations for a marriage are being made reassures Charinus, and he is dismissed with the vague advice that he should approach the friends of Chremes in an effort to arrange the match. Pamphilus is then very reluctantly persuaded to consent to his father's plans for his marriage. This consent violently contradicts the promises which he has made to Glycerium. Pamphilus apparently has no intention of deliberately renouncing these former promises; indeed he later repeats them in most solemn language (694–97), as he also repeats his consent to do his father's will (898). Perhaps Pamphilus gives his consent to his father with mental reservations, thinking that he will not be called upon to fulfill this promise. Nevertheless both promises are given and, once given, only the grace of Heaven or the cleverness of the playwright can save Pamphilus.

Now for the first time Simo hears of the childbirth. But ironically enough he considers this a mere farce which Davus is putting on for his benefit. He makes various references to players and the theater, and in particular he criticizes Lesbia's coming out of the house and calling back directions from the street. Although such action is a common device for informing the audience of what has been going on within—. indeed this device seems almost inevitable in social comedy that is limited to a street scene—still it is admittedly a little ridiculous. The dramatist himself would have done well to take Simo's criticism more seriously and eliminate such action elsewhere; but in point of fact this device is used again in the *Woman of Andros* (684–85) and in Menander's own *Shearing of Glycera* (176–77). Equally pertinent to good dramaturgy is Simo's later criticism of the pat arrival of Crito (916), but that criticism too—unfortunately—was without effect on New Comedy.

The climax of Pamphilus' dilemma is skillfully accentuated by Terence's own Charinus, who comes on just as Pamphilus is berating Davus for the predicament into which he has been inveigled. The emotional turmoil of this scene is nicely brought out by the use of excited meters and by the nervously rapid shift in meters. Even this turmoil is not enough, however, and Mysis must appear to report Glycerium's trepidation.

The solution of all these complications is very rapidly accomplished. Davus puts on a clever little scene for Chremes, the convenience of whose entrance is adeptly glossed over—the dramatist has Davus imply that he is laying the scene for an entirely different farce when Chremes is suddenly seen approaching. Chremes then no sooner goes in to find Simo and renounce the engagement than Crito appears, with something of the suddenness of a *deus ex machina,* for he has received no preparation except the vaguest passing reference to kinsmen of Chrysis in the opening scene (71).

By these happy events the honor of Pamphilus is saved. But such events are purely external, and this solution has been sharply criticized for that reason. A contrast unfavorable to Terence has been drawn between this solution and that of Menander's *Arbitration*. There is not the slightest justification, however, for thinking that the solution of the *Woman of Andros* is due to Terence rather than to Menander.[30] The complication of the play is built upon Pamphilus' contradictory promises. External solutions, furthermore, are frequent in New Comedy. Indeed the *Arbitration* itself depends on an external solution though it does have an internal solution as well. Each play, like many another of New Comedy, leans heavily upon the long arm of coincidence.

2. *SELF-TORMENTOR* (*HEAUTON TIMORUMENOS*)

(Festival in honor of Cybele, 163 B.C.)

The incidents of the *Self-Tormentor* are typical of New Comedy, but the emphasis upon character and the generalization of the particular incidents into a serious theme are extraordinary. The *Self-Tormentor* resembles the *Brothers* in these respects but is somewhat inferior to it. An interesting technical detail is the passage of a night during the action (410).

Terence's play is taken from Menander's play of the same name. It is often assumed that the original action has not been altered in any important respect, although an omniscient prologue has probably been omitted.

Discussion.—The *Self-Tormentor* is based upon a double plot of love affairs, intrigue, and recognition. Chremes' son, Clitipho, is ensnared by a grasping courtesan, Bacchis, for whom his personal slave Syrus defrauds the father of a certain amount of money. In the end, however, Clitipho is forced to break off this affair and to agree to marriage—with a girl of whom we have heard nothing before. Menedemus' son, Clinia, is in love with a very virtuous girl who is discovered to be the daughter of Chremes. The connection between these series of events is hardly more than one of mere juxtaposition. Still, the recognition is made to serve as a complication for the major phase of the plot, since it threatens the exposure of Clitipho's affair, and as a means of defrauding Chremes, since the daughter is said to be indebted to Bacchis. The triteness of these situations is camouflaged by the usual type of minor variation. More important, however, is the focusing of the plot not upon the sons but upon the fathers. Chremes is certainly the main character of the play, and he is delightfully individualized.

That Chremes is interested in all human affairs, especially the affairs of other people, is clearly brought out in the opening scene. So is his penchant for offering free advice on the most intimate subjects and his smug confidence in the usual moral clichés. Since this play has no omniscient prologue, the irony of all this does not become evident until the third scene, wherein Clitipho, soliloquizing, complains of his father's treatment and reveals his own difficult situation with Bacchis. The reader who is acquainted with Menander need hardly go on in order to discover that in the end Chremes will find that he too has not learned the lesson of the Golden Mean, and that he will have his own advice thrown back at him with interest. He, like Menedemus, must learn the hard way. Every father is to some extent, at least, a self-tormentor.

The opening scene is a very picturesque one and is remarkable in that it apparently begins with a "set": Menedemus swinging his heavy mattock into the earth, while Chremes leans over the fence, so to speak, and addresses him. Here the exposition is given with unusual deftness. Loss of irony at the very beginning can hardly be considered a blemish, for enlightenment follows almost immediately, and this technique, if it is not positively preferable, certainly furnishes a refreshing variation, especially in a play which, even as it stands, thoroughly exploits the usual methods of dramatic irony.

As in the *Brothers,* contrast plays a most important part in the portrayal of the characters. That between the studiedly morose Menedemus and the affable, inquisitive Chremes is a main interest throughout the play. The two girls, though distinctly minor roles, are nicely characterized, Bacchis as the hardened courtesan, and Antiphila as the naïve girl so virtuous that we immediately recognize her good birth and anticipate her recognition. Clinia is the typically fearful and rapturous young lover, and Clitipho the typically colorless young blood enamored of a grasping courtesan and terrified at the thought of his father's discovering the affair.

3. *EUNUCH

(Festival in honor of Cybele, 161 B.C.)

The *Eunuch* was Terence's most successful play and is said to have brought a greater price than any previous Roman comedy.[31] Its technical execution is admirable. It has always been held in high respect until recent times, when certain critics, judging the play according to standards which were not those of the authors or those of the society about which New Comedy was written, have roundly condemned it on moral grounds.[32] If judged without moral prejudice, however, the play appears gay and spirited and amusing—much more so than Terence's other comedies, with the possible exception of the *Phormio*. But we should not forget that to prefer an author's least characteristic work is to reject the author's own criteria.

The *Eunuch* has exerted considerable influence on modern comedy, and its adaptations include *Ralph Roister Doister* by Nicholas Udall, the earliest English comedy (before 1553, indebted also to the *Braggart Warrior* of Plautus). Lines 74–75 are quoted in part in the *Taming of the Shrew* (I. i. 167).

Sources and originality.—The *Eunuch* is for the most part a translation of the *Eunouchos* of Menander, but the braggart soldier, Thraso, and his parasite, as we are told in the prologue, are taken from Menander's *Toady* (*Kolax*). The plot of the original Greek *Eunouchos* is not known, but it is unnecessary to assume that the addition of these two characters has changed that plot. Certainly a rival of Phaedria for the love of Thais may have existed in the original *Eunouchos* and is essential to Terence's play. Phaedria must presumably be absent when his younger brother assumes the disguise; the confusion caused by Chremes is highly desirable; and the uncertainty of Thais' securing and retaining Pamphila is a main source of dramatic suspense. In Terence's play, therefore, the soldier Thraso plays an essential role from the beginning of the play to the recognition of Pamphila, and if we were not expressly so told, we should never suspect that Thraso is an addition of Terence. Soldier and parasite, it is true, are farcical characters; but the disguise of Chaerea, also, belongs to the realm of farce, and so does the deluding of Parmeno near the end of the play. The additional characters, therefore, are thoroughly at home in this play, and on the whole Terence has done an admirable job of incorporating them.[33]

Another excellent feature of the play owes its existence to the originality of Terence. In Menander's play, we are told by the ancient commentator, Chaerea's triumphant narration of his conquest was a monologue.[34] Terence has made this a dialogue by adding Antipho. Though of course this new character should have been worked into the action more intimately, the gain of a dialogue over a monologue here is very great. Nor is Terence's change a mechanical one. He has introduced humor of his own: Chaerea fears that someone will ask the very questions with which Antipho greets him. Further characterization of these naïve adolescents also has been added in their dialogue (e.g., 604).

Discussion.—The *Eunuch* is based upon a double plot of love affairs, disguise and intrigue, and recognition. But the whole is skillfully fused and unified.

The opening scenes are as delightful as they are dramatically adept.

Parmeno, a wiser Aristotelian than his young master, Phaedria, insists that one should not expect any more rationality in an activity than the activity admits, and that the activity of love, like other forms of insanity, admits of none. This self-evident truth is nicely illustrated in the ensuing scene wherein Thais and her way with a man are introduced. Phaedria's consequent promise to retire for two days initiates the dramatic action. Further exposition is here added, especially for that phase of the plot which deals with the virtuous young Pamphila, whose recognition as an Attic citizen is clearly foreshadowed. Especially neat is Thais' anticipation of Chremes' later appearance; for Chremes, though essential only for identifying Pamphila, is thus worked into the exposition. With equal deftness he is later to be worked into the complication.

After Thais has been allowed a monologue at the end of the scene —in order, of course, that we may clearly distinguish between the fact and the fiction which she has told Phaedria—there follows a short farewell scene between Phaedria and Parmeno. Though repetitious, this nicely emphasizes the vain effusiveness of the lover and prepares for his moral collapse and early return. More important is Parmeno's first description of Pamphila at the end of the scene. His praise of her ladylike beauty foreshadows a love affair and along with the earlier information of Thais assures her eventual recognition as a citizen.

The portrayal of Chaerea is masterly. He is the very incarnation of irrepressible adolescent exuberance. Most effective is his excitement at first falling in love, his naïve conceit of being a connoisseur of feminine beauty, his dash and determination, and the virgin innocence of his companion Antipho (604)—this last an addition of Terence that is quite apposite to the picture. A nice subtlety in Chaerea's description of the seduction is found in the use of phrases suggesting the ceremonies of marriage.[35] His enthusiasm for possessing Pamphila in the future (613–14), furthermore, is as natural to his character as it is necessary to the plot.

Another effective scene occurs when Thraso ("bold") comes to lay siege to the house of Thais. Here the only brave person proves to be Thais herself. The young Chremes is only less afraid than the braggart Thraso, whose culinary "army" has come equipped with—a sponge! The whole scene is so well done that we forget that the "siege" is a stock motif in plays containing a soldier.[36]

The poetic justice which Pythias later metes out to Parmeno also is highly amusing. It is well worked into the plot mechanism, however, for it serves to introduce the father of Chaerea and Phaedria, who in turn brings about the very rapid solution.

Noteworthy throughout these later scenes are the rapid shifts in emotional tone. At times these are accompanied by amusing irony. Parmeno enters with great self-satisfaction and is anticipating his rewards, when he is terrified by the false news of the seizure of Chaerea. The father, too, enters in a very bland mood only to join in the same terror. Later Thraso comes on wholly crushed, and he is immediately followed by the ecstatically happy Chaerea.

4. *PHORMIO*

(Roman Games, 161 B.C.)

The *Phormio* is an adaptation of a Greek comedy (*Epidikazomenos*) by Apollodorus of Carystus. Few if any important innovations, according to the usual assumption, have been made by Terence except that the original probably had an expository prologue in which the secret marriage of Chremes was explained.

The characters and events of this play are in general typical of New Comedy. Phormio himself and Nausistrata are delightfully portrayed, and the contrast between the two old men is effective. But the real virtues of the play lie elsewhere. Its structure is unusually deft; much of the action, especially in the final scenes, is very delightful farce. It has always been popular and famous; and this reputation, though somewhat exaggerated in modern times because of the total absence of obscenity or suggestiveness, is well deserved.

The *Phormio* has also been of considerable influence in modern literature. The most important adaptation is doubtless Molière's *Les Fourberies de Scapin* (1671).

Discussion.—The *Phormio* is based upon a double plot of two— one might include old Chremes and say three—lovers and their difficulties, which are solved, as usual, one by recognition and one by artfully securing money. The minor phase concerning Phaedria and his girl Pamphila is elaborately and intimately bound with the major phase concerning Antipho and his marriage to a penniless girl. Series of scenes dealing now with one phase now with the other are most skillfully interwoven.

The *Phormio*, like the *Woman of Andros*, opens with a "maid-and-butler" scene of exposition. Geta, the confidential slave of Antipho, relates his young master's goings-on to friend Davus. But Davus is more colorful than Sosia in the *Woman of Andros*, and Davus' appearance only in the opening scene is more plausibly motivated. Geta's account nicely combines the two phases of the plot: he relates that the young men were waiting to conduct Pamphila home from music school when they first heard of Phanium. The recognition of Phanium as the daughter of a good Athenian family is clearly foreshadowed in Geta's account. There is not the slightest hint, however, that the supposed fiction by which Phormio has legally "forced" Antipho to marry this penniless girl is not really fiction but fact—that Antipho is in truth obligated to marry this girl.[37] In regard to Phaedria, also, Geta does not tell the whole story: he fails to mention that Phaedria's friends have promised to lend him money and that a day has already been set for the purchase—information which might well have been used to suggest that his affairs too are soon to reach a climax. Thus the exposition leaves ample room for suspense and surprise. Indeed, perhaps no ancient comedy employs suspense and surprise more effectively than does the *Phormio*.

The two young men are nicely characterized in their first scene. Antipho regrets having embarked upon such a rash course as his marriage proves to be, and he looks forward with dread to the return of his father. He is certainly given no consolation by Phaedria, who is rudely impatient with his cousin, being incapable of sympathy for anyone who actually possesses his love and is still unhappy. The action of the play begins with Demipho's sudden arrival and the flight of Antipho, who can see nothing but suicide ahead if he loses his Phanium. He leaves his fate in the hands of Geta and Phaedria—a nice device for maintaining suspense and for having Phaedria play an important role in this phase of the action which really concerns only Antipho and Phanium.

The first clash between Demipho and the resourceful Phormio is excellent comedy, and not all the amusement is at the expense of the older man. But the best comedy comes with the hopeless equivocation of the *advocati* whom Demipho has so cautiously provided as legal witnesses. Thus Demipho is in the end left angry but undecided, though he has threatened to throw Phanium out of his house.

While the fate of Antipho hangs thus precariously in the balance —the complication of his affairs is arrested at its point of greatest tension—a crisis now arises for Phaedria. Another man will purchase his sweetheart on the morrow unless he can today raise the necessary funds. Demipho has rightly said that these young men are accustomed to lend each other mutual aid (267), for as Phaedria became the advocate of Antipho in a crisis so now Antipho persuades the reluctant Geta to devise a plan for securing the money. This alone, it seems, saves Phaedria in his desperation from a fate only slightly less tragic than the contemplated suicide of Antipho!

At this point Demipho reappears with his brother Chremes, and

now for the first time we are told the story of Chremes' secret polygamy
—a refreshingly unusual item in New Comedy—and of his daughter
from Lemnos. Up to this point we have assumed that Demipho's only
objection to the marriage of Antipho is based, as Geta has suggested
(120), on his unwillingness to accept a girl without a dowry; but now
it appears that there are even more serious considerations, for if
Chremes is forced to marry off his daughter to a stranger he must
explain her origin and risk a major scandal. A divorce would ruin
him, for his wife has all the money in the family! This complication
comes as a complete and effective surprise. Naturally under these circumstances the old men fall easy victims to the machinations of Geta
when the prospect of a separation of Antipho and Phanium is held
out as bait. These machinations, however well intended by Geta, appear seriously to jeopardize the future of Antipho's marriage. Here
both phases of the plot, therefore, are fused at their simultaneous
climaxes.

Antipho, whose eavesdropping, though awkward, facilitates rapidity
of dramatic action, is terrified when he learns to what desperate means
Geta and Phormio have resorted to secure money for Phaedria. This
terror comes as the climax of a carefully developed crescendo of comic
fear. Indeed, the *Phormio* furnishes a model example of the use of
pessimism in comedy, for comedy employs false pessimism as effectively
as tragedy employs false optimism. Even in the opening scene of the
play Geta has expressed misgivings, and in the succeeding scene Antipho
has been characterized by timorous remorse. Misgivings and remorse
have grown to terror with the sudden arrival of Demipho. Later
Antipho has somewhat recovered when he comes back on stage to learn
of Phaedria's difficulties with the slave dealer. But now when he overhears Geta apparently arrange for breaking up his marriage, he is more
terrified than ever.

The very pat entrance of Sophrona, like the eavesdropping of Antipho, is somewhat awkward. But the author has more than redeemed
himself by the plan of having Nausistrata prepare Phanium for the
divorce. This not only furnishes a further link between the two phases
of the plot. Nausistrata's introduction here serves to characterize her
and to show Demipho's influence with her. Incidentally it furnishes a
very amusing scene between these two and husband Chremes.

Before the recognition of Phanium, which solves Antipho's difficulties, an important minor interest has been built up about Chremes.
The recognition itself, furthermore, merely heightens the danger of
Chremes and apparently that of his son also. Comic fear is one of the
chief devices for maintaining suspense, and in place of the fear of

Antipho, which has turned into ecstasy, there now appears the terror of Chremes. Long before, however, ample preparation for this has been made, for at Chremes' first appearance his anxiety was only too evident. The final scenes with Phormio are the best of the play and indeed among the most lively and amusing scenes in Roman comedy. All the earlier fears of Geta and Antipho, like those of Phaedria and Chremes, serve by contrast to emphasize their relief and happiness in the end.

5. *MOTHER-IN-LAW* (*HECYRA*)

(Roman Games [?], 160 B.C.)

Attempts were made to produce the *Mother-in-Law* at the festival in honor of Cybele in 165 B.C. and at the funeral games of Lucius Aemilius Paullus in 160; but on these occasions the audience, excited by rumors of gayer sports, refused to remain for the end of the play.

Dramatically the *Mother-in-Law* is weak. Its main appeal is found in the tender pathos of the story which it tells.

Source.—The *Mother-in-Law* is adapted from a Greek original written probably in the first half of the third century by Apollodorus of Carystus. The original play seems to have derived its basic plot from Menander's *Arbitration,* for in both plays a husband is estranged from his wife over the birth of a child which he thinks not his own. Eventually it turns out that the violator of the wife before her marriage was the husband himself. In both plays this recognition is brought about by a kindly courtesan, but the process is much more subtle and entails much more dramatic action in Menander. Indeed, the borrowings of Apollodorus are for the most part limited to the highly improbable incidents, which of course are the worst features of Menander's play.

Discussion.—Unlike the other plays of Terence, the *Mother-in-Law* presents a very simple plot of one young man and his difficulties in love. The play is almost wholly one of discovery.

The original Greek play doubtless opened with an omniscient prologue in which the coming childbirth was announced and the real identity of the child's father made known. This allowed the original audience from the very first of the play to appreciate the irony of the situation and to understand the various "errors" to which the characters of the play are subject. The omission of the prologue results in a plot in which mystery and suspense play a major role.

Terence's play opens with an expositional scene between two courtesans and the confidential slave Parmeno. The two women do not reappear in the play, and their use here seems awkward, especially since no significant motivation for the whole scene is given and no vital interest is generated in it. In both these respects the similar expositional scene of the *Phormio* is much superior. Still these two women were certainly employed by Apollodorus.[38] Incidentally, of course, they serve by contrast to heighten the attractiveness of the character of Bacchis and to suggest her milieu. This preparation softens the abruptness of her entrance near the end of the play where she takes the role of a *deus ex machina*.

If Terence had so chosen he could have presented Parmeno as cognizant of Philumena's pregnancy and skeptical of its legitimacy. Thus Parmeno could have gone far to replace the omniscient prologue. In Menander's *Arbitration,* it will be recalled, the confidential slave Onesimus is already cognizant of the wife's secret, and this very knowledge makes Onesimus' situation more difficult and joins him more intimately with the action. The mystification of Parmeno becomes amusing later in Terence's play; but near the opening, where it is so important to arouse the interest of the audience, the detachment of Parmeno is unfortunate. His laziness and curiosity, both of which he is continually prevented from indulging, form an amusing incidental leitmotif throughout the play.

The first scene with the father and mother of Pamphilus makes the situation as puzzling for the spectator as it is for the characters involved. Nor does this scene arouse any keen interest, as the opening scenes in a play of discovery by Sophocles or Ibsen would do. First of all the friction between Philumena and her mother-in-law seems trivial, as Parmeno himself later states (292, 313). In this scene no hint of graver problems is given, and Laches and Sostrata are not portrayed with the seriousness and depth that might elicit any real sympathy with them. Indeed, they are here the stereotyped ridiculous old married couple of New Comedy, and Laches indulges in the usual jokes on married life (207).

The whole series of misunderstandings among the old people has only a slight connection with the concatenation of events which forms the real plot of the play—Pamphilus' discovery of the birth of the child and his recognition of the child as his own. He makes the discovery of the birth quite independently. But from this point forward the irony of these errors is interesting and amusing. They also motivate the main tension at the climax of the play, because Laches, seeing that the avowed excuses of Pamphilus are so flimsy, is on the point of compelling his son to take back Philumena and recognize the child. The quarrel between Laches and Pamphilus, furthermore, leads to the introduction of

Bacchis, through whom the recognition of the child is accomplished. Thus the series of errors has its functions, but these develop only in the later part of the play and the amusing irony which might have sustained interest earlier has been lost. Terence's use of mystification and surprise in this play, therefore, cannot be considered a success.

The *Mother-in-Law* has other faults. It is sadly lacking in dramatic action. Indeed, the most important scenes of the play are monologues. Pamphilus reports his initial discovery of the birth in a long recitation of fifty-four lines, and this recitation is primarily one of facts and not a true soliloquy; for, except at the very last, Pamphilus shows no inclination to ponder his fate and commune with his soul concerning a future course of action. The plea of Myrrina which he recounts could have been presented much more effectively upon the stage. The author has missed another good scene in connection with Bacchis. In the *Arbitration* of Menander, wife and courtesan effectively meet on stage. Perhaps the recognition might have been managed with Myrrina in Terence's play. Certainly Bacchis' monologue of twenty-five lines is much less effective than a dialogue would have been, especially for the presentation of the solution. Perhaps Terence himself is at fault here.[39]

Finally, the situation dramatized in the *Mother-in-Law* is proper to serious drama; but the solution—the discovery that Pamphilus unknowingly married the very girl whom he had previously violated— is a fantastic coincidence proper only to light comedy or melodrama. Greek tragedy, it is true, could employ such a coincidence, but only if it was guaranteed by accepted legend or, as in Euripides' *Ion*, hedged about by divine providence. Even so, the real effectiveness of such plays depends largely on dramatic irony, portrayal of character, lyric poetry, and other incidental features. The coincidence in this play of Terence has no external support, the characters are of no great interest in themselves, and the situation is not dramatized in such a manner as to become of great significance. The failure of the play at its first two presentations, therefore, was primarily the fault of the author and not that of the audiences.

6. *BROTHERS (ADELPHOE)*

(Funeral games of Aemilius Paullus, 160 B.C.)

The *Brothers* is the most intellectual of the plays of Terence and in a way, therefore, the most interesting. It is a serious consideration of the eternal problem of the proper education of children—and parents. This subject is superficially treated also in the *Self-Tormentor*. Indeed, since the original of that play is thought to have been one of the earliest plays of Menander,[40] it may be that the original of the *Brothers* was a later and more serious effort to do justice to this subject. Certainly the *Brothers* is a more successful play.

The *Brothers* has always been well known and has inspired many adaptations in modern literature, such as Molière's *L'École des Maris* (1661) and Fielding's *The Fathers*.

Sources and originality.—For the most part, the *Brothers* is a translation of a similarly named play of Menander (*Adelphoi*), but the scene of Aeschinus' abducting the slave girl is taken from the *Suicide Pact* (*Synapothneskontes*) of Diphilus. This insertion nicely illustrates the action that has been under discussion in the previous scenes. It also characterizes Aeschinus and introduces a lively dramatic scene. But it detracts from the serious problem of Menander's play and throws the emphasis awry. A minor blemish is found in Aeschinus' contention that the girl is really a free woman. In the play of Diphilus this doubtless served as foreshadowing of recognition, as such references invariably do elsewhere in New Comedy. Apparently Terence, frightened by the attacks of his critics, has been too conservative in adapting this scene to the play of Menander. Still we are told that the Roman critic and polymath of Cicero's day, Varro, preferred the opening of Terence's play to that of Menander.[41]

Several minor changes made by Terence have been noted in the ancient commentary. Among these are a more abrupt first entrance for Demea, who in the Terentian version does not return the polite greeting of his brother—a bit of apt characterization. Again, in Menander, Ctesipho threatened suicide rather than exile if he lost his sweetheart (see line 275 and the commentary of "Donatus"). Perhaps Terence thought suicide too bold a threat for such a spineless and timid young man.[42] Finally, in Menander, Hegio (or his equivalent) was the brother of Sostrata (see line 351), and Micio made no protest against marrying her (see line 938). By making Hegio more distant Terence has presented Sostrata as more alone in the world; by making Micio protest he has presented the urban brother as a weaker character who is unable to refuse a request even when he really desires to do so. All of these changes, then, seem to have been made to sharpen and improve the characterizations.

Discussion.—"Every father is a fool." So runs a fragment (144, Kock) of Menander's original of the *Self-Tormentor* (line 440), and this might be taken as the motto of the *Brothers*. But the serious subject of the play, of course, is the role of discipline in education. The play does have a conventional double plot concerning two young men in love; the plot is skillfully unified, and some interest in it is maintained throughout the play. But in masterly fashion the dramatic action—except the inserted scene of abduction—has been made wholly subservient to the portrayal of Demea and Micio and to the discussion of the intellectual problem. Indeed, the two young men themselves are subservient to these ends. Here more than in any other extant play of New Comedy, not external events but the reactions of characters—especially of Demea—are the main concern of the play, and many scenes have little or nothing to do with the progression of the plot.

Portrayal of character by contrast is elaborately developed in this play. The contrast of the two old brothers is the center of interest, but the young brothers differ as violently. The sons are contrasted with the fathers, also, and in a way the liberally educated Aeschinus resembles Demea more than he does Micio; the country-bred Ctesipho certainly has the urban Micio's love of luxury. Even the slaves are contrasted—the strait-laced Geta and the dissolute Syrus.

It is not inappropriate that such a serious and contemplative play should open with a true soliloquy: Micio reviews his life and his theory of education, pointing out the contrast between his own ideas and those of his older brother. This soliloquy is effectively interrupted by the abrupt entrance of the older brother, and a dramatic illustration of their basic conflict follows. In the absence of an omniscient prologue one might at first miss the irony of Demea's position. But the spectator acquainted with Menander must have smiled when Demea repeatedly praises the son whom he has raised as the very model of a thrifty and assiduous young man, since in Menander young men are never painted in such unadulterated colors without irony. Perhaps the spectator who was an experienced father also smiled when Micio insisted that love and kindness are discipline enough for raising a young man and when both older brothers are presented as quite sure that they know how to be perfect fathers. Certainly the problem of the play is brilliantly set forth in these opening scenes.

The scenes with Aeschinus and Ctesipho which follow initiate the action of the plot and furnish varied dramatic business. Their real importance, however, is found in the portrayal of the two young men. In this regard the scene from Diphilus makes a real contribution, for it presents Aeschinus as a young man of great self-reliance and force of character. After this Ctesipho appears very much a weakling. Ctesipho's fear that his father may hear of this affair creates some suspense (283). It also gives an external justification for the later scenes where the presence of Demea seems to threaten discovery. Thus it forms a link between the plot action and the characterization of Demea, for characterization is the basic function of these later scenes.

With the exception of minor details, the *Brothers* lacks those conventional improbabilities that are so frequent in New Comedy and that tend so strongly to preclude the development of serious drama. In this respect the *Brothers* is much superior to the *Self-Tormentor*. The day of Pamphila's delivery, however, coincides with the day of the abduction of Ctesipho's sweetheart. Such telescoping of chronology is unavoidable if the unity of time is to be maintained.

A series of scenes is now introduced to show the effect of the news of the abduction upon the family of Pamphila. They misinterpret Aeschinus' motives, of course, as Micio and Demea both have done, and thus the two phases of the plot are fused. The consternation caused by the supposed treachery of Aeschinus greatly complicates matters.

At this point of tension the action of the plot is suspended and the portrayal of Demea is resumed. In the light of the previous events, the irony of his position is now unmistakably plain. This of course is comic irony, for the slave Syrus knows the truth better than anyone, and he makes merciless sport of the old man. Still Demea is far from being a stupid old man of the usual comic type. He is saved from this by his profound sincerity and his great concern for the welfare of the young men. The scene of Demea and Hegio continues this characterization and serves to inform Demea concerning the affair of Aeschinus and Pamphila. Its connection with the action of the plot, however, is only superficial. One of the ironic aspects of Demea's character is that he is continuously busy trying to straighten out affairs but actually never accomplishes anything. Indeed, despite his opinion to the contrary (546), he is usually the last to be correctly informed. So here he undertakes to find Micio and to settle this matter, but he does not succeed in doing either.

The following scenes with Ctesipho, Syrus, and Demea likewise have little to do with the action of the plot. Ctesipho's fear of his father does serve to continue the suspense over his eventual discovery; but far more important is the portrayal of his attitude toward his father—which is one of respectful hatred. Again Syrus amusingly deceives the old man by praising virtues in Ctesipho which do not exist; and again the result carries with it pathos as well as comedy.

Micio now returns with Hegio, and all the difficulties of Aeschinus are solved. But Aeschinus himself does not know this, and hence a delicate irony is thrown over the following scene in which he enters with a true soliloquy expressing his dilemma and his remorse at not having been quite frank with his father. Indeed, the hesitant young man here hardly seems the same person who acted so aggressively in solving the difficulties of his brother Ctesipho; but perhaps his modesty where his own affairs are concerned is sufficient to account for the difference. Though Aeschinus does not prove as honest in his own affairs as Micio had believed him to be, still the relationship of Aeschinus to Micio as here brought out is touchingly affectionate and is far preferable to that of Ctesipho to Demea, which has been so unattractively portrayed in the immediately preceding scenes.

Now that the two sons have been proved in action and the portrait of the two older brothers has been completed, the basic problem is taken up again with the clash of Micio and Demea. But their first scene here is only sparring. Demea must learn the facts concerning Ctesipho, and it is highly desirable that he should learn these for himself in the course of the dramatic action. It is only poetic justice, furthermore, that Ctesipho and Syrus should give themselves away. The effect of this discovery upon Ctesipho is not portrayed, and this omission is indicative of the comparative unimportance of the young men in the play.

Demea, having the moral wind taken out of him by such a blow, is forced to compromise. He grudgingly submits to allowing Ctesipho his youthful foibles. Thus the last complication of the plot is solved; but the play does not end here—indeed, the real climax is yet to come.

For the third time in the play we now have a true soliloquy. This one of Demea corresponds with that of Micio at the opening of the play. Demea reviews his life and finds that it has been somewhat futile. In a way he summarizes the lessons which the action of the play has taught him. Now he decides to change, and he proceeds to do so with a vengeance. This vengeance falls so squarely and so heavily upon Micio that he too in the end is forced to admit that his theories need rectification. Menander is too enlightened to be satisfied with a compromise from only one side. Indeed, after all, perhaps it is Micio who is forced to make the greater concessions; for in the final arrangement Demea resumes his stern dignity, and all admit the desirability of a certain amount of discipline along with timely complacence.

Part Five
ROMAN TRAGEDY

XII

SENECA

LIFE[1]

Lucius Annaeus Seneca, called "the philosopher" to distinguish him from his father, "the rhetor," was born a few years before the Christian era at Cordoba, Spain. He was brought to Rome at an early age and educated in the usual rhetorical manner. He also applied himself to philosophy. Chronically ill, he records that he contemplated suicide but (like Hercules at the end of his *Mad Hercules*) refrained out of consideration for his father.[2] He visited Pompeii and Egypt. Returning to Rome to become an important official, he incurred the enmity of the Emperor Caligula, who was not too mad to characterize the literary style of Seneca most aptly as "all sand and no mortar."[3] Caligula is said to have been restrained from putting Seneca to death only because it seemed obvious that he would soon die of natural causes.

Messalina, wife of Claudius, encompassed Seneca's banishment in A.D. 41 by alleging an affair between him and Julia Livilla, sister of Agrippina and the then dead Caligula. It is usually assumed, however, that political considerations were the real cause of his banishment. Seneca withdrew to Corsica until Agrippina replaced Messalina as the wife of Claudius and had him recalled in A.D. 49 to become praetor and the tutor of her promising young son by another husband. When this son, Nero, thanks to his mother's machinations and crimes, was made emperor in A.D. 54, Seneca and the city prefect Burrus became very powerful and gave the empire excellent government. Maintaining their positions under such a prince, however, was difficult; and with the death of Burrus in A.D. 62 Seneca and his moderation were forced into the background. He had already seen the murder of Claudius, that of the son of Claudius, and finally that of Agrippina herself— "father," "brother," and mother. Now, according to the *Octavia*, Seneca tried to dissuade Nero from putting his wife to death—the role of the dissuading and unsuccessful subaltern that appears so frequently in his tragedies. Not long afterward the conspiracy of Piso was discovered in A.D. 65, and Seneca was forced to commit a Stoic suicide. There is no evidence that he had any connection with the plot, but some thought that he was to become emperor if the plot succeeded.

Seneca, then, was a man of the highest social, political, and economic status. He early distinguished himself in literature, as his father had done in rhetoric, and he left an impressively large body of writings. Much of this has survived to make him the most influential Latin prose writer after Cicero. His primary interest was clearly moral philosophy; but his activity in letters, as in business, extended far and wide. Among his lost works was one on the geography of India, one on the form and one on the movement of the earth. These, like his extant work entitled *Natural Questions,* are noteworthy here because the scientific interests which they reveal are observable in his tragedies.

Nine tragedies of Seneca have been preserved. These are all written on the conventional Greek tragic subjects. Influence of intermediate adaptations, sometimes demonstrable, may be assumed in most cases, and always Seneca has himself made important changes that are apparently original. In general, however, five of his tragedies are modeled primarily after Euripides (the *Mad Hercules,* the *Trojan Women,* the *Phoenician Women,* the *Medea,* and the *Phaedra*), two after Sophocles (the *Oedipus* and the *Hercules on Oeta* [*Trachiniae*]), and one after Aeschylus (the *Agamemnon*). Seneca's *Thyestes* is the only tragedy for which no corresponding Greek original has survived.

A tenth play, the *Octavia,* is preserved. This tragedy concerns a contemporary historical situation and presents Seneca himself as an important character. For various reasons it is often assumed that this play was written after the death of both Seneca and Nero.

TRAGEDY UNDER SENECA

The leap from Greek tragedy to Seneca is one of almost five hundred eventful years. Of the extensive corpus of tragedies produced in both Greece and Italy during this period, however, only a series of names and titles and a few hundred short fragments have survived. Probably one Greek play, the *Rhesus,* also belongs to this period. In the field of tragedy changes were certainly enormous, but no approach to an adequate picture can be obtained. One point of interest in connection with Seneca may be mentioned: "philosophical" tragedy not designed for production in the theater seems occasionally to have been written.[4]

Turning to Seneca's tragedies from the extant Greek plays, we appear to be on familiar ground. The same old subject material is being mulled over once more: Oedipus and Agamemnon are still stamping across the scene. If we are satisfied with this first appearance, or if we insist upon absolute literary criteria, we shall find the plays of Seneca so far inferior to the Greek tragedies that we may be tempted to view the Roman plays as the worthless product of an incompetent writer.

Judged by the criteria of Aristotle, however, some of the plays of Shakespeare himself would come off poorly. The comparison of Seneca's plays with the very best Greek masterpieces is likely to obscure more than it reveals unless designed primarily to discover the intent of Seneca in making his changes. Such comparison is so obvious, furthermore, that one never thinks of comparing Seneca's best with the only other plays that have survived from this half-millennium, the *Rhesus* and the *Octavia,* to which either Seneca's *Trojan Women* or his *Phaedra* is much superior. Critics forget, also, that many Senecan faults are found in plays such as the *Rhesus* or Euripides' *Orestes.*[5]

It is unnecessary here to point out all the respects in which the Greeks wrote better Greek tragedies. Certainly if Seneca's purpose had been to imitate the Greeks of the fifth century, a man with far less talent could have done a much more competent job. Nor is it likely that one who was such a competent writer in other fields should continue writing tragedy unless he felt that he was achieving his purpose, or that he would be so conceitedly prejudiced that he could not perceive something of the true qualities of his work. The inevitable conclusion is that most critics condemn Seneca for not doing what he never had the slightest intention of doing. Actually his plays are vastly different from the Greek tragedies of the fifth century, though they are doubtless not masterpieces judged by any standard. His strong personality has left its impress on every phase of them, and they are thoroughly Roman productions.

The primary purpose of Seneca in writing his tragedies is one of the most disputed problems in classical drama. Any attempt at a satisfactory solution, therefore, must be conjectural. The various interests of Seneca can be determined from his tragedies, from his other writings, and perhaps from a knowledge of his life. Obviously the plays must be interpreted in the light of these interests, more so with Seneca than with the previous classical dramatists. These were all practical men of the theater or at least had intimate contact with actual production. They were all professional dramatists in the best sense of that term. But Seneca was not. Most critics would call him a dilettante. His tragedies are marked not so much by the superficiality of the dilettante, however, as by the disproportion of the amateur. The perfection of the artistic whole is sacrificed to the author's special interests. This characteristic is a vice which he shared with many in a nervous and intellectually chaotic age. These special interests of Seneca, furthermore, were sometimes incompatible with dramatic effectiveness.

Several of Seneca's interests have a tinge of pedantry. He is inordinately fond of detailed geographical descriptions. The Romans of his day had achieved a far larger world than any previous people, and they were conscious and justifiably proud of this. Even now it is thrilling to read Seneca's references to the antipodes or his prediction of the discovery of America in the *Medea* (375–79). Such a bold stretch of the human imagination, though anticipated by others, is undeniably admirable. His detailed catalogue of the districts of Attica at the opening of the *Phaedra,* however, must have been almost as boring to the Roman as it is to the modern reader. Many another catalogue is equally so, as are his lists of hunting dogs and his series of rare wild animals. He could well have been more sparing also with his vast mythological lore—his plays require a far more detailed knowledge of Greek legends than the Greek tragedies do.

All critics recognize one interest and one effect consistently achieved in Seneca's tragedies: rhetorical display. Brilliant sophistic argument, arresting epigrammatic point, vivid description of sensational events —these qualities were highly prized in Seneca's day, and these he achieved undeniably well. It is often concluded, therefore, that the tragedies were designed merely as a vehicle for this rhetorical display and that they were written not for actual production but for reading.[6] Still we should not be too ready to assume that a man of Seneca's stature—history and his other writings prove that this was not small— should indulge in mere display and should write tragedies as a schoolboy's exercise.

The question of production is an old and still hotly disputed one. There is no external proof that any of his plays were ever produced. Most critics who analyze from the point of view of Greek tragedy and Roman rhetoric are convinced that the plays were written for reading or recitation. The extreme violence of many scenes is cited. Certainly the slaughter which the mad Hercules wreaks would tax modern stagecraft to the utmost—we need not assume that Roman stagecraft of this period was much less skillful.[7] But this slaughter may be enacted behind the scenes. Certainly the assembling of the body of Hippolytus is done on stage, and some critics cite this as a scene impossible of presentation. But the scene at the end of Euripides' *Bacchae,* now lost, may have been almost as gory. In short, there is no proof here.

The strongest indication that the plays were not intended for the theater, in the opinion of the present writer, lies in the minuteness with which the actions of characters on stage are described. When Phaedra rushes up to Hippolytus and faints, for instance, the Nurse does not cry out in a natural fashion and come to her aid; but in the fashion of a medical casebook she describes how Phaedra's body falls lifeless to the ground and how a deathlike pallor spreads over her face. Even plainer are the words of Hippolytus when he is on the point of slaying Phaedra: "See, I have grasped your hair and forced your shameless head back with my left hand . . . . " Though a certain amount of such description is natural in ancient drama where stage directions were not explicitly added, this description is so much commoner in Seneca than in other extant plays that it seems designed to replace the action of the real theater.[8] The assumption that the plays were not written for production appears attractive, therefore; but it is by no means proved, and the plays should be read without prejudice on the point.

Certain dramatic qualities are sadly lacking in the plays of Seneca, especially dramatic action. This is most clearly brought out by a comparison of the number of scenes in the extant tragedies. The seven plays of Aeschylus have an average of approximately eight and one-half scenes each, the plays of Sophocles and Euripides fifteen scenes, and those of Seneca approximately nine scenes.[9] Seneca is careless of motivation of entrances and exits, realistic dialogue, preparation for subsequent events, and the various other details of technique which the Greek masters had developed to such perfection. The plays tend to seem collections of scenes, therefore, rather than dramatically articulated units. Often action is managed awkwardly. Medea calls for her children who are within the house, and one line later they seem to be standing before her awaiting her orders. Such unnatural, schematic action is characteristic of the informality of Old Comedy. Still more important, the characters often are implausibly or desultorily presented, unity of subject seems to be violated by apparently extraneous material, and the plays usually open on such a shrill note of horror that no opportunity remains for an effective reversal of fortune.

In contrast to these various undramatic features, extremely theatrical and spectacular scenes are not infrequent. The opening scene of the *Phaedra* seems to be designed as colorful pageantry—thoroughly according to the Roman tradition of overelaborate stage effects.[10] The scene between Andromache and Ulysses in the *Trojan Women* is splendid theater. So is the scene between Phaedra and Hippolytus. Many of the final scenes, however horrible, are eminently spectacular.

That rhetorical display is one of Seneca's most striking characteristics is obvious; but sometimes it may serve as a means to a less obvious end. The first choral song of the *Phaedra*, for instance, is pertinent to the situation and its poetry would be very acceptable if the whole passage did not end with the point that love overcomes even a stepmother. Again Hippolytus, delivering a fine Stoic speech excoriating civilized man and his crimes, cites all sorts of crime within the family except the crimes of the stepmother. It would be unfair, he intimates, to argue from such an extreme and indisputable example. But this seems a jarring note in his characterization; for hitherto Hippolytus has revealed no prejudice or cause for such at least against his own stepmother, and in the ensuing scene with her he seems to have no prejudice.[11] Consistency of character appears here to have been sacrificed to rhetorical point. But many sententious pronouncements on stepmothers are found in this tragedy of Seneca as in several others, and although the stepmother theme was a rhetorical commonplace we must consider the possibility that Seneca was interested not primarily in rhetorical display but in stepmothers. Nor is this alternative as ridiculous as it at first seems; for the mother of the Emperor Nero as a stepmother had run the gamut of crimes, and this theme is very properly an important one in the historical tragedy *Octavia.*

The theme of the tyrant is even more frequent in Seneca. Those speeches in which the Nurse tries to dissuade Phaedra from pursuing Hippolytus, for instance, read like a lecture of Seneca to his pupil Nero urging him not to embark upon a career of crime. "I am not unaware," she says (136–39), "how unwilling to be guided to an honorable course is royal pride, callous and unaccustomed to the truth. But I shall bear whatever fate may chance to be mine; courage is given to one who is old by the thought that death soon will bring freedom." Unfortunately, however, this play like all the others cannot be dated.[12] The assumption of any reference to the ruling family, therefore, is purely conjectural.

The use of drama as more or less subtle political criticism had a long tradition in Rome.[13] Extended allegory was not necessary; a single line even of an old play was often interpreted in the light of contemporary events and greeted with applause or hissing. During the time of Seneca, when the tyrannies of the emperors made open criticism of political policies extremely dangerous, all genres of literature were used for covert criticism. A certain Cremutius Cordus wrote a history in order, perhaps, to praise Brutus and to call Cassius "the last of the Romans." Cordus was forced to commit suicide. Another contemporary of Seneca, Curiatius Maternus, wrote tragedies with a political purpose and sometimes on Roman historical figures. These were publicly read by the author and were apparently not intended for production in the theater.[14] One of the men under whom Seneca in his youth mastered rhetoric, Mamercus Aemilius Scaurus, is said to have incurred the wrath of the Emperor Tiberius by writing a tragedy, *Atreus,* in which a commonplace from Euripides' *Phoenissae* (393) was included —"One must bear the follies of his rulers."[15]

Every play of Seneca has somewhat similar lines. It is not inconceivable that Seneca, though no extremist, should write a whole play for one well-placed line of this type. The subject material of Greek tragedy was ideal for such application. The more commonplace a theme might be there or in contemporary rhetoric, such as the theme of the tyrant or that of the stepmother, the safer the author would feel in dwelling upon it; and the audience would doubtless be no less keen in applying it where it seemed most apposite in the contemporary situation. That Seneca had a political purpose in writing his tragedies, therefore, is an easily conceivable, though at present not widely accepted, hypothesis.

Inextricably bound up with a possible political end are Seneca's very certain moral and philosophical interests. The inevitability that one dreadful crime will lead to another, for instance, is an obvious theme in the *Thyestes* and the *Agamemnon,* and indeed this is the theme of Aeschylus himself in his trilogy on Orestes. Not only interpretation of the legends is affected by philosophical concepts but portrayal of characters also, the choral lyrics, the action, and perhaps even the form of the play. If crime must lead to crime, then the individual characteristics of those who come late in the vicious cycle do not determine the course of events and so need not be dwelt upon. Indeed, if determinism is accepted, then tragedy of character becomes meaningless. Perhaps this in part is the explanation of the very desultory treatment which is given the character of Oedipus or that of Clytemnestra.

Many of Seneca's figures are almost ideal Stoics. Even his women and children face disaster and die with a fortitude which may well stifle pathos and preclude dramatic effectiveness. The choral lyrics, where intensity of feeling is most desirable, are emotionally reserved. Such stringent inhibition of the softer emotions results in a lack of genuine pathos in Seneca's plays—perhaps their one greatest shortcoming.

Violent emotions and their outrageous crimes, however, are most frequent and constitute another obvious special interest of Seneca. His portrait of Medea is not, like that of Euripides, a detailed psychological study of a more or less normal woman driven by a series of events to abnormal crime. It is rather a livid exaggeration of the conventional barbaric sorceress. His motive is apparently not to explain an abnormal action but to display a sensational figure who is more than abnormal from the first line of the play. He deliberately strives to create a climax that is fantastically horrible; and no one will deny that he succeeds.

Closely allied with Seneca's interest in the horrible is his enthusiasm for the mystic.[16] This appears superficially in rites of magic, ghosts, and concern with the underworld. The pathetic fallacy, also, is carried to mystical lengths. The whole cosmos reacts to the crime of Atreus. But these external manifestations are merely the dark background for the mysticism of man's own soul. Thyestes is overwhelmed with the consciousness of his guilt (*Thyestes* 513), and an inexplicable premonition of ill chokes his enjoyment of the banquet. Even more significant is the obsession of death which many Senecan characters display. This obsession was the author's own, as may be observed also in his prose works—and justifiably so, for his health was extremely delicate and, in an age precarious for all of his class, he lived in unusually close and dangerous relation to the tyrannical emperors. In his tragedies death is at once the ultimate of the horrible and the supreme release from toil and suffering.[17] This avid mysticism and obsession of death is the intellectual ground that later proved so fertile a seed plot for Christianity.

Seneca has chosen his material with a keen regard for his special interests. There must be no romantic recognitions and no sweetness— no *Alcestis* or *Iphigenia in Tauris*. All his plays with the possible exception of the mystic *Hercules on Oeta* are tragedies in the modern sense of that word. All are filled with the qualities for which he was famous in the Renaissance—*atrocitas, gravitas, maiestas*.[18] The Greeks of the fifth century were the youths—eternal youths—of the ancient world; Seneca was its disillusioned old age.

Interpreted as expressions of his intellectual interests, we conclude, the tragedies of Seneca are successful productions. The author was a serious thinker and an eloquent writer despite his many faults. He was not a great dramatist and made no attempt to be; but his plays have certain dramatic virtues, and their historical importance as drama has been tremendous. Largely neglected in ancient and in medieval times, they emerged in the fourteenth century as the only well-known classical tragedy, and their rule over Italian and French drama continued for many centuries.[19] In the England of Shakespeare's day, too, they were immensely popular. Nor should we be too ready to deplore history's preference for Seneca, because of his language, above the Greeks. His intellectual outlook, like his language, was a part of the immediate tradition of Italy and France: the Greeks were essentially foreign. Even as drama, Greek tragedy with its chorus and with its Greek divinities, though vastly superior, could never have been so readily and so thoroughly assimilated.[20]

Structure.—By the time of Seneca, dramatists as well as critics seem to have approved the rule of five acts, for all his plays except possibly the *Oedipus* have four divisional choral songs.[21] The rule of three speaking characters, too, is observed, though some scenes, as that at the end of the *Agamemnon*, would require four actors. The unities of time and place are normally respected. A change of scene, however, seems to occur in the *Hercules on Oeta* and possibly elsewhere. The background of the *Medea*, furthermore, seems vague and uncertain. Strict unity of subject is often sacrificed to the author's peculiar interests.

In metrical usage Seneca is conservative. His characters almost invariably speak in simple iambic verse. Three short passages in trochaic verse of seven and one-half feet occur. Occasionally a character, such as Hecuba at the opening of the *Trojan Women*, is given anapestic or other lyric measure. The choral meters are monotonously simple.

The tragedy often begins with a monologue-prologue delivered by the main character. This form is doubtless descended from the Euripidean prologue; but Seneca does not use it primarily for purposes of exposition. Indeed, lack of adequate exposition is a typical feature of a Senecan play. One can hardly avoid the impression that the audience and even the characters themselves are thoroughly acquainted with their past, present, and future before the action begins. Any exposition given often appears inevitable or fortuitous. The Senecan prologue is normally used to create the mood of the play, and this mood is frequently that of horror. A dire note is struck at the very first and is maintained throughout. The prologue may develop into a semblance of a dialogue, but usually it constitutes the whole first act. Ghosts and spirits are used twice in prologues and a major divinity is used once.

The chorus in Seneca is primarily an interlude. It is sometimes withdrawn after a lyric, as apparently in earlier Roman tragedy, but again it may remain on stage and even engage in conversation with a messenger or some character. This is rare, however, and occurs only when no other speaking character is on stage.[22] Sometimes two different choruses are used. In the *Agamemnon,* for instance, a group of Trojan captives constitutes the second chorus. The lyrics themselves occasionally rise to poetic heights of real beauty, but too often they are pedestrian. A distinct effort is still made to give them at least a superficial connection with the action. In general, however, little of the Greek subtlety in adapting the chorus to the needs of the play can be observed, and it is regrettable that the chorus was not wholly eliminated.

The absence of an organic chorus creates certain difficulties of staging to which Seneca is not wholly impervious. On the huge Roman stage, as in Roman comedy, the entrance of a character in mid-scene becomes a distinct problem. Such entrances are accompanied by a soliloquy, which is often an aside. Asides are not unnatural under these conditions, and they are accordingly much more common than in Greek tragedy. Such soliloquies are employed to reveal information which it might be difficult to convey in the ensuing dialogue. Indeed, Seneca is inordinately fond of soliloquies of every type.

Usually at the beginning of the second act the dramatic action is initiated. Frequently this takes the form of a subaltern's attempting to deter the main character from crime. Such a scene is designed, of course, to bring out the criminal determination of the main character. The entrance of a new character may develop a complication. The act usually ends with the formation of a definite criminal plan.

The third act, as in the *Thyestes,* may be given over to the presentation of the victim and may end with his entrapment. The fourth act may give a description of the catastrophe and the fifth a vivid illustration of it. Normally there is no sharply marked peripety or any strong emotional contrast between the opening and the close of the action. The situation is very bad at the beginning, and it rapidly becomes much worse.

Seneca uses no *deus ex machina,* unless the appearance of Hercules at the end of the *Hercules on Oeta* can be called such. Far from having any prejudice against violent deeds on stage, he delights in making his finale fantastically horrible and bloody. So we see Jocasta stab herself in her "capacious womb," and so we hear the thud of the bodies of Medea's children as she flings them from the housetop.

1. *MAD HERCULES (HERCULES FURENS)*

The *Mad Hercules* shows many dramatic faults and much overdone rhetoric, but individual scenes in it are very impressive. The subject doubtless made a strong appeal to Seneca for several reasons. It is perfectly adapted to the themes of the stepmother and the tyrant. Both these were dear to his heart, and they furnish some of his finest rhetorical effects. "No greater victim can be sacrificed to Jupiter and no richer one than a king who is unjust," says Hercules as he is about to sacrifice while his hands still drip the blood of Lycus.[28] Effective also is Hercules' apostrophe to his own hands as the tools of his stepmother (1236). The fantastic exaggeration of his labors also must have teased the imagination of Seneca, and the long description of the underworld is well fitted to serve both moralist and rhetorician. Seneca obviously took delight also in depicting the growing frenzy of Juno and especially the seizure of Hercules—a magnificent scene. Still more attractive perhaps was the contemplation of the sufferings of this Stoic saint which so clearly emphasize Fortune's envy of virtue and her ironic fickleness in bestowing her favors (esp. 524–32).

Sources.—Euripides introduced this subject into tragedy in his still extant *Heracles;* and, though there were later Greek versions and perhaps one Roman adaptation, Seneca seems to have followed the original

play.[24] The incidents, at least, are the same, but fundamental changes in treatment and interpretation have been made. Since these affected every part of the play they may best be noted in the general consideration.
Discussion.—Seneca has added a conventional prologue spoken by Juno. Her catalogue of the various loves of Jupiter and their mementos in the sky seems a little ridiculous but is a part of the stepmother theme. More important is her recitation of the great accomplishments of Hercules and her great anger at his success.[25] Finally, raising her voice to the screech of hysteria, she foretells his madness and adumbrates its results. Thus the loud note of horror which usually characterizes the opening of a Senecan tragedy is here clearly sounded.

Another effect of the prologue is even more important.[26] The foreknowledge here imparted casts a shade of irony upon the glory of Hercules' return, and thus Euripides' magnificent contrast between the returning hero and the murderer of wife and children is largely lost. No such contrast really exists in the life of Hercules as Seneca presents it. All has been and still remains a titanic struggle against a superior power.[27] The climax of this struggle and Hercules' inevitable ruin is the subject of Seneca's tragedy. In the prologue and throughout the play the fantastic exaggeration of Hercules' accomplishments raises the hero so far above human accomplishment that he loses much of his human appeal. But he gains the superhuman stature requisite for contest with divinity. Juno's prologue, therefore, serves the Senecan interpretation of Hercules well, however far this may be from the Aristotelian concept of the most effective tragic character. The prologue also concentrates attention upon Hercules alone, whereas the opening of Euripides' play emphasizes the plight of his family.

As an explanation of Hercules' madness, Juno's conventional prologue replaces the very unconventional scene of Iris and Lyssa in the center of Euripides' play. The elimination of that scene allows the gradual seizure of Hercules to be depicted on stage without supernatural interference in its presentation. But while Iris and Lyssa poetically symbolize the madness which at that moment is at work within the palace, Juno's prologue, though ending on the pitch of frenzy, comes long before the actual madness and is immediately followed by the chorus' idyllic description of dawn and Stoic praise of the simple life!

The second act begins in no less declamatory fashion than the prologue. Amphitryon now prays for relief from misfortune and holds forth on the eleven previous labors—the securing of Cerberus is still in progress—for some seventy-five verses, and Megara closes the series with a mere thirty on much the same subject. Both invoke Hercules as if he were a god. Thus the first three hundred and eight verses pass in only four units. This disturbingly awkward opening is caused by Seneca's failure to recast the first of his play—or rather the first of Euripides' play—after he has added the prologue by Juno. The endless repetition of the labors has its justification—emphasis on the endless struggle which Hercules' life has been. The effect is well designed, therefore, but it is not well executed. The repetition is too monotonous and boring.

The scene with Lycus, except for the further intrusion of the labors, is far better. Seneca gives the tyrant the very plausible motivation of wishing to marry Megara in order to make his reign a more legitimate one. This is an improvement over Euripides, designed no doubt to facilitate Seneca's theme of the tyrant. If the play was written during the reign of Nero, however, it was an obvious motivation; for Nero himself had a somewhat similar reason for marrying Octavia, the daughter of Claudius. Nero's relation to Octavia also was somewhat similar, for Claudius and his son were to be or had been murdered for the benefit of Nero, and according to Seneca he who derives the benefit from a crime is the guilty party.[28] After Lycus has withdrawn, Amphitryon at the end of the scene foresees the return of Hercules.

The labors are now once more attempted, this time by the chorus, and special emphasis is given the return from the underworld. Following their fanfare, Hercules appears. After an entrance monologue in which he boasts of his triumph over death, he hears of Lycus' outrages and immediately goes off to slay him. He has shown no tenderness in greeting wife and children; and, since Theseus has entered with him as a speaking character, Megara can say nothing if the rule of three speaking actors is to be maintained. Thus one of the most pathetic episodes of Euripides' play is eliminated. But this is consistent with Seneca's procedure; for he makes no effort to humanize Hercules, at least before the climax, and Megara and the children are carefully kept in the background throughout.

Theseus has been brought on with Hercules in order, no doubt, that he may declaim on the underworld and Hercules' accomplishments there. This description enables the author to bring out the Stoic conception of retribution after death and to apply it especially to the tyrant. Such a conception is a natural counterpart or consolation for a view of life as a laborious and finally unsuccessful struggle, but no effort is made to bring out this connection with the theme of the play and so to justify the inclusion of the scene. Theseus' description itself, of course, is sensational and colorful.

Dramatically Theseus' entrance with Hercules is very plausible and avoids the abruptness of his appearance later, as in Euripides. But this advantage is small gain and apparently involves the extreme inconvenience of removing him at the climax when Hercules is about to slaughter wife and children. After a choral song contemplating the underworld and death but ending on an ironically joyful note concerning the success of Hercules, the hero returns with the blood of Lycus upon his hands. As he prepares to sacrifice in spite of this defilement, the madness gradually comes over him. The actual presentation of this scene has been made possible by having Lycus slain somewhere off stage and not trapped within the palace as in Euripides. This, too, is a distinct gain for Seneca, but precisely how the following carnage could have been portrayed in the theater is quite uncertain.[29] Some assume that it was not designed ever to be portrayed, others that the carnage takes place behind the scenes while Amphitryon views and reports it. Amphitryon's detailed description does not necessarily decide the matter, for contemporary action on stage is often so described in Seneca. The seizure itself is plausibly managed and does not include those manifestations which the comic poets considered a little puerile and ridiculous in Euripides.[30]

After a choral lyric of grief that is too rhetorical to be very effective, Hercules awakens, and through his own deductions he is made to realize what he has done. His gradual enlightenment and his desire to die are depicted with genuine pathos. He is finally persuaded to live, not so much by Theseus' exhortation to withstand adversity, the prime consideration in Euripides, as by Amphitryon's appeal to filial piety. This, too, is as we should expect in Seneca, where suicide is often praised as the one escape from misfortune.

2. *TROJAN WOMEN (TROADES)*

The *Trojan Women* has often been considered the best of Seneca's plays. It is certainly an impressive spectacle of the mutability of fortune, the woes of the vanquished, and the insolence of the victorious. The whole is overcast by the irony of the victors' own coming destruction. The outlook of the play, then, is similar to that of the *Trojan Women* of Euripides; so is the structure, which achieves a certain unity of tone and theme even though the two main incidents of the play are only superficially connected. The scene between Andromache and Ulysses, an important source for Racine, is brilliantly written and would doubtless be very effective in any theater. On the whole, however, the play lacks that consummate finish of dramatic technique which usually characterizes Greek tragedies.

Sources.—The murder of Astyanax and the grief of Andromache

form one of the main episodes in Euripides' *Trojan Women*. The death of Polyxena is an important part of his *Hecuba*. Seneca follows the main outlines of Euripides in relating these events, and distinct echoes of both plays are found; but major changes have been made. The question of sacrificing Polyxena is here made the subject of a spirited and dramatic debate; Andromache has a premonition of the danger and hides Astyanax in Hector's tomb, but eventually she is forced by the crafty Ulysses to reveal his whereabouts. This hiding of Astyanax occurred also in a Latin tragedy of Accius entitled *Astyanax*, in which also Calchas seems to have motivated the murder.[31] But the use of the tomb of Hector for this, considered fantastic by some critics,[32] may be original with Seneca.

Various other important changes have been made: Hecuba is not the center of Seneca's play; more speaking characters are brought on stage; the choral songs though effective do not have the beauty or depth of pathos of those in Euripides. Seneca's play may well be the product of contamination, since this combination of Astyanax and Polyxena is not known to have occurred in any previous play.

Various other plays may have been drawn upon for details. Sophocles wrote a *Polyxena* and also a *Captive Women* (*Aichmalotides*), which may possibly have covered some of the same material as Euripides' *Trojan Women*. Accius wrote a *Hecuba* and apparently a *Trojan Women* besides the *Astyanax* just mentioned. Still other plays had been written on these subjects in both Greek and Latin.

Discussion.—Hecuba, at once the most venerable and the most pathetic survivor of the destruction of Troy, opens and closes the play. Her prologue emphasizes the mutability of fortune, the sacrilegious violence of the conquerors, and the enslavement awaiting the women. These thoughts very naturally develop into an antiphony between her and the chorus, which contains genuine tears for the dead and for the even more unfortunate living. Emotionally, this is an effective opening of the play. From the dramatic point of view, however, we should have expected some significant reference to Polyxena, Andromache, and Astyanax, the characters about whom the main incidents of the play devolve. Actually Hecuba twice refers to Cassandra, who does not appear as a character in the play. At the end of this lyric exchange, furthermore, Hecuba very ineffectively withdraws (or becomes silent).

The Herald now comes on for a more typical Senecan prologue of horror reporting the appearance of the ghost of Achilles. Since the Herald immediately departs when his report is given, his speech also has that detachment which usually characterizes a Senecan prologue. The creation of Senecan atmosphere is doubtless the main purpose of this sensational speech, for the information which it gives could easily have been worked into the conversation between Pyrrhus and Agamemnon.

Agamemnon here, reminiscent of the Agamemnon of Euripides' *Hecuba*, is a very cautious and restrained conqueror. He is keenly aware that the Greeks have gone to excesses and that the momentary whim of fortune is just as formidable as an armada of a thousand ships or a struggle of ten long years. Indeed he forebodes the disasters which actually overtake the Greeks and himself. Thus the ominous theme of Hecuba's prologue is elaborated to cast a grim irony over the present insolence of the victors. With such farsighted Stoic characters, Seneca's play has no need of a divine prelude like that of Euripides' *Trojan Women*. This substitution of vague human foreboding for supernatural explicitness might be considered a distinct improvement.

The quarrel between Pyrrhus and Agamemnon over the sacrifice of Polyxena begins with long and comparatively restrained speeches. But it soon develops into a rapid and excited contest of abuse which is one of the most dramatic dialogues in Seneca. Finally Calchas is called in to settle the matter like a *deus ex machina*. All critics have laid the severest strictures upon the abruptness here, and perhaps this, like the appearance of the children in the *Medea* (845), is another example of that dramatic awkwardness which is not infrequent in Seneca. Still this scene could be staged very effectively by having Calchas and various other figures enter along with Pyrrhus and Agamemnon at the beginning of the scene. The sacred insignia would clearly mark out the priest who sacrificed Iphigenia. He would stand by ominously silent and contemptuously superior to this futile logomachy over reason and justice —the priest waiting for the kings to appeal to him as he knows they eventually must. The end of this act is admittedly abrupt, but Agamemnon can say nothing after Calchas' pronouncement ex cathedra.

The pronouncement of Calchas not only settles the dispute over Polyxena; the fate of Astyanax, also, is brusquely determined in three short lines.[33] Thus the action of the remainder of the play is foretold. The following chorus on death as the end of all is not inapposite, and this pagan conviction is here expressed with depressing certainty.

The third act is masterly. The appearance of the ghost of Hector to Andromache, corresponding to that of the ghost of Achilles to the Greeks, is well conceived. Andromache's finding the features of her dead husband in the face of her son is both moving and significant for the dilemma which she is soon to have thrust upon her.[34] The genuine pathos here and the obviously inevitable tragic outcome prevent any semblance of melodrama in the spectacular scene with Ulysses. Andromache's turmoil of spirit is depicted with keen psychological insight, though the incoherency of her lines is sometimes destroyed by benighted modern editors. In these scenes, furthermore, Seneca has placed at least some restraint upon his inveterate fondness for rhetorical effect.[35]

In the ensuing lyric the chorus contemplate to what homes they may be taken in Greece. This adaptation of a Euripidean choral theme is not well done, but the suggestion of imminent departure is effective.

The fourth act moves rapidly but lacks the brilliance of the third. Andromache's wrangling with Helen immediately after Astyanax has been taken off to die detracts from the pathos of her suffering. Euripides chose the wiser course when he allowed her to make her final exit along with Astyanax, for anything that she can say after this must appear anticlimactic. Nor is the defense of Helen really pertinent to this scene, although the pity of an enemy adds to the pathetic tragedy of Polyxena. Significant for the play as a whole, however, is the resumption of the theme of the destruction to be visited upon the Greeks. Hecuba prophesies woes for Ulysses (994), and prays that the seas may be as savage to the Greeks as the Greeks are to their suppliants (1006).

The fifth act combines the stories of Astyanax and Polyxena, but only in an external fashion. The speech of the Messenger must be divided between these two unrelated events—a division not characteristic of messenger speeches in Greek tragedy—and the resultant awkwardness is aggravated by the Messenger's offering a choice as to whose misfortune he should relate first. Incidentally both Astyanax and Polyxena die like Stoics. The play ends effectively with Hecuba's ironic *propempticon* to the Greeks amounting to a curse and a prophecy that the sea will give them the welcome which they deserve.

3. *PHOENICIAN WOMEN (PHOENISSAE)*

Scholars have not agreed on an explanation of the scenes preserved under this title. Perhaps they are mere independent studies; perhaps they are parts of a complete or projected tragedy.

Doubtless Euripides' *Phoenissae* was Seneca's chief model. That play was one of the most famous of all Greek tragedies and contained perhaps the most widely known discussion of tyranny in classical literature. It was a dangerous play during Seneca's day, as Mamercus Scaurus, his contemporary and one of his rhetorical models, had discovered under Tiberius.[36] The general subject had been treated in various other Greek and Roman tragedies, including Sophocles' *Oedipus at Colonus,* and in epic verse. The Roman historical legend of Coriolanus as related in Livy (2. 39–40) may well have contributed to the scene with Jocasta.[37]

The first scene is one between Oedipus and Antigone. Oedipus asks that he be allowed to go the way which, even in his blindness, he will find more easily alone—the way of death. But Antigone replies that she will never leave him. Incidentally she reveals that Polynices is leading his army against Thebes, and that Jocasta is still alive.[38] This conversation develops into a Senecan discussion of suicide somewhat like that in the *Mad Hercules*.

The scenes with Jocasta either include a change of locale from Thebes to the battleground or else Jocasta leads the brothers on stage in a unique manner. Here Jocasta does most of the talking, making a passionate appeal especially to Polynices and ending on the Senecan theme of the folly of kinghood. The attitudes of the two brothers are much the same as in Euripides.

4. *MEDEA*

This is a tragedy of revenge written with special emphasis upon the inhuman fury and weird sorcery of a barbaric Medea. Indeed this play is an important source of knowledge of ancient magic, and a comparison with the witches' scenes in *Macbeth* is sufficient to prove that in literature, at least, ancient magic was not so very different from modern.

Sources.—The story of Medea was one of the most popular among both Greek and Latin dramatists, and it was treated in various other genres as well. Especially famous in Latin literature was the tragedy which the brilliant young Ovid wrote. Seneca, an admirer of Ovid,[39] seems to have been influenced considerably by that play as he doubtless was by still other treatments.[40]

The plot of Seneca's play, however, is essentially that of the *Medea* of Euripides; and doubtless this famous masterpiece was his chief source and model. But fundamental changes, as usually in Seneca, have been made in the characters and tone of the play, and much of its dramatic action has been deleted. Aegeus and the Paedagogus are eliminated. Jason appears only twice; and he is very different from the Jason of Euripides. Here he is weaker, more ingenuous, and more appealing. He has been forced into the marriage; and his entreaties alone, as Creon himself reveals, have saved Medea from being put to death. Jason here is also extremely fond of his children. Indeed, he insists that he chose submission to Creon rather than death only in order to save his sons. In part this more human portrayal of Jason is designed to bring out the inhumanity of Seneca's Medea; for whereas

Euripides' great achievement had been to make Medea entirely human and understandable, Seneca deliberately presents her as a fantastic exaggeration of that barbaric sorceress which she is normally represented as being in ancient literature.

Discussion.—Medea herself opens the play with a hysterical monologue. She screeches for vengeance. She prays that death may come upon Creon and his daughter and that life may be made a miserable burden for Jason. She flagellates herself and casts about for a crime worthy of her maturity. Thus is sounded the usual Senecan note of horror. Entirely gone is the careful emotional preparation for the appearance of Medea which the prologue of Euripides' play contains, as well as its vague and uncertain forebodings. Gone too is the effective scene with the children, who do not appear in Seneca's play until they are sent with the poisoned gifts, when they are present for only four lines. All this, of course, is in strict accord with Seneca's desire to present Medea in a very unfavorable but very intense light.

Seneca's chorus, as might be expected, is bitterly opposed to Medea and sympathetic with Jason and their king. So the first choral lyric is a gay song in honor of the marriage which is now to be consummated.

Naturally the strains of this festive song gall Medea and stimulate her to greater fury. She recalls in detail the crimes which she has committed for Jason's sake. Still she is obviously in love with him, as she reveals by her conviction that Creon alone is responsible and by her momentary resolve to take vengeance only upon him. The Nurse makes a desperate attempt to curb Medea's wrath, but this serves merely to reveal her determination more sharply. The next scene with the imperious Creon allows Medea a spirited defense. It also adds direct description of her character and her witchcraft. She is one, says Creon, who combines the natural deceit of a woman with the aggressiveness of a man (267–68). After finally granting her one more day within the realm, Creon hastens off to the marriage—an effective detail.

The chorus deprecates the impious boldness of man in inventing ships and overcoming those barriers which the gods placed between the lands. Medea was worthy freight for the first vessel! Then, by a shocking anachronism, Seneca marvels at the vast extent to which man's ingenuity has expanded the world of his own day, and predicts that in a day to come new continents will be revealed—his famous prediction of the discovery of America.[41]

After her Nurse has described her utter madness, Medea comes on again for more self-flagellation. This soliloquy reveals a hardening of her attitude toward Jason and prepares for his entrance just as her former soliloquy has prepared for the entrance of Creon. The scene with Jason gives Medea another opportunity for a brilliant speech justifying her position and incriminating Jason. But Jason stands up well against all her charges, and the sincerity of his defense has been carefully guaranteed by his entrance monologue as well as by the previous statements of Creon and by the free admissions of Medea. Jason resolutely refuses Medea's plea to return to her and seek life elsewhere. Only at this point does Medea, who has never shown much regard for her children,[42] give up hope of recovering him and begin definitely to plot for a vengeance upon him far worse than that upon Creon. In the course of this scene, when Medea asks that the children be allowed to go with her Jason very naturally reveals his great love for them. Medea immediately realizes where her vengeance upon him can strike deepest. Thus Seneca skillfully works into this scene the main function of Euripides' scene of Medea and Aegeus. Seneca has no other use for that scene, for he is wholly unconcerned with any semblance of a realistic escape at the end of the play. As soon as Jason departs, Medea plunges into a tantrum and announces her plan to send the poisoned gifts.

Remarking the limitless fury of a woman spurned, the chorus ponder the ill fate of those who sailed on the first ship and pray that Jason, their leader, may be spared. So this lyric harks back to the previous choral song and sounds an effectively ominous note.

The scenes of witchery, like the sacrifice and the raising of the ghost in Seneca's *Oedipus,* are essentially a digression. Still they are not so very much out of place here, since Medea's sorcery has been emphasized from the first and an atmosphere of horror and diabolical crime has been consistently maintained.[43] The metrical variation in this scene is noteworthy. She enters with excited trochaics, lists her magical accomplishments in staid iambics (well suited to the realm of facts!), shifts to lyric iambics in making her offerings, and then to anapests for her "prayers." At the end of the scene, which reaches its climax with Medea's barbaric gashing of her own arms, the children are abruptly dispatched with the gifts.

After a short choral lyric describing Medea's fury, a messenger reports the catastrophe. For once Seneca rejects the opportunity of making a long glowing description of horror. Indeed, so short a report is unique in ancient tragedy; but the innovation is as welcome as it has been long awaited. A conventional messenger's speech here, furthermore, would be quite useless, for Medea in her incantation has directed with revolting detail the effects which the gifts are to have upon the bride.[44]

Medea's last soliloquy, in which she finally determines upon the slaughter of her children, is an amazing confusion of natural human emotions, including even remorse, of the mysticism of madness, and of sophistry strained almost to the ridiculous. She wishes that she, like Niobe, had borne fourteen children instead of two in order that her vengeance might be greater! There is here no thought of saving the children from destruction at the hands of her enemies, as in Euripides. Here all is vengeance.

Jason enters with soldiers, coming not to save his children primarily, as in Euripides, but to punish Medea. As Medea has just slain one of her children before the eyes of the audience in order to satisfy the Avenging Furies of her brother, so now, having mounted to the roof of her dwelling, she slays the other before Jason and despite his most abject entreaties. Then she apparently flings the bodies down to him. This ghastly scene is most dramatic and is a fitting climax to a play that from the very first has sounded the note of horror. It is less effective than the final scene in Euripides, because Medea is less human and the children here have never been effectively presented. It is less tragic, too, because the heavy grief that falls upon life, which must go on even after such a catastrophe, is really more tragic than the catastrophe itself. But Seneca has undeniably achieved a harrowing and spectacular finale.

5. *PHAEDRA (HIPPOLYTUS)*[45]

The *Phaedra* is one of Seneca's best plays. His interpretation is very different from that of Euripides in his extant *Hippolytus*. No effort is made to soften the character of Phaedra. This villainess plays the main role of the tragedy, and perhaps Seneca's primary interest lay in the study of her character. There is nothing mystical about Seneca's Hippolytus, who worships Diana as any other huntsman would and who is a more normal human being than the Hippolytus of Euripides, though he does hate women and civilization for various philosophical reasons. The theme of the stepmother is prominent in the play,[46] and it is conceivable that certain passages are directed toward the imperial family.[47]

Source.—Euripides wrote two plays on the story of Phaedra and Hippolytus, of which only the later *Hippolytus Crowned* has been preserved. Seneca's *Phaedra* shows certain similarities to this play but in the main appears to be an adaptation of Euripides' earlier *Hippolytus Veiled*. Several other dramatists, however, are known to have treated the subject. Various lines in Seneca's play, especially in the first scene between Phaedra and her Nurse, loosely correspond to certain fragments of Euripides' earlier play, although it is sometimes assumed that there was no Nurse in that play. Seneca's treatment has many points in common with an imaginary love letter of Phaedra written by Ovid. We know that on some points Ovid is following Euripides' earlier play, and it may be that both Seneca and Ovid are independently following Euripides rather than that Seneca is following Ovid.[48]

Influence.—In his *Phèdre* (1677) Racine used to the best advantage not only Seneca's *Phaedra* but Euripides' extant *Hippolytus* as well. A complete analysis of Racine's indebtedness is beyond the limits of the present consideration,[49] but the following motives may be mentioned as due to Seneca: Phèdre dominates the action throughout the play; the infidelity of Theseus is stressed; Phèdre confesses her love to Hippolytus in person, and her words are at times very close to those of Seneca; Phèdre beseeches the contemptuous Hippolytus to slay her and retains his sword; Phèdre dies on stage after confessing the truth.

The subject has been dramatized also by Gabriele d'Annunzio (*Fedra*, 1909).

Structure.—The play opens with a long passage in anapestic recitative by Hippolytus. Although his catalogues of places, dogs, and animals are elaborated with brilliant pedantry—witness the inclusion of the bison—still this scene could be staged as a colorful and spectacular extravaganza. It is more proper to the pageantry of modern opera, however, than it is to an exposition scene in serious drama. It is wholly a prelude. The lines of Hippolytus do end with a prayer to Diana; but this prayer is no more than that of an ordinary huntsman, and there is not, as in Euripides, any suggestion that Hippolytus is guilty of sacrilege toward Venus. After this prelude, Phaedra comes on with her Nurse. Her languishing complaints strongly contrast with the animal exuberance of Hippolytus and emphasize the gulf between these two. The conversation between Phaedra and the Nurse furnishes the real exposition of the play. Here the Nurse is already acquainted with Phaedra's passion, and the scene consists not of the Nurse's seducing Phaedra, as in Euripides, but of Phaedra's seducing the Nurse.[50] Like a Stoic philosopher the Nurse preaches restraint and continency. She inveighs against royal license. She systematically eliminates every possibility of committing such a crime successfully. But Phaedra will not hear her, and by artfully threatening suicide, mistress bends servant to her will. The Nurse agrees to approach Hippolytus—the first step in the complication—and here the act ends (first act, 273 lines).

The subsequent choral song (84 lines) is strictly pertinent to the situation: love is supreme master of all the world. The poetry of the song is spoiled by the epigram at the end—love overcomes even the savage stepmother.

The second act (378 lines) opens with a realistic description of the manifestations of Phaedra's passion by the Nurse. Phaedra herself comes on, and her words and actions corroborate the description. This scene is reminiscent of the scene between Phaedra and the Nurse in Euripides' extant play; but its function here is somewhat different, for it is preparing for Phaedra's madly throwing herself at Hippolytus and perhaps for her madly taking revenge upon him. The action moves into new ground with the entrance of Hippolytus, who comes on at precisely the most convenient moment. The gross efforts of the Nurse to seduce him to a life of luxurious wantonness only offend him. After the Nurse has failed, Phaedra rushes up to faint in Hippolytus' arms. As she is revived, or pretends to be so, she steels her determination and makes her confession in a brilliantly written scene. She begs Hippolytus not to call her by the name of mother but rather by that of slave. She urges him to take her royal power—and herself. She tries to convince him that his father is dead. In Hippolytus she sees the more ideal Theseus. Finally she throws herself at his feet; but he is frightened and revolted by her crude advances. He abandons his sword and flees as Phaedra pretends to swoon and the Nurse comes to her rescue and calls for help in an effort to save her mistress by indicting Hippolytus.

The second choral song (88 lines) describes the flight of Hippolytus, dwells upon his beauty, and forebodingly suggests that flight will not bring him safety.

The leader of the chorus denounces Phaedra for her false charge and her base artifice. He then introduces Theseus. Theseus enters expressing his great relief at having escaped from Tartarus. He is startled by the sounds of grief. The Nurse appears and abruptly warns him that Phaedra is on the point of suicide. At the command of Theseus the doors of the palace are opened and Phaedra is revealed. But she artfully refuses to confess her secret until Theseus threatens to put the Nurse to torture. Refusing to name Hippolytus, Phaedra indicts him by means of his sword—an effective dramatic gesture. In a long monologue Theseus then calls upon his father Neptune to destroy Hippolytus. This short third act (135 lines) constitutes the climax of the play and practically the reversal of fortune for Hippolytus.

The choral song which follows (30 lines) loftily ponders why the universe is so marvelously controlled but mankind is left to the mere whims of chance. This is a not unnatural reaction to the apparent triumph of the wicked Phaedra and to the ruin of the innocent Hippolytus.

The fourth act (134 lines) consists of the Messenger's report of the destruction of Hippolytus. This strikes the modern reader as too long and too much concerned with the miraculous. Significant description of Hippolytus himself and of the reaction of friends and servants is not as effectively emphasized as in Euripides; but occasional phrases (1005, 1067) do reveal Hippolytus' pathetic admiration for his father. The last choral song (31 lines) opines that Fortune is most likely to strike down the great, as it has struck down Theseus. He has returned from the underworld only to meet even worse calamity in his own house.

The fifth act (127 lines) begins with the appearance of Phaedra. She calls down imprecations upon herself; but her dominant emotion is grief at the death of her beloved Hippolytus. She confesses her guilt and commits suicide. In excited trochaic meter Theseus, overwhelmed with remorse, curses himself in the most extravagant manner. He finally attempts to compose the mangled body of his son and with his last words curses Phaedra.

Discussion.—Structurally Seneca's play is not very different from Euripides' extant *Hippolytus*. Some scenes in the Greek play, however, have no equivalent in the Latin. The divinities of prologue and epilogue have been entirely eliminated. Seneca's play develops wholly on the human level, and he manages to reveal the truth to Theseus without divine revelation—a weak and often criticized device in Euripides' play. In Seneca, furthermore, there is no choral song between the opening scene with Hippolytus and the first appearance of Phaedra. This is awkward. Indeed the whole beginning of this play with its interminable speeches is very poorly managed.

Seneca has added some excellent scenes. That between Phaedra and Hippolytus is the best of these. Its psychology is keen and subtle. Its theatrical effectiveness is equal to almost anything in ancient drama. The scene wherein Phaedra indicts Hippolytus, furthermore, is a brilliant one. Lastly, the scene of Phaedra's confession and suicide is spectacular, though the lack of any effective exchange between Phaedra and Theseus perhaps robs this scene of the dramatic effectiveness which it might be made to possess.[51]

But Seneca has suffered the very serious loss of the scenes between Hippolytus and Theseus which play so important a part in Euripides.

A comparison of one other item of structure in each play is very significant—the "curtain" of the second act. In Euripides' extant play, when Hippolytus denounces Phaedra and flees the scene, Phaedra bursts into a short lyric lament, and this is immediately followed by the scene in which Phaedra dismisses the Nurse as her bane and determines to die in a last resort to save her good name and the honor of her children, and also to punish Hippolytus for his haughty disdain. Thus Euripides at the exit of Hippolytus refuses a spectacular curtain and its consequent suspense. He prefers to end the episode with ominous foreshadowing of the tragedy, but not before he has thoroughly motivated the most dreadful of Phaedra's actions—her denunciation of Hippolytus. Seneca omits this motivation. Here the Nurse hastily forms the plan for denouncing Hippolytus. His act ends so quickly after the departure of Hippolytus that his curtain is a spectacular one, though the suspense has been spoiled by the Nurse's announcement of her plan. Racine, as we might expect, has this spectacular curtain; but he also maintains the greatest suspense by ending his second act before Phaedra has had time to consider her future course.

Phaedra is drawn with great skill.[52] Forced into marriage with a man notorious for mistreatment of his wives, and now deserted and betrayed, she is intensely miserable in her solitude. Small wonder is it, then, that this Phaedra, the undisciplined child of a royal house whose women were distinguished for their worse than licentious conduct, should fall in love with her beautiful stepson. Almost incredibly selfish, this Phaedra shows no hesitation in making known her passion to the Nurse, and she complains only that she does not, like her mother, have the inventive genius of a Daedalus to pander to her desires. She freely admits the criminal nature of such a union, but her moral consciousness is so obtuse that she feels no obligation to struggle against her passion or even to rationalize away its criminal aspect. Madness rules over her, as she herself expresses it (184). She cannot bring herself rationally to consider the possibility of her husband's return or the impossibility of seducing Hippolytus. She is driven by a passion that is reckless of everything but its own desire.

Still, Phaedra maintains enough equilibrium to practice deceit most artfully. She wins over the Nurse to her aid by an apparently insincere resolve to commit suicide. She faints most opportunely in the arms of Hippolytus (cf. 426). She begs Hippolytus to slay her, but this device —if it is device—is unfortunately without result. Seneca has not given Phaedra any expressed motivation for denouncing Hippolytus to Theseus. The Nurse in first suggesting such a course is motivated by the desire to cover their guilt. Perhaps Seneca felt that Phaedra's selfishness and her passionate weakness make further motivation unnecessary, or perhaps this is another instance of Seneca's tendency to write a collection of scenes and not a dramatically articulated play. But Phaedra goes to such extremes of artfulness in her deception of Theseus (cf. 826–28) that she must be considered morally responsible for this course of action even though the Nurse has been the first to suggest it.

In her final scene Phaedra is still the same. She taunts Theseus with his guilt, though this guilt is very slight compared to her own. She commits suicide not so much because of remorse as in a last desperate effort to be with Hippolytus and satisfy her insatiable passion. The final scene has been severely condemned as an atrocious violation of propriety. This gory handling of the limbs of Hippolytus, however, seems to be not so very different externally from the original final scene of Euripides' *Bacchae*. Such matters are largely governed by superficial convention, though it must be admitted that for the modern reader Seneca's scene, far from achieving any great pathos, is revolting.

6. *OEDIPUS*

In his *Oedipus* Seneca appears most interested in presenting the portrait of a tyrant who from first to last was a curse upon his people and who himself was strangely obsessed with a premonition of his dreadful guilt.[53] As a background for this mystic consciousness of sin, all the horror of the play is apposite, and even the callous sensibilities of one who has seen the slaughter of war or gladiatorial combats must be stimulated by this remarkable display. Those of more delicate sensibilities are likely to be repelled by it.

Source.—Seneca follows the main lines of Sophocles' famous tragedy, but his purpose is so very different that the two plays are hardly comparable. His minor details may come from other sources. A host of Greek dramatists had treated the subject, and the young Julius Caesar, also, had taken a fling at it.[54]

Discussion.—Seneca has not only exhausted the natural possibilities of the subject for sensational and dreadful effects. He has introduced extraneous scenes, also, and germane and extraneous alike are strung together by the flimsiest dialogue in order to retain the semblance of a drama. Seneca makes no attempt to construct a logical and inevitable progression of events or to individualize the characters into something more than puppets of fate. Since the career of Oedipus is to be interpreted as an illustration of determinism (980–94), portrayal of character is superfluous for Seneca except that he wishes to present Oedipus as a tyrant obsessed with a consciousness of his guilt. Only the curtest respects, furthermore, are paid to details of dramatic technique. The most difficult problem in dramatizing the material is to avoid the embarrassment of two discoveries. Sophocles accomplished this only by the implausible expedient of identifying the shepherd who exposed Oedipus with the one survivor of Laius' struggle with the "robbers." Seneca has eliminated this implausibility, but he has two discoveries.[55] Jocasta's revelation of the nature of Laius' death convinces Oedipus that he is the murderer.[56] Mechanical haste in bringing

on the Corinthian, however, prevents this untimely climax from becoming disturbingly obvious. But smooth articulation of the dramatic
action also appears to be of little concern for Seneca; it is hardly pertinent to his chief interests.

"Seneca . . . ," we read in the preface of the *Oedipus* of Dryden
and Lee, "as if there were no such thing as nature to be minded in a
play, is always running after pompous expression, pointed sentences,
and philosophical notions, more proper for the study than the stage:
the Frenchman followed a wrong scent; and the Roman was absolutely
at cold hunting." Certainly the material furnishes Seneca an excellent
excuse for delivering Stoic sermons on several of his favorite subjects,
especially the principle that a king who inspires fear must himself be
subject to it—a good theme for Seneca's pupil Nero. The quarrel of
Oedipus and Creon, so nicely prepared for and worked into the progression of events in Sophocles, is here used for this sermon and has no
important effect upon the action.

The play opens with a long soliloquy—though Jocasta may be present—in which Oedipus reveals the horror of his own conscience and his
dark past. The consumption of the plague, also, is dwelt upon. Finally,
another harrowing picture out of Oedipus' past, his clash with the
Sphinx, is presented.

The chorus now continue with a depressingly vivid description of
the plague.

Creon's chilling account of receiving the oracle brings more horror,
and the oracle itself is all too plain. Like several other references, the
oracle foretells the misfortunes of Oedipus' sons as well as those of
the king himself. These references contribute to the general gloom of
the play, but being extraneous they tend to disrupt its logical unity. The
fearful curse which Oedipus pronounces upon the murderer is no less
obvious than the oracle, thus losing the simple and effective irony of
the curse in Sophocles. But the revolting details of an unnatural marriage have been added.

At this point the Sophoclean tradition of events is abandoned in
order to insert the account of the sacrifice. This is gory in the extreme
and doubtless original with Seneca. The bull's fleeing the light of day,
of course, suggests Oedipus' blinding himself, as the manner of the
heifer's death suggests the suicide of Jocasta. The splanchnology, too,
is painfully clear in its application to the house of Oedipus.

Here, perhaps as temporary relief, Seneca has kindly introduced a
choral dithyramb to Bacchus, which constitutes a fine display of geographical erudition.[57]

The dreadful sacrifice leads only to a still more harrowing episode, the exorcism of the ghost of Laius. Returning from this ordeal, Creon is very loath to reveal its results to Oedipus. His reluctance is nicely brought out in the assignment of lines. Oedipus is given precisely two lines and Creon precisely one during several exchanges—a dramatic subtlety used in the opening scene of Aeschylus' *Prometheus.* But of course Creon is eventually brought to his gruesome description. It begins in the best classic manner with an account of the place where the rite was performed. But the best classic manner quickly gives way to more of the magic, the supernatural, and the horrible.

At first glance Seneca would appear to have lost an opportunity for exploiting the horrible by not having Jocasta on stage when the discovery of Oedipus' identity is made, or at least by not portraying her reactions when this point is being approached. In Seneca's version, it is the Corinthian who tries to deter Oedipus from pursuing this knowledge. In Sophocles the Corinthian is characterized by optimistic eagerness, which effectively contrasts with Jocasta's efforts to deter Oedipus and with the reluctance of the shepherd of Laius. In Seneca the loss of Jocasta's reactions is a serious one; but it is apparently necessary, for they must be reserved intact for the final scene.

The Messenger's description of Oedipus' blinding himself is another masterpiece in depicting the horrible. It is almost forgotten, however, after we have seen what Seneca has in store for us and what he can accomplish when he extends himself; for the final scene is horrible beyond all words. Jocasta commits suicide by plunging Oedipus' sword into her "capacious womb,"[58] and the blinded Oedipus seems to stumble over her corpse as he shuffles off into miserable exile.

7. *THYESTES*

The *Thyestes* in its own crude way is a powerful tragedy of revenge. A secondary theme, crime's perpetuation of crime, is given strong emphasis especially in the opening scenes and at the very close of the play. This theme is carried on in the *Agamemnon,* where vengeance for vengeance is foreshadowed. Such a theme was a timely one for the court of Nero. That Emperor had murdered or was soon to murder his stepbrother Britannicus and his own mother, who incidentally had murdered her husband, the Emperor Claudius. Uncertainty as to the dates of these plays, however, precludes any assumption of a definite reference to these contemporary events.

The *Thyestes* surpasses many of Seneca's plays in its technical execution and theatrical qualities. Dramatic dialogue is maintained throughout. Only one iambic speech extends to fifty lines. The dramatic action is straightforward, though it could hardly be otherwise in a plot of such simplicity. The tone, as usually in Seneca, is dire and unrelieved. Great care has been taken to integrate the choral lyrics with the dramatic action, but these are somewhat too long and at times too boring.

Source and influence.—The story of Atreus and Thyestes was one of the most frequently dramatized Greek legends. Sophocles wrote an *Atreus*. We know of some nine Greek plays entitled *Thyestes,* including one tragedy by Euripides and perhaps two by Sophocles. Still other titles were used, such as Euripides' *Cretan Women,* and various phases of this complicated story were covered; but the banquet was its most famous event. Among the Romans this story was easily the most popular for tragedy. Four tragedies entitled *Atreus* and perhaps seven entitled *Thyestes* are known to have been written. These included plays by the masters Ennius and Accius, but most famous of all was the *Thyestes* of Lucius Varius Rufus, the intimate friend of Vergil and Horace, which Quintilian (10. 1. 98) thought comparable to any Greek tragedy.

Only fragments of a few of these Greek and Latin plays have been preserved, however, and they furnish little of interest in connection with Seneca's play. One point is noteworthy: in some versions Thyestes returned of his own accord. Hence Atreus might well be afraid of him and thus be driven to crime. In Seneca, however, Atreus invites the return in order to obtain his vengeance. In any treatment the banquet must have been gory and dreadful.

The *Thyestes,* a model play of revenge, has exerted more influence on English drama than any other play of Seneca.

Discussion.—In form the prelude between Tantalus and the Fury is somewhat reminiscent of various scenes in Greek tragedy, such as the prelude of the *Alcestis* or that of the *Trojan Women* and the scene between Iris and Lyssa in the *Heracles* of Euripides. In content, however, this scene is typically Senecan. The Fury lays grim stress on crime's passing from one generation to another in this house, and her words foreshadow every remarkable event and every dreadful future crime in the whole saga; but her most vivid prediction is reserved for the coming feast of Thyestes. After this it is small wonder that the ghost of Tantalus prefers his Hell.

The first choral song completes the saga by dwelling upon the past atrocities of Pelops and Tantalus and Tantalus' punishment in the underworld. Thus this lyric is bound to the previous scene. Cessation of the house's perpetual crime is the theme of the chorus' prayer.

Atreus now comes on to flagellate himself to fury and revenge. The efforts of his subaltern to deter him bring out his determination and the viciousness of tyranny—a favorite theme with Seneca—and again the inevitable progression from crime to greater crime. Finally, Atreus forms his plan: Thyestes will be lured into his clutches by his own desire for revenge. The prospect of return to power and escape from poverty will overcome all scruples if not of the father at least of his sons!

The chorus, who have apparently not been present during this scene, note the renewed harmony of the house. The main theme of their lyric, however, is the Stoic principle that the true king is he who has no fear and who rules his own soul—a theme that has real significance for the subsequent episode.

True to the prediction of Atreus, Thyestes does return. But he seems to have no desire to harm Atreus. His extreme reluctance to entrust himself to his brother and his desire to go back to the simple life of the free exile give him the Stoic virtue of which the chorus have just sung.[59] Like them, Thyestes preaches against the life of the tyrant. The palace and the customs which he describes are those of the Palatine and the Roman emperors, especially Nero (455–67). Thyestes as a Stoic philosopher is hardly consistent with his actual return or with the motives predicted by Atreus; but this characterization does facilitate an excellent scene of irony when his son pleads with Thyestes to trust Atreus and restore them to wealth and power. Such a retiring Thyestes, furthermore, causes Atreus by contrast to appear all the more monstrous.

Irony plays a still more important role in the reunion of the two brothers, neither of whom can restrain his hatred without a great effort, as we observe in their grim asides. The innocent children of Thyestes are given as pledges of his faith, and Atreus in his last line promises to offer the destined victims to the gods! This last is reminiscent of Electra's similarly appalling line as she receives Clytemnestra in Euripides' play (1141).

The irony continues as the chorus celebrate the strength of family ties and the wonder of concord after war. But, as an introduction to the peripety, their lyric ends on the mutability of fortune. Afterward, the Messenger enters to give a gruesome description of this palace and a harrowing account of the "sacrifice." The chorus respond with a description of the turning aside of the sun and the apparently imminent destruction of the world—a strange motive in classical poetry, but a favorite one with Seneca.

Like Aeschylus' Clytemnestra after the murder of Agamemnon, Atreus appears to gloat over his deed. An interior scene, a rarity in Roman tragedy, now reveals the lonely Thyestes trying to drown his years of grief in the joys of the banquet. But strange misgivings rise up to choke his pleasure. Throughout he sings his lines in lyric anapests. The effect of this eerie scene is very powerful.

Atreus comes up to mock Thyestes and finally presents the heads of his sons for the ghastly climax of the play. The one defense of Atreus is that moderation should be shown in crime and not in revenge. Thus again the theme of perpetuation of crime is emphasized, and the play ends with Thyestes' resigned prediction of vengeance.

8. *AGAMEMNON*[60]

The story of the *Agamemnon* is a continuation of that of the *Thyestes*. Like the *Agamemnon* of Aeschylus, this play deals mainly with the return and murder of Agamemnon. Many other Greek and early Roman tragedies dramatized the fate of the house of Atreus, however, and Seneca seems to have been influenced by some of these.[61] Noteworthy points of difference from Aeschylus are found in the introduction of the ghost of Thyestes for the prologue and the escape of Orestes at the end of the play. Besides suggesting the larger framework of the action, these innovations stress the perpetuation of crime in this royal house. The central section of Seneca's play is given over to the messenger's speech and to Cassandra. The first brings out the destruction of the sacrilegious Greeks by the storm, the second the destruction of the victor himself by his wife and her paramour. The play lacks a central figure; but again Seneca shows little interest in character. The action progresses naturally, and there is more dramatic dialogue than usually in Seneca.

A few words from this play (line 730) are scratched on a wall in Pompeii,[62] and it is not impossible that the play was produced in one of the two theaters there. But Seneca had sojourned at Pompeii in his youth and visited there later in life; it was the home of his great friend Lucilius.[63]

Discussion.—As the *Thyestes* opens with the ghost of Tantalus, so the *Agamemnon* opens with the ghost of Thyestes, and this ghost like that one would prefer its place in Hell to this palace of dreadful crimes. The whole series is again recounted, and the coming slaughter of Agamemnon is foretold. Finally the ghost encourages his wavering son Aegisthus, though later in the play no reference is made to the ghost and Aegisthus seems never to have heard it.

Clytemnestra's wavering, the ominous admonitions of the Nurse, and the bickerings with Aegisthus—all these have distinct dramatic possibilities. They suggest a new and interesting approach to this old material. Properly they belong to a treatment which makes Clytemnestra a very ordinary human being caught in the trap of adultery and forced to murder her husband. Seneca's primary interest seems to lie not in a study of her character but in the moral theme that one crime must inevitably lead to another and that any woman caught in this situation must act in similar fashion. The alternative for Clytemnestra here, as Atreus claims in the *Thyestes* (203), also, is to kill or be killed. When Aegisthus enters, Clytemnestra plays the foil for him as the Nurse has earlier done for her in order that the inevitability of this crime may be further emphasized with rhetorical point and cogency. Any emphasis on her vacillation would be wholly pointless in view of her minor role in the remainder of the play; and the question whether her sudden change is genuine or pretended, long debated among critics, is not, therefore, of any real importance.

Disregard for character, however, has involved Seneca in certain inconsistencies. Aegisthus is craven and base. He can plausibly become extremely cruel to Electra after the murder. But his Stoic readiness to commit suicide (304–5) certainly does not seem consistent with such a character. Clytemnestra's talk of saving her children from a mad stepmother (198–99), furthermore, seems ridiculous in the light of her later desire to put Orestes and Electra out of the way.

At the mid-point of the play, the rhetorical fury of the messenger's storm is unleashed and threatens to blow the dramatic action quite away. Aeschylus had the natural elements run their course in some twenty lines; but Seneca, challenged also by Vergil's famous storm in the first book of the *Aeneid* and by many another such tour de force, adds a hundred to this score.[64]

Cassandra's scenes are effective, and the use of a second chorus of Trojan captives is noteworthy.[65] Madness is realistically suggested by the speeches of Cassandra—German scholars' complaints of illogicality and their tamperings with the text are sufficient proof of this.[66] In her repartee with Agamemnon, however, Cassandra is much too smart for Greek or modern taste. The king himself, on stage for only a few lines, plays a very minor role in the action. After he has gone into the palace, the chorus sing a long interlude on the labors of Hercules. Although, at the end, a reference to Hercules' taking Troy in ten days brings this into superficial connection with Agamemnon, this distant subject may have been chosen in order not to jeopardize the suspense at the climax of the play—a Euripidean technique.

After the murder Strophius appears "pat .... like the catastrophe of the old comedy." Thus Orestes is spirited away, but Electra is left to the fury of Clytemnestra and Aegisthus.[67] Forced by one crime to another, they are now utterly heartless villains. But Cassandra's final prediction, the last words of the play, is one of vengeance and more crime to come with the return of Orestes.

9. *HERCULES ON OETA*

Like the earliest dithyrambic tragedy, perhaps, the *Hercules on Oeta* glorifies the passion of a divinity—the death and rebirth of Hercules. But the moral spirit of this play looks to the Christian future rather than to the Greek past. The triumph of this laboring Stoic over suffering and death, the feeling that the world should end with his destruction, and his epiphany to his mother—all this breathes a mystical allegory not unlike that of the story of Seneca's contemporary, Jesus of Nazareth. Hercules furnished the outstanding example of persecuted virtue in Greek legend. Long before the origin of formal Stoicism, he was the ideal Stoic hero. It is not surprising, then, that the Stoic Seneca reworked both of the plays on Hercules known to have been written by the leading Greek tragic poets. The very features which made Hercules a poor subject for Greek tragedy made him a splendid one for Seneca.

The shortcomings of the play are typically Senecan.[68] One needs the devotion of a saint and the endurance of a martyr to bear up under the endless repetition of Hercules' toils. Every section of the play is too lengthy, and the whole is over two hundred verses longer than any other ancient drama. It has been called the most formless product having the pretense of art which has been preserved from ancient times.[69] Indeed, its formlessness, like its change of scene and length, is almost Elizabethan. Still, the play, though as crude and rough as Hercules himself, has its virtues. The description of Hercules' death, however extravagant, is imaginative and powerful. One may recall the magnificent description of the death of Oedipus in Sophocles' *Oedipus at Colonus*. Hercules' epiphany, last of all, and the chorus' invocation of the new divinity furnish a glorious finale.

Sources.—The main source of the play is doubtless Sophocles' *Trachiniae*, although plays on Hercules were written by minor Greek dramatists. The story was told also in other genres, and the influence of Ovid seems to be undeniable. He had treated the subject in his *Metamorphoses* (9. 134–272) and in his *Heroides* (9). So much of Seneca's play is original, however, that these dependencies are of little significance.

Discussion.—The *Hercules on Oeta* opens apparently in Euboea. Hercules declares that he has fulfilled his mission on earth, and for his reward he now asks Jupiter to raise him to the stars. Other than this prayer, there is no indication, such as the oracle in Sophocles, that a crisis in his life has been reached. At the end of his monologue-prologue, the chorus of captives are driven off singing of their fallen city, of death, and of the might of Hercules. Iole follows with a monody which incidentally gives some exposition and thus prepares for the coming scene. This prelude fixes attention upon Hercules and also prepares for the sacrifice at which the poisoned robe will do its work.

The locale now apparently shifts from Euboea to Trachis. Deianira, "like a mother tigress," rages with jealous wrath against Iole and Hercules. Nothing that the Nurse can say consoles her. Seneca has made no effort to exalt the character of Deianira. His interest, as we should expect, lies rather in depicting her in violent emotional upheavals. Seneca also emphasizes the irony of Deianira's being able to cause the death of Hercules, a thing which all the monsters and Juno herself have so far failed to do.[70] The Nurse, however, finally prevails upon her mistress to resort to the use of magic to regain the love of Hercules. Deianira then abandons any intention of harming Hercules and determines, as in Sophocles, to anoint a robe with the blood of Nessus.

After a lyric of Horatian praise of the simple life sung by the chorus of handmaidens, Deianira enters in great consternation. The idea that Nessus could wish Hercules no good has occurred to her, and she has observed the consuming effect of the blood upon the fleece.[71] Hyllus appears and describes the destruction of his father. He does not, however, upbraid his mother, nor does she without a word retire— we might forgive her more readily if she did! Indeed her remorse now becomes as insanely violent as her jealous wrath has formerly been. Hyllus, of course, must play the foil and attempt to dissuade her from her lengthily avowed purpose of suicide. Her fate is left uncertain at the end of the act, when she rushes off and Hyllus follows to prevent her.

The choral song does not jeopardize this suspense, though it dwells on mortality and predicts the end of the world now that Hercules has been destroyed. Hercules upon his entrance continues this same theme and bemoans the irony of his dying at the hands of a mortal woman. The chorus express their sympathy in short verses. Alcmena, his mother, now appears to console him. In Sophocles, it will be remembered, the hero called for his mother but was told that she was not in Trachis (*Trachiniae* 1148–54). She is essentially an extraneous figure, but her wild grief nicely plays the foil for the Stoic heroism of Hercules and effectively motivates his final epiphany. At Hyllus' announcement of the innocence of Deianira, Hercules recognizes his fate. The theme of the irony of his downfall is now dropped. His mystical triumph over death begins. After the chorus initiates the crescendo of Hercules' apotheosis, a Messenger enters to report the majestic end of the hero. Alcmena follows to bewail the small compass of the ashes of her colossal son. Even these ashes, however, will protect her and terrify kings.[72] Her hymn of mourning is ended by the epiphany of her son. His virtue has again conquered death; the prayer of his first lines in the play has been answered.

10. *OCTAVIA*

(Authorship uncertain.)

The *Octavia* is the only Roman tragedy on a historical subject that has been preserved, although this type of play had occasionally been written since the time of Naevius. The language, style, outlook, and general structure of the *Octavia* seem to justify its inclusion among Seneca's plays, and some scholars accept its traditional assignment to him.[73] Other scholars see in the play a work by an unknown author shortly after the death of Nero. Seneca himself takes part in the play; some details of the manner of Nero's actual death, which occurred in A.D. 68, three years after the death of Seneca, are foretold; reference is made to events, such as the burning of Rome in 64, which occurred only shortly before Seneca's death; and certain metrical peculiarities are sometimes alleged to indicate that Seneca did not write the play. The composition or possession of such a document during the later years of Nero, of course, would have constituted a certain death warrant if known, whereas immediately after the revolution it would have done honor to its author.

Discussion.—This play appears to be an important historical document. It records events with accuracy as well as with monotonous repetition.[74] Chronology has been telescoped primarily in order to secure unity of time. Thus in the play Nero marries Poppaea on the day after his divorce, whereas actually he waited until several days afterward.[75] In order further to vilify Nero, the house of Claudius, especially Octavia herself, is presented somewhat more favorably than historical accuracy warrants, though sooner or later most of the crimes of the women of the whole Julian line are adequately covered.

As drama the *Octavia* suffers from a too close adherence to historical fact. Doubtless the events were too well known to be distorted. Perhaps also it was the tradition in Roman historical plays to adhere very strictly to the known facts, especially since such plays had often been written on contemporary events.[76] The author of the *Octavia*, furthermore, is obviously desirous of painting Nero in colors as black as possible. Dramatic effects are not his primary concern. The play lacks action and an integral plot. Poppaea's misgivings, though historically significant, lead to nothing in the play; the civil strife introduces an exciting complication, but it is quickly resolved; Octavia is wholly passive and is never brought face to face with Nero. For a contemporary Roman, reading or viewing historical events, however, the play must have had a powerful effect.

Noteworthy is the emphasis placed upon the theme of the stepmother in reference to Agrippina's crimes. This suggests but does not prove that the theme of the stepmother in so many of Seneca's plays may have been something more than a rhetorical commonplace. The tendency of the chorus to break up into mere groups of followers, also, is striking. Their songs are invariably written in simple anapests. Indeed, of all classical tragedies this play perhaps shows the most informal handling of the chorus. From this it is only a short step to the modern form of tragedy.

Octavia opens the play with her mourning anapests, reviewing the crimes of the house and bewailing her fate very much like the Electra of Sophocles. She wanders off as the Nurse comes on with staid iambics to tell again the story of criminal deeds. Octavia returns with more anapests. She now likens herself to Electra—Electra without a brother and avenger. The Nurse tries in vain to console her. As the conversation develops into iambics, Octavia relates her dreams of Nero's slaughtering both her brother and herself. The theme of Poppaea is now brought in, and Nero's crimes are repeated. Again like Electra, Octavia thinks of attempting herself to slay Nero, but the Nurse reminds her that she does not have the strength (174–75).

A chorus of Octavia's partisans deprecate the rumor of her divorce and vilify Nero. A new character, identified as Seneca by an early reference to his exile on Corsica, now enters to deplore his high fortune and ruminate on the corruption of man. Nero makes his entrance, deftly characterized by his ordering the death of two famous kinsmen in his first lines. Seneca protests, only to bring out the tyrannical cruelty of Nero. The tyrant claims the divine right of kings (492). A contention over his proposal to marry Poppaea ensues. The scene closes with Nero's imperiously commanding silence and announcing his wedding on the morrow.

As if in response to this announcement, the ghost of Agrippina appears with an ominous torch for the accursed marriage. After a gruesome reference to her murder, she effectively predicts the miserable death of Nero. This appearance of a ghost nicely symbolizes the passage of a night.

Octavia comes on to caution her partisans, but they as chorus respond by calling on the people to rise against the Emperor. A short scene between Poppaea and her Nurse follows. Instead of happiness in the arms of Nero, Poppaea has found dreadful apparitions of Agrippina, of her own former husband, and of her son—all of whom had already met or were soon to meet violent death, as was Poppaea herself.

After a choral lyric by those who praise Poppaea, the Messenger hastens in to report a popular uprising in favor of Octavia. The same chorus responds with a lyric on the invincibility of Love. Nero appears in a rage. He will slay Octavia and burn Rome.

After the chorus of the partisans of Octavia remark the irony of popular favor's bringing ruin, citing examples from Roman history, the play ends as it began with a lyric lament of Octavia. In the concluding lines her partisans, with annihilating bitterness, denounce the barbarism of Rome and its delight in the blood of citizens.

ADDENDUM

All the complete Greek and Roman plays extant have been treated in this volume except certain late works which are not usually included in treatments of classical drama. The most noteworthy of these late works is the miserable comedy entitled *Querolus*. This has been translated with an introduction by George E. Duckworth in his *The Complete Roman Drama*. There exists also a Vergilian cento entitled *Medea*, probably by Hosidius Geta (perhaps about A.D. 200). This has been edited and translated by J. J. Mooney, *Hosidius Geta's Tragedy* Medea (Birmingham, Cornish Bros., 1919). Cf. *Anthologia Latina*, I, 1^2 No. 17, Riese (Leipzig, Teubner, 1894).

NOTES AND BIBLIOGRAPHY

NOTES

Bibliographical data are normally not given if the work is listed below in the Bibliographies. A superior index number after the title of a work denotes the edition used. Extant fragments of Greek and Roman writers are cited with the name of the editor of the edition used, sometimes with a superior index number after the editor's name to indicate the specific edition; for example: Aeschylus, frag. 161 Nauck.² Bibliographical data concerning this edition of Nauck will be found in the Bibliography under Aeschylus, Greek text of fragments.

I. INTRODUCTION TO GREEK TRAGEDY

1 One school of modern critics denies the existence of important themes consistently maintained in Greek tragedy, and sees merely a succession of effective dramatic scenes as the poets' chief concern. For instance, Ernst Howald, *Die Griechische Tragödie* (Munich and Berlin, Oldenbourg, 1930), esp. pp. 15–16. In general, Howald's interpretations, at once too subtle and too naïve, reduce tragedy to the level of melodrama.

For a discussion of the philosophical content of Greek tragedy and of the contributions of Aeschylus and Sophocles to the development of Greek thought, see Helmut Kuhn, "The True Tragedy: On the Relationship between Greek Tragedy and Plato," *Harvard Studies in Classical Philology*, 52 (1941), 1–40 and 53 (1942), 37–88. See also, Greene, *Moira: Fate, Good, and Evil in Greek Thought*, pp. 89–219.

2 Cf. Flickinger, *The Greek Theater and Its Drama*⁴, pp. 1–56; Bieber, *The History of the Greek and Roman Theater*, pp. 1–25; Pickard-Cambridge, *Dithyramb, Tragedy, and Comedy*; Max Pohlenz, "Das Satyrspiel und Pratinas von Phleius," *Nachrichten der Gesellschaft der Wissenschaften zu Göttingen*, Philologisch-Historische Klasse (1926), pp. 298–321.

3 Cf. Martin P. Nilsson, *Geschichte der Griechischen Religion* (Munich, Beck, 1941), pp. 532–68.

4 This is a highly disputed point. Cf. Aristophanes, *Thesmophoriazusae* 396; Haigh and Pickard-Cambridge, *The Attic Theatre*³, pp. 324–29.

5 Cf. Haigh and Pickard-Cambridge, *op. cit.*, pp. 31–38. On the powerful influence which popular reception exerted on both judges and poets, see Plato, *Laws* 659 A–C. The influence of the choregus and the manner in which he equipped the chorus might greatly affect the judges' decision. The wealthy and influential Nicias (died 413 B.C.), for instance, is said never to have been choregus without having the plays which he sponsored win the first prize (Plutarch, *Nicias* 3).

6 Herodotus 6. 21. The decree may have been intended to prevent anyone else from producing a play on the same subject. So Gilbert Murray, *Aeschylus*, p. 162.

7 See below, p. 446, note 19.

8 Compare certain remarks of Eugene O'Neill, taken from "Working Notes and Extracts from a Fragmentary Work Diary" on *Mourning Becomes Electra* (printed proofs in the library of Stanford University; cf. "O'Neill's Own Story of 'Electra' in the Making," *New York Herald-Tribune*, November 8, 1931, Sec. vii, p. 2 [cited by H. C. Montgomery, "Some Later Uses of the Greek Tragic Chorus," *Classical Journal*, 38 (1942), 159, note 35]): ". . . . World War too near and recognizable in its obstructing (for my purpose) minor aspects and superficial

character identifications (audience would not see fated wood because too busy recalling trees)—needs distance and perspective—period not too distant for audience to associate itself with, yet possessing costume, etc.—possessing sufficient mask of time and space, so that audiences will unconsciously grasp at once . . . ."

9   For an example of this fallacious but effective reasoning in oratory, see Cicero, *Pro Sestio* 143.

10   Aristotle, *Poet.* 1451 b. Cf. Horace, *Ars Poetica* 119; J. E. Spingarn, *A History of Literary Criticism in the Renaissance*[2] (New York, Columbia University Press, 1908), pp. 45–46. So Aristophanes (*Frogs* 1052–53) has his Aeschylus admit that the story of Phaedra is true.

11   Aristotle (*Poet.* 1460 a) thinks that the marvelous is a source of pleasure and is required in tragedy. Cf. A. C. Bradley, *Shakespearean Tragedy*[2] (London and New York, Macmillan, 1905), p. 71 (". . . . the story, in most of the comedies and many of the tragedies of the Elizabethans, was *intended* to be strange and wonderful").

12   Cf. A. W. Verrall, *Euripides the Rationalist* (Cambridge University Press, 1895).

13   Gilbert Murray, *Euripides and His Age*, p. 186.

14   The Roman Pacuvius, for instance, wrote a play entitled *Orestes as a Slave* (*Dulorestes*), in which doubtless Orestes returned for vengeance in the disguise of a slave.

15   Greek legend was a vast source, but instead of working into new material as time went on, the later dramatists tended to limit themselves to the old, now threadbare stories. Aristotle (*Poet.* 1453 a) says that in his day the finest tragedies are always on the stories of some few houses, such as the stories of Alcmaeon, Oedipus, Orestes, Meleager, Thyestes, Telephus, and others of similar experiences. We can only deplore his enthusiasm for this decadent practice.

16   Cf. Aristotle, *Poet.* 1451 b; 1456 a. The nature of Agathon's innovation in writing fictional tragedy has been disputed in spite of Aristotle's apparently clear statement; cf. Seymour M. Pitcher, "The *Anthus* of Agathon," *American Journal of Philology*, 60 (1939), 145–69. A few cases of later Greek tragedies on historical subjects are recorded; cf. Schmid and Stählin, *Geschichte der Griechischen Literatur*, II, 101, note 2.

17   The verse is called trimeter, not hexameter, because iambic verse, like trochaic and anapestic, was counted in double feet. These meters are Greek in origin, and the Latin dramatists in adopting them make many changes. The whole subject is far too complicated for adequate treatment here, and a knowledge of the languages is essential to it.

18   *Achilles* 1, Warmington (quoted by Plautus, *Carthaginian* 11).

19   Cf. J. Descroix, *Le Trimètre Iambique*, Paris, Klincksieck [Macon, Protat Frères], 1931; E. B. Ceadel, "Resolved Feet in the Trimeters of Euripides and the Chronology of the Plays," *Classical Quarterly*, 35 (1941), 66–89.

20   *Achilles* 12, Warmington.

21   Aristotle, *Poet.* 1449 a.

22   Cicero, *Tusculan Disputations* 1. 106.

23   Haigh and Pickard-Cambridge, *The Attic Theatre*[3], p. 270. For a consideration of lyric forms in Euripides, see Decharme, *Euripides and the Spirit of His Dramas*, pp. 318–78.

24   See Athenaeus 21 F–22 A; Plato, *Laws* 816 A. Choral movements can be followed somewhat in Aristophanes, *Thesmophoriazusae* 655–85, 947–1000 (see the discussion of this play) and *Ecclesiazusae* 478–503. On dancing with the hands, see La Meri [Russell Meriwether Hughes], *The Gesture Language of the Hindu Dance* (Columbia University Press, 1941); Fritz Weege, *Der Tanz in der Antike* (Halle, Niemeyer, 1926).

25 Since the main character's determination is already formed, we are nearer the climax in a classical tragedy than in most modern tragedies. A large part of *Hamlet*, for instance, is taken up with the gathering of proof and the forming of Hamlet's determination.

26 It may be significant that the *Ion*, the *Iphigenia in Tauris*, and the *Helen* are each divided into five sections. At least, each has only three complete (responsive) choral songs after the entrance song; but each has duets and other lyric passages. These melodramatic plays had great influence upon New Comedy. A lyric exchange or kommos is often considered by modern scholars equal to choral songs in marking off episodes, but this seems contrary to the definition of Aristotle and—much more important—it often confuses rather than reveals the dramatic structure. The important criterion is continuity or interruption of the dramatic action: a kommos continues, a choral lyric interrupts.

27 Cf. Walther Kranz, *Stasimon: Untersuchungen zu Form und Gehalt der Griechischen Tragödie* (Berlin, Weidmann, 1933), pp. 14–15.

28 Certain generalizations on the use of divinities as such are made in considering foreknowledge and suspense.

29 A chorus of fifty, as may be observed in the Passion play at Oberammergau, is an impressive sight. Naturally it is somewhat unwieldy.

30 The chorus also wore a special white shoe, said to have been the innovation of Sophocles. (*Life of Sophocles*, §6.)

31 On the arrangement of the chorus, see Haigh and Pickard-Cambridge, *The Attic Theatre*[3], pp. 298–305 (to which add Athenaeus 152 B, Aeschylus, *Choephoroe* 983, scholiast on Aristophanes, *Frogs* 548). On the position of actors, see Flickinger, *The Greek Theater and Its Drama*[4], pp. 75–117. Flickinger's account, however, gives insufficient consideration to those plays, such as the *Philoctetes*, which demand the use of a raised position.

32 Professor Hermann F. Fränkel called the writer's attention to the importance of this training.

33 Cf. Plato, *Republic* 395 A; contrast *Symposium* 223 D. Some passages in tragedy approach comic relief. Such are the scenes with the Guard in Sophocles' *Antigone* and those with the Phrygian in Euripides' *Orestes*. Consistency of tone and style also prevented the use of language for characterization in almost all ancient literature, although hints of this use are found in the opening scene of the *Prometheus* and elsewhere.

34 Shakespeare regularly uses the term chorus to mean simply a speaker who comments on the action as the dramatist's mouthpiece. Cf. *Hamlet*, III. ii. 255. The Chorus in *Henry the Fifth* performs the function of a prologue, as is pointed out in his first speech, explains intervening action at certain points as a Greek chorus might indirectly do, and apologizes for the inadequacy of the play.

35 See Gilbert Murray, *Euripides and His Age*, pp. 236–37.
    Critics often blame the presence of the chorus for awkward scenes like that at the opening of Euripides' *Orestes*. Here the chorus enters and sings a lyric exchange with Electra while the deranged Orestes lies asleep on stage. Singing is certainly implausible under such circumstances, but the basic difficulty here lies not with the chorus—sleep is impossibly undramatic and cannot be maintained for long on any stage if the audience is to be kept awake. Cf. Sophocles, *Trachiniae* 971–82.

36 The writer is indebted to Professor Hermann F. Fränkel for this keen observation.
    We should view as a part of this focusing process the one or two lines of transition which are conventionally spoken by the chorus between the long speeches of a "debate" and which have annoyed some critics because of their inevitable triteness. The focusing process is even more obvious in the "agon" of Old Comedy.

37 In the *Helen*, Menelaus and Helen depart at line 1450, and hence this point at first glance seems to correspond to line 1233 in the *Iphigenia in Tauris*. But on more careful examination it becomes evident that the point of greatest danger in the *Helen* comes earlier, where Menelaus is forced to go within the palace. In his final scene Menelaus is already armed; Theonoe has refused her last opportunity to reveal his identity to her brother; and when he leaves the scene with Helen the audience feels sure that his escape is made.

38 So Flickinger, *The Greek Theater and Its Drama*⁴, pp. 144-46.

39 *Archiv für Papyrusforschung*, V (1913), 570; Page, *Greek Literary Papyri*, p. 158. On the chorus in later Greek drama, see Weissinger, *A Study of Act Divisions in Classical Drama*, p. 49, note 5, and the literature there cited, esp. Maidment in *Classical Quarterly*, 29 (1935), 1-24.

40 Because of the brief extent of the play and the regular occurrence of lyric relief, the ancient audience doubtless felt no need of intermissions. Extant tragedies range from 996 lines (*Rhesus*) and 1,047 (*Eumenides*) to 1,779 (*Oedipus at Colonus*); the one extant satyr-play has only 709 lines; the comedies of Aristophanes range from 1,183 (*Ecclesiazusae*) to 1,765 (*Birds*).

On rare occasions, it seems, a dramatist presented only two tragedies; cf. Flickinger, *The Greek Theater and Its Drama*⁴, p. 204.

41 *Œuvres Complètes de Voltaire* 2, Théâtre I (Paris, Garnier, 1877), p. 38.

42 The chorus of the *Alcestis* become the funeral procession and leave the scene for a short time; the choruses of the *Helen* and the *Rhesus* are withdrawn primarily, it seems, to allow certain scenes to take place without the hindrance of their presence. The choruses of the *Choephoroe* (872) and the *Heracles* (1081) seem to retire for a very brief space.

43 Terence, *Self-Tormentor* 409. A night passes also in Aristophanes, *Plutus* 626, a play in which the chorus seems to remain on the scene but is very loosely attached. In the *Clouds*, also, several days are presumed to elapse during the second parabasis (1114-30). Perhaps these cases are best explained as due to the informality of Old Comedy, although, in the second case, the elemental nature of clouds prevents any appearance of incongruity in their continued presence. Considerable time passes also in the *Lysistrata*.

44 The accuracy of Aristotle's observation is questioned by E. G. O'Neill, Jr. (*Transactions of the American Philological Association*, 72 [1941], 291, note 6). We should of course grant Aristotle's opinions no more weight than those of any other keen critic, but it is surely bold to reject his observations on his own civilization. O'Neill cites a fragment of Antiphanes (191 Kock) as contradicting Aristotle. Antiphanes cites Oedipus and Alcmaeon, Peleus and Teucer; and these most famous stories were doubtless known to many especially in the fourth century, but the dramatists of the fifth century did not limit themselves to the most famous stories. The evidence of the plays themselves is the best.

45 Norman T. Pratt, Jr., *Dramatic Suspense in Seneca and in His Greek Precursors*, pp. 110-15.

46 Donald Clive Stuart (*The Development of Dramatic Art* [New York, Appleton-Century, 1928], p. 87) insists that the resurrection of Alcestis comes as a surprising *coup de théâtre*.

47 Surprise is essentially comic. Cf. A. C. Bradley, *Shakespearean Tragedy*² (London, Macmillan, 1905), p. 63: "Shakespeare very rarely makes the least attempt to surprise by his catastrophes."

48 Bradley, *op. cit.*, p. 67.

49 Cf. William W. Flint, Jr., *The Use of Myths to Create Suspense in Extant Greek Tragedy* (Princeton University Dissertation, 1922), pp. 84-87.

50 *Poetics* 1454 a. This translation is taken from Ingram Bywater, *Aristotle, On the Art of Poetry* (Oxford, At the Clarendon Press, 1909). (By permission of the publishers.) On the *Cresphontes*, compare the plays of Voltaire (*Mérope*, 1743) and Alfieri (*Merope*, 1783).

51 This subject was treated by all three of the great dramatists. On the original authorship of this scene, which is uproariously parodied by Aristophanes in the *Acharnians* (331–46), see Séchan, *Études sur la Tragédie Grecque* . . . , pp. 121–23. For similar scenes, see the *Medus* of Pacuvius (Warmington, II, 248–49), the *Agamemnonidae* of Accius (Warmington, II, 330–31) and the plays cited by Alfred Gudeman, *Aristoteles: Poetik* (Berlin and Leipzig, De Gruyter, 1934), pp. 257–58 (on *Poetics* 1453 b 19).

52 On the Greek conception of fate, see p. 470, n. 191, and Index, s. v. "Fate."

53 Cf. P. W. Harsh, "Deeds of Violence in Greek Tragedy," *Stanford Studies in Language and Literature* (Stanford University, 1941), pp. 59–73.

54 Cf. Flickinger, *The Greek Theater and Its Drama*[4], pp. 168–82. Some of the examples cited by Flickinger are not really pertinent: the silence of Iole in the *Trachiniae* is much more effective than anything that she could say; Xuthus must be absent from the final scene in the *Ion*, for he is to be spared the disconcerting knowledge that his wife had given birth to a child before she married him.

55 Pollux 4. 133–42; for a list with references to illustrations, see Bieber in Pauly-Wissowa, *Real-Encyclopädie* . . . . Vol. 14 (1930), cols. 2077–82, s.v. "Maske."

II. AESCHYLUS

1 For documentation, see Schmid and Stählin, *Geschichte der Griechischen Literatur*, II, 182–94.

2 *Ibid.*, II, 183.

3 In the *Frogs* of Aristophanes (911–17), Euripides complains of the long silences of Aeschylean characters "on stage," but Dionysus responds that he prefers such silences to the incessantly talking characters of Euripides' day.

4 Cf. Aristophanes, *Frogs* 963, 1061.

5 It is the current fashion of scholars to deny Aeschylus the use of elaborate machines, but this is contrary to ancient tradition and, indeed, has no sound basis whatever.

6 Cf. Aristophanes, *Frogs* 1004–5; *Life of Aeschylus*, §§ 2, 5, 14. Cf. Aristotle, *Poet.* 1449 a.

7 Cf. J. E. Harry, *Aeschylus: Prometheus* (New York, American Book Co., 1905), on *Prometheus* 90.

8 Aristophanes, frag. 677, 678, Kock, quoted by Athenaeus, 21 F. The intimate concern of Aeschylus with every phase of the production of his plays is similar to the contention of Richard Wagner that the composer must write the words, direct, and even design the stage-settings for his productions. Cf. J. T. Sheppard, *Aeschylus and Sophocles*, p. 187.

SUPPLIANTS

9 For an account of what these plays may have contained, cf. Smyth, *Aeschylean Tragedy*, pp. 43–45. See also notes 12 and 14, below. Phrynichus, too, dramatized this subject (*Aigyptioi* and *Danaides*).

10 Note the eloquent plea for justice among states rather than appeal to arms which the chorus make in their song in praise of Argos (698–703). Legal processes at Argos were said to have been founded with the trial of Danaus; cf. Euripides, *Orestes* 871–73. On the right of sanctuary as a step to legal process, cf. *Eumenides* 258–60.

11   Cf. Schmid and Stählin, *Geschichte der Griechischen Literatur*, II, 196.

12   In the second play of the trilogy, the daughters had been forced to marry their cousins. Subsequently, at their father's command, each slew her husband on their wedding night except Hypermnestra, who was overcome with love and refused to obey this command.

13   Cf. Thomson, *Aeschylus and Athens*, pp. 298–309. The main weaknesses of Thomson's arguments are, first, that there seems no reason to assume that Aeschylus would term endogamy sacrilegious ("asebes," 9; cf. 228, where the violence justifies similar condemnation) ; and, secondly, that the case of the Danaids is not morally the same as the case of an "heiress" at Athens and no amount of Thomson's sarcasm and dogmatism can make it so. Nor is it legally the same, since the father of the Danaids is still alive and opposed to the marriages. On the Attic law, see "Demosthenes" 43. 51 (1067), 46. 14 (1133) ; Georg Busolt, *Griechische Staatskunde*[3], I (Munich, Beck, 1920), p. 240.

     For an extended discussion of Thomson's views and rejection of them, see Grace Harriet Macurdy, "Had the Danaid Trilogy a Social Problem?" *Classical Philology*, 39 (1944), 95–100.

14   Cf. Kurt von Fritz, "Die Danaidentrilogie des Aeschylus," *Philologus*, 91 (1936), 121–36 and 249–69. But any contention that the trilogy did not include Hypermnestra's trial is rash. Cf. Pausanias 2. 19. 6.

15   Cf. Max Pohlenz, *Die Griechische Tragödie: Erläuterungen* (Leipzig and Berlin, Teubner, 1930), p. 11 (crediting Hermann Fränkel).

16   There seem to be two distinct positions and levels upon which the chorus and actors are deployed. One is spoken of as a smooth lawn (508) ; here the chorus sing their stasima. The other is a mound upon which are located the altar and the symbols of various gods (189). Danaus apparently stands here during the first part of the play, and from this place he sights the ships of his adversaries (713). The chorus seem to take refuge here on the entrance of the king Pelasgus.

17   Cf. *Suppliants* 71, 234–36, 432, 719–20.

PERSIANS

18   Some scant fragments of the *Glaucus Potnieus* have only recently appeared; cf. *The Oxyrhynchus Papyri*, XVIII (edited by E. Lobel and others, London, Egypt Exploration Society, 1941), 5–8.

19   The choregus was normally assigned after plays were accepted for presentation, but since production involved a large private outlay of money, perhaps anyone might become choregus if he so desired. Bribery and manipulation, furthermore, were frequent in Athenian politics. Themistocles was struggling for his political existence during these years and was finally banished, perhaps some months after the *Persians* was produced.

20   The scene of the play, since it includes the tomb of Darius, has caused some difficulty. A. M. Harmon (*Transactions of the American Philological Association*, 63 [1932], 7–19) thinks the action is laid not before the royal palace but at the city gates, and this opinion has been very favorably received (Morel in Bursian's *Jahresbericht* . . . . , 259 [1938], 14).

21   *Persians* 175, 214, 248, 758. This dancing trochaic meter is earlier in drama than the iambic; cf. Aristotle *Poet.* 1449 a. In this trochaic meter, also, are the two main passages in "stichomythia," in which each speaker is given precisely one full line (232–45; 715–38). The more usual iambic stichomythia was used in the *Suppliants*.

22   Cf. Wilamowitz, *Aischylos: Interpretationen*, pp. 45–46. On the ghost of Darius, see Ruby Mildred Hickman, *Ghostly Etiquette on the Classical Stage*, Iowa Studies in Classical Philology, Vol. 7 (Cedar Rapids, The Torch Press, 1938), pp. 18–31.

23 The first line is paraphrased from Phrynichus. Aeschylus uses a more obviously ironic word, though irony was probably intended by Phrynichus.

24 Cf. Denys L. Page, *Actors' Interpolations in Greek Tragedy* (Oxford, At the Clarendon Press, 1934), pp. 80–81.

25 This awkwardness may possibly be due to difficulties involved in the movements of actors: the actor of the role of Atossa may take the role of Xerxes, and if so, he must somehow get off into the west wing. There may have been no stage building to shield his movement.

SEVEN AGAINST THEBES

26 For a sketch of these lost plays, see Smyth, *Aeschylean Tragedy*, pp. 127–29.

27 Thomson (*Aeschylus and Athens*, p. 313) makes a similar interpretation. Compare the repeated emergence of the Athenian point of view in the *Persians*, where the gods invoked are Greek (532, etc.) and the adjective "foreign" is used for "Persian" (187, etc.).

28 The staging of this, as of the other early plays, presents interesting problems. On entering, the chorus flee to a sacred precinct containing statues of various gods, which they term "this acropolis" (240). Such a setting is reminiscent of the *Suppliants*.

29 Cf. Schmid and Stählin, *Geschichte der Griechischen Literatur*, II, 212, note 1. Lines 710–11 ("Too true are the visions seen in my dreams") are possibly a reference to something in a previous play of the trilogy.

PROMETHEUS BOUND

30 For discussion of the lost plays, see Thomson, *Aeschylus: The Prometheus Bound*, pp. 1–46; Gilbert Murray, *Aeschylus*, pp. 99–104.

31 "Every romantic poet at this time [the beginning of the nineteenth century] turned instinctively to the *Prometheus*, just as every would-be classicist had turned to the *Oedipus* a century earlier."—Sheppard, *Aeschylus and Sophocles*, p. 176. Cf. Heinemann, *Die Tragischen Gestalten der Griechen in der Weltliteratur*, I, 12–39.

32 For a detailed account of the legends concerning Prometheus and for documentation, see L. Preller and Carl Robert, *Griechische Mythologie*, Vol. I, *Theogonie und Götter*,[4] Berlin, Weidmann, 1894, pp. 91–102.

33 Wooden figures may have been used in other plays. Cf. Séchan, *Études sur la Tragédie Grecque ...*, pp. 153–54.

34 The aesthetic effectiveness of Prometheus' silence is sufficient to account for it, although Aeschylus was here making a virtue of necessity if the play was produced before Sophocles introduced the third actor (probably 468 B.C.). A period of silence comes also before verse 436. (Cf. Wilamowitz, *Aischylos: Interpretationen*, p. 122.) Aeschylus was famous for his use of silence. Compare the silence of Cassandra as long as Clytemnestra is on stage in the *Agamemnon*. Cf. Aristophanes, *Frogs* 911–26.

35 Cf. Murray, *Aeschylus*, pp. 38–43. One would like, however, to have Io on the cliff when she contemplates casting herself from "this rugged crag" (748). The location is called a hill (*pagos*, vs. 20) as the raised position in the *Suppliants* (189). The staging of the *Prometheus*, however, is disputed. See Flickinger, *The Greek Theater and Its Drama*[4], pp. 289–91.

36 Wilhelm Schmid (*Untersuchungen zum Gefesselten Prometheus*, Tübinger Beiträge zur Altertumswissenschaft, 9 [Stuttgart, Kohlhammer, 1929], 89–90) insists that the maturing of a god, as assumed in the present interpretation, would be contrary to Greek thought. But just such a change in character as is here assumed for Zeus occurs in the case of the Furies (Erinyes) in the *Eumenides*.

37 Cf. David Grene, *"Prometheus Bound," Classical Philology,* 35 (1940), 22–38; also *Three Greek Tragedies in Translation,* pp. 18–36. The association of fire and wisdom is not peculiar to Greek mythology. Forethought is a common surname for Agni (*ignis*) in the Rig-Veda, who is called "the friend of man, the immortal among mortals, who is brought down from heaven to human kind."—J. E. Harry, *Aeschylus: Prometheus* (New York, American Book Co., 1905), p. 99.

38 Zeus' restraint in regard to this woman contrasts effectively with his license in regard to Io. Cf. Max Pohlenz, *Die Griechische Tragödie* (Leipzig and Berlin, Teubner, 1930), p. 75.

TRILOGY ON ORESTES

39 Cf. R. C. Jebb, *Sophocles: The Electra* (Cambridge University Press, 1894), p. xxxii.

40 *Odyssey* 1. 29–43; 3. 263–312; 4. 512–37; 11. 405–34; and other minor references.

41 Pindar, *Pythian Ode* 11. 22–28. (Dated 474 B.C.)

42 Cf. Schmid and Stählin, *Geschichte der Griechischen Literatur,* II, 237, 244, 255.

43 Cf. Séchan, *Études sur la Tragédie Grecque ...,* pp. 86–101; Pliny, *Natural History* 33. 156; David M. Robinson, "Illustrations of Aeschylus' *Choephoroi* and of a Satyr-Play on Hydrias by the Niobid Painter," *American Journal of Archaeology,* 36 (1932), 401–7; Hetty Goldman, "The *Oresteia* of Aeschylus as Illustrated by Greek Vase-Painting," *Harvard Studies in Classical Philology,* 21 (1910), 111–59.

44 Cf. H. S. Scribner, "The Treatment of Orestes in Greek Tragedy," *Classical Weekly,* 16 (1922–23), 105–9.

45 Cf. K. Heinemann, *Die Tragischen Gestalten der Griechen in der Weltliteratur,* I, 68–100; Schmid and Stählin, *Geschichte der Griechischen Literatur,* II, 397.

46 Cf. Sheppard, *Aeschylus and Sophocles,* pp. 126–27. The text of Euripides' *Iphigenia at Aulis,* also, is very faulty, perhaps more so than that of these plays of Aeschylus at the present time.

47 Sheppard, *op. cit.,* pp. 186–87.

48 Eugene O'Neill, *Mourning Becomes Electra* (New York, Liveright, 1931). Among other contemporary plays adapted from this trilogy of Aeschylus may be mentioned *The Tower beyond Tragedy* by Robinson Jeffers, and the *Daughters of Atreus* by Robert Turney.

49 O'Neill, *op. cit.,* pp. 39, 165, and 212; 55 and 225.

50 *Ibid.,* pp. 75–76, 82 ("Homecoming," Act III, Ezra's remarks on death).

51 *Agamemnon* 1019–21; *Choephoroe* 48, 66–67, 514–21; *Eumenides* 261–63, 647–48.

52 Compare Sophocles, *Oedipus the King* 1227 (p. 128, above); Seneca, *Phaedra* 715–18, *Mad Hercules* 1323–29; Shakespeare, *Macbeth,* II. ii. 60.

53 *Agamemnon* 533, 1527–29 ("the penalty matches the deed"—Clytemnestra's defense), 1562–64 ("the doer must pay the penalty"—the chorus predict the punishment of Clytemnestra in practically her own words), 1658; *Choephoroe* 313; *Eumenides* 490–565. Individual words meaning "do," "exact" (*prasso*), or "execute" (*drao*) recur independently and suggest this same idea.

54 *Agamemnon* 177–78, 250–51, 1425; *Eumenides* 276, 520–21, 1000.

AGAMEMNON

55 Wilamowitz, *Aischylos: Interpretationen,* p. 171.

56 *Agamemnon* 83, 248 or 254, 585, 850 (or possibly earlier).

57 George Thomson, *The Oresteia of Aeschylus,* II, commentary on *Agamemnon* 69–71.

58 Wilamowitz (*Aischylos: Interpretationen*, pp. 167–68) seems entirely to miss the irony of these lines and attributes to "naïve dramaturgy" the fact that Clytemnestra, who is planning murder, should warn against sacrilege.

59 The sacrilege of the Greeks is stressed in the corresponding speech in Seneca's *Agamemnon* (448).

60 The phrase "for a woman's sake" (line 823) might possibly be considered a lapse in character, reflecting the opinion of Aeschylus and the chorus rather than the proper view of Agamemnon. Cf. 62, 447–48, 800, 1455–61.

61 Cf. Schmid and Stählin, *Geschichte der Griechischen Literatur*, II, 231, note 2. Cornford (*Thucydides Mythistoricus*, p. 146, quoted by Flickinger, *The Greek Theater and Its Drama*[4], p. 267) is talking nonsense, of course, when he says that Agamemnon is "simply Hybris typified in a legendary person." Agamemnon is an individual as skillfully characterized as possible in one brief appearance.

62 Orestes is said to be absent, doubtless because the dramatist did not wish to be concerned with his escape after the death of his father (the usual version of the story) and because the dramatist wishes to add his exile later to the guilt of Clytemnestra. Cf. *Choephoroe* 130–34, 915. But contrast the views of F. M. B. Anderson on this point ("The Character of Clytemnestra in the *Agamemnon* of Aeschylus," *Transactions of the American Philological Association*, 60 [1929], 144–45).

63 So the manuscripts, but some editors refuse to believe that the chorus have been carrying arms and so assign line 1651 to the captain of Aegisthus' guard.

CHOEPHOROE

64 Cf. Hetty Goldman, "The *Oresteia* of Aeschylus as Illustrated by Greek Vase-Painting," *Harvard Studies in Classical Philology*, 21 (1910), 135, note 2.

65 Compare *Iliad* 9. 485–95. Cf. George Thomson, *The* Oresteia *of Aeschylus*, I, 43.

66 This materialistic point of view is mentioned, but not emphasized, by Sophocles (*Electra* 71–72, 960) and by Euripides (*Electra* 304–18). The squandering or loss of one's patrimony was a disgrace of the first magnitude. Another characteristic feature of the Aeschylean Orestes is the frank bargaining of his prayers (esp. 255–57). But this is characteristic of Greek religion, indeed of all popular religions, and the modern reader should not be offended by it.

67 This is the most elaborate chant in Greek tragedy; for an analysis, see George Thomson, *op. cit.*, I, 35–41. In their intense moments at the end of the chant, Electra and Orestes may kneel on the mound and beat upon the earth with their hands; cf. Ulrich von Wilamowitz-Moellendorff, *Aeschyli Tragoediae* (Berlin, Weidmann, 1914), p. 264 on verse 479.

68 For a study of the character of Clytemnestra in the *Choephoroe* and the *Eumenides*, see F. M. B. Anderson, in *American Journal of Philology*, 53 (1932), 301–19.

69 *Agamemnon* 1497–1504.

70 For a study of the two characters, see Gilbert Murray, "Hamlet and Orestes," *Proceedings of the British Academy*, 1913–14, pp. 389–412 (also, New York, Oxford University Press).

71 The fact that Orestes suffers after his execution of the command of Apollo may seem to some extent a criticism of the god, but actually no criticism is intended. The orthodoxy of Aeschylus in comparison to Euripides is well brought out in the speech of Apollo in the *Eumenides* in which the stamp of infallibility is placed on the all-too-human Delphic oracle. Cf. *Choephoroe* 559, *Eumenides* 19, 616–18, 797–99.

EUMENIDES

72 The precise manner of staging this scene is much disputed; cf. Roy C. Flickinger, "Off-Stage Speech in Greek Tragedy," *Classical Journal*, 34 (1938–39), 355–59.

73 Cf. Wilamowitz, *Aischylos: Interpretationen*, p. 189; Albin Lesky in Pauly-Wissowa, *Real-Encyclopädie* ...., 18. 1 (1939), col. 980, s.v. "Orestes."

74 Euripides, *Electra* 1258–63.

75 See *Agamemnon* 463, etc. If the Furies are concerned with blood kin only, it is because in normal cases of homicide the kinsmen of the murdered person take revenge, but when homicide occurs within a family the kinsmen may naturally refuse to slay one of their own members. Punishment by the blood feud breaks down in such cases and so is left to divine agents. Similar was the case of strangers murdered by a host. See *Eumenides* 545–49.

"Axine" and "Euxine" have here been explained as the Greeks themselves understood them. Actually, this explanation may be incorrect.

76 Orestes was not, of course, the only matricide in Greek legend. Alcmaeon slew his mother, Eriphyle, to avenge his father Amphiaraus. (Eriphyle, bribed with a necklace, had compelled Amphiaraus against his will to take part in the expedition against Thebes.) Aristotle (*Nicomachean Ethics* 1110 a; cf. 1136 a) considers absurd the arguments which Euripides' Alcmaeon used in his attempt to show that he was forced to slay his mother.

77 E. M. Walker in *The Cambridge Ancient History*, V (1927), 100.

78 Aristotle, *Constitution of Athens* 4. 4; cf. 25. 2.

79 C. P. Bill (in *Transactions of the American Philological Association*, 61 [1930], 111–129) contends that Aeschylus and the other dramatists locate the palace of Agamemnon in Mycenae. If so, in the opinion of the present writer, political considerations necessitated the omission of all reference to Mycenae in the trilogy. In general, Bill does not give sufficient consideration to the political purpose of the *Eumenides*.

80 Cf. Herodotus 7. 148–52.

81 Wilamowitz, *Aischylos: Interpretationen*, pp. 226–27.

82 Orestes is no longer accompanied by his elsewhere inseparable companion Pylades, and no explanation is offered for Pylades' absence.

83 Cf. Euripides, *Electra* 1270.

84 Thomson, *The Oresteia of Aeschylus*, I, 63; II, 293–94.

85 Schmid and Stählin, *Geschichte der Griechischen Literatur*, II, 238, note 6.

86 Cf. *Iphigenia in Tauris* 1005–6.

87 Cf. F. M. B. Anderson in *American Journal of Philology*, 53 (1932), 318–319; George Thomson, *Aeschylus and Athens*, p. 288.

III. SOPHOCLES

1 For documentation, see Schmid and Stählin, *Geschichte der Griechischen Literatur*, II, 309–25; Bates, *Sophocles: Poet and Dramatist*, pp. 1–13; Webster, *An Introduction to Sophocles*, pp. 1–17.

2 Plutarch, *Numa* 4.

3 Schmid and Stählin, *op. cit.*, II, 318.

4 Cf. P. W. Harsh, "Deeds of Violence in Greek Tragedy," *Stanford Studies in Language and Literature* (Stanford University, 1941), pp. 70–73.

5 Plutarch, *Moralia* 79 B. Cf. C. M. Bowra, "Sophocles on His Own Development," *American Journal of Philology*, 61 (1940), 385–401.

6 See below, note 78, in this sequence (Sophocles, *Electra*).

7 *Electra* 1015–16 and 1058–97; *Philoctetes* 676–729 and 827–38. Compare Aeschylus, *Prometheus* 1036–39 and 1063–70.

8 Plutarch, *Solon* 17.

9 Ancient critics found many Homeric qualities in Sophocles' plays. Cf. Schmid and Stählin, *Geschichte der Griechischen Literatur*, II, 315, note 2.

AJAX

10 Herodotus, 8. 64 and 121. Cf. Jebb, *Sophocles: The Ajax*, pp. xviii, xxx–xxxi. Critics sometimes insist that the status of Ajax as a hero at Athens is impertinent to any consideration of the play because it is nowhere referred to by Sophocles. This is unsound reasoning, though such references are common in Greek tragedy.

11 Cf. Haigh, *Tragic Drama of the Greeks,* p. 448, note 4; scholiast on *Ajax* 864.

12 Cf. Jebb, *Sophocles: The Ajax,* pp. xlviii–xlix.

13 Cf. Jebb, *ibidem;* Sheppard, *Aeschylus and Sophocles,* pp. 128–30.

14 See p. 173, on the *Medea* of Euripides. Cf. Séchan, *Études sur la Tragédie Grecque ...,* pp. 128–31.

15 In the epic tradition, Athena diverted the mad Ajax from the Greek leaders, but Sophocles appears to be the first to ascribe the madness itself to Athena. (So Karl Reinhardt, *Sophokles* [Frankfurt-am-Main, Klostermann, 1933], p. 247.)

16 This change of scene, of course, necessitates the removal of the chorus, which is excellently motivated by the prophecy of Calchas. Indeed, this is the main purpose of the prophecy. The chorus is divided into two semichoruses for its exit and re-entrance. Some scholars are of the opinion that the prophecy maintains the suspense created by the joyful song of the chorus at Ajax' pretended change of purpose. But the prophecy is immediately interpreted by messenger, chorus, and Tecmessa as foretelling the death of Ajax, since the all-important condition that Ajax must be kept within his tent has already been broken. Cf. Schmid and Stählin, *Geschichte der Griechischen Literatur,* II, 338; Tycho von Wilamowitz-Moellendorff, *Die Dramatische Technik des Sophokles* (Berlin, Weidmann, 1917), pp. 52–53. (These scholars think that the prophecy maintains the suspense.)

17 So Jebb, *Sophocles: The Ajax,* p. xxii.

18 Cf. P. W. Harsh, "Deeds of Violence in Greek Tragedy," *Stanford Studies in Language and Literature* (Stanford University, 1941), pp. 59–73.

19 "Argument" of the *Ajax*. Although Athena is not seen by Odysseus, she may well have been visible to the audience. So an ancient commentator (on line 14) insists "because this was necessary for the gratification of the spectator."

20 Cf. Apuleius, *Metamorphoses* 10. 29.

21 Cf. Pausanias, 4. 22. 7; A. C. Pearson, "Sophocles, *Ajax* 961–973," *Classical Quarterly,* 16 (1922), 133–34.

22 An ancient commentator remarks that sophisms such as those of lines 1123 and 1127 are more proper to comedy than to tragedy and that the poet, wishing to prolong the play after the death of Ajax, falls into frigidity and destroys the tragic pathos. But this is probably not in accordance with the tastes of the fifth century. Bitter debates are frequent in tragedy. In Aeschylus' *Judgment of the Arms* (frag. 175, Nauck²), Ajax cast aspersions on the mother of Odysseus, as Teucer here does on the mother of Agamemnon.

23 Cf. Kitto, *Greek Tragedy,* pp. 119–20.

ANTIGONE

24 Cf. Schmid and Stählin, *Geschichte der Griechischen Literatur,* II, 345. A fuller discussion of the legend and documentation may be found in this work. For an extensive study and bibliography, see Minnie Keys Flickinger, *The 'ΑΜΑΡΤΙΑ of Sophocles' Antigone,* Iowa Studies in Classical Philology, No. 2, 1935.

25 This is the subject of Euripides' *Suppliants.*

26 So the ancient commentator on Euripides, *Phoenissae* 1760.

27 Cf. Schmid and Stählin, *op. cit.,* II, 359–60; Heinemann, *Die Tragischen Gestalten der Griechen in der Weltliteratur,* II, 50–58.

452 GREEK TRAGEDY [Pages 103-14]

28 Socrates' discussion is found in Plato's dialogue, the *Crito*. When the Thirty Tyrants had seized power in Athens and ordered Socrates to arrest a certain man who was to be put to death unjustly, however, Socrates refused to obey their command. Obviously he did not allow such a command the status of law. Cf. Plato, *Apology* 32 C–D.

29 Cf. Diodorus Siculus, 12. 17. 1–2.

30 Plato, in his *Republic* (568 A–B), contends that the writers of tragedy (especially Euripides) are the eulogists of tyrants. This contention is false. By wrenching a few words out of their context, however, almost anything can be "proved" for any dramatist. (The quotation which Plato here and in the *Theages* [125 B] attributes to Euripides possibly occurred in some lost play of Euripides; it certainly occurred in Sophocles' lost play, *Locrian Ajax*, frag. 14, Pearson. See Pearson's commentary.)

31 Cf. Norwood, *Greek Tragedy*, p. 141.

32 *Antigone* 471–72; cf. 853–56.

33 The author is indebted to Professor Hermann Fränkel for this keen observation. Cf. George Thomson (*Aeschylus: The Prometheus Bound*, pp. 41–42, note), who considers this passage one of the finest pieces of characterization in Sophocles; if verses 909–12 are weak and halting, he explains, it is because Antigone feels that they are unconvincing.

34 *Antigone* 940–43, Jebb; cf. 927–28. Ismene is here ignored perhaps because, as Jebb explains, Antigone "feels that, in spirit at least, she herself is indeed the last of the race." But compare lines 599–600, where the chorus, too, considers Antigone the last of her house. The old curse of the race of Labdacus is mentioned in the play (593–625; cf. 1–6); but, like the anger of Athena in the *Ajax*, it is really a secondary motivation and is easily rationalized: Antigone has inherited the too fierce spirit of her ancestors.

Desire for fame is not a prime motivation with Antigone, as various critics have insisted; compare line 839 and Aeschylus, *Agamemnon* 1303. Postmortem fame, it is intimated in these passages, is poor compensation for an unjust death.

35 Aelian, *Variae Historiae* 5. 14.

36 Diodorus Siculus, 16. 25. 2; cf. Plato, *Laws* 873 A–C.

37 Euripides in his *Heracles* (1232), produced some twenty years after the *Antigone*, defends this claim. Cf. Wilamowitz, *Euripides: Heracles²*, commentary on line 1232.

38 Schmid and Stählin, *Geschichte der Griechischen Literatur*, II, 315–16.

39 *Ibid.*, p. 356.

40 Kitto, *Greek Tragedy*, pp. 124–25. The great actors of the fourth century, as pointed out above, chose the role of Antigone as their own and left the role of Creon to the third actor.

OEDIPUS THE KING

41 This defeat need occasion no surprise. On the strange manner of awarding prizes, see above, p. 4.

42 Cf. Heinrich Weinstock, *Sophokles²* (Leipzig, Teubner, 1937), p. 162.

43 Jebb, *Sophocles: The Oedipus Tyrannus³*, pp. xiii–xv. For an exhaustive treatment of the legend and its use in Greek literature, see Carl Robert, *Oidipus*, two volumes (Berlin, Weidmann, 1915).

44 Jebb, *op. cit.*, p. xviii.

45 Cf. Suetonius, *Julius Caesar* 56. 7; Cicero, *Letters to His Brother Quintus* 3. 5(6). 7; Suetonius, *Augustus* 85. 2.

46 Suetonius, *Nero* 21. 3. Canace was the leading feminine character in one of Euripides' most scandalous plays, the *Aeolus*. The father of her child was her brother. See Aristophanes, *Clouds* 1371–72.

47 Schmid and Stählin, *Geschichte der Griechischen Literatur*, II, 373–74. Cf. Heinemann, *Die Tragischen Gestalten der Griechen in der Weltliteratur*, II, 29–50.

48 J. T. Sheppard (*The Oedipus Tyrannus of Sophocles*, p. ix) condemns Reinhardt's production in the most severe terms.

See, also, Henry Norman, *An Account of the Harvard Greek Play* (Boston, Osgood, 1882).

49 Cf. Georg Brandes, *Voltaire* (New York, A. and C. Boni, 1930), I, 99–104.

50 Some scholars contend that this error (*hamartia*) is one of intellectual judgment and has no ethical implications. So Ingram Bywater, *Aristotle, On the Art of Poetry* (Oxford, At the Clarendon Press, 1909), p. 215; Alfred Gudeman, *Aristoteles: Poetik* (Berlin, De Gruyter, 1934), pp. 241–42. But Aristotle's sentence, which begins with the statement that the most effective tragic character is one not pre-eminently virtuous or just, implies a degree of ethical delinquency. Only if this is included, furthermore, does the generalization have any validity for the extant tragedies. "The underlying observation is that a disproportion exists between cause and effect, between guilt and resulting catastrophe."—Helmut Kuhn, "The True Tragedy: On the Relationship between Greek Tragedy and Plato, I," *Harvard Studies in Classical Philology*, 52 (1941), 21. See also Euripides' *Bacchae* 1346.

51 Cf. M. L. Barstow in Lane Cooper, *The Greek Genius and Its Influence* (Yale University Press, 1917), p. 162.

On the Delphic oracle, see Herbert W. Parke, *A History of the Delphic Oracle* (Oxford, Blackwell, 1939). On the Greek idea of fate, see Aeschylus, *Agamemnon* 1025–27 (conflicting fates), p. 470, n. 191, and Index, s.v. "Fate."

52 J. T. Sheppard, *The Oedipus Tyrannus of Sophocles*, p. xxxvi. Cf. Weinstock, *Sophokles*², pp. 166, 193.

53 The story is told in Thucydides, 1. 126–28. If Sophocles had wished to put any such political design into his play, doubtless he would have retained the Avenging Furies as a motivation in the legend; for these acts of sacrilege at Athens consisted in part of slaying certain men who had taken refuge at the altars of the Avenging Furies. Still, lines 863–910 have recently been interpreted as referring to Pericles and his opponent Thucydides, son of Melesias (not the historian). Cf. Grace H. Macurdy in *Classical Philology*, 37 (1942), 307–10.

54 For other minor inconsistencies or difficulties, see A. S. Owen, "The Oedipus Tyrannus on the Stage," *Greece and Rome*, 2 (1932–33), 155–60.

55 Norman T. Pratt, Jr., *Dramatic Suspense in Seneca and in His Greek Precursors*, p. 103.

56 Cf. Plato, *Republic* 571 A–572 B.

57 Compare Aeschylus, *Choephoroe* 72–74, and note 52, p. 448.

58 Lines 1455–57, Jebb's translation. This is a much disputed passage.

59 The last seven lines of the play, usually assigned to the chorus, are similar to six lines in the same meter spoken by Oedipus at the end of Euripides' *Phoenissae*. Some scholars assume that the verses in Sophocles' play are spurious; others, that Euripides is echoing the ending of Sophocles' famous play.

TRACHINIAE

60 Schmid and Stählin, *Geschichte der Griechischen Literatur*, III, 436.

61 Jebb, *Sophocles: The Trachiniae*, p. xxxi. The recent interpretation of Gordon M. Kirkwood ("The Dramatic Unity of Sophocles' *Trachiniae*," in *Transactions of the American Philological Association*, 72 [1941], 203–11) seems to be made from a point of view that is too romantic and that has too little sympathy for the heroic code. Heracles certainly is selfish and self-centered. He is the greatest man in the world; for him to fail to recognize this fact would be stupid, to fail to admit it would be dishonest. To him, Deianeira is just a woman. It is not surprising that such severity offends the modern critic.

62 See Clyde Pharr, "The Interdiction of Magic in Roman Law," in *Transactions of the American Philological Association*, 63 (1932), 269–95, esp. p. 278. Philters sometimes resulted in death. Such was the end, according to an uncertain tradition, of the poet Lucretius.

63 Deianeira has employed an unusually coarse line to describe her situation: "And now two of us await his embrace beneath one blanket" (539–40). Cf. Norwood, *Greek Tragedy*, p. 160.

64 Cf. Arthur B. Cook, *Zeus: A Study in Ancient Religion*, II (Cambridge University Press, 1925), p. 903.

65 *Trachiniae* 200, 436, 635.

66 Cf. Wilamowitz, *Euripides: Herakles²*, I, 152–56.

67 Compare *Trachiniae* 1101 and *Heracles* 1353. Such quotations among ancient writers, far from constituting plagiarism, are actually an acknowledgment of indebtedness and a compliment to the original author. See Seneca Rhetor, *Suasoria* 3. 7. (I am indebted to Professor Hermann Fränkel for this very apt reference.)

68 *Trachiniae* 416 and *Suppliants* 567.

69 Cf. Norwood, *Greek Tragedy*, pp. 159–60; Schmid and Stählin, *op. cit.*, II, 375 (note 3), 383–84.

ELECTRA

70 Many scholars now assume that Sophocles' play preceded the *Electra* of Euripides. But A. S. Owen thinks that Sophocles' play was later and produced about 410 B.C. (cf. "The Date of the *Electra* of Sophocles," *Greek Poetry and Life, Essays Presented to Gilbert Murray* [Oxford, At the Clarendon Press, 1936], pp. 145–57).

Owen's use of Chrysothemis as a criterion for dating is risky, however, for it is the regular practice of the dramatists to ignore those phases of the legend which are inconsistent with or not pertinent to the play in hand. There is no place for Chrysothemis in Euripides' play; Orestes himself furnishes a sufficient foil for Electra. It is true, however, that she is mentioned in the *Orestes* (23), where she plays no role. The reference to her might well be expected in the *Iphigenia at Aulis* (1164), for there Clytemnestra is trying to make as strong an appeal to Agamemnon as possible.

Albrecht von Blumenthal, also, thinks Sophocles' play was the later one, pointing out that Euripides' criticism of Aeschylus would have been very flat if Sophocles' play had preceded it. (Cf. Bursian's *Jahresbericht* . . . ., 259 [1938], p. 95 and pp. 103–4.)

71 Cf. Ulrich von Wilamowitz-Moellendorff, "Die Beiden Elektren," *Hermes*, 18 (1883), 236–37. This article is an outstanding contribution to the subject, although its conclusions were later repudiated by its author. For further consideration of the legend and documentation, see Jebb, *Sophocles: The Electra*, pp. ix–xxiv.

72 See above on Aeschylus' trilogy on Orestes (*Oresteia*).

73 This detail (484–85) would not seem grotesque to an Athenian. At Athens inanimate objects which caused the death of human beings were brought to trial and on conviction formally cast beyond the borders of Athenian territory. A somewhat similar English law of "deodands" was repealed only in 1846, as Jebb points out in his commentary on these lines.

74 The attempt of J. T. Sheppard (*Classical Review*, 41 [1927], "*Electra*: A Defence of Sophocles," pp. 2–9 and "*Electra* Again," pp. 163–65) to demonstrate that Sophocles is really condemning the matricide is unsuccessful, in the opinion of the present writer, though his view is enjoying a certain vogue among scholars; cf. Kitto, *Greek Tragedy*, pp. 128–37; Thomson, *Aeschylus and Athens*, pp. 354–60; Gordon M. Kirkwood, "Two Structural Features of Sophocles' *Electra*," *Transactions of the American Philological Association*, 73 (1942), 86–95. This view assumes that the Sophoclean Apollo did not approve of the matricide, and it is true that Sophocles' references to the oracle are not unequivocably explicit on this point. Vagueness is permissible, especially for a poet, when a well-established tradition is being followed. But when a well-established tradition is being changed or renounced, the Attic dramatists are regularly very explicit. Thus in the *Oedipus at Colonus*, when Sophocles wishes to make Polyneices the older son so that his appeal to his father may be stronger, it is repeatedly and explicitly pointed out that Polyneices is the older son. That Apollo approved Orestes' matricide was at this time the accepted legend, and the very vagueness of Sophocles in referring to the oracle is sufficient to indicate that he is following the accepted legend. If Orestes' matricide seems severe and cruel, so does Oedipus' curse of his sons in the *Oedipus at Colonus*. Punishment of the guilty as a deterrent from crime is stressed in both plays (*Electra* 1505–7; *Oedipus at Colonus* 1372–79).

75 Gellius, 6. 5.

76 Cf. Ingram Bywater, *Aristotle, On the Art of Poetry* (Oxford, At the Clarendon Press, 1909), commentary on 1460 a, 31, p. 321.

77 Cf. Schmid and Stählin, *Geschichte der Griechischen Literatur*, II, 392, note 1.

78 The idea of the dead slaying the living, used with such magnificent effect by Aeschylus (*Choephoroe* 886), occurs twice in this play (1420–22 and 1477–78) and frequently elsewhere in Sophocles (*Ajax* 901, 1027; *Antigone* 871; *Oedipus the King* 1453–54; *Trachiniae* 1163). As Aeschylus has Clytemnestra driven within to die by the side of Aegisthus, so Sophocles has Aegisthus driven within to be slain where Agamemnon was slain.
    Both Euripides (*Electra* 62, 626) and Sophocles (*Electra* 589) refer to children of Clytemnestra by Aegisthus. Sophocles wrote plays concerning these (*Aletes* and *Erigone*).

79 It is sometimes assumed, however, that this sacrifice was deliberately ignored in the *Iliad* in order to spare Agamemnon and his line. Cf. Th. Zielinski, *Tragodumenon Libri Tres* (Krakow, 1925), pp. 242–43 (a strong contention).

80 Cf. Schmid and Stählin, *op. cit.*, II, 386–88.

81 Cf. Max Pohlenz, *Die Griechische Tragödie* (Leipzig, Teubner, 1930), pp. 331–32.

82 Lines 811–12, 987, 1319–21, 1426–27, 1483–90.

83 Aristotle, *Poetics* 1451 b, translated by Ingram Bywater (*Aristotle, On the Art of Poetry* [Oxford, At the Clarendon Press, 1909]. Quoted by permission of the publishers.)
    Similar in its implications, perhaps, is the remark in the ancient *Life of Sophocles* (section 6) that he wrote plays with a view to the actors, although Owen (article cited above in note 70, pp. 148–55) is inclined to interpret this

remark as meaning that Sophocles distributed the lyric parts with a view to the actors so that they might be carried properly.

84 Cf. Tycho von Wilamowitz-Moellendorff, *Die Dramatische Technik des Sophokles*, Philologische Untersuchungen, 22 (Berlin, Weidmann, 1917), pp. 165–268. This scholar frequently goes astray. Thus he assumes (p. 193) that the audience is supposed to share Electra's reactions to the false report of Orestes' death. Such a childishly naïve attitude would rob Sophocles' plays of many of their finest effects.

85 Cf. *Electra* 191–92, 1181; *Anthologia Palatina* 7. 37.

86 In writing the *Trachiniae*, Sophocles was probably inspired by Euripides' *Heracles*, and in writing the *Oedipus at Colonus*, possibly by Euripides' *Phoenissae*. Cf. Ulrich von Wilamowitz-Moellendorff, "Die Beiden Elektren," *Hermes*, 18 (1883), 239–40.

PHILOCTETES

87 Cf. Jebb, *Sophocles: The Philoctetes*[2], pp. ix–xiii.

88 Dio Chrysostomus, 52 and 59.

89 Cf. Nauck, *Tragicorum Graecorum Fragmenta*[2], p. 79.

90 Aristotle (*Poetics* 1458 b) cites a poor line from Aeschylus' *Philoctetes* which Euripides has changed into a fine one by the substitution of a single poetic word for a prosaic one. This improvement of Aeschylus is obviously a criticism.

91 Dio Chrysostomus, 52. 16.

92 *Ibid.*, 52. 15.

93 In certain versions of the story, this procedure is followed and succeeds; cf. Dio Chrysostomus, 52. 2; Apollodorus, *Epitome* 21 (5. 8).

94 In a speech in Thucydides (4. 86, Jowett), Brasidas is made to say: "For to men of character there is more disgrace in seeking aggrandisement by specious deceit than by open violence; the violent have the justification of strength which fortune gives them, but a policy of intrigue is insidious and wicked."

For a stimulating literary study of Neoptolemus in this play and Achilles in Euripides' *Iphigenia at Aulis*, see A. R. Bellinger, "Achilles' Son and Achilles," *Yale Classical Studies*, 6 (1939), 3–13.

95 *Philoctetes* 82; cf. 1050–51. This reasoning of Odysseus is very similar to that of the unscrupulous politician, Cleon, as represented in a speech to the Athenians by Thucydides (3. 40, Jowett): ". . . . when virtue is no longer dangerous, you may be as virtuous as you please."

96 Thucydides, 1. 138, Jowett.

97 Neoptolemus' original promise to Philoctetes was a part of the original intrigue and was very sophistically worded (524–29), but that it was a promise to take Philoctetes home (cf. 459–60) only sophistry could dispute. Neoptolemus, once changed, does not resort to such sophistry.

98 Compare *Philoctetes* 1046 with *Antigone* 472 and *Prometheus* 320.

OEDIPUS AT COLONUS

99 Cf. Wilhelm Dittenberger, *Sylloge Inscriptionum Graecarum*[3] (Leipzig, Hirzel, 1920), III, No. 1083. Cf. Albrecht von Blumenthal in Pauly-Wissowa, *Real-Encyclopädie* . . . . , Zweite Reihe, 3 (1929), col. 1090, s.v. "Sophokles (aus Athen)."

100 Schmid and Stählin, *Geschichte der Griechischen Literatur*, II, 324. Although the play was written at a time of war, no general vilification of the Thebans is made (cf. 919). Again the honesty of Athenian patriotism is remarkable.

101 Schmid and Stählin, *op. cit.*, II, 409. Some scholars have interpreted certain lines of *Oedipus the King* as referring to this legend, especially lines 454–56 and 1456–57 (a disputed passage). The passage cited from the *Phoenissae* is sometimes considered spurious.

102 Triptolemus, son of a legendary king of Eleusis, was said to have been one of the founders of the Eleusinian Mysteries.

103 *Oedipus at Colonus* 592, 855, 1192–98.

104 W. Rhys Roberts, *Longinus, On the Sublime*[2] (Cambridge, Cambridge University Press, and New York, Macmillan, 1907). An ancient commentator (on line 1725) remarks on the pathos and the naturalness of the grief of Antigone.

105 Any attempt to compare the structure of this play with that of *Oedipus the King* (cf. Kathleen Freeman, "The Dramatic Technique of the *Oedipus Coloneus*," *Classical Review*, 37 [1923], 50–54) is likely to result in fallacious conclusions. *Oedipus the King* is a play of tragic discovery and its use as a canon for plays of action and decision, like the *Oedipus at Colonus*, has caused endless confusion in dramatic criticism.

IV. EURIPIDES

1 For documentation, see Schmid and Stählin, *Geschichte der Griechischen Literatur*, III, 309–38; Bates, *Euripides*, pp. 1–21; Decharme, *Euripides and the Spirit of His Dramas*, pp. 1–16.

2 On athletics, see *Electra* 883, frags. 199, 282, Nauck.[2]

3 Cf. frag. 492, Nauck.[2]

4 Cf. Schmid and Stählin, *op. cit.*, III, 330–31.

5 Cf. Satyrus' *Life of Euripides*, column 19. 1 (in H. von Arnim, *Supplementum Euripideum* (Marcus and Weber, Bonn, 1913), p. 8, or in *The Oxyrhynchus Papyri*, IX (edited with notes and translations by Arthur S. Hunt, London, Egypt Exploration Fund, 1912), 124–82. Compare Plutarch, *Nicias* 29. According to another story in Plutarch (*Lysander* 15), the city of Athens itself was saved from destruction after the Peloponnesian War by the poetry of Euripides (*Electra*).

6 Gilbert Murray, *Euripides and His Age*, p. 18.

7 Aristotle, *Poetics* 1460 b.

8 "Longinus," 15. 3, translated by W. Rhys Roberts, *Longinus, On the Sublime*[2] (Cambridge, Cambridge University Press, and New York, Macmillan, 1907).

9 *Philoctetes* 308–9. Cf. Shakespeare, *The Tempest*, I. ii. 164–65.
   When the musician Timotheus was thoroughly disheartened because of the unfavorable public reception of his work, Euripides is said to have encouraged him and to have quieted his concern over mere popularity. Cf. Satyrus' *Life of Euripides*, column 22.

10 *Hecuba* 1199–1201.

11 *Hecuba* 243.

12 Aristotle, *Poetics* 1454 a (Melanippe).

13 Cf. Aristophanes, *Frogs* 945–47; cf. W. Schadewaldt, *Monolog und Selbstgespräch* (Berlin, Weidmann, 1926), p. 11. Euripides' lost *Stheneboea*, written perhaps about the same time as the *Medea*, also opened with a very natural and effective soliloquy. Cf. D. L. Page, *Greek Literary Papyri*, I, 127–29. The lost *Andromeda* opened with a beautiful monody (anapests).

458	GREEK TRAGEDY	[Pages 164–69

ALCESTIS

14 Cf. L. Séchan, *Le Dévouement d'Alceste* (Paris, Boivin, 1927), p. 6.

15 Wilamowitz, *Griechische Tragoedien*, III, 73.

16 But Sophocles may have written a satyr-play or something like it on this subject; cf. frag. 851, Pearson.

17 Cf. E. M. Butler, "Alkestis in Modern Dress," *Journal of the Warburg Institute,* I (1937), 46–60; Heinemann, *Die Tragischen Gestalten der Griechen in der Weltliteratur,* I, 117–53.

18 Schmid and Stählin, *Geschichte der Griechischen Literatur,* III, 349.

19 Cf. *Heracleidae* 735, 739; *Orestes* 1369–1536. Aristotle (*Poetics* 1449 a) says that tragedy passed through the satyric stage and only late achieved a serious tone. Hence the comic elements of this play are traced by some scholars to the older tradition of tragedy. Cf. Leo Weber, *Euripides: Alkestis* (Leipzig, Teubner, 1930 [larger edition]), p. 33.

20 Cf. A. W. Verrall, *Euripides the Rationalist* (Cambridge University Press, 1913 [1895]), pp. 1–137. The article by D. L. Drew, "Euripides' *Alcestis*," in *American Journal of Philology,* 52 (1931), 295–319, is unconvincing.

21 Wilamowitz, *Griechische Tragoedien*, III, 94. In such a case, the music was of the greatest importance.

22 "The poet through the mask of the chorus," remarks the ancient scholiast on line 962, "wishes to display how much education he has acquired." Cf. Pollux, 4. 111. This beautiful choral song is reminiscent of a fragment of Aeschylus' *Niobe* (161, Nauck²) translated by Swinburne in his *Phaedra*.

23 *Alcestis* 55, 466–75, 711.

24 Compare the praise of Ajax' silence in the *Odyssey* (11. 563) by "Longinus," *On the Sublime* 9. 2. Euripides' own explanation (*Alcestis* 1144–46), however, may have real point; cf. Erna P. Trammell, "The Mute Alcestis," *Classical Journal,* 37 (1941), 144–50.

25 Cf. Plato, *Symposium* 179 B–D.

26 Alcestis' concern over the marriage of her daughter (313–16) is a nice feminine touch.

27 Cf. Heinrich Dörrie, "Zur Dramatik der Euripideischen Alkestis," *Neue Jahrbücher für Antike und Deutsche Bildung,* 1939, p. 175. In the *Agamemnon* of Aeschylus Agamemnon himself is dramatically a minor character, almost wholly overshadowed by the sinister towering figure of Clytemnestra.

28 Compare the adaptations of Herder, Wieland, and Alfieri; cf. Butler, "Alkestis in Modern Dress," *Journal of the Warburg Institute,* I (1937), 48–54.

29 Cf. Butler, article cited in note 28 above, p. 59.

30 Dörrie, article cited in note 27 above, pp. 174–89.

31 To view Admetus' reception of Heracles as "stupidly excessive hospitality," as does Schmid (*Geschichte der Griechischen Literatur,* III, 343, cf. 346), inevitably leads to misinterpretation. The chorus do call Admetus foolish (552), but the audience is supposed to realize the irony of their words. Indeed the chorus corrects itself in the following lyric, which indicates that this same hospitality—and not mere religious *"Korrektheit,"* as Schmid (*op. cit.,* p. 347, note 7) assumes—won the favor of Apollo. That hospitality was the moral of Admetus' story is shown by the drinking song quoted in Aristophanes' *Wasps* (1238).

32 So Wilamowitz, *Griechische Tragoedien,* III, 91, note 1. Compare the story of Protesilaus and Laodameia (the niece of Alcestis; cf. *Alcestis* 732–33), which Euripides also dramatized in his lost *Protesilaus.* H. J. Rose ("Euripides, *Alcestis* 340 ff.," *Classical Review,* 41 [1927], 58) thinks that Admetus is half-

mad with grief in this scene; a modern parallel for the making of such a statue is cited. Again, Grube (*The Drama of Euripides,* p. 136) thinks that the protestations of Admetus are extravagant and unnatural and so intended by the poet, because Admetus is beginning to realize his own unheroic conduct.

33 The brutal frankness of this quarrel between father and son does not, as some have thought (cf. Flickinger, *The Greek Theater and Its Drama*[4], p. 199), suggest the spirit of the old satyric drama. This frankness is typical of such quarrels. It is found in the *Antigone* (Creon and Haemon), in the *Hippolytus,* in the *Medea,* and elsewhere. See above, p. 451, n. 22.

34 Pheres' statement that he cares not what people may say of him after his death (726) is extremely base according to Greek morality.

35 *Alcestis* 382, 861 ff., 1084; cf. 363–68.

36 *Alcestis* 238–43 (chorus), 274 (Admetus).

37 One's attitude toward hospitality was of far greater moral import in ancient times than in modern times. Travel was slow, difficult, and dangerous; there were no respectable hotels or inns and few of any sort; in most countries a foreigner had no legal rights and was afforded little or no protection. Pericles repeatedly boasted of Athens' enlightened attitude toward foreigners and contrasted it with the banishment of foreigners from Sparta. (Cf. Thucydides 1. 144; 2. 39.) Such pride accounts for the stress which Euripides places upon the hospitality of Athens in the *Medea,* the *Heracleidae,* and other plays.

38 Cf. Weber, *Euripides: Alkestis* (see note 19 above), p. 45.

MEDEA

39 For further details, D. L. Page, *Euripides: Medea,* pp. xxi–xxx. An excellent appreciation of the *Medea* is found in Grube, *The Drama of Euripides,* pp. 147–65.

40 Scholiast on *Medea* 9.

41 That this scene was a famous example of an episode that was unmotivated, or, as Aristotle calls it, irrational, seems to be indicated by the cryptic way in which Aristotle cites it ("as Euripides employs Aegeus") without any mention of the title of the play in which it occurs, which is all the more striking, since Euripides wrote a play entitled *Aegeus.*

42 Another point of difference is found in the manner of death predicted for Jason. In Neophron (frag. 3, Nauck[2]), Medea tells Jason that he will hang himself in a most shameful death. Hanging, of course, was a woman's manner of committing suicide and ill befitted a hero. Cf. Euripides, *Helen* 299–300 (often considered spurious); Gellius 15. 10.

43 A mere title does not necessarily reveal the subject of a play. We know that the play of the Roman dramatist Accius, entitled *Medea,* for instance, did not treat the same subject as the *Medea* of Euripides. A remark of Aristotle (*Rhetoric* 2. 23 [1400 b]) is usually interpreted as meaning that the dramatist Carcinus wrote a *Medea* in which the children were sent away and not slain by Medea.

44 Cf. Léon Mallinger, *Médée: Étude de Littérature Comparée* (Louvain; Paris, Boccard, 1897); Grace Knopp, "The Motifs of the 'Jason and Medea Myth'" in Modern Tradition" (unpublished Stanford University dissertation, 1933); Heinemann, *Die Tragischen Gestalten der Griechen in der Weltliteratur,* II, 1–28.

45 Cf. D. L. Page, *Euripides: Medea,* pp. lvii–lxviii; Bieber, *The History of the Greek and Roman Theater,* figs. 72–75; Séchan, *Études sur la Tragédie Grecque* ..., pp. 396–422.

46 Pliny, *Natural History* 7. 126.

47   Cf. Schmid and Stählin, *Geschichte der Griechischen Literatur*, III, 371.

48   D. L. Page, *Euripides: Medea*, p. xiv. In Seneca's play, the first words show that revenge is there the problem of the play. The interpretation of Aristotle's criticism is disputed. Some refer it to Aegeus; cf. Schmid and Stählin, *op. cit.*, III, 361, note 7; 365, note 9.

49   It is often stated that the *Medea* requires only two actors. It could be so presented, but perhaps three actors are used in the opening scenes. See the scholiast on line 112. Medea's costume doubtless marked her as a foreigner. See Bieber, *op. cit.*, p. 146.

50   Compare Medea's own outbursts to Zeus and Earth and Light (143), and the prologue of the *Agamemnon* of Aeschylus. Still, the motivation of the prologue in the *Medea* was parodied by Philemon (frag. 79, Kock). Compare Athenaeus 288 D. (Cf. Friedrich Leo, *Der Monolog im Drama*, Abhandlungen der Königlichen Gesellschaft der Wissenschaften zu Göttingen, Philologisch-Historische Klasse, Neue Folge X, 5 [Berlin, Weidmann, 1908], pp. 1–6.) One of Euripides' most famous plays, the *Andromeda*, which was produced in 412 along with the *Helen*, opened with the heroine crying in lyric (anapestic) measure (frag. 114, Nauck²): "Oh Night divine, how long the course that you pursue . . . ."

51   The lines of the prologue containing these fears are sometimes interpreted somewhat differently and sometimes considered spurious (38–43), especially since lines 40–41 recur with slight change as lines 379–80. Both occurrences are accepted by P. W. Harsh, "Repetition of Lines in Euripides," *Hermes*, 72 (1937), 438–39, and by Norman T. Pratt, Jr., "The Euripidean *Medea* 38–43," *Classical Philology*, 38 (1943), 33–38. D. L. Page (*Euripides: Medea*, pp. 68–69) rejects lines 38–43, saying that he is in complete disagreement with the methods and conclusions of Harsh. Such disagreement in method is obvious from the fact that Page in considering the general problem of lines repeated within a given play of Euripides (*Actors' Interpolations in Greek Tragedy* [Oxford, At the Clarendon Press, 1934], pp. 103–5) presents only about half of the evidence —about half of the number of lines so repeated within a given play. It is obvious also in Page's dogmatic assumption that *Medea* 786 (see his commentary on this line in his edition of the *Medea*), which recurs as line 949, "must be an interpolation" in one of the two passages. Another striking feature of Page's method is his acceptance of line 786 in his text of the *Medea* but rejection of it in his commentary, and vice versa, his rejection of line 949 in his text and acceptance of it in his commentary. On these two lines, see the remarks of Gilbert Murray, below, in note 61.

52   See note 41, above.

53   Abrupt and poorly motivated entrances of important characters are found elsewhere in Euripides. Compare the entrance of Heracles in the *Alcestis*, which, however, is foretold in the prologue, and that of Orestes in the *Andromache*, and that of Theseus in the *Heracles*. Cf. Schmid and Stählin, *op. cit.*, III, 365, note 9.

54   Noteworthy here are certain conceptions of Greek popular morality. Medea says (807–9): "Let no one consider me a person weak and of no consequence, or a retiring woman, but a character of a different mold, baleful to my enemies and kindly to my friends." To do harm to one's enemies seemed as natural as to do good to one's friends. This is a commonplace in Greek literature; it is contradicted, of course, by Plato. Another popular conception is important in this speech of Medea: to be made an object of laughter and ridicule by one's enemies is a most dreadful humiliation, to be avoided at almost any price. This is one of the motives of Phaedra, also, in her cruel revenge upon Hippolytus. Cf. *Hipp.* 728–31 (cited by Schmid and Stählin, *op. cit.*, III, 359, note 11).

55 Cf. Gilbert Murray, *The Medea of Euripides* (London, Allen, and New York, Oxford University Press, 1907), note on line 731.

56 "Let Medea be savage and invincible," says Horace (*Ars Poetica* 123), "let Ino be full of tears." The most famous cases of mothers who slew their children are Althaea, whose act, according to legendary chronology, was subsequent to this (her son was Meleager; *Iliad* 9. 565–72), and Procne (*Odyssey* 19. 518–23). For a few other instances, see Hyginus, *Fabula* 239. Schmid strangely overlooks all these cases. Here as elsewhere he exaggerates the differences between Greeks and barbarians as portrayed in Euripides. It is Jason who claims that no Greek woman would have committed Medea's deed, and his opinion here is worthless (*Med.* 1339). Procne was an Athenian! Nor does Schmid seem justified in saying that Euripides has recourse to Medea's legendary status of barbarian and witch to add plausibility to her actions. Cf. Schmid and Stählin, *op. cit.*, III, 359–60.

57 Medea's speech on the hardships of woman's life (230–51) gives a good picture of the position of women at Athens during the fifth century—sometimes considered an important theme of the play.

58 If line 468 is rejected (it is repeated without change as line 1324 and is rejected by most editors), then both the speech of Medea and that of Jason have exactly fifty-four lines. Such consciously balanced speeches are not uncommon in Euripides, although precise numerical equality is rare.

59 Gilbert Murray, *The Medea of Euripides* (London, Allen, and New York, Oxford University Press, 1907), p. ix.

60 A noteworthy subtlety in the play is the fact that the name of the bride, Creusa ("Princess") or Glauce, is never used by Medea or anyone else throughout the play.

61 Cf. *Medea* 899–905. There may be an ominous second meaning in *Medea* 957, where an adjective is applied to the bride which, though usually referring to the living, is sometimes applied to the dead. On *Medea* 949, Murray (*op. cit.*, p. 92) remarks: "Repeated from 1. 786, ... where it came full in the midst of Medea's avowal of her murderous purpose. It startles one here, almost as though she had spoken out the word 'murder' in some way which Jason could not understand."

HIPPOLYTUS

62 Pausanias, 2. 32. 1. Such dedication of a lock of hair to some divinity or heroine was a regular Greek custom. Cf. Seneca, *Phaedra* 1181–82. A fuller account of this legend and documentation may be found in Pauly-Wissowa, *Real-Encyclopädie* . . . . , Vol. 8 (1913), col. 1865, s.v. "Hippolytos."

63 Pausanias, 2. 32. 3; *Inscriptiones Graecae*, IV, 754.

64 Scholiast on Euripides, *Alcestis* 1.

65 Cf. Pausanias, 2. 32. 1 (popular denial). The destruction of Hippolytus as described in Seneca (*Phaedra* 1093–1114), therefore, may be closer to the popular legend than the destruction according to Euripides in the extant play, where a still living Hippolytus is desired for the final scene.

66 Scholiast on Theocritus, 2. 10.

67 Plutarch, *Moralia* 28 A; cf. Seneca, *Phaedra* 91–92.

68 For fragments of this lost play and other evidence, see Nauck, *Tragicorum Graecorum Fragmenta*², pp. 491–96; Leo, L. *Annaei Senecae Tragoediae*, I, 173–83. (Fragment 446, Nauck² is assigned not to Artemis but to the chorus in Schmid and Stählin, *Geschichte der Griechischen Literatur*, III, 378.)

69   Sophocles, fragments 686 and 679-80, Pearson.

70   Cf. Schmid and Stählin, *op. cit.*, III, 389-90.

71   Cf. Schmid and Stählin, *ibidem;* Winifred Newton, *Le Thème de Phèdre et d'Hippolyte dans la Littérature Française* (Bibliothèque de la Faculté de Philosophie et Lettres de l'Université de Liége, LXXXII, Paris, Droz, 1939); Louis Méridier, *Hippolyte d'Euripide* (Paris, Librairie Mellottée, no date); Heinemann, *Die Tragischen Gestalten der Griechen in der Weltliteratur*, II, 69-79.

72   So Ister, quoted by Athenaeus, 557 A; cf. *Hippolytus* 1082. Theseus was notorious for his many affairs.

73   This line is usually translated inadequately. The literal rendering here given would be adequate only if delivered in a contemptuous manner.

74   Euripides, *Iphigenia at Aulis* 1049-53; cf. *Ion* 517-26; Plato, *Symposium* 179 E-180 E (Aeschylus, *Myrmidones*); Cicero, *Tusculan Disputations* 4. 71 (Euripides, *Chrysippus*); Athenaeus, 601 A (Aeschylus, *Myrmidones;* Sophocles, *Niobe*). Doubtless even greater freedom in such matters characterized the satyr-plays; cf. Sophocles, *Lovers of Achilles* (A. C. Pearson, *The Fragments of Sophocles,* I, 103-9); Euripides, *Cyclops* 581-89.

75   Plato, *Symposium* 179 E-180 E; Petronius, 85. 5.

76   Being a vegetarian is a strange custom for a hunter and athlete, and earlier in the play (108-10), Hippolytus has been represented as taking delight in a good meal after the hunt. Possibly Euripides is criticizing Orphic fanatics of his own day. Cf. scholiast on 953. For a scholarly discussion, however, see Ivan M. Linforth, *The Arts of Orpheus* (University of California Press, 1941), pp. 50-60.

77   Some scholars think that this point is impertinent to the present play and the result of a confusion of this version with the earlier one. In Seneca (*Phaedra* 617-22), where Phaedra thinks her husband dead, she holds out the prospect of acquiring the rule of the land as an enticement to Hippolytus. On the characterization of Hippolytus by his language, compare that of Jason in the *Medea*.

78   The author is indebted to Professor G. M. A. Grube for this point, made in a personal letter. See now his book, *The Drama of Euripides*, p. 189.

79   Cicero (*De Officiis* 3. 108) approves the famous line of Hippolytus, "My tongue swore, but my conscience is unsworn." It was this line that Aristophanes thought so scandalous (*Thesmophoriazusae* 275) and put to such clever use in the *Frogs* (1471). Cf. Plato, *Symposium* 199 A; *Theaetetus* 154 D. Aristotle (*Rhetoric* 3. 15 [1416 a]) says that this line was cited as evidence of impiety against Euripides in an actual law suit. But in the *Iphigenia at Aulis* (394 a-395) Euripides again asserts the validity of his point.

80   According to the *Odyssey* (11. 324-25) Ariadne was slain by Artemis on the island of Dia at the instance of Dionysus. Later accounts deified her as the wife of Dionysus. Compare the famous painting of Titian, *Bacchus and Ariadne*, in the National Gallery, London.

81   This scene is taken over bodily by Racine, *Phèdre*, I. iii. Note Euripides' use of the divided iambic line (*antilabe*) when the name Hippolytus is spoken by the Nurse (310, 352). This device is used elsewhere in the play only twice: line 724, in Phaedra's last, impassioned words; line 1325, in Theseus' grief at the realization of what he has done.

82   Compare the second poem of Theocritus (cf. note 66 above). The translation of lines 491-92 in the version of Coleridge (Oates and O'Neill, *The Complete Greek Drama*) or the version of Wodhull (Everyman's Library) is apparently not justified, although the original text here is uncertain.

HERACLEIDAE

83 For conjectures on the play of Aeschylus, see Schmid and Stählin, *Geschichte der Griechischen Literatur,* III, 418, note 2. It is misleading, however, to say that Euripides places the maidens within the temple for reasons of modesty. Modesty, as so often in life, is here only an excuse. The real reason lies in the economy of roles: since three actors appear in the early scenes, Macaria could obviously not be represented on the scene. Compare the scholiast on *Phoenissae* 93, a passage in which modesty again is only an excuse.

84 Schmid and Stählin, *op. cit.,* III, 418, note 5.

85 The Heracleidae were the leaders of the Dorian Greeks in their conquest of the Peloponnesus, and their descendants existed not only at Argos but at Sparta, where they were the kings, and in various other cities of the Peloponnesus. Cf. Thucydides, 1. 12.

86 The self-sacrifice of a youth or maiden is a favorite theme with Euripides. Compare Menoeceus in the *Phoenissae* and Iphigenia in *Iphigenia at Aulis.* Euripides' lost *Erechtheus,* also, was a famous play of sacrifice and patriotism.

87 See above, p. 443, n. 33.

88 This motif anticipates that of Sophocles' *Oedipus at Colonus.*

ANDROMACHE

89 Cf. Schmid and Stählin, *Geschichte der Griechischen Literatur,* III, 404–5; Gilbert Murray, *Euripides and His Age,* p. 110 (Argos); D. L. Page, in *Greek Poetry and Life: Essays Presented to Gilbert Murray* (Oxford, At the Clarendon Press, 1936), p. 228 (Argos). Olympias, the mother of Alexander the Great (died 323 B.C.), belonged to the house of the Molossian kings, as did Pyrrhus (died 272 B.C.), the brilliant opponent of the Romans.

90 Cf. Schmid and Stählin, *op. cit.,* III, 406.

91 Thucydides, 1. 118.

92 See above, p. 118.

93 Thucydides, 4. 78, Jowett.

94 Cf. Grube, *The Drama of Euripides,* p. 206.

95 Cf. Schmid and Stählin, *op. cit.,* III, 398–400.

96 Orestes' close kinship to Menelaus makes him practically a Spartan, at least in this play. To contend that Orestes' character is not villainous, as one scholar has recently done, is to confess oneself unable to cope with the subtlety of Euripides.

97 Cf. line 964, where the manuscripts vary.

98 Peleus' indictment of Spartan morals is perhaps intended by Euripides in part as an answer to Hermione's earlier tirade against the morals of "barbarians." Since only Spartans refer to Andromache as a barbarian, the charge can be of no significance.

HECUBA

99 In the *Hecuba* and the *Trojan Women,* the events are much the same, but the plot structure is somewhat different. In the *Iphigenia in Tauris* and the *Helen,* the plot structure is practically the same, but the events are entirely different.

100 So Schmid (Schmid and Stählin, *Geschichte der Griechischen Literatur,* III, 465); some scholars think otherwise.

101 Surprising developments take place also in the *Ion.*

102   In the *Hecuba*, as occasionally elsewhere, Euripides changes the accepted legends
in certain details for the purposes of specious logic. Odysseus is here said to owe
his life to Hecuba, since Helen had discovered him in disguise in Troy and had
revealed him to Hecuba (239–50); but in the *Odyssey* (4. 240–64) Helen alone
discovers him and reveals him to no one. Proper characterization, also, is here
sometimes dropped for the sake of argument (cf. 1199–1201).

103   Cf. Schmid and Stählin, *Geschichte der Griechischen Literatur*, III, 473–74.

104   In the *Trojan Women*, Hecuba silently collapses when Cassandra is taken away,
though she is quickly revived. When Polyxena here goes to her death, however,
Hecuba's faintness does not prevent her speaking and cursing Helen. This curse,
though perhaps abrupt, furnishes a nice bit of characterization—Hecuba will
have vengeance!

105   Polymestor foretells the future like a *deus ex machina*. Similar are the final
pronouncements of Medea, of Eurystheus in the *Heracleidae*, and of Polyphemus
in the *Cyclops*.

106   An effective bit of irony occurs in the *Hecuba*, however, when Agamemnon expresses incredulity that women could take vengeance on men (883).

CYCLOPS

107   It is sometimes assumed that the final scene of Aristophanes' *Wasps* is being
followed by Euripides in his presentation of the drunken Cyclops. Cf. Schmid
and Stählin, *Geschichte der Griechischen Literatur*, III, 533, note 2. Schmid
accepts the dating after 415 B.C. But to the present writer it seems more likely
that Aristophanes is parodying Euripides in the *Wasps*.

108   Cf. Flickinger, *The Greek Theater and Its Drama*[4], pp. 23–24; Max Pohlenz,
"Das Satyrspiel und Pratinas von Phleius," *Nachrichten der Gesellschaft der
Wissenschaften zu Göttingen*, Philologisch-Historische Klasse (1926), pp. 298–321.

109   Euripides, *Autolycus* frag. 282, Nauck[2]. Cf. Schmid and Stählin, *op. cit.*, III, 624.

110   Only one other satyr-play, the *Trackers* (*Ichneutae*) of Sophocles, remains in
sufficient part to show anything of its structure. In this play, considered to be
earlier than the *Cyclops*, extended use is made of the construction with interlarded lyrics (epirrhematic).

111   Cf. Schmid and Stählin, *op. cit.*, III, 537, note 4; Walther Kranz, *Stasimon:
Untersuchungen zu Form und Gehalt der Griechischen Tragödie* (Berlin,
Weidmann, 1933), p. 262. Gilbert Murray, however, rearranges the lines of the
choral song and assumes that it was originally responsive and included a refrain.

112   This type of lyric exchange, in which one lyric form is repeated three times
(495–518), is quite foreign to tragedy, but similar lyrics are found in comedy
(e.g., *Frogs* 416–39).

HERACLES

113   Schmid and Stählin, *Geschichte der Griechischen Literatur*, III, 433, 436.
Heracles was a frequent figure in comedies and satyr-plays. Euripides was the
first poet, it seems, to present him as a tragic hero. The transformation was not
easy, and Euripides has shown subtle skill in making it. If the paternity of
Heracles seems a little confused, we may recall that within five lines of the
Iliad (5. 392–96) Heracles is termed both the child of Amphitryon and the
son of Zeus.

114   This is the manner in which Voltaire uses Oedipus and Jocasta in his *Oedipe*.
Cf. Aristotle, *Poetics* 1452 b.

115   Schmid and Stählin, *op. cit.*, III, 433.

116 This was a favorite chorus with Richard Porson and Ulrich von Wilamowitz-Moellendorff, two of the greatest Greek scholars of modern times. Cf. Wilamowitz, *Euripides: Herakles²*, II, 147.

117 Cf. Euripides, *Suppliants* 1080–93.

118 Cf. G. L. Hendrickson, "The Heracles Myth and Its Treatment by Euripides," in *Classical Studies in Honor of Charles Forster Smith* (University of Wisconsin Studies in Language and Literature No. 3, Madison, 1919), pp. 11–29. (This is an excellent appreciation of the play.)

SUPPLIANTS

119 The comic poets protest against the lucrative neutrality and wavering uncertainty of Argos at about this time. See Aristophanes, *Peace* 475–77; Pherecrates, frag. 19, Kock. An alliance of Athens, Argos, Mantinea, and Elis was formed in 420 B.C., largely through the machinations of Alcibiades. But after an unsuccessful campaign, Argos made a treaty with Sparta in 418.

120 Cf. Plutarch, *Theseus* 29.

121 Thucydides, 4. 97. The Thebans were notorious for this propensity. Cf. Xenophon, *Hellenica* 3. 5. 24 (Haliartus), Pausanias, 9. 13. 11 (Leuctra).

122 Schmid and Stählin, *Geschichte der Griechischen Literatur*, III, 452. Cf. J. S. Morrison, "The Place of Protagoras in Athenian Public Life (460–415 B.C.)," *Classical Quarterly*, 35 (1941), 15, who thinks that the play advocates the policy and leadership of Alcibiades.

123 *Suppliants* 229–37; Thucydides, 6. 12–15 (in part a speech of Nicias).

124 *Suppliants* 748–49, 949–54.

125 *Suppliants* 496 (Theban Herald), 639 (Messenger), 861 (Adrastus), 934–38. Cf. Schmid and Stählin, *op. cit.*, III, 459, note 1. It is assumed that the chorus consists of five mothers and ten servants (*ibid.*, p. 455, note 3). This would well suit the usual arrangement of the chorus in three files of five each. (Cf. Haigh and Pickard-Cambridge, *The Attic Theatre³*, p. 298.) The number seven is used in reference to the chiefs and to the mothers because it was so firmly established in tradition.

This episode shows an interesting use of local color, since there was actually a cliff behind the temple at Eleusis from which one might easily commit suicide. (But it is a mistake to try to determine anything about the topography of Eleusis, as some archaeologists have done, from *Suppliants* 87–97, where the entrance technique is a regular one when the chorus is grouped about a central figure. Cf. *Heracles* 1163–77.)

ION

126 Cf. H. von Arnim, *Supplementum Euripideum* (Bonn, Marcus and Weber, 1913), p. 26, lines 9–11; D. L. Page, *Greek Literary Papyri*, p. 118, lines 9–11. A fuller discussion and documentation may be found in A. S. Owen, *Euripides: Ion*, pp. ix–xli.

127 Cf. *Helen* 16–21; *Iphigenia at Aulis* 790–800; frag. 210, Nauck². This subject was a favorite one with later satirists; cf. Juvenal, 6. 58–59.

128 Creusa's denunciations of the god are in the end found to be based almost wholly on error. The charge of violence is not refuted, but it is given too much importance by modern critics. This is a frequent situation in New Comedy, and it is viewed rather lightly even by the guardians or parents of the abused girl, though of course the young man is expected to marry the girl. Cf. Terence, *The Brothers* 469–74. It was the custom to guard maidens with extreme vigilance, and the duty of maidens to see that they were so protected. The use of violence is stressed in literature to keep the moral intention of the girl unsullied,

but a certain amount of skepticism is not unwarranted here. Cf. Menander, *Arbitration* 256–312, Jensen (297–353, Körte³).   In general, see Felix Martin Wassermann, "Divine Violence and Providence in Euripides' *Ion*," *Transactions of the American Philological Association,* 71 (1940), 587–604.

129   A bit of local color may possibly be found in the Old Man's complaints of the steepness of the grade leading up to the temple (735–46). The grade at Delphi is a very trying one. But cf. Euripides, *Electra* 489–90.

130   Ulrich von Wilamowitz-Moellendorff, *Euripides: Ion* (Berlin, Weidmann, 1926), p. 12 (the German adjective used is "zarteste").

131   Justification for this interference of the chorus, as in the *Choephoroe* of Aeschylus (766–82), is found in their devotion to the character concerned. In the *Ion* all the songs of the chorus are intimately connected with the action. The chorus are presumed to share the mortal danger of Creusa at the climax and thus add to the excitement.

132   *Poetics* 1453 b.

133   Cf. Owen, *op. cit.,* on line 988.

134   The final lines of *Oedipus the King,* also, are trochaic.

TROJAN WOMEN

135   Cf. Schmid and Stählin, *Geschichte der Griechischen Literatur,* III, 474–76.

136   *Ibid.,* 476–78, esp. 477, note 4.

137   Paris, for instance, has often been thought to represent Alcibiades. Cf. Schmid and Stählin, *op. cit.,* III, 478.

138   Euripides apparently is the first poet to present Athena as taking vengeance upon the whole Greek force for the crime of Ajax, son of Oïleus. (So Wilamowitz, *Griechische Tragoedien,* III, 263, note 1; see, however, Aeschylus, *Agamemnon* 649.) This extension and generalization of the guilt obviously serves the theme of the play.

139   See especially *Trojan Women* 131–37, 498 (Hecuba); 368–69 (Cassandra); 766–73 (Andromache); 781 (chorus); 210–13, 357. Grube (*The Drama of Euripides,* pp. 87–88, 291–92) goes astray in finding the theme of vengeance of primary importance in the scene with Helen. It is hardly more than an external motivation. The scene must be interpreted in the light of the *Alexander.* Compare Ennius, *Alexander* 75, Warmington: . . . . Lacedaemonia mulier furiarum una adveniet.

140   So Kitto, *Greek Tragedy,* p. 212. Schmid (*op. cit.,* III, 479, 484–85) seems somewhat to miss the point of this scene. It will be recalled that Aristophanes claimed that Pericles started the Peloponnesian War over two sluts belonging to Aspasia (*Acharnians* 526–34).

141   Aristophanes, *Lysistrata* 155–56.

ELECTRA

142   On the later influence of this play, see above on the trilogy on Orestes (*Oresteia*) of Aeschylus.

143   *Phoenissae* 751 (possibly a criticism of the long descriptions in Aeschylus, *Seven against Thebes*); *Philoctetes* (see above on Sophocles' play of the same title). Euripides' improvement of a line of Aeschylus in the *Philoctetes,* as cited by Aristotle (*Poetics* 1458 b), seems an undeniable instance of the younger poet's criticizing his predecessor. Still Gilbert Murray (*The Electra of Euripides* [London, Allen, and New York, Oxford University Press, 1905], p. 90) contends that Electra's rejection of the signs is not an attack on Aeschylus. "No parallel for such an artistically ruinous proceeding," he says, "is quoted from any Greek tragedy."

144 Even in the *Electra,* the conventional attitude comes out elsewhere in the play (633). In certain lines before his recognition, Orestes is somewhat of a swaggering young aristocrat; but this, it seems, is merely a part of his disguise (397–98; 553–54). So the disguised Odysseus speaks rudely to his father (*Odyssey* 24. 244–79).

145 Lines 969–70 are essentially the same as two lines in the first scene between the disguised Orestes and Electra (278–79). Somewhat similar use of repetition is found in Sophocles (*Electra* 279, 588, 1495–96). Note that in Aeschylus also the chorus exhort Orestes to answer Clytemnestra's "my son" with "father" (or "father's," *Choephoroe* 829).

146 Gilbert Murray, *op. cit.,* p. 94.

147 *Electra* 524–26. Cf. Denniston, *Euripides: Electra,* p. 116.

148 In his excellent appreciation of this play, Grube (*The Drama of Euripides,* p. 302) thinks that Orestes is very reluctant in identifying himself because Electra has shown herself so violent and bloodthirsty.

149 Lines 9–10, but in lines 1155–61 reference is made to Clytemnestra's wielding the ax. Cf. 160–66, 279.

150 Gilbert Murray, *op. cit.,* p. 91.

151 Clytemnestra's hypothetical case of the sacrifice of Orestes if Menelaus had been abducted is extremely bizarre, but no more so than many another sophistic argument in the debates in Euripides or, in Sophocles' *Electra,* the contention of Electra that an enemy should not be married for a daughter's sake (593–94, rejected as spurious by Ulrich von Wilamowitz-Moellendorff, "Die Beiden Elektren," *Hermes,* 18 [1883], 219, note 1).

IPHIGENIA IN TAURIS

152 Book 4. 103 (Rawlinson). Herodotus probably died before this play of Euripides was written. It goes without saying that the studious Euripides, like Aristophanes and other educated Athenians, was well acquainted with Herodotus' famous work.

The Taurians inhabited what is now called the Crimea, on the northern coast of the Black Sea.

153 Cf. Wilhelm Schmid in Schmid and Stählin, *Geschichte der Griechischen Literatur,* III, 520–23.

154 A similar contest seems to have taken place in the *Chryses* of Pacuvius (frag. 100, Warmington) and possibly in another play of Pacuvius (frag. 163–66, Warmington). The *Chryses* of Sophocles, of course, may possibly have been the original source of this scene.

155 Cf. Schmid, *op. cit.,* III, 530–31. Fragments of a mime parodying this play have been discovered in papyri (see below, p. 487, note 65, on Plautus, *Carthaginian*). These give some idea of ancient popular theatrical entertainments. These fragments are written in both prose and verse, and foreign characters are given some lines apparently in their native dialect.

156 *Ibid.,* III, 531–33.

157 A minor item that may here be noticed is the miraculous escape of Orestes and Pylades from harm when they are attacked by the herdsmen (cf. 328–29), so that the two young men may appear unscathed. (Cf. Gilbert Murray, *The Iphigenia in Tauris of Euripides* [London, Allen, and New York, Oxford University Press, 1910], p. 94.) Earlier in his career, for example in his *Philoctetes* (431 B.C.), Euripides was notorious for presenting even his heroes in sordid garb; but here he wishes them to appear as handsome as possible. Noteworthy, also, is the fact that the herdsman has caught only the name Pylades, which Iphigenia does not know (cf. 60; 920).

158   Compare the *Ion.*

159   Cicero, *De Finibus* 5. 63 (Pacuvius, 163–66, Warmington).

160   This passage is often cited to prove that the actors in Greek tragedy stood not upon a raised stage but on the same level with the chorus.

161   This type of plot is frequent and probably very old; see on the *Helen.*

HELEN

162   Lucian, *The Way to Write History* 1–3. Cf. Aristophanes, *Frogs* 52–54. In his *Thesmophoriazusae,* Aristophanes parodies both the *Helen* and the *Andromeda.*

163   Cf. Schmid and Stählin, *Geschichte der Griechischen Literatur,* III, 502. Helen was rendered divine honors also at Athens and in Egypt. Cf. W. H. Roscher, *Ausführliches Lexikon der Griechischen und Römischen Mythologie,* Vol. I, col. 1950, s.v. "Helena."

164   *Helen* 603, 706, 718, 1107–64, 1220.

165   Plutarch, *Nicias* 13. 1; Thucydides, 8. 1.

166   Cf. Tycho von Wilamowitz-Moellendorff, *Die Dramatische Technik des Sophokles,* Philologische Untersuchungen, 22 (Berlin, Weidmann, 1917), pp. 265–68.

167   See the treatment of Plautus' *Braggart Warrior.* The plot of Euripides' *Cyclops,* also, concerns a Greek's deception of a barbarian and his escape.

PHOENISSAE

168   Oenomaus, king of Elis, required suitors for the hand of his daughter, Hippodameia, to contend with him in a chariot race, and as he overtook them, he slew them with his spear. Pelops, however, promised a bribe to the charioteer of Oenomaus to tamper with the wheels of his master's chariot. After this plot succeeded and Oenomaus was slain, the charioteer was so rash as to ask for his reward. Pelops threw him into the sea, and this unjust act became a curse to the house of Pelops. Chrysippus, his son, excited the passion of Laius, who kidnaped him. Pelops then prayed that Laius might never have a son, or if he did have one, that his son might slay him. This story of Chrysippus, possibly the invention of Euripides, connects the two greatest houses of legendary Greece. Cf. Schmid and Stählin, *Geschichte der Griechischen Literatur,* III, 571–73.

169   Cf. Schmid and Stählin, *op. cit.,* III, 588–90. The references to Colonus at the end of the play, if genuine, perhaps inspired Sophocles' *Oedipus at Colonus.*

170   Euripides avoids and perhaps even criticizes (751–52) the long static scene in which Aeschylus describes the various heroes before the battle.

171   Cicero, *De Officiis* 3. 82 (*Phoenissae* 524–25). Augustus, too, took a motto from this debate, but his was the cautious dictum of Polyneices (599) : "A conservative general is better than a rash one." Cf. Suetonius, *Augustus* 25. 4. The contentions of Eteocles in this debate remind one of those of Thrasymachus in the first book of Plato's *Republic.*

172   Cf. Wilamowitz, *Aischylos: Interpretationen,* p. 93, note; Wilhelm Kroll in Pauly-Wissowa, *Real-Encyclopädie* . . . . , Vol. 15 (1932), col. 918, lines 17–40, s.v. "Menoikeus."

173   So Grube, *The Drama of Euripides,* pp. 364, 370.

174   This was the subject of Euripides' lost *Erechtheus.*

175   Schmid's discussion of the final scene is on the whole satisfactory except in one particular : his assumption that Antigone is supposed to abandon the burial of Polyneices is certainly wrong. Such a famous act, here so carefully prepared for throughout the play, could not be omitted. (Cf. Schmid and Stählin, *op. cit.,* III, 585–87, 862–68.)

176   "Hypothesis" of the *Phoenissae* (I, 243, line 1, Schwartz).

ORESTES

177   One may compare the ending of Plautus' *Amphitryon* and *Haunted House* (where Callidamates plays the role of the *deus ex machina*). See the "hypothesis" of the *Orestes* attributed to Aristophanes of Byzantium and the scholiast on line 1691. Grube (*The Drama of Euripides*, p. 396) seems unjustified in insisting that even here the god does not come to the rescue of the poet; this ending would be utterly intolerable in a serious play if it were not brought about by divine fiat. The god seems to have rescued the poet also in Euripides' lost *Antiope*, which was written at about this same time. (For fragments of this play, see D. L. Page, *Greek Literary Papyri*, pp. 61–71.)

178   Grube, *op. cit.*, p. 397.

179   This vilification contributes to the theme of the contrast between the fate of Agamemnon and that of Menelaus: war has taken the good and left the evil.

180   See below, note 201, on Euripides, *Bacchae*.

181   Grube, *The Drama of Euripides*, p. 376.

182   *Ibidem*. This is similar to the main theme of the *Andromache*.

183   Cf. Schmid and Stählin, *Geschichte der Griechischen Literatur*, III, 611.

BACCHAE

184   Cf. Sandys, *The Bacchae of Euripides*[4], pp. xxxvii f.; Ulrich von Wilamowitz-Moellendorff, *Griechische Verskunst* (Berlin, Weidmann, 1921), p. 577.

185   Carl Robert, *Oidipus* (Berlin, Weidmann, 1915), I, 495; Willi Göber in Pauly-Wissowa, *Real-Encyclopädie* . . . . , Vol. 19 (1938), col. 546, s.v. "Pentheus."

186   In supporting the claim that Athens spent more money on the theater than in maintaining her empire and her freedom by warring upon the barbarians, Plutarch (*De Gloria Atheniensium* 6 [*Moralia* 349 a]) cites the following titles as those of typical plays: *Bacchae, Phoenissae, Oedipus, Antigone, Medea, Electra.* Schmid (Schmid and Stählin, *Geschichte der Griechischen Literatur*, III, 631. note 1; 681) seems to misinterpret this passage as indicating that an unusually lavish outlay was made in producing the *Bacchae* [of Euripides].

187   For details, consult the index to Sandys' edition of the *Bacchae* under these proper names.

188   Plutarch, *Crassus* 33, translated by Bernadotte Perrin (*Plutarch's Lives*, Loeb Classical Library, London, Heinemann, and New York, Putnam, 1916 [now handled at Cambridge, Mass., by Harvard University Press]).

189   Cf. Bieber, *The History of the Greek and Roman Theater*, fig. 68, p. 57, and the various woodcuts in Sandys' edition. For the influence of the play on Christian writers, see Schmid and Stählin, *op. cit.*, III, 682.

190   Gilbert Murray, *Euripides and His Age*, pp. 186–88. Euripides' usual attitude toward popular religion remains unchanged in the *Iphigenia at Aulis*, where he reiterates his heretical opinion that oaths evilly exacted are not binding (*Iphigenia at Aulis* 394 a–395). This play may possibly have been written earlier than the *Bacchae;* it resembles the *Orestes* in many ways, including a certain nervousness that is not characteristic of the *Bacchae*.

Still other critics have found in the *Bacchae* a powerful argument for prohibition! Again, it has been contended that the play centers about the problem of the state and religion (Schmid and Stählin, *op. cit.*, III, 679–81); but this is not a valid contention, for too much of the play is taken up with the portrayal of Pentheus as an abnormal character, and Pentheus as here presented certainly cannot be taken as a fair representative of the state.

191 See above, pp. 101–2. The *deus ex machina* often resorts to fatalism at the end of the play. Cf. Euripides, *Electra* 1247–48; *Helen* 1646, 1660; *Hippolytus* 1436 (here at the beginning, also, but for certain effects). Cf. *Alcestis* 962–83; contrast *Ion* 71, 1566–68. On Greek conceptions of fate, see Greene, *Moira: Fate, Good, and Evil in Greek Thought.*

192 See, for example, "Theocritus," poem 26. Cf. Göber (article cited in note 185, above), 548–49.

193 Cf. *Bacchae* 402–15, 769–74.

194 Cf. *Hippolytus* 20. On this view of Dionysus, see Grube, "Dionysus in the *Bacchae*," *Transactions of the American Philological Association*, 66 (1935), 53–54 (an eloquent passage). The present discussion owes much to this article of Grube. See also his book, *The Drama of Euripides*, pp. 398–420.

195 The phrase "ancestral traditions" (201) refers not to the worship of Dionysus but to the traditional attitude of submission to any and all divinities, new or old. This is a widespread concept in both Greek and Roman religion. Only religions intolerant of other beliefs, such as Christianity, evoked real opposition. The Athenians raised an altar even to the "Unknown God" for fear of omitting any possible divinity. This passage in the *Bacchae* is misinterpreted by many critics, including even Wilamowitz (*Griechische Tragoedien*, IV, 141).

196 But compare Hecuba's rationalizations on the judgment of Paris (*Trojan Women* 969–86), and the bitter exchange between Pheres and Admetus in the *Alcestis*.

197 The fate of Actaeon is recalled elsewhere in the *Bacchae* (1227, 1291). He was torn to pieces by his own hounds after offending Artemis.

198 The translations of *Bacchae* 358 are usually inaccurate, failing to bring out the idea of wicked persistence in the epithet applied to Pentheus.

199 The whole stage building obviously does not collapse. For similar stage effects, see *Heracles* 905; *Trojan Women* 1295–1325; Aeschylus, frag. 58, Nauck²; Plautus, *Amphitryon* 1052–71.

200 Dionysus introduces this messenger (658–59), doubtless judging the origin of the man from his leather jerkin, wallet, and staff. Messengers usually enter after a choral song and are introduced by the chorus at the first of an episode. Another instance of effective entrance in mid-episode is found in the *Iphigenia at Aulis* (414). It is noteworthy also that this episode in the *Bacchae* falls into five distinct scenes—an unusually large number.

201 In "Longinus" (*On the Sublime* 15. 3) Euripides is considered to have been most assiduous and most successful in dramatizing two emotions, those of madness and of love. Intoxicated characters were introduced into tragedy by Aeschylus, according to Athenaeus (428 F–429 A).

202 Elsewhere in legend Cadmus had a son Polydorus and a grandson Labdacus. These are here ignored in order that Pentheus may be presented as king and Cadmus may be utterly forlorn at the end of the play.

203 Cf. Apsines, IX. 590, Walz (I. 322, Spengel and Hammer), confirmed by *Christus Patiens* 1466 ff. The last choral lines of the *Bacchae* are the same as those at the end of the *Alcestis,* the *Medea,* the *Andromache,* and the *Helen.*

204 A decree of the Roman Senate forbidding Baccanalia is still extant (186 B.C.); cf. Warmington, *Remains of Early Latin*, IV (1940), 254–59. Cf. Pliny, *Natural History* 14. 89; Livy, 39. 15; Schmid and Stählin, *op. cit.,* III, 660, note 5. Bacchic revels as described in the *Bacchae* were not a part of the worship of Dionysus in Attica (*ibid.,* 660) but were practiced at Delphi (cf. Euripides, *Ion* 550–53; the immorality of the rites is here attested).

205 Cf. *Bacchae* 354, 487, 1062, and 314–18, 680–88, 1048 ff. Milman's translation (Everyman's Library) of *Bacchae* 37 is incorrect.

206 Cf. Aristotle, *Poetics* 1453 a.

207 Cf. Gilbert Murray, *Euripides and His Age,* p. 185.

208 The hostile composition of the chorus here as in the *Antigone* is in part designed to isolate the main character. Pentheus usually ignores the presence of the chorus. This emphasizes his intense busyness, but it is not otherwise significant. The same technique is used in the *Iphigenia at Aulis.*

IPHIGENIA AT AULIS

209 Cf. *Iphigenia at Aulis* 1547–50 (possibly later than Euripides), *Heracles 323, Ion 967,* and Aeschylus, *Agamemnon* 184–249. See also Séchan, *Études sur la Tragédie Grecque* . . . . , fig. 19; p. 373, note 2. (Séchan seems to accept the explanation given by Cicero and Pliny.)

210 Wilamowitz (*Griechische Tragoedien,* IV, 122, note) thinks both prologues genuine alternative drafts. But compare Schmid and Stählin, *Geschichte der Griechischen Literatur,* III, 640–41. Ennius chose the anapestic dialogue for the opening of his adaptation. Euripides' very popular *Andromeda* began with an anapestic monody.

211 The *deus ex machina* is not used by Seneca except, perhaps, in the *Hercules on Oeta,* 1940–82.

212 Cf. Flickinger, *The Greek Theater and Its Drama*⁴, p. 310; Gilbert Murray, *Euripides and His Age,* pp. 172–73 (other innovations mentioned).

213 Similar use is made of an infant in Menander's *Arbitration* 85–88, Jensen (126–29, Körte³). In a romantic melodrama of Euripides, the *Hypsipyle,* the leading woman sings to a baby using castanets. This scene outraged Aristophanes' sense of tragic propriety (*Frogs* 1305–7). For fragments of the *Hypsipyle,* see D. L. Page, *Greek Literary Papyri,* I, 83–109.

214 Horace, *Ars Poetica* 120–22. A. R. Bellinger ("Achilles' Son and Achilles," *Yale Classical Studies,* 6 [1939], 3–13) views the character of Achilles as very lofty, however, and thinks that his portrayal here has been influenced by that of Neoptolemus in Sophocles' *Philoctetes.*

215 Grube, *The Drama of Euripides,* pp. 426–27.

216 Cf. Schmid and Stählin, *op. cit.,* III, 645.

217 Grube, *op. cit.,* p. 424.

RHESUS

218 For a recent brief summary of the vast literature on this problem, see J. Geffcken, "Der Rhesos," *Hermes,* 71 (1936), 394–408. Cf. W. H. Porter, *The Rhesus of Euripides*² (Cambridge University Press, 1929).

219 In a drama on these same events, however, Accius seems to have laid the scene in the Greek camp. Cf. Accius, *Night Patrol (Nyctegresia),* frag. 488, 491, Warmington.

220 So John C. Rolfe, "The Tragedy Rhesus," *Harvard Studies in Classical Philology,* 4 (1893), 69, note 2.

221 Another instance of possible imitation of the *Hippolytus* is found in the use of a strophe widely divided from its antistrophe. But in the *Hippolytus* (362–72 and 669–79) the rhythmical repetition emphasizes similar emotional crises, and the two lyrics, so to speak, bracket the duel between Phaedra and Hippolytus. In the *Rhesus* (454–66 and 820–32) the repetition seems pointless. Perhaps this misuse of the interlarded construction reveals a decadent tendency of archaizing. The interlarded construction is used also in the first episode. Here it is effective—but somewhat unusual, since the episode is so short.

222 This motive is apparently taken from Pindar; cf. scholiast on *Iliad* 10. 435.

223 In the Homeric version Dolon wears but is not disguised in the wolf skin, and Odysseus and Diomedes leave Dolon's belongings in a conspicuous spot to mark the route back to their own camp. The assumption of Gilbert Murray (*The Rhesus of Euripides* [London, Allen, and New York, Oxford University Press, 1913], p. 63) that the wolf skin is left in Hector's tent is mere romanticizing. Murray's whole translation is so bedizened that it falsifies the simplicity of the original.

V. INTRODUCTION TO OLD COMEDY

1 Cf. Flickinger, *The Greek Theater and Its Drama*[4], p. 38. For fuller discussion, see A. E. Haigh and A. W. Pickard-Cambridge, *The Attic Theatre*[3], pp. 20–28; Edward Capps, "The Introduction of Comedy into the City Dionysia," *The Decennial Publications,* The University of Chicago (1903), VI, 261–88.

2 The word comedy means "revel-song," as tragedy means "goat-song." For more details, see the works of Flickinger and Pickard-Cambridge (cited in the Bibliography).

3 The phallic symbol is an exaggerated representation of the male generative organ. Such symbols, as any visitor to Pompeii has seen for himself, were found on almost every street corner in ancient cities—charms against sterility and bad luck in general. In Athens, a "herm" was placed at the side of most doorways. A large number of these little columns surmounted by a head of Hermes and having a phallus were mutilated by a band of conspirators in 415 B.C. Unexpurgated representations of comic actors and choruses may be found in Bieber, *The History of the Greek and Roman Theater,* figs. 76–138.

4 For illustrations, see Bieber, *op. cit.*

5 Cf. above, p. 15. The lyrics in these epirrhematic forms are frequently termed "ode" and "antode," but the terms "strophe" and "antistrophe" are used in the present work.

6 For an analysis of the parabases of the extant comedies and a discussion of various theories, see P. W. Harsh, *Transactions of the American Philological Association,* 65 (1934), 178–97.

7 Cf. Walther Kranz, *Stasimon: Untersuchungen zu Form und Gehalt der Griechischen Tragödie* (Berlin, Weidmann, 1933), pp. 19–20.

8 Cf. p. 15, above.

9 *Ecclesiazusae* 582.

10 In the *Helen,* the chorus makes no comment before Helen's passionate appeal to Theonoe—to do so would be artificial and stilted—but after her speech, the chorus express their sympathy and desire to hear what Menelaus will say in defense of his life (944–46). After he has spoken, they urge Theonoe to be favorable (996–97), and after she has delivered her decision, they praise justice (1030–31). A similar technique is used in the *Phoenissae* (465–589; here Jocasta bids the first speaker begin his address), and in the *Trojan Women* (911–1041; here Menelaus bids the first speaker begin; the decision goes to the second speaker).

Epirrhematic *kommoi* (lyrics with anapestic verse interlarded) are common in all periods of tragedy.

11 Kranz, *op. cit.,* p. 31. Kranz's assumption that the parabasis is the original epirrhematic form in comedy and the agon a later addition is unlikely for several reasons: the epirrhematic form is found in debate (between chorus and actor) in the earliest tragedy; it has a natural dramatic function here, whereas the parabasis, as Kranz points out, is "pure form." The functional use in the agon, it seems reasonable to assume, is the earlier.

12 Serious anapests are sometimes spoken by the coryphaeus in other parts of the play; cf. *Frogs* 354–71.

13 The chorus speaks as the poet: *Acharnians* 300–301; 1150–73; *Frogs* 389–93; Eupolis, frag. 357, Kock (perhaps part of an epirrhema of the parabasis). An actor speaks as the poet: *Acharnians* 377–82; 502–7; perhaps frag. 471, Kock; Plato Comicus, frag. 107, Kock (cf. Cyril Bailey, in *Greek Poetry and Life: Essays Presented to Gilbert Murray* [Oxford, At the Clarendon Press, 1936], pp. 234–35). See also Plautus, *Two Bacchides* 214–15.

14 Aristophanes in his middle period shows a peculiar tendency to maintain one theme through a series of lyrics near the end of the play; see, for example, *Lysistrata* 1043–71 and 1189–1215 (double lyrics interlarded).

VI. ARISTOPHANES

1 Convenient documentation for the facts of Aristophanes' life may be found in Victor Coulon, *Aristophane*, I (1923), i–vi.

2 This is the implication of *Knights* 541–44.

3 Cf. *Frogs* 416–30; Athenaeus, 622 D.

4 Aristotle, *Poetics* 1449 b.

5 Scholiast on *Acharnians* 67 (ca. 440–437 B.C.) ; *Knights* 1274–77.

6 This is not to say that Euripides did not produce great poetry; there is nothing in Aristophanes as truly magnificent as the chorus on youth and old age in Euripides' *Heracles* (637–700).

7 *Knights* 743 (literal; cf. 846), 1166–67 (allegorical).

8 Cf. Plutarch, *Nicias* 11. Plutarch (*Nicias* 9), furthermore, indicates that the theater played some part in bringing about the Peace of Nicias (421 B.C.).

9 Throwing grains of barley or sweetmeats to the audience is condemned, *Wasps* 58, *Plutus* 797–99; cf. *Clouds* 540–52; but Aristophanes makes this very thing the basis of a good joke in the *Peace* (962). The stock figure of the glutton Heracles is condemned, *Peace* 741, but is used incidentally in the *Birds* and in the *Frogs*. The slaves who are beaten and complaining of blows are condemned in the *Peace* (743–44), though one has been used just the year before in the *Wasps* (1292–96).

10 The reader who does not know Greek should have a key to the significant names in each play. The best translations usually include this. (In Oates and O'Neill, *The Complete Greek Drama*, this is given in the Glossary.)

11 *Acharnians* 659–64, however, is a parody of Euripides (frag. 918, Nauck²) ; the first person was used in the original passage.

12 Pherecrates' *Corianno* seems to have been a play about a courtesan with whom both a father and his son were in love, as in the *Mercator* of Plautus, and to have been written somewhat in the homely manner of later comedy. But it seems also to have had some of the characteristics of Old Comedy: father and son quarrel violently, and Corianno was probably the actual name of a contemporary woman at Athens. Cf. Athenaeus 567 C.

13 See below, pp. 309–10.

ACHARNIANS

14 So Cyril Bailey, "Who Played 'Dicaeopolis'?" *Greek Poetry and Life: Essays Presented to Gilbert Murray* (Oxford, At the Clarendon Press, 1936), pp. 231–40.

15 Cf. Thucydides, 1. 19.

16 Cf. Plutarch, *Pericles* 12.

17 Cf. Thucydides, 2. 20. On the crowded quarters of the city, cf. *Knights* 792–93.

18 A part of this emotional appeal is the celebration of the Rural Dionysia which Dicaeopolis undertakes. The appeal of this would be all the stronger if the Lenaean festival, at which the play was being produced, was the urban equivalent of the Rural Dionysia. (Martin P. Nilsson [*Geschichte der Griechischen Religion* (Munich, Beck, 1941), p. 559] seems to reject the identification of these two festivals.)

19 But these lines, including the use of the first person, are taken from Euripides (frag. 918, Nauck²) with slight change.

20 Telephus, wounded by the spear of Achilles, had been told by an oracle that the wounder must be the healer; and so he had come as a suppliant to the court of Agamemnon. Aeschylus, also, had treated the story of Telephus; but Aristophanes obviously is parodying Euripides' version.

21 Cf. Starkie, *The Acharnians of Aristophanes*, p. 117, commentary on lines 566 ff.; p. 250.

22 Cf. Starkie, *op. cit.*, p. 182, commentary on lines 885–86. The extant plays of Euripides with such recognitions, however, are subsequent to the date of this comedy. See also Aeschylus, *Choephoroe* 235–45.

KNIGHTS

23 Athenian citizens were divided into four classes according to their property for purposes of taxation and of determining military service (cf. *Knights* 925–26). The second of these classes, the knights, served as cavalry, furnishing their own horses, as did some members of the first class also. It will be recalled that the *Acharnians* opens with a reference to the knights' successful prosecution of Cleon on a charge of bribery. The composition of the *Knights* was definitely in prospect at that time (*Acharnians* 301).

24 Scholiast on *Knights* 1291; on *Clouds* 554. Cf. Eupolis, frag. 78, Kock. In the *Clouds* (553–54) Aristophanes claims that Eupolis misused the *Knights* in his attack upon Hyperbolus (*Maricas*, 421 b.c.). The parabasis of the *Knights* constitutes an interesting sketch of early comedy.

25 This account is taken almost wholly from Thucydides, 4. 1–45.

26 Thucydides, 5. 16, Jowett; this is the same explanation—fishing in troubled waters—as that offered by Aristophanes, *Knights* 801–9; 864–67.

27 Such a speech is essentially an informal adaptation of the Euripidean prologue. Aristophanes' frankness is effectively imitated in Molnar's *The Play's the Thing*.

28 The *Knights* parodies the lyric poets at several points; but the most amusing instance occurs with the first entrance of Demos, who comes on to the rescue of his lover Paphlagon as if he were Aphrodite answering the beautiful prayer of Sappho (1. 19–20). This is especially apt here, since the motive of the lover runs throughout the passage.

29 The length of the war (thrice nine years) was the "solitary instance," says Thucydides (5. 26, Jowett), "in which those who put their faith in oracles were justified by the event."

30 It is a mistake to contend that this last episode with the cookery is an after-thought. (Cf. Rogers, *The Knights of Aristophanes*, p. 154, on line 1098.) The stealing of the hare is too neat a climax; and, besides, talk of feasting and wenching regularly occurs at the end of an Old Comedy.

31 *Knights* 154, but cf. 234. If either Demosthenes or Nicias appears later—this is a matter of dispute—then a supernumerary actor was used for the role and spoke only a line or two.

CLOUDS

32 Connus was a musician and an instructor of Socrates in music. An account of Cratinus' *Flask* is given by Norwood, *Greek Comedy*, pp. 116–18.

33 The passage in which an attack is made upon the election of the Paphlagonian tanner as general (*Clouds* 575–94) was apparently written to come soon after the *Knights* and in this revised edition is jarringly inconsistent with the almost immediately preceding reference to Cleon's death (550). (These points, however, are subject to dispute.)

34 Whether the debate between the Just and the Unjust Argument and the burning of Socrates' school are wholly new in the revised edition is a matter of uncertainty.

35 Here as elsewhere Aristophanes fails to maintain a consistent point of view. Fun is poked at Socrates for being unwashed (837), but later the Just Argument is presented as unwashed (920) and contemptuous of the hot baths of the "moderns" (991 ; 1045). The real Socrates was physically as tough as any of the tough men of Marathon.

Critics are lacking in a sense of humor when they take seriously Aristophanes' excessive praise of the *Clouds* (*Wasps* 1047). This is of a piece with his usual slander of his rivals and praise of his own virtues. Other writers of Old Comedy indulged in these same extravagances; cf. Cratinus, frag. 306, Kock. (Wilamowitz [*Aristophanes: Lysistrate* (Berlin, Weidmann, 1927), p. 11, note 1] assigns this fragment to Eupolis.)

36 Cf. Starkie, *The Clouds of Aristophanes*, pp. xlvi–l; Lord, *Aristophanes*, pp. 116–33; Süss, *Aristophanes und die Nachwelt*, pp. 104–14; W. D. Ross, "The Problem of Socrates," *Proceedings of the Classical Association*, 30 (1933), 9–10.

37 Cf. Starkie, *op. cit.*, p. 61, commentary on *Clouds* 230.

Many scholars are of the opinion that Socrates was interested in physical science in his younger days. The fact remains, however, that the theories here cited were definitely attached to the names of others.

38 Cf. Starkie, *op. cit.*, p. 99, commentary on *Clouds* 378; scholiast on *Clouds* 361.

39 Aristotle, *Rhetoric* 2. 24 (1402 a) ; Aulus Gellius, 5. 3. 7. Later, in the *Wasps* (1037–1042) Aristophanes seems to imply that the evil forces attacked in the *Clouds* were the real school of the sycophants. (Starkie [*The Wasps of Aristophanes*, p. 316, commentary on line 1037] must be wrong in thinking that these lines do not refer to the *Clouds*.)

40 Compare *Clouds* 362–63, and Plato, *Symposium* 221 B, *Phaedo* 117 B.

41 Plato, *Apology* 19 C.

42 For further discussion, see the literature cited above, note 36.

43 An excellent sketch of Athens during this period is found in Forman, *Aristophanes: Clouds*, pp. 17–55.

44 Some scholars think that Alcibiades is being satirized in the figure of Pheidippides. But see Starkie, *The Clouds of Aristophanes*, index, s.v. "Alcibiades."

45 In this debate, as in the debate between Euripides and Aeschylus in the *Frogs* and in the second debate between Cleon and Agoracritus in the *Knights*, the disputants speak their main speeches in different meters. The Just Argument and Aeschylus and Cleon speak in dignified anapests, the Unjust and Euripides and Agoracritus speak in pert iambic tetrameters. Cf. John Williams White, *The Verse of Greek Comedy* (London and New York, Macmillan, 1912), pp. 368–69.

46 The burning of the "Think-Shop" may have been inspired by a mob's actual burning of the Pythagorean school in Croton, a town of southern Italy. Many persons were here burned to death. Cf. Starkie, *op. cit.*, pp. 308–9, commentary on lines 1489 ff.

47   This is the earliest example of a practice which later becomes the rule in New Comedy. (This example is not admitted by Coulon and others, but Socrates retires at line 887 in order that his actor may take the role of the Unjust Argument in the following debate, and a lyric or interlude of some sort is necessary to allow time for this change of roles.)

48   This is especially true of Pheidippides.

WASPS

49   Some days before the actual presentation of plays, a preliminary ceremony or preview was held in the Odeum. Cf. Haigh and Pickard-Cambridge, *The Attic Theatre*[3], p. 67. In the *Preview* of Aristophanes, Euripides played a role (so the scholiast on *Wasps* 61), and possibly the feud of the *Clouds* was continued. In the first edition of the *Clouds*, it seems, Aristophanes had intimated that Socrates was the real author of Euripides' clever and argumentative tragedies (frag. 376, Kock; cf. *Frogs* 1491–99). Other comic poets intimated the same thing. Cf. Diogenes Laertius, 2. 18.
     Racine borrowed from the *Wasps* for his one comedy, *Les Plaideurs* (1668).

50   The huge size of Athenian juries, which always numbered hundreds and sometimes even thousands of individuals, was designed to prevent bribery and is the point of an amusing passage in the *Clouds* (208). On legal procedure, see Robert J. Bonner and Gertrude Smith, *Administration of Justice from Homer to Aristotle* (2 vols., University of Chicago Press, 1930, 1938).

51   See, for instance, the historical sketch included in the treatment of the *Frogs*.

52   Cf. Thucydides, 5. 10.

53   The precise divisions of structural units in the comedies varies with each authority. In the present work, divisions are made primarily according to content and function rather than according to meter or external form, but satisfactory treatment is impossible within brief limits. See the commentaries of Starkie and also the following works: John Williams White, *The Verse of Greek Comedy* (London and New York, Macmillan, 1912), pp. 422–58; Th. Zielinski, *Die Gliederung der Altattischen Komoedie* (Leipzig, Teubner, 1885).

PEACE

54   In his *Toadies*, Eupolis satirized Callias, the son of Hipponicus, and the "parasites" (Sophists) who had collected about him. He was one of the richest of all Athenians at that time (but not when he died!). Protagoras was a character in the play and an especial object of attack. Leucon's play is thought to have been primarily an attack upon Hyperbolus, who is incidentally satirized in the *Peace* and in every other extant play of Aristophanes during this period. Hyperbolus was finally ostracized in 417 B.C., in part perhaps because of this merciless satire. Melanthius, a writer of tragedies, was attacked in the *Toadies*, the *Peace*, and the *Clansmen*.

55   Cf. *Knights* 390, 1057.

56   Thucydides, 5. 20.

57   The precise manner of staging the *Peace* has long been a disputed question. Cf. Roy C. Flickinger, "The Staging of Aristophanes' 'Pax,'" *Mélanges Offerts à M. Octave Navarre* . . . . (Toulouse, Edouard Privat, 1935), pp. 191–206.
     Aristophanes' use of the colossal figure of Peace was as unfitted to the careless informality of Old Comedy as Euripides' use of a mechanical Pegasus was to the dignity of tragedy. Both Eupolis and Plato "Comicus" satirized this clumsy device of Aristophanes. (Cf. the scholiast on Plato, *Apology* 19 C.) The Aetnean beetle is reminiscent of Epicharmus (frag. 76, Kaibel).

58   The theory that war is caused by the makers of armament, so widely publicized after the war of 1914–18, is well enunciated by Aristophanes here and elsewhere. Compare Robert E. Sherwood's *Idiot's Delight*.

59 The reference to the miserliness of Sophocles, lines 695–99, has puzzled many scholars. This, like the following reference to Cratinus, probably is a mere joke directed against Sophocles' easy irresponsibility in financial matters. Cf. Cicero, *Cato on Old Age* (*De Senectute*), 22; *Life of Sophocles*, 13 (but here the complaint is against his generosity to his illegitimate family).

60 Cf. *Wasps* 1030–36. The repetition of these lines is not, as has been claimed, an indication of hurry or evidence that the parabasis was written after the remainder of the play was finished. The primary concern of the play is to combat the policy of the dead Cleon.

61 Popular superstition had been greatly abused by soothsayers and oracle-mongers during the war (and before!). See above, p. 227. Perhaps the present attack is made especially to combat the prediction that the war must last thrice nine years (cf. Plutarch, *Nicias* 9).

BIRDS

62 No fragment or information about Ameipsias' play has been preserved. Phrynichus' hermit may have borne some resemblance to Pisthetaerus, as he had fled from active life and was living like Timon. (Cf. *Birds* 1549; Shakespeare's *Timon of Athens*.) Several individuals were mentioned both in the *Hermit* and in the *Birds*: Teleas, Peisander, Meton, Execestides, Nicias, and Heracles.

63 "Utopia" is a word of Greek origin, the original meaning "nowhere."

64 Hypothesis II.

65 *Birds* 145–48, 1204, 640 (but compare 363).

66 Cf. *Birds* 1583–85. The *Lysistrata*, which might be taken to advocate a revolution, was produced under very different conditions.

67 The ideal of having a city of festivity and easy-going life is not wholly forgotten; compare lines 127–42 and 1318–22.

68 Victor Coulon and Hilaire Van Daele, *Aristophane*, III (Paris, "Les Belles Lettres," 1928), 11–15. Arthur Bernard Cook (*Zeus: A Study in Ancient Religion*, III [Cambridge University Press, 1940], 44–68) thinks that Basileia is really Hera Basileia and reference is being made in the play to Argos. This apparently rather pointless suggestion is rejected by Campbell Bonner (*American Journal of Philology*, 64 [1943], 208–10), who thinks that Aristophanes had Athena somewhat in mind and that he may have remembered Peisistratus' return to power (Herodotus 1. 60). So Bonner is inclined to think the hero of the *Birds* should be called Peisetaerus.

69 Especially the mutilation of the hermae (see above, p. 472, note 3) and the desecration of the mysteries.

70 This technique is repeated later (1269–70).

LYSISTRATA

71 The *Lysistrata* in an adaptation by Dmitry Smolin, translated by George S. and Gilbert Seldes, was produced in Philadelphia in 1930 and later had an extended run in New York and on tour. For other modern adaptations and performances, see the introduction to the Seldes' work (listed below in the Bibliography).

72 See Euripides, *Andromache* 595–600.

73 Anxious as Aristophanes was for peace and thoroughgoing political reform, he doubtless had no stomach for the party who carried out a briefly successful revolution perhaps some months after the *Lysistrata* was produced. One of the chief leaders of this, Peisander, is attacked bitterly as one favoring the war because troubled times aid his thieveries (*Lysistrata* 489–91; cf. *Peace* 395). On this revolution, see p. 299.

74 Both these names were in actual use at Athens, but it is usually assumed that no individuals are here being satirized and that these names were chosen for the very suggestive verbal connotations which they have in Greek.

75 The Athenian magistrate enters here at precisely the right moment with no motivation.

76 Cf. Ulrich von Wilamowitz-Moellendorff, *Aristophanes: Lysistrate* (Berlin, Weidmann, 1927), pp. 29, 61.

THESMOPHORIAZUSAE

77 The title means "women celebrating the Thesmophoria." This was a festival in honor of Demeter and Persephone, the "law-givers" (*thesmophoroi*), who were the goddesses of grain and of stabilized civilization. This festival celebrated especially the disappearance of the seed (Persephone) beneath the earth at the time of the fall planting of winter wheat, the mourning of mother Demeter at this apparent death of her daughter, and finally their joyous reunion (the emergence of the new grain). This cult of death and rebirth was the religion most revered at Athens.

78 Scholars think that the *Lysistrata* was presented at the Lenaea, this play at the City Dionysia in 411 B.C. Cf. Paul Geissler, *Chronologie der Altattischen Komödie*, Philologische Untersuchungen, 30 (Berlin, Weidmann, 1925), 55-56. Cf. Ulrich von Wilamowitz-Moellendorff, *Aristoteles und Athen* (Berlin, Weidmann, 1893), II, 343-55. But Lamachus died not in the winter of the archonship of Charias (Chabrias), as Wilamowitz (p. 343) states, but in the summer of that of Teisander (cf. Diodorus, 13. 7-8; Thucydides, 6. 101).

79 Cf. *Frogs* 52-53 and the scholiast on line 53. See above, pp. 225-26.

80 Other plays, such as the *Clouds* and Aeschylus' *Agamemnon,* are presumed to open at night.

81 *Frogs* 83-84. Agathon was attacked in still other plays of Aristophanes, such as the *Gerytades.*

82 The very amusing scene in which Mnesilochus is shaved and singed is said by ancient commentators to have been taken from a comedy of Cratinus. Cf. Theodor Kock, *Comicorum Atticorum Fragmenta* (Leipzig, Teubner, 1880), I, 32.

83 Compare the parodos of the *Frogs,* which reflects the invocations at the Eleusinian festival.

FROGS

84 A good-natured fling is taken at Phrynichus in the first lines of the *Frogs.* Later a quite different Phrynichus, the leader of the oligarchical revolution of 411 B.C., is mentioned in the parabasis (689), and still another Phrynichus, the very early tragic poet, is cited by "Euripides" (910).

85 *Life of Aristophanes* 8.

86 Scholiast on *Peace* 741.
  For recently discovered fragments of Eupolis' *Demes,* see D. L. Page, *Greek Literary Papyri,* pp. 202-17.
  A lost play of Aristophanes, the *Gerytades,* may have been very similar to the *Frogs.* Cf. A. M. Young, "The *Frogs* of Aristophanes as a Type of Play," *Classical Journal,* 29 (1933), 23-32.

87 Cf. Thucydides, 8. 63-end; Xenophon, *Hellenic History* 1. 1. 1—2. 2. 24. The precise chronology of this period, however, is uncertain; cf. Lenschau in Bursian's *Jahresbericht* . . . . , 244 (1934), 68.

88 Cf. Ulrich von Wilamowitz-Moellendorff, *Aristoteles und Athen* (Berlin, Weidmann, 1893), II, 212-16.
  This fund was founded by Cleophon, and Aristophanes seems to imply that it

was being misused, as we should expect, to acquire political power. Other authors make the fare across the Styx one obol; ancient skulls found by modern archaeologists (as at Olynthus) usually have one, but sometimes two, three, or four coins in their mouths. (Cf. David M. Robinson in *American Journal of Archaeology*, 39 [1935], 228.) Aristophanes appears to have made the fare two obols (270) in order to facilitate the political reference.

89 On the *Andromeda*, one of the most popular plays of Euripides, see above, on the *Thesmophoriazusae* of Aristophanes and the *Helen* of Euripides.

90 The adjective here used for "well-disposed" (359) is the same as that used to describe Sophocles earlier (82). In line 358, a ban is laid upon those who indulge in untimely coarseness; the important word here is applied to Euripides at the end of the play (1521; cf. 1085).

91 *Frogs* 416–21, 534–41. The choral ribaldry, lines 416–30, suggests the ritualistic abuse—a purificatory rite—which characterized the Eleusinian procession when it reached the bridge over the Cephisus River. The verses on Theramenes are cleverly inserted where Dionysus is changing from one role to another. This change would include the heroic half-boots of Dionysus' original costume (*cothurni*, which were worn on either foot indiscriminately) and thus suggests the nickname, "Cothurnus," which had been given the shifty Theramenes.

92 Cf. Xenophon, *Hellenic History* 1. 4. 20; Plutarch, *Alcibiades* 34. Aristophanes himself, apparently, had attacked Alcibiades in his *Triphales*, perhaps in 410 or 409 B.C. (Cf. Paul Geissler, *Chronologie der Altattischen Komödie*, Philologische Untersuchungen, 30 [Berlin, Weidmann, 1925], 59. Geissler [p. 60] dates the return of Alcibiades as the spring of 408 B.C.)

93 *Frogs* 1391–92; Aeschylus, frag. 161, Nauck², Swinburne's translation (see above, p. 458, n. 22).
    Interesting criticism of the style of the three great dramatists is found in "Longinus," especially chapters 3, 15, 23, 40. Cf. John W. H. Atkins, *Literary Criticism in Antiquity* (Cambridge University Press, 1934), I, 27–32. Aristophanes was accused of imitating Euripides by Cratinus (frag. 307, Kock), and Aristophanes (frag. 471, Kock) admitted the charge to some degree. Aristophanes is joined with Euripides by "Longinus" (40) as securing dignity by skillful use of ordinary words.

94 On *Hippolytus* 612, see above, p. 462, n. 79.

95 The Greek word here translated "stop-at-nothing" is used as a proper noun by Cicero (*Pro Roscio Comoedo* 27) and by Rabelais, *Panurge*. Cf. *Acharnians* 603. Aristophanes exerted a strong influence on Rabelais; cf. Lord, *Aristophanes*, p. 135.

96 *Frogs* 1491–99; I *Clouds*, frag. 376, Kock. Other comic poets made the same charge; cf. Diogenes Laertius, 2. 18.

97 Thucydides, 2. 40.

98 In this debate, Aeschylus speaks in dignified anapestic meter, whereas Euripides' main speech has been in pert iambic tetrameter. See note 45 above.

99 In a comedy cited as the *Second Thesmophoriazusae*, Aristophanes had the nurse of Demeter speak the prologue, possibly parodying Euripides' *Medea*. (See the scholiast on *Thesmophoriazusae* 299 and Photius, *Lexicon*, s.v. Kalligeneia.) The Euripidean prologue nevertheless became the rule in later comedy—even the prologues of the latest plays of Aristophanes himself approach the Euripidean type.

100 Cf. John Williams White, *The Verse of Greek Comedy* (London and New York, Macmillan, 1912), pp. 145–47.

101 See above, p. 471, note 213, on Euripides, *Iphigenia at Aulis*.

102   For ancient theory of the bearing of music on morality, see Plato, *Republic* 398 C–402 E.

103   See above, p. 457, note 9, on Euripides.

ECCLESIAZUSAE

104   "Women Holding an Assembly (*ecclesia*)." Paul Geissler dates the play 391 B.C. (*Chronologie der Altattischen Komödie,* Philologische Untersuchungen, 30 [Berlin, Weidmann, 1925], 73.)

105   Cf. *Ecclesiazusae* 220, 456–57, 571–87, 812–29.

106   Cf. Aristotle, *Politics 2*. 5 (1263 a) ; but compare *Ecclesiazusae* 579.

107   Vague preparation for some extravagant proposal is found in lines 229–32.

108   Some scholars think that there was originally an interlude after line 1111.

109   The identity here is much disputed.

PLUTUS

110   Plutus was the proverbially blind god of wealth.

111   *Life of Aristophanes* 10. The *Cocalus* may have been in part or whole a parody of Sophocles' *Kamikoi.* The *Cocalus* was produced perhaps in 387 B.C. at the City Dionysia. Cf. Paul Geissler, *Chronologie der Altattischen Komödie,* Philologische Untersuchungen, 30 (Berlin, Weidmann, 1925), 2.

112   Hyphothesis I (edition of F. W. Hall and W. M. Geldart, *Aristophanis Comoediae,* Oxford, At the Clarendon Press, 1907).

     Descriptions of earthly paradises, however, were frequent in Old Comedy.

113   In the tragedies of Seneca, the leader of the chorus regularly takes no part in the dialogue if two or more speaking characters are present.

114   Compare *Plutus* 802–22 and Plautus, *Captives* 498–515. The evils of slavery, the topic on which Cario opens the prologue, is a commonplace in New Comedy (somewhat in Old Comedy also; cf. *Peace* 744); so is the scene of the ill-humored slave answering the door (*Plutus* 1097–1107).

115   *Plutus* 40, 75, 83, 414, 453; 275–76 (cited by Norwood, *Greek Comedy,* p. 273).

116   As Poverty is driven off she declares that Chremylus and his companion will one day recall her; but this prediction finds no fulfillment in the action.

VII. INTRODUCTION TO NEW COMEDY

1   Haigh and Pickard-Cambridge, *The Attic Theatre*³, pp. 18–19.

2   Körte in Pauly-Wissowa, *Real-Encyclopädie* . . . . , Vol. 15 (1932), cols. 754–55, s.v. "Menandros."

     Cf. Weissinger, *A Study of Act Divisions in Classical Drama,* p. 59.

3   Ovid, *Tristia 2*. 369.

4   Accius, frag. 78, Warmington (II. 352). See above, p. 465, n. 128.

5   L. A. Post in Oates and O'Neill, *The Complete Greek Drama,* II, 1123. See, also, Post's article, "Menander in Current Criticism," *Transactions of the American Philological Association,* 65 (1934), 13–34.

6   See page 332.

7   Translations of the plays should include explanations of significant names, as does W. A. Oldfather's translation of the *Brothers* (see the Bibliography). Only the most important cases are noted in this Handbook. Learned commentaries of the plays usually explain the names. See also James Curtiss Austin, *The Significant Name in Terence,* University of Illinois Dissertation, University of Illinois Studies in Language and Literature, Vol. VII, No. 4 (1921).

8   For documentation, see the various accounts under these names in Pauly-Wissowa, *Real-Encyclopädie* . . . .

VIII. MENANDER

ARBITRATION

1 This story is told by Hyginus, *Fabula* 187. The precise events dramatized in Euripides' play are unknown.

2 Syriscus' insistence that everyone must be concerned with the administration of justice is a commonplace but perhaps is also a conscious reminiscence of Euripides' *Hecuba* 844-45.
Although the scene of arbitration is taken from tragedy, one should not forget that Athenians in actual life were notorious for their litigiousness, as Aristophanes shows in the *Wasps*, and that formal arbitration was a well-recognized method of settling disputes, especially for slaves, since they had no legal rights and could take nothing to court. The use of a baby to make an appeal to the opponent or judge, furthermore, was frequent in ancient Athens.

3 E.g., the original of Plautus' *Casket*, and the original of Caecilius' *Necklace* (*Plocium*).

4 Improbable coincidence is found in tragedy but usually under extenuating circumstances. It is often based upon well-established legend or is outside the action proper of the play.

5 The use of assonance emphasizes the impudence of the slave (669 Jensen [745 Körte³]).

IX. INTRODUCTION TO ROMAN COMEDY

1 For a discussion of this subject and the various authors whose works have not been preserved, see J. Wight Duff, *A Literary History of Rome, From the Origins to the Close of the Golden Age²*, pp. 124-32, 156-223; Lily Ross Taylor, "The Opportunities for Dramatic Performances in the Time of Plautus and Terence," *Transactions of the American Philological Association*, 68 (1937), 284-304.

2 Cf. Warmington, *Remains of Old Latin*, II, 141, frag. 7-8 (126-27, Ribbeck³).

3 *Ibid.*, p. 75 (*Acontizomenos*).

4 *Ibid.*, pp. 75-79 (*Agitatoria*).

5 *Ibid.*, p. 75 (*Acontizomenos*).

6 *Ibid.*, p. 79 (*Agrypnuntes*), p. 99 (*Tarentilla*). It is not certain that these passages come from prologues.

7 Terence, *Woman of Andros*, prologue 18.

8 At one point in the *Two Bacchides* (106-8), a character suggests withdrawing, for she sees someone coming on and raising a disturbance. This seems to announce the arrival of a chorus. Such an announcement of the chorus' first appearance is frequent. One may compare Euripides, *Phoenissae* 196, Alexis, frag. 107, Kock, Menander, *Arbitration* 33-35, Jensen and Körte³, *Shearing of Glycera* 71-76. This appears to be a case where an interlude chorus was used in Plautus, for we can hardly assume, as some scholars do in similar cases, that Plautus was asleep when he translated this passage—and the actors asleep when they produced it. The frequency of such choral interludes in Plautus and Terence is a much disputed point. See Clinton C. Conrad, *The Technique of Continuous Action in Roman Comedy* (University of Chicago Dissertation, Menasha, Wisconsin, Banta, 1915), and the review of this work by Roy C. Flickinger in *Classical Weekly*, 10 (1916-17), 147-51. Incidentally one may note that the modern act division does not occur at line 108 of the *Two Bacchides*, as of course it should.
The basis for the division into acts in Terence is found in the ancient commen-

tators, who divided his plays into five acts, but not without misgivings. On this whole question, see Weissinger, *A Study of Act Divisions in Classical Drama*.

9 Cf. Körte in Pauly-Wissowa, *Real-Encyclopädie* . . . . , Vol. 11 (1922), cols. 1272–73, s.v. "Komödie."

10 Gellius (2. 23) quotes some sixteen iambic lines of Menander and compares the version of Caecilius (died 168 B.C.), which is written in anapestic and elaborate lyric meters.

11 In general, see Bieber, *The History of the Greek and Roman Theater*, pp. 315–25. W. Beare believes masks were used at an early period ("Masks on the Roman Stage," *Classical Quarterly*, 33 [1939], 139–46).

X. PLAUTUS

1 Gellius (3. 3. 14) is our main source of information. For fuller discussion, see J. Wight Duff, *A Literary History of Rome, From the Origins to the Close of the Golden Age*², pp. 159–66. Cf. Tenney Frank, "Notes on Plautus," *American Journal of Philology*, 58 (1937), 348–49.

2 Gellius 1. 24. 3.

3 For a discussion of chronology see Charles Henry Buck, Jr., *A Chronology of the Plays of Plautus* (Johns Hopkins Dissertation, Baltimore, 1940). Buck (p. 105) dates the plays as follows: *Comedy of Asses*, 207; *Merchant*, 206; *Braggart Warrior*, 205; *Casket*, 202; *Stichus*, 200; *Pot of Gold*, 194 or after; *Curculio*, 193 or after; *Haunted House*, 193 or after; *Carthaginian*, 191; *Pseudolus*, 191; *Epidicus*, 190; *Two Bacchides*, 189; *Rope*, 189; *Captives*, 188; *Three Bob Day*, 187; *Truculentus*, 186; *Amphitryon*, 186; *Twin Menaechmi*, 186; *Persian*, 186; *Casina*, 184. See also the review of Buck's work by George E. Duckworth, *American Journal of Philology*, 64 (1943), 348–52.

4 The monotonous repetition of a rhythmical pattern is sometimes found in Plautine cantica just as it is characteristic of American popular songs. Indeed some identical patterns can be cited. Thus the delightful lyric of the terrified Pardalisca in the *Casina* (621–27) has essentially the same rhythm as "Wintergreen for President" from *Of Thee I Sing*, by G. S. Kaufman and M. Ryskind; music by G. Gershwin and I. Gershwin. The Latin runs as follows (a final vowel standing before an initial vowel is slurred):

> Nulla sum, nulla sum, tota tota occidi,
> cor metu mortuomst, membra miserae tremunt, ...

This is cretic meter. Bacchiac lyrics are also frequent in Plautus, such as that of Menaechmus (*Men.* 571–79) on the nuisances of clientage. A modern song written perhaps in this rhythm is the second verse of the anonymous American song entitled, "Oh Dear, What Can the Matter Be?"

5 An effort has been made to trace systematic development in Plautus' handling of intrigue, his use of obscenity, and various other features. Such studies have usually been based on analysis that is too mechanical. One should not expect more precision in a subject, as Aristotle says, than the subject admits. It is impossible, for instance, significantly to measure the precise number of times obscenity occurs in Plautus, since a scene such as that at the end of the *Braggart Warrior* may outweigh ten or a hundred mildly indecent jests. No trustworthy conclusions, therefore, have resulted.

6 *Epistles* 2. 1. 170–76.

7 *Woman of Andros*, prologue, 18–21, *Brothers*, prologue, 6–11. Some, however, denied the Plautine authorship of the *Suicide Pact* (*Commorientes*), the play which Terence cites. Cf. Gellius 3. 3. 9.

8 *De Oratore* 3. 45; *De Officiis* 1. 104. Cf. Quintilian, 10. 1. 99.

AMPHITRYON

9   Heracles was eight months old when he strangled the serpents according to Apollodorus (*Bibliotheca* 2. 62), ten months according to Theocritus (24. 1).

10 There is no evidence that these elements were combined before Plautus. On the problem, see Henry W. Prescott, "The *Amphitruo* of Plautus," *Classical Philology*, 8 (1913), 14–22. Conversion of the long night into one of dalliance has involved the poet in various improbabilities and inconsistencies.

11 Andreas Thierfelder ("Die Motive der Griechischen Komödie im Bewusstsein Ihrer Dichter," *Hermes*, Vol. 71 [1936], p. 327, note 1) assigns the original play to New Comedy because of the scene of the "running slave" (984–1008) and the references to the motive of the parasite (515–21, 993).

12 Cf. *Pot of Gold* 181.

13 Note how Amphitryon's idea of appealing to the king (1042) is elaborated in Rotrou, Molière, and others.

14 Cf. Adam E. A. K. Roeder, *Menechmi und Amphitruo im Englischen Drama bis zur Restauration 1661*, Leipzig Dissertation (Leipzig, Glausch, 1904), pp. 28–36; in general, see Reinhardstoettner, *Plautus: Spätere Bearbeitungen* . . . . , pp. 115–229.

15 This scene may conceivably have been suggested by the lines of Plautus which report that Jupiter within is recounting to Alcmena the happenings of the war (133–34). It was a stroke of genius, however, to change this martial braggadocio to marital, and to produce the scene on stage.

16 This irony may be lost in some translations, such as that of Allison in Duckworth's *The Complete Roman Drama*, but it is cleverly preserved in the superior translation of Nixon. The lyric nature of many passages is lost in both these translations.

17 *Amphitryon* 516–17 and 1146 in the translation of Paul Nixon, *Plautus*, I (1916), in Loeb Classical Library (London, Heinemann, and New York, Putnam [now handled at Cambridge, Massachusetts, by Harvard University Press]). Line 508 is given in the present writer's translation.

COMEDY OF ASSES

18 Louis Havet and Andrée Freté, *Pseudo-Plaute: Le Prix des Ânes* (Paris, "Les Belles Lettres," 1925).

19 This motive, of course, is found elsewhere. In the *Fishes* (*Ichthyes*) of Archippus, for instance, an agreement between the fishes and the Athenians occurred; and the famous courtesan Gnathaena, mistress of Diphilus, drew up a code for the conduct of her admirers at dinner in imitation of such codes among the philosophers. Cf. Athenaeus, 329 B–C, 585 B.

POT OF GOLD

20 The *Querolus*, an anonymous comedy from the period of the late Roman Empire, takes some superficial details from the *Pot of Gold*.
    In general, see Reinhardstoettner, *Plautus: Spätere Bearbeitungen* . . . . , pp. 255–324.

21 Cicero, *De Oratore* 3. 45.

22 The long list of caterers to feminine luxury which Megadorus recites is somewhat reminiscent of Aristophanes. Cf. Aristophanes, frag. 320, Kock (52 articles of toilet). But such lists belong to the inalienable rights of satirists; Rabelais expanded them to prodigious lengths. Reminiscent of Old Comedy also is Euclio's direct address to the audience—including direct insults—as he rages over the loss of his treasure.

TWO BACCHIDES

23 In a strange lapse of the dramatic illusion (lines 214–15), the actor Pellio is at-tacked, and his performance of the *Epidicus* cited. There is an external record of Pellio's having performed the *Stichus*, also. When the *Two Bacchides* was produced, Plautus was evidently no longer on good terms with his former actor. Cf. Friedrich Leo, *Geschichte der Römischen Literatur*, I (Berlin, Weidmann, 1913), 94–95.

24 Cf. Alfred Ernout, *Plaute*, II (Paris, "Les Belles Lettres," 1933), 7 (an excellent appreciation of the play).

25 Ernout, *op. cit.*, II, 9.

CAPTIVES

26 Gotthold Ephraim Lessing, *Beyträge zur Historie und Aufnahme des Theaters*, 4, in *Sämtliche Schriften*³, edited by Karl Lachmann (Stuttgart, Göschen, 1889), IV, 191–92. The purpose of comedy, Lessing thought, is to instruct and to improve the ethics of its spectators, a purpose achieved by making virtue attractive and vice odious and, even more, by having virtue rewarded and vice confounded in the outcome of the action. In these respects he considered the *Captives* unsurpassed— the first example of a play to show how comedy could be raised to a higher level. We must remember that the recently discovered fragments of Menander were unknown to Lessing.

27 Cf. Reinhardstoettner, *Plautus: Spätere Bearbeitungen . . . . ,* pp. 324–55.

28 The fifth section properly begins with line 922. Between lines 908 and 909, there was only a succession of crash and clatter of crockery from within. Cf. W. M. Lindsay, *The Captivi of Plautus* (London, Methuen, 1900), p. 323; Henry W. Prescott, "Three *Puer*-Scenes in Plautus, and the Distribution of Rôles," *Harvard Studies in Classical Philology*, 21 (1910), 37–39.

29 Lindsay, *op. cit.*, p. 273.

30 The failure of Philopolemus to appear and welcome his long-lost brother, however, is due not to classic restraint but probably to a desire of producing the play with as small a cast as possible. The roles of Tyndarus and Philopolemus may both have been played by the same actor. Cf. Carrie May Kurrelmeyer, *The Economy of Actors in Plautus* (Johns Hopkins University Dissertation, 1929, printed in Austria, 1932), p. 60.

CASINA

31 Line 980 refers to the suppression of the worship of Bacchus at Rome in 186 B.C. Since the Bacchae seem to be mentioned only in order to make this reference, and since the reference would be most pointed immediately after the decree, it is not likely that these lines are a later insertion.

32 Alfred Ernout, *Plaute*, II (Paris, "Les Belles Lettres," 1933), 155.

33 Cf. *Rope* 429, Athenaeus, 451 B–C.

34 Cf. Ulrich von Wilamowitz-Moellendorff, "Die Kunst des Menander," in *Menander: Das Schiedsgericht (Epitrepontes)* (Berlin, Weidmann, 1925), p. 166.
    Scholars are not warranted in assuming from the reference to Plautus in line 65 that things were different in the Greek play, since "Plautus" may here be used merely for "the author" as "Terence" is used in the ancient commentaries (for example, "Donatus" on *Andria* 9, 119, *Eunuchus* 360).

35 See note 73, below, on Plautus, *Rope*.

CASKET

36 Line 202 refers to the expected victory of the Romans over the Carthaginians, which actually occurred in 202 B.c. A better English title for this play perhaps would be "The Jewel Box."

37 Cf. Ernst Wüst in his review of Greek Comedy for 1931–37 in Bursian's *Jahresbericht* . . . . , 263 (1939), 87.

38 For discussion and bibliography of this mosaic, see Wüst, in *Jahresbericht*, cited above, pp. 82–83; for an illustration, see Bieber, *The History of the Greek and Roman Theater*, p. 179, fig. 242.

39 Richard Mahrenholtz, *Molières Leben und Werke* . . . . , *Französische Studien*, 2 (Heilbronn, Henninger, 1881), 272.

CURCULIO

40 See also the *Merchant* 409.

41 Cf. Reinhardstoettner, *Plautus: Spätere Bearbeitungen* . . . . , p. 361.
    This play is thought to have been written in part by Fletcher. Cf. *The Cambridge History of English Literature*, VI (1910), 132.

42 This passage is often compared to the parabasis of Old Comedy. The only significant resemblance, however, is found in the informality of introducing such an address. It appears to be a Plautine addition designed to replace the Greek interlude chorus. But some scholars think that a similar address may have occurred in the Greek original. See Henry W. Prescott, "Inorganic Rôles in Roman Comedy," *Classical Philology*, 15 (1920), 269–71.

EPIDICUS

43 Cf. *Two Bacchides* 214–15. Plautus' praise of the *Epidicus* in that passage, like Aristophanes' praises of his own plays, amounts to little more than a press agent's blurb and does not, as is often stated, prove that the *Epidicus* was a favorite play.

44 Cf. Reinhardstoettner, *Plautus: Spätere Bearbeitungen* . . . . , p. 406.

45 For an excellent discussion of the vexed question of Plautine changes in this play, see Clinton W. Keyes, "Half-Sister Marriage in New Comedy and the *Epidicus*," *Transactions of the American Philological Association*, 71 (1940), 217–229. Some scholars think that a Plautine prologue has been lost from the play. The reason for Epidicus' talk of a Rhodian soldier (300) rather than the Euboean soldier previously mentioned (153), explains Keyes (*ibid.*, p. 223), lies in the too close proximity of Euboea to Athens. His scheme calls for the removal of the girl from the vicinity.

46 Cf. George E. Duckworth, *T. Macci Plauti Epidicus* (Princeton University Press, 1940), pp. 277–79.

TWIN MENAECHMI

47 Especially the version of Hyde and Weist (see Bibliography below). Some of the metrical variation of Plautus is here preserved, as also in the much more formal version of Rogers. The metrical variety of *The Comedy of Errors* is thought by some to reflect that of Plautus. (So George Lyman Kittredge, *The Complete Works of Shakespeare* [Boston, Ginn, 1936], p. 134.)

48 Most recent editors and translators take *peniculus* to mean "brush." Brushing the dinner table and brushing shoes sounds more natural to the modern ear. Editors cite Festus (260. 15 [W. M. Lindsay, Leipzig, Teubner, 1913]), who says that "the ancients" used animal tails for brushing shoes; but the present writer, without disputing this, prefers the evidence of Homer (*Odyssey* 1. 111, etc.) for wiping

a table with a sponge, and that of Aristophanes (*Wasps* 600) and Athenaeus (351 A) for wiping shoes with a sponge. The name *peniculus* also has an obscene undertone; and sponges were put to certain obscene uses when paper had not yet been invented, as we may observe in Aristophanes' *Frogs* (484) and elsewhere.

49   Cf. Reinhardstoettner, *Plautus: Spätere Bearbeitungen* . . . . , pp. 490–594; Adam E. A. K. Roeder, *Menechmi und Amphitruo im Englischen Drama bis zur Restauration 1661*, Leipzig Dissertation (Leipzig, Glausch, 1904).

50   Shakespeare avoided the omniscient prologue here but only by the desperate expedient of introducing Aegeon and Aemilia—more implausibility.

51   The similarity of the twins was doubtless facilitated in the Greek original by the use of identical masks, but masks perhaps were not used in the presentation of Plautus' plays.

52   Athenaeus, 621 D. Cf. Legrand, *The New Greek Comedy*, p. 100.

MERCHANT

53   The dream of Demipho is similar to the dream of Daemones in the *Rope*, and certain generalizing lines are identical. The explanation of this is highly disputed. Cf. P. W. Harsh, *Studies in Dramatic "Preparation" in Roman Comedy* (University of Chicago Dissertation, University of Chicago Press, 1935), p. 78, note 23.

54   Some scholars think that the departure from home is a parody of a tragedy concerning Teucer. Cf. Tenney Frank, "Two Notes on Plautus. 1. Parody in Act V of Plautus' *Mercator*," *American Journal of Philology*, 53 (1932), 243–48.

BRAGGART WARRIOR

55   Cf. Julius Brix, Max Niemeyer, Oskar Köhler, *Ausgewählte Komödien des T. Maccius Plautus: IV Miles Gloriosus*[4] (Leipzig, Teubner, 1916), p. 26.

56   *Bellum Alexandrinum* 24 (an anonymous work in the corpus of Julius Caesar).

57   For the Albanian tale, see Gustav Meyer and Reinhold Köhler, "Albanische Märchen," *Archiv für Litteraturgeschichte*, 12 (1884), 134–37. For a somewhat similar story, see that of Kamar al-Zaman and the Jeweller's Wife, in Richard F. Burton, *Arabian Nights' Entertainments, Thousand Nights and a Night* (London, Printed by the Burton Club, no date), IX, 246–304, Nights 963–78. Cf. Blanche Brotherton, "The Plot of the *Miles Gloriosus*," *Transactions of the American Philological Association*, 55 (1924), 128–36.

58   Cf. Reinhardstoettner, *Plautus: Spätere Bearbeitungen* . . . . , pp. 595–680; Herman Graf, *Der Miles Gloriosus im Englischen Drama bis zur Zeit des Bürgerkrieges* (Rostock Dissertation, Schwerin i.M., Herberger, 1892).

HAUNTED HOUSE

59   Cf. Reinhardstoettner, *Plautus: Spätere Bearbeitungen* . . . . , pp. 444–89.

60   Cf. Edwin W. Fay, "Further Notes on the Mostellaria of Plautus," *American Journal of Philology*, 24 (1903), 245–48. Fay (pp. 248–60) also has an interesting discussion of the significant names in the play.

61   The story of the ghost is similar to those told by Pliny the Younger (*Letters* 7. 27) and Lucian (*Liar* [*Philopseudes*] 29–31 [55–58]).

62   The use of Callidamates to facilitate the plot is noteworthy. At his first entrance he directs slaves to come for him later, and it is these slaves who reveal the true state of affairs to Theopropides. It is his drunkenness, furthermore, which makes immediate dispersion of the carousal impossible.

PERSIAN

63   Alfred Ernout, *Plaute*, V (Paris, "Les Belles Lettres," 1938), 97.
64   *Ibid.*, p. 94.

CARTHAGINIAN

65 This use of an unintelligible foreign language is really quite different from Aristophanes' use of dialect or nonsense sounds. Compare the mime *Charition*, D. L. Page, *Greek Literary Papyri*, I, 337–49.

PSEUDOLUS

66 The name Pseudolus means "trickster" or "liar." It is a mistake to assert, as many scholars do, that the ancients considered the role of Ballio the leading one of the play because Roscius, a famous actor of Cicero's day, played Ballio (Cicero, *Pro Roscio Comoedo* 20). Possibly Roscius, already of mature age and already or soon to become a Roman knight, rejected the role of Pseudolus because he felt that drunken dancing and belching in another's face was beneath his dignity. One may recall the case of Decimus Laberius, a Roman knight who was forced by Caesar to act one of his own mimes (Macrobius, *Saturnalia* 2. 7) and the dignified lines of Cicero perhaps in reference to this incident (*De Officiis* 1. 114).
Obviously the *Pseudolus* was still a popular play in the time of Cicero.

67 Cf. Terence, *Woman of Andros* 168–71; Euripides, *Ion* 77, *Electra* 297–99.

68 Cf. Alfred Ernout, *Plaute*, VI (Paris, "Les Belles Lettres," 1938); 11. For an extensive discussion, see John Newbold Hough, *The Composition of the* Pseudolus *of Plautus* (Princeton University Dissertation, 1931).

ROPE

69 Cf. P. W. Harsh, *Studies in Dramatic "Preparation" in Roman Comedy* (University of Chicago Dissertation, University of Chicago Press, 1935), p. 33, note 11.

70 Cf. Athenaeus, 351 C–352 B. Hedonism was one of the best-known exports of Cyrene, the home of the philosopher Aristippus.

71 The story is told (Athenaeus, 589 A) that Diphilus, being served a deliciously cold cup of wine by the famous hetaera Gnathaena, remarked on the excellence of her cistern. Gnathaena replied that her cistern was very cold indeed, since she was always careful to throw the prologues of his plays into it! (The wine had really been chilled with snow, the costly gift of another admirer.)

72 Sceparnio is apparently the only instance of a character in New Comedy who wears the phallus (*Rope* 429, often expurgated). Note that he is a slave. The phallus—reminiscent of the ultimate origin of comedy in phallic worship—was not invariably worn even in Old Comedy. Cf. Aristophanes, *Clouds* 538–39 (but contrast 734). Cf. Bieber, *The History of the Greek and Roman Theater*, p. 70.

73 Ennius, *Andromache Captive*, frag. lines 95–100, Warmington (75–80, Ribbeck³, 86–91, Vahlen).

74 Cf. Salomon Reinach, *Répertoire des Vases Peints* (Paris, Leroux, 1923–24), I, 161 (illustration). For discussion, see Friedrich Marx, *Plautus: Rudens*, Abhandlungen der Sächsischen Akademie der Wissenschaften zu Leipzig, 38. 5 (Leipzig, Hirzel, 1928), commentary on line 688; illustrated on p. 1.

75 Other instances of parody occur in the *Rope*, especially the dream of Daemones and its use to foretell the coming action.

76 This appears the most apt interpretation of a disputed line.

STICHUS

77 This type of notice has been preserved only for the *Stichus* among all the plays of Plautus, though a fragment of such a record is preserved also for the *Pseudolus*.

78 This play, *Adelphoi A*, was a quite different comedy from the original of Terence's *Brothers, Adelphoi B*.

79   Breaking the dramatic illusion to notice the musician is found in Aristophanes, *Ecclesiazusae* 890–92. Cf. Plautus, *Pseudolus* 573 A.

THREE BOB DAY

80   Tenney Frank ("Some Political Allusions in Plautus' *Trinummus*," *American Journal of Philology*, 53 [1932], 152–56) thought that this play was produced in 187 B.C., and that it contains many veiled references to contemporary events of that time. This may be so; but most of the references in question, complaints of the corruption and abuses of the day, are commonplaces.

81   Gotthold Ephraim Lessing, *Beyträge zur Historie und Aufnahme des Theaters*, 1, in *Sämtliche Schriften*³, edited by Karl Lachmann (Stuttgart, Göschen, 1889), IV, 81.

82   Friedrich Leo (*Geschichte der Römischen Literatur*, I [Berlin, Weidmann, 1913], 117) is inclined to think that radical changes have been made by Plautus, but his grounds for this are not convincing. He fails to appreciate the humor of certain lines of Stasimus (413, 727), and so he misinterprets them. Indeed, in comparing this play with the *Haunted House* and in assuming that an affair of Lesbonicus played a larger role in the original, Leo seems to mistake the essential features of this plot.

83   Cf. Reinhardstoettner, *Plautus: Spätere Bearbeitungen* . . . . , pp. 757–63.

84   This monody is reminiscent of the equally delightful song of Philolaches in the *Haunted House*.

85   For a possible explanation of this feature, see note 80, above.

TRUCULENTUS

86   Critics ancient ("Donatus" on Terence, *Brothers* 986) and modern have complained of the sudden change in the truculent slave. A modern scholar has also assumed that the original had an omniscient prologue in which the story of Callicles' daughter was told. (Friedrich Leo, *Plautinische Forschungen*² [Berlin, Weidmann, 1912], p. 206.) Such a prologue would throw the whole emphasis of the play askew. The role of the truculent slave and its significance, too, would be spoiled by any elaboration of the obvious. The structure of the play is extraordinary, somewhat resembling that of Euripides' *Trojan Women;* but it is very skillfully managed and very effective. Reminiscent of Euripides is the attitude of this dramatist, also, for he certainly portrays men as they are and not as they ought to be.

XI. TERENCE

1   Most of this information comes from a biography of Terence by Suetonius. For documentation, see Günther Jachmann in Pauly-Wissowa, *Real-Encyclopädie* . . . . , Zweite Reihe, 5 (1934), cols. 598–650, s.v. "Terentius."

2   Reference is made to this rumor (in regard to Laelius) by Cicero (*Letters to Atticus* 7. 3. 10) and others beside Suetonius. Most modern scholars think that these great men may have given the benefit of their criticism but not that they actually collaborated with Terence. Except in this connection, we hear of no poetic activity by them. Cf. Schanz and Hosius, *Geschichte der Römischen Literatur*⁴, I, 104.

3   This story is suspect, since Caecilius died in 168 B.C.

4   Cf. Schanz and Hosius, *op. cit.*, I, 104.

5   Cf. Thomas Ashby, *The Roman Campagna in Classical Times* (London, Benn, 1927), p. 177.

6 For bibliography, see Schanz and Hosius, *op. cit.*, I, 122. An instructive sketch in English is found in F. G. Ballentine, *P. Terenti Afri Hauton Timorumenos* (New York, Sanborn, 1910), pp. vii–xviii. Two recent works may be cited: Katherine E. Wheatley, *Molière and Terence: A Study in Molière's Realism,* University of Texas Bulletin, No. 3130 (1931); Bernard Stambler, *Terence in Europe to the Rise of Vernacular Drama* (Cornell University Dissertation, 1938). See also Marie Delcourt, *La Tradition des Comiques Anciens en France avant Molière*, pp. 7–21.

7 Cf. Leslie Webber Jones and C. R. Morey, *The Miniatures of the Manuscripts of Terence Prior to the Thirteenth Century* (Princeton University Press, 1930); Margarete Bieber, *The History of the Greek and Roman Theater* (Princeton University Press, 1939), pp. 400–403.

8 Cf. Varro, *Saturae Menippeae* 399, Bücheler.

9 The *Mother-in-Law* has eighteen scenes, the *Self-Tormentor* twenty-two, and the other plays each from twenty-five to twenty-seven. Nine plays of Plautus have seventeen or less, the *Captives* has eighteen, and the *Twin Menaechmi* twenty-one, although the *Rope* has twenty-nine and the *Pot of Gold* originally had more than twenty-eight. (All these figures are according to the division into scenes of the standard Latin texts.)

10 For evidence of shortening, see the commentary of "Donatus" on *Mother-in-Law* 825, *Eunuch* 1001. Some fragments of the original plays, furthermore, have no equivalents in the plays of Terence. Certain partly recovered plays of Menander are thought to have extended to about eleven hundred lines. (Cf. Alfred Körte in Pauly-Wissowa, *Real-Encyclopädie* ...., Vol. 15 [1932], col. 724, s.v. "Menandros.")

11 Tenney Frank, *Life and Literature in the Roman Republic* (University of California Press, 1930), pp. 104–23. Cf. Philip W. Harsh, "A Study of Dramatic Technique as a Means of Appreciating the Originality of Terence," *Classical Weekly,* 28 (1934–35), 161–65.

12 *Brothers* 22–24, *Woman of Andros* 6; Evanthius, *De Fabula* 3. 2, Wessner. The fragmentary *Vidularia* (see line 11) of Plautus contained concealed identity but had no omniscient prologue.

13 Cf. W. E. J. Kuiper, *Grieksche Origineelen en Latijnsche Navolgingen* (Amsterdam, 1936), p. 9.

14 Cf. *Brothers* 9–10. Turpilius, a writer of comedy subsequent to Terence, changed an opening soliloquy into a dialogue in adapting Menander's *Heiress* (*Epicleros*).

15 Commentary of "Donatus" on *Hecyra* 825 (a much disputed comment).

16 Cf. Heinz Haffter, *Untersuchungen zur Altlateinischen Dichtersprache,* Problemata 10 (Berlin, Weidmann, 1934), p. 127.

17 Wolfgang Schadewaldt, *Monolog und Selbstgespräch,* Neue Philologische Untersuchungen, 2 (Berlin, Weidmann, 1926), p. 31, note. See *Self-Tormentor* 531. (This is found, however, also in Plautus' *Carthaginian,* line 1206.)

18 Cf. Euripides, *Iphigenia at Aulis* 414 (here the first words of an entering character perhaps interrupt the speaker). Menander, *Arbitration* 165, Jensen (206, Körte[3]).

19 Evanthius, *De Fabula* 3. 8, Wessner.

20 A possible parallel for this change of Terence is found in a fragment of the *Medea* of Ennius (266–68, Warmington [219–21, Ribbeck[3]; 259–61, Vahlen]). Here in translating Euripides, *Medea* 214–18, Ennius has eliminated what he may have taken for a woman's apology for appearing actively in public. Such an apology would seem pointless or ridiculous in the freer atmosphere of Rome. (On this interpretation of Euripides' difficult lines, see the scholiast on *Medea* 214 in Eduard Schwartz, *Scholia in Euripidem,* II (Berlin, Reimer, 1891), p. 156, line 26.

21 Both these "epigrams" are quoted by Suetonius in his *Life of Terence*. The precise interpretation of Caesar's lines has been much disputed; suffice it here to say that Caesar does not, as so often is stated, call Terence a "half Menander," but rather "halved Menander," or in English perhaps "Menander's double." Both epigrams are certainly highly complimentary. Cf. Roy C. Flickinger, "Terence and Menander," *Classical Journal*, 26 (1930–31), 686–89.

22 The best consideration of these perhaps is that of Günther Jachmann in Pauly-Wissowa, *Real-Encyclopädie* . . . . , Zweite Reihe, 5 (1934), cols. 613–18, s.v. "Terentius."

WOMAN OF ANDROS

23 There is no sound basis for the assumption, which is often made, that a previous exhibition of this play had been unsuccessful.

24 Cf. Plautus, *Pseudolus* 549–60; Euripides, *Ion 77, Electra* 297–99.

25 In the *Three Bob Day* of Plautus a young gentleman, Lysiteles, wishes to marry a girl of good family and succeeds in doing so, but there is no hint of a strong romantic attachment.

Whether the characters Charinus and Byrria are wholly original with Terence or were taken from Menander's *Perinthia* or some other Greek comedy is still a disputed point. Cf. Edmund Bigott, *Die Komposition der Andria des Terenz* (Bochum-Langendreer, 1939) (not available to the present writer).

26 Byrria's assurance that Philumena is a beautiful girl, as the ancient commentator notes (line 428), cancels out the earlier remarks of Pamphilus in which, without ever having seen her, he surmises that she is some dreadful unmarriageable creature. This is a nice point and obviously Terence's own.

27 Menander used this situation not only in his *Andria* and *Perinthia* but also in the original from which Plautus' *Casket* is taken. Traces of its use in another play are found; cf. Otto Schroeder, *Novae Comoediae Fragmenta in Papyris Reperta* (Bonn, Marcus and Weber, 1915), p. 38; D. L. Page, *Greek Literary Papyri*, I, 281–87.

28 This passage is praised by Cicero (*De Oratore 2. 326–28*).

29 Pamphilus' description of how Chrysis gave him Glycerium suggests the Roman marriage ceremony. This was culminated by a matron's joining the right hands of the bride and groom, and the bride under certain circumstances was spoken of as coming into the hand of the groom.

30 The original Greek for line 611 is quoted by the commentator. This seems to make probable, though it does not prove, that the situation at this point in the original was the same.

EUNUCH

31 Suetonius, *Life of Terence 3*, Wessner. This play seems to have been reproduced in Terence's lifetime and later.

The best extended treatment of the *Eunuch* is still the introduction (French) of Philippe Fabia, *P. Terenti Afri Eunuchus* (Paris, Colin, 1895), pp. 1–72. See also Edward Kennard Rand, "The Art of Terence's *Eunuchus*," *Transactions of the American Philological Association*, 63 (1932), 54–72. This is an excellent appreciation, but Rand goes too far in finding Terentian originality. Specifically the assumption (Rand, pp. 59–66) that the Chaerestratus of Menander's *Eunouchos* is Chaerea in Terence's play can hardly be accepted, for the vacillation of Chaerestratus, which we know (from Persius, *Satire 5*. 161–75) to have been very much like that of Phaedria in the first scene of Terence's play, is wholly foreign to the very determined character of Chaerea. Even if we allow, with Rand (p. 59), that the character has been refashioned, the difference here is too great, and the events themselves seem to call for one vacillating and one determined character.

32   Chaerea's violation of Pamphila, as we are repeatedly reminded by Terence, takes place in the house of a courtesan (esp. 382, 960). It is no more brutal than the violation which forms the background for Menander's *Arbitration* (273 Jensen [314, Körte³]). In such cases the reported violence of the man keeps the moral intention of the girl above reproach. See above, p. 465, note 128, on Euripides' *Ion*, and p. 319.
     For other cases of the sharing of a sweetheart, such as occurs at the end of the *Eunuch*, see Philip W. Harsh, "Certain Features of Technique Found in Both Greek and Roman Drama," *American Journal of Philology*, 58 (1937), 285–87.

33   The proper names of the characters have been changed by Terence; he has given the name Chremes to a young man, whereas it seems to have been used in Greek New Comedy only of old men.

34   Commentary of "Donatus" on line 539. Günther Jachmann (Pauly-Wissowa, *Real-Encyclopädie* . . . . , Zweite Reihe, 5 [1934], cols. 636–37, s.v. "Terentius") considers this scene one of the best in Terence and refuses to believe that it is original with him. Following certain other scholars, Jachmann assumes that the commentary has been interpolated. This is possible; but the use of the word *poeta* by the commentator on line 607 is not a sound criterion, for this word may be used of either Terence or Menander. See chapter X. Plautus, note 34. Cf. P. W. Harsh, *Studies in Dramatic "Preparation" in Roman Comedy* (University of Chicago Dissertation, University of Chicago Press, 1935), p. 55, note. On the origin of Antipho, see also Alfred Klotz, *Philologische Wochenschrift*, Vol. 52 (1932), cols. 358–59.

35   This is a frequent literary device. So Vergil suggests the marriage ceremony in his beautiful description of the "cave scene" in the *Aeneid* (4. 160–172), and, partially in parody of Vergil, Petronius (112. 3) in his famous story of the widow of Ephesus.

36   Cf. Menander, *Shearing of Glycera (Perikeiromene)* 217–235; Lucian, *Dialogues of the Hetaerae*, No. 9.
     A phrase from the last line of this scene, "animus est in patinis" (my mind is in my pans), has been taken by a famous restaurant in San Francisco as one of its Latin mottoes.

PHORMIO

37   The dramatist might possibly have given a hint of the true situation by having Geta mention that Phanium had come to Athens from Lemnos and that Chremes had made many long visits there.

MOTHER-IN-LAW

38   Commentary of "Donatus" on line 58.

39   Commentary of "Donatus" on line 825. The meaning of this comment, however, is highly disputed.

BROTHERS

40   Cf. Schanz and Hosius, *Geschichte der Römischen Literatur⁴*, I, 112.

41   Suetonius, *Life of Terence* 3, Wessner. To how much of the play this refers and what criteria Varro was using are disputed points. Terence is a master of expository style, but to assume with Drexler that Varro preferred Terence's style to Menander's would be rash indeed. (Cf. Hans Drexler, *Die Komposition von Terenz' Adelphen und Plautus' Rudens, Philologus*, Supplementband 26, Heft 2 [1934], p. 32.)

42   Cf. Karl Dziatzko and Robert Kauer, *Ausgewählte Komödien des P. Terentius Afer: II. Adelphoe²* (Leipzig, Teubner, 1903 [1921]), p. 16.

XII. SENECA

1 For documentation, see J. Wight Duff, *A Literary History of Rome in the Silver Age*, pp. 196–208; Schanz and Hosius, *Geschichte der Römischen Literatur*⁴, II, 679–82.

2 Seneca, *Epistles* 78. 2.

3 Suetonius, *Caligula* 53. 2.

4 For later Greek tragedy, see Haigh, *The Tragic Drama of the Greeks*, pp. 403–61. For early Roman tragedy, see J. Wight Duff, *A Literary History of Rome, From the Origins to the Close of the Golden Age*, pp. 224–33 and index, s.v. "Tragedy"; Tenny [*sic*] Frank, "The Decline of Roman Tragedy," *Classical Journal*, 12 (1916–17), 176–87. For philosophical tragedy, see Haigh, *op. cit.*, pp. 426–29; Diogenes Laertius, 6. 98 (on Crates), and remarks in Nauck, *Tragicorum Graecorum Fragmenta*², p. 808 (on Diogenes of Sinope).

5 The *Orestes* tends to fall into a series of sensational individual scenes (so Ernst Howald, *Die Griechische Tragödie* [Munich and Berlin, Oldenbourg, 1930], p. 167); the characters tend to be melodramatic villains or heroes, etc. On the melodramatic effects of Seneca, see Moses Hadas, "The Roman Stamp of Seneca's Tragedies," *American Journal of Philology*, 60 (1939), 220–31.

6 Public readings by an author of his latest work (*recitationes*) had become one of the most marked—and terrifying—features of the literary activity at Rome. Mendell (*Our Seneca*, pp. 88–90) has suggested that the lack of proper introduction of characters indicates that the plays were designed to be recited and that the performers would simply read out the name of the speaker, at least in the case of a new character. This may be correct. If so, however, we should expect that the speakers would be clearly named in the original text and that the characters of a given scene would be listed at the head of that scene. But the variation and uncertainty of our manuscripts in these listings seem to indicate that the original text of Seneca did not contain any such scene headings and that assignments were none too clearly marked. (See manuscripts on the first scene of the *Thyestes*; see also Friedrich Leo, *L. Annaei Senecae Tragoediae*, I, 86–87.)

7 Cf. Apuleius, *Metamorphoses* 10. 29–34.

8 A certain amount of such description, usually well-motivated, is found in previous dramatists. Cf. Euripides, *Trojan Women* 462–65; Plautus, *Three Bob Day* 622–25, *Braggart Warrior* 200–216 (the most extreme example). Elaborate description is found in the fragments of a "mime," possibly written for recitation by one person. Cf. Page, *Greek Literary Papyri*, I, 369.

9 These figures are computed from the analyses of Demetrius Detscheff, *De Tragoediarum Graecarum Conformatione Scaenica ac Dramatica* (Göttingen Dissertation, Sofia, 1904).

10 Cf. Cicero, *Letters to His Friends* 7. 1. 2.

11 Cf. Pratt, *Dramatic Suspense in Seneca and in His Greek Precursors*, p. 84, note 181. Pratt perhaps rightly thinks that Hippolytus' long speech is a philosophical discourse divorced from personal considerations and that consistency should not be expected.

12 Scholars are in hopeless disagreement concerning the dates of the plays. For summaries and bibliography, see Schanz and Hosius, *Geschichte der Römischen Literatur*⁴, II, 458. Herrmann (*Le Théâtre de Sénèque*, p. 147) dates them all A.D. 54–62. (Hosius has badly mistaken the view of Herrmann.)

13 Cf. Ludwig Friedländer, *Roman Life and Manners* (London, Routledge), II (1909), 93–94; F. Warren Wright, *Cicero and the Theater*, Smith College Classical Studies, No. 11 (Northhampton, 1931), pp. 4–9.

14   Schanz and Hosius, *op. cit.*, II, 524–25.

15   Dio Cassius, 58. 24.

16   Cf. Otto Regenbogen, "Schmerz und Tod in den Tragödien Senecas," *Vorträge der Bibliothek Warburg*, VII (1927–28), 167–218 (Leipzig, 1930).

17   Noteworthy also is Seneca's frequent theme of the end of the world, which occurs also in his prose writings; e.g., *Natural Questions* 3. 27–30. Cf. Regenbogen, *op. cit.*, p. 213.

18   See Regenbogen, article cited in note 16, p. 177.

19   The first edition of Seneca was published about 1481, that of Sophocles in 1502, that of Euripides in 1503, that of Aeschylus in 1518. (Cf. Duff, *A Literary History of Rome in the Silver Age*, p. 247, note 5; Schmid and Stählin, *Geschichte der Griechischen Literatur*, II, 309.)

20   Imitation of the Greek tragedies was not unknown in this period; but imitation of them, we should note, is perhaps no more successful than imitation of Seneca. (Cf. Lucas, *Euripides and His Influence*, pp. 105–6.)
       For a recent opinion on the vexed question of Seneca's influence on Shakespeare, see T. W. Baldwin, *William Shakspere's Small Latine and Lesse Greeke* (University of Illinois Press, 1944), II, 553–61.

21   Cf. Horace, *Ars Poetica* 189 (five acts), 192 (three speaking characters). In the *Hercules on Oeta* choral verses occur within an act and also at the end of the play.

22   *Mad Hercules* 1032–34 is a disputed passage, but some modern editors do not give this to the chorus.

MAD HERCULES

23   Lines 922–24. The effect of these lines is ruined in the verse translation of F. J. Miller (in Duckworth, *The Complete Roman Drama*) but entirely adequate in his prose translation (in the Loeb Classical Library).

24   The use of intermediate plays, of course, is possible, but the arguments of Wolf H. Friedrich ("Euripideisches in der Lateinischen Literatur," *Hermes*, 69 [1934], 303–10) are unconvincing.

25   Lines 34–36 play upon the etymological meaning of the name Hercules (Greek Heracles, apparently "made glorious by Hera," but really of doubtful meaning).

26   Various explanations of this prologue have been offered. Some think Seneca wished to secure greater unity than Euripides' play, in their opinion, possesses. Seneca, however, never seems greatly concerned over ordinary unity, and he has here admitted a long description of the underworld. Others assume that Seneca wished to make the madness appear a natural phenomenon and to prepare for it. So Richard M. Haywood, "Note on Seneca's *Hercules Furens*," *Classical Journal*, 37 (1941–42), 421–24.

27   Cf. Wolf-Hartmut Friedrich, *Untersuchungen zu Senecas Dramatischer Technik* (Freiburg Dissertation, Borna-Leipzig, Noske, 1933), p. 58.

28   Compare the anonymous *Octavia*, below. For the epigram, see *Medea* 500–501.

29   The Emperor Nero himself played the role of the mad Hercules as he did that of Orestes and that of the blinded Oedipus. Suetonius (*Nero* 21. 3) tells the amusing story that when the end of this scene was reached—possibly Seneca's play somewhat modified was being produced—and Nero as Hercules was stripped of his arms and loaded with chains, a stupid military guard rushed out on the stage to rescue the Emperor!

30   Cf. Plautus, *Merchant* 931–50.

TROJAN WOMEN

31 Cf. Warmington, *Remains of Old Latin*, II, 371–77.

32 Schmid and Stählin, *Geschichte der Griechischen Literatur*, III, 486, note 2. The general situation here—Andromache trying to protect her child from an unscrupulous Greek leader—is found in Euripides' *Andromache*.

33 The greatness and importance of Hector, however, has already been repeatedly expressed and runs like a leitmotif through the play; the same rhetorical identification of Hector and Troy, indeed, occurs several times. But the mystical interpretation of William Francis Jackson Knight ("Magical Motives in Seneca's *Troades*," *Transactions of the American Philological Association*, 63 [1932], 20–33) is not convincing, failing to take sufficient account of Senecan rhetoric and straining the interpretation of certain lines (e.g., 322–24).

34 The dilemma of Andromache would appear more important to an ancient audience because tombs were sacred and the obligation of surviving kindred to protect and honor them was extremely severe.

35 The scene of Andromache and Ulysses, perhaps as Accius presented it, is depicted on an interesting Roman relief. Cf. Bieber, *The History of the Greek and Roman Theater*, fig. 421, p. 317.

PHOENICIAN WOMEN

36 See above, p. 406. The quarrel of two brothers might suggest Nero's murder of his stepbrother.

37 So Umberto Moricca, "Le 'Fenicie' di Seneca," *Rivista di Filologia*, 45 (1917), 491.

38 Schmid (Schmid and Stählin, *Geschichte der Griechischen Literatur*, III, 589, note 1) thinks that Shakespeare may well have taken inspiration from this scene for his *King Lear*.

MEDEA

39 Cf. Seneca, *Natural Questions* 3. 27. 13.

40 Cf. H. L. Cleasby, "The Medea of Seneca," *Harvard Studies in Classical Philology*, 18 (1907), 39–71. In general, see Herrmann, *Le Théâtre de Sénèque*, pp. 280–88. On modern adaptations, see the treatment of Euripides' play.

41 Lines 375–79. Ferdinand Columbus in his copy of Seneca's tragedies is said to have written (in Latin) opposite these lines: "This prophecy was fulfilled by my father, Admiral Christopher Colón, in the year 1492."

42 But see line 283. Jason (441–43) pathetically says that Medea herself, he presumes, would prefer the welfare of her children to that of her marriage.

43 Note also the reference to Sisyphus (747; cf. 512); who forever casts an ominous shadow over the royal house of Corinth.

44 This keen observation is made by George E. Duckworth in his *The Complete Roman Drama*, II, 583.

PHAEDRA

45 The title of this play varies in the manuscripts; but *Phaedra* is better attested, and Phaedra is certainly the main character of this play.

46 *Phaedra* 356–57, 555–58, 638, 684, 697, 1191–92, 1200.

47 One passage (981–88) is thought by some scholars to be a specific reference to Messalina. Cf. Schanz and Hosius, *Geschichte der Römischen Literatur*[4], II, 462.

48 Leo, *L. Annaei Senecae Tragoediae*, I, 176. See above on Euripides' *Hippolytus* for an outline of the lost play. Cf. Wolf H. Friedrich, "Euripideisches in der Lateinischen Literatur," *Hermes*, 69 (1934), 310–15.

49 Cf. Méridier, *Hippolyte d'Euripide*, pp. 329–34; for more elaborate treatments, see works cited by Herrmann, *Le Théâtre de Sénèque*, pp. 13–14.

50 The Nurse first addresses Phaedra, not sympathetically with "child," as in Euripides, but with "wife of Theseus."

51 Cf. Méridier, *op. cit.*, p. 313.

52 Cf. Sten G. Flygt, "Treatment of Character in Euripides and Seneca: The Hippolytus," *Classical Journal*, 29 (1933–34), 507–16.

OEDIPUS

53 Cf. Herrmann, *Le Théâtre de Sénèque*, pp. 304–5.

54 Cf. Suetonius, *Julius* 56. 7. For remarks on modern adaptations, see the treatment of Sophocles' play above.

55 Seneca's change has eliminated also the implausibility of the lone Oedipus fighting at the crossroads with five men. (So Herrmann, *op. cit.*, p. 297, where the count is six men.) Such "corrections" of the tradition are not uncommon in Seneca. Cf. Wilhelm Marx, *Funktion und Form der Chorlieder in den Seneca-Tragoedien* (Heidelberg Dissertation, 1932), p. 60.

56 Friedrich's opinion that this conversation should continue and Oedipus' reactions be brought out is not correct. The structure here is awkward, but haste is imperative. Cf. Wolf-Hartmut Friedrich, *Untersuchungen zu Senecas Dramatischer Technik* (Freiburg Dissertation [Borna-Leipzig, Noske, 1933], pp. 81–90).

57 The account of Bacchus and the pirates was doubtless a favorite dithyrambic subject and is charmingly illustrated on a monument in Athens celebrating the dithyrambic victory of a certain Lysicrates in 334 B.C. Cf. Bieber, *The History of the Greek and Roman Theater*, fig. 10, p. 6; text, p. 8.

58 A similar motive occurs in the death of Agrippina, mother of Nero, but this may be a coincidence. Cf. *Octavia* 369; Tacitus, *Annals* 14. 8. The unpleasant word *uterus*, of somewhat wider meaning than the English, occurs some 16 times in eight of Seneca's nine plays.

THYESTES

59 See also Olof Gigon, "Bemerkungen zu Senecas Thyestes," *Philologus*, 93 (1938), 176–83. Gigon seems to go too far in making Thyestes the perfect Stoic sage. He (p. 181) overlooks a reference to the vengeance of Thyestes which is included in line 42 (the birth of Aegisthus from the incestuous union of father and daughter). If Thyestes includes himself in the ruin which he calls down upon Atreus (1015), so has Atreus included himself in his earlier imprecation (191). (Cf. Seneca, *Medea* 535–36.) At the end of the play Thyestes' referring Atreus' punishment to the gods, furthermore, may be not the resignation of a Stoic philosopher but a rhetorical reference to Apollo's command to beget Aegisthus as an avenger (cf. Seneca's *Agamemnon* 294) and a rhetorical preparation for Atreus' last epigram.

AGAMEMNON

60 The conventional order of the plays of Seneca places the *Agamemnon* immediately before the *Thyestes*. This order has been reversed by the present writer because the story of the *Agamemnon* is a continuation of that of the other play.

61 Herrmann, *Le Théâtre de Sénèque*, pp. 305–12.

62 *Corpus Inscriptionum Latinarum* 4. 6698. This quotation, of course, disproves Leo's contention that lines 730–33 are spurious. Hardly justified is the implication in Schanz and Hosius (*Geschichte der Römischen Literatur*[4], II, 464) that the occurrence of the name Seneca near by strengthens the assurance of the authenticity of the play (*C.I.L.* 4. 4418; actually in a different block of houses).

ROMAN TRAGEDY   [Pages 430–35

Seneca, *Epistles* 70. 1.

Cf. Aeschylus, *Agamemnon* 527, on the sacrilege committed by the Greeks.

The description of the fall of Troy is somewhat after Vergil's. Compare *Aeneid*
      2. 239 and *Agamemnon* 638–39.

See Leo's critical notes on lines 730–33.

The movements of Clytemnestra, lines 588–780, are awkwardly obscure.

HERCULES ON OETA

The authenticity of this play in whole or in part has sometimes been questioned.
      Seneca's authorship is defended by various scholars, including Arthur Stanley
      Pease, "On the Authenticity of the *Hercules Oetaeus*," *Transactions of the Amer-
      ican Philological Association,* 49 (1918), 3–26.

Friedrich Leo in *Göttingische Gelehrte Anzeigen,* 1903, p. 7.

The name Deianira means "man (husband) slayer." Possibly Seneca is playing
      upon this in lines 315, 436. Deianira's statement that slaughter is Hercules'
      method of divorce (line 432) might have a political significance if this play was written
      after Nero's divorce from Octavia. Compare Claudius' divorce from Messalina.

This reversal of the Sophoclean sequence adds plausibility to the character of
      Deianira. Similarly Seneca perhaps changed the story of Oedipus' murder of Laius
      at the crossroads in order to secure greater plausibility of detail.

Lines 1828–31. Cf. Euripides, *Heracles* 495.

OCTAVIA

Cf. Arthur Stanley Pease, "Is the *Octavia* a Play of Seneca?" *Classical Journal,*
      15 (1919–20), 388–403; "The *Octavia* Once More," *Classical Philology,* 19 (1924),
      80–83.

The *Octavia* requires an intimate knowledge of contemporary events. Most
      translations include a sketch of these. The main sources are Suetonius' lives of
      Claudius and Nero, and Tacitus, *Annals* XI–XVI.

Suetonius, *Nero* 35. 3.

A good sketch of the few known Roman historical dramas is given by Miller in
      the introduction to his translation in the Loeb Classical Library.

BIBLIOGRAPHY

KEY TO ABBREVIATIONS

LCL Loeb Classical Library
A series containing original texts and English translations. London, Heinemann, and formerly New York, Putnam, now Cambridge, Massachusetts, Harvard University Press

ODGR Our Debt to Greece and Rome
A series of literary studies with short bibliographies. Formerly Boston, Marshall Jones, now New York, Longmans

(p) A translation in prose

(v) A translation in verse

* A translation especially recommended

A superior index number after the title denotes the latest edition now available.

The following lists are intended only as a brief introduction to the subject, primarily for the general reader in English. An attempt has been made to include the most important works, the most recent noteworthy works, and, in the case of translations, the most readily available ones. Learned commentaries on individual plays are listed only when they include introductions or other material useful to the general reader. If a book was first published in the United States, only the original publisher is given; if first published abroad, the original publisher and usually also the publisher in the United States, if any, are given. A few of the items, not available to the present writer, are listed as they occur in announcements and catalogues.

These lists are divided into the following sections:

I. Bibliographical Works and Histories of Literature
II. Mythological Dictionaries and Background Material
III. General Works on Classical Drama
IV. Dramatic Antiquities
V. Translations: Bibliography and Collections
VI. Authors

I. BIBLIOGRAPHICAL WORKS AND HISTORIES OF LITERATURE

BURSIAN, CONRAD (founder). *Jahresbericht über die Fortschritte der Klassischen Altertumswissenschaft.* Leipzig, O. R. Reisland.
This massive work consists of two different types of material: a bibliographical list of important works on classical philology in all languages, which is published yearly; and comprehensive reviews of works in the separate fields published at irregular intervals. The most recent of the reviews, as far as present information is available, is listed within each of the sections below dealing with specific authors or fields. Various other yearly bibliographies of the classical field are published, but none compares with this one.

DUFF, J[OHN] WIGHT. *A Literary History of Rome, From the Origins to the Close of the Golden Age².* London, Unwin, and New York, Scribner, 1910.

———. *A Literary History of Rome in the Silver Age.* London, Unwin, and New York, Scribner, 1927.

GEFFCKEN, JOHANNES. *Griechische Literaturgeschichte* I. Heidelberg, Winter, 1926.
Useful especially for Aristophanes.

SCHANZ, MARTIN, AND HOSIUS, CARL. *Geschichte der Römischen Literatur⁴.* Handbuch der Altertumswissenschaft. Munich, Beck.
Plautus and Terence are treated in the "Erster Teil," 1927; Seneca in the "Zweiter Teil," 1935.

497

SCHMID, WILHELM, AND STÄHLIN, OTTO. *Geschichte der Griechischen Literatur.* Handbuch der Altertumswissenschaft. Munich, Beck.

Aeschylus (except the *Prometheus*) and Sophocles are treated in the "Erster Teil, Zweiter Band," 1934; the *Prometheus* and Euripides in the "Erster Teil, Dritter Band, Erste Hälfte," 1940. These volumes are written by Schmid alone. Extensive bibliographical material is given; the section on Euripides is especially good.

II. MYTHOLOGICAL DICTIONARIES AND BACKGROUND MATERIAL

HARVEY, SIR PAUL. *The Oxford Companion to Classical Literature.* Oxford, At the Clarendon Press, 1937.

Often too brief.

HOWE, GEORGE, AND HARRER, G. A. *A Handbook of Classical Mythology.* New York, Crofts, 1929.

There are many modern works in the field of Greek life and thought, but none perhaps is as interesting and few if any will be as instructive as the original works of Herodotus and Thucydides. In the translations of Rawlinson and Jowett, these are available in various editions including Francis R. B. Godolphin, *The Greek Historians,* 2 vols., New York, Random House, 1942. The student should, of course, be acquainted with the Homeric poems. The prose translation of Andrew Lang, Walter Leaf, and Ernest Myers for the *Iliad,* and that of S. H. Butcher and Andrew Lang for the *Odyssey* are perhaps the most satisfactory. A complete edition is available in the Modern Library.

III. GENERAL WORKS ON CLASSICAL DRAMA

DELCOURT, MARIE. *La Tradition des Comiques Anciens en France avant Molière.* Bibliothèque de la Faculté de Philosophie et Lettres de l'Université de Liége, LIX. Paris, Droz, 1934.

FLICKINGER, ROY C. *The Greek Theater and Its Drama*[4]. University of Chicago Press, 1936 (1938).

An excellent work when first published in 1918; now in need of revision, especially the archaeological sections.

GOODELL, THOMAS DWIGHT. *Athenian Tragedy: A Study in Popular Art.* Yale University Press, 1920.

GREENE, WILLIAM CHASE. *Moira: Fate, Good, and Evil in Greek Thought.* Harvard University Press, 1944.

Separate chapters are devoted to each of the three tragic poets.

HAIGH, A[RTHUR] E. *The Tragic Drama of the Greeks.* Oxford, At the Clarendon Press, 1896.

Although in need of revision, this standard work is still useful.

HEINEMANN, KARL. *Die Tragischen Gestalten der Griechen in der Weltliteratur.* Das Erbe der Alten. 2 vols. Leipzig, Dieterich, 1920.

KITTO, H[UMPHREY] D. F. *Greek Tragedy: A Literary Study.* London, Methuen, 1939.

Kitto's interpretations are stimulating but at times erratic.

LEGRAND, PH[ILIPPE] E. *The New Greek Comedy.* Translated by James Loeb. London, Heinemann, and New York, Putnam, 1917.

An excellent analysis. The learned reader should use the unabridged original listed below.

LEGRAND, PH[ILIPPE] E. *Daos: Tableau de la Comédie Grecque Pendant la Période Dite Nouvelle.* Annales de l'Université de Lyon, Nouvelle Série, II, 26. Lyon, A. Rey, and Paris, A. Fontemoing, 1910.

LITTLE, ALAN M. G. *Myth and Society in Attic Drama.* Columbia University Press, 1942.

MAHR, AUGUST C. *The Origin of the Greek Tragic Form: A Study of the Early Theater in Attica.* New York, Prentice-Hall, 1938.

MATTHAEI, LOUISE E. *Studies in Greek Tragedy.* Cambridge University Press, 1918. Treats especially *Prometheus, Ion, Hippolytus, Hecuba.*

MURRAY, GILBERT. "Greek and English Tragedy: A Contrast," in G[eorge] S[tuart] Gordon's *English Literature and the Classics* (Oxford, At the Clarendon Press, 1912), pp. 7–24.

NORWOOD, GILBERT. *Greek Comedy.* London, Methuen, and Boston, Luce, 1932.

———. *Greek Tragedy²*. London, Methuen, and Boston, Luce, 1928.
Norwood's works are written in a brilliant English style; his opinions are stimulating but often bizarre.

PICKARD-CAMBRIDGE, A[RTHUR] W. *Dithyramb Tragedy and Comedy.* Oxford, At the Clarendon Press, 1927.
A learned work.

PLUGGÉ, DOMIS E. *History of Greek Play Production in American Colleges and Universities from 1881 to 1936.* Teachers College Contributions to Education No. 752. Teachers College, Columbia University, 1938.

PRENTICE, WILLIAM KELLY. *Those Ancient Dramas Called Tragedies.* Princeton University Press, 1942.

SÉCHAN, LOUIS. *Études sur la Tragédie Grecque dans ses Rapports avec la Céramique.* Paris, Champion, 1926.
Generously illustrated.

SHEPPARD, J[OHN] T[RESIDDER]. *Greek Tragedy.* Cambridge Manuals. Cambridge University Press, 1911.

WEISSINGER, REINHARD T. *A Study of Act Divisions in Classical Drama.* Iowa Studies in Classical Philology No. IX, 1940. University of Iowa Dissertation.

WILAMOWITZ-MOELLENDORFF, ULRICH VON. *Griechische Tragoedien.* 4 vols. Berlin, Weidmann, 1899–1923.
The introductions to these translations and the supplementary essays are important.

IV. DRAMATIC ANTIQUITIES

ALLEN, JAMES TURNEY. *Stage Antiquities of the Greeks and Romans and Their Influence.* ODGR, 1927.

BIEBER, MARGARETE. *The History of the Greek and Roman Theater.* Princeton University Press, 1939.
The five hundred sixty-six illustrations are well chosen, unexpurgated, and extremely valuable; the text is very brief and the sections dealing with the plays as literature are not good; bibliography.

FIECHTER, E[RNST]. *Das Dionysos-Theater in Athen,* I–III. Stuttgart, Kohlhammer, 1935–36.
This possibly is the definitive publication of the theater at Athens.

FLICKINGER, ROY C. *The Greek Theater and Its Drama*⁴ (see III above).

HAIGH, A[RTHUR] E., AND PICKARD-CAMBRIDGE, A[RTHUR] W. *The Attic Theatre*³. Oxford, At the Clarendon Press, 1907.

This work is in need of revision, but it contains a vast storehouse of information.

Review

FENSTERBUSCH, CURT. Review for 1896–1926. Bursian, *Jahresbericht* . . . . , 253 (1936), 1–57.

V. TRANSLATIONS: BIBLIOGRAPHY AND COLLECTIONS

Some material has never been translated, such as the fragments of many Greek and Roman writers and the remarks of ancient commentators (scholiasts). Translations of almost all important Greek and Roman writers, however, are now included in LCL. Translations of the dramatists which are listed by F. Seymour Smith (see below) are normally not listed below.

Bibliography

SMITH, F. SEYMOUR. *The Classics in Translation: An Annotated Guide to the Best Translations of the Greek and Latin Classics into English.* London and New York, Scribner's, 1930.

Collections

COOPER, LANE. *Fifteen Greek Plays.* With an introduction and a supplement from the "Poetics" of Aristotle. New York, Oxford University Press, 1943. (v).

The plays included and their translators are as follows: Aeschylus, *Prometheus,* Whitelaw; *Agamemnon, Choephoroe, Eumenides,* Gilbert Murray; Sophocles, *Oedipus the King,* Gilbert Murray; *Antigone,* Whitelaw; *Oedipus at Colonus, Electra,* Lewis Campbell; Euripides, *Electra, Iphigenia in Tauris, Medea, Hippolytus,* Gilbert Murray; Aristophanes, *Clouds, Birds, Frogs,* Rogers. Bibliography.

DUCKWORTH, GEORGE E. *The Complete Roman Drama.* 2 vols. New York, Random House, 1942.

A variety of prose and verse translations by various hands with notes and glossary. Sketches of the plays are usually contained in the introductions. Modern adaptations are noted.

GRENE, DAVID. *Three Greek Tragedies in Translation.* [*Prometheus, Oedipus the King, Hippolytus*]. University of Chicago Press, 1942. (p and v).

Grene's appreciations of these plays are somewhat too subjective. Generalizations of higher criticism must be based on the minutiae of lower criticism.

HAMILTON, EDITH. *Three Greek Plays.* [*Prometheus, Agamemnon, Trojan Women*]. New York, Norton, 1937. (v).

OATES, WHITNEY J., AND O'NEILL, EUGENE, JR. *The Complete Greek Drama.* 2 vols. New York, Random House, 1938.

A variety of prose and verse translations by various hands with notes and glossary. Sketches of the plays are usually contained in the introductions.

PAGE, D[ENYS] L. *Greek Literary Papyri.* Vol. I. LCL, 1942.

WARMINGTON, E[RIC] H. *Remains of Old Latin.* 4 vols. LCL, 1935–40.

VI. AUTHORS
AESCHYLUS
Greek Text

MURRAY, GILBERT. *Aeschyli Septem Quae Supersunt Tragoediae.* Oxford, At the Clarendon Press, 1937.

Greek Text of Fragments

NAUCK, AUGUST. *Tragicorum Graecorum Fragmenta²*. Leipzig, Teubner, 1889.

See also D. L. Page, *Greek Literary Papyri* (see V above), and the translation of H. W. Smyth (see below).

Review

MOREL, WILLY. Review for 1930–33. Bursian, *Jahresbericht* . . . . , 259 (1938), 1–34.

Translations of More than One Play

CAMPBELL, LEWIS. *Aeschylus: The Seven Plays*. The World's Classics. Oxford University Press. (v).

First published in 1890.

*MORSHEAD, E[DMUND] D. A. *The Suppliant Maidens, The Persians, The Seven against Thebes, The Prometheus Bound of Aeschylus*. Golden Treasury Series. London and New York, Macmillan, 1908. (v).

The Suppliants and *The Seven against Thebes* are in Oates and O'Neill, *The Complete Greek Drama*.

*———. *The House of Atreus: Being the Agamemnon, Libation-Bearers and Furies of Aeschylus*. Golden Treasury Series. London and New York, Macmillan, 1901. (v).

In Oates and O'Neill, *The Complete Greek Drama*.

MURRAY, GILBERT. [Separate volumes of various dates.] London, Allen and Unwin, and New York, Oxford University Press. (v).

Agamemnon, Choephoroe, Eumenides in Cooper, *Fifteen Greek Plays*.

SHEPPARD, J[OHN] T[RESIDDER]. *Aeschylus: Oresteia. The Greek text as arranged for performance at Cambridge* . . . . , *with an English verse translation*. Cambridge, Bowes, 1933.

*SMYTH, HERBERT WEIR. *Aeschylus*. 2 vols. LCL, 1922, 1926. (p).

Bibliography of editions and translations. Selected fragments included in the second volume. Index.

See also·Oates and O'Neill, *The Complete Greek Drama*, and Cooper, *Fifteen Greek Plays*.

Translations of Single Plays

PROMETHEUS

GRENE, DAVID. *Three Greek Tragedies in Translation*. See V above.

HAMILTON, EDITH. *Three Greek Plays*. See V above.

*THOMSON, GEORGE. *Aeschylus: The Prometheus Bound*. See below.

TREVELYAN, R[OBERT] C. *Aeschylus: Prometheus Bound*. Cambridge University Press, 1939. (v).

AGAMEMNON

CAMPBELL, ARCHIBALD Y. *The Agamemnon of Aeschylus*. University Press of Liverpool, 1940. (v).

HAMILTON, EDITH. *Three Greek Plays*. See V above.

MACNEICE, LOUIS. *The Agamemnon of Aeschylus*. London, Faber, 1936, and New York, Harcourt, 1937. (v).

*THOMSON, GEORGE. *The* Oresteia *of Aeschylus*. See below

Commentaries

PROMETHEUS

*THOMSON, GEORGE. *Aeschylus: The Prometheus Bound.* Cambridge University Press, 1932.

Includes introduction and verse translation.

TRILOGY ON ORESTES (*ORESTEIA*)

*THOMSON, GEORGE. *The Oresteia of Aeschylus.* 2 vols. Cambridge University Press, 1938.

First volume includes good introduction and verse translation; the text is at times too boldly emended, and the line numbering is not the one now commonly used.

Criticism

CROISET, MAURICE. *Eschyle: Études sur l'Invention Dramatique dans son Théâtre.* Paris, "Les Belles Lettres," 1928.

MURRAY, GILBERT. *Aeschylus: The Creator of Tragedy.* Oxford, At the Clarendon Press, 1940.

This work, like all Murray's criticism, is beautifully written and stimulating; but its value is somewhat vitiated by an incorrigible romanticism.

POST, CHANDLER RATHFON. "The Dramatic Art of Aeschylus," *Harvard Studies in Classical Philology,* 16 (1905), 15–61.

SHEPPARD, J[OHN] T[RESIDDER]. *Aeschylus and Sophocles: Their Work and Influence.* ODGR, 1927.

Excellent.

SMYTH, HERBERT WEIR. *Aeschylean Tragedy.* University of California Press, 1924.

Excellent.

THOMSON, GEORGE. *Aeschylus and Athens. A Study in the Social Origins of Drama.* London, Lawrence, 1941.

This work may be ignored. It is written apparently for urging the author's own social and political theories (see p. 346), and it obscures more of Aeschylus than it enlightens (e.g., *Choephoroe* 887, p. 189).

WILAMOWITZ-MOELLENDORFF, ULRICH VON. *Aischylos: Interpretationen.* Berlin, Weidmann, 1914.

Indispensable for scholars.

SOPHOCLES

Greek Text

PEARSON, A[LFRED] C. *Sophoclis Fabulae².* Oxford, At the Clarendon Press. [Preface to original edition dated 1923.]

Fragments

PEARSON, A[LFRED] C. *The Fragments of Sophocles.* 3 vols. Cambridge University Press, 1917.

See also D. L. Page, *Greek Literary Papyri* (see V above).

Review

BLUMENTHAL, ALBRECHT VON. Review for 1931–35. Bursian, *Jahresbericht* . . . . , 259 (1938), 67–139.

Translations of More than One Play

CAMPBELL, LEWIS. *Sophocles: The Seven Plays in English Verse*. The World's Classics. Oxford University Press.
First published in 1883. *Oedipus at Colonus* and *Electra* in Cooper, *Fifteen Greek Plays*.

*JEBB, RICHARD C. *The Tragedies of Sophocles: Translated into English Prose*. Cambridge University Press, 1904.
Oedipus the King, Antigone, Trachiniae, Electra, and *Oedipus at Colonus* in Oates and O'Neill, *The Complete Greek Drama*.

STORR, F[RANCIS]. *Sophocles*. 2 vols. LCL, 1912, 1913. (v).
Bibliography of editions and translations.

See also Oates and O'Neill, *The Complete Greek Drama*, Cooper, *Fifteen Greek Plays*.

Translations of Single Plays

ANTIGONE

FITTS, DUDLEY, AND FITZGERALD, ROBERT. *The Antigone of Sophocles*. New York, Harcourt, 1939. (p and v).

MORRISON, LENNOX J. *Sophocles: Antigone*. London, Christophers, 1938. (v).

MURRAY, GILBERT. *Sophocles: The Antigone*. London, Allen and Unwin, and New York, Oxford University Press, 1941. (v).

TREVELYAN, R[OBERT] C. *Sophocles: Antigone. The Greek text as arranged for performance at Cambridge . . . . with an English verse translation*. Cambridge, Bowes, 1939.

OEDIPUS THE KING

GRENE, DAVID. *Three Greek Tragedies in Translation*. See V above.

*MENDELL, CLARENCE W. *Our Seneca*. Yale University Press, 1941, pp. 201–250. (v).

MURRAY, GILBERT. *Oedipus King of Thebes, by Sophocles*. London, Allen and Unwin, and New York, Oxford University Press, 1911. (v).
In Cooper, *Fifteen Greek Plays*.

SHEPPARD, J[OHN] T[RESIDDER]. *The Oedipus Tyrannus of Sophocles*. See below.

YEATS, W[ILLIAM] B[UTLER]. *Sophocles' King Oedipus. A Version for the Modern Stage*. London and New York, Macmillan, 1928. (p and v).
Good but too free—the last line rings a false note; music for the chorus is included.

TRACHINIAE

BARLOW, [LADY] E[STHER] S. *The Trachiniae of Sophocles*. Preface by T. B. L. Webster. Manchester University Press, 1938. (v).

ELECTRA

FERGUSSON, FRANCIS. *Sophocles: Electra. A Version for the Modern Stage*. New York, W. R. Scott, 1938. (v).
This translation, like the translations of many American men of letters, falls short because the author is not thoroughly acquainted with the language of the original. English men of letters are usually much superior in this regard.

OEDIPUS AT COLONUS

FITZGERALD, ROBERT. *Sophocles: Oedipus at Colonus*. New York, Harcourt, 1941. (v).

504 A HANDBOOK OF CLASSICAL DRAMA

Commentaries

*JEBB, RICHARD C. [Separate volumes of various dates.] Cambridge University Press, 1883–1908.
All plays. Excellent introductions and prose translation.

OEDIPUS THE KING

SHEPPARD, J[OHN] T[RESIDDER]. *The Oedipus Tyrannus of Sophocles.* Cambridge University Press, 1920.
Introduction and verse translation.

Criticism

BATES, WILLIAM NICKERSON. *Sophocles: Poet and Dramatist.* University of Pennsylvania Press, 1940.
Accounts of extant plays, and sketches of lost plays. List of fragments on papyri.

BOWRA, C[ECIL] M[AURICE]. *Sophoclean Tragedy.* (Announced for publication, 1944.)

CROISET, MAURICE. *Oedipe-Roi de Sophocle: Étude et Analyse.* Paris, Librairie Mellottée, no date.

POST, CHANDLER RATHFON. "The Dramatic Art of Sophocles," *Harvard Studies in Classical Philology,* 23 (1912), 71–127.

———. "The Dramatic Art of Sophocles as Revealed by the Fragments of the Lost Plays," *ibid.,* 33 (1922), 1–63.

SHEPPARD, J[OHN] T[RESIDDER]. *Aeschylus and Sophocles: Their Work and Influence.* ODGR, 1927.

WEBSTER, T[HOMAS] B. L. *An Introduction to Sophocles.* Oxford, At the Clarendon Press, 1936.
A stimulating analysis.

EURIPIDES

Greek Text

MURRAY, GILBERT. *Euripidis Fabulae.* 3 vols. Oxford, At the Clarendon Press, 1901–13.

Greek Text of Fragments

NAUCK, AUGUST. *Tragicorum Graecorum Fragmenta²*. Leipzig, Teubner, 1889.
See also D. L. Page, *Greek Literary Papyri* (see V above).

Review

MOREL, WILLY. Review for 1930–33. Bursian, *Jahresbericht* . . . . , 259 (1938), 35–66.

Translations of More than One Play

HADAS, MOSES, AND MCLEAN, JOHN HARVEY. *The Plays of Euripides.* Including: *Alcestis, Medea, Hippolytus, Andromache, Ion, Trojan Women, Electra, Iphigenia among the Taurians, The Bacchants, Iphigenia at Aulis.* New York, Dial Press, 1936. (p).
Sometimes criticized as too prosaic.

MEREDITH, HUGH OWEN. *Four Dramas of Euripides. Hecuba, Heracles, Andromache, Orestes.* London, Allen and Unwin, 1937. (v).

MURRAY, AUGUSTUS TABER. *Four Plays of Euripides. Alcestis, Medea, Hippolytus, & Iphigenia among the Taurians.* Stanford University Press, 1931. (p).

MURRAY, GILBERT. [*Alcestis, Medea, Hippolytus, Trojan Women, Electra, Iphigenia in Tauris, Bacchae, Rhesus.* Published in separate volumes and various collections of various dates.] London, Allen and Unwin, and New York, Oxford University Press or Longmans. (v).

Not recommended; see the remarks of Grube, *The Drama of Euripides*, pp. 13–14. *Electra, Iphigenia in Tauris, Medea, Hippolytus* in Cooper, *Fifteen Greek Plays. Trojan Women, Bacchae, Rhesus* in Oates and O'Neill, *The Complete Greek Drama.*

NEWHALL, JANE PEERS. *The Lyric Portions of Two Dramas of Euripides, Iphigenia at Aulis, Iphigenia among the Taurians, Set to Music.* Smith College Classical Studies, No. 5, 1924. Boston, C. W. Thompson & Co.

Music and Greek text; no translation.

WAY, ARTHUR S. *Euripides.* 4 vols. LCL, 1912. (v).

Revised form of translations published 1894–98.

See also Oates and O'Neill, *The Complete Greek Drama.* (The selections for Euripides, mainly the prose translations of E. P. Coleridge, are good.) Also, Cooper, *Fifteen Greek Plays.*

Translations of Single Plays

ALCESTIS

*ALDINGTON, RICHARD. *Euripides: Alcestis.* London, Chatto and Windus, 1930. (p and v).

Also in Oates and O'Neill, *The Complete Greek Drama.*

FITTS, DUDLEY, AND FITZGERALD, ROBERT. *The Alcestis of Euripides.* New York, Harcourt, 1936. (p and v).

MEDEA

TREVELYAN, R[OBERT] C. *Euripides: Medea.* Cambridge University Press, 1939. (v).

HIPPOLYTUS

GRENE, DAVID. *Three Greek Tragedies in Translation.* See V above.

ION

H. D. [HILDA DOOLITTLE]. *Euripides: Ion.* Translated with notes. London, Chatto and Windus, and New York, Houghton, 1937. (v).

An extremely free exotic translation; some passages are omitted.

TROJAN WOMEN

HAMILTON, EDITH. *Three Greek Plays. See* V above.

IPHIGENIA AT AULIS

STAWELL, F[LORENCE] MELIAN. *Euripides: Iphigenia in Aulis.* Preface by Gilbert Murray. London, Bell, 1929, and New York, Oxford University Press, 1930. (v). In Oates and O'Neill, *The Complete Greek Drama.*

Commentaries

MEDEA

PAGE, DENYS L. *Euripides: Medea.* Oxford, At the Clarendon Press, 1938.

HIPPOLYTUS

KER, A[LAN]. *Euripides: Hippolytus.* Oxford, At the Clarendon Press. (Announced.)

HERACLES

WILAMOWITZ-MOELLENDORFF, ULRICH VON. *Euripides: Herakles²*. Berlin, Weidmann, 1895.

A monumental work. Important introductory chapters of the first edition were reprinted various times under the title, *Einleitung in die Griechische Tragödie*, Berlin, Weidmann.

ION

OWEN, A[RTHUR] S. *Euripides: Ion.* Oxford, At the Clarendon Press, 1939.

ELECTRA

DENNISTON, J[OHN] D. *Euripides: Electra.* Oxford, At the Clarendon Press, 1939.

IPHIGENIA IN TAURIS

PLATNAUER, M[AURICE]. *Euripides: Iphigenia in Tauris.* Oxford, At the Clarendon Press, 1938.

BACCHAE

DODDS, E[RIC] R. *Euripides: Bacchae.* Oxford, At the Clarendon Press, 1944.

SANDYS, JOHN EDWIN. *The Bacchae of Euripides*[4]. Cambridge University Press, 1900.

Includes interesting woodcuts.

Criticism

APPLETON, R[EGINALD] B. *Euripides the Idealist.* London, Dent, and New York, Dutton, 1927.

BATES, WILLIAM NICKERSON. *Euripides: A Student of Human Nature.* University of Pennsylvania Press, 1930.

Accounts of the extant plays and sketches of lost plays; list of fragments on papyri, supplemented in *American Journal of Philology,* 52 (1941), 469–75.

DECHARME, PAUL. *Euripides and the Spirit of His Dramas.* Translated by James Loeb. London and New York, Macmillan, 1906.

GRUBE, G[EORGE] M. A. *The Drama of Euripides.* London, Methuen, 1941.

Grube's introduction and critical analyses of the plays are excellent, though occasionally vitiated by a too great concern with the bizarre theories of A. W. Verrall. List of books.

LUCAS, F[RANK] L. *Euripides and His Influence.* ODGR, 1923.

MÉRIDIER, LOUIS. *Hippolyte d'Euripide.* Paris, Librairie Mellottée, no date.

MURRAY, GILBERT. *Euripides and His Age.* Home University Library. London, Williams and Norgate, New York, Holt, 1913.

Very stimulating and interesting little book, essential to every student of Euripides, but to be read with critical reserve.

ARISTOPHANES

Greek Text

COULON, VICTOR. *Aristophane.* 5 vols. Paris, "Les Belles Lettres," 1923–30.

Greek Text of Fragments

KOCK, THEODOR. *Comicorum Atticorum Fragmenta.* Vol. I. Leipzig, Teubner, 1880.

See also D. L. Page, *Greek Literary Papyri* (see V above).

Review

WÜST, ERNST. Review of Greek Comedy for 1931–37. Bursian, *Jahresbericht* . . . . , 263 (1939), 1–99.

Translations of More than One Play

ANONYMOUS. *Aristophanes: The Eleven Comedies*. London, Athenian Society, 1912, and New York under various dates and publishers. (p).

Most of the frank indecency is retained, but the poetic beauty is lost in this translation. Useful notes. Except the *Frogs*, in Oates and O'Neill, *The Complete Greek Drama*.

FRERE, JOHN HOOKHAM. *Aristophanes: Four Plays*. [*Acharnians, Knights, Birds, Frogs*] The World's Classics. Oxford University Press. (v).

These old translations, first printed in 1839, are very free, but spirited. Expurgated.

*ROGERS, BENJAMIN BICKLEY. *Aristophanes*. 3 vols. LCL, 1924. Various later revised impressions. (v).

Published earlier in separate volumes listed below under "Editions." Aristophanes cannot be read intelligently with fewer notes than are included in the edition in LCL. Indecency is here toned down, but this is an inspired verse translation. Indices. Rogers' translations of *Clouds, Birds, Frogs* are also in Cooper, *Fifteen Greek Plays*.

WAY, ARTHUR S. *Aristophanes in English Verse*. 2 vols. London and New York, Macmillan, 1927, 1934.

See also Oates and O'Neill, *The Complete Greek Drama*, and Cooper, *Fifteen Greek Plays*.

Translations of Single Plays

LYSISTRATA

MURPHY, CHARLES T. In Whitney Jennings Oates and Charles Theophilus Murphy, *Greek Literature in Translation*, New York, Longmans, 1944, pp. 387–418. (p and v).

Significant names explained.

SMOLIN, DMITRY. *Lysistrata. In three acts.* English translation from the Russian by George S. and Gilbert Seldes. With an Introduction by Oliver M. Sayler. Morris Gest Edition of Librettos. New York, Brentano's, 1925. (v).

This is a free adaptation.

FROGS

MURRAY, GILBERT. *The Frogs of Aristophanes*. London, Allen, 1908. (v).

Indecency is toned down or eliminated. In Oates and O'Neill, *The Complete Greek Drama*.

Commentaries

ROGERS, BENJAMIN BICKLEY. [Separate volumes of various dates.] London, Bell, 1902–16.

All plays.

Each volume contains, besides the translation, an introduction, text, and notes. This material is not particularly scholarly and is somewhat antiquated; some of it was written much earlier than the dates given. For example, the original edition of the *Clouds* was published in 1852.

ACHARNIANS

STARKIE, W[ILLIAM] J. M. *The Acharnians of Aristophanes*. London and New York, Macmillan, 1909.

Introduction, translation, commentary, scholarly bibliography.

CLOUDS

FORMAN, LEWIS LEAMING. *Aristophanes: Clouds*. New York, American Book Co., 1915.

Forman's introduction is an excellent general consideration of Aristophanes and the Athens of his day. Bibliography.

STARKIE, W[ILLIAM] J. M. *The Clouds of Aristophanes.* London and New York, Macmillan, 1911.

Uniform with the edition of *The Acharnians.*

WASPS

STARKIE, W[ILLIAM] J. M. *The Wasps of Aristophanes.* London and New York, Macmillan, 1897.

Introduction, scholarly bibliography. Expurgated.

Criticism

CROISET, MAURICE. *Aristophanes and the Political Parties at Athens.* Translated by James Loeb. London, Macmillan, 1909.

EHRENBERG, VICTOR. *The People of Aristophanes: A Sociology of Old Attic Comedy.* Oxford, Blackwell, 1943.

LORD, LOUIS E. *Aristophanes: His Plays and His Influence.* ODGR, no date.

Includes brief accounts of the extant plays; bibliography.

MURRAY, GILBERT. *Aristophanes: A Study.* Oxford, At the Clarendon Press, 1933.

This is the least attractive of Murray's portraits of the dramatists. Aristophanes cannot convincingly be made an admirer of Euripides.

NAVARRE, OCTAVE. *Aristophane: Les Cavaliers. Étude et Analyse.* Paris, Librairie Mellottée, no date.

RICHARDS, HERBERT. *Aristophanes and Others.* London, Grant Richards, 1909.

SÜSS, WILHELM. *Aristophanes und die Nachwelt.* Das Erbe der Alten. Leipzig, Dieterich, 1911.

MENANDER

Greek Text

JENSEN, CHRISTIAN. *Menandri Reliquiae in Papyris et Membranis Servatae.* Berlin, Weidmann, 1929.

KÖRTE, ALFRED. *Menandri Quae Supersunt³.* Pars Prior. Leipzig, Teubner, 1938.

Greek Text of the Older Fragments

KOCK, THEODOR. *Comicorum Atticorum Fragmenta.* Vol. III. Leipzig, Teubner, 1888.

See also D. L. Page, *Greek Literary Papyri* (see V above), and the translation of Allinson, below.

Review

WÜST, ERNST. Review of Greek Comedy for 1931-37. Bursian, *Jahresbericht* . . . . , 263 (1939), 1-99.

Translations of More than One Play

ALLINSON, FRANCIS G. *Menander: The Principal Fragments².* LCL, 1930. (p and v).

Bibliography; index to proper names.

*POST, L[EVI] A[RNOLD]. *Menander: Three Plays.* Broadway Translations. London, Routledge, and New York, Dutton, 1929. (p).

In revised form this excellent translation is included in Oates and O'Neill, *The Complete Greek Drama.*

Translations of Single Plays

SHEARING OF GLYCERA (PERIKEIROMENE)

MURRAY, GILBERT. *The Rape of the Locks. The Perikeiromenê of Menander. The fragments translated and the gaps conjecturally filled in.* London, Allen and Unwin, 1942. (v).

Criticism

LEGRAND. *The New Greek Comedy* (see III above).

POST, L[EVI] A[RNOLD]. "Aristotle and Menander," *Transactions of the American Philological Association,* 69 (1938), 1–42 (and the literature there cited).

––––––. "Menander in Current Criticism," *Transactions of the American Philological Association,* 65 (1934), 13–34.

PLAUTUS

Latin Text

LINDSAY, W[ALLACE] M. *T. Macci Plauti Comoediae²*. Oxford, At the Clarendon Press, 1910.

Review

CONRAD, FRITZ. Review for 1926–34. Bursian, *Jahresbericht . . . .* , 247 (1935), 63–90.

Translations of More than One Play

NIXON, PAUL. *Plautus.* 5 vols. LCL, 1916–38. (p).

The best translation for most of the plays. Includes selected fragments in the fifth volume, and in each volume an index to proper names.

See also Duckworth, *The Complete Roman Drama.* Duckworth's own prose translations are good.

Translations of Single Plays

MENAECHMI

*HYDE, RICHARD W[HITNEY], AND WEIST, EDWARD C[ILLEY]. *The Menaechmi of Plautus. With a preface by E. K. Rand.* Harvard University Press, 1930. (p and v).

A spirited translation for a performance at Harvard. Also in Kevin Guinagh and Alfred P. Dorjahn, *Latin Literature in Translation* (New York, Longmans, 1942, pp. 43–79). In a slightly different version also in Duckworth, *The Complete Roman Drama.*

ROGERS, BENJAMIN BICKLEY. *The Menaechmi of Plautus.* London, Bell, 1907. (v).

Often bound with Rogers' *The Comedies of Aristophanes.* Vol. VI. *The Plutus.*

HAUNTED HOUSE (MOSTELLARIA)

BUTCHER, MARY LOUISE. *Music for Plautus' Mostellaria.* Vassar College, 1928.

Criticism

COULTER, CORNELIA C. "The Plautine Tradition in Shakespeare," *Journal of English and Germanic Philology,* 19 (1920), 66–83.

LEGRAND. *The New Greek Comedy* (see III above).

NORWOOD, GILBERT. *Plautus and Terence.* ODGR, 1932.

Norwood's opinions in this book are often bizarre and sometimes founded on inaccurate data. Brief appendix on modern adaptations; bibliography.

REINHARDSTOETTNER, KARL VON. *Plautus. Spätere Bearbeitungen Plautinischer Lustspiele.* Leipzig, Friedrich, 1886.

See also the review of this, "Plautus and His Imitators," *Quarterly Review,* 173 (No. 345, 1891), 37–69.

TERENCE
Latin Text

KAUER, ROBERT, AND LINDSAY, WALLACE M. *P. Terenti Afri Comoediae.* Oxford, At the Clarendon Press, 1926.

Review

No review in Bursian, *Jahresbericht* . . . . , since 1909.

Translations of More than One Play

SARGEAUNT, JOHN. *Terence.* 2 vols. LCL, 1912. (p).

See also Duckworth, *The Complete Roman Drama.*

Translations of Single Plays

PHORMIO

*OLDFATHER, WILLIAM ABBOTT. In GUINAGH AND DORJAHN, *Latin Literature in Translation* (see under Plautus, *Menaechmi,* above), pp. 83–120. (p).

BROTHERS (ADELPHOE)

*OLDFATHER, WILLIAM ABBOTT. *Ibid.,* pp. 121–61. (p).

Brilliant introduction; significant names explained.

Criticism

NORWOOD, GILBERT. *The Art of Terence.* Oxford, Blackwell, 1923.

To be read with caution.

See also under Plautus (Criticism), above.

SENECA
Latin Text

LEO, FRIEDRICH. *L. Annaei Senecae Tragoediae.* 2 vols. Berlin, Weidmann, 1878, 1879.

PEIPER, RUDOLF, AND RICHTER, GUSTAV. *L. Annaei Senecae Tragoediae²*. Leipzig, Teubner, 1902 (1921).

Review

MÜNSCHER, KARL. Review for 1915–21. Bursian, *Jahresbericht* . . . . , 192 (1922), 185–214.

Translations of More than One Play

HARRIS, ELLA ISABEL. *The Tragedies of Seneca.* Oxford University Press, 1904. (v).

Phoenician Women, Thyestes, and *Hercules on Oeta* in Duckworth, *The Complete Roman Drama.*

MILLER, FRANK JUSTUS. *Seneca's Tragedies.* 2 vols. LCL, 1917. (p).

Bibliographies, comparative analyses, and in second volume index with identification of mythological and historical characters.

See also Duckworth, *The Complete Roman Drama.* (Verse translations of Miller and Harris. Miller's prose translation is preferable.)

Translations of Single Plays
OEDIPUS
*MENDELL, CLARENCE W. *Our Seneca.* Yale University Press, 1941, pp. 251–85. (v).

Criticism

BRAGINTON, MARY V. *The Supernatural in Seneca's Tragedies.* Yale University Dissertation. Menasha, Wisconsin, Banta, 1933.

CUNLIFFE, JOHN W. *The Influence of Seneca on Elizabethan Tragedy.* London, Macmillan, 1893, and New York, Stechert, 1907.

GODLEY, A. D. "Senecan Tragedy," in G[eorge] S[tuart] Gordon's *English Literature and the Classics* (Oxford, At the Clarendon Press, 1912), pp. 228–47.

HERRMANN, LÉON. *Octavie: "Tragédie Prétexte."* Paris, "Les Belles Lettres," 1924.

———. *Le Théâtre de Sénèque.* Paris, "Les Belles Lettres," 1924.
Elaborate bibliographies.

LUCAS, F[RANK] L. *Seneca and Elizabethan Tragedy.* Cambridge University Press, 1922.

MENDELL, CLARENCE W. *Our Seneca.* Yale University Press, 1941.

PRATT, NORMAN T., JR. *Dramatic Suspense in Seneca and in His Greek Precursors.* Princeton University Dissertation. Princeton University Press, 1939.
Bibliographical index.

REGENBOGEN, OTTO. "Schmerz und Tod in den Tragödien Senecas," *Vorträge der Bibliothek Warburg,* VII (1927–1928), Leipzig, 1930, pp. 167–218.
This article represents perhaps the most important modern attempt at profound interpretation of the plays.

INDEX

General entries are arranged alphabetically, but subentries under each author and each play are arranged as discussed in the text.

Main entries, alphabetized under nouns, are cited in bold-faced type. Sections (and their notes) covered by main entries are not analyzed with regard to the subject of the main entry. For example, the various items concerning *Oedipus the King* covered on pages 111–29 are not listed in the Index, for they can readily be located by referring to that systematically arranged section of the text. Important references to this play which occur elsewhere in the book, however, are listed in the Index under Sophocles, *Oedipus the King*. Notes are included in the Index, but no note is cited that is a mere explanation of a specific item in the text that has been cited.

Plays are listed only under the names of their authors.

Documentary references are not cited.

Accius
Agamemnonidae, 445 (n. 51)
Alcestis, 164
Amphitryon, 338
Antigona, 103
Astyanax, 414
Atreus, 428
Bacchae, 237
Hecuba, 414
Medea, 459, n. 43
Night Patrol (*Nyctegresia*), 471 (n. 219)
Philocteta, 143
Phoenissae, 229
Prometheus, 52
Trojan Women, 414, 494 (n. 35)
Actors: change of costume and economy of roles, 22, **33–35**, 98, 278, 311 *bis*, 319, 463 (n. 83), 476 (n. 47), 484 (n. 30); limited to three in Greek tragedy, 4, 25, 154, 230, 460 (n. 49); men, 20; mutes, 98; plays written with a view to actors, 91, 140; position in theater, 17, 332; in Roman tragedy, 408; scenic composition, 34, 174; second actor innovation of Aeschylus, 38; third actor innovation of Sophocles, 38, 90–91
Acts: division of Roman comedies not authentic, 332; origin of five acts, 14, 163, 197, 310 (six), 316, 325, 347, 408, 443 (n. 26)
Aemilius Scaurus, Mamercus, 406 (*Atreus*), 416
Aeschylus, **36–87**; life, **36–37**; tragedy under, **37–42**; and Aristophanes, 301–6; silence, use of, 447 (n. 34); orthodoxy, 449 (n. 71), cf. 188. Mentioned, 3–35, 88–95, 156–63 *passim,* 119, 196, 295

Extant plays:
Agamemnon, 60–63, **63–73**, 73–87, 430–32; shift in meter, 12; tragic atmosphere, 18, 30; chorus social background, 19; inconsistency of chorus, 20; composition of chorus, 20–21; double chronology, 27; suspense, 30; choral lyrics, 39; character portrayal, 40–41; exposition elaborate, 58; prologue, 460 (n. 50); opens at night, 478 (n. 80). Mentioned, 38, 41, 54, 55, 106, 112, 177, 202, 210, 215, 429, 458 (n. 27)
Choephoroe, 60–73, **73–81**, 81–87, 132–41, 212–19; recognition criticized in *Electra* of Euripides, 10, 117; chorus, 21, 39, 466 (n. 131); text faulty, 37. Mentioned, 38, 107
Eumenides, 60–81, **81–87**; glorification of Attica, 9, 40; chorus, 21, 39; changes of scene, 26; interior scene, 39; informality of background, 73. Mentioned, 40, 43, 163, 218, 236, 261
Persians, **45–48**; no prologos, 13, 44; messenger's speech, 16; not part of a trilogy, 24; ghost, 28, 77; in Byzantine selection, 37; encomium of Athens, 40; character portrayal, 40; no peripety, 59; background, 73. Mentioned, 5, 6, 39, 52, 55, 66, 68, 71, 447 (n. 27)
Prometheus Bound, **52–59**; time covered in trilogy, 26; influence, 37; in Byzantine selection, 37; "stage" effects, 39, 142; character portrayal, 40–41; ends at high pitch of excite-

233, 259, 265, 310, 462 (n. 79), 471 (n. 213), 475 (n. 45)
Knights, 274–78; parody of Prometheus Bound, 52; interior prologue, 352. Mentioned, 259–68, 278, 283–85, 287, 289–90, 475 (n. 45)
Lysistrata, 292–94; advocates revolution (?), 477 (n. 66). Mentioned, 183, 259–69, 308, 473 (n. 14)
Peace, 286–88. Mentioned, 259–68, 465 (n. 119)
Plutus, 309–12. Mentioned, 81, 259–69, 315, 340
Thesmophoriazusae, 295–98. Mentioned, 259–69
Wasps, 282–85; and Cyclops, 464 (n. 107). Mentioned, 14, 259–68, 287, 481 (n. 2)
Lost plays:
Babylonians, 272
Banqueters (Daitales), 272, 280
Cocalus, 264, 269, 309
Gerytades, 478 (n. 81; n. 86)
Preview (Proagon), 282
Thesmophoriazusae, Second, 479 (n. 99)
Triphales, 266, 479 (n. 92)
Aristophanes of Byzantium, 232
Aristotle's criticisms: character, 8, 26, 168, 234, 249, 411, 453 (n. 50); chorus, 91, 224; criteria proper to Greek tragedy, 403; criticism of Euripides, 172–75, 457 (n. 12); fiction, 6–7; interludes, 23; Iphigenia in Tauris, 219; knowledge of audience, 27; marvelous, 442 (n. 11); Oedipus the King, 116–17; origins, 4, 258, 458 (n. 19); prefers Sophocles, 157; recognition, 134, 223; tragic situations, 32, 207, 222, 373, 442 (n. 15); unities, 25–27, 140
Artemis Tauropolos, 219–20
Asides, 22, 379, 409, 429
Assonance, 167, 481 (n. 5)
Astydamas, 36, 103
Athenaeus, 325, 355
Athens, political situation, 270–72, 475 (n. 43); career resembles tragedy, 300
Atilius, 133
Audience
Greek: presence of women and children doubtful, 81
Roman: adults, 369; described, 364
Augustus, 468 (n. 171); Ajax, 114

Baïf, Jean Antoine de, Le Brave, 361

Beaumarchais, Pierre Augustin Caron de, Mariage de Figaro, 351
Bellamy, Daniel, the Elder and Younger, The Perjured Devotee, 381
Bergerac, Savinien Cyrano de, Le Pédant Joué, 345
Bridges, Robert Seymour, 52
Browning, Elizabeth Barrett, 52
Browning, Robert, 52, 169
Aristophanes' Apology, 199
Balaustion's Adventure, 165
Byron, George Gordon Noël, 52
Byzantine selections, see Manuscript tradition

Caecilius, 375–76, 482 (n. 10); Necklace, 481 (n. 3)
Caesar, Julius, 114, 172–73, 230, 360, 487 (n. 66); criticism of Terence, 381; Oedipus, 425
Caligula, 401 bis
Callistratus, 270, 272 bis, 288, 292
Carcinus, Medea, 459 (n. 43)
Catullus, 237
Characters, protatic, see Protatic
Charition, a fragmentary mime, 487 (n. 65), cf. 467 (n. 155)
Chinese drama, 39
Choerilus, 37
Choregus, 4, 6, 441 (n. 5), 446 (n. 19)
Chorus, see Comedy; Tragedy
Christus Patiens, a Medieval cento, 470 (n. 203)
Chronology, double, defined, 27
Cicero, Marcus Tullius, 230, 344; on Plautus, 337; on Terence, 381
Cicero, Quintus Tullius, 114, 133
claqueurs in ancient theater, 340
Claudius, 401, 412, 427, 434, 496 (n. 70)
Cleon, 266–68, 272–87, 304, 456 (n. 95)
Collaboration, 274
Comedy, Middle, 307–12, 315, 363, 364
Large number of plays, 355
Structure similar to tragedy, 282
Subject matter, 309
See Comedy, Old and Middle
Comedy, New and Roman (definitions, 257–58, 315):
Character portrayal, 322, 326–27, 343–45, 376–77, 382–83, 388, 396–98; change in character during play, 327, 398, 488 (n. 86); by contrast, 386; individualized characters in generalized situations, 318; by language, 344; types, 318

Tragedy, Greek (cont.):
Themes (cont.):
of sanctuary, 40, 42, 189, 202; sins
of fathers visited upon sons, 49, 113,
184; unjust judge, 104, 182, 242;
vengeance, see Revenge, tragedy of;
violence vs. justice, 54; war, 199
Trilogy, 23–24, 38, 60, 94, 208–12, 229;
no unity of time or place, 26; abandoned by Sophocles, 91; possibly
used by Sophocles, 96
Unities of time and place, 25–27, 74;
change of scene, 60, 81, 98; informality during early period, 39, 81; passage of time, 82
Unity of action, 24–25, 60, 92, 141, 163,
190, 191–92, 194, 199, 210–12; lacking,
232–33, 251; minor plot, 230–31
Violent deeds "off stage," 32, 33; "on
stage," 98
Tragedy, Roman (Seneca):
Character portrayal, immaterial if determinism accepted, 407, 425, 430–31;
inconsistencies, 431
Chorus, 409; coryphaeus silent if two or
more speaking characters on stage,
480 (n. 113); informal, 435; primarily
interlude, 409, 426, 431
Divinities, 409–10, 432–34; eliminated,
378, 415, 423, 471 (n. 211)
Foreknowledge, 28, 409, 411
Ghosts, 409, 428, 430
Informality and carelessness in dra-
matic technique, 405, 413, 415, 425,
432
Leitmotif, 494 (n. 33)
Meter and music, 409, 430, 435; shifts
in meter, 419, 423
Preparation, 422
Production of plays, 404–5; difficulties
in presentation, 404
Relief, lyric, 426
Rhetorical motives, 404–6
Scenery: interior scene, 429; screen
used, 99
Significance: allegory, 432; moral and
philosophical, 407; political, 406–7;
psychological, 234, 407
Staging: spectacular effects, 405
Structure, 408–10; climax, 422; inter-
lude at, 431, 433; peripety, 429; peri-
pety slight or lacking, 405, 410; pre-

lude, 421, 428, 433; prologue, Euripidean, 409; scenes, number of, 405;
soliloquy, 409, 418
Subjects:
Greek, 402
Roman, sometimes contemporary, 10,
402, 406, 432–36
Themes: crime leads to crime, 427–30,
430–31; life unsuccessful struggle,
411–12; passion overwhelms reason,
418, 424; stepmother, 405, 410–11,
420, 421, 431, 435; triumph over
death, 432–34; tyrant, 406, 410–12,
425–26, 429, 435; see Revenge,
tragedy of
Unities of time and place, 408; change
of scene, 408–9, 417; passage of a
night, 436
Unity of action violated, 405, 419
Violent deeds on stage, 404, 413, 420,
423, 427
Trissino, Giovanni Giorgio:
I Simillimi, 356
Sofonisba, 6, 164
Tullius, see Cicero
Turney, Robert, Daughters of Atreus,
246, 448 (n. 48)
Turpilius, Heiress (Epicleros), 489 (n.
14)

Udall, Nicholas, Ralph Roister Doister,
360, 387

Varius Rufus, Lucius, Thyestes, 428
Varro, Marcus Terentius, 395
Vergil, 33, 237, 431, 491 (n. 35), 496 (n.
65)
Voltaire, François Marie Arouet de: re-
marks on length of modern plays, 25
Mérope, 445 (n. 50)
Oedipe, 116, 464 (n. 114)
Oreste, 62

Wagner, Richard, 62, 445 (n. 8)
Wieland, Christoph Martin, 165, 458 (n.
28)
Wilder, Thornton Niven, The Woman of
Andros, 381

Xenocles: Oedipus, Lycaon, Bacchae,
Athamas, 208 (236)
Xenophon, 103